DATE DUE

AP 25 '96			

THEORETICAL ISSUES
IN BEHAVIOR THERAPY

THEORETICAL ISSUES IN BEHAVIOR THERAPY

EDITED BY

STEVEN REISS

Department of Psychology
University of Illinois
Chicago, Illinois

RICHARD R. BOOTZIN

Department of Psychology
Northwestern University
Evanston, Illinois

1985

ACADEMIC PRESS, INC.

(Harcourt Brace Jovanovich, Publishers)

Orlando   San Diego   New York   London
Toronto   Montreal   Sydney   Tokyo

ACADEMIC PRESS, INC.
Orlando, Florida 32887

United Kingdom Edition published by
ACADEMIC PRESS INC. (LONDON) LTD.
24–28 Oval Road, London NW1 7DX

Library of Congress Cataloging in Publication Data

Main entry under title:

Theoretical issues in behavior therapy.

   Includes index.
   1. Behavior therapy. 2. Anxiety. 3. Depression,
Mental. I. Reiss, Steven. II. Bootzin, Richard R.,
Date   . [DNLM: 1. Anxiety Disorders--therapy.
2. Behavior Therapy . 3. Depressive Disorders--therapy.
WM 425 T396]
RC489.B4T52   1985   616.89'142   84-21613
ISBN 0-12-586360-8 (alk. paper)

PRINTED IN THE UNITED STATES OF AMERICA

85 86 87 88   9 8 7 6 5 4 3 2 1

CONTENTS

II. THEORIES OF ANXIETY AND FEAR

3. Implosive Theory: A Comprehensive Extension of Conditioning Theory of Fear/Anxiety to Psychopathology

DONALD J. LEVIS

4. Incubation Theory of Fear/Anxiety

H. J. EYSENCK

5. Expectancy Model of Fear

STEVEN REISS AND RICHARD J. MCNALLY

III. SELECTED THEORETICAL ISSUES

IV. THEORIES OF DEPRESSION

CONTRIBUTORS

Numbers in parenthesis indicate the pages on which the authors' contributions begin.

LAUREN B. ALLOY (379), Department of Psychology, Northwestern University, Evanston, Illinois 60201

DONALD M. BAER (179), Department of Human Development, The University of Kansas, Lawrence, Kansas 66405

RICHARD R. BOOTZIN (35), Department of Psychology, Northwestern University, Evanston, Illinois 60201

EDWARD G. CARR (219), Department of Psychology, State University of New York at Stony Brook, Stony Brook, New York 11794

CAROLINE CLEMENTS (379), Department of Psychology, Northwestern University, Evanston, Illinois 60201

HIKARU DEGUCHI (179), Department of Human Development, The University of Kansas, Lawrence, Kansas 66405

ULF DIMBERG (123), Institutionen for Tillampad Psykologi, Uppsala Universitet, 751 42 Uppsala, Sweden

V. MARK DURAND (219), Department of Psychology, State University of New York at Albany, Albany, New York 12222

H. J. EYSENCK (83), Department of Psychology, Institute of Psychiatry, London, SE5 8AF, 01-703, England

SUE M. HAGERMAN (3), Department of Psychiatry, Dartmouth College Medical School, Hanover, New Hampshire 03755

MARTIN HAUTZINGER (331), Universität Konstanz, FG Psychologie, D-7750 Konstanz, Federal Republic of Germany

ELAINE M. HEIBY (279), Department of Psychology, University of Hawaii, Honolulu, Hawaii 96822

HARRY M. HOBERMAN[1] (331), Department of Psychology, University of Oregon, Eugene, Oregon 97403

L. ROWELL HUESMANN (361), Department of Psychology, University of Illinois at Chicago, Chicago, Illinois 60680

FREDERICK H. KANFER (3), Department of Psychology, University of Illinois, Urbana, Illinois, 61801

GREGORY KOLDEN (379), Department of Psychology, Northwestern University, Evanston, Illinois 60201

DONALD J. LEVIS (49), Department of Psychology, State University of New York at Binghamton, Binghamton, New York 13901

PETER M. LEWINSOHN (331), Department of Psychology, University of Oregon, Eugene, Oregon 97403

RICHARD J. McNALLY (107), University of Health Sciences/The Chicago Medical School, North Chicago, Illinois 60601

SHARON MORIKAWA (361), Department of Psychology, University of Illinois at Chicago, Chicago, Illinois 60680

ARNE ÖHMAN (123), Institutionen For Tillampad Psykologi, Uppsala Universitet, 751 42 Uppsala, Sweden

LARS-GÖRAN ÖST (123), Institutionen For Tillampad Psykologi, Uppsala Universitet, 751 42 Uppsala, Sweden

STEVEN REISS (107), Department of Psychology, University of Illinois at Chicago, Chicago, Illinois 60680

ARTHUR W. STAATS (279), Department of Psychology, University of Hawaii at Maoa, Honolulu, Hawaii 96822

LINDA TERI (331), Department of Psychology, University of Oregon, Eugene, Oregon 97403

AUBREY J. YATES (255), Department of Psychology, The University of Western Australia, Nedlands, Western Australia 6009, Australia

[1] Present address: Division of Child and Adolescent Psychiarty, University of Minnesota Medical School, Minneapolis Minnesota 55455.

PREFACE

Although the field of behavior therapy is almost 30 years old, there have been very few books exclusively devoted to a discussion of theoretical issues. This is unfortunate because theories add a dimension of intellectual depth and interest to the behavior therapy field. Moreover, there is an important historical relationship between theoretical positions and the development of important clinical techniques. For example, the theoretical position that many abnormal behaviors are maintained by reinforcing environmental consequences led to the development of reinforcement therapy. The view that anxiety is a conditioned Pavlovian response led to the development of systematic desensitization and implosive therapy. The theoretical position that depression is caused by irrational ideas and other faulty cognitions led to the development of cognitive therapy. As these examples show, advances in theory have often led to advances in treatment.

The primary purpose of this book is to stimulate interest in the theoretical aspects of behavior therapy and to encourage theoretically relevant research. Original theories are presented in some chapters, and established theories are updated and revised in others. Critical reviews of influential theoretical issues are also included. The book as a whole demonstrates some of the intellectual excitement of the field, while providing a state-of-the-art summary of thinking on important theoretical issues.

The book is divided into four parts. Part I consists of two chapters on ways of accommodating the widespread interest in cognitive processes while retaining a basic behavioral orientation. Part II consists of four chapters on the nature and treatment of anxiety problems, and Part III consists of chapters on imitation, severe behavior problems, and biofeedback. Part IV consists of four chapters on the nature and treatment of depression.

We would like to express our appreciation to our contributing authors for having made our work on this volume a pleasurable and stimulating experience. We also would like to thank the editorial staff of Academic Press for their assistance in publishing this volume.

S. R.
R. R. B

PART I

INTEGRATING COGNITIONS INTO BEHAVIOR THERAPY

Behavior therapy, with its emphasis on directly changing observable behavior, developed as an exciting alternative to psychodynamic, primarily verbal, therapies. It was not that behavior therapy excluded cognition. From the beginning, behavior therapists were interested in changing cognition and affect in addition to behavior. Nevertheless, there was a difference. Psychodynamic therapists used dysfunctions, whether behavioral, cognitive, or affective, as signs of underlying psychodynamic disturbance, while behavior therapists developed strategies to ameliorate those dysfunctions directly.

Within the behavioral perspective, cognition has been used in two different ways. First, and noncontroversially, cognition has been used to refer to thoughts, images, and verbal behavior that accompany behavioral dysfunctions. Treatment interventions can be directed at changing dysfunctional behavior, affect, or cognition. Second, and controversially, cognition has been used to refer to processes within the individual that mediate or cause subsequent behavior. It is on this issue that there remains considerable disagreement. Cognitive behavior therapists assert that an understanding of cognitive mediation is essential for a complete analysis of an individual's dysfunctional behav-

ior. Some behavior therapists, on the other hand, consider the label "cognitive behavior" therapist to be a contradiction in terms. They consider a focus on observable behavior to be behavior therapy's major contribution.

The two chapters in this section explore ways of bringing cognitive processes into behavior therapy. Frederick Kanfer and Sue Hagerman review the accomplishments of behavior therapy and the reasons for the reluctance to include cognitive processes. They propose that the information-processing paradigm that has developed in modern cognitive psychology can usefully supplement the models used by behavior therapists. They illustrate the applicability of the information-processing paradigm for clinical practice by describing some implications of automatic versus controlled-processing models, temporal and sensory sources of information in interviews, and the importance of the perceived origin of information.

Richard Bootzin further describes the contributions of cognitive mediation mechanisms to theories of learning, emotion, and behavior. He cautions, however, that the role of affect should not be neglected. He reviews evidence from hemispheric lateralization and other areas that indicate that affect may be automatic, holistic, and autonomous from cognition.

1

Behavior Therapy and the Information-Processing Paradigm

FREDERICK H. KANFER
SUE M. HAGERMAN

Introduction

Behavior therapy as currently practiced is harvesting the fruit of nearly a century of philosophical and methodological developments. Its achievements, much like those of psychoanalysis earlier in this century, resulted in a social movement rather than in the development of specific methods (London, 1972). The impact of the behavioral credo resulted in a new perspective on human activities, both normal and pathological, and behaviorism dominated American psychology for several decades. More recently, behavior therapy has come under heavy criticism as a social movement and a therapeutic enterprise. The most strident attacks have focused on the limitations of behaviorism to account for human cognitive functions. These attacks come from researchers who are interested in developing models for unobservable, "private events," yet who use behavioral methods to test these models. Although the cognitive revolution seems still at its peak, there are already some who forecast its decline (Averill, 1983). Nevertheless, cognitive science and the information-processing paradigm (IPP) are contributing to a reevaluation of traditional views about human behavior. Essentially, the current ferment in clinical psychology reflects a wider problem. The task that psychologists face is one of accommodating in one comprehensive science the growing body of knowledge on the acquisition and organization of information on the one hand, and the traditional contents of a science dealing with environmental, social, and biological determinants of behavior on the other hand.

In this chapter we discuss ways in which research data from the IPP can be integrated into behavior therapy. Although many epistemological and practical issues separate behavior modifiers from cognitive scientists, we argue that data from the IPP, obtained in methodologically sound experiments, have the same status as data from learning studies or other areas as a basis for developing behavior therapy methods. In fact, these data may suggest innovative ways to conduct assessment and treatment, to conceptualize cases, and to decide among target behaviors. First, however, we present a broad historical overview of the developments and accomplishments of the behavioral movement, particularly for clinical practice. We next discuss several criticisms of behavior therapy and describe some attempts within the behavioral camp to address and accommodate them. In particular, we highlight some of the dissatisfactions with behavior therapy that have given rise to efforts to incorporate concepts and data of cognitive science into an expanded clinical model. We use several research models from cognitive psychology to illustrate possible ways in which such an integration might occur. Finally, we present our view of limitations and cautions necessary in any attempt to integrate findings from cognitive science with clinical practice. These caveats are needed to retain a nondualistic, neobehavioral stance toward the human organism, and to counter the temptation to relinquish the advances made by behavior therapy.

History and Achievements of Behavior Therapy

In the history of the treatment of mental disorders, the most striking theme is the rejection of philosophical and theological thought in the models that guide therapeutic interventions (Frank, 1961; Zilboorg, 1941). The spirit of scientific inquiry and pragmatism began in the late nineteenth century with efforts to approach abnormal behavior and the treatment of mental illness in a systematic manner. Leaning heavily on developments of medicine and biology, psychiatry attempted to free itself from the influences of religion and morality. Freud's work represents the pinnacle of such efforts in what Zilboorg (1941) has called the "second psychiatric revolution." Despite the enormous impact of psychodynamic theory on Western culture, the psychoanalytic model failed to meet the criteria of a testable and empirically based scientific theory. Freudian theory was increasingly criticized, and general dissatisfaction was expressed, both with the theoretical formulation and its application to psychotherapy (Eysenck, 1959; Kazdin,

1978). By the mid-1960s, the rapid growth of research and theory in learning psychology, coupled with social factors that increasingly relegated responsibility for assessment and treatment to psychologists, culminated in the ascendance of behavior therapy as a strong contender for a dominant position in the field of therapeutic intervention.

The behavioral movement in clinical psychology was characterized by a shift of emphasis from inner resources to environmental determinants of behavior. Despite disagreements within the behavioral movement that had roots in such divergent approaches as those of Skinner (1953), Hull (1943), Rotter (1954), Guthrie (1935), and Tolman (1932), early behavioral clinicians shared the following tenets: (1) an underlying acceptance of logical positivism; (2) a faith in the utility of extrapolation of conclusions of the animal laboratory to complex human social situations; and (3) a conceptualization of behavior disorders as learned phenomena.

The behavioral movement resulted in an unprecedented trend toward experimentation and research as the basis for assessment and treatment concepts. Excellent results were obtained in areas that had previously defied the ingenuity of therapists (e.g., mental retardation and autism), and excellent track records were established in the treatment of phobias, interpersonal problems, and other neurotic disorders. Behavior therapy's achievements fall into four basic areas: (1) emphasis on overt, concrete behaviors instead of syndromes in conceptualizing and treating problems in living; (2) individualized analysis and treatment approaches; (3) demonstration of effectiveness and accountability in treating specific target behaviors; and (4) development of a number of effective treatment packages for previously recalcitrant problems (e.g., phobias, sexual dysfunctions) and for application to nonclinical populations. These achievements are reviewed below.

Emphasis on Observables

The basic view of radical behaviorism (and logical positivism generally) that only observable behavior and events constitute the data of science implied that the clinician should treat maladaptive behavior directly, rather than treat its presumed underlying pathological process. The demonstration that symptom substitution rarely, if ever, occurred after the removal of maladaptive behaviors (Rachman, 1963) enhanced the clinical respectability of behavior modification. Observable, quantifiable behavior change, rather than testimony of therapist or client, became the focus of assessment strategies (Ferster, 1965; Kanfer & Saslow, 1965; Lindsley, 1964) and treatment approaches.

Individualized Analysis

The behaviorist's insistence that behavior disorders be described in terms of the relationship between stimuli, responses, and consequences (S–R–C) led to the adoption of the functional analysis as the basis for case formulation. The earlier focus on "inner causes" was replaced by an emphasis on environmental influences. As a result of the idiographic nature of the behavioral analysis (and treatment prescriptions based on it), strategies for examining treatment effects were developed, most notably those adapted to single cases (Barlow, Hayes & Nelson, 1984; Hersen & Barlow, 1976; Kazdin, 1982).

Accountability

The emphasis on individualized analysis, and on demonstrable treatment effects, also resulted in an awareness of the importance of therapeutic accountability. By their stress on assessment and verification of progress through measurement of target behaviors, behavior therapists intensified the earlier efforts of Carl Rogers and his group to open the double doors of the psychoanalyst's consulting room and encouraged public and peer scrutiny of therapeutic methods. Although the optimistic claims of the early behaviorists have not been realized fully in practice, the importance of outcome evaluation and individualized assessment has become widely accepted.

Expanded Scope of Behavior Therapy

Behavior therapists have emphasized the continuity of behavioral principles for human activities ranging from pathological to everyday actions. Consequently, the scope of clinical psychology has been extended to such common problem areas as parent training, social skills, sexual behavior, and stress management. Techniques originally developed for neurotic clients have been widely used by the general population, and the behavioral analysis approach has been extended beyond individual problems. For example, applied behavior analysts have contributed to problem resolution in such social areas as city and office planning; community organization; and school, industrial, and health provision systems (Kanfer, 1984). Further contributions were made by behavioral psychologists who focused on the physical and social environment. Environmental and community problems (Rogers-Warren & Warren, 1977; Winett, 1974, 1980; Zifferblatt & Hendricks; 1974), school and day-care environments (Doke & Risley, 1972; Krasner & Krasner, 1973), inpatient facility designs (Kanfer, May, Oberberger, & Brengelman, 1978), family systems (Patterson, Reid, Jones, & Conger, 1975), and partner relationships (Gottman, Notarius, Gonzo, &

Markman, 1976; Weiss, 1980) were targeted by behaviorists for analysis and change.

In summary, the behavior therapy movement made a number of important contributions to clinical psychology. Standardized and effective treatment packages for a wide number of problems in living (pathological and nonpathological) were developed. Most important, a set of assessment and intervention strategies that are generalizable outside of a strictly behavioral approach, an emphasis on competencies rather than deficits, and parsimony in explanation and intervention have been the lasting contributions made by the behavioral movement. These contributions have resulted in the compilation of books that could qualify almost as virtual "psychologist's desk reference."

Shortcomings of Behavior Therapy

Critics of the behavioral movement emerged early. In the year the first edited volume on research in behavior modification was published in the United States (Krasner & Ullmann, 1965), there also appeared the first widely noted criticism (Breger & McGaugh, 1965). The attacks articulated by various writers—relatively unchanged over the last 15 years—focused on several main themes:

1. Behavior therapists do not practice what they preach. They are not "behavioral" in their operations and, consequently, their practice is incompatible with the professed conceptual framework (Locke, 1971).
2. The classical and operant conditioning models are insufficient to account for change processes in humans (Bandura, 1974; Ellis, 1962).
3. Logical positivism, the backbone of behavior therapy, and its stringent operational procedural rules, are outmoded and untenable. In particular, sound, scientific procedural rules are not violated when constructs about unobservable behaviors and processes are invoked (Suppes, 1975).
4. Behavior therapy must be expanded to accommodate the cognitive revolution in psychology (Mahoney, 1977).
5. Behavior therapy neither has nor needs a philosophical foundation, nor do its roots in learning theory and scientific research go beyond heuristic utility (Erwin, 1978).

The limitations of a therapy model based on conditioning and the central role of the clinical interview as a mediating instrument, especially in outpatient therapy, led Kanfer and Phillips (1966) to distinguish between *interven-*

tion therapy and *instigation therapy*. In the former, the sole focus of treatment is the in situ application of a particular conditioning principle to a target behavior. The token economy or systematic contingency arrangements illustrate intervention therapy as a direct extrapolation of principles derived from animal learning studies. In these situations, the role of interpersonal and cognitive factors is minimal. Moreover, the clinician can operate very much like the laboratory experimenter in selecting variables and contingencies to match the conditions under which the paradigm was first developed.

Instigation therapy denotes the more common form of intervention in which the therapist does not have extensive control over the client's environment. As the clinician deals with clients who move freely in their daily environment, a host of obstacles to direct application of the laboratory conditioning paradigms emerge. In place of direct control over the antecedents and consequences of a target behavior, the therapist must rely heavily on the client to mediate the change process. Both for formulating the task of therapy and for encouraging the client to initiate new behaviors, the verbal–symbolic dimension and the client's cooperation emerge as indispensible features. In 1953, even Skinner viewed the role of the therapist as an instigative one. He described the client's change as a direct result of a carefully structured verbal and interpersonal relationship. Twenty years later, Skinner again emphasized the critical role of the therapist as instigator: "Behavior therapy is often supposed to be exclusively a matter of contriving reinforcement contingencies, but it quite properly includes giving a patient warnings, advice, instructions, and rules to be followed." (Skinner, 1974, p. 185)

In this section, we review several limitations of behavior therapy associated with its origins in the animal laboratory. The limitations fall into four major categories: (1) difficulties arising from ignoring cognitive and verbal–symbolic processes in the interview, (2) difficulties in extrapolating findings from laboratories to settings involving free living organisms in dynamic interplay with natural environments, (3) differences in the aims and methods of the lab and the clinic, and (4) difficulties arising from the assumption that the clinician has the degree of control and objectivity that the experimenter has.

THE ROLE OF COGNITION AND "HIGHER MENTAL PROCESSES"

Two major learning paradigms have served as foci for the development of behavior therapy techniques: Skinner's Operant Conditioning model and Hull's Drive Reduction theory. Neither system lent itself easily to an analysis of the relationship of the client and therapist, particularly its strong verbal–symbolic and cognitive components. In addition, neither approach offered a framework for dealing with inner events, such as thoughts, beliefs, and intentions, or fantasies, as possible moderators of simple input–output relationships.

During the period in which behavior therapy evolved, the need to incorporate "higher mental processes" in learning theories persisted as an undertone. For example, Dollard and Miller (1950) asserted, "we are not denying the fact that the organism must possess certain capacities, the exact nature of which is still unknown, before such responses can operate in this way. A parrot can learn to imitate words but not to become a great thinker" (1950, p. 101). The monumental efforts of the "big four" (Guthrie, Hull, Skinner, and Tolman) to develop learning theories that would encompass all of human behavior gave way to approaches that were less ambitious. This trend gradually weakened adherence to the original assumptions and procedural rules that characterized the early behavioral movement. Most important, it foreshadowed the current "cognitive revolution" (Dember, 1974). Unfortunately, as the applied behavioral movement moved away from the mainstream of experimental psychology, it also lost touch with concurrent developments in learning theory (e.g., Atkinson, Bower, & Crothers, 1965; Kendler, 1961; Spence & Spence, 1968). As it concentrated on issues related to its own development, the behavior therapy movement became isolated from the growing body of research in verbal learning. One consequence of this dissociation of behavior modification from learning theory was a continued distrust of verbal behavior as a reliable source of information. In particular, self-reports and change methods involving verbal learning were viewed with suspicion.

Although regarded as suspect or unnecessary in an explanation of human behavior by radical behaviorists, the capacity of humans (as opposed to other organisms) to utilize the verbal–symbolic system in regulating their own behavior has important clinical implications. In addition, in both Hullian and Skinnerian psychology, the power of a reinforcer or a cue is attributed mainly to its effect on a response and its relevance (even if only by remote association or earlier conditioning) to a biological advantage or threat to the organism (e.g., preparedness). Challengers of the behavioral position, including its own proponents (see Estes, 1972), have pointed to the crucial function of information processing in regulating behavior. Further, as Lang (1983), Kanfer and his collegues (Kanfer, 1975; Kanfer & Grimm, 1980; Kanfer & Hagerman, 1981), and others have indicated, the ability of humans to set goals and to evaluate and change their own behavior is an important source of control unheeded by radical behaviorists. Other information-processing capacities of humans, critical to instigation therapy (Kanfer & Phillips, 1969), were also eschewed by early behavior therapists for both explanation and application, thereby relegating important segments of human behavior to theoretical and practical limbo.

Current arguments by cognitive behavior therapists to reintroduce the constructs of cognition and self-regulation to clinical practice resulted from the perceived inadequacy of extrapolating from simple S–R–C conceptions to account for both psychopathological behavior and the change process. As we argue below, once the human information-processing system is introduced into explanations about learning, conditioning models alone can no longer be considered sufficient to account for behavioral changes.

THE ORIGINS IN THE ANIMAL LABORATORY

The Dynamic Nature of Organisms

Human interactions with the environment (including other persons) are varied and complex, occur over time, and are rarely accompanied by the precisely defined and potent incentive states or specific demands produced in laboratory subjects. Extensions of laws from carefully controlled environments to free-field settings may be epistemologically unsound. That the laws hold to the degree that they seem to in everyday interactions is perhaps remarkable, given the difference between the outside world and the laboratory. If anything, frequent successes in the clinic demonstrate the robustness of the laboratory-based theories.

A related critique of the application of relationships observed in the laboratory to everyday behavior is based upon their static nature. Adoption of a static model of behavior clouds the episodic and dynamic nature of human behavior. The temporal dimension of most human interactions is poorly modeled in laboratory experiments, yet it is critical in most clinical interventions. Indeed, it is likely that not even the behavior of rats in nature is adequately explained by the relationships observed from the behavior of their laboratory cousins. The lab represents a closed system in a fixed environment; human behavior in the field exists in a continually changing, open system. This difference limits the range of critical variables that can be tested in a controlled setting and carries the danger of oversimplifying interventions or even aggravating a client's situation (Reppucci & Saunders, 1974).

The contrived setting of the lab permits control of the environment so that only a limited set of experimenter-determined contingencies are allowed to occur. This restriction of possible outcomes and response options can limit attention to other, possibly more ecologically valid, outputs and parameters of behavior. When Bernstein and Paul (1971) warned against common sources of threats to external validity in clinical analogue studies, they raised this issue of ecological validity. The ability of humans to alter inputs and outputs over time, even in the face of constant environments, can be easily overlooked in time and response-limited studies of clinically relevant behavior (e.g., anxiety).

The Difference in Goals and Methods between the Lab and the Clinic

The goals and methods of the laboratory are often different from those of the clinic (Manicas & Secord, 1983; Mook, 1983). Rigid attempts to apply research findings directly to natural settings fail to recognize the need to use other knowledge, outside of psychological science, to guide such applications (Kaminski, 1970). Precise and long-term predictions of behavior in the clinic on the basis of laboratory data are impossible due to differences in time span, the complexity of critical variables, and the setting and aims of the endeavor. At best, scientific knowledge can provide clinicians with broad guidelines to alert them to important sources of variation that must be examined again in the clinical context as the task and the settings change (Cronbach, 1975).

Despite the fact that lab-based "mini-theories" cannot encompass all of human behavior, laboratory research is an excellent tool for developing theories, testing hypotheses, and suggesting possible procedures for clinical application. The perspicacity and skill of the clinician in recognizing salient clinical variables and relating them to relevant research data is the critical nexus between the clinic and the lab (Kaminski, 1970; Kanfer, 1984; Kanfer & Busemeyer, 1982). We inveigh only against the unwitting attempts to translate lab methods and lab data directly to the clinic that characterized many early behavioral programs.

The Difference in Amount of Control between the Lab and The Clinic

Early behavior therapy successes were achieved mostly in institutionalized populations under nearly complete environmental control. In the clinic, behavior therapists quickly discovered the limits under which they worked. Behaviorists intially had hoped that therapists could be trained as standardized instruments (Kanfer, 1966) or virtual reinforcing machines (Krasner, 1962), and that assessment and treatment strategies could be applied without regard to interpersonal influences. The presumed objectivity of the lab (now called into question by many philosophers and sociologists of science (Gergen, 1982; Kuhn, 1970) was to be transferred to the clinic. Research on client–therapist variables in outcome studies has demonstrated that, in fact, interpersonal variables can be critical in therapy (Garfield &

Bergin, 1978) and has restored attention to the interpersonal and verbal–symbolic dimensions in therapy (Goldstein, 1980; Wilson & Evans, 1977).

In addition to the goal of eliminating therapist variance in applying behavioral treatments, behavior therapists attempted to investigate optimal matches between classes of problem behaviors (e.g., fears) and techniques (e.g., systematic desensitization). It was assumed that specificity in assessment and treatment could develop to the extent that it could be known which treatment to apply for which kinds of clients with which kinds of problems in living (Paul, 1969). Unfortunately, the potential promised has not been realized, nor may it be possible.

Attempts to Address Criticisms of Behavior Therapy

Within the behavior modification camp, several early attempts were made to address these criticisms. Theorists such as Bandura, Kanfer, Mischel, Rotter, Staats, and others worked independently to incorporate variables that they believed broadened the applicability of laws of learning to human behavior. These and other workers used the label "social learning theory" to emphasize the importance of verbal, mediational, and interpersonal aspects of human behavior. A second generation of behaviorally trained theorists emphasized cognitive mediational variables in their criticisms and attempts to broaden behavior modification (Kendall & Hollon, 1979; Meichenbaum, 1977) and adopted the "cognitive–behavioral" label.

Initially, social learning theorists believed that cognitive events could be incorporated into a behavioral framework by assuming that learning principles are equally applicable to overt, observable and covert, unobservable responses (Bandura, 1969; Dollard & Miller, 1950; Homme, 1965; Kanfer, 1966; Shoben, 1949; Skinner, 1953; Ullmann, 1970). As early as 1965, the study of vicarious learning (modeling) was viewed as a "glimpse into the black box" (Kanfer, 1965) and raised questions concerning the role of symbolic processes in learning (Bandura, 1965). A decade of research on verbal learning and conditioning (Kanfer, 1968), vicarious learning (Bandura, 1969), and the interactions among person, situation, and environment in personality (Mischel, 1973) illustrate the efforts of early behavioral clinicians to wrestle with these issues in a clinically and methodologically sophisticated manner.

In the early 1970s, social learning theorists moved even further from a radical behavioral position over the role of internal events. Research indicating the capacity of humans to develop heuristics for conduct (rule-based learning), challenges to the automaticity assumption in operant conditioning (Dulany, 1961) and classical conditioning (Wilson, 1968), the superiority of predictability over sheer number of pairings in classical conditioning (Rescorla, 1966, 1967), the potency of some classes of CSs over others for different organisms, and the ability of organisms to persist in their pursuit of incentives over long periods of time without external reinforcement (Kanfer, 1970, 1971) raised questions about the completeness of radical behavioral explanations of learning and behavior. In particular, Kanfer (1970, 1971), Bandura (1969), and Mischel (1973; 1979) saw the need to come to grips with the notion that knowledge guides and directs motivated behavior. These researchers began to address that need, yet they remained reluctant to abandon old mediational S–R notions completely.

Other workers began to incorporate ideas from social psychology and person-perception experiments into research on the clinical process. For example, Goldstein, Heller, and Sechrest (1966) attempted to expand the data base of behavior therapy from strict learning theory and to incorporate social psychology data in their thinking about therapeutic technique. Examples of this continuing effort include work by Fisher, Nadler, and DePaulo (1983) and Willis (1982) on the helping relationship, and by Brehm (1976) and Weary and Mirels (1982) on the application of social psychology to clinical practice. These attempts focus not only on the mechanisms of change, but also on important social variables that influence the therapy process.

Cognitive behavior modification arose in the early 1970s as an attempt to address the inadequacies of applying a strictly S–R–C model to clinical problems and processes. Some cognitive behavior therapists assumed that observed verbal behaviors were essentially similar to the inferred mediational (internal) cognitive events, while others assumed that cognitions, events of a different nature, were causal determinants of behavioral responses. While cognitive behavior modifiers disagree about the causal role of cognitions, they agree on the need to modify these poorly understood events (behaviors or processes) in therapy, and the utility of changing cognitive "behavior" using traditional behavioral techniques. This assumption, discussed by Mahoney (1974), provided the basis for a variety of cognitive behavioral approaches. Following Skinner (1953), Homme (1965) and Cautela (1971) postulated that internal events were determined by the same S–R laws that govern external events. On this basis, they proposed the techniques of covert rehearsal, covert modeling, and covert sensitization. Others (Beck, 1976; Goldfried, 1980; Kendall & Hollon, 1979; Meichenbaum, 1977) have reported various clinical methods that combine cognitive and overt behaviors as therapy targets. These attempts did not take full account of the accumulating research in information processing relating to perception, memory, and the organization of information. Nevertheless, they are significant first steps in recognizing and dealing with the criticisms of conceptual narrowness of a conditioning model of therapy.

In summary, early cognitive behavior therapy can be considered an important, but limited, first attempt to accommodate intrapersonal processes while remaining behavioral in method. Several issues still remain to be considered, however, in evaluating early cognitive–behavioral models. First, the dynamic, iterative nature of information processing has been ignored. Cognitive processes continually affect the nature of the input, and the consequences of information processing affect further processing. Second, perception of input signals, organization of information, and recall are interdependent. Third, the links from external events and behavior to internal events are not always clearly specifiable in the manner assumed by many cognitive–behavior modifiers. Fourth, the manner in which cognitive–behavior modifiers attempted to incorporate cognition constituted a return to the use of mentalistic constructs (e.g., cognitive distortions) not clearly linked to observable events and acting in an unspecified and unspecifiable way on information. Instead of attempting a neobehavioral "liberalization" of radical behaviorism as advocated by Miller (Dollard & Miller, 1950; Miller, 1959), cognitive–behavior modifiers created an internally inconsistent system of assumptions and methods by the reintroduction of mentalistic, and often dualistic, constructs.

The Behavioral Clinician's Dilemma

Lacking a firm conceptual framework for dealing with such phenomena as language, memory, thinking, and self-regulation, many behavior therapists have tended to rely on personal experience, cultural norms, and "common knowledge" in dealing with verbal and cognitive behaviors. These shortcomings have led contemporary writers in clinical psychology to strive for an integration of cognitive and behavioral views to provide a comprehensive model for what happens in therapy. But the task is not simply to combine two research areas to remedy the insufficiency of conditioning models in dealing with the clinical process. The opposition of S–R learning theories and cognitive theories has been viewed widely as a paradigm clash. The contestants differ not only in the explanation of focal psychological phenomena; they also differ sharply in their philosophical and methodological bases. Cognitive theories do not eschew constructions of complex analogues and models. Radical behaviorists have avoided the use of such devices and methodological and analytic behaviorists have used them very sparingly. But the most crucial issue that separates adherents of behavioral and cognitive perspectives are (1) the central versus peripheral explanation of behavior, and related to it, (2) the degree to which active organisms impose structure and organization on their environment and experiences.

These differences can be reduced by the neobehavioral approach advocated here. If one admits data-level findings from the information processing area, one can adopt them as descriptions of the characteristics of the human organism as information processor (called gamma variables in Kanfer, 1970, 1971) yet remain skeptical about the models of information processing proposed to explain the data. One can therefore remain skeptical about constructs that are not firmly anchored by observables, but can use them for their heuristic and research-generating value.

Of the many cognitive approaches, the information-processing model lends itself most readily to integration with learning-based behavioral views because it (1) meets stringent methodological requirements for data collection, (2) deals with well-controlled variables affecting clearly defined behavioral measures, (3) deals with universal characteristics of the human organism in the encoding, storage, and retrieval of information that act by facilitating or constraining both acquisition and performance of various behaviors, and (4) uses a physicalistic analogy reminiscent of the assumptions of classical behaviorists about the automaticity of stimulus–response sequences. Simon (1981) describes it as an approach that focuses "on the problem of how strategies and neurophysiological constraints interact to produce effective behavior in task situations that require thinking" (p. 301). Thus, the IPP centers on the study of cognitive mediators, the causes and consequences of behavior, rather than on the study of the behaviors by which organisms adapt to their environments. Before illustrating how we believe an integration of IPP data with behavior therapy strategies and tactics can occur, we first sketch some of the essential epistemological and practical issues that divide cognitive scientists and behavior therapists.

Cognitivism and Behaviorism

Contemporaneous with the development of the behavior therapy movement, the learning paradigms on which it was founded have been modified. In addition, cognitive models of human verbal learning are increasingly dominant in the domain of learning psychology. A rapprochement of behavior therapy and cognitive models in clinical practice may be possible at some levels, but antagonistic stands taken by the two approaches at other levels yield differing implications for epistemology, theory construction, and research methodology. These differences make a full integration an unrealistic hope and require a distinction between levels at which integration is feasible. For example, today it is trivial to say that both cognitive and behavioral scientists accept only behavioral events as the critical data in their experiments. This similarity at the level of operations is in sharp contrast to the difference with regard to the legitimacy of data usage for inferences about conceptual models and their nature. Furthermore, within each camp, proponents differ among themselves almost as much as between modal representatives of each of the two camps with regard to the inferential leap that can be taken.

It would be wrong to presume that the cognitive revolution had its banners hoisted by a band of opponents to the traditional view. Greeno (1980) notes the gradual, progressive shift made by learning psychologists from a focus on behavior to a focus on learning "as asquisition of knowledge, in which modification and combination of cognitive structures are basic processes" (Greeno, 1980, p. 713). As the subject matter shifted from animal conditioning studies to human verbal learning, stochastic process models developed, and probability of responding was viewed as the central (derived) dependent variable directly related to observable independent variables. Estes (1955) argued that model building, even if only provisional, is essential to direct empirical investigations in a field in which there is danger in collecting increasing numbers of facts that are not useful without an organizing framework. The analytic power of a model thus became a more desirable goal than the accumulation of isolated empirical findings and low-level relationships. But attainment of breadth and generality required models in which the construct–data relationships are rigorously defined, even though the constructs may be distant from the data. Suppes clearly articulated the need for extension of the S–R learning theories:

> I want to make the essential behavioral feature of neobehaviorism the retention of stimuli and responses as central on the one hand, and the introduction of unobservable internal structure as the "neo" component on the other. Thus, in neobehaviorism as opposed to classical behaviorism, it is quite appropriate to postulate a full range of internal structures, ranging from memory hierarchies to language production and language comprehension devices that cannot be, from the standpoint of the theory, directly observed. (1975, p. 270)

The shift toward models of increased complexity and distance from the data is not simply a minor adjustment. Simplicity of models, and minimal use of constructs, from the earliest model of the reflex arc to the current model of Skinner, has been a hallmark of behaviorism. Behaviorism stresses a constructional or inductive view. Analysis and integration of S–R units is

the basis for generating higher level principles. In contrast, cognitive theorists employ central explanatory constructs. They stress complex organizing principles that affect levels of human functioning lower (more peripheral) in the hierarchy. The models represent the human organism as actively
imposing structure and organization on both the environment and its own
experience. To know the processes and rules by which such organization is
developed, rather than to sample observable activities and interactions, is
the road to formulating a model of the person. In clinical terms, a person's
belief systems, perceptual schemata (Kelly, 1955), or ego structure
(Loevinger, 1969), rather than functional analyses of environment–organism interactions, are seen as critical in formulating a case.

Both approaches look to the behavioral level for supporting evidence.
Further, the shift toward the admission of constructs and intervening variables in neobehaviorism (such as internal structures or covert responses)
blurs the distinction between neobehaviorism and cognitivism. The increase
in complexity of constructs was surely not fortuitous as the interests of
learning psychologists shifted from animal learning to verbal learning; it is
in the study of what Dollard and Miller have called "higher mental processes" that pure S–R relationships are particularly unsatisfying unless mediational constructs are added.

Cognitive theorists are interested in the architecture of the cognitive system, that is, the capabilities and processes of the human organism that
determine how environmental inputs are perceived, organized, stored, and
retrieved for later action (Bower, 1978). The overlap of substantive interest
with behavioral psychologists lies in their attempts to study the "software"
of the cognitive system, that is, the relationships between various independent variables and human performance, and the various conditions of exposure and recall. The renewed interest in studying complex human activities
to make inferences about human cognitive structures is not restricted to
learning (Hilgard, 1980). It is reflected in developmental psychology by the
work of Piaget and his followers, and in social psychology by research on
cognitive dissonance, attribution, self-awareness, and other phenomena. In
the area of personality, Mischel (1973, 1979) has also introduced the concept
of cognitive structures to assist in the integration of empirical findings.

From a behavioral perspective, a critical epistemological difference exists
in that cognitivists, to varying degrees, posit that the human organism (1)
actively imposes order on the world, (2) engages in interaction with the
environment, primarily in conjunction with (or as a result of) organized
knowledge structures about the world, and therefore, (3) is best understood
(i.e, predicted) by knowledge of cognitive structures and content. In contrast, the radical behavioral position has usually been linked to a Lockean
tabula rasa empiricism, associationism, and physicalistic monism. Our view

is close to a contemporary version of the field or systems approach of interbehavioral psychology as proposed by Kantor (1924). We conceptualize the organism as a subsystem in the natural environment, interacting with its external and internal environment in a dynamic, ever-changing transaction. Both the environment and the organism are reciprocally affected by these transformations. The human organism is vastly flexible and adaptive. Its biological characteristics and its past experiences prescribe its functions and behavioral capacities, and its cultural heritage codetermines the content of behavior and "experience." The capacity to organize, store, and utilize knowledge (information) affects the total behavioral pattern, some of it observable in interaction with other components of the larger (social and physical) system, some of it occurring within the individual. No assumptions are made of an isomorphism between the nervous system (as an electrical field or biological structure) and the real world, nor of an active, constructive recreation of the world resulting from an innate preparedness to grasp, organize, or select special features of the world.

Instead, human infants learn within the limits and opportunities provided by biology (and culture) to interact with the world and to utilize their capacity for use of symbolic and sensorium-based activities (e.g., language, visual imagery) for self-generation and maintenance of behaviors that are relatively free of concurrent external influence. This capacity vastly extends the repertoire of the human in dealing with the environment. Whether such "cognitive" processes are innately focused on the organism's inner experiences and based on some universal structures (as in the presumption of self-awareness as a given) or developed under social tutelage is unclear and has been a central issue in theories of language development and personality.

What can be agreed upon is that universal rules (associated with human biological potentials) govern the *processes* involved in organizing, retaining, and retrieving experiences in a manner that permits their effective utilization in later action. Just as human biology defines the range of motor acts that can be carried out by an organism with two arms and legs, it also defines the range of remembering acts that a person can perform. From this perspective, research based on the IPP is an especially useful complement to neobehavioral models. Epistemologically, theorists in both fields accept the reality of the world. Both view the organism as an active operator on inputs from the environment, capable of selecting those inputs that are compatible with the structures (hardware) or program of the processor. Neither group requires an internal representation model of the world, an isomorphism of "inside" and "outside," or presumes that the processor operates on the input to impose structure on the outside world. The IPP, as the behavioral model, strives for continuity with other natural sciences and requires no special assumption of dualism for human functioning. A dynamic systems or field-oriented neobehavioral psychology can therefore utilize data from the IPP as complementary to its domain, suggesting processing parameters and limits that affect behavior.

Some central issues remain, however. Information defies definition in behavioral terms. Radical behaviorists have attempted to deal with the organism's actions in processing information (e.g., Skinner's 1957 approach to verbal behavior), but it is unclear what is acted upon. In contrast, contemporary cognitive–behavior therapists often deal with cognition as contents, rather than with processes. But knowledge only guides and directs action; knowledge does not constitute action. To use a somewhat extended parallel for illustration, consider the task of developing a strategy for assembling a picture puzzle to match a criterion picture. Algorithms for action can be developed, but the impact of the content, for example, recognition of a house form or a vague face outline, is not accounted for by the rules. In the clinical literature, content dimensions often are classified on the basis of the experiences of the observer and confounded with processing features. Thus, a depressed client's "cognitions" of a dysphoric nature have been too readily explained by content, rather than processing differences in dealing with objective events. Only since the late 1970s have there been experiments that attempt to separate the source of such dysfunctions.

By contrast, models of schizophrenic speech have long attempted to relate content to processing, and in turn, to neurophysiological variation from the norm. Current work on neurophysiology and in rehabilitation of patients with CNS damage is continuing the centuries-old efforts to correlate behavior deviations with structural or functional biological variations. A neobehavioral view may be able to accommodate data that define the biological and social parameters of human functions, including those that affect attention, organization of sensory data, memory, and decision making. It cannot, however, give up its insistence on empirical data as the only admissible source of scientific knowledge, on operational rules of verification, and on rejection of epistemological views that prejudge the capacities and the nature of the human organism.

Clinical Applications: The Interview

Behavior therapists have long been reluctant to deal with the cognitive (covert) part of the interview. Some writers have summarily labeled the cognitive antecedents and consequences of overt verbalizations as "cognitions" and dismissed them. Others have assumed that overt and covert verbal behaviors are continuous (Mahoney, 1974). This attempt to treat all of the mediating events and their determinants as identical fails to recognize the relevance of structural characteristics in information processing, the widely different processes associated with different types of cognitive events (e.g., visual imagery, decision making, or memory), and the different methodological problems in studying these diverse events. Skepticism about the adequacy of self-reports as true representations of past or current experiences is still widespread. It has led behavior therapists and others to stress that self-reports must be treated as interpersonal behaviors in their own right, varying in the degree with which the contents correlate with actual events as a function of the specific social and interpersonal variables acting at the time of the interview. Yet behavioral interviewers rely heavily on information obtained from interviews, even though they usually supplement it with behavioral observations on episodes first reported in interviews. It therefore is logical to turn to the research of cognitive psychology in an attempt to understand the contributions of cognitive processes in determining information obtained in interviews.

Our main purpose is to demonstrate the pragmatic advantage of a systematic differentiation among various cognitive–verbal operations and the source (external–internal) of their controlling variables. For the practicing clinician, the implications of already existing research in these areas have not yet been adequately related to clinical content. Particularly lacking are guideposts for use of different procedures based on the different demands on information processing that are inherent in the structure and content of particular interview strategies. An awareness of the difference among the controlling variables that affect many cognitive events may help clinicians to select specific interview operations for assessment and change of cognitive behaviors and their associated verbal reports. We provide three examples to illustrate these suggestions. Obviously, if the implications of most major research findings from cognitive psychology are to be spelled out for clinical application, a great deal of tedious and detailed work will be required before substantial bodies of data are patched into clinical procedures.

AUTOMATIC VERSUS CONTROLLED-PROCESSING MODELS

Although it is recognized that clients frequently produce "superficial," stereotyped replies in clinical interviews, insufficient attention has been paid to the crucial importance of distinguishing between such responses and a class of much more complex cognitive events. Simple verbal responses that are highly overlearned, stereotyped, and occur under close control of specific events have been distinguished in earlier behavioral theory as verbal operants, differing from the output resulting from autoclitic, self-editing, and self-strengthening behaviors (Skinner, 1957). Automatic responses have also been viewed as significant pathogenic features in depressed patients by Beck (1976). Langer (1978) has referred to such automatic responses as "mindless thought." Schneider and Shiffrin (1977; Shiffrin & Schneider, 1977) have distinguished between automatic and controlled processing and described different characteristics of the products of these two cognitive processes.

Essentially, automatic processing yields well-learned, quick responses that have long-term stability and make little demand on the person's cognitive capacity. Consequently, such automatic responses can occur simultaneously with other activities. They require a large amount of training, are stored in long-term memory, and the capacity limits for such responses are relatively high. Reproduction requires little attention or concentration. In contrast, controlled processing deals with behaviors that demand much of the person's attention, can only be handled serially, are held in short-term memory, require little training, and deal with momentary content that constantly changes during the process. Controlled processing requires much effort. It occurs in novel situations calling for the integration of information and requires relatively little training or change in specific content. The two processes are assumed to be interactive. For example, when a client attempts to elicit support or compassion from an interviewer, he or she may verbalize well-practiced, "automatic," self-deprecatory statements or other descriptive responses that have effectively elicited support from others on previous occasions. The distinction between controlled and automatic processes has been made with regard to memory as well as attention and perception (Posner & Snyder, 1975). It has far-reaching implications both for the conduct of clinical interviews and for the structure of cognitive–behavioral treatment methods.

In general, automatic responses, whether they are verbal or motor, represent an effective repertoire for dealing with most everyday situations. They reduce cognitive demands and simplify execution of myriads of daily routines. In clients, however, some of these responses have become well established and automatic even though they are ineffective and have social effects that mark them as pathological. The clinician's task is to alter such problematic automatic behaviors. Inadequate or symptomatic (motor or verbal) responses are usually overlearned, stereotyped, and rigid. They can be viewed as well-established conditioned responses or automatic responses that need to be changed. These overlearned responses also frequently serve to avoid confronting a problem or to escape from recognizing the need for change.

When a behavior change is attempted, automatic responses impede progress since their alteration is a prerequisite to the change process and they are difficult to change. To change them, controlled processing is required. But this requires substantial effort and is demanding (and sometimes aversive) to both client and therapist. If a universal rule for therapy can be stated at all, it is that during the change process the client must be aided to produce verbal and motor behaviors in interactions and self-reactions that are predominatly nonstereotyped, relatively novel, initially low in frequency of occurrence, and have the characteristics of controlled processing. Control of cognitive and verbal responses is then shifted so that the behavior becomes rule governed, rather than elicited by specific stimuli. Put in common language, the client must learn to think and act differently, more flexibly and more daringly during the transition process.

This change from automatic to controlled processing characterizes initial progress in interview or instigation therapy (Kanfer & Phillips, 1969). For lasting therapeutic effectiveness, the newly learned responses must again become stereotyped, overlearned, and elicited quickly by environmental or self-generated stimuli without intervening complex cognitive behaviors. Thus, starting with the disruption of ineffective or self-defeating automatic responses, the clinician guides the client through a process that utilizes self-regulatory behaviors, problem solving, decision making, and similar complex activities, until new and more satisfactory behavior patterns are found, overlearned, and stabilized.

Clinical interviews yield mostly automatic responses when an interviewer uses questions or instructions to which the client can respond with minimum effort or concentration, and without infraction of common social rules of courtesy. Responses such as "I feel nervous"; "I like my job"; "I just don't remember what happened"; "I don't know what made me do it" illustrate automatic responses that are obstacles to the process of change. These behaviors are highly effective in day-to-day communication. Automatic responses, of course, are also established in self-reactions and in narration of past events. Their use is well illustrated in the client's "cover story," as described by H. S. Sullivan (1954).

In interviews, automatic responses serve to shift responsibility for the next transaction back to the interviewer. Progress in interviews can therefore be enhanced by strategies that activate controlled processing. Cues requiring the client to reframe and integrate memories and verbal behaviors from new perspectives can provide the structure within which the change process proceeds. In general, interview procedures in which novel responses are generated tend to yield more controlled processing than approaches in which the client can depend on long-established verbal or cognitive sequences or on often-rehearsed standard responses to maintain the interaction.

TEMPORAL AND SENSORY SOURCES OF
INFORMATION IN THE INTERVIEW

Interview information can refer to events occurring at different points in time in relation to the interview. The accuracy of self-reports is presumed to vary as a function of time elapsed since occurrence of the described event and the comprehensiveness, specificity, and observability of the contents. Many interviewers have developed techniques for assisting clients to report accurately and to incorporate sensory, autonomic, motoric, and cognitive domains in their reports. Role-play, think-aloud procedures, self-monitoring assignments, and interpersonal process recall are examples of such aids. Their use is often based on the assumption that both information for the interviewer and constructive feedback for the client can further the change process.

Ericsson and Simon (1980) provided a model of the mechanisms by which verbal reports are generated. The model is based on information-processing theory (Anderson & Bower, 1973; Bower, 1978; Simon, 1979) and assumes that information is held for a brief time in short-term memory (STM), then either lost or shifted to long-term memory (LTM). Ericsson and Simon distinguish two dimensions in categorizing verbalizations: (1) the time of the report and (2) the requirement either for direct articulation of stored information (e.g., talking aloud) or for reports requiring intermediate processing (e.g., explaining an impression or an action). Differences in underlying processes on the first dimension are attributed to whether STM or LTM is involved in retrieval. On the second dimension, direct reports differ from those requiring intermediate processing because the latter require transformation (verbal encoding) from information to which a person attends in another mode, as in making judgements or describing emotional states. This view is consistent with models that presume differences in semantic memory (for language-encoded information) and for episodic memory (for information about specific events).

The model suggests refinements in the manner in which interview probes are set up. For example, recognizing that requests for general information about a past event yield less comprehensive information with a lower order of accuracy than specific information or present events can guide the interviewer to ask specific questions. On the other hand, such a probe can yield information about the client's intermediate processing, such as the manner in which inferences are made. Further, probes for information about any point in time or in any mode yield different answers when they concern inputs to which the client had attended, rather than when they require reconstructions about behavioral dimensions that were not attended to (e.g., "Where were you sitting when you first got anxious?"). By structuring probes, the clinician can thus guide reports to enhance production of information about events, the client's own cognitive processes, or the client's inferences about experiences. Finally, as we have previously indicated, probes may be structured to reference automatic or controlled processes, thereby indicating the specificity of the reply to the unique occurence of the event under examination.

The model proposed by Ericsson and Simon suggests that inconsistencies between verbal reports and events are likely when the required information had not been attended to at the time the event occurred (therefore not stored in STM). For the clinician, it is of particular interest to note that automatic responses (both interactional and self-reactive), often the most critical elements in reports of problematic episodes, are presumed to leave no trace in STM (Fisk & Schneider, 1984). Therefore, veridical reports can hardly be expected, except when retrospective reconstructions and inferences happen to coincide with the event. Of course, clinical experience has long taught us to observe symptomatic behaviors or problematic interactions, rather than to rely on client reports. The authors, as others, have often experienced gross distortions in reports about problematic situations and assisted clients to correct their perceptions by instructed self-monitoring or video replays. The laboratory-based model of Ericsson and Simon points to the type of studies needed to yield more systematic and precise rules about clinical inferences on the veridicality of verbal reports. It also suggests the need for integrating knowledge of the limitations and strengths imposed by the characteristics of human information processing in interviews and related prescripted experiences.

THE PERCEIVED ORIGIN OF INFORMATION

A growing set of experiments has demonstrated the advantages of a self-management approach to therapeutic change: perceived control over behavior (Langer, 1978, 1983; Perlmuter & Monty, 1979), opportunities for choices (Brigham, 1979; Kanfer & Grimm, 1978), participation in goal setting and program execution (Locke, Shaw, Saari, & Latham, 1981), and attributions of outcomes to one's own actions or abilities (Kopel & Arkowitz, 1975; Sonne & Janoff, 1979) have been shown to enhance motivation, performance, and treatment adherence. Continued self-regulation has also been suggested for enhancing the durability of treatment effects (Kirschenbaum & Tomarken, 1982). In the interview, the self-management approach advocates that clients take responsibility for making commitments (Kanfer, 1980; Kanfer & Grimm, 1980; Kanfer & Karoly, 1972). In all phases of therapy, generation of new experiences in imagination and reality are viewed as critical for developing and maintaining motivation and change. It is presumed that clients act more readily on specific ideas, information, and insights that *they* verbalize, than when offered similar contents offered by the clinician. For optimal use of this strategy, it is important for clinicians to use interview techniques that enable clients to differentiate sources of control as internal or external in the analysis of their problem behaviors. Additionally, clinicians should encourage attributions of decisions and actions to clients in the planning and execution of behavioral changes.

Johnson and Raye (1981) deal with these problems in a model of "reality monitoring." The model proposes that memories generated by external events differ from internally generated memories. The latter have more contextual and sensory attributes, and more semantic details; paradoxically, less information about cognitive operations is available. When a person attempts to decide whether information initially was obtained from an external or internal source, the decision is influenced by the attributes of the memory, as well as by reasoning processes relating the specific content to class characteristics of the two types and to general assumptions about memory processes. The Johnson and Raye model offers suggestions about variables that would make attributions to external or internal origins difficult or easy.

Many clinical procedures attempt to shift the locus of attributions. Careful prompting of a client to attend to specific dimensions (attributes) of an episode, or the prescription of a heuristic for decisions about the source of memories, may help to guide the client's attributions (in either direction) toward therapeutic objectives. Since recalled events often form the motivational and decisional basis for further behavior, the development of methods for altering the evaluation of memories or for creating memories that facilitate change appears a promising clinical application of the Johnson and Raye model.

The research conducted by Johnson, Raye, and their coworkers (e.g., Johnson, Taylor, & Raye, 1977; Raye, Johnson, & Taylor, 1980) to support the model assumption about the differences between memories of perceived and self-generated events clearly demonstrated the superiority of self-generated over externally provided information. For example, in one study college students were exposed to two word lists; one prepared by the experimenter, the other generated by the subjects. Words were presented with varying frequencies. Subjects made more accurate frequency estimates for self-generated words. In other studies similar results were obtained for identification of the sources of generation and free recall. These findings are also consistent with a self-management framework for behavior change (Karoly & Kanfer, 1982). They strongly suggest giving systematic attention to structuring therapeutic procedures and tasks so that information is better remembered and accurately attributed. In some situations, the blurring of the distinction may be useful. For example, daydreams or images can be supplemented by concrete actions (acting out in role play) to provide additional specific (perceptual) information, thus aiding recall and attributions for subsequent decisions. Other techniques include requesting clients to review interview content in their own words. Role play (or creating in vivo situations) is used to create motoric, sensory, and autonomic cues and responses that are congruent with the new ways of talking and thinking learned in therapy.

While clinicians have long used techniques that fit the conceptualizations described here, a better understanding of the research underlying these working models should permit refinement of clinical procedures by taking advantage of the most effective variables and processes to increase the rate of change, and to maximize the durability of therapeutic effects. The foregoing discussion is intended as an illustration of the need for increased attention by behavior therapists to the rapidly growing body of empirical findings on cognitive processes.

There are numerous other examples from experiments in information processing that invite translation of data to clinical procedures. Increasingly, such isolated translations are appearing. There is a growing literature that reflects an awareness of the need to incorporate cognitive research into the mainstream of clinical psychology (Arnkoff, 1980; Cantor & Kihlstrom, 1980; Goldfried, 1980; Greenberg & Safran, 1980; Mahoney, 1980; Safran & Greenberg, 1982; Turk & Speers, 1983; and others). A firm grounding of the current generation of clinicians in both cognitive research and clinical practice promises to narrow the gap between clinical model and experimental and social psychology.

What will eventually be needed, however, is a coherent framework that provides practical guidelines for the clinician on dealing with the various stages of information processing in the context of clinical interactions. The characteristics of perception, organization, and memory need to be called on to develop more efficient therapy methods, just as learning principles have served to improve clinical technology. Given the demands and complexity of the clinician's tasks, a broad philosophical and scientific base is needed from which short-term intervention strategies are quickly and easily derived. In fact, none of the existing therapy models fits this requirement. One resolution to this problem appears to be a trend toward models of the clinical change process that cut across theories. Such systems-oriented approaches (Kanfer & Grimm, 1980; Prochaska & DiClemente, 1982; Sundberg, Taplin, & Tyler, 1983; Taplin, 1980) integrate various domains of psychological research, irrespective of their theoretical origins, into a comprehensive working model of the clinical process. These models could provide the general framework for the type of integration of data from the IPP and other subfields of psychology we have proposed here.

Summary

Behavior therapists have long been reluctant to make use of data from cognitive psychology. To a large extent the conceptual and methodological differences lie not only in the appeal to environmental or internal events as causes of behavior and the use of mental (internal) constructs (Skinner, 1977). These schisms also arise out of differences in objectives. While behaviorists have aimed for prediction and control of organism–environment interactions, cognitivists leaned toward the study of organizing processes involved in perception, language, and memory. With this difference in focus, early attempts to apply cognitive paradigms to the entire clinical enterprise (e.g., Breger, 1969) clashed with basic behavioral tenets. But they also demonstrated that the theory-oriented research of the cognitivists at that time did not yield directly applicable clinical procedures. Its thrust was aimed mainly at the underlying framework within which clinicians operate. Recent work in cognitive psychology is increasingly attending to variables encountered in day-to-day behaviors, while behavior therapists are stressing the role of cognitive events in new assessment and treatment procedures. This convergence of interest facilitates an integration of data from the behavioral and cognitive literatures, yet it should allow a synthesis to occur without abandonment of a focus on behavior, the centrality of learning processes, or the overarching theoretical framework of the behavioral clinician.

In this chapter, we attempted to demonstrate that behavior therapy's early attempts to exclude unobservable behavior and constructs was found to be too limited for application to the entire clinical enterprise. For the core of behavioral models to remain viable, the models must be supplemented by variables and data from other subfields of psychology besides conditioning. We have attempted to show why this is necessary and to highlight particular clusters of variables and findings that are pertinent to such a broadening of the behavioral clinician's range. Instead of simply abandoning the entire conceptual foundation of behavior therapy, we proposed an alternative, an integration of variables that constitute parameters on the biological and social information processing functions of the human organism. Examples of particular IPP variables were chosen and strategies and tactics in the interview based on them were described. Finally, while we presented some limitations of an over-encompassing adoption of theory and data from the IPP, we argued that the resulting integration shows greater promise for a "liberalized" science and technology of human behavior than either the behaviorists or cognitivists can provide alone.

References

Anderson, J. R., & Bower, G. H. (1973). *Human associative memory*. Hillsdale, NJ: Lawrence Erlbaum & Associates.

Arnkoff, D. B. (1980). Psychotherapy from the perspective of cognitive theory. In M. J. Mahoney (Ed.), *Psychotherapy process: Current issues and future directions* (pp. 339–361). New York: Plenum Press.

Atkinson, R. C., Bower, G. H., & Crothers, E. J. (1965). *An introduction to mathematical learning theory*. New York: John Wiley & Sons.

Averill, J. R. (1983). Studies on anger and aggression: Implications for theories of emotion. *American Psychologist, 38,* 1145–1160.

Bandura, A. (1965). Behavioral modification through modeling procedures. In L. Krasner & L. P. Ullmann (Eds.), *Research in behavior modification: New developments and implications.* Holt, Rinehart, & Winston.

Bandura, A. (1969). *Principles of behavior modification.* New York: Holt, Rinehart, & Winston.

Bandura, A. (1974). Behavior theory and the models of man. *American Psychologist, 29,* 859–869.

Barlow, D. H., Hayes, S. C., & Nelson, R. O. (1984). *The scientist practitioner.* New York: Pergamon Press.

Beck, A. T. (1976). *Cognitive therapy and the emotional disorders.* New York: International Universities Press.

Bernstein, D. A., & Paul, G. (1971). Some comments on therapy analogue research with small animal "phobias." *Journal of Behavior Therapy and Experimental Psychiatry, 2,* 225–237.

Bower, G. H. (1978). Contacts of cognitive psychology with social learning theory. *Cognitive Therapy and Research, 2,* 123–146.

Breger, L. (Ed.). (1969). *Clinical-cognitive psychology.* New York: Prentice-Hall.

Breger, L., & McGaugh, J. L. (1965). A critique and reformulation of "learning theory" approaches to psychotherapy and neurosis. *Psychological Bulletin, 63,* 338–358.

Brehm, S. S. (1976). *The application of social psychology to clinical practice.* Washington, D.C.: Hemisphere Publishing.

Brigham, T. A. (1979). Some effects of choice on academic performance. In L. C. Perlmuter & R. A. Monty (Eds.), *Choice and perceived control* (pp. 131–142). Hillsdale, NJ: Lawrence Earlbaum & Associates.

Cantor, N. A., & Kihlstrom, J. F. (Eds.). (1980). *Personality, cognition, and social interaction.* Hillsdale, NJ: Lawrence Earlbaum & Associates.

Cautela, J. R. (1971). Covert conditioning. In A. Jacobs & L. B. Sachs (Eds.), *The psychology of private events.* New York: Academic Press.

Cronbach, L. J. (1975). Beyond the two disciplines of scientific psychology. *American Psychologist, 30,* 116–127.

Dember, W. N. (1974). Motivation and the cognitive revolution. *American Psychologist, 29,* 161–168.

Doke, L. A., & Risley, T. R. (1972). The organization of day-care environments: Required vs. optional activities. *Journal of Applied Behavior Analysis, 5,* 405–420.

Dollard, J., & Miller, N. E. (1950). *Personality and psychotherapy.* New York: McGraw-Hill.

Dulany, D. E. (1961). Hypotheses and habits in verbal "operant conditioning". *Journal of Abnormal and Social Psychology, 63,* 251–263.

Ellis, A. (1962). *Reason and emotion in psychotherapy*. New York: Stuart.

Ericsson, K. S., & Simon, H. A. (1980). Verbal reports as data. *Psychological Reports, 87*, 215–251.

Erwin, E. (1978). *Behavior therapy: Scientific, philosophical, and moral foundations*. Cambridge: Cambridge University Press.

Estes, W. K. (1955). Theory of elementary predictive behavior: An exercise in the behavioral interpretation of a mathematical model. In *Mathematical models of human behavior: Proceedings of a symposium*. Stanford, CT: Dunlap & Associates.

Estes, W. K. (1972). Reinforcement in human behavior. *American Scientist, 60*, 723–729.

Eysenck, H. J. (1959). Learning theory and behavior therapy. *Journal of Mental Science, 105*, 61–75.

Ferster, C. B. (1965). Classification of behavioral pathology. In L. Krasner & L. P. Ullmann (Eds.), *Research in behavior therapy*. New York: Holt, Rinehart, & Winston.

Fisher, J. D., Nadler, A., & DePaulo, B. M. (Eds.). (1983). *New directions in helping, Vol. 1*. New York: Academic Press.

Fisk, A. D., & Schneider, W. (1984). Memory as a function of attention, level of processing, and automatization. *Journal of Experimental Psychology: Learning, Memory, and Cognition, 10*, 181–197.

Frank, J. D. (1961). *Persuasion and healing*. Baltimore, MD: John Hopkins Press.

Garfield, S. L., & Bergin, A. E. (Eds.). (1978). *Handbook of psychotherapy and behavior change*. New York: Wiley.

Gergen, K. J. (1982). *Toward transformation in social knowledge*. New York: Springer.

Goldfried, M. R. (1980). Toward the delineation of therapeutic change principles. *American Psychologist, 35*, 991–999.

Goldfried, M. R. (1980). Psychotherapy as coping skills training. In M. J. Mahoney (Ed.), *Psychotherapy process: Current issues and future directions* (pp. 89–119). New York: Plenum Press.

Goldstein, A. P. (1980). Relationship-enhancement methods. In F. H. Kanfer and A. P. Goldstein (Eds.), *Helping people change, Revised 2nd Edition*. New York: Pergamon Press.

Goldstein, A. P., Heller, K., & Sechrest, L. B. (1966). *Psychotherapy and the psychology of behavior change*. New York: Wiley.

Gottman, J., Notarius, C., Gonzo, J., & Markman, H. (1976). *A couples' guide to communication*. Champaign, IL: Research Press.

Greenberg, L. S., & Safran, J. D. (1980). Encoding, information processing, and the cognitive behavioural therapies. *Canadian Psychology, 21*, 59–66.

Greeno, J. G. (1980). Psychology of learning 1960–1980: One participant's observations. *American Psychologist, 35*, 713–728.

Guthrie, E. R. (1935). *Psychology of learning*. New York: Harper.

Hersen, M., & Barlow, D. H. (1976). *Single case experimental designs*. New York: Pergamon Press.

Hilgard, E. R. (1980). Consciousness and contemporary psychology. In M. Rosenzweig & L. Porter (Eds.), *Annual review of psychology*. Palo Alto, CA: Annual Reviews.

Homme, L. E. (1965). Perspectives in psychology, XXIV: Control of coverants: The operants of the mind. *Psychological Record, 15*, 501–511.

Hull, C. L. (1943). *Principles of behavior*. New York: Appleton-Century-Crofts.

Johnson, M. K., & Raye, C. L. (1981). Reality monitoring. *Psychological Review, 88*, 67–85.

Johnson, M. K., Taylor, T. H., & Raye, C. L. (1977). Fact and fantasy: The effects of internally generated events on apparent frequency of externally generated events. *Memory and Cognition, 5*, 116–122.

Kaminski, G. (1970). *Verhaltenstheorie und verhaltensmodifikation.* Stuttgart: Klett.

Kanfer, F. H. (1965). Vicarious human reinforcement: A glimpse into the black box. In L. Krasner & L. P. Ullmann (Eds.), *Research in behavior modification: New developments and implications.* New York: Holt, Rinehart, & Winston.

Kanfer, F. H. (1966). Implications of conditioning techniques for interview therapy. *Journal of Counseling Psychology, 13,* 171–177.

Kanfer, F. H. (1968). Verbal conditioning: A review of its current status. In T. R. Dixon & D. L. Horton (Eds.), *Verbal behavior and its relation to general S–R theory* (pp. 254–290). Englewood Cliffs, NJ: Prentice-Hall.

Kanfer, F. H. (1970). Self-regulation: Research, issues, and speculations. In C. Neuringer & K. L. Michael (Eds.), *Behavior modification in clinical psychology.* New York: Appleton-Century-Crofts.

Kanfer, F. H. (1971). The maintenance of behavior by self-generated stimuli and reinforcement. In A. Jacobs & L. B. Sachs (Eds.), *The Psychology of private events* (pp. 39–57). New York: Academic Press.

Kanfer, F. H. (1975). Self-management methods. In F. H. Kanfer & A. P. Goldstein (Eds.), *Helping people change* (pp. 309–356). New York: Pergamon Press.

Kanfer, F. H. (1980). Self-management methods. In F. H. Kanfer & A. P. Goldstein (Eds.), *Helping people change, Revised 2nd Edition.* New York: Pergamon Press.

Kanfer, F. H. (1984). Self-management in clinical and social interventions. In R. P. McGlynn, J. E. Maddux, C. D. Stoltenberg, & J. H. Harvey (Eds.), *Interfaces in Psychology, Vol. 2.* Lubbock, TX: University of Texas Tech. Press.

Kanfer, F. H., & Busemeyer, J. R. (1982). The use of problem-solving and decision-making in behavior therapy. *Clinical Psychology Review, 2,* 239–266.

Kanfer, F. H., & Grimm, L. G. (1978). Freedom of choice and behavioral change. *Journal of Consulting and Clinical Psychology, 46,* 873–878.

Kanfer, F. H., & Grimm, L. G. (1980). Managing clinical change: A process model of therapy. *Behavior Therapy, 4,* 419–444.

Kanfer, F. H., & Hagerman, S. (1981). The role of self-regulation. In L. P. Rehm (Ed.), *Behavior therapy for depression: Present status and future directions.* New York: Academic Press.

Kanfer, F. H., & Karoly, P. (1972). Self-control: A behavioristic excursion into the lion's den. *Behavior Therapy, 3,* 398–416.

Kanfer, F. H., May, M., Oberberger, M., & Brengelman, J. C. (1978). Planning an institution for behavior therapy: A project report. *Behavioral Analysis and Modification, 2,* 146–162.

Kanfer, F. H., & Phillips, J. S. (1966). Behavior therapy: A panacea for all ills or a passing fancy? *Archives of General Psychiatry, 15,* 114–128.

Kanfer, F. H., & Phillips, J. S. (1969). A survey of current behavior therapies and a proposal for classification. In C. Franks (Ed.), *Behavior therapy: Appraisal and status* (pp. 445–475). New York: McGraw-Hill.

Kanfer, F. H., & Saslow, G. (1965). Behavioral analysis: An alternative to diagnostic classification. *Archives of General Psychiatry, 12,* 529–538.

Kantor, J. R. (1924). *Principles of psychology.* Bloomington, IN: Principia Press.

Karoly, P., & Kanfer, F. H. (Eds.). (1982). *Self-management and behavior change.* New York: Pergamon Press.

Kazdin, A. (1978). *History of behavior modification.* Baltimore, MD: University Park Press.

Kazdin, A. E. (1982). *Single case research designs: Methods for clinical and applied settings.* New York: Oxford Press.

Kelly, G. (1955). *The psychology of personal constructs.* New York: W. W. Norton.

Kendall, P. C., & Hollon, S. D. (Eds.). (1979). *Cognitive behavioral interventions.* New York: Academic Press.

Kendler, T. S. (1961). Concept formation. *Annual Review of Psychology, 12,* 447–472.

Kirschenbaum, D. S., & Tomarken, A. J. (1982). On facing the generalization problem: The study of self-regulatory failure. In P. C. Kendall (Ed.), *Advances in cognitive-behavioral research and therapy, Vol. 1* (pp. 119–200). New York: Academic Press.

Kopel, S., & Arkowitz, H. (1975). The role of attribution and self-perception in behavior change: Implications for behavior therapy. *Genetic Psychology Monographs, 92,* 175–212.

Krasner, K. L. (1962). The therapist as a social reinforcing machine. In H. H. Strupp & L. Luborsky (Eds.), *Research in psychotherapy, Vol. 2.* Washington, DC: American Psychological Association.

Krasner, K. L., & Krasner, K. M. (1973). Token economies and other planned environments. *Behavior Modification—an overview.* (pp. 351–384). Washington, DC: The National Society for the Study of Education.

Krasner, K. L., & Ullmann, L. P. (1965). *Research in behavior modification: New developments and implications.* New York: Holt, Rinehart, & Winston.

Kuhn, T. S. (1970). *The structure of scientific revolutions, Second edition.* Chicago: University of Chicago Press.

Lang, P. (1983). Psychophysiology of anxiety disorders. Paper presented at the NIMH conference on Anxiety and Anxiety Disorders. Sterling Forest, New York.

Langer, E. J. (1978). Rethinking the role of thought in social interaction. In J. H. Harvey, W. J. Ickes, & R. F. Kidd (Eds.), *New directions in attribution research, Vol. 2.* Potomac, MD: Earlbaum.

Langer, E. J. (1983). *The psychology of control.* Beverly Hills, CA: Sage.

Lindsley, O. R. (1964). Direct measurement and prosthesis of retarded behavior. *Journal of Education, 147,* 62–81.

Locke, E. A. (1971). Is "behavior therapy" behavioristic? *Psychological Bulletin, 76,* 318–327.

Locke, E. A., Shaw, K. N., Saari, L. M., & Latham, G. P. (1981). Goal setting and task performance. *Psychological Bulletin, 90,* 125–152.

Loevinger, J. (1969). Theories of ego development. In L. Breger (Ed.), *Clinical cognitive psychology* (pp. 83–135). New York: Prentice-Hall.

London, P. (1972). The end of ideology in behavior modification. *American Psychologist, 27,* 913–920.

Mahoney, M. J. (1974). *Cognition and behavior modification.* Cambridge, MA: Ballinger.

Mahoney, M. J. (1977). Reflections on the cognitive-learning trend in psychotherapy. *American Psychologist, 32,* 5–13.

Mahoney, M. J. (Ed.). (1980). *Psychotherapy process: Current issues and future directions.* New York: Plenum Press.

Manicas, P. T., & Secord, P. F. (1983). Implications for psychology of the new philosophy of science. *American Psychologist, 38,* 399–413.

Meichenbaum, D. (1977). *Cognitive-behavior modification: An integrative approach.* New York: Plenum Press.

Miller, N. E. (1959). Liberalization of basic S–R concepts: Extensions to conflict behavior, motivation, and social learning. In S. Koch (Ed.), *Psychology, a study of a science, Vol. 2.* New York: McGraw-Hill.

Mischel, W. (1973). Toward a cognitive social learning reconceptualization of personality. *Psychological Review, 80,* 252–283.

Mischel, W. (1979). On the interface of cognition and personality. *American Psychologist, 34,* 740–754.

Mook, D. G. (1983). In defense of external invalidity. *American Psychologist, 38,* 379–387.

Patterson, G. R., Reid, J. B., Jones, R. R., & Conger, R. E. (1975). *Social learning approach to family intervention.* Eugene, OR: Castalia Publishing.

Paul, G. (1969). Behavior modification research: Design and tactics. In C. M. Franks (Ed.), *Behavior therapy: Appraisal and status*. New York: McGraw-Hill.

Perlmuter, L. C., & Monty, R. A. (Eds.). (1979). *Choice and perceived control* (pp. 131–142). Hillsdale, NJ: Lawrence Earlbaum & Associates.

Posner, M. I., & Snyder, C. R. (1975). Attention and cognitive control. In R. L. Solso (Ed.), *Information processing and cognition*. Hillsdale, NJ: Lawrence Earlbaum & Associates.

Prochaska, J. O., & DiClemente, C. O. (1982). Transtheoretical therapy: Toward a more integrative model of change. *Psychotherapy: Theory, Research, and Practice, 19*, 276–288.

Rachman, S. (Ed.) (1963). *Critical analysis of psychoanalysis*. Oxford: Pergamon Press.

Raye, C. L., Johnson, M. K., & Taylor, T. H. (1980). Is there something special about memory for internally generated information? *Memory and Cognition, 8*, 141–148.

Reppucci, N. D., & Saunders, J. T. (1974). Social psychology of behavior modification: Problems of implementation in natural settings. *American Psychologist, 29*, 649–660.

Rescorla, R. A. (1966). Predictability and number of pairings in Pavlovian fear conditioning. *Psychonomic Science, 4*, 383–384.

Rescorla, R. A. (1967). Pavlovian conditioning and its proper control procedures. *Psychological Review, 74*, 71–80.

Rogers-Warren, A., & Warren, S. (Eds.). (1977). *Ecological perspectives in behavioral analysis*. Baltimore, MD: University Park Press.

Rotter, J. B. (1954). *Social learning and clinical psychology*. New York: Prentice-Hall.

Safran, J. D., & Greenberg, L. S. (1982). Cognitive appraisal and reappraisal: Implications for clinical practice. *Cognitive Therapy and Research, 6*, 251–258.

Schneider, W., & Shiffrin, R. M. (1977). Controlled and automatic human information processing: I. Detection, search, and attention. *Psychological Review, 84*, 1–66.

Shiffrin, R. M., & Schneider, W. (1977). Controlled and automatic human information processing: II. Perceptual learning, automatic attending, and a general theory. *Psychological Review, 84*, 127–150.

Shoben, E. J., Jr. (1949). Psychotherapy as a problem in learning theory. *Psychological Bulletin, 46*, 366–392.

Simon, H. A. (1979). Information processing models of cognition. *Annual Review of Psychology, 30*, 363–396.

Simon, H. A. (1981). Studying human intelligence by creating artificial intelligence. *American Scientist, 69*, 300–309.

Skinner, B. F. (1953). *Science and human behavior*. New York: Macmillan.

Skinner, B. F. (1957). *Verbal behavior*. New York: Appleton–Century–Crofts.

Skinner, B. F. (1974). *About behaviorism*. New York: Alfred A. Knopf.

Skinner, B. F. (1977). Why I am not a cognitive psychologist? *Behaviorism, 5*, 1–10.

Sonne, J. L., & Janoff, D. (1979). The effect of treatment attributions on the maintenance of weight reduction: A replication and extension. *Cognitive Therapy and Research, 3*, 389–398.

Spence, K. W., & Spence, J. T. (Eds.). (1968). *The psychology of learning and motivation: Advances in research and theory*. New York: Academic Press.

Sullivan, H. S. (1954). *The psychiatric interview*. New York: W. W. Norton.

Sundberg, N. D., Taplin, J. R., & Tyler, L. E. (1983). *Introduction to clinical psychology*. New York: Prentice-Hall.

Suppes, P. (1975). From behaviorism to neobehaviorism. *Theory and Decision, 6*, 269–285.

Taplin, J. R. (1980). Implications of general systems theory for assessment and intervention. *Professional Psychology, 11*, 722–727.

Tolman, E. C. (1932). *Purposive behavior in animals and man*. New York: Century.

Turk, D. C., & Speers, M. A. (1983). Cognitive schemata and cognitive processes in cognitive-behavioral interventions: Going beyond the information given. *Advances in Cognitive-Behavioral Research and Therapy, 2,* 1–31.

Ullmann, L. P. (1970). On cognitions and behavior therapy. *Behavior Therapy, 1,* 201–204.

Weary, G., & Mirels, H. L. (Eds.). (1982). *Integration of clinical and social psychology.* New York: Oxford University Press.

Weiss, R. L. (1980). Strategic behavioral marriage therapy: Toward a model for assessment and intervention. In J. P. Vincent (Ed.), *Advances in family intervention, assessment, and theory, Vol. 1.* Greenwich, CT: Jai Press.

Willis, T. A. (Ed.). (1982). *Basic processes in helping relationships.* New York: Academic Press.

Wilson, G. D. (1968). Reversal of differential GSR conditioning by instructions. *Journal of Experimental Psychology, 76,* 491–493.

Wilson, G. T., & Evans, I. M. (1977). The therapist-client relationship in behavior therapy. In A. S. Gurman & A. M. Razin (Eds.), *Effective psychotherapy.* New York: Pergamon Press.

Winett, R. A. (1974). Behavior modification and social change. *Professional Psychology, 5,* 244–256.

Winett, R. A. (1980). An emerging approach to energy conservation. In D. M. Glenwick & L. Jason (Eds.), *Behavioral community psychology.* New York: Praeger.

Zifferblatt, S. M., & Hendricks, C. G. (1974). Applied behavioral analysis of societal problems: Population change, a case in point. *American Psychologist, 29,* 750–761.

Zilboorg, G. (1941). *A history of medical psychology.* New York: Norton.

Affect and Cognition in Behavior Therapy

RICHARD R. BOOTZIN

During the past 15 years, there has been a cognitive revolution in psychology in which explanatory models have increasingly relied upon cognitive variables. In the process, the role of affect has often been neglected or relegated to a role subordinate to cognition. The purpose of this chapter is to explore the role of affect and its relationship to cognition in psychopathology and treatment.

Behavior therapy, which developed during the 1950s and 1960s, drew primarily upon those theories of learning that minimized the role of cognitive mediation. Thus, behavioral models of psychopathology and treatment consisted of (1) Pavlovian conditioning to explain the acquisition and extinction of anxiety, (2) Mowrer's two-factor theory (Pavlovian conditioning of anxiety and the reinforcing effects of anxiety reduction) to explain the persistence of avoidance behavior, and (3) operant conditioning to explain the acquisition and extinction of instrumental behavior. A noteworthy aspect of early behavioral theories of clinical phenomena was the central role accorded affect. Aversive affect, such as anxiety, was assumed to be conditioned by means of Pavlovian principles. Treatments, such as systematic desensitization, were developed to countercondition anxiety.

35

Cognition and Theories of Learning

Increasingly, the learning theories upon which behavior therapy was based were modified to include cognitive mediating mechanisms. In one of the first studies of cognitive mediation, Miller (1935) demonstrated that a physiological response could be conditioned to a cognitive stimulus. Miller electrically shocked subjects when the letter *T* but not the number *4* was read out loud. Subjects were then instructed to think *T* and *4*, alternately, in a series of trials. Subjects had galvanic skin responses when they thought *T*, but not when they thought *4*.

Although Miller's research expanded Pavlovian conditioning to include cognitive stimuli, it did not challenge the basic model. Conditioned responses (CRs) would be elicited by conditioned stimuli (CSs) whether the stimuli were cognitive or overt. However, contemporaries of Miller, such as Tolman (1948), proposed a more explicit cognitive learning theory, and, thus, they are predecessors of the present–day cognitive behavior therapists. According to Tolman, learning resulted in a new cognitive organization that in turn mediated subsequent performance. In experiements on latent learning with rats in mazes, Tolman (1948) proposed that rats constructed cognitive maps of the maze during unreinforced exploratory trials. In later trials, when reinforcement was present, the rats ran the maze faster than those who did not get the earlier nonreinforced trials. From these experiments, Tolman concluded that reinforcement affected only the speed of performance, not the degree of learning. Learning, which, according to Tolman, was a cognitive process, took place without reinforcement.

Research in modeling and observational learning is the modern descendent of Tolman's research on latent learning. Modeling and observational learning experiments demonstrate that reinforcement is not necessary for learning, just as Tolman's research did. It has been found repeatedly that individuals can learn by observing others being reinforced (Rosenthal & Bandura, 1978). The person observing does not overtly engage in the response to be learned and is not directly reinforced for the response. Thus, observational learning must involve symbolic processes.

The type of learning proposed to be most relevant for the acquisition of emotional responses is Pavlovian conditioning. Even its most basic mechanisms have had cognitive reinterpretations. Recent theories of Pavlovian conditioning have focused on the information contained in the stimulus rather than on the traditional association of CS and UCS (unconditioned stimulus) through contiguity. For example, Wagner and Rescorla (1972) proposed that Pavlovian conditioning of a CS depends on the new information that the CS provides about the magnitude or occurrence of the UCS. This model explains findings such as the Kamin blocking effect that are contradictory to contiguity theories. Kamin (1969) found that if an animal is given a series of conditioning trials in which a particular CS (*B*) is always followed by a UCS, and then another series of conditioning trials with a compound CS (*A* and *B*) followed by the UCS, a CR is not elicited by *A* alone. According to the Wagner and Rescorla information model, *A* did not acquire associative strength when it was paired with *B* because it provided no new information about the occurrence of the UCS.

This type of cognitive model of conditioning has been generalized to fear acquisition and maintenance. Reiss (1980, Reiss & McNally, this volume, Chapter 5) proposed an expectancy model of fear acquisition in humans that derived from Wagner and Rescorla's information model. According to Reiss, Pavlovian conditioning is itself a cognitive process. "what is learned in Pavlovian conditioning is an expectation regarding the occurrence or nonoccurrence of a UCS onset or a change in UCS magnitude or duration" (1980, p. 387). However, conditioning is only one way to change expectancies. Cognitive learning and the observation of models change expectancies just as associative learning does.

In applying this model to phobias, Reiss (1980) identified two types of expectancies, danger and anxiety expectancies. Danger expectancy is the anticipation of physical danger or social rejection. Anxiety expectancy is the anticipation of anxiety, or the person's fear of becoming anxious. This is a useful distinction that may have important therapeutic consequences, not only for phobias, but for other emotional disorders, as well. Frequently a large component of a client's problem is that the individual is afraid of being anxious or depressed. Since it is not possible to develop a therapy that prevents the individual from ever experiencing aversive affect, it would be important to help reduce the fear of anxiety and depression. The identification of fear of anxiety is an apt illustration of how cognitive approaches can supplement traditional, noncognitive approaches to treatment.

The previous examples have dealt with ways in which the basic processes of learning involve cognitive or central processes. There has also been considerable interest in developing models for how the mind organizes and processes information. Many of these models rely upon the computer as their inspiration. As indicated by Kanfer and Hagerman (Chapter 1), information-processing models of attention, memory, and decision processes provide a rich source of hypotheses that may also lead to important modifications of theory and treatment in behavior therapy.

Cognition and Theories of Emotion

Just as theories of learning became more cognitive, so did theories of emotion. An important watershed was the proposal by Schachter and

Singer (1962) that emotion consisted of two components: (1) generalized physiological arousal, and (2) cognitive evaluation of the social context of the arousal. As proposed by Schachter and Singer, different emotions elicit the same pattern of physiological arousal. Consequently, it is the social context, and not the physiological arousal, that allows the person to distinguish anger from fear from elation. The experience of emotion, then, depends upon an ongoing cognitive appraisal and inference process. Schachter and Singer's two component theory of emotion generated considerable research and continues to be influential (see Mandler, 1984).

Theory and research on clinically disturbed affects, such as anxiety and depression, have also emphasized a cognitive component. For example, Beck (1967, 1976) and Ellis (1962) have articulated theories and developed therapies focused on helping depressed or anxious patients correct their perceptions and inferences about their social worlds. Similarly, Alloy, Clements, and Kolden (Chapter 13) explore the role of congitive attributional styles as constituting a diathesis for depression, and Reiss and McNally (Chapter 5) propose an expectancy theory of anxiety. These theorists agree with the maxim stated by Epictetus, "Men are disturbed not by things, but by the views they take of them."

Further demonstrations of the capacity of symbolic processes to elicit emotional responses have been documented by research in many areas including hypnosis, verbally induced anxiety (Lang, 1977; Sipprelle, 1967), verbally induced depression and elation (Velten, 1968), and aversive conditioning procedures such as covert sensitization that employ imagined CS–UCS pairs (Cautela, 1967).

Symbolic processes are also involved in the transmission of information about feared objects or events. Although there is little formal evidence, experience from everyday life clearly indicates that anxiety can be induced by information alone (Rachman, 1978). Information and instructions are constantly used—by parents, for example—to teach individuals to avoid situations that are dangerous and, therefore, to be feared. A boy walking alone at night in parts of a city that he has been told are dangerous may become anxious even if he has never previously been mugged or observed a mugging. The anticipation of feared consequences is likely to lead to cognitive rehearsal of the feared event, thereby inducing emotional arousal (Bootzin & Max, 1980).

As the preceding paragraphs indicate, the evidence that cognition can elicit and modulate the expression of emotion is overwhelming. This has led to the development of an information-processing model of emotional imagery that illustrates how the various components of affect could be centrally controlled (Lang, 1977, 1979). In this model, Lang (1979) assumes that images, including images with emotional content, are not represented in the brain as pictures. Rather he assumes that images are represented by logical propositions that indicate the interrelationships between sensory information, previous knowledge, and responses. This propositional network about an emotional image contains many connections, including knowledge about the components of the image, information about perceptual responses such as sense organ adjustments and body orientation to the stimulus, and response propositions about verbal behavior, autonomic responses, and avoidance behavior. The unique aspect of Lang's model is that the person's response is considered to be part of the emotional image. "The image is *not* a stimulus in the head to which we respond; it is itself an active response process" (Lang, 1979, p. 500).

It follows from this theory that an image would be likely to evoke an emotional response to the extent that propositions leading to that response have been activated. This position is in sharp contrast to theories of emotion based upon traditional associative conditioning. According to traditional conditioning theories, a stimulus can be conditioned to elicit a response by repeated pairings. Thus, a sensory image of the stimulus should elicit the response. According to Lang, however, what we learn through repeated pairings is a network of propositional statements regarding the relationships between stimuli, responses, and consequences. While repeated pairings may be one way to construct a network of propositional statements, it is not the only way. Thus, propositional networks could be constructed, maintained, and modified by means of symbolic processes.

The research to evaluate different means of constructing propositional networks has yet to be done. Thus far, Lang (1979) has focused primarily on evaluating the characteristics of images that engage the response propositions of the network. He found that descriptions of an image that focus entirely on the stimulus properties of a scene are not as effective in eliciting physiological responses as are descriptions that include response statements.

Lang's theory is an important integrative step. Although dealing only with imagery, it presents a model for affect in which verbal, physiological, and behavioral responses are controlled by a central mechanism. While the model could be characterized as cognitive because it relies upon the processing of propositional information, this does not imply that the person is aware of the process. In fact, some of the propositions of the network could deal with subjective awareness leading the individual to be either aware or unaware of aspects of the stimuli, responses, and their relationships. This type of model might be usefully extended to deal with the interrelationships between cognition, affect, and behavior more generally.

Cognition and Theories of Behavior Change

As theories of learning and emotion have become more cognitive, there has been a corresponding increase in the role of cognitive variables in theories of behavior change. Among the cognitive variables, expectancy has been the particular focus of many theories. Without attempting a comprehensive review, suffice it to say that of the different types of expectancies investigated, many are variations of expectancies of predictability and control. Both predictable aversive events and aversive events over which the organism can exert control are experienced as less stressful than those that are unpredictable or uncontrollable (Thompson, 1981).

Controllability, in particular, has been found to have wide-ranging psychological and physiological effects. For example, uncontrollable aversive events can affect the immune system and facilitate the growth of cancerous tumors (Laudenslager, Ryan, Drugan, Hyson, & Maier, 1983; Sklar & Anisman, 1979; Visintainer, Volpicelli, & Seligman, 1982). The organism's response to uncontrolled aversive events has also been used as a model for the psychological as well as the neurobiochemical features of depression (Miller, Rosellini, & Seligman, 1977; Weiss, 1982). Further, Bandura (1977, 1982) has made expectations of control (efficacy expectations) the central concept in his theory of avoidance behavior.

To understand the contributions of cognition to behavior change, it is important to ask how expectancy changes behavior (see Bootzin, 1985; Bootzin & Lick, 1979; Lick & Bootzin, 1975). A number of theories propose that behavior change is mediated directly by changes in expectancy (Bandura, 1977; Reiss, 1980; Shapiro, 1981). If a person expects to be able to cope with a problem, he or she will be better able to cope. If a person expects anticipatory anxiety to be diminished, emotional reactivity will be diminished. According to these theories, the final common pathway to predicting subsequent therapeutic change is the person's expectancy. However, not all expectancy manipulations are equally effective. Expectancy theories acknowledge that there are many ways that expectancies can be changed including performance feedback, associative learning, observational learning, information, persuasion, feedback from autonomic responses, and other symbolic processes. The more reliable the information upon which the expectancies are based, such as performance feedback (Bandura, 1977) or associative learning over many trials (Reiss, 1980), the stronger the expectancy and the more likely that subsequent behavior will correspond.

Expectancy is only one of many cognitive variables that have been investigated. Others include goals, plans, strategies, motives, and values (e.g., Mischel, 1973, 1979). Rather than limit discussion to one cognitive variable, expectancy, and its relationship to behavior, it may be useful to consider the broader context of cognitive organization. One way of conceptualizing the relationship of cognitive variables and behavior is by means of hypothesized cognitive structures such as schemas.

A schema is a knowledge structure that specifies the defining features of some stimulus domain. Schemas "help to structure, organize, and interpret new information; they facilitate encoding, storage, and retrieval of relevant information; they can affect the time it takes to process information, and the speed with which problems can be solved" (Crocker, Fiske, & Taylor, 1984). It may be useful to consider schemas, particularly self-schemas (Markus, 1983), as the organizing structure determining the interrelationships between cognitive structure, affect, and behavior (Bootzin, 1985). To illustrate, a common goal of therapy is to help change the patients' views of themselves from people who are victims of a problem to people who are capable of coping with the problem. The self-schemas of "victim" versus "coper" would have different implications regarding efficacy expectations, anticipatory affect, and willingness to confront the problem. It would be the organization of the schema that would determine the interrelationship between cognitive variables, affect, and behavior.

This proposal shares some similarities with the therapeutic use of "scripts" (i.e., stereotypical ways of interacting with others in particular situations) as suggested by Bower and Bower (1976). Bower and Bower proposed that individuals rewrite their own dysfunctional scripts to help learn new ways of behaving. Although scripts contain response components and are, thus, one way of integrating action and cognition, they are not as general as schemas, particularly self-schemas. As described by Markus (1983), "Self-schemas are knowledge structures about the self that derive from the past experience and organize and guide the processing of the self-relevant information contained in the individual's social experiences." They describe not only the past self, but also define future, possible selves. Self-schemas are active cognitive structures that frame situations, encode experience, and include generalizations about the self such as expectancies, values, and plans. Thus, scripts might be one of the many components included in self-schemas.

As indicated throughout this chapter, the contributions of cognitive mediating variables to theories of learning, emotion, and behavior change have been substantial. During the past decade, the change in underlying theory has been accompanied by the development of cognitive-behavior therapeutic interventions (e.g., Kendall & Hollan, 1979; Mahoney & Arnkoff, 1978; Meichenbaum, 1977). Further, many of the cognitive theoretical developments discussed here such as expectancies, propositional networks, and schemas will lead to new interventions. This reflects the coming of age of behavior therapy. Behavioral treatments have become comprehensive, multicomponent interventions that include attention to perceptions, inferences, and attitudes, in addition to dysfunctional behavior (e.g., Bootzin, in press; Lewinsohn, Hoberman, Teri, & Hautzinger, Chapter 11; Staats & Heiby, Chapter 10).

While the current focus on cognitive variables has been beneficial for both psychology and behavior therapy, care should be taken that noncognitive determinants of affect and behavior not be ignored. While cognition may have been neglected in earlier accounts of affect, it does not follow that affect is determined solely by cognitive variables. In fact, there is much to suggest that affect may be a primitive, automatic reaction under the control of variables other than cognition.

The Autonomy of Affect

There has been a vigorous debate about the temporal and causal sequence of affect and cognition. We have already discussed some of the evidence that cognition can produce and influence affect. However, such demonstrations do not indicate that this is the typical way that affect and cognition interact. In fact, our introspections often indicate that affect precedes cognition. We may feel angry, anxious, or elated without knowing why. It is only after reflection that we come up with a post hoc explanation. In addition, Schachter and Singer's (1962) proposition that the same physiological response underlies different emotions may have been wrong. In the past 20 years, knowledge has advanced in two areas that have implications for their theory. First, advances in biofeedback indicate that individuals can learn highly patterned physiological reactions (Schwartz, 1982). Thus, fear and anger have differential impact on heart rate, blood pressure, muscle tension, respiration rate, and numerous other physiological responses (Schwartz, Weinberger, & Singer, 1981). Second, there has been an explosion of research during the past 20 years in neurotransmitters and psychopharmacology. Drug effects have become increasingly specific and are often targeted to specific moods such as depression. As a result, it is unlikely that generalized, undifferentiated arousal underlies all emotions. Instead, it is likely that in many situations there are specific physiological reactions for specific emotions, and an ongoing cognitive appraisal process may not be necessary.

In contrast to the cognitive view, Zajonc (1980) has proposed that affect is precognitive, automatic, holistic, irrevocable, and substantially independent of cognition. In order to sharpen the contrast between affect and cognition, Zajonc uses *cognition* to refer primarily to conscious reflection. While others (e.g., Lazarus, 1982) would view cognition more broadly to involve attention, perception, and appraisal processes that could occur out-side of awareness, the unique feature of Zajonc's proposal for this chapter is his description of affect, not his description of cognition.

Further support for the relatively autonomous nature of affect comes from research on hemispheric lateralization. In general, the left hemisphere controls language and processes information in a logical, sequential fashion while the right hemisphere appears more involved in visual and spatial skills and processes information more intuitively and holistically. The under-standing and expression of affect are associated with right hemisphere func-tioning. Patients with lesions in the right cerebral hemisphere are often impaired in both the understanding (Geschwind, 1979) and display of emo-tion (Buck & Duffy, 1980). In addition, the left side of the face, which is controlled by the right hemisphere, communicates emotion more fully than does the right side (Sackheim & Gur, 1978).

Thus, the primitive, holistic, automatic, irrevocable nature of affect de-scribed by Zajonc (1980) may be a function of emotion being more under the control of the right, than the language-dominant left, hemisphere. It may be that we will need to develop treatments that are not as dependent upon language as are most of our current treatments. In this regard, it is noteworthy that exposure- and performance-based treatments are often more effective than verbal treatments. It may be that affect is more effec-tively altered by feedback from nonverbal aspects of treatment that can be processed directly by the right hemisphere.

On balance, there is considerable evidence for a system of emotional processing that is separate from cognitive processing. While more research is needed to sort out the reciprocal influences of cognition and affect, it is important not to neglect the investigation of affect. It should be remem-bered that frequently it is aversive affect that brings the client to therapy and it is the reduction of aversive affect that ultimately determines whether the therapy was successful. If the client remains anxious or depressed, it is little consolation that he or she is able to analyze misperceptions and identify biases in thinking more accurately. Cognitive therapies, while useful, are not always sufficient. In fact, it is often acknowledged that they have not fully delivered on their promise (Rachman, 1981). Part of the difficulty may be that cognitive therapies have not taken the autonomous nature of affect sufficiently into account.

References

Bandura, A. (1977). Self-efficacy: Toward a unifying theory of behavioral change. *Psychological Review, 84,* 191–215.

Bandura, A. (1982). Self-efficacy mechanism in human agency. *American Psychologist, 37,* 122–147.

Beck, A. T. (1967). *Depression: Clinical experimental, and theoretical aspects.* New York: Harper & Row.

Beck, A. T. (1976). *Cognitive therapy and the emotional disorders.* New York: International Universities Press.

Bootzin, R. R. (1985). The role of expectancy in behavior change. In L. White, G. E. Schwartz, & B. Tursky (Eds.), *Placebo: Clinical phenomena and new insights.* New York: Guilford Press.

Bootzin, R. R. (In press). Insomnia. In M. Hersen & C. G. Last (Eds.), *Behavior therapy casebook.* New York: Springer Publishing.

Bootzin, R. R., & Lick, J. R. (1979). Expectancies in therapy research: Interpretive artifact or mediating mechanism? *Journal of Consulting and Clinical Psychology, 47,* 852–855.

Bootzin, R. R., & Max, D. (1980). Learning and behavioral theories. In I. L. Kutash & L. B. Schlesinger (Eds.), *Handbook on stress and anxiety.* San Francisco: Jossey-Bass.

Bower, S. A., & Bower, G. H. (1976). *Asserting yourself: A practical guide for positive change.* Reading MA: Addison-Wesley.

Buck, R., & Duffy, R. (1980). Nonverbal communication of affect in brain-damaged patients. *Cortex, 16,* 351–362.

Cautela, J. R. (1967). Covert sensitization. *Psychological Reports, 20,* 459–468.

Crocker, J., Fiske, S. T., & Taylor, S. E. (1984). Schematic bases of belief change. In J. R. Eiser (Ed.), *Attitudinal judgment.* New York: Springer.

Ellis, A. (1962). *Reason and emotion in psychotherapy.* New York: Lyle Stuart.

Geschwind, N. (1979). Specialization of the human brain. *Scientific American, 241,* 180–201.

Kamin, L. J. (1969). Predictability, surprise, attention, and conditioning. In B. A. Campbell & R. M. Church (Eds.), *Punishment and aversive behavior.* New York: Appleton-Century-Crofts.

Kendall, P. C., & Hollon, S. D. (Eds.) (1979). *Cognitive-behavioral interventions: Theory, research, and procedures.* New York: Academic Press.

Lang, P. J. (1977). Imagery in therapy: An information processing analysis of fear. *Behavior Therapy, 9,* 962–886.

Lang, P. J. (1979). A bio-informational theory of emotional imagery. *Psychophysiology, 16,* 495–512.

Laudenslager, M. L., Ryan, S. M., Drugan, R. C., Hyson, R. L., & Maier, S. F. (1983). Coping and immunosuppression: Inescapable but not escapable shock suppresses lymphocyte proliferation. *Science, 221,* 568–570.

Lazarus, R. S. (1982). Thoughts on the relations between emotions and cognition. *American Psychologist, 37,* 1019–1024.

Lick, J., & Bootzin, R. R. (1975). Expectancy factors in the treatment of fear: Methodological and theoretical issues. *Psychological Bulletin, 82,* 917–931.

Mahoney, M. J., & Arnkoff, D. (1978). Cognitive and self-control therapies. In S. L. Garfield & A. E. Bergin (Eds.), *Handbook of psychotherapy and behavior change: An empirical analysis* (2nd ed.). New York: Wiley.

Mandler, G. (1984). *Mind and body: Psychology of emotion and stress.* New York: Norton.

Markus, H. (1983). Self-knowledge: An expanded view. *Journal of Personality, 51,* 543–565.

Meichenbaum, D. H. (1977). *Cognitive behavior modification: An integrative approach.* New York: Plenum Press.

Miller, N. E. (1935). *The influence of past experience upon the transfer of subsequent training.* Unpublished doctoral dissertation, Yale University.

Miller, W. R., Rosellini, R. A., & Seligman, M. E. P. (1977). Learned helplessness and depression. In J. D. Maser & M. E. P. Seligman (Eds.), *Psychopathology: Experimental models*. San Francisco: Freeman.

Mischel, W. (1973). Toward a cognitive social learning reconceptualization of personality. *Psychological Review, 80*, 252–283.

Mischel, W. (1979). On the interface of cognition and personality: Beyond the person-situation debate. *American Psychologist, 34*, 740–754.

Rachman, S. (1978). *Fear and courage*. San Francisco: Freeman.

Rachman, S. (1981). The primacy of affect: Some theoretical implications. *Behaviour Research and Therapy, 19*, 279–290.

Reiss, S. (1980). Pavlovian conditioning and human fear: An expectancy model. *Behavior Therapy, 11*, 380–396.

Rosenthal, T., & Bandura, A. (1978). Psychological modeling: Theory and practice. In S. L. Garfield & A. E. Bergin (Eds.), *Handbook of psychotherapy and behavior change: An empirical analysis* (2nd ed.). New York: Wiley.

Sackheim, H. A., & Gur, R. C. (1978). Lateral asymmetry in intensity of emotional expression. *Neuropsychologia, 16*, 473–481.

Schachter, S., & Singer, J. E. (1962). Cognitive, social, and physiological determinants of emotional state. *Psychological Review, 69*, 379–399.

Schwartz, G. E. (1982). Physiological patterning and emotion: Implications for the self-regulation of emotion. In K. R. Blankstein & J. Polivy (Eds.), *Self-control and self-modification of emotional behavior*. New York: Plenum Press.

Schwartz, G. E., Weinberger, D. A., & Singer, J. A. (1981). Cardiovascular differentiation of happiness, sadness, anger, and fear following imagery and exercise. *Psychosomatic Medicine, 43*, 343–364.

Shapiro, D. A. (1981). Comparative credibility of treatment rationales: Three tests of expectancy theory. *British Journal of Clinical Psychology, 20*, 111–122.

Sipprelle, C. Induced anxiety. *Psychotherapy: Theory, Research, and Practice, 4*, 34–40.

Sklar, L. S., & Anisman, H. (1979). Stress and coping factors influence tumor growth. *Science, 205*, 513–515.

Thompson, S. C. (1981). Will it hurt less if I control it? A complex answer to a simple question. *Psychological Bulletin, 90*, 89–101.

Tolman, E. C. (1948). Cognitive maps in rats and men. *Psychological Review, 55*, 189–208.

Velten, E. (1968). A laboratory task for induction of mood states. *Behaviour Research and Therapy, 6*, 473–482.

Visintainer, M. A., Volpicelli, J. R., & Seligman, M. E. P. (1982). Tumor rejection in rats after inescapable or escapable shock. *Science, 216*, 437–439.

Wagner, A. R., & Rescorla, R. A. (1972). Inhibition in Pavlovian conditioning: Applications of a theory. In R. A. Boakes & M. S. Halliday (Eds.), *Inhibition and learning*. New York: Academic Press.

Weiss, J. M. (1982). A model for neurochemical study of depression. Paper presented at the annual meeting of the American Psychological Association, Washington, DC, August.

Zajonc, R. (1980). Feeling and thinking. *American Psychologist, 35*, 151–175.

PART II

THEORIES OF ANXIETY AND FEAR

Behavior theory holds that fear and anxiety are conditioned emotional responses that are learned and unlearned in accordance with the principles of Pavlovian conditioning. Under this view, anxiety disorders are initiated when a neutral stimulus is associated with a traumatic event or conflict, and treatment (extinction) should be a simple matter of repeatedly presenting the anxiety-eliciting stimulus in the absence of traumatic events and conflict. The fact that therapy is not this simple is a central theoretical issue in the field of behavior therapy today.

Donald Levis' implosive theory is a defense of the long-standing behavioral position that fear and anxiety are Pavlovian conditioned responses. Levis argues the hypothesis of anxiety conservation to explain the persistence of anxiety reactions, and he critically examines some of the alternative views. Levis' chapter is a challenging reminder of the viability and sophistication of the conditioning theories that led to the development of effective behavioral therapies for anxiety disorders.

H. J. Eysenck addresses the problem of persistence of anxiety symptoms by invoking the concepts of incubation and preparedness. The former suggests circumstances under which anxiety reactions can become stronger in the absence of envi-

ronmental reinforcement, and the latter implies a biological reason for the persistence of certain fears. Eysenck shows how this theory permits predictions of interactive effects between the level of anxiety aroused by a stimulus and the length of time the stimulus needs to be exposed for extinction to occur.

Steven Reiss and Richard J. McNally explain the persistence of anxiety symptoms in terms of the concepts of anxiety expectancy and a personality variable called "anxiety sensitivity." In this view, some people suffering from anxiety disorders are overreacting to anticipations of becoming anxious because they have a high sensitivity for becoming anxious and fear the real or imagined consequences of anxiety symptoms. The expectancy model stands as a call for research on anxiety expectancies and the personality variable of anxiety sensitivity.

Arne Öhman, Ulf Dimberg, and Lars-Göran Öst explain the persistence of anxiety symptoms in terms of the concept of preparedness and other biological factors. They provide a fascinating discussion of the possible role of instincts in human anxiety and fear. Since behavior therapists sometimes overlook the possible role of biological factors, the chapter serves as a timely reminder of the need for more research on the interaction of biological and behavioral factors in the development of fear and anxiety.

3

Implosive Theory: A Comprehensive Extension of Conditioning Theory of Fear/Anxiety to Psychopathology

DONALD J. LEVIS

Introduction

Since Pavlov's (1927) original and ingenious experimentation with dogs on the conditioned reflex, thousands upon thousands of research articles have been devoted to the scholarly search to uncover laws of learning and behavior. The vast majority of data upon which the established principles of behavior are based, emanated largely from laboratory studies with infrahuman subjects. Yet, from the start there was little doubt that Pavlov and those who followed him believed that these principles developed from infrahumans were applicable to our understanding of both human adaptive and maladaptive behavior. Pavlov (1928, p. 361), himself concluded from work in his laboratory that a paradigm for studying neurosis can be developed by producing a conflict between excitatory and inhibitory response tendencies. Thus for Pavlov, human neurotic and psychotic symptoms were seen as behavioral manifestations of the organism's attempt to reduce the conflict. Gantt (1942, 1971) replicated and extended Pavlov's work on neurosis with dogs, while others found similar effects with cats (Masserman, 1943, 1971), sheep (Liddell, 1944, 1965), rats (Maier & Ellen, 1952), and human children (Krasnogorski, 1925).

THEORETICAL ISSUES
IN BEHAVIOR THERAPY

ISBN 0-12-586360-8

Stimulated by the above work on experimental neurosis, more and more infrahuman paradigms emerged in the attempt to understand human clinical phenomena. For example, N. E. Miller (1951) conducted a series of studies using the approach–avoidance paradigm that established the experimental foundation for the learning and maintenance of such conflicts. Masserman (1943), Dollard and Miller (1950), Wolpe (1958), and more recently Eysenck (1968), Seligman (1975, and Stampfl and Levis (1969) have extended this learning literature to explain symptom formation involved in the development and maintenance of human psychopathology. Extensive infrahuman work also has been carried out on the etiology of frustration, persistence, and regression (Amsel, 1967, 1971); on dominance and aggression (Logan, 1971); on social isolation (Harlow, 1964); and on the psychophysiology of emotion (Brandy, 1970). Furthermore, other experimental models have been offered to explain the etiology of obesity (Rodin, 1977), depression (Abramson, Seligman, & Teasdale, 1978; Suomi & Harlow, 1977), phobias and obsessions (Marks, 1977), psychosomatic disorders (Weiss, 1977), epilepsy and minimal brain dysfunctions (Gaito, 1979; Sechzer, 1977), catatonia (Gallup & Maser, 1977), and schizophrenia (Paul, 1977).

The extrapolation of principles to human psychopathology from controlled laboratory studies with infrahumans may well be perceived as a bold, imaginative, gigantic, if not a totally unwarranted leap. In science, however, such generalizations of principles from a highly controlled environment to a less controlled one tends to be the rule rather than the exception. For example, theory in astronomy has been enhanced greatly by studying movements of electrons here on earth. In genetic biology, until recently, it would be difficult to list even one fundamental genetic discovery in this field that was based on human research. Most of the past work in this field was conducted with plants or fruit-flies, subjects not considered close to humans on the evolutionary scale. Such dramatic leaps in extrapolation are not uncommon, as even a cursory review of the history of science will attest to the successfulness of this approach. Yet, in psychology, a growing reluctance is building against this strategy. The argument made is that humans are unique and complex and that laws largely based on infrahuman research and sterile paradigms of human learning are not generalizable.

This controversy over whether the human is indeed "unique" or simply an extension of the evolutionary process can not be resolved on philosophical grounds. The merit of any model of behavior must be based on its utility and scientific support. Few argue against the proposition that maladaptive behavior is tied in part to conditioning of emotional or autonomic responses. If such responses involve mediated internal cues such as words, thoughts, images, and memories, and if it turns out they follow essentially the same conditioning laws as exteroceptive stimuli, the case for extrapolating principles based on infrahuman research becomes much stronger. The laboratory rat not only provides a less complex organism that appears to be more advantageous for deciphering basic laws but it is also equipped with an emotional system not unlike that of a human. Moreover, animals are expendable and subject to control and manipulations that would be difficult if not unethical to conduct with humans (Levis, 1970a).

Despite the obvious need for confirmation at the clinical level, the extension of principles based on infrahuman and human conditioning research to account for and treat human psychopathology has already resulted in considerable achievement over the last 25 years (Kalish, 1981). The success of the behavioral therapy movement, which is founded on this strategy, attests to the potential promise of the learning-conditioning approach. It is somewhat disconcerting, given the above accomplishments, that a growing dissatisfaction within the behavior therapy field exists for abandoning a learning interpretation. If the learning theory era of behavior is over it will not be because the learning field lacks creative models reflective of clinical phenomena. Learning theorists' work on self-punitive behavior (Brown, 1965); frustration (Amsel, 1958), serial CS conditioning (Levis, 1979a), memory reactivation (Spear, 1978), and S–R analysis of cognitive variables (Mowrer, 1960b) have been almost totally ignored by a vast majority of the writers in the behavioral therapy field. Their ignorance of these and numerous other important developing models from the experimental literature represents the heart of the problem.

Stampfl (1983), in addressing the above topic, suggested that the growing dissatisfaction and lack of imagination in the behavior therapy field is most likely a consequence of the growing neglect of clinical training programs to require general–experimental courses in learning and conditioning combined with expanded economic opportunities for purely clinical skills. As he correctly observed, the advances made by the pioneers of behavior therapy were made by individuals thoroughly familiar with the infrahuman learning and conditioning literature available at that time. Stampfl concluded that it is ironic that this current state of affairs should exist precisely at a time when marvelous opportunities for solidly based theoretical innovations to the human condition may readily be inferred from the contemporary learning and conditioning literature. As Eysenck (1960, p. 5) reasoned, if the laws of behavior that have been formulated are at least partially correct, then it must follow that deductions can be made from them to (1) cover the type of behavior represented by neurotic patients, (2) construct a model that will duplicate the important and relevant features of the patient, and (3) suggest new and possibly helpful methods of treatment along lines laid down by learning theory.

In an attempt to reverse the current trend to abandon a conditioning interpretation, the main objective of this chapter is to provide a review of a comprehensive theory and treatment technique of psychopathology that hopefully will highlight the power and usefulness of adopting modern learning principles to explain and treat clinical phenomena. The model to be described was originally conceptualized by Thomas G. Stampfl and has led to the development of the behavioral treatment technique of Implosive (Flooding) Therapy (Stampfl & Levis, 1967). The theory, which was stimulated in large part from experience with clinical patients, accounts for critical data at the infrahuman and human level and most importantly provides an S–R analysis of avoidance maintenance that does not require the addition of nontraditional concepts like partial irreversibility (Solomon & Wynne, 1954), incubation (Eysenck, 1968, 1979), preparedness (Seligman, 1971), or cognitive variables (e.g., expectancy; Seligman & Johnston, 1973). This part of the theory is especially important because it addresses those critics (see Stampfl, 1983) who maintain that a learning interpretation can not account for the extreme resistence to extinction of human symptoms. The theory is also unique among behavioral theories of psychopathology in that it provides a detailed analysis of the CS complex motivating human symptoms and stresses the important roles that memory encoding and reactivation play in maintaining pathology. Besides adopting the avoidance theory of Mower (Mower, 1960a, 1960b; Rescorla & Solomon, 1967), the model to be described incorporates the contributions of Miller's (1951) and Brown's (1961) theory of conflict, Solomon and Wynne's (1954) conservation of anxiety hypotheses, Amsel's (1958) theory of frustration, and the learning conceptualizations of psychopathology suggested by Dollard and Miller (1950).

Since the position to be presented has been described in detail elsewhere (Levis, 1979a, 1980a, 1981; Levis & Hare, 1977; Stampfl, 1970; Stampfl & Levis, 1967, 1969, 1973, 1976), an attempt is made to state the main points of the theory in a more formal framework. The purpose for adopting this objective is to highlight the key statements of the theory in the hope of fostering increased research interest and critical scrutiny. This review presents the overall theoretical principles of the model. It should be noted that Implosive Theory has resulted in the development of specific models for each clinical nosology that are derived from the main tenets of theory. These submodels of the theory are not covered. Unfortunately, not all of these specific models of nosology have appeared in print, but the interested reader can evaluate such extrapolations from the general therapy by reviewing the models of depression (Boyd & Levis, 1980; Levis, 1980b; Stampfl & Levis, 1969) and pervasive anxiety (Hare & Levis, 1981).

For a theory of psychopathology to be comprehensive, it is critical that the basic principles for the development of maladaptive emotional states be outlined, as well as the relationship between such emotional states and symptom formation. It is also important to understand what role cognitive variables play in this development and whether or not they are important to consider when addressing issues of symptom maintenance and symptom removal. However, the paramount issue for any conditioning theory revolves around delineating the factors responsible for maintaining human symptoms over time. As will become apparent, the theory to be discussed maintains that for techniques of symptom removal to be maximally effective, it is essential that they take into account the factors responsible for symptom maintenance. It is the intent of this chapter to outline the critical principles responsible for symptom development, maintenance, and removal.

The Development of Psychopathology

Under this section, the key variables believed to be responsible for maladaptive emotional learning and symptom formation are discussed. Central to this discussion are the issues of the nature of the CS complex conditioned and the relationship of a given complex to symptom formation.

EMOTIONAL CONDITIONING

POSTULATE 1.   Psychopathology is learned behavior resulting from the organism's exposure to past, specific aversive conditioning experiences. Inherent in the development of psychopathology is the learning of two response classes. The first response class involves the conditioning of an aversive emotional state and second involves learned behavior designed to reduce the negative effects of the first response class.

The above stated proposition follows a two-factor theoretical framework (Mowrer, 1947, 1960a, 1960b) that conceptualizes psychopathology as an emotional as opposed to a cognitive disorder. Aversive emotional learning is based on the well-established laws of classical conditioning. Fear conditioning, for example, results from the pairing of initially nonfearful stimuli with an inherent aversive event producing pain. This biological reactive, pain-producing stimulus is referred to as an unconditioned stimulus (UCS). With sufficient repetition of the neutral stimulus with the UCS, the nonfearful stimulus acquires the capability of eliciting a fear response in the absence of the UCS. When this occurs the previous nonfearful stimulus is labeled a conditioned stimulus (CS). The aversive emotional reaction elicited by the presentation of conditioned fearful stimulus is referred to as the conditioned fear response (CR). Some theorists (Mowrer, 1947; Wolpe, 1958) maintain that the fear response solely reflects conditioning of the autonomic nervous system while others question this assumption (Rescorla & Solomon, 1967). However, it is safe to assume that in most cases of emotional conditioning the autonomic nervous system is probably affected directly. It is also clear that fear response itself does not involve a unitary well-defined set of response topographies (Levis & Hare, 1977).

POSTULATE 2.   Conditioning of an aversive emotional reaction involves the elicitation of primary drive states by a UCS involving pain, fear, frustration, or severe states of deprivation. Through conditioning, the CS is also capable of eliciting motivational or secondary drive states such as fear or anxiety.

This viewpoint of psychopathology clearly represents a motivational position. Primary or innate drives states like hunger, thirst, sex, and pain are those that produce their effects through the action of inherited bodily mechanisms and are not dependent on learning (UCSs). Secondary drives are learned and include the striving for prestige, social mobility, money, power, love, and status. But in terms of motivating maladaptive behavior, learned fear or anxiety appears to be the most dominant secondary drive (CSs). Considerable experimental evidence exists that aversive CSs do function as a secondary source of drive, possessing motivational or energizing effects (Amsel & Maltzman, 1950; Brown, Kalish, & Farber, 1951).

POSTULATE 3.   All conditioning events associated with psychopathology are encoded in long-term memory, and the resulting representations are capable of being reactivated.

As will be seen later, memory storage of past conditioning events is a critical factor for providing an explanation of symptom maintenance and in analyzing the total CS complex motivating symptom behavior.

THE CS COMPLEX

POSTULATE 4.   Conditioned cues eliciting aversive emotional responses involve a complex set of stimuli comprising both external and internal CS patterns.

Postulate 4 needs to be stressed since some theorists take a rather myopic viewpoint in analyzing what CSs are motivating maladaptive behavior. They frequently make the naive assumption that the CS patterns conditioned only involve those cues correlated with the onset of emotional responding. For example, for a patient reporting a strong emotional reaction to driving a car or flying in an airplane, the assumption may be made that the car or the airplane is the critical stimulus in need of extinction. Yet, in the vast majority of such cases a careful histoy reveals no direct conditioning events to these stimuli. Based on clinical experience and theory it is a probable assumption that the cues correlated with symptom onset represent in many cases only generalized conditioned reactions. The CS complex being avoided by most clinical symptoms is conceptualized as involving a complex set of cues including anticipated cues elicited by exposure to the phobic stimulus (e.g., bodily injury, death, or loss of control cues). Again, laboratory evidence has demonstrated quite convincingly that conditioning occurs not simply to a discrete stimulus but to a stimulus complex potentially including all the cues that immediately precede the UCS, generalized cues, and cues that have undergone secondary conditioning effects (see McAllister & McAllister, 1971).

> POSTULATE 4, COROLLARY 1. The external and internal set of cues comprising the total CS complex eliciting emotional responding can represent a complicated set of associative interactions. However, the origin of this process must involve a primary, biological UCS.

The above correlate seems redundant if one postulates a conditioning framework but unfortunately some theorists confuse the difference between a CS and UCS. The CS acquires the ability to elicit an emotional reaction in the organism by being paired with another aversive stimulus involving either a secondary (learned) or primary (unlearned) stimulus. Furthermore, the conditioning effects to a CS are capable of being unlearned by repeated exposure in the absence of further UCS presentations. On the other hand, an aversive UCS is a primary drive stimulus. It involves a biological aversive reaction such as that produced by physical pain arising from harmful external stimuli or inherently painful states within the organism resulting from the blocking of another primary drive (e.g., severe states of hunger deprivation). It is also possible that stimuli that are not considered inherently aversive when presented to an adult organism may function as UCSs during certain critical developmental stages of the organism. For example, loud noises (Watson & Rayner, 1920) or lack of physical contact (Harlow, 1964) may function as a UCS for an infant. Unlike the CS, repetition of the UCS will either increase the strength of the aversive reaction or at least maintain the aversive-eliciting strength of stimulation correlated with it (excluding temporary effects of habituation or adaptation). A UCS does not extinguish with exposure.

> POSTULATE 4, COROLLARY 2. Central state constructs such as images, thoughts, and memories can function as conditioned cues and in many cases represent the major part of the stimulus complex maintaining human psychopathology.

In theory, images, thoughts, and memories can become part of the conditioned complex in at least three ways: (1) Repeated fear-conditioning trial may elicit images and thoughts directly. For example, punishment may be preceded by sexual fantasies, images, or thoughts of parental acceptance, or with anticipatory images or memories of repeated punishment trials. When these internal events are directly followed by punishment, such internal cues will become part of the CS complex. (2) The external stimuli associated with a conditioning trial (e.g., punishment administered by a parent) may reactivate imaginal representations of past punishment trials stored in memory that not only add to the fear level of the conditioning sequence but if followed by pain become strengthened through reconditioning. (3) Anticipated images of the punishment to be received may involve cues associated with an emotional feeling that is in excess of the pain produced in the actual conditioning trial. For example, an anticipatory image may develop in a child that the angry parent may kill or seriously injure the child. Although the actual UCS may not involve serious bodily injury, these anticipatory cues, because they have been followed by aversiveness, can become part of the CS complex.

> POSTULATE 4, COROLLARY 3. Internal cognitive processes labeled thoughts, images, and memories that produced an aversive reaction function as CSs not UCSs.

Images, thoughts, and memories are not inherently aversive primary reinforcers and if they possess aversive properties the effect has been imposed by a conditioning sequence. Considerable confusion exists on this point in the behavior therapy literature where writers like Morganstern (1973) and Foa, Blau, Prout, and Latimer (1977) have expressed concern over the implosive therapist's attempts to present to their clients aversive images that they labeled as "horrifying" and "cruel". This viewpoint represents a gross misunderstanding of both the implosive procedure and the conditioning approach offered here. What is a "horrifying" scene to one person is not to another, and the difference in reactivity can be found in differences in conditioning histories. If a subject does differentially respond to such material the assumption is made that conditioning to these cues has occurred. The greater the response, the greater the degree of assumed past conditioning effects. Words, thoughts, memories, or images that elicit fearful responses are not, in and of themselves, capable of eliciting unconditioned responses (i.e., producing physical pain). They acquire their affective aversive reactions by being paired with another CS or CS sequence that was at some point in time paired with a UCS. However, it should be noted that such CSs, if not extinguished, can produce, upon exposure, strong conditioned reactions that, in turn, can function as powerful secondary motivators for the learning of new behavior to remove such stimulation.

POSTULATE 5.   A great deal of human aversive emotional learning becomes conditioned through association or pairing with other aversive CSs. The learning principles involved in this transfer include the process of secondary conditioning, higher-order conditioning, primary stimulus generalization, response-mediated generalization, semantic and symbolic mediated conditioning, and memory reactivation or reintegration of past aversive agents.

The above postulate is needed to explain, for example, why children fear ghosts and skeletons, although they have not been directly hurt by them, or why many adults fear riding in an airplane, being exposed to a spider, rat, or snake, when such an experience has never been followed by bodily injury or physical pain. Such principles as stated in Postulate 5 also provide an explanation for the development of symbolism and displacement (Miller & Kraeling, 1952). If, for example, the sight of a knife has been conditioned to elicit a strong fear reaction, the fear may generalize to all sharp objects or to objects that can potentially produce bodily injury, such as cars, guns, unprotected high places, airplanes, and so forth. If the sight of feces is associatively chained to the fear of disease, the cue transference may include such items as dirt, money, water fountains, and public toilets. In a like manner, fear of a penis may generalize or be displaced to other objects like snakes, telephone poles, and knives, which have some generalized properties similar to those involved in the original feared objects (Kimble, 1961; Levis & Hare, 1977; Stampfl & Levis, 1969).

SYMPTOM DEVELOPMENT

Laboratory evidence suggests that a reduction in or removal of conditioned aversive stimulation results in a decrease in drive that, in turn, serves as a positive reinforcing state of affairs (Brown & Jacobs, 1949; Kalish, 1954; Miller, 1948). Any behavior that reduces conditioned aversive stimulation sets the stage for learning of the second class of responses correlated with psychopathology, referred to as avoidance behavior. Maladaptive behaviors, labeled symptoms, are viewed from this model as being equivalent to avoidance behavior and governed by the laws of instrumental learning. As is the case with conditioned emotional responses, symptoms produce varied response topographies.

POSTULATE 6.   Learned behaviors labeled psychological symptoms are functionally designed to avoid or escape conditioned aversive stimulation that signals the potential occurrence of a catastrophic event (the occurrence of a UCS). They are reinforced by a reduction in aversive stimulation.

POSTULATE 6, COROLLARY 1.   Emotional aversive conditioning and subsequent avoidance attempts are not, in and of themselves, a sign of psychopathology. Rather, human survival is in large part dependent upon emotional learning and subsequent avoidance responding that protects the individual from a potential source of physical pain and tissue damage (UCS presentation).

POSTULATE 6, COROLLARY 2.   Psychopathology is assumed to occur when a very low, or zero, correlation exists between the occurrence of the above response classes (Postulate 6, Corollary 1) and the potential presence of physical danger (UCS presentation) to the organism.

For example, the failure of an obsessive-compulsive individual to wash his hand over and over after touching a door knob would not increase the probability of physical danger to himself. For this viewpoint, such behaviors are labeled maladaptive because their occurrence is not biologically protective, is usually not under the individual's control, and frequently interferes with the functioning of desired, socially adaptive responses.

POSTULATE 7.   Human psychological symptoms and maladaptive avoidance behavior comprise response topographies that involve the skeletal nervous system and can be classified as external, overt, or behavioral; the higher mental processes of the central nervous system (cognitive processes) that can be classified as internal or covert; and, the autonomic nervous system. (In most clinical cases at least two of the above response systems are interacting.)

Overt avoidance behaviors involving the skeletal nervous system can be seen in flight responses, aggressive acts, and compulsive rituals. These behaviors are overt and subject to direct measurement. Covert avoidance behavior mainly involves the classic cognitive defense mechanisms such as repression (not thinking or remembering), rationalization, intellectualization, projection, suppression, and denial. Unfortunately, direct or indirect measurement of covert activity represents a difficult methodological hurdle for the behaviorist.

Perhaps the least understood and least studied avoidance behavior is that which involves the autonomic nervous system. Most therapists look at the repeated occurrence of an autonomic reaction as a failure in avoidance such as occurs with cases of pervasive anxiety. But clinical experience suggests that in such cases the anxiety reaction itself helps the individual turn his or her attention away from confronting the cue patterns responsible for eliciting the reaction (for a detailed analysis of pervasive anxiety see Hare & Levis, 1981). The use of autonomic reactions as avoidance behavior also occurs in cases where anger is continually felt and expressed. When one is angry, cues associated with rejection, failure, individual responsiblity, and guilt can be masked and avoided (see Levis, 1980b). The emotional reaction of the depressive response can also function in this matter by preventing an individual from avoidance feelings of anger, guilt, or rejection (see Boyd & Levis, 1980).

POSTULATE 7, COROLLARY 1.   The topography of overt and covert human avoidance behavior can be classified as active or passive avoidance responding and follows the corresponding established experimental laws for these behaviors.

Active overt avoidance responding can be seen in the flight response of a phobic, the rituals of an obsessive, and in the conversion reaction of an hysteric. Active covert responding is seen in activation of cognitive defense like rationalization, intellectualization, and projection. Passive overt avoidance responding can be seen in individuals who fail to engage in behaviors that elicit fear, and in depressive responding. Covert passive avoidance responding is seen in the execution of cognitive defense mechanisms such as denial and repression.

POSTULATE 7, COROLLARY 2.   The response topography of a given avoidance behavior makes sense in a functional way if the source of conditioned aversive stimulation and reinforcement effects are taken into consideration.

The most obvious examples of symptom utility can be found in cases of hysterical conversion reactions where a combat soldier, for example, develops a paralyzed leg or a combat aviator develops blindness or a disturbance in depth perception or night vision. Another example is seen in an obsessive who counts his heartbeats in order to avoid fearful sexual thoughts or in cases of depression or agoraphobia where an individual attempts to avoid cues associated with rejection, sexuality, or fears of failure in work or interpersonal relationships. Symptoms are not an effect or outgrowth of anxiety but rather a stratagem to circumvent, suppress, or avoid painful CS cues (see Levis, 1980a). They can be understood more easily following a thorough analysis of the array of CSs driving the individual's symptomatology.

POSTULATE 7, COROLLARY 3.   Ideational recognition, as indexed by verbal report, need not be present for conditioned associations to function as an aversive stimulus. Thus, a subliminal area of neural functioning is necessary to account for all of the phenomena associated with the defensive avoidance patterns of the individual.

POSTULATE 8. The etiology of human symptom formation can be motivated by more than a single drive state and in most cases can be best described in the context of a multiprocess approach–avoidance conflict paradigm involving two or more primary drive states.

In many cases, psychopathology is conceptualized as involving learning paradigms more complex than that suggested by the simple fear-elicited, avoidance model. Levis and Hare (1977) have outlined four conflict models believed responsible for generating psychopathology. Each of these is presented in the form of a corollary followed by a brief description.

POSTULATE 8, COROLLARY 1. Symptom formation can be motivated by a conflict involving the primary drives of hunger and fear.

As Dollard and Miller (1950, p. 132) noted, if a child is repeatedly left to "cry itself out" when hungry, the child may learn that no matter what is tried the painful experience of hunger is still felt. Such training may lay the basis for the habit of apathy or helplessness, the behavior of not trying to avoid when in pain (Seligman, 1975). Following the development of intense hunger, the responses involved can attach fearfulness to situational cues like the bedroom, darkness, quietness, being alone, or to the absence of parental stimuli. An approach-avoidance conflict may then develop between the primary drives of hunger and fear. This can occur if the child cries when hungry and is subsequently punished for crying or is directly punished for certain eating behaviors that meet the displeasure of the parents. When the desire to eat and the fear of being punished for eating are pitted against each other, the resulting conflict can heighten fearfulness and the conditionability of situational cues associated with the stressful situation.

POSTULATE 8, COROLLARY 2. Symptom formation can be motivated by a conflict involving the primary drives of sex and fear.

Perhaps no other primary drive is so inhibited and punished in our society by parents as that involved in a child's expression of sexual behavior. It is also not uncommon for parents to create an approach–avoidance conflict by directly stimulating their child sexually and then punishing the child's response. It is little wonder that the conflict and guilt associated with the response of sexual feelings are actively avoided and contribute to the etiology and maintenance of most psychopathology.

POSTULATE 8, COROLLARY 3. Symptom formation can be motivated by the conflict of fear and the withdrawal of positive reinforcing cues labeled "affection" of "love."

As is the case with fear conditioning, stimuli made contingent with positive reinforcement can acquire the capacity to elicit a positive emotional response. A decrease in the positive emotional state experienced occurs as a direct function of eliminating or reducing the cues eliciting the positive affect. If sufficient loss of positive affect occurs, the experience will generate a negative emotional state resulting in the aversive conditioning of those situational cues correlated with the reduction in stimulation of the positive affective cues. The compounding of negative affective stimuli from withdrawal of love cues or through direct punishment of approach behavior for affection can generate strong negative emotional states frequently described by clinicians as representing feelings of guilt, worthlessness, and depression. Therefore, the goal-directed behavior designed to elicit a positive emotional state may become inhibited by fear that the goal will not be met (rejection). This anticipated fear can result in an inhibition of such approach behavior in an attempt to avoid the possible negative outcome. This conflict is seen clinically when a patient reports feeling anxious after experiencing feelings of pleasure. The reader is referred to an article by Stampfl and Levis (1969) for a description of a fairly typical childhood conditioning sequence depicting the above conflict.

POSTULATE 8, COROLLARY 4.   Symptom formation can be motivated by a conflict between fear and the emotion labeled anger.

When a goal-direct behavior is paired with punishment, the goal-directed behavior becomes thwarted. The blocking of the goal behavior can produce frustration in addition to the pain felt by punishment and lead to aggressive behavior. If the latter is also punished, the aggressive response will become inhibited by conditioned anxiety.

The anger response can be partially discharged by channeling the aggressive behavior into internal cues involving thoughts, images, or ruminations toward the punishing agent. However, when the punishing agent is a source of considerable positive primary and secondary reinforcement, such as is the case of a parent, the stage is set for an additional conflict. By the child's harboring aggressive impulses toward the parent, the reinforcement incurred from viewing the parent as a supporting, loving figure will be decreased. This conflict is frequently resolved by avoiding or suppressing the aggressive behavior and fantasies. Such avoidance also reduces additional secondary anxiety (guilt) over expressing the internal aggressive cues. When the avoidance pattern is not completely successful in removing the conflict, cognitive defense mechanisms such as displacement, reaction formation, and projection may develop. Depression is also believed to result from the above conditioning sequences (see Boyd & Levis, 1980; Levis & Hare, 1977; Stampfl & Levis, 1969).

Symptom Maintenance

Perhaps no other issue is more problematic for an S–R avoidance theory of psychopathology than that of symptom maintenance. This issue represents a major theoretical paradox because it is well recognized that maintenance of human symptoms can last for years while infrahuman and human avoidance learning tends to extinguish fairly rapidly following removal of the UCS (Mackintosh, 1974). Thus, until the principles for generating extreme avoidance maintenance in extinction are isolated and demonstrated in the laboratory, extrapolation from existing avoidance theories represents a tenuous strategy. Theorists concerned with addressing this issue recognize the above paradox (Eysenck, 1976; Rachman, 1976; Seligman, 1975). For example, Eysenck (1976) concluded that the classical law of extinction fails to explain why with many neuroses, the unreinforced CS appears not to extinguish but rather results in an enhancement of symptom maintenance. Theoretical attempts at explaining extreme avoidance maintenance have largely abandoned a traditional S–R viewpoint in favor of such concepts as partial irreversibility (Solomon & Wynne, 1954); automatization (Kimble & Perlmuter, 1970); CS incubation (Eysenck, 1976); uncontrollability (Seligman, 1975); and cognitive expectancy (Seligman & Johnston, 1973).

Clinical observation appears to confirm that symptomatic behavior can last for years without any significant signs of extinction. Clinical evidence also suggests that when a patient attempts to block symptomatic behavior, the failure to avoid it usually results in an unbearable increase in anxiety that frequently progresses to a panic-like intensity. Rather than producing a decrease in anxiety as theory would suggest, it appears that the resulting increase in anxiety punishes the individual (Stampfl & Levis, 1976).

Although the above observations appear to be damaging to an S–R avoidance position, further inspection of the clinical setting by Stampfl revealed some interesting findings. Although symptoms did appear to last for long periods of time, the cue eliciting symptom onset seemed to change over time with the earlier fear-eliciting cues frequently failing to trigger the symptom. Further, when a given patient directly fought symptom occurrence, new cues were introduced that appeared to result in the intensification of the anxiety reaction. This led Stampfl to conclude that a network of cues were involved in motivating a given symptom and that these cues were ordered in a sequential or serial arrangement in terms of accessibility with the more aversive part of the cue pattern being less accessible. Stampfl ingeniously translated this discovery into S–R terminology by incorporating the, now classic, Solomon and Wynne (1954) conservation of anxiety hypothesis.

Solomon and his colleagues (Solomon, Kamin, & Wynne, 1953; Solomon & Wynne, 1953) demonstrated in a laboratory avoidance study with dogs that following a few intense shocks during acquisition, the dogs' mean latency of responding following the removal of shock was still getting shorter 200 trials later. Although most animals were stopped at trial 200 if they had not extinguished, one subject was reported to have made 490 extinction trials before a punishment procedure was introduced. These findings were important in that they demonstrated that extreme resistance to extinction was possible with infrahumans.

According to Solomon and Wynne (1954) there emerged three important observations that required explanation: (1) The avoidance latencies of the dogs shortened considerably with training, with response latencies of 2 to 4 seconds being common; (2) overt signs of anxiety appeared to diminish with training and at times seemed nonexistent in extinction; and (3) if a long-latency response occurred in extinction, behavioral signs of anxiety became apparent and short latency responses returned for the next few trials. To explain these observations, Solomon and Wynne reasoned that overt signs of anxiety rapidly disappeared because the short exposure to the CS resulting from a quick avoidance response did not permit the time required for the full elicitation of the classically conditioned fear reaction. The habit strength of the avoidance response should become weakened without fear elicitation and subsequent fear reduction. Longer response latencies would then occur. The longer response latency allows sufficient time for the elicitation of the fear response explaining the reoccurrence of fear. The return of short latency responses was explained by the resulting increase in avoidance habit followed by the fear reduction occurring to the long latency response.

Solomon and Wynne (1954), however, felt compelled to rely on yet another principle, that of partial irreversibility to explain why for some dogs little extinction was noted after 200 trials. They attributed this finding to the use of traumatic shock. The partial irreversibility principle is predicated on the proposition that a very intense pain–fear reaction to a given CS pattern results in a permanent fear-reaction.

Based on the finding of Brush (1957) that the extreme resistance to extinction reported in the Solomon studies was not dependent on the use of traumatic shock, Stampfl abandoned the partial irreversibility hypothesis and focused on expanding the conservation of anxiety principle. According to the conservation hypothesis, a short latency avoidance response to a given CS interval prevents CS exposure to the total interval and results in fear extinction effects only to the part of the CS actually exposed. The remaining part of the CS interval is blocked from exposure by the avoidance behavior, and fear occurring to the unexposed part of the interval is conserved. Complete fear extinction to the CS interval will only occur with sufficient exposure to the total CS–UCS interval. When that part of the CS interval eliciting the short latency avoidance behavior undergoes an extinction effect, a longer CS exposure will be required to elicit the avoidance behavior. Solomon and Wynne hypothesized that the fear loading to a given CS segment increases as the CS duration approaches the length of the original CS–UCS interval. In other words, there is less fear conditioned to the onset of the CS and more fear to the part of the CS directly paired with UCS onset. When a long latency avoidance response occurs, more of the CS interval is exposed resulting in a stronger fear response. The elicitation of a strong fear response to a long CS exposure can secondarily recondition or recharge the shorter extinguished part of the interval re-establishing short-latency avoidance response. This process repeats itself until all the fear conditioned to the CS interval is extinguished.

By incorporating the clinical observation of serial cues, Stampfl (see Levis, 1966a) reasoned that one could maximize the principle of anxiety conservation in the laboratory by dividing the CS–UCS interval into distinctive CS components and ordering them sequentially. He hypothesized that after the attainment of short latency responses to the first stimulus component of the sequence S_1 subsequent extinction effects to this component would result in less generalization of extinction effects to the second component in the sequence S_2 if the S_2 segment is highly dissimilar to the S_1 segment. The greater the reduction in generalization of extinction effect from the early part of the CS–UCS interval to the later portions, the greater the amount of anxiety that will be conserved to the components closer to the UCS onset. With extinction of fear to the S_1 stimulus, the avoidance response latencies will become longer, resulting in the exposure of S_2. The stimulus change from a low fear state to a high fear state results in a secondary conditioning effect, recharging the S_1 segment. This process will continue to repeat itself until S_2 is sufficiently exposed to produce a full extinction effect. By adding additional distinctive cues (S_3, S_4) to the CS chain, the probability of increasing resistance to extinction will be maximized by generating a greater percentage of short latency avoidance responses via the principles of anxiety conservation and secondary intermittent reinforcement. Considerable research has been conducted in support of the above theory and the interested reader is referred to the following articles (Boyd & Levis, 1976; Dubin & Levis, 1973; Kostanek & Sawrey, 1965; Levis, 1966a, 1966b, 1970b; Levis & Boyd, 1973, 1979; Levis & Dubin, 1973; Levis & Stampfl, 1972; Levis, Bouska, Eron, & McIlhan, 1970; Shipley, 1974).

Thus, human conditioning resulting in psychopathology is not viewed as a function of a simple conditioning episode to one CS element but rather comprises many CS components that are ordered in a serial or sequential manner in terms of accessibility. By adding the concept of memory encoding of conditioning sequences, memory summation, and memory reactivation, a powerful explanatory model can be put in place that not only explains symptom maintenance but parallels existing clinical observations. The model of symptom maintenance can be more formally stated as follows:

> POSTULATE 9.   Symptoms are maintained by a network of previously conditioned cue patterns stored in memory that interconnect in a sequential linkage. This chain of cue patterns is ordered in terms of retrieval from least to most aversive with the most aversive patterns representing stored memories of past conditioning sequences involving UCS presentation.

> POSTULATE 9, COROLLARY 1.   According to this viewpoint, the role of external stimuli correlated directly with symptom onset is seen mainly as a mediator or reactivator (retrieval cue) involving a network of stored memories of past-conditioning events that are affectively encoded and represented in the form of images, thoughts, or impulses.

The implosive procedure can be viewed as a memory reactivation technique and numerous clinical examples reflecting the position adopted in the above corollary already have been reported (see Levis, 1980a; Stampfl & Levis, 1969, 1976; Stampfl, 1970). What is interesting is that the content of the avoided memories is frequently correlated with a particular symptom. Following exposure to the phobic object, phobic individuals often report memories of past conditioning events where the fear of bodily injury or death was heightened. Handwashers frequently report the recall of past sexual memories (e.g., semen on the hand) that elicit thoughts of being exposed and punished and that they attribute to the start of their handwashing compulsion. Hysterics (following therapy) frequently report memories in which they experience strong sexual feeling for the opposite sex parent, and so on (Levis, 1980a, 1980b; Levis & Hare, 1977).

> POSTULATE 10.   Excluding effects from generalization of extinction, all unexposed components of the conditioning complex associated with maladaptive behavior will maintain or conserve their aversive loading until such exposure occurs.

> POSTULATE 11.   Extinction of the cues correlated with symptom onset can result in the reactivation of the next set of cues in the chain. Their exposure can lead to an increase in emotional responding and, if paired with the earlier part of the chain, can produce a secondary conditioning effect that re-establishes responding of the symptomatic behavior to the previously extinguished cues.

Clinically this is seen when patients try to stop their symptoms by not engaging in them when fear is elicited. Such attempts frequently result in an unbearable increase in anxiety, forcing the patient to return to the symptomatic behavior in order to reduce this new increase in anxiety.

POSTULATE 11, COROLLARY 1.   Although the reactivated stimulus increases the level of aversiveness and although it can recondition the early part of the chain, any exposure to this stimulus results in a weakening effect (extinction) of the secondary drive source attached to this stimulus. With sufficient exposure, a new part of the stimulus chain will be exposed.

POSTULATE 12.   Although symptom behavior is primarily reinforced by the resulting reduction in aversive stimulation, such behavior also can be reinforced if it produces a positive secondary gain effect.

Many patients are positively reinforced for symptom behavior. Such behavior may elicit in significant others behavior that demonstrates support, love, or caring feelings. In other cases the patient's work load may be reduced or direct financial gain may be received because of the disability. Still in other cases, symptom behavior may be reinforced because it hurts an individual toward whom the patient feels anger. Such reinforcement can help perpetuate the maintenance of maladaptive behavior.

Unlearning Symptom Behavior

One of the most established and time-honored principles of psychology is the Pavlovian principle of direct experimental extinction. This basic principle states that the presentation of the CS in the absence of the UCS will lead to extinction of the conditioned response. From a two-factor position one needs only to extinguish the conditioned emotional response. According to Mowrer's theory (1947, 1960a), the repeated presentation of the total CS complex will result in extinction of the conditioned emotional response. Once the drive value of the CS has been eliminated, CS presentation will cease to motivate the avoidance behavior. Ample experimental research has corroborated this interpretation (Baum, 1970; Black, 1958; Denny, Koons, & Mason, 1959; Hunt, Jernberg & Brady, 1952; Knapp, 1965; Weinberger, 1965). Stong evidence at the infrahuman level exists that suggests force exposure to the total CS markedly extinguishes both fear and avoidance behavior (Shipley, Mock, & Levis, 1971). It is maintained that this extinction principle of the laboratory can be readily applied to the treatment of maladaptive behavior by using the techniques of implosive therapy.

POSTULATE 13.   Repeated exposure to the CS patterns motivating maladaptive behavior will result in extinction of the emotional response, which, in turn, will result in the elimination of symptom behavior.

POSTULATE 13, COROLLARY 1.   To maximize the extinction effect, repeated exposure should be given not only to CS patterns directly correlated with symptom onset but also to all the cues reactivated by the exposure procedure and those hypothesized to be responsible for symptom development.

POSTULATE 13, COROLLARY 2.   It is not essential that all external or encoded conditioning patterns be presented or that their presentation be completely accurate. Extinction effects resulting from the presentation of one cue pattern can generalize as a function of stimulus similarity to other unexposed patterns. The principle of generalization of extinction appears to be a powerful principle that helps facilitate the extinction process.

POSTULATE 14.   Extinction of the conditioned emotional response appears to be directly related to the total amount of CS exposure.

Although this principle of total amount of CS exposure is still debated at the infrahuman level, experimental support for the principle has been obtained (e.g., Shearman, 1970; Shipley, 1974; Shipley, et al., 1971).

POSTULATE 15.   The stronger the emotional responses elicited by the presentation of a CS pattern, the greater the degree of emotional extinction obtained.

POSTULATE 15, COROLLARY 1.   The more clearly the subject perceives the aversive-eliciting stimuli when followed by nonreinforcement, the more rapid the extinction of the emotional response.

The above corollary is supported by the experimental work of Lowenfeld, Rubenfeld, and Guthrie (1956) and by Wall and Guthrie (1959).

POSTULATE 15, COROLLARY 2.   Greater emotional responding and extinction will occur with the presentation of cues directly correlated with the development of symptomatic behavior.

This is the main reason the implosive therapist introduces cues reactivated in memory by the implosive procedure and cues that are hypothesized to be correlated with symptom development. An attempt is made to get the subject to re-experience the original and generalized conditioning events through the use of an imagery technique. To obtain the best results it is important to represent an image of the subject being exposed to the hypothesized UCS. A mental or imaginal representation of the UCS functions as a

CS and is capable, by repeated exposure, of being extinguished. This is why implosive therapists frequently introduce scenes in which the subject imagines himself or herself being exposed to punishment or bodily injury cues.

POSTULATE 15, COROLLARY 3.   If CS exposure fails to elicit emotional responding, extinction of the emotional response will not occur.

It is critical that the emotional responses be elicited if extinction of this response is to occur. Failure to achieve this objective should result in failure of the technique to remove symptom behavior.

Therapeutic Extension of the Model

Unlike many behavioral models of psychopathology that were primarily stimulated by laboratory data, Implosive Theory and the resulting technique was developed from extensive clinical experience, especially with cases involving severe pathology. Laboratory research was instrumental, however, in providing a testing ground and support for critical features of the theory. The technique of Implosive Therapy is based primarily on one principle, direct experimental extinction. The technique is designed to maximize this principle in a clinical setting. The task of the therapist is to extinguish the conditioned stimulus complexes that provide the motivation for symptom occurrence and maintenance. This is achieved by representing, reinstating, or symbolically reproducing in the absence of physical pain (UCS) the cue pattern to which the symptomatology has been conditioned. In those cases where symptom-correlated cue patterns involve discrete external stimuli, in vivo exposure to these cues has been found very effective and may be the only form of cue presentation necessary. This is especially true in cases where psychopathology is not severe. In vivo CS exposure should function as an activator of other internally coded cues that if elicited will themselves undergo an extinction effect upon repeated exposures mitigating the need for presentation by the therapist. It will be recalled that extinction effects to one set of cues can generalize to other nonpresented sets of cues. The extent of the generalization of extinction effect is a function of the degree of stimulus similarity between the sets of cues. If sufficient generalization of extinction effects occurs, in vivo exposure may be the only intervention necessary.

In many cases, especially those involving severe psychopathology, presentation of the external cues correlated with symptom onset will not be sufficient to produce symptom removal. In such cases or in cases where in vivo exposure is difficult, an imagery method of cue presentation is used. Such a method is especially needed for the presentation of those internal cues believed to include neural representation of specific past events involving pain and punishment. Through verbal instruction to imagine, scenes are presented to the patient that include the various stimuli (visual, auditory, tactual) hypothesized to be linked to the original conditioning events. According to theory all cues reproduced in imagery that elicit negative affect do so because of previous learning and thus are extinguishable. Images function as CSs since they are not inherently aversive.

The therapist's task is to present to the client as many of the cue patterns as possible that comprise the total avoided CS complex. Complete accuracy in reconstructing the original conditioning events is not essential since some effect, through the principle of generalization of extinction would be expected when an approximation is presented. In the interest of efficiency and to reduce resistance, symptom-correlated cues are presented first, followed by cues reported by the patient, and then by hypothesized cues. Belief or acceptance of the themes introduced in a cognitive sense is not required. The task of the therapist is to maximize emotional arousal (anxiety, anger, guilt, etc.) by describing the avoided cues as vividly and realistically as possible. By repeating the scene over and over again the emotional resonse elicited should become less and less until complete extinction occurs. Repetition of the main components of the avoided CS complex introduced is critical and is followed by progressive expansion to other sets of cues hypothesized to be related to the patient's symptom. Any attempt on the patient's part to avoid the imagined aversive stimuli is matched by the therapist's attempt to circumvent or discourage such behavior. The essence of the procedure is to repeatedly expose the aversive stimuli underlying the patient's difficulties until an extinction effect is obtained and symptomatic behavior is markedly reduced or eliminated. To increase CS exposure and maximize the extinction effect, the patient is assigned "homework" scenes. These assignments also help to bring the process under personal control.

Prior to administering the technique, a session of "neutral" imagery training is given to help establish a baseline for the ability of the client to imagine various stimuli. Since it is critical that the therapist has a clear understanding of what cues are being avoided, a good historical work-up and behavioral assessment of the patient's problem is needed prior to starting therapy. The therapist should also remember that since the original aversive conditioning events are assumed to result from contiguity of stimuli with physical injury or pain, it would follow that cues immediately associated with these events will carry a greater weight in evoking the anxiety response.

It should be understood that the implosive procedure is an operational procedure involving feedback from the patient. The validity of the content of a given scene is determined by the patient's emotional response to the scene. The greater the emotional responding elicited, the stronger the support for introducing the cues presented. By soliciting verbal feedback following a given scene as to what feelings and thoughts were experienced, new material for additional scenes can be obtained. It is common following scene presentations to have patients report new memories and feelings associated with their symptom development.

Since the focus of this chapter is on theory only, the above cursory review of the technique is presented. The brief description provided is taken from Levis (1980a) and Levis and Boyd (in press). A more comprehensive description of the technique can be found in Levis (1980a) and in Boudewyns and Shipley (1983) (also see Stampfl, 1970; Stampfl & Levis, 1967, 1969, 1973, 1976). Since the initial conceptualization of the technique in 1958 by Stampfl, over 40 research studies using clinical patients have appeared using this or a similar direct extinction approach. In all but one study where no difference emerged, the exposure-based extinction approach was found to be reliably superior to a controlled condition. Because outcome studies tend to be plagued with methodological inadequacies, caution in making strong claims for effectiveness should be adhered to. Yet, the growing weight of evidence in support of an extinction approach also can not be denied. After almost 20 years of research activity on this technique, the approach has also been demonstrated to be safe and nonharmful (see Shipley & Boudewyns, 1980). The reader is referred to Levis and Hare (1977) and Levis and Boyd (in press), for a comprehensive review of the research literature.

Alternative Viewpoints

Although faced with the problem of generalizing across species and situational variables, the conditioning laws established in the laboratory do rest upon considerable research data. Such a state of affairs does not appear to be the case for many nonlearning-based, clinical theories. The strategy of theory construction is also not the same. Learning theorists tend to start from the more well-defined and controllable examples of behavior and then systematically and progressively work to build on these. In contrast, nonbehavioral theories tend to be all encompassing theories riddled and interlaced with so many surplus meaning concepts that experimental analyses become difficult if not impossible. Such theories provide their followers with an illusory and sophistic sense of understanding at the expense of clarity, precision, and predictability.

For theory to be useful and contributory, it should lead to a systematic expansion of our knowledge mediated by specific empirical propositions, statements, hypotheses, and predictions that are subject to empirical test. Although a function of theory is to order and interpret data, the field is not lacking for explanatory models. As Campbell (1952) stressed, the critical function of theory is to predict and explain in advance laws that were unknown before. The strength of any theory is the ability of the theory to provide differential predictions.

The main theoretical contribution of Implosive Theory centers on its explanation of symptom maintenance, which as noted earlier represents the Achilles' heel of most contemporary S–R avoidance theories (Eysenck, 1976; Gray, 1971; Rachman, 1976; Seligman & Johnston, 1973). The importance of the serial CS hypothesis in explaining symptom maintenance is that the theory does not require the introduction of any new, nontraditional learning constructs. Furthermore, implications of the theory have been successfully tested at the infrahuman (e.g., Levis & Boyd, 1979) and human levels (Malloy, 1979) providing empirical confirmation for the conservation of anxiety hypothesis as a paradigm for generating extreme avoidance maintenance in extinction. The model also reflects what appears to be reported at the clinical level and has resulted in the enhancement of an extinction approach to treatment of severe pathology.

Implosive Theory also makes a number of differential predictions with other behavioral attempts to explain symptom maintenance. Most of these positions are presented in this volume. Over the last 5 years, this writer has been actively involved in providing tests of these differential predictions. This section is devoted to providing a discussion of how the alternative models differ from the Implosive Theory and the outcome of the data that bear on these differences. The alternative models of symptom maintenance that will be discussed are Solomon and Wynne's partial-irreversibility hypothesis, Seligman's concept of preparedness, Eysenck's theory of incubation, and Seligman's theory of cognitive "expectancy" and learned helplessness.

THE SOLOMON AND WYNNE
PARTIAL-IRREVERSIBILITY HYPOTHESES

Clinical evidence can attest to the observation that adults with serious psychopathology report histories involving very cruel and traumatic conditioning events. It is little wonder that some behavior therapists (Eysenck, 1979, Wolpe, 1958), as well as traditional clinicians, appeal to the effects during conditioning of intense UCS presentations to account for symptom maintenance. It will be recalled that Solomon and Wynne (1954), in an attempt to explain why some of their dogs didn't extinguish, suggested that their use of "traumatic" shock produced a pain–fear reaction to the CS that resulted in a permanent increase in the probability of occurrence of a fear reaction to the CS. They labeled their hypothesis the Principle of Partial

Irreversibility and suggested that this principle explains why human symptoms (avoidance behavior) fails to extinguish.

Their concept is like Gordon Allport's functional autonomy (1937) and, if correct, has profound implications at both the theoretical and applied levels. Most importantly the principle of partial irreversibility suggests that avoidance behavior can be impervious to the laws of extinction and, therefore, untreatable by such principles. Fortunately, Brush (1957) tested the implication of the theory directly by manipulating the levels of UCS intensity in Solomon's laboratory. He found that subtraumatic shock levels could also produce the extreme resistance to extinction reported by Solomon, Kamin, and Wynne (1953) and that traumatic shock was not effective if a drop-gate that prevented intertrial responding was not used.

Although it is recognized that there is a direct relationship between the intensity of the conditioned fear-reaction and UCS intensity, direct evidence for the partial-irreversibility hypothesis does not exist. Further, prolonged avoidance responding in extinction following the use of moderate shock levels and few shock trials have been reported by other investigators (Levis, 1966a, 1966b, 1979a; Maatsch, 1959), which suggests that UCS intensity may not be the critical factor.

SELIGMAN'S CONCEPT OF PREPAREDNESS

Seligman (1971) has criticized the two-factor theory's account of fear acquisition on the grounds that the concept of CS equipotentiality inherent in the model needs to be modified. The notion of CS equipotentiality suggests, according to Seligman, that one CS is as good as another. The argument is made that the notion of equipotentiality is weakened by the "taste-aversion" studies (e.g., Garcia, McGowan, & Green, 1971) and by the clinical observation that phobias concern a limited set of objects such as fear of specific animals and insects, heights, and dark. As Seligman observed (1971, p. 312): "And only rarely, if ever, do we have pajama phobias, grass phobias, electric-outlet phobias, hammer phobias, even though these things are likely to be associated with trauma in our world".

Seligman (1971) maintains that the most frequently experienced phobic fears are attached to situations that threatened the survival of our ancestors. He argues that there is a genetic predisposition or "preparedness" for acquiring these fears, a position not unlike that proposed by Carl Jung's (1925) concept of archetypes. Cues associated with biological threats like dark, snakes, and spiders are "prepared" stimuli as opposed to "unprepared" stimuli like tones, shoes, and clothes that are not linked to any ancestoral threats. According to Seligman, prepared stimuli are more readily acquired and more resistant to extinction.

First, it should be noted that it is incorrect to suggest that the concept of euqipotentiality states that one CS is as good as another. This is only true when everything else is held equal, a situation that rarely occurs. For example, animals sensory systems frequently differ, which is why visual CSs are usually presented to pigeons and tactical stimuli to rats. Further, differences exist in nonreinforced pre-exposure to a CS and such an occurrence can significantly interfere with subsequent conditioning to that stimulus. This finding is referred to as "latent inhibition," and according to Levis (1979b) may explain why certain phobic stimuli are conditioned more readily and maintain their effect longer. Finally, it should be noted that the interpretation of the taste-aversion studies are very controversial (Bitterman, 1975; 1976; Delprato, 1980).

An alternative interpretation of preparedness theory has been offered by Levis (1979b). Considering the issue that phobias of electric outlets and hammers are rare, despite the possibility that such objects may well be a source of aversive conditioning, Levis argues that unprepared stimuli are frequently exposed throughout life in nonaversive settings. Therefore, past conditioning effects to these stimuli have a chance to undergo extinction effects and any new conditioning trials may be retarded because of latent-inhibition effects. Further, unprepared stimuli that are potentially dangerous usually are subjected to early discrimination training on how to use these objects to avoid danger. Prepared stimuli, on the other hand, are infrequently pre-exposed, exposed following conditioning for long durations, or subject to discrimination training. Finally, little experimental support for preparedness theory can be found. Seligman's own studies (De-Silva, Rachman, & Seligman, 1977; Rachman & Seligman, 1976) with patients provide damaging negative evidence. The concept of preparedness currently provides little threat to a conditioning position like two-factor theory and does not appear to enhance our theoretical understanding of the issue at hand.

EYSENCK'S THEORY OF INCUBATION

Aware that the issue of symptom maintenance is problematic for conditioning fear-theory, Eysenck (1968, 1979) introduced the concept of "fear incubation." Eysenck's use of the term "incubation" refers to an increase in the fear response that results from additional short exposure or exposures to the CS. According to theory this can occur because under certain conditions the CRs of fear and pain, which Eysenck's labeled "nocive responses," or NRs, themselves have reinforcing properties. When paired on extinction trials, the habit strength associating CSs and NRs may increase, especially when NRs are particularly strong. According to Eysenck (1979), the development of incubation is favored when the following conditions are met:

(1) Pavlovian conditioning in which the CR is a drive, (2) a strong UCS, (3) short exposure of the CS only, and (4) individual differences in neuroticism and introversion.

The observation that fear appears to increase following a short CS exposure, however, does not require the concept of incubation. Also, the data cited by Eysenck in support of incubation has been challenged as not being directly related or relevant to the concept (see the comments of 25 leading experts immediately following the publication of Eysenck's 1979 paper). Criticism (Levis, 1979b, 1981) has been leveled especially at the Napalkov (1963) study, which greatly influenced Eysenck, who labeled the finding as the "Napalkov phenomenon." Napalkov reported that, following a single conditioning trial, repeated administration of the CS brought about increases in blood pressure of dogs from 30–40 mm Hg to 190–230 mm Hg, which in some cases lasted for over a year. Clearly such an effect is incredible and difficult to reconcile with the existing literature. It makes it even more difficult to accept these findings because Napalkov only provided a one-paragraph summary of this work without citing a primary source of reference. Thus, it is impossible to determine and evaluate exactly what experimental procedures were used. Ten years have also passed without a replication. It is little wonder why researchers in the area are either unfamiliar with the Napalkov study or seriously question the validity of the findings.

In a recently completed study in our laboratory, Malloy (1981) provided a direct test of Eysenck's incubation theory. Human adult subjects ($N = 110$) were tested using a mixed factorial design, with three crossed and one repeated factor. Subjects were exposed to a classical, fear acquistion and extinction procedure. The intensity of the UCS was the first crossed factor, with groups receiving 2.0 ma or 6.0 ma of shock during conditioning. Duration of postconditioning unreinforced CS exposure (extinction trials) was the second crossed factor, with groups receiving 0, 2, 5, 10, or 50 second trials. Neuroticism–introversion was a blocked factor, with subjects assigned to blocks based on Eysenck's Personality Inventory scores (Eysenck & Eysenck, 1968). Trials were the repeated factor with one shock trial being administered during acquisition. In addition, a pseudoconditioning control group was included.

As can be deduced from the above design, the conditions for maximizing an incubation effect were present: one-trial; Pavlovian fear-conditioning; high UCS intensity (6 ma); brief CS exposure during extinction (2 sec); and high neuroticism–introversion scores. During "incubation" testing (extinction), all groups were equated for total CS exposure. Thus, subjects were exposed to 25 trials of 2 second duration, 10 trials of 5 second duration, 5 trials of 10 second duration, or 1 trial of 50 second duration. Skin conduc-

tance, heart rate, and self-report measures of fear were monitored continuously throughout the experiment.

The results were consistent and easily interpretable. Contrary to the predictions of incubation theory, it was found that: (1) neuroticism–introversion levels had no effect on initial conditionability; (2) high shock, brief
exposures to the unreinforced CS, and high neuroticism–introversion did
not result in incubation of fear, even when subjects received several manipulations favoring incubation; and (3) monotonic fear extinction occurred for
all subjects as a direct function of total CS exposure. It is also important to
note that even highly fearful subjects extinguished, although they required
longer durations of exposure to extinguish more rapidly. These results are
very consistent with prediction made from Implosive Theory.

SELIGMAN'S MODEL OF COGNITIVE "EXPECTANCY" AND LEARNED HELPLESSNESS

Seligman (1975) and Maier and Seligman (1976) have outlined a theory of
learned helplessness that they believe is applicable to understanding the
development and maintenance of human reactive depression. Learned helplessness occurs when a human or infrahuman is repeatedly exposed to an
aversive situation in which the conditional probability of an outcome, given
a specific response, does not differ from the conditioned probability of
reinforcement in the absence of that response. In other words, the subject is
exposed to an outcome that cannot be changed or controlled by the subject's
behavior. According to Maier and Seligman (1976), the subject learns that a
contingency exists concerning the indepence of responding and outcome
and the subject develops an expectation that responding and outcome will
remain independent of future trials. Once developed, a "why try" attitude
tends to generalize or transfer to new learning situations.

This concept of "expectancy" has also been extended by Seligman and
Johnston (1973) to account for issues related to avoidance maintenance.
According to their theory, animals (humans) continue to avoid because a
cognition has developed that failure to respond will result in the occurrence
of a physical harmful event, the UCS. They argue that although fear is
needed to explain avoidance acquisiton, it diminishes shortly after learning.
Since fear isn't present to explain avoidance maintenance, a cognitive variable like expectancy must be operative. In making the case that fear is easily
unlearned, they cite the available evidence from the classical-conditioning
literature that suggests that fear-related behavior extinguishes rapidly. They
note in particular a study by Annan and Kamin (1961), which reported that
rats extinguished within 40 trials following conditioning with a strong
UCS. They also note that many of Solomon's dogs showed no signs of

avoidance extinction after 200 trials, with one subject responding for 490 without extinguishing.

One of the problems with the above argument was noted by Levis (Levis, 1981; Levis & Boyd, 1979), who argued that Seligman and Johnston failed to equate for total CS exposure when comparing 490 avoidance trials (Solomon, Kamin, & Wynne, 1953) with 40 classical-conditioning trials (Annan & Kamin, 1961). Levis reasoned that the dog that responded for 490 trials with short-latency responses probably averaged around a 2 second pretrial response latency. Thus, for this animal, the total CS exposure would be a little under 1000 seconds. In the Annan and Kamin (1961) study, extinction of fear followed 40 trials but each trial involved 60 seconds of CS exposure giving an average of 2400 seconds of CS exposure. Thus, if one extrapolates between studies as Seligman and Johnston did, then it is apparent that the dog that was stopped at trial 490 (under 1000 seconds of CS exposure) did not receive even half the amount of CS exposure required to produce an extinction effect in the Annan and Kamin study. The critical point is that CS exposure, not trials to extinction, should be considered when addressing the issue of fear extinction and fear maintenance.

Cognitive interpretations of avoidance behavior have not been popular historically, in large part because they lack theoretical precision and testability. Levis (1976) in his critical critique of learned-helplessness theory, highlights some of the unanswered questions raised by the use of a cognitive construct like expectancy: How does one determine, independent of measuring the outcome variable, when or whether a given procedural manipulation has been registered cognitively? Once registered, what are the rules and measurement criteria for determining whether or not an "expectation" will, or has, developed, and whether or not it will generalize to future trials? What are the parameters responsible for facilitating this generalization process, and what are the rules that determine its boundary conditions? What exactly are expectations; how are they identified; how do they link up to behavior; and how do they change? In other words, how are these constructs linked operationally to antecedent conditions?

Despite the above reservations, a cognitive interpretation may be needed out of necessity if an alternative fear position cannot handle the questions raised by Seligman and Johnston. The main reason cited for introducing an expectancy construct was Seligman and Johnston's conclusion that fear extinguishes shortly after avoidance acquisition. Levis and Boyd (1979) were the first to test this observation directly. They conditioned animals to make 50 consecutive short-latency responses. Following this phase, the CS used to elicit avoidance responding was transferred to a conditional emotional response (CER) paradigm to determine the presence or absence of fear. Seligman and Johnston (1973, p. 95) state that autonomic responses, like skin conductance, would not be present to the short-duration CS during asymptotic responding. The fear CER test conducted by Levis and Boyd strikingly supported the contention that the initial onset of the CS elicited fear after 50 consecutive short-latency responses. The recent findings of Starr and Mineka (1977) are also consistent with the fear interpretation as are the findings of Malloy (1979). Malloy, using human subjects, reported the presence of conditioned skin conductance responses following hundreds of trials of avoidance responses in extinction.

As can be seen from the above review of the alternative theories of symptom maintenance, Implosive Theory appears to be the most strongly empirically supported position. The serial CS model of symptom maintenance is faithful to an S–R orientation, requires no new or specialized constructs, and is supported by clinical observation and human and infrahuman research. Many propositions from the theory, especially those involving memory reactivation, however, are still in need of experimental confirmation. Hopefully, this paper will serve as a catalyst in generating the necessary research interest.

References

Abramson, L. Y., Seligman, M. E. P., & Teasdale, J. D. (1978). Learned helplessness in humans: Critique and reformulation. *Journal of Abnormal Psychology, 87*, 49–74.

Allport, G. W. (1937). The functional autonomy of motives. *American Journal of Psychology, 50*, 141–156.

Amsel, A. (1958). The role of frustrative nonreward in noncontinuous reward situations. *Psychological Bulletin, 55*, 102–119.

Amsel, A. (1967). Partial reinforcement effects on vigor and persistence: Advances in frustration theory derived from a variety of within-subjects experiments. In K. W. Spence and J. T. Spence (Eds.), *The psychology of learning and motivation, Volume, I.* New York: Academic Press.

Amsel, A. (1971). Frustration, persistence, and regression. In H. D. Kimmel (Ed.), *Experimental psychopathology,* New York: Academic Press.

Amsel, A., & Maltzman, I. (1950). The effect upon generalized drive strength of emotionality as inferred from the level of consummatory response. *Journal of Experimental Psychology, 40*, 563–569.

Annan, Z., and Kamin, L. J. (1961). The conditioned emotional response as a function of intensity of the US. *Journal of Comparative and Physiological Psychology, 54*, 428–430.

Baum, M. (1970). Extinction of avoidance responding through response prevention (flooding). *Psychological Bulletin, 74*, 276–284.

Bitterman, M. E. (1975). The comparative analysis of learning. *Science, 188*, 699–709.

Bitterman, M. E. (1976). Flavor version studies. *Science, 192*, 266–267.

Black, A. H. (1958). The extinction of avoidance responses under curare. *Journal of Comparative and Physiological Psychology, 51*, 519–525.

Boudewyns, P. A., & Shipley, R. H. (1983). *Flooding and implosive therapy.* New York: Plenum Press.

Boyd, T. L., & Levis, D. J. (1976). The effects of single-component extinction of a three-component serial CS on resistance to extinction of the conditioned avoidance response. *Learning and Motivation, 7,* 517–531.

Boyd, T. L., & Levis, D. J. (1980). Depression. In R. J. Daitzman (Ed.), *Clinical behavior therapy and behavior modification, volume I.* New York: Garland STPM Press.

Brady, J. V. (1970). Endocrine and autonomic correlates of emotional behavior. In P. Black (Ed.), *Physiological correlates of emotion* (pp. 95–125). New York: Academic Press.

Brown, J. S. (1961). *The motivation of behavior.* New York: McGraw-Hill.

Brown, J. S. (1965). A behavioral analysis of masochism. *Journal of Experimental Research in Personality, 1,* 65–70.

Brown, J. S., & Jacobs, A. (1949). The role of fear in the motivation and acquistion of responses. *Journal of Experimental Psychology, 39,* 747–759.

Brown, J. S., Kalish, H. I., & Farber, I. E. (1951). Conditioned fear as revealed by magnitude of startle response to an auditory stimulus. *Journal of Experimental Psychology, 41,* 317–328.

Brush, F. R. (1957). The effect of shock intensity on the acquisition and extinction of an avoidance response in dogs. *Journal of Comparative and Physiological Psychology, 50,* 547–552.

Campbell, N. (1952). *What is science?* New York: Dover Publications.

Delprato, D. J. (1980). Hereditary determinants of fears and phobias: A critical review. *Behavior Therapy, 2,* 79–103.

Denny, M. R., Koons, P. B., & Mason, J. E. (1959). Extinction of avoidance as a function of the escape situation. *Journal of Comparative and Physiological Psychology, 52,* 212–214.

DeSilva, P., Rachman, S., & Seligman, M. E. P. (1977). Prepared phobias and obsessions: Therapeutic outcome. *Behaviour Research and Therapy, 15,* 65–77.

Dollard, J., & Miller, N. E. (1950). *Personality and psychotherapy.* New York: McGraw-Hill.

Dubin, W. J., & Levis, D. J. (1973). Influence of similarity of components of a serial CS on conditioned fear in the rat. *Journal of Comparative and Physiological Psychology, 85,* 304–312.

Eysenck, H. J. (Ed.) (1960). *Behaviour therapy and the neuroses.* New York: Pergamon.

Eysenck, H. J. (1968). A theory of the incubation of anxiety/fear responses. *Behaviour Research and Therapy, 6,* 309–322.

Eysenck, H. J. (1976). The learning theory model of neurosis—A new approach. *Behaviour Research and Therapy, 14,* 251–267.

Eysenck, H. J. (1979). The conditioning model of neurosis. *the Behavioral and Brain Sciences, 2,* 155–166.

Eysenck, H. J., & Eysenck, S. B. G. (1968). *Eysenck personality inventory manual.* San Diego: Educational and Industrial Testing Service.

Foa, E. B., Blau, J., Prout, M., & Latimer, P. (1977). Is honor a necessary component of flooding (implosion)? *Behaviour Research and Therapy, 15,* 397–402.

Gaito, T. (1979). The kindling effects: An experimental model of epilepsy. In J. D. Keehn (Ed.), *Psychopathology in animals. Research and clinical implications.* New York: Academic Press.

Gallup, G. G., & Maser, J. D. (1977). Tonic immobility: Evolutionary underpinnings of human catalepsy and catatonia. In J. D. Maser and M. E. P. Seligman (Eds.), *Psychopathology: Experimental models.* San Francisco: W. H. Freeman and Company.

Gantt, W. H. (1942). Origin and development of nervous disturbances experimentally produced. *American Journal of Psychiatry, 98,* 475–481.

Gantt, W. H. (1971). Experimental basis for neurotic behavior. In H. D. Kimmel (Ed.), *Experimental psychopathology: Recent research and theory.* New York: Academic Press.

Garcia, J., McGovan, B., & Green, K. (1971). Sensory quality and integration: Constraints on conditioning. In A. H. Black and W. F. Prokasy (Eds.), *Classical conditioning*. New York: Appleton-Century-Crofts.

Gray, J. (1971). *The pychology of fear and stress*. London: Weidenfeld and Nicholson.

Hare, N., & Levis, D. J. (1981). Pervasive ("free-floating") anxiety: A search for a cause and treatment approach. In S. Turner, K. Calhoun, and H. Adams (Eds.), *Handbook of clinical behavior therapy*. New York: John Wiley and Sons, Inc.

Harlow, H. F. (1964). Early social deprivation and later behavior in the monkey. In H. H. Garner and J. E. P. Toman (Eds.), *Unfinished tasks in the behavioral sciences*. Baltimore, MD: Williams and Wilkins.

Hunt, H. F., Jernberg, P., & Brady, J. V. (1952). The effect of electroconvulsive shock (E.C.S.) on a conditioned emotional response: The effects of post-E.C.S. extinction on the reappearance of the response. *Journal of Comparative and Physiological Psychology, 45,* 589–599.

Jung, C. G. (1925). *Psychology of the unconscious*. New York: Dodd.

Kalish, H. I. (1954). Strength of fear as a function of the number of acquisition and extinction trials. *Journal of Experimental Psychology, 47,* 1–9.

Kalish, H. I. (1981). *From behavioral science to behavior modification*. New York: McGraw-Hill Co.

Kimble, G. A. (1961). *Hilgard and Marquis' conditioning and learning*. New York: Appleton-Century-Crofts, Inc.

Kimble, G. A., & Perlmuter, L. C. (1970). The problem of volition. *Psychological Review, 77,* 361–384.

Kostanek, D. J., & Sawrey, J. M. (1965). Acquisition and extinction of shuttlebox avoidance with complex stimuli. *Psychonomic Science, 3,* 369–370.

Knapp, R. K. (1965). Acquisition and extinction of avoidance with similar and different shock and escape situations. *Journal of Comparative and Physiological Psychology, 60,* 272–273.

Krasnogorski, N. I. (1925). The conditioned reflexes and children's neurosis. *American Journal of Diseases of Children, 30,* 753–768.

Levis, D. J. (1966a). Effects of serial CS presentation and other characteristics of the CS on the conditioned avoidance response. *Psychological Reports, 8,* 755–766.

Levis, D. J. (1966b). Implosive therapy, Part II: The subhuman analogue, the strategy, and the technique. In S. G. Armitage's (Ed.), *Behavioral modification techniques in the treatment of emotional disorders* (pp. 22–37). Battle Creek, MI: V. A. Publication.

Levis, D. J. (1970a). Behavioral therapy: The fourth therapetuc revolution? In D. J. Levis (Ed.), *Learning approaches to therapeutic behavior change*. Chicago: Aldine Publishing Company.

Levis, D. J. (1970b). Serial CS presentation and the shuttlebox avoidance conditioning: A further look at the tendency to delay responding. *Psychonomic Science, 20,* 145–147.

Levis, D. J. (1976). Learned helplessness: A reply and an alternative S–R interpretation. *Journal of Experimental Psychology: General, 105,* 47–65.

Levis, D. J. (1979a). The infrahuman avoidance model of symptom maintenance and implosive therapy. In J. D. Keehn (Ed.), *Psychopathology in animals*. New York: Academic Press.

Levis, D. J. (1979b). A reconsideration of Eysenck's conditioning model of neurosis. *The Behavioral and Brain Sciences, 2,* 172–174.

Levis, D. J. (1980a). Implementing the technique of implosive therapy. In A. Goldstein and E. B. Foa (Eds.), *Handbook of behavioral interventions: A clinical guide*. New York: John Wiley & Sons, Inc.

Levis, D. J. (1980b). The learned helplessness effects: An expectancy, discrimination deficit, or motivational induced persistence? *Journal of Research in Personality, 14,* 158–169.

Levis, D. J. (1981). Extrapolation of two-factor learning theory of infrahuman avoidance behavior to psychopathology. *Neuroscience and Biobehavioral Review, 5,* 355–370.

Levis, D. J., Bouska, S., Eron, J., & McIlhon, M. (1970). Serial CS presentation and one-way avoidance conditioning: A noticeable lack of delayed responding. *Psychonomic Science, 20,* 147–149.

Levis, D. J., & Boyd, T. L. (1973). Effects of shock intensity on avoidance responding in a shuttlebox to serial CS procedures. *Psychonomic Bulletin, 1,* 304–306.

Levis, D. J., & Boyd, T. L. (1979). Symptom maintenance: An infrahuman analysis and extension of the conservation of anxiety principle. *Journal of Abnormal Psychology, 88,* 107–120.

Levis, D. J., & Boyd, T. L. (in press). The CS exposure approach of implosive (flooding) therapy: A review of the theoretical model and treatment literature. In M. Aschev, P. Latimer and R. M. Turner (Eds.), *Evolutionary behavior therapy outcome,* New York: Springer Publishing Co.

Levis, D. J., & Dubin, W. J. (1973). Some parameters affecting shuttle-box avoidance responding with rats receiving serially presented conditioned stimuli. *Journal of Comparative and Physiological Psychology, 82,* 328–344.

Levis, D. J., & Hare, N. (1977). A review of the theoretical rationale and empirical support for the extinction approach of implosive (flooding) therapy. In M. Hersen, R. M. Eisler, and P. M. Miller (Eds.), *Progress in behavior modification.* New York: Academic Press.

Levis, D. J., & Stampfl, T. G. (1972). Effects of serial CS presentation on shuttlebox avoidance responding. *Learning and Motivation, 3,* 73–90.

Liddell, H. S. (1944). Conditioned reflex method and experimental neurosis. In J. J. Hunt (Ed.), *Personality and the behavior disorders* (Vol. 1). New York: Ronald Press.

Liddell, H. S. (1965). The challenge of Pavlovian conditioning and experimental neuroses in animals. In J. Wolpe, A. Salter, and L. J. Reyna (Eds.), *The conditioning therapies.* New York: Holt, Rinehart and Winston, Inc.

Logan, F. A. (1971). Dominance and aggression. In H. D. Kimmel (Ed.), *Experimental psychopathology.* New York: Academic Press.

Lowenfeld, J., Rubenfeld, S., & Guthrie, G. M. (1956). Verbal inhibition in subception. *Journal of General Psychology, 54,* 171–176.

Maatsch, J. L. (1959). Learning and fixation after a single shock trial. *Journal of Comparative and Physiological Psychology, 52,* 408–410.

McAllister, W. R., & McAllister, D. E. (1971). Behavioral measurement of conditioned fear. In F. R. Brush (Ed.), *Aversive conditioning and learning.* New York: Academic Press.

Mackintosh, N. J. (1974). *The psychology of animal learning.* New York: Academic Press.

Maier, N. R. F., & Ellen, P. (1952). Studies of abnormal behavior in the rat. XXIII. The prophylactic effects of guidance in reducing rigid behavior. *Journal of Abnormal and Social Psychology, 47,* 109–116.

Maier, S. F., & Seligman, M. E. P. (1976). Learned helplessness: Theory and evidence. *Journal of Experimental Psychology: General, 105,* 3–46.

Malloy, P. F. (1979). Human avoidance responding to serial and nonserial conditioned stimuli: Support for a model of psychopathology. M. A. Thesis, SUNY, Binghamton, NY.

Malloy, P. F. (1981). Incubation of human fear effects of UCS intensity, CS exposure, and individual differences. Ph.D. Dissertation, SUNY, Binghamton, NY.

Marks, I. M. (1977). Phobias and obsessions: Clinical phenomena in search of a laboratory model. In J. D. Maser and M. E. P. Seligman (Eds.), *Psychopathology: Experimental Models.* San Francisco: W. H. Freeman and Company.

Masserman, J. H. (1943). *Behavior and neurosis.* Chicago: University of Chicago Press.

Masserman, J. H. (1971). The principle of uncertainty in neurotigenesis. In H. D. Kimmel (Ed.), *Experimental psychopathology: Recent research and theory.* New York: Academic Press.

Miller, N. E. (1948). Studies of fear as an acquirable drive: I. Fear as motivation and fear-reduction as reinforcement in the learning of a new response. *Journal of Experimental Psychology, 38,* 89–101.

Miller, N. E. (1951). Learnable drives and rewards. In S. S. Stevens (Ed.), *Handbook of experimental psychology.* New York: Wiley.

Miller, N. E., & Kraeling, D. (1952). Displacement: Greater generalization of approach than avoidance in generalized approach-avoidance conflict. *Journal of Experimental Psychology, 43,* 217–221.

Morganstern, K. P. (1973). Implosive therapy and flooding procedures: A critical review. *Psychological Bulletin, 79,* 318–334.

Mowrer, O. H. (1947). On the dual nature of learning—A re-interpretation of "conditioning" and "problem-solving". *Harvard Educational Review, 17,* 102–148.

Mowrer, O. H. (1960a). *Learning theory and behavior.* New York: Wiley.

Mowrer, O. H. (1960b). *Learning theory and the symbolic processes.* New York: Wiley.

Napalkov, A. V. (1963). In N. Wisner and J. C. Sefade, *Progress of Brain Research, 2,* 59–69.

Paul, S. M. (1977). Movement, mood and madness: A biological model of schizophrenia. In J. D. Maser and M. E. P. Seligman (Eds.), *Psychopathology: Experimental models.* San Francisco: W. H. Freeman and Company.

Pavlov, I. P. (1927). *conditioned reflexes.* London: Oxford University Press.

Pavlov, I. P. (1928). *Lectures on conditioned reflexes.* New York: International Publishers.

Rachman, S. (1976). The passing of the two-stage theory of fear and avoidance: Fresh possibilities. *Behaviour Research & Therapy, 14,* 125–131.

Rachman, S., & Seligman, M. E. P. (1976). Unprepared phobias. "Be prepared." *Behaviour Research and Therapy, 14,* 333–338.

Rescorla, R. A., & Solomon, R. L. (1967). Two process learning theory: Relationships between Pavlovian conditioning and instrumental learning. *Psychological Review, 74,* 151–182.

Rodin, J. (1977). Bidirectional influences of emotionality, stimulus responsivity, and metabolic events in obesity. In J. D. Maser and M. E. P. Seligman (Eds.), *Psychopathology: Experimental models.* San Francisco: W. H. Freeman and Company.

Sechzer, J. A. (1977). The neonatal split-brain kitten: A laboratory analogue of minimal brain dysfunction. In J. D. Maser and M. E. P. Seligman (Eds.), *Psychopathology: Experimental models.* San Francisco, W. H. Freeman and Company.

Seligman, M. E. P. (1971). Phobias and preparedness. *Behaviour Therapy, 2,* 307–320.

Seligman, M. E. P. (1975). *Helplessness; On depression, development and death.* San Francisco: W. H. Freeman and Company.

Seligman, M. E. P., & Johnston, J. C. (1973). A cognitive theory of avoidance learning. In F. J. McGuigan and D. B. Lumsden (Eds.), *Contemporary prospectives in learning and conditioning.* Washington: Scripta Press.

Shearman, R. W. (1970). Response-contingent CS termination in the extinction of avoidance learning. *Behaviour Research and Therapy, 8,* 227–239.

Shipley, R. H. (1974). Extinction of conditioned fear in rats as a function of several parameters of CS exposure. *Journal of Comparative and Physiological Psychology, 87,* 699–707.

Shipley, R. H., & Boudewyns, P. A. (1980). Flooding and implosive therapy: Are they harmful? *Behavior Therapy, 11,* 503–508.

Shipley, R. H., Mock, L. A., & Levis, D. J. (1971). Effects of several response prevention procedures on activity, avoidance responding, and conditioned fear in rats. *Journal of Comparative and Physiological Psychology, 77,* 256–270.

Solomon, R. L., Kamin, L. J., & Wynne, L. C. (1953). Traumatic avoidance learning: The outcomes of several extinction procedures with dogs. *Journal of Abnormal and Social Psychology, 48,* 291–302.

Solomon, R. L., & Wynne, L. C. (1953). Traumatic avoidance learning: Acquisition in normal dogs. *Psychological Monographs, 67* (354), 1–19.

Solomon, R. L., & Wynne, L. C. (1954). Traumatic avoidance learning: The principle of anxiety conservation and partial irreversibility. *Psychological Review, 61,* 353–385.

Spear, N. E. (1978). *The processing of memories: Forgetting and retention.* New Jersey: Lawrence Erlbaum Associates.

Stampfl, T. G. (1970). Implosive therapy: An emphasis on covert stimulation. In D. J. Levis (Ed.), *Learning approaches to therapeutic behavior change.* Chicago: Aldine.

Stampfl, T. G. (1983). Exposure treatment for psychiatrists? Review of J. C. Boulougouris (Ed.), *Learning theory approaches to psychiatry. Contemporary Psychology, 28,* 527–529.

Stampfl, T. G., & Levis, D. J. (1967). The essentials of implosive therapy: A learning-theory based on psychodynamic behavioral therapy. *Journal of Abnormal Psychology, 72,* 496–503.

Stampfl, T. G., & Levis, D. J. (1969). Learning theory: An aid to dynamic therapeutic practice. In L. D. Eron and R. Callahan (Eds.), *Relationship of theory to practice in psychotherapy.* Chicago: Aldine.

Stampfl, T. G., & Levis, D. J. (1973). Implosive therapy. In R. M. Juyevich (Ed.), *Direct Psychotherapy: 28 American Originals.* Coral Gables: University of Miami Press.

Stampfl, T. G., & Levis, D. J. (1976). Implosive therapy: A behavioral therapy. In J. T. Spence, R. C. Carson, and J. W. Thibaut (Eds.), *Behavioral approaches to therapy.* Morristown, NJ: General Learning Press.

Starr, M. D., & Mineka, S. (1977). Determinants of fear over the course of avoidance learning. *Learning and Motivation, 8,* 332–350.

Suomi, S. J., & Harlow, H. F. (1977). Production and alleviation of depressive behaviors in monkeys. In J. D. Maser and M. E. P. Seligman (Eds.), *Psychopathology: Experimental models.* San Francisco: W. H. Freeman and Company.

Wall, H. N., & Guthrie, G. M. (1959). Extinction of responses to subceived stimuli. *Journal of General Psychology, 60,* 205–210.

Watson, J. B., & Rayner, R. (1920). Conditioned emotional reaction. *Journal of Experimental Psychology, 3,* 1–4.

Weinberger, N. M. (1965). Effects of detainment on extinction of avoidance responses. *Journal of Comparative and Physiological Psychology, 60,* 135–138.

Weiss, J. (1977). Ulcers. In J. D. Maser and M. E. P. Seligman (Eds.), *Psychopathology: Experimental models.* San Francisco: W. H. Freeman and Company.

Wolpe, J. (1958). *Psychotherapy by reciprocal inhibition.* Stanford: Stanford University Press.

Incubation Theory of Fear/Anxiety

H. J. EYSENCK

Theory versus Eclecticism

Kurt Lewin is credited with saying that there is nothing as practical as a good theory. Most psychotherapists and behavior therapists tend to be pragmatic, eclectic, and antitheoretical; they prefer to use and adapt any methods that they feel may benefit their patients, regardless of theoretical underpinning, and they like to use such methods even though the theories on which they are based may be contradictory to each other. The "broad spectrum" approach apparently has a good deal of appeal, but equally there are many things to be said against it.

In the first place, a therapist's belief that the methods he is using and combining in various ways are effective is no proof that they are in fact so. It is well known that there is a strong spontaneous remission effect in neurosis (Rachman & Wilson, 1980), and even the fact that a patient improves is no proof that this improvement has been brought about by the therapist. Even if the therapist has succeeded better than chance (where chance is represented by the level of spontaneous remission), this does not prove that he has succeeded *because* of the methods of treatment he has employed; it is equally possible that he has succeeded because of some placebo or suggestion effect. To accept an eclectic or "broad spectrum" approach, without attempts to prove by means of clinical control groups and follow-up experiments the efficacy of the particular mix of therapies involved, is to leave science behind and to adopt what is essentially the position of the quack. All sciences pass through an ordeal by quackery;

83

astronomy had to slough off its early association with astrology, just as chemistry had to slough off its early association with alchemy. Psychology is in the same position; if it wishes to be a science, it must behave as the sciences do, which means that it must ask for proof and not accept speculation unsupported by acceptable evidence.

It is quite obvious that there is little theory concerning the origins and treatments of neurosis. Gossop (1980), in his book *Theories of Neurosis,* was surprised at the absence of clearly stated and empirically testable theories; he found it difficult even to obtain a sensible statement of the psychoanalytic theory, where one would have expected after some 80 years of endeavour by literally thousands of psychoanalysts to find such a statement. The only theory that compiled with the usual standards of scientific testability was Watson's hypothesis that neurotic symptoms originated in a process of Pavlovian conditioning, and that treatment consisted of a process of Pavlovian extinction (Watson & Rayner, 1920). However, Watson failed to state his theory in sufficient detail; it appears more or less as an appendage to the case history of Little Albert, the 11-month old infant whom he conditioned to demonstrate a lasting fear of rats and other furry animals. Watson was handicapped in developing his theory by the fact that Pavlov's work on conditioning had not yet been translated into English, and that little empirical work was available to Watson to base his theories on. His "theory" was clearly a felicitous and serendipitous hunch, but little more; it is not detailed or extensive enough to be properly called a theory in the usual sense.

Weakness in Watson's Conditioning Theory

Eysenck (1968, 1977, 1979) has pointed out a number of weaknesses in the theory tentatively suggested by Watson—weaknesses that are so destructive that the theory in its original form becomes completely untenable. In order to make it acceptable, these weaknesses had to be removed, and the theory had to be updated with the modern developments in conditioning theory and practice. In order to do this, Eysenck developed his incubation theory of fear/anxiety, which will be described in more detail later on. To understand better the nature and purpose of this theory in relation to the development and treatment of neurosis, we must consider first of all the weaknesses in Watson's original theory, which these new developments were meant to avoid.

A detailed statement of the development of Watson's theory is given elsewhere (Eysenck, 1982) and will not be repeated here. The major objections to the theory are the following.

1. Watson's experiment with Little Albert involved only a single case, which, when studied in detail, is less impressive than it may seem at first sight (Harris, 1979). Furthermore, other authors (e.g., Bregman, 1934; English, 1929) have failed to replicate Watson's results. The experimental support for Watson's theory is obviously inadequate to bear the large structure that he erected upon it. Watson himself seems to have been uneasily aware that his experiment might not be easily replicable, because, remarking upon the persistence of the CRs in Little Albert, he also stated that: "One may possibly have to believe that such persistence of early conditioned responses would be found only in persons who are constitutionally inferior" (Watson & Rayner, 1920, p. 14). Watson was quite right in assuming that personality differences would be important in future work on the conditioning of anxiety, although his notion of "constitutional inferiority" seems odd, particularly in view of his general disregard of individual differences and genetic causes. But the fact remains that his experiment proved difficult to replicate and in itself is obviously faulty.

2. Phobias, which are perhaps the most clear-cut instances of emotional CRs, are relatively restricted in the kinds of conditioned stimuli that give rise to them. Seligman (1971) has pointed out that phobias comprise a relatively nonarbitrary and limited set of objects; they tend to be restricted to fear of specific animals, fear of heights, fear of the dark, fear of open and closed spaces, and so on. The set of potentially phobic stimuli thus seems to be highly selected and related to the survival of the human species through the long course of evolution. Such a finding contradicts the postulate of equipotentiality, which was commonly accepted by Watson and Pavlov, that is, the notion that one CS is as good as another in producing conditioned responses. The nonarbitrary and limited choice of objects and situations that predominantly produce phobic fears in humans is difficult to explain along the lines of equipotentiality.

3. The dependence of the typical laboratory CS-US connection on very refined and precise experimental conditions, particularly the exact timing is difficult to achieve. For eyeblink conditioning, for instance, the CS has to precede the US by between 500 and 2500 msec; very little conditioning will be found if the timing is outside these limits. But such precision is generally unobtainable, especially in real-life situations, and the problem arises as to how conditioning can be made responsible for the growth of neurotic disorders under conditions where precise time relations do not pertain.

The Contribution of "Preparedness"

These difficulties can be overcome, as I have pointed out elsewhere (Eysenck, 1982), by adopting Seligman's theory of "preparedness." This concept is dealt with in detail by Öhman, Dimberg, and Öst (Chapter 6), and I will not say a great deal about it here. Seligman (1971) suggests that phobias are highly prepared to be learned by humans, are selective and resistant to extinction, can be learned even with degraded input, and are probably noncognitive. In other words, some contingencies are learned much more readily than others, that is, with highly degraded input, such as single-trial learning, long delays of reinforcement, and so forth. This view integrates well with the hypothesis of innate fears (Breland & Breland, 1966; Hinde & Stevenson-Hinde, 1973). The theory of preparedness stops at a midpoint between the environmentalist notions of Watson and many other behaviorists and a simple genetic theory suggesting that phobic fears are fully innate (Gray, 1981).

Such a position agrees well with the empirical data on the importance of genetic factors in phobic fears. Rose and Ditto (1983) have published data based on comparisons between MZ and DZ twins, related to seven different types of phobic fear (negative social interaction, social responsibility, dangerous places, small organisms, deep water, loved one's misfortune, personal death) for which they calculated heritabilities. These averaged around .6, suggesting that genetic factors play a very important but not exclusive part in the genesis of neurotic disorders.

It should not, however, be assumed that these fears are necessarily inherited directly. First, heritability is far from total; 60% of the variance accounted for by genetic factors leaves 40% to be accounted for by environmental factors. Second, the analysis of the data was faulty in that the seven types of phobic fear were derived from a factor analysis of a larger number of items, in which the rotation was performed by means of the Varimax paradigm, which insists on orthogonal factors; this eliminates the usually strong intercorrelations among the various types of phobic fears. Third, there was no attempt to measure or estimate a general factor of neuroticism, which, as a major personality variable, has been shown to be powerfully determined by genetic factors and to underlie many different types of phobic fears (Fulker, 1981). Thus the empirical evidence, while definitely indicating the importance of a genetic contribution, leaves in doubt the precise way in which this genetic contribution affects the differential growth of phobic fears. My own assessment would be that some combination of genetic factors and Pavlovian conditioning, as postulated in Seligman's theory, is involved in the production of phobic and other types of fears. Thorndike (1935) anticipated such concepts in his notion of "belongingness," and future experimental work in this field, like the admirable studies done by the Upsala school and described by Reiss and McNally in Chapter 5, will undoubtedly throw much light on this concept.

Let us merely note here that it explains adequately the criticisms of Watson's original theory listed so far. Other authors failed to replicate Watson's experiment because the stimuli they used were not "prepared," as were his. Wooden ducks and other toys that were used in these replications are not prepared in the sense that rats are. The nonarbitrary and limited choice of objects in phobias is obviously explained by the notion of preparedness, which was indeed advanced percisely to account for this fact. Finally, the fact that laboratory investigations of conditioned responses require precise timing does not apply to ordinary life situations if stimuli are in fact pre-pared in Seligman's sense, as under those conditions degraded input is acceptable.

Let us now turn to other difficulties of Watson's paradigm, which cannot so easily be dismissed by reference to Seligman's theory of preparedness.

Other Criticisms of Watson's Model

These difficulties arise partly from clinical research, and partly from ex-perimental investigations. The first to be mentioned arises from Watson's assumption that neurotic disorders start with a single traumatic condition-ing event, or with a series of relatively traumatic events of this nature. This assumption does not find any support with peace-time neurotic subjects. Traumatic events are relatively rare in these patients, and their neurosis seems to have graduated insidiously over a period of time, starting possibly with events that while emotionally disturbing were certainly not traumatic in the usual sense of that term. War-time neuroses often start with traumatic events; however, war-time neuroses are quite different from peace-time neuroses in many ways, and quite atypical in this sense. In any case, from the psychiatric point of view Watson's theory fails in its most important and obvious requirement. This may be one of the reasons that psychiatrists have been rather reluctant to adopt a conditioning point of view. The failure of traumatic USs to occur in peace-time neuroses is of course well known and has frequently been documented (Gourney & O'Connor, 1971; Lautsch, 1971), as is the insidious onset of many neuroses (Marks, 1969; Rachman, 1968). The rather more frequent occurrence of traumatic USs in war-time has been well documented by Grinker and Spiegel (1945).

While this objection has often been raised by clinical experts, the next objection is one that is more frequently made by experimental psychologists (e.g., Kimmel, 1975). It is well known that unreinforced CRs extinguish quickly (Kimble, 1961), and if neurotic symptoms and reactions are indeed conditioned responses, then it should follow that they too would extinguish quickly when following a CS-only (i.e., unreinforced) experience. There is no doubt that such CS-only experiences are quite common in the lives of neurotics, where feared objects and situations can not always be avoided, and where they frequently occur in vivo, in the imagination, or portrayed in the theatre, the cinema, or on the television screen. A patient suffering from a cat phobia may encounter cats in vivo, he may read about cats, see them in one of the media, or even imagine encounters with cats; all these experiences would be CS-only, and hence should lead to extinction. Yet in the usual long-term neurotic illness, such extinction is notably missing.

Eysenck and Rachman (1965) have suggested that the well-documented presence of spontaneous remission in neurosis may be due to extinction of this type, and indeed this seems to be a reasonable explanation for what is of course a very common phenomenon. Yet obviously not all neuroses remit spontaneously, and we would still be faced with the task of explaining (1) the causal differences between remitting and nonremitting neurotic disorders and (2) what happens in the case of nonremitting neuroses.

These are the two major objections put forward by experimentalists and clinicians, respectively, to the Watson paradigm. A possible solution is suggested in another clinical observation related to that already mentioned, that is, the failure of a traumatic beginning to the neurotic disorder. In many neuroses, therapists not only fail to oberve the expected extinction of the unreinforced CS, but they find an incremental (enhancement) effect, such that the unreinforced CS actually produces increased anxiety (CR) with each presentation of the CS-only. Thus we have the difficulty, combining clinical and experimental experiences, of how it is possible that such mild US can give rise to CRs that are much stronger than the unconditioned response? Mackintosh (1974) has pointed out that CRs, even if they resemble the UR very closely, are usually weaker and of lesser amplitude. Yet the notion of subtraumatic USs implies that the final CR (neurotic breakdown) is stronger (involves more anxiety) than the UR! This counters all the known facts of the URs; they are known to habituate rather than to increase in strength. These, then, are major objections to Watson's theory that, if they cannot be answered on a factual basis, render it unacceptable to clinicians and experimentalists alike.

Incubation of Anxiety

The model suggested here for a modern conditioning theory of neurosis (Eysenck, 1976, 1979) is based on two facts. First, many of the difficulties with Watson's original formulation are due to faults in the generally accepted notions about extinction. A drastic revision of the law of extinction seems necessary before we can begin to cope with the experimentally observed facts in this area. The simple belief that the presentation of the unreinforced CS inevitably leads to extinction was shown to be erroneous as early as the 1950s by Razran (1956), who stated in his review of 40 years of American and Russian experimentation that extinction has always been found to be a less than 100% phenomenon, with instances of difficult and even impossible extinction constantly reported for classical conditioning experiments. The notion of "incubation of anxiety" is one attempt to change the law of extinction in the direction of being more responsive to experimental and clinical facts. This restatement obviously makes the position very much more complicated, as a new law is required to state in detail under what conditions extinction and incubation take place when the CS-only is presented to the individual.

Second, we clearly need some firm theoretical basis in conditioning to lead to a theory that can be used to explain the lack of extinction in certain circumstances.

I suggest that the conditioning involved in the genesis of neurotic disorders is to be identified with Pavlovian B conditioning (Grant, 1964) rather than, as is more usual, with Pavlovian A conditioning. It is symptomatic of the lack of interest in theoretical considerations that characterizes both psychotherapist and behavior therapist that neither the former, usually critical of a conditioning theory, nor the latter, often favorable to it, have ever considered either the importance of making this distinction or the vital consequences that follow from it. It is clear that no realistic criticism of a theory is possible without taking into account major conceptual differences such as these, and as the distinction is possibly not as well known in clinical circles as it ought to be, a few words regarding it may be required.

Pavlovian A conditioning is exemplified by the typical example that usually comes to readers' minds when talking about Pavlovian conditioning, namely the dog's salivary response conditioned to the sound of a bell by pairing the bell and feeding the animal. Two points are vitally involved in Pavlovian A conditioning. The first of these is that motivation has to be manipulated externally to the conditioning paradigm and is not produced by the conditioning paradigm itself. The dog has to be hungry before the conditioning experiment is performed; otherwise no conditioning occurs. Equally, he has to be hungry again when called upon to produce the conditioned response, otherwise the response again will not be forthcoming. Thus motivation is external to the conditioning paradigm.

The second point relates to the similarity between CRs and URs. Normally these are rather different, and may be quite dissimilar. Typically, the UR involves eating, the CR involves salivation; these two responses are quite dissimilar. This point has often been mentioned by critics of the conditioning approach, as it clearly contradicts the hypothesis that the CS is simply substituted for the US in producing identical responses. Here let us merely note it as a fact that is usually demonstrated in Pavlovian A type conditioning experiments; as we will see, Pavlovian B type conditioning is very much different in respect both to the motivational factor and to the similarity relations involved between UR and CR.

As Grant (1964) puts it, in Pavlovian B conditioning, stimulation by the US is not contingent on the subject's instrumental acts, and hence has less dependence upon the motivational state of the organism. Furthermore, the CR appears to act as a partial substitute for the UR. Another differentiation, less important from our point of view, is that the US elicits a complete UR in Pavlovian B conditioning, whereas in Pavlovian A conditioning, the organism emits the UR of approaching and ingesting the food. As Grant points out, a great deal of interoceptive conditioning (Bykov, 1957) and autonomic conditioning (Kimble, 1961) apparently follows the Pavlovian B paradigm.

The reference experiment for Pavlovian B conditioning cited by Grant is that of an animal that is given repeated injections of morphine. The UR in this case involves severe nausea, profuse secretion of saliva, vomiting, and then profound sleep. After repeated daily injections, Pavlov's dogs would show severe nausea and profuse secretion of saliva at the first touch of the experimenter (Pavlov, 1927, pp. 35–36). In the human field, the well-known experiment by Campbell, Sanderson, and Laverty, (1964) in which the US was the injection of a muscle-paralyzing drug, produced very similar results and may be used as a reference experiment.

One major difference between Pavlovian A and Pavlovian B conditioning, therefore, is the fact that in the latter the US acts as a drive—it has, of course, been known for many years that anxiety/fear in fact acts as a drive. This immediately links Pavlovian B conditioning with anxiety, and indeed Grant points out that this subclass of classical conditioning could well be called Watsonian conditioning, after the Watson and Rayner (1920) experiment conditioning fear responses in Albert; but as he also points out, Pavlov has priority. Grant thus recognizes the relevance of Pavlovian B, not Pavlovian A conditioning for the learning of anxiety responses.

It seems likely that the other property of Pavlovian B conditioning, namely that the CS appears to act as a partial substitute for the US, is a consequence of the fact that the US acts as a drive. If the US acts as a drive, then the CS, by being associated with the US, can also act as a drive and will thus produce CRs similar to the URs produced by the US. Profound differences are thus apparent between Pavlovian A conditioning, in which presentation of the CS only leads to extinction, and Pavlovian B conditioning, in which presentation of the CS-only may, under certain circumstances (to be specified later), lead to incubation (enhancement of the CR).

We may now consider the reasons for this prediction. Extinction normally occurs because the CS-only is not followed by the UR for a number of trials. The absence of the UR weakens the US–CS connection, and hence the CR, until the latter is finally eliminated. In the case of Pavlovian B conditioning, however, the presentation of the CS-only evokes a CR that is similar to or identical with the UR. Hence an entirely different situation now arises. The CS-only is *not* followed by the absence of reinforcement, but by a CR that itself may act as a reinforcing agent by virtue of its similarity to the UR. The experimenter, of course, knows the difference between the CS and the US, but to the animal the identical consequences suggest a similarity or identity of stimuli. What is being suggested, therefore, is that conditioning sets in motion a positive feedback cycle in which the CR provides reinforcement for the CS-only. Usually the extinction process will be stronger than this form of reinforcement, leading to overall extinction and making the action of CR reinforcement for the CS-only unobservable. However, under certain circumstances, for example, when the US is exceptionally strong, the extinction process may be weaker than the reinforcement process, and observable incubation will result, demonstrated by an incrementation in the strength of the CR when the animal or the human subject is presented with a CS-only a number of times.

I have suggested that URs that fit the Pavlovian B conditioning model particularly well are those related to fear/anxiety, by virtue of the fact, pointed out above, that fear/anxiety can act as a drive, and hence, that responses of this kind are likely to obey the precepts of Pavlovian B conditioning. It seems possible that sexual responses may also fall within the purview of this model; certainly sexual stimuli can elicit a complete UR, and CSs are particularly likely here to act as partial substitutes for the US. Many stimuli conditioned to sexual USs produce erection, that is, CR = UR in this case. Unfortunately too little work has been done in the field of sex, as compared with that of anxiety, to pursue this analogy further.

Animal Experiments

Let us consider an experiment that I have often quoted to illustrate the way incubation works (Eysenck, 1968). I purposely say "illustrate" rather than "prove," because clearly no single experiment can prove an important and complex theory of this kind, and the experiment itself has not been reported in sufficient detail to make replication easy. Nevertheless the results are in good accord with other animal experiments, and we are now beginning to accumulate evidence from human subjects to demonstrate that there also similar effects can be observed.

The study in question has been reported by Napalkov (1963), who

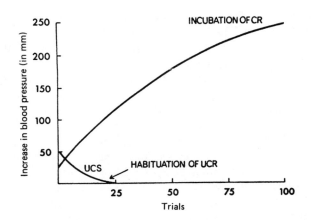

FIGURE 4.1   Reduction of unconditioned response through habituation, and enhancement of conditioned response through incubation, in dogs.

worked with dogs in a Pavlovian paradigm. He fired a pistol behind the ear of the dog as the US and used the increase in blood pressure in millimeters as the UR. Figure 4.1 shows the fate of the UCR after a number of repetitions of the experiment. A relatively slight increase in blood pressure of 50 mm at the beginning is gradually reduced to nothing after 25 repetitions; habituation of the UR is complete. There is here no traumatic event; increases in blood pressure of the order here observed are quite common in the life of the dog.

Consider now the fate of the CR when a conditioned stimulus is used to precede the US just once. Napalkov worked with a single-trial conditioning paradigm, and in the conditioning part of the experiment the dogs were never exposed to the US (the pistol shot) more than once; thereafter only CS presentations without reinforcement were employed.

The figure shows the process of repeated elicitation of the CS-only; it will be seen that there is a gradual (insidious) rise in the CR, until it reaches the very high figure of 250 mm. Napalkov reports that in some dogs blood pressure at this height became chronic; that is, it did not go back to 0 once the stimulation by the CS had been removed. This may serve as an index of the way that conditioning processes may result in hypertension and other types of psychosomatic disorders. The dogs in the experiment behaved just as the theory demands.

Other animal experiments have demonstrated similar results, such as the work of Lichtenstein (1950), Dykman, Mack, and Ackerman, (1965), Dykman and Gantt (1958, 1960a,b), and Galbrecht, Dykman, and Peters,

(1960). Of human studies we may mention the work of Bridger and Mandel (1964), Cook and Harris (1937), and Maatsch (1959). Studies of "partial irreversibility" of conditioned fear responses, such as those of Solomon, Kamin, and Wynne, (1953) and Solomon and Wynne (1953, 1954) may also be relevant, as is the already mentioned study of Campbell *et al.* (1964). These investigators found enhancement effects after a single, traumatic experience of respiratory paralysis; despite repeated extinction trials (30 trials administered 5 minutes after conditioning, 30 one week later, and 40 two weeks after that), CRs continued to gain strength over time. This is a particularly important and impressive study relevant to the concept of incubation.

Other more recent studies are quoted in Eysenck (1982), such as those of Reynierse (1966), Baum (1970), Sartory and Eysenck (1976), Rohrbaugh and Riccio (1970), Silvestri, Rohrbaugh, and Riccio, (1970), Rorbaugh, Riccio, and Arthur, (1972), Sartory and Eysenck (1978), Morley (1977), and Siegeltuch and Baum (1971). Reviews of the literature by Woods (1974) and Eysenck (1979) and critiques such as that of Bersh (1980) suggest that while there is a good deal of evidence compatible with the incubation theory, many of the studies supporting it have certain weaknesses that make them inconclusive proof of the theory. One reason of course is that many of the older studies, in particular, were not carried out to test the theory, which was developed relatively recently. It would seem highly desirable for further studies, specifically designed to investigate the parametric predictions of the model, to be carried out with both animals and humans in order to resolve this ambiguity. The problem is clearly a very important one for general psychology, where the law of extinction has been a vital part of the conditioning paradigm, and for behavior therapy in particular, where extinction may be the major variable mediating therapeutic success.

Before describing the parameters that determine whether in a given situation we will observe extinction or incubation, the classical differentiation between US and UR should be discussed. The classical account of conditioning links the CS with the US, but I would suggest partly ignoring the US and concentrating largely on the UR. The differentiation between US and UR is usually somewhat artificial from the point of view of the organism being conditioned. In an experiment using shock, for instance, the shock is the US, and pain plus fear the UR. This makes sense from the point of view of the experimenter, who administers the US, while the subject experiences the pain. However, from the subject's point of view, he does not feel the shock (US) that produces pain (UR). He experiences a painful shock; that is, US and UR are experienced simultaneously and not as separate, consecutive entities. It is this Gestalt-like NR (nocive response) that is being linked with the CS through contiguity, and to which the CR eventually adds another increment of pain/fear that is introspectively very difficult or even impossible to differentiate from the original NR. Conditioning clearly can occur when there is no observable US at all, as in the previously mentioned experiment by Campbell *et al.* (1964) in which temporary interruption of respiration (UR) was produced by intravenous injection of succinylcholine chloride dihydrate (US). The subjects were in fact unaware of the process of injection, which was part of a lengthy process of injection of saline solution and sometimes of atropine (to reduce salivation). The CS was so timed as to precede the first sign of UR, usually a sudden drop in skin resistance. Here the patients were thus completely unaware of the US; furthermore, the US preceded the CS, thus suggesting a case of backward conditioning. This has usually been declared to be weak or impossible (Kimble, 1961), but as Eysenck (1975) has pointed out, there is much relevant literature in the Soviet countries to demonstrate that backward conditioning can be quite strong under certain conditions. Certainly in the Campbell *et al.* (1964) experiment, the CRs produced were exceptionally strong and long-lasting, giving support to the view voiced here, which emphasizes the importance of the UR and plays down the importance of the US. The point is an important one for the understanding of the process of conditioning as a whole and of incubation in particular.

There are other ways in which the theory presented here differs from the orthodox and largely animal-based presentation usually found in textbooks. These differences are discussed in detail elsewhere (Eysenck, 1982). Here let me merely mention the fact that the theory of incubation agrees in important points with views that have already been voiced by other authors, although in different contexts and in a different form. Thus Razran (1956) had already stated that the automatic deconditioning in the early stage of extinction is a direct result of the loss of the interoceptive and the proprioceptive conditional stimuli that in the original conditioning situation were an integral part of the CR situation and that, when the unconditioned stimulus is withheld and the evoked reaction is induced, cease to be present. In the case of anxiety conditioning, the introceptive and proprioceptive CSs remain, if in somewhat reduced form, and this alone would be sufficient to avoid extinction and instead to produce enhancement under certain conditions to be specified later.

There is also some common ground between the concept of incubation in conditioning theory and that of "sensitization" in habituation theory (Groves & Thompson, 1970) although this similarity is mentioned with some caution in view of the clear differences in methodology and conceptualization involved. Nevertheless, the differentiation between extinction and habituation is easier to make in theory than to apply in practice.

Parameters of Incubation

Let us now consider the parameters involved in the crucial question of whether extinction or incubation will take place. Consider Figure 4.2, which shows the relationship between the strength of CR on the ordinate, and the duration of CS-only exposure on the abscissa. Curve A shows the typical decline in CR with duration of CS-only exposure; it is well known that in general, the longer the exposure to CS-only, the weaker the CR (Borkovec, 1972, 1974; Marks & Huson, 1973; Mathews, Johnston, Shaw, and Gelder, 1974; Mathews & Shaw, 1973; Nunes & Marks, 1975; Stern & Marks, 1973; Rachman & Hodgson, 1980; Watson, Gaind, and Marks, 1972). What the theory suggests is that, in Pavlovian B conditioning, a strong CR is evoked that is felt as fear/anxiety by the patient or the experimental animal. This CR habituates or extinguishes, as shown in Figure 4.2, Curve A, as CS-only presentation is prolonged. When strong, the CR can act as reinforcement in much the same way as the UR. Below a critical point, the CR is too weak to act in this manner, and hence below this point

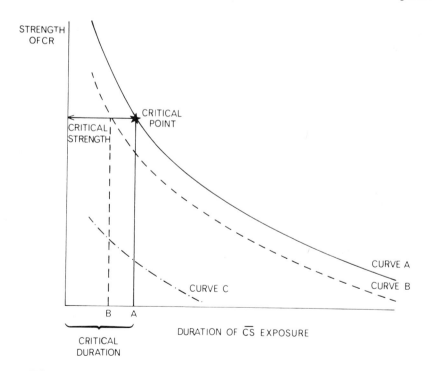

FIGURE 4.2   Strength of CR as a function of duration of CS-only exposure.

only extinction, rather than enhancement of the CR, is obtained. Above the critical point, incubation is obtained.

Figure 4.2 also shows the critical importance of duration of CS-only exposure. Where the CR is strong to begin with, short exposures of CS-only will lead to incubation of anxiety, prolonged exposure to extinction. If we agree that extinction is a crucial element in the treatment of neurotic disorders by behavior therapy (and, as Eysenck, 1979, has argued, by psychotherapy), clearly the theory has great importance from the point of view of behavior therapy generally and treatment by means of flooding, in particular.

In the figure, Curve B shows the effect of long-term duration of CS-only exposure; extinction takes place and displaces Curve A to a lower level. Curve C illustrates the later stages of this procedure, that is, after several extinction experiments have already been performed. Alternatively we can regard Curve C as illustrating the process of desensitization, where ideally the critical point is never reached, and successive presentation of CS only are given at a low level of CR, that is, with little anxiety present.

The main parameters in our model, therefore, are strength of CR and duration of CS-only exposure. These should never be considered in isolation, but always in conjunction. There is some interesting clinical-experimental work to support the adequacy of this model. Rachman (1966) has shown that the flooding treatment of certain types of phobias, when duration of CS-only exposure is short, results not in extinction but in incubation. On the whole, patients got worse rather than better. On the other hand, when in another series of studies long-term exposure to CS-only was attempted, Rachman and Hodgson (1980) obtained excellent curative results. There is thus good evidence that the theory here suggested can be applied to the treatment of human neurotic disorders.

Eysenck (1978) has suggested what is both a crucial experiment and a recommendation for improved methods of treatment. It is well known that in desensitization, when the therapist makes a mistake and uses a stimulus on the hierarchy that elicits too strong an anxiety, the patient loses all the gains previously accomplished and reverts to a much earlier stage of fear/anxiety reactions. The usual recommendation in such a case is to stop desensitization at once and to go back to simple relaxation. The theory here advocated suggests that this is the wrong type of procedure, and that the bad effects commonly observed are due to the shortness of the presentation of the CS-only, which produces incubation. What the theory suggests would be to transform the treatment session from desensitization into flooding and to continue exposure of the anxiety-provoking stimulus for a lengthy period of time rather than curtailing it at a point where the CR is above the critical point. This, according to the theory, should obviate the regression to an earlier stage of the neurotic illness, and should, if anything, have a curative effect.

Habituation and Incubation

The theory in its present form has one curious weakness that requires a solution. The problem is in understanding the fact that while the UR *habituates*, the CR *augments* when repeated exposures to the US or the CS-only are presented to the subject. The problem of how this can be possible is a crucial one for any theory of neurosis, and it is equally crucial for an understanding of the conditioning process in the laboratory. Eysenck (1982) has suggested an answer along the following lines.

Let us call the typical UR "PFA", a mixture of pain, fear, and anxiety, and let us consider what the fate is of the CR accompanying a CS-only. Consider Figure 4.3, where the abscissa denotes the duration of CS-only exposure, the ordinate the strength of the CR, and *a* the moment when CS-only exposure is discontinued. As we have already seen, the strength of the CR declines from a maximum that is presumably equal to or less than the UR. We now have to explain why the reinforcement produced by the CR, that is, the PFA effect mediated by the CS, is apparently more powerful than the UR and leads to incubation rather than to habituation and extinction.

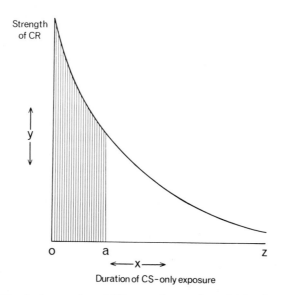

FIGURE 4.3   Summation of CR strength over time of CS-only exposure.

The most obvious reason would seem to be that because the CS-only exposure is continued over a period of time, the PFA effects build up, so that what we should take into account is not just the strength of the CR at 0, but rather the whole area under the curve, as indicated by vertical lines. This suggestion therefore amounts simply to an hypotheses that after CS-only exposure the PFA effects, extending over a long period of time, will sum-mate to produce a stronger effect than the UR effects, which occupy a much shorter period of time. In the case of Napalkov's dogs, the US lasts only a few milliseconds (i.e., the shot fired from a pistol), but the CR extends over a period of time. The position is rather similar to the old story about the man who could not go to sleep when the neighbor living in the room above dropped one shoe on the floor when going to bed. He kept awaiting the drop of the other shoe! The noise produced by the first shoe is a momentary phenomenon, but the waiting for the second shoe is continued over a much longer period of time.

This model, as it stands, is of course insufficient. It would suggest that if exposure of the CS only were to be continued to point z, then the incuba-tion effect should be even stronger than if it terminated at point a. This is clearly implausible, and in fact untrue; if it were true, then flooding treat-ment could not work, as it is known to do. We have to introduce one further step, namely the proviso that for the summation of the area under the curve, recency is an important variable, so that events at or close to point a count much more heavily than points remote from a in the direction of z. Thus as we approach point z the very weak CRs recorded there outweight the very strong CRs found at or near the point of the CS-only exposure, so that the total effect is very weak. Only termination of CS-only exposure relatively close to point 0, would, through integration of the area under the curve with this proviso, provide us with a CR stronger than the UR generated by the US. Eysenck (1982) suggests that the hypothesis in question could be expressed in terms of a formula:

$$I = \int_0^a \alpha(1 - e^{\beta\alpha})e^{-[\gamma(a - x)]} \, dx$$

where I is the total PFA experienced after exposure of the CS only, alpha the strength of the CR at point 0, beta the decay factor or slope of the CR strength over time, and a the termination of the exposure of CS-only. It would also seem to be important to introduce a backward weighting factor, gamma, which may differ from person to person. Broadbent (1958) has suggested that introverts weight events distant in time more heavily than do extraverts, who are more likely to weight heavily quite recent exposures.

It will be seen that this model makes adequate provision for individual differences, a feature that to my knowledge no other model of the development of neurosis and treatment has incorporated. Such individual differences would manifest themselves in terms of either alpha, beta, or gamma, and from general personality theory (Eysenck, 1981) it should not be difficult to make quite specific predictions for the interrelation of these three factors, extraversion–introversion, and neuroticism–stability. It would seem to me that the search for the interaction between personality variables and treatment should not be random, but governed by specific hypotheses related to a definite model, such as the one presented here. This general hypothesis may serve to account for the facts of neurosis and experimental extinction; there is no direct evidence one way or the other, and indeed it would seem quite difficult to design an experiment to obtain such evidence. Nevertheless such an experiment would seem crucial to the development of the theory, and it to be hoped that work along these lines will be carried out in the near future.

To summarize, I have altered Watson's original theory by suggesting the use of Pavlovian B instead of Pavlovian A conditioning; I have suggested that the theory of extinction requires reworking; and I have suggested that under certain circumstances the presentation of CS-only can lead to the enhancement of the CR (incubation) rather than to extinction. In addition, I have specified some of the parameters involved in deciding whether extinction or incubation should take place. I have also suggested that the theory in question is of considerable concern to behavior therapists insofar as it specifies the events taking place in the genesis of a neurotic disorder and specifies the features responsible for successful treatment of the neurosis, namely Pavlovian extinction. I have previously suggested (Eysenck, 1980) that this general theory is capable of unifying all the known facts, not only of behavior therapy but also of psychotherapy and spontaneous remission. I now turn to a discussion of this last suggestion.

Application of the Theory

What, in fact, is known with some degree of certainty in these various fields? First, spontaneous remission, or rather the events taking place during nontreatment that produce spontaneous remission, can be extremely effective in curing neurotic disorders within a time space of 2 years or so. Rachman and Wilson (1980) have documented this point exhaustively, and it is an interesting fact that the majority of psychiatric treatises and textbooks, including psychoanalytic works, do not even mention this vitally important variable, in spite of the fact that spontaneous remission probably contributes all, or nearly all, of the effectiveness that is claimed for psychotherapeutic, psychoanalytic, and other methods of treatment.

Second, psychotherapy of the traditional kind (including psychoanalysis) is effective in improving the condition of neurotic patients, but it has not been shown to be superior to spontaneous remission (Eysenck, 1984; Rachman & Wilson, 1980). Claims have been made (e.g., Bergin & Lambert, 1978; Smith & Glass, 1977; Smith, Glass, & Miller, 1980) that there now exists such evidence, but as the above references make clear, these claims are essentially unfounded.

The third point to be explained is the existence of a possible biphasic effect of psychotherapy, particularly of the Freudian kind. It appears that although some patients are benefited, others may be made worse (Hadley & Strupp, 1976; Strupp, Hadley, & Gomes-Schwartz, 1977). The evidence is far from conclusive (Mays & Franks, 1980), but is it sufficient to suggest that such negative effects do occur, at least occasionally.

This suggestion is supported by evidence pointing to the importance of the personality and approach of the therapist, irrespective of theoretical position (Truax, 1963; Truax, Frank, & Imber, 1966). The work summarized in these studies suggests that empathy, genuineness, and warmth appear to be favorable qualities in therapists, whereas their absence would seem to produce negative effects in patients.

The final point requiring explanation is that behavior therapy is significantly better in its effect than is spontaneous remission, orthodox psychotherapy, or psychoanalysis (Kazdin & Wilson, 1978). These authors discuss all the qualifications needed to make this generalization acceptable and also discuss the difficulties of research in this field. Eysenck (1984) discussed the large-scale review of all work in this field by Smith et al. (1980) and has shown that their own data and calculations support this conclusion, although they themselves fail to realize the import of their analyses.

Unification of Treatment Methods

Any proper theory of anxiety and neurosis must be able to explain these facts, and it is suggested that the revised Watsonian model, incorporating both the notion of "preparedness" and the new extinction model involving the incubation of anxiety, is capable of fulfilling this function. I begin with an explanation of spontaneous remission. It is well known that people suffering from neurotic disorders who are denied psychiatric attention tend to seek help from priests, teachers, friends, or relatives; in doing so they can discuss their problems endlessly with these persons who could be regarded as lay therapists. The essential feature is the presentation of the causes of their troubles, that is, the CSs in our theory, without reinforcement, and in the presence of a sympathetic listener who will reduce the general level of anxiety (and hence the general level of Curve A in Figure 4.2). Under these conditions we would expect extinction to take place, although the unsystematic presentation of the CSs, partly resembling desensitization, partly flooding, but without any preconceived plan to govern the presentation, would make the whole process much less successful than proper behavior therapy, following a theoretically justifiable mode of procedure.

Psychotherapy and psychoanalysis, essentially, are similar in this respect to the procedures used by the lay therapists in spontaneous remission. Here too the patient talks about his troubles, usually in an ascending kind of hierarchy, and here too he is reassured by the presence of a kind, sympathetic, and helpful listener. Under these conditions, as in the case of spontaneous remission, extinction should take place, but the effect should be less marked than in the case of behavior therapy because of the unplanned nature of the exercise. This will also explain the last point above, namely the fact that behavior therapy is significantly better in its effect than is spontaneous remission, orthodox psychotherapy, or psychoanalysis. Behavior therapists, by using consciously paradigms of extinction that have been shown in the laboratory and in the clinic to be successful, clearly should do better than therapists of other persuasions who do not consciously make use of extinction methodology but use it implicitly and without proper planning.

The possible biphasic effect of psychotherapy, and particularly psychoanalysis, may be explained by the methods used by certain types of therapists, as suggested in our fourth point above. Empathy, genuineness, and warmth have been found to be favorable qualities in therapists, presumably because they lower the general anxiety present in the situation and thus make it much less likely that the crucial point on our curve in Figure 4.2 would be reached. In other words, a good therapists keeps patients' anxiety below this point and hence makes extinction rather than incubation more likely.

Some analysts, particularly of the Freudian kind, quite consciously avoid sympathy and explanations to the patient and restrict themselves to interpretation; this would increase the anxiety of the patient and hence make it more likely that during the therapy session the critical point would be reached and surpassed, hence leading to incubation and to a worsening of the patient's condition. Sutherland (1977) gives an interesting account of how the behavior of the therapist and the negative effects of treatment may have been linked in a particular case. Other interesting accounts of a similar kind are given by York (1966). These accounts bear out in considerable detail the hypothesis outlined above.

The unification of theories of treatments outlined above has been discussed previously in much greater detail (Eysenck, 1980), and no attempt is made here to repeat this work. However, it may be useful to point out that if the theory is correct, we have an important counterpoint to the frequent suggestion that we should not talk about "behavior therapy," but rather about behavior therapies, that is, a multiplicity of methods having no theoretical justification or unification. I would suggest that this notion is entirely false, and that all the methods used, for example, desensitization, flooding, and modeling, can be derived directly from the general theory outlined in this chapter. I have always made the point that behavior therapy is an applied science (e.g., Eysenck, 1976) and that it is only when it applies general principles discovered in the laboratory, and theories based upon these principles, that it is of potential use to psychiatrists and clinical psychologists. This view, which is clearly opposed to the Lazarus-type of "broad spectrum" treatment, finds support in the facts outlined above, and in the possibility of extending this unification beyond behavior therapy to psychotherapy, psychoanalysis, and even spontaneous remission.

We can see that Watson's theory, in its revised form, is still viable and explains many detailed facts that cannot be accounted for at the moment by any alternative theory. This applies not only to Freudian and other "dynamic" theories, but also to so-called cognitive theories; it would be difficult to see how such theories could account for the many observational and experimental facts dealt with in this chapter. How, one would like to ask, can a cognitive theorist account for the exceptional effectiveness of flooding with response prevention in the treatment of handwashing and other obsessive–compulsive disorders (Rachman & Hodgson, 1980), where previously methods of treatment using cognitive methods fail to effect any kind of improvement whatsoever? It is factual questions of this kind that we should always be asking when evaluating a method of therapy or a general theory; theories are useful in the degree to which they govern and suggest improvements in practice. It is by this criterion that the present theory also will in due course be judged.

References

Baum, M. (1970). Extinction of avoidance responding through response prevention (flooding). *Psychological Bulletin, 74,* 276–284.

Bergin, A. E., & Lambert, M. J. (1978). The evaluation of therapeutic outcomes. In S. L. Garfield & A. E. Bergin (Eds.), *Handbook of psychotherapy and behavior change.* (2nd ed.). New York: Wiley.

Bersh, P. J. (1980). Eysenck's theory of incubation: A critical analysis. *Behaviour Research and Therapy, 18,* 11–17.

Borkovec, T. D. (1972). Effects of expectancy on the outcome of systematic desensitization in implosive treatment for analogue anxiety. *Behavior Therapy, 3,* 29–40.

Borkovec, T. D. (1974). Heart rate process during systematic desensitization and implosive therapy for analogue anxiety. *Behavior Therapy, 5,* 636–641.

Bregman, E. (1934). An attempt to modify the emotional attitudes of infants by the conditioned response technique. *Journal of Genetic Psychology, 45,* 169–198.

Breland, K., & Breland, M. (1966). *Animal behavior.* New York: Macmillan.

Bridger, W., & Mandel, I. J. (1964). A comparison of GSR fear responses produced by threat and electric shock. *Journal of Psychiatric Research, 2,* 31–40.

Broadbent, D. E. (1958). *Perception and communication.* London: Academic Press.

Bykov, K. M. (1957). *The cerebral cortex and the internal organs.* (W. H. Gantt, trans.). New York: Chemical Publishing.

Campbell, D., Sanderson, R., & Laverty, S. G. (1964). Characteristics of a conditioned response in human subjects during extinction trials following a simple traumatic conditioning trial. *Journal of Abnormal and Social Psychology, 68,* 627–639.

Cook, S. W., & Harris, R. E. (1937). The verbal conditioning of the galvanic skin reflex. *Journal of Experimental Psychology, 21,* 202–205.

Dykman, R. A., and Gantt, W. H. (1958). Cardiovascular conditioning in dogs and humans. In W. H. Gantt (Ed.), *Physiological basis of psychiatry.* Springfield, IL: Charles C. Thomas.

Dykman, R. A., & Gantt, W. H. (1960a). A case of experimental neurosis and recovery in relation to the orienting response. *Journal of Psychology, 50,* 105–110.

Dykman, R. A., & Gantt, W. H. (1960b). Experimental psychogenic hypertensions: Blood pressure changes conditioned to painful stimuli (schizokinesis). *Bulletin of John Hopkins Hospital, 107,* 72–89.

Dykman, R. A., Mack, R. L., & Ackerman, P. T. (1965). The evaluation of autonomic and motor components of the unavoidance conditioned response in the dog. *Psychophysiology, 1,* 209–230.

English, H. B. (1929). Three cases of the "conditioned fear response". *Journal of Abnormal and Social Psychology, 34,* 221–225.

Eysenck, H. J. (1968). A theory of the incubation of anxiety/fear response. *Behaviour Research & Therapy, 6,* 319–321.

Eysenck, H. J. (1975). A note on backward conditioning. *Behaviour Research & Therapy, 13,* 2101–2202.

Eysenck, H. J. (1976). Behavior therapy: Dogma or applied science? In M. P. Feldman & A. Broadhurst (Eds.), *Theoretical and experimental bases of the behaviour therapies.* London: Wiley.

Eysenck, H. J. (1977). *You and neurosis.* Los Angeles: Sage.

Eysenck, H. J. (1978). What to do when desensitization goes wrong? *Australian Behaviour Therapist, 5,* 15–16.

Eysenck, H. J. (1978). The conditioning model of neurosis. *The Behavioral and Brain Sciences, 2,* 155–199.

Eysenck, H. J. (1980). A unified theory of psychotherapy, behaviour therapy and spontaneous remission. *Zeitschrift für Psychologie, 188,* 43–56.

Eysenck, H. J. (1981). *A Model for Personality.* New York: Springer Verlag.

Eysenck, H. J. (1982). Neobehahvioristic (S–R) theory. In G. Terence Wilson & Cyril M. Franks (Eds.), *Contemporary Behaviour Therapy.* (pp. 205–276). New York: The Guilford Press.

Eysenck, H. J. (1984). Meta-analysis: An abuse of research integration. *The Journal of Special Education, 18,* 41–59.

Eysenck, H. J., & Rachman, S. (1965). *The causes and cures of neurosis.* London: Routledge & Kegan Paul.

Fulker, D. W. (1981). The genetic and environmental architecture of psychoticism, extraversion and neuroticism. In H. J. Eysenck (Ed.), *A model for personality*. (pp. 88–122). New York: Springer.

Galbrecht, C. D., Dykman, R. A., & Peters, J. (1960). The effect of traumatic experiences on the growth and behavior of the rat. *Journal of Genetic Psychology. 50*, 227–251.

Gossop, M. (1980). *Theories of neurosis*. New York: Springer.

Gourney, A. B., & O'Connor, P. J. (1971). Anxiety associated with flying. *British Journal of Psychiatry, 119*, 159–166.

Grant, D. A. (1964). Classical and operant conditioning. In A. W. Melton (Ed.), *Categories of human learning*. New York: Academic Press.

Gray, J. (1981). Alternative theories of personality. In H. J. Eysenck (Ed.), *A model for personality*. London: Springer.

Grinker, R., & Spiegel, J. (1945). *Men under stress*. London: Churchill.

Groves, P. M., & Thompson, R. F. (1970). Habituation: A dual-process theory. *Psychological Review, 77*, 419–450.

Hadley, S. W., & Strupp, H. H. (1976). Contemporary views of negative effects of psychotherapy. *Archives of General Psychiatry, 33*, 1291–1303.

Harris, B. (1979). Whatever happened to little Albert? *American Psychologist, 34*, 151–160.

Hinde, R. A., & Stevenson-Hinde, J. (1973). *Constraints on learning*. London: Academic Press.

Kazdin, A. E., & Wilson, G. T. (1978). *Evaluation of behavior therapy. Issues, evidence, and research strategies*. Cambridge, MA: Ballinger.

Kimble, G. A. (1961). *Hilgard and Marquis' conditioning and learning*. New York: Appleton-Century-Crofts.

Kimmel, H. D. (1975). Conditioned fear and anxiety. In C. D. Spielberger & I. G. Sarason (Eds.), *Stress and anxiety* (Vol. 1). New York: Wiley.

Lautsch, H. (1971). Dental phobia. *British Journal of Psychiatry, 1119*, 151–158.

Lichtenstein, P. E. (1950). Studies of anxiety: I. The production of a feeding inhibition in dogs. *Journal of Comparative and Physiological Psychology, 43*, 16–29.

Maatsch, J. L. (1959). Learning and fixation after a single shock trial. *Journal of Comparative and Physiological Psychology, 52*, 408–410.

Mackintosh, N. J. (1974). *The psychology of animal learning*. London: Academic Press.

Marks, I. M. (1969). *Fears and phobias*. London: Academic Press.

Marks, I. M., & Huson, J. (1973). Physiological aspects of neutral and phobic imagery: Further observations. *British Journal of Psychiatry, 122*, 345–356.

Mathews, A. M., Johnston, D. W., Shaw, P. M., & Gelder, M. G. (1974). Process variables and the prediction of outcome in behaviour therapy. *British Journal of Psychiatry, 125*, 256–264.

Mathews, A. M., & Shaw, P. (1973). Emotional arousal and persuasion effects in flooding. *Behaviour Research and Therapy, 11*, 587–598.

Mays, D. T., & Franks, C. M. (1980). Getting worse: Psychotherapy or no treatment. The jury should still be out. *Professional Psychology, 11*, 78–92.

Morley, S. (1977). The incubation of avoidance behaviour: Strain differences in susceptibility. *Behaviour Research and Therapy, 15*, 365–367.

Napalkov, A. V. (1963). Information process of the brain. In N. Wiener & J. P. Schade (Eds.), *Progress in brain research* (Vol. 2: Nerve brain and memory models). Amsterdam: Elsevier.

Nunes, J. S., & Marks, I. M. (1975). Feedback of true heart-rate during exposure *in vivo*. *Archives of General Psychiatry, 32*, 983–994.

Pavlov, I. P. (1927). *Lectures on conditioned reflexes*. New York: International Publishers.

Rachman, S. (1966). Studies in desensitization: II. Flooding. *Behaviour Research and Therapy, 4*, 1–6.

Rachman, S. (1968). *Phobias: Their nature and control*. Springfield, IL: Charles C. Thomas.

Rachman, S., & Hodgson, R. J. (1980). *Obsessions and compulsions.* New York: Appleton-Century-Crofts.

Rachman, S., & Wilson, G. T. (1980). *The effects of psychotherapy.* New York: Pergamon.

Razran, G. (1956). Extinction re-examined and re-analysed: A new theory. *Psychological Review, 63,* 39–52.

Reynierse, J. H. (1966). Effects of CS-only trials on resistance to extinction of an avoidance response. *Journal of Comparative and Physiological Psychology, 61,* 156–158.

Rohrbaugh, M., & Riccio, D. V. (1970). Paradoxical exhancement of learned fear. *Journal of Abnormal Psychology, 75,* 210–216.

Rohrbaugh, M., Riccio, D. V., & Arthur, S. (1972). Paradoxical enhancement of conditioned suppression. *Behaviour Research and Therapy, 10,* 125–130.

Rose, R. J., & Ditto, W. B. (1983). A developmental-genetic analysis of common fears from early adolescence to early adulthood. *Child Development, 54,* 361–368.

Sartory, G., & Eysenck, H. J. (1976). Strain differences in acquisition and extinction of fear responses in rats. *Psychological Reports, 38,* 163–187.

Sartory, G., & Eysenck, H. J. (1978). Fear conditioning and extinction in rats at different times of day. *Journal of General Psychology, 99,* 87–92.

Seligman, M. E. P. (1971). Phobias and preparedness. *Behavior Therapy, 2,* 307–320.

Siegeltuch, M. B., & Baum, M. (1971). Extinction of well-established avoidance through response prevention (flooding). *Behaviour Research and Therapy, 9,* 103–108.

Silvestri, R., Rohrbaugh, M., & Riccio, D. V. Conditions influencing the retention of learned fear in young rats. *Developmental Psychology, 2,* 389–395.

Smith, M. L., & Glass, G. P. (1977). Meta-analysis of psychotherapy outcome studies. *American Psychologist, 32,* 752–760.

Smith, M. K., Glass, G. V., & Miller, T. I. (1980). *The Benefits of Psychotherapy.* Baltimore: The John Hopkins University Press.

Solomon, R. L., Kamin, L. J., & Wynne, L. C. (1953). Traumatic avoidance learning: The outcome of several extinction procedures with dogs. *Journal of Abnormal and Social Psychology, 48,* 291–302.

Solomon, R. L., & Wynne, L. C. (1953). Traumatic avoidance learning. *Psychological Monography, 67(4).*

Solomon, R. L., & Wynne, L. C. (1954). Traumatic avoidance learning. The principles of anxiety conservation and partial irreversibility. *Psychological Review, 61,* 353–385.

Stern, R., & Marks, I. M. (1973). Brief and prolonged flooding. *Archives of General Psychiatry, 28,* 270–276.

Strupp, H. H., Hadley, S. W., & Gomes-Schwartz, B. (1977). *Psychotherapy for better or worse.* New York: Jason Aronson.

Sutherland, S. (1977). *Breakdown.* London: Temple Smith.

Thorndike, E. L. (1935). *The psychology of wants, interests and* attitudes. New York: Appleton-Century-Crofts.

Truax, C. (1963). Effective ingredients in psychotherapy. *Journal of Counseling Psychology, 10,* 256–263.

Truax, C., Frank, I., & Imber, S. (1966). Therapist empathy, genuineness, and warmth and patient outcome. *Journal of Consulting Psychology, 30,* 395–401.

Watson, J. B., & Rayner, R. (1920). Conditioned emotional reactions. *Journal of Experimental Psychology, 3,* 1–14.

Watson, J. P., Gaind, P., & Marks, I. M. (1972). Physiological habituation to continuous phobic stimulation. *Behaviour Research and Therapy, 10,* 269–278.

Woods, D. J. (1974). Paradoxical enhancement of learned anxiety response. *Psychological Reports, 35,* 295–304.

York, C. (1966). *If Hopes Were Dupes.* London: Hutchinson.

5

Expectancy Model of Fear

STEVEN REISS
RICHARD J. MCNALLY

Three important assumptions underlie the expectancy model of fear and anxiety. The first assumption is that almost everyone is motivated to avoid stimuli that arouse expectations of environmental danger. The second assumption is that anxiety sensitivity can be regarded as a personality variable along which stable individual differences can be measured. These differences may be related to biological factors such as autonomic reactivity, and they may be related to learning about the real and imagined consequences of becoming anxious. The third assumption is that people learn that certain environmental stimuli make them anxious. The expectancy model holds that these assumptions have important implications for understanding exposure therapies, placebos, and how people can be phobic for stimuli they recognize to be harmless.

Statement of Expectancy Theory

A formula statement of expectancy theory follows. As with many theoretical formulas in behavioral science, there is no suggestion of mathematical precision. The formulas permit general predictions in which increases (or decreases) in one variable cause increases (or decreases) in another variable. The purpose of the formula statement is conceptual clarity regarding the number of variables in the model and the general ways in which these variables may influence one another.

The central tenet of the expectancy model can be expressed by the following, Formula 1:

$$Fb = Ed + (Ea \times Sa),$$

where Fb (fear behavior) denotes a theoretical tendency to avoid a feared stimulus; Ed (danger expectancy), the theoretical tendency of a feared stimulus to elicit expectations of harm in the environment; Ea (anxiety expectancy), the theoretical tendency of a feared stimulus to elicit expectations of becoming anxious; and Sa (anxiety sensitivity), the degree to which an individual is afraid of becoming anxious.

Formula 1 proposes a two-component analysis of fear in terms of three variables. One fear component is the danger expectancy (Ed) in which a person learns that a given stimulus is a reliable signal of danger in the environment. The other fear component ($Ea \times Sa$) is the product of the anxiety expectancy and anxiety sensitivity. The total amount of fear, or more precisely, the total theoretical tendency to avoid any specific stimulus, is the sum of the avoidance motivation associated with the danger component and the avoidance motivation associated with the anxiety component. Some phobias may be sustained primarily by danger expectancies, others by anxiety expectancies, and still others by various degrees of both danger and anxiety expectancies.

The significance of Formula 1 is that it implies two categorically different reasons for avoiding a given stimulus. Viewing a stimulus as dangerous motivates people to avoid that stimulus (e.g., The snake will bite me; the airplane will crash; I will fall from the top floor of the building). Viewing a stimulus as anxiety-arousing motivates at least some people to avoid that stimulus (e.g., the snake will make me so nervous I could have a heart attack; I will faint in the elevator before I get to the top floor of the building).

(The distinction between danger and anxiety expectancies should not be confused with the psychodynamic distinction between fear and anxiety. The terms *fear* and *anxiety* will be used interchangeably in accordance with the behavioral tradition of regarding anxiety as a fear of its eliciting stimuli.)

DANGER EXPECTANCY

The expectancy model holds that phobias usually are initiated by danger expectancies (Ed). In this process, a person reacts to a given stimulus as a reliable signal of environmental harm, negative social condition, or loss. For example, danger expectancies include an airplane flight eliciting anticipations of a crash, a snake eliciting anticipations of a snake bite, and a school examination eliciting anticipations of failure and social rejection. The expectancy model holds that people generally are motivated to avoid stimuli that are viewed as signals of physical or social harm.

The following comments concern the nature, initiation, and measurement of danger expectancies.

1. How are danger expectancies initiated? The early behavior therapists explained the initiation of fear in terms of Mowrer's (1947) theory of avoidance learning. This view holds that initially neutral stimuli become conditioned elicitors of fear when experienced in temporal contiguity with such aversive events as conflict, trauma, pain, and confinement. A phobic stimulus is regarded as a conditioned stimulus (CS), acquired fear is regarded as a conditioned response (CR), and aversive (dangerous) events are regarded as unconditioned, reinforcing stimuli (UCSs). Under this view, danger expectancies are initated by Pavlovian conditioning.

Although the early behavior therapists made an important contribution in their argument that phobic anxiety could be a result of Pavlovian conditioning, the view that all phobias can be explained in this manner is questionable. Pavlovian conditioning (repeated CS–UCS experience) is only one of a number of methods by which a person can learn to fear an initially neutral stimulus. Fear also can result from cognitive learning (e.g., an adult tells a child that a house is haunted), covert conditioning (repeated associations of imaginations or words), observational learning, and deductive reasoning (e.g., a scientist presents a mathematical analysis suggesting the existence of dangerous "black holes"). Given that the world population is about four billion, and that almost everyone has at least one fear, the view that all of these fears were learned in the same way (Pavlovian conditioning), and that none were learned in other possible ways (observational learning, instructions, deductive reasoning), seems inconsistent with the varied nature of human experience.

Expectancy theory differs from some previous behavioral models in its explicit recognition that Pavlovian conditioning is only one of several possible ways in which fear can be initiated. The model also includes the possibility of covert conditioning, observational learning, and cognitive learning. Generally, it is assumed that if it is possible for a fear to be learned in a particular way, the possibility will account for at least some examples of real-world fears.

2. As shown in Table 5.1 danger expectancies are measured by the frequencies with which the feared stimulus elicits anticipations of a variety of harmful events. For example, consider an individual who is afraid of flying in an airplane. In reflective moments, the individual may realize that airplane flying is safe, but when the person actually is in flight, the person

TABLE 5.1

Measure of Danger Expectancy

Below are some ideas that might pass through your mind before or during an airplane flight. Indicate how often each thought usually occurs. Rate each item 1-5 by using the scale below:

1. Thought never occurs.
2. Thought rarely occurs.
3. Thought occasionally occurs.
4. Thought occurs with some frequency.
5. Thought often occurs.

_____ The plane might collide with another plane.
_____ The landing gear might not operate when it is time to land.
_____ The plane might fall from the sky and crash.
_____ One or more of the plane's engines might stall.
_____ The plane might run out of fuel in mid-air.
_____ A wing might fall off.
_____ An engine might catch on fire.
_____ An engine might fall off the plane.
_____ The plane might be struck by lightning.
_____ The plane might be hijacked.

might worry that the plane will crash, the wings will fall off the plane, the landing gear might not work, and so on. The greater the degree to which a person experiences such anticipations, the greater the motivation to avoid airplane flying, and the higher the individual's score on the measure of danger expectancy shown in Table 5.1.

3. Each fear requires its own separate measure of danger expectancy. Whereas danger expectancy in a fear of flying might include anticipations of the engine falling off the wing, danger expectancies in a fear of heights might include slipping under the guard rail of the observation deck. Since specific dangerous events such as a wing falling off and slipping under a guard rail obviously are relevant to some fears and not others, a separate measure of danger expectancy is needed for each specific fear.

ANXIETY EXPECTANCY

An anxiety expectancy (Ea) is an anticipation of becoming anxious when a certain stimulus is encountered. The stimulus may be any cue that people can learn to fear, and the anticipatory responses are expectations of anxiety sensations (see Table 5.2). One example of an anxiety expectancy is an airplane flight eliciting anticipations of other people noticing that you are afraid of flying. Another example is a school examination eliciting anticipations of fainting in the classroom.

TABLE 5.2

Measure of Anxiety Expectancy

Imagine that you are about to take an airplane flight. Below some feelings, thoughts, and sensations you might experience. Indicate how likely you would be to experience these feelings at some point before or during the flight. Rate each item 1–5 by using the scale below:

1. Experience very unlikely to occur.
2. Experience unlikely to occur.
3. 50/50 chance that experience would occur.
4. Experience likely to occur.
5. Experience very likely to occur.

_____ You might perspire excessively
_____ You might feel faint
_____ You might feel nauseous
_____ Your heart might pound or beat rapidly
_____ Your stomach might growl
_____ You might tremble or feel shaky
_____ You might not be able to keep your thoughts clear
_____ You might feel nervous
_____ You might experience unusual body sensations (such as tingling)
_____ You might lose control of your feelings

The following comments concern the nature, initiation, and measurement of anxiety expectancies.

1. Recognition of a fear (e.g., I am afraid of snakes) implies the presence of an anxiety expectancy. Since people generally can self-report their fears and identify the stimuli that make them anxious, anxiety expectancies are present in many phobias and anxiety disorders. Anxiety expectancies differ in the amount of anxiety anticipated, the number of stimulus elements eliciting expectations of anxiety, and the associative strength between the eliciting stimuli and the anticipation of anxiety.

2. Both observational and cognitive learning can result in an anticipation of becoming anxious. In the vast majority of instances, however, anxiety expectancies are probably learned as a result of associative experiences. Having learned that a given stimulus signals danger, the person should experience either in vivo or covert associations between the feared stimulus and anxiety. Through stimulus expectancy learning, the person should learn to anticipate becoming anxious when the phobic stimulus is encountered. The expectancy model holds that the laws governing the learning of stimulus expectations resulting from associative experiences are essentially the same as the laws governing Pavlovian conditioning (Reiss, 1980). Thus, the principles of Pavlovian conditioning are held to be especially relevant to the learning and unlearning of anxiety expectancies.

3. Recent attempts to modify the applied Pavlovian theory of fear have focused on the stimulus properties of anxiety responses, and this has led to at least three theories in which a two-component analysis of fear was proposed. In addition to expectancy theory, both Eysenck's (1979) incubation theory and Evans' (1972) theory propose a two-component analysis of fear. However, the three theories differ in terms of the proposed nature of the second component. The expectancy model, for example, suggests certain measures for anxiety sensitivity that are not included in the other models. The various two-component models also permit different predictions. Nevertheless, all three theories can be contrasted with Mowrer's (1947) influential view in which only one Pavlovian component is postulated to explain fear behavior. A central issue for future research in this area is whether fear should be analyzed in terms of one or two distinguishable components.

4. Experimental evidence supporting the concept of anxiety expectancy has been reported by Kirsch, Tennen, Wickless, Saccone, and Cody (1983). The investigation compared the effects of systematic desensitization, therapeutically-credible placebo, and waiting-list control conditions on fear in snake-phobic subjects recruited by a newspaper advertisement. Of primary interest here are the interrelated findings that expected anxiety was highly correlated with behavioral and self-report measures of fear at both pre- and posttreatment assessments. It appears that the anticipation of fear may lead to both subjectively experienced fear and to avoidance motivation.

ANXIETY SENSITIVITY

Under the model proposed here, danger and anxiety expectancies are situation-specific factors, whereas anxiety sensitivity is a person-specific factor. In other words, anxiety sensitivity is proposed as a new personality variable that is relevant to the development of phobias, fears, and anxiety disorders. Anxiety sensitivity (fear of anxiety) is a clinically salient aspect of many case examples of anxiety disorders, especially phobias and agoraphobia (Beck, Laude, & Bohnert, 1974; Fenichel, 1945; Mathews, Gelder, & Johnston, 1981; Mavissakalian & Barlow, 1981).

The Reiss–Epstein–Gursky Anxiety Sensitivity Scale is shown in Table 5.3. This scale includes 16 items intended to measure concern about the real or imagined consequences of anxiety. These consequences include additional anxiety (incubation), physical and mental illness, loss of control, and embarrassment. The scale is scored by assigning 0,1, . . . 4 points, respectively, to the response alternatives *very little, a little, some, much,* and *very much.* The scale has been found to have sound psychometric properties and is a valid measure of anxiety sensitivity (Reiss, Peterson, Gursky, & McNally, 1984).

TABLE 5.3

Reiss–Epstein–Gursky Anxiety Sensitivity Scale

Respond to each item by circling one of the five corresponding phrases. Circle the phrase which best represents the extent to which you agree with the item. If any of the items concern something that is not part of your experience (i.e., "It scares me when I feel shaky" for someone who has never trembled or had the "shakes"), answer on the basis of how you think you might feel *if you had* such an experience. Otherwise, answer all items on the basis of your own experience. Be careful to make only one choice for each item and please answer all items.

1. It is important to me not to appear nervous.
2. When I cannot keep my mind on a task, I worry that I might be going crazy.
3. It scares me when I feel "shaky" (trembling).
4. It scares me when I feel faint.
5. It is important to me to stay in control of my emotions.
6. It scares me when my heart beats rapidly.
7. It embarrasses me when my stomach growls.
8. It scares me when I am nauseous.
9. When I notice that my heart is beating rapidly, I worry that I might have a heart attack.
10. It scares me when I am short of breath.
11. When my stomach is upset, I worry that I might be seriously ill.
12. It scares me when I am unable to keep my mind on a task.
13. Other people notice when I feel shaky.
14. Unusual body sensations scare me.
15. When I am nervous, I worry that I might be mentally ill.
16. It scares me when I am nervous.

The following comments concern the concept of anxiety sensitivity and its role in expectancy theory.

1. Equivalent levels of anxiety should be more salient, and more reinforcing, for individuals who are highly sensitive to becoming anxious than for those who are not. Factors that increase the salience of anxiety and its reinforcing value are factors that favor fear conditioning. Hence, there should be a positive correlation between anxiety sensitivity and the number of different stimuli feared. This prediction was supported in a study in which the Reiss–Epstein–Gursky scale was found to be a better predictor of college students' Fear Survey Schedule-II scores than were the Taylor Manifest Anxiety Scale and a reliable measure of the frequency of anxiety symptoms (Reiss, Peterson, Gursky, & McNally, 1984). These results support expectancy theory.

2. The expectancy model provides a conceptual basis for the importance of the *Ea* and *Sa* variables. The implication is to study the role of these

variables in human fear and other psychopathological anxiety conditions. Ultimately, the importance of the model may be related more to the importance of the *Ea* and *Sa* variables than to the validity of the model in its current form. Almost all psychological theories are invalid. The good theories stimulate research on important variables, whereas the bad ones stimulate research on trivial variables.

LEARNING PRINCIPLES

Expectancy theory posits two learning principles, one for danger expectancies and one for anxiety expectancies, both of which apply only under conditions of associative experience. These principles reflect the authors' adaptation of Wagner and Rescorla's (1972) theory of Pavlovian conditioning to the phenomenon of human fear. This adaptation is consistent with the modified statements of the Wagner–Rescorla theory (Wagner, 1978, 1981); the principles presented here are based primarily on the well-established findings that surprising events are processed differently than expected events (e.g., Kamin, 1969; Wagner & Rescorla, 1972).

The expectancy model holds that danger expectancies are strengthened and weakened as a function of the discrepancy between the levels of danger experienced and anticipated when the person is exposed to a specific stimulus complex. Danger expectancies are strengthened (acquired) when the level of danger is surprisingly higher than the person expected; danger expectancies are weakened (extinguished) when the level of danger is surprisingly lower than the person expected. Anxiety expectancies are strengthened and weakened as a function of the level of anxiety experienced and anticipated when the person is exposed to a specific stimulus complex. Anxiety expectancies are strengthened when the level of anxiety is surprisingly higher than the person expected to experience; anxiety expectancies are weakened when the level of anxiety is surprisingly lower than anticipated. For each expectancy, the critical factors are discrepancies between experience and expectations elicited by the total stimulus complex as opposed to expectations elicited by the phobic stimulus alone.

The expectancy model predicts a therapeutic exposure only when the reduction in anxiety is surprising to the subject. For example, it should be therapeutic when a person with agoraphobia remains in a situation and the panic attack subsides. On the other hand, it should not be therapeutic when a person with agoraphobia is not surprised by the absence of a panic attack ("Oh, this doesn't count. It was cloudy outside and I always do better on cloudy days. That's why I didn't get scared and have something bad happen. The next time I'll panic.")

Although the expectancy model posits associative learning formulas for danger and anxiety expectancies, the model does not specify any similar formulas to explain anxiety sensitivity. This is because anxiety sensitivity is not thought of as an associative process and instead is viewed as a set of learned beliefs about the consequences of anxiety symptoms. This learning may result from any of a number of factors. Moreover, there may be a biological basis to anxiety sensitivity; that is, people who are highly reactive autonomically may develop more concerns about becoming anxious than people who are less reactive autonomically.

Implications

The expectancy model has broad implications for behavior therapy and models of anxiety.

TWO-COMPONENT ANALYSIS OF EXPOSURE THERAPIES

The behavioral treatments for fear were developed in accordance with the principles of applied contiguity theory (Reiss, 1980). These principles include the view that Pavlovian conditioning occurs when a CS and a UCS are paired, that Pavlovian extinction occurs when an effective CS is presented alone (without the UCS), and that Pavlovian counterconditioning occurs when an effective CS is paired with behaviors that are antagonistic to the CR. Applied to fear phenomena, the contiguity model specifies that fear is learned when a real or imagined stimulus is associated with a real or imagined traumatic (aversive) event, and that fear is diminished when a real or imagined phobic stimulus is presented in a harmless manner. The contiguity model also holds that fear can be diminished through counterconditioning in which the phobic stimulus is paired with fear antagonistic responses such as relaxation.

Systematic desensitization and flooding are among the behavior therapy techniques based on the principles of applied contiguity theory. In systematic desensitization, a mildly feared stimulus is paired with relaxation in an effort to countercondition relaxation to the feared stimulus. In flooding therapy, a highly feared stimulus is presented in a harmless manner for a sustained time period in an effort to produce extinction of the fear. The term "exposure therapy" has been used widely to refer to these and other therapies (such as modeling) in which the subject is exposed to feared stimuli in vivo, in observation, or through imagination.

The expectancy model suggests certain modifications in the fundamental principles underlying exposure therapies. Under expectancy theory, the harmless presentation of a feared stimulus can be insufficient to produce extinction, and the pairing of a feared stimulus with relaxation does not necessarily produce counterconditioning. This is because the expectancy model provides a two-component analysis of the learning and unlearning of fear. Whereas applied contiguity theory treats fear acquisition and extinction in terms of danger expectancies only, the expectancy model requires consideration of the effects of stimulus exposures on both danger and anxiety expectancies. Since different events (danger and anxiety) reinforce danger and anxiety expectancies, it is theoretically possible for one process (e.g., danger expectancy) to be weakened while the other process (e.g., anxiety expectancy) is strengthened.

The expectancy model provides four theoretically possible outcomes to a trial in which a feared stimulus is exposed. Both the danger and the anxiety expectancies can be strengthened, both expectancies can be weakened, the danger expectancy can be strengthened while the anxiety expectancy is weakened, and the danger expectancy can be weakened while the anxiety expectancy is strengthened. Under Formula 1 of the model, the effects of danger and anxiety expectancies are additive. Thus, total avoidance motivation is increased when both danger and anxiety expectancies are strengthened or when one of these expectancies is strengthened more than the other is weakened. Similarly, total avoidance motivation is weakened when both expectancies are weakened or when one of the expectancies is weakened more than the other is strengthened. Under the expectancy learning principles described previously, danger expectancies are strengthened and weakened as a function of the discrepancy between the levels of danger anticipated and experienced, whereas anxiety expectancies are strengthened and weakened as a function of the discrepancy between the levels of anxiety that are anticipated and experienced.

The expectancy model suggests that therapeutic exposure is most effective when both danger and anxiety expectancies are reduced. This should occur when the stimulus is presented harmlessly (extinction of danger expectancy) and when there is a surprising (unexpected) reduction in anxiety in the presence of the feared stimulus (extinction of anxiety expectancy, or the placebo effect).

FEARING HARMLESS STIMULI

The two-component analysis provides a plausible explanation of the well-known phenomenon of people fearing harmless stimuli. For example, why might a person say, "I am afraid of garden snakes even though I know they are harmless." This statement is confusing under the view that fear results from the association of neutral stimuli with traumatic experience. This view suggests that the fear of snakes should be associated with anticipations of being bitten, strangled, or harmed by snakes. Yet some people insist that they fear garden snakes even though they know that garden snakes are harmless.

Expectancy theory permits the possibility that what was once feared as a signal of danger can now be feared as a signal for becoming anxious. For example, a person may assume as a child that snakes are dangerous and experience associations between snake stimuli and actual anxiety. Over time, the person may have learned that garden snakes are harmless; however, the person still may be motivated to avoid garden snakes because of the expectation of becoming anxious in the presence of any snake.

PLACEBO EFFECT

The expectancy model may be relevant to understanding the placebo effect. This effect is associated with anxiety disorders (Shapiro, 1971) and occurs after a therapeutically credible procedure has been experienced (Kirsch, 1978). Apparently, the placebo induces the belief that therapeutic benefits have occurred, and this belief is sometimes a self-fulfilling prophecy.

How is it possible that the mere belief that one has improved can be sufficient to produce real therapeutic improvement? Perhaps it is because the belief that one has improved from an anxiety condition implies an expectation of responding less anxiously in the future than in the past. Effective placebos should diminish anxiety expectancies. Since anxiety expectancies may be important components of anxiety disorders, placebos that effectively diminish anxiety expectancies should produce real therapeutic gains.

Under expectancy theory, systematic desensitization and other exposure therapies should reduce both danger and anxiety expectancies, whereas effective placebos should reduce anxiety expectancies but not danger expectancies. The two conditions should have approximately equivalent effects when avoidance of the feared object is motivated primarily by the expectation of becoming anxious. Systematic desensitization, however, should be more effective than placebos when avoidance is motivated by expectations of physical danger, harm, or loss. Moreover, when subjects are not preselected for fears sustained primarily by danger versus anxiety expectancies, as has been the case with research studies comparing the effectiveness of CS exposure therapy and credible placebo, some studies should find that systematic desensitization is more effective than placebos, others should find no difference; however, no studies should find that credible placebos are more effective than systematic desensitization (except, of course, by chance when large number of studies are conducted). The contradictory results from credible placebo studies, in which some studies found that desensitization was more effective than credible placebo and others found no differences (Kazdin & Wilcoxon, 1976), suggest that an important variable has been left uncontrolled. Under expectancy theory, the uncontrolled variable is the degree to which the initial fears were sustained primarily by danger versus anxiety expectancies.

Although the expectancy model has implications for understanding placebos, the model does not permit predictions regarding the effectiveness of any particular placebo. There is nothing in the model to evaluate whether or not a particular placebo procedure will induce a belief in therapeutic gain and diminish anxiety expectancies. Moreover, the expectancy model does not predict that placebos can cure agoraphobia or any other anxiety condition. However, if a placebo procedure were found to improve an anxiety condition, the expectancy model holds that the therapeutic improvement would be strongly associated with a reduction in anxiety expectancy as opposed to a reduction in danger expectancy.

ROLE OF SAFETY SIGNALS IN BEHAVIOR THERAPY

A well-established principle of conditioning is that extinction of a neutral stimulus in compound with a feared stimulus can condition fear-inhibiting properties to the initially neutral stimulus (Wagner & Rescorla, 1972). This suggests that some situational stimuli present during exposure therapies may become safety signals (Rizley & Reppucci, 1976). Reiss (1980) has suggested that the therapist, who is one of the most salient stimuli present during behavior therapy, can become a conditioned safety signal. In other words, during exposure therapy, the therapist can be regarded as a salient and initially neutral stimulus extinguished in compound with feared stimuli.

The potential implications of safety-signal conditioning during exposure therapy include the possibility of interactive effects among safety signals, neutral stimuli, and feared stimuli. For example, the protection phenomenon implies that the conditioning of safety-signal properties to a therapist would impede the extinction of a feared stimulus. Although the individual would continue to show fear reduction in the therapist's office, this would be because the therapist had become a safety signal actively inhibiting fear as opposed to the feared stimulus having been extinguished. The progress in fear reduction evident in the therapist's office would not be matched by similar gains outside the therapy situation.

Possible examples of safety signals in clinical situations include people with an obsessive–compulsive disorder who fail to become anxious when exposed to an obsessional stimulus (e.g., an unchecked lock) in the presence of the therapist (Roper & Rachman, 1976). Although these clients say they transfer responsibility for any imminent disasters to the therapist, the mechanism underlying this phenomenon may be the establishment of the therapist as a conditioned inhibitor of fear. Similarly, many otherwise housebound agoraphobics can travel with a trusted companion, a vial of valium, or some other talisman (Foa, Stekete, & Young, 1984).

These considerations support Bandura's (1977, p. 202) advice of removing external aids during in vivo desensitization. Bandura's concern is with developing in the client a sense of self-efficacy as opposed to the attribution of fear reduction to the therapist or to other agents of help. The expectancy model provides an alternative rationale for the advice to phase out salient, external aids. Both the therapist and other external aids during in vivo desensitization might become safety signals blocking extinction to feared stimuli, and unless they are at some point removed or reduced in salience, the treatment effect should be less complete and less likely to show desired levels of generalization.

TURNING PHOBIC STIMULI INTO SAFETY SIGNALS

Another issue for future research is the possibility of establishing an initially phobic stimulus as a safety signal that actively suppresses fear to other phobic stimuli. The potential advantage of safety-signal therapy may be related to evidence that safety signals can be extremely resistant to extinction. A safety signal may indicate learning that the CS signals a period of absence from the UCS. The repeated presentation of the CS alone, as in extinction, would be consistent with the anticipation of a period of nonoccurrence of the UCS. Future research is needed to evaluate the therapeutic potential of safety-signal conditioning procedures.

ANXIETY SENSITIVITY AS A PERSONALITY VARIABLE

The expectancy model posits the existence of a personality variable (Sa) that is a predisposing factor in the development of anxiety-mediated disorders. A high sensitivity for anxiety should be associated with tendencies to show exaggerated anxiety reactions. A high sensitivity for becoming anxious also may have implications for behavioral treatments of agoraphobia and obsessive–compulsive disorders.

Several investigators have reported that people with agoraphobia are capable of conducting self-exposure programs with minimal therapeutic guidance (e.g., Ascher, 1981; Emmelkamp, 1974). Yet others have questioned whether this approach is suitable for all people with agoraphobia (Holden, O'Brien, Barlow, Stetson, & Infantino, 1983). Holden et al. (1983) found that clients often failed to comply with self-help manual instructions, and one woman not only failed to do travel work but also avoided reading the manual because it made her too anxious. Patients in this study subsequently improved with therapist-assisted exposure.

These findings suggest that a certain degree of anxiety tolerance may be necessary for the success of self-exposure programs. Clients with very low tolerance for anxiety may need the additional support of a therapist, at least in the early stages of therapy; otherwise, they may quit treatment before experiencing therapeutic gains.

The concept of anxiety sensitivity may have implications for exposure therapy in the treatment of phobia. As Marks (1978) has noted, most successful psychological treatments for phobia involve exposure to the fear-eliciting stimuli. These procedures are based on the assumption that prolonged contact will produce decrements in anxiety. However, the mere presentation of a phobic stimulus does not imply functional exposure because the client may not attend to the stimulus. As Borkovec (1982) has noted, clients must attend to stimuli for exposure to work. Thus, Borkovec has advised therapists to be alert for subtle forms of avoidance that undermine therapeutic exposure. Subtle avoidance may be more likely in individuals who have a high sensitivity for becoming anxious compared to those who have a low sensitivity.

References

Ascher, L. M. (1981). Employing paradoxical intention in the treatment of agoraphobia. *Behaviour Research and Therapy, 19,* 533–542.

Bandura, A. (1977). *Social learning theory.* Englewood Cliffs, N.J.: Prentice-Hall.

Beck, A. T., Laude, R., & Bohnert, M. (1974). Ideational components of anxiety neurosis. *Archives of General Psychiatry, 31,* 319–325.

Borkovec, T. (1982). Facilitation and inhibition of functional CS exposure in the treatment of phobias. In J. Boulougouris (Ed.), *Learning theory approaches to psychiatry* (pp. 95–102). New York: Wiley.

Emmelkamp, P. M. G. (1974). Self-observation versus flooding in the treatment of agoraphobia. *Behaviour Research and Therapy, 12,* 229–237.

Evans, I. M. (1972). A conditioning model of a common neurotic pattern: Fear of fear. *Psychotherapy: Theory, Research, and Practice, 9,* 238–241.

Eysenck, H. J. (1979). The conditioning model of neurosis. *The Behavioural and Brain Sciences, 2,* 155–199.

Fenichel, O. (1945). *The psychoanalytic theory of neurosis.* (Chapter 11). New York: W. W. Norton.

Foa, E. B., Stekete, G., & Young, M. (1984). Agoraphobia: Phenomenological aspects, associated characteristics, and theoretical considerations. *Clinical Psychology Review, 4,* 431–457.

Holden, A. E., O'Brien, G. T., Barlow, D. H., Stetson, D., & Infantino, A. (1983). Self-help manual for agoraphobia: A preliminary report of effectiveness. *Behavior Therapy, 14,* 545–556.

Kamin, L. (1969). Predictability, surprise, attention, and conditioning. In B. A. Campbell and R. M. Church (Eds.), *Punishment and aversive behavior*. New York: Appleton-Century-Crofts.

Kazdin, A. E., & Wilcoxon, L. A. (1976). Systematic desensitization and nonspecific treatment effects: A methodological evaluation. *Psychological Bulletin, 83*, 729–758.

Kirsch, I. (1978). The placebo effect and the cognitive-behavioral revolution. *Cognitive Therapy and Research, 2*, 255–264.

Kirsch, I., Tennen, H., Wickless, C., Saccone, A. J., & Cody, S. (1983). The role of expectancy in fear reduction. *Behavior Therapy, 4*, 520–533.

Marks, I. (1978). Behavioral psychotherapy of adult neurosis. In S. L. Garfield & A. E. Bergin (Eds.), *Handbook of psychotherapy and behavior change* (2nd ed., pp. 493–547). New York: Wiley.

Mathews, A. M., Gelder, M. G., & Johnston, D. W. (1981) *Agoraphobia: Nature and treatment*. New York: Guilford.

Mavissakalian, M., & Barlow, D. H. (1981). *Phobia: Psychological and pharmacological treatment*. New York: Guilford.

Mowrer, O. H. (1947). On the dual nature of learning—A reinterpretation of "conditioning" and "problem-solving". *Harvard Educational Review, 17*, 102–148.

Reiss, S. (1980). Pavlovian conditioning and human fear: An expectancy model. *Behavior Therapy, 11*, 380–396.

Reiss, S., Peterson, R. A., Gursky, D. M., & McNally, R. J. (1984). The fear of anxiety as a personality variable. Unpublished manuscript, University of Illinois at Chicago.

Rizley, R., & Reppucci, N. D. (1976). Pavlovian conditioned inhibition processes in behavior therapy. In B. Maher (Ed.), *Progress in experimental personality research, 74*, 209–263.

Roper, G., & Rachman, S. (1976). Obsessional–compulsive checking: Experimental replication and development. *Behaviour Research and Therapy, 14*, 25–32.

Shapiro, A. K. (1971). Placebo effects in medicine, psychotherapy, and psychoanalysis. In A. E. Bergin & S. L. Garfield (Eds.), *Handbook of psychotherapy and behavior change*. New York: Wiley.

Wagner, A. R. (1978). Expectancies and priming of STM. In S. H. Hulse, H. Fowler, & W. K. Honig (Eds.), *Cognitive processes in animal behavior*. Hillsdale, NJ: Erlbaum.

Wagner, A. R. (1981). SOP: A model of automatic memory processing in animal behavior. In N. E. Spear & R. R. Miller (Eds.), *Information processing in animals: Memory mechanisms*. Hillsdale, NJ: Erlbaum.

Wagner, A. R., & Rescorla, R. A. (1972). Inhibition in Pavlovian conditioning: Applications of a theory. In R. A. Boakes & M. S. Halliday (Eds.), *Inhibition and learning*. New York: Academic Press.

6

Animal and Social Phobias: Biological Constraints on Learned Fear Responses

ARNE ÖHMAN
ULF DIMBERG
LARS-GÖRAN ÖST

Introduction

The basic suggestion in this chapter is that phobias provide examples of biologically prepared learned responses (see Seligman, 1971). The core assumption is that humans have a biological readiness to associate fear with some events and situations that once provided threats to the well-being of their ancestors. The primary purpose of the chapter is to take this theory one step further with a perspective on behavior inspired by evolutionary biology (see Öhman & Dimberg, 1984). In so doing, we are able to develop a theoretical framework that promises to explain a number of characteristics of and differences between various phobias that until now have been theoretically intractable.

THE DEFINITION OF PHOBIAS

Phobias may be described as intense fear reactions evoked by fairly specific stimulus situations. From an objective point of view, the intensity of the reaction does not seem to match the real dangers involved. Thus, to the

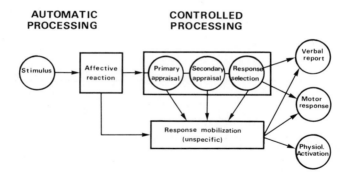

FIGURE 6.1   A schematic model of emotional processing (after Öhman, in press).

observer, phobic reactions often appear strikingly irrational. This impression is further strengthened by the victim's lack of voluntary control over
the fear, as well as by the rapid and unconditional avoidance responses it
provokes (see e.g., Marks, 1969).

   Following Lang (1984, in press), we view phobias as cases of intense
emotions. As such, they involve a series of manifestations organized around
an action set of avoidance. More specifically, phobias can be observed
through three different and partially independent response domains: overt
motor acts, physiological responses, and verbal reports of emotional experience. These different fear indices often fail to covary (e.g., Lang, 1968),
which may make the particular patterning of responses informative (e.g.,
Rachman, 1978).

A HEURISTIC MODEL OF EMOTION

   For the present analysis, it is convenient to view phobias (as well as other
emotions) as composed of a series of external and internal events. Some of
these events are illustrated in Figure 6.1. This model (see Öhman, in press,
for a more extensive discussion) takes advantage of a distinction between
two different modes of information processing that has been endorsed by
leading theoreticians (e.g., LaBerge, 1981; Posner, 1978; Shiffrin & Schneider, 1977). Basically these two modes denote unconscious and conscious
information processing. *Automatic processing* occurs unconsciously, rapidly,
and effortlessly; it can operate on input in parallel, is holistic rather than
analytical, and reflects overlearning or genetically given mechanisms to
such an extent that it reflects routinized processing acts. *Controlled processing,*
on the other hand, requires conscious attention; that is, it occurs in the
center of awareness and depends on volitional intentions; it is slow, sequential, analytical, effort-demanding, and "creative" rather than routinized.

An emotionally relevant stimulus evokes an immediate and automatic affective reaction, the characteristics of which have been well described by Zajonc (1980). Some of its clinical implications have been discussed by Rachman (1981). We suggest that one of the functions of this affective reaction is to prime efferent systems so that the organism is prepared for efficient action if necessary. Part of this priming involves physiological responses innervated by the autonomic nervous system, which prepare the metabolic foundation for activating the motor system. In the case of phobias, this affective reaction has a core position. Indeed, phobic responses have been regarded as prime examples of automatically controlled responses (Dawson & Schell, 1985).

The affective reaction provides part of the input to the controlled processing mechanisms. Following Lazarus (e.g., Lazarus, Averill, & Opton, 1970; Lazarus, Kanner, & Folkman, 1980) at least two controlled processes of emotional activation can be distinguished. *Primary appraisal* refers to a fuller analysis of the stimulus than does the automatic process resulting in the affective reaction. Thus its meaning, ramifications, and consequences are related to memories of past experience. Partly overlapping this process is *secondary appraisal,* which assesses the stimulus in relation to the individual's behavioral capacity. That is, during threatening events, it seeks answers to the question "what can be done about the threat?". To obtain these answers, characteristics of the threat, such as its predictability (Miller, 1981) and controllability (Miller, 1979), as well as characteristics of the individual, such as perceived self-efficacy (Bandura, 1982), are of paramount importance. Both types of appraisals feed into the efferent priming, which includes autonomic activation, and form the basis for selecting a particular response. Aspects of the appraisal processing also may be manifested in verbal reports.

Although automatic processing routines deliver information to controlled processing routines, these two systems are quite independent of each other (see particularly Zajonc, 1980). In the case of phobias, we propose that the automatic affective reaction more or less overrides the controlled processing routines, so that their more "rational" analyses have only a weak impact on efferent priming and the selection of overt (typically avoidance) responses (see Rachman, 1981). In order to explain phobias, therefore, we must understand this affective response.

TRADITIONAL APPROACHES TO PHOBIAS

Typically, learning-theory analyses of phobias have dealt with a concept of fear responses that has much in common with the affective reaction outlined above. With few exceptions, such as social-learning theorists (e.g.,

Bandura, 1977b), little interest has been directed toward controlled cognitive processes. Basically, learning theorists have suggested that phobias are instances of Pavlovian conditioned responses. According to this type of analysis, a phobic fears snakes, for example, because on a previous occasion the phobic has experienced intense but unrelated fright while exposed to a snake. Given that this simple analysis could marshal support from one of the most famous (and misquoted, Harris, 1979) experiments in psychology, Watson and Raynor's (1920) "Little Albert" study, it is not surprising that it for a long time held the championship as the paradigmatic example of successful learning-theory interpretations of psychopathology.

More recently, the simple Pavlovian conditioning interpretation of phobias has come under fire (e.g., Eysenck, 1979; Seligman, 1971). Seligman (1971) pointed out several important discrepancies between phobias and conditioned fear responses as observed in the laboratory. Whereas phobias appear to be acquired quickly, laboratory fear typically requires a series of trials before it is established. Similarly, whereas phobias often are extremely persistent and need special curative measures to become extinguished, laboratory-conditioned fear weakens quickly when the conditioned stimulus (CS) is presented without reinforcement from the unconditioned stimulus (UCS). One aspect of the irrationality of phobias is their refractoriness to verbal persuasions regarding the lack of real danger involved. Conditioned fear responses in humans, on the other hand, are strongly influenced by reassuring verbal instructions (e.g., Grings, 1973, Öhman, 1983). Finally, perhaps the most strategic discrepancy is that phobias are typically seen to a nonarbitrary set of situations that differ markedly from what one would expect from learning theory. Rather than seeing phobias for events related to painful experience in modern life, such as electrical equipment or dental treatment, one often sees fears and phobias for relatively rare and often harmless events such as small animals. In fact, fear of snakes was about twice as prevalent as fear of dental treatment in a normal population, although presumably many more persons have actual pain experiences in the latter context (Agras, Sylvester, & Oliveau, 1969).

THE PREPAREDNESS THEORY OF PHOBIAS

According to Seligman (1971) the common theme in the various categories of events associated with phobias is that they reflect potential dangers to the survival of pretechnological man and his mammalian ancestors. In fact, objects and circumstances like snakes, heights, and large open or small enclosed spaces may involve some degree of danger. Seligman's main thesis, then, was that during the evolution of our species these dangers have been severe enough to put an adaptive premium on those individuals who easily learned to avoid them. Thus, consistent with an earlier general analysis (Seligman, 1970), Seligman (1971) suggested that phobias were cases of biologically prepared learning. That is, humans have a biologically derived readiness to easily associate fears to typical phobic situations. In agreement with results from previous studies of another case of biologically prepared learning, the acquisition of taste aversions (see Seligman & Hager, 1972 for reviews), phobias were presumed to be (1) rapidly acquired, (2) resistant to extinction, (3) insensitive to cognitive factors, and (4) selective to stimulus situations. In effect, then, this preparedness model was able to handle all the difficulties that, according to Seligman's (1971) analysis, plagued traditional accounts.

In the present chapter we depart from Seligman's (1971) preparedness theory in a biologically inspired analysis of phobias. In some respects, our analysis provides a more radical departure from traditional learning theory than Seligman's. Thus, rather than suggesting that the problem of general process learning theory can be alleviated by postulating an abstract dimension of general biological preparedness, we analyze phobias, and the differences between, for example, animal and social phobias, in terms of the behavioral systems within which the fear components have likely evolved (see Johnston, 1981, with associated debate).

The Biology of Animal and Social Phobias

EVOLUTION AND LEARNING

By concentration on learning, with few considerations of its evolutionary underpinnings, traditional psychology more or less explicitly assumed a dichotomy between "learning" and "instinct." Seligman's postulation of the preparedness dimension was an explicit attempt to relate these two categories across a continuum (see Seligman & Hager, 1972). However, the question is whether one continuum suffices or, indeed, whether dimensional thinking is relevant at all. The behavior of a particular organism reflects an intricately interwoven network of causal factors, which defy any simplistic attempts at easy categorization of what is innate and what is learned (see Delprato, 1980). Evolution opportunistically equips the gene pools of populations with capacity for learning when the cost–benefit ratio favors it (Johnston, 1982) and when the individuals of the population are faced with particular types of ecological problems (Plotkin & Odling-Smee, 1979). The learning capacity that evolves is specifically tailored to the biology and ecology of the particular population, rather than being of unlimited flexibility (e.g., Johnston, 1981). Thus, learning capacities are likely to be biologically constrained (Hinde & Stevenson-Hinde, 1973).

Broadly speaking, the causal factors for behavior can be grouped in three categories, reflecting widely different time spans of environmental influence (Johnston & Turvey, 1980). Behavior that, first, is central for adaptation, second, is dependent on environmental factors that remain stable over many generations, and third, involves relatively fixed behavior sequences to well-defined environmental stimuli, is likely to be controlled from the gene pool. Thus its control reflects events accumulated over very extended time scales. For behavior that is dependent on environmental changes occurring within lifetimes of individuals, learning often provides a better solution (e.g., Plotkin & Odling-Smee, 1981). Learning, then, may be understood as causal factors reflecting events cumulating over the life-span of an individual. For still shorter time spans, reflecting the moment-to-moment adjustment of behavior according to ecological events, various mechanisms of perception and action have evolved (Johnston & Turvey, 1980).

Some aspects of the interaction between these three types of factors can be illustrated by paraphrasing and elaborating a metaphor originally used by Waddington (1957) in a slightly different context. Behavioral ontogeny can be viewed as the course of a ball rolling down a mountain slope. The fact that the ball has a potential of rolling down the slope and characteristics of its journey, like its average speed and lifetime, is dependent on the underlying bedrock. Originally the bedrock may have been shaped by dramatic events like folding due to continental plate movement or volcanic activity, but over eons of time the effects of these events may have been gradually modified by erosion processes, for example. By providing the underlying structure, the bedrock shapes the mountain: its ridges, valleys and passes; thus it determines a number of characteristics of the rolling ball's route. In some respects it corresponds to the effects of the gene pool in the control of behavior.

However, the shape of the bedrock is modified by the distribution of the overlying strata and the soil, which is dependent on factors other than those shaping the bedrock. In particular, they reflect the cumulative effects of water and wind erosion, as well as the history of vegetation. While the shape of strata and soil is heavily dependent on the shape of the underlying bedrock, it can nevertheless modify the route of the ball by masking or enhancing bedrock shapes, for example, leveling ridges and smoothing out passes and valleys. These causal factors operating over intermediate time spans would correspond to learning.

The details of the ball's route, finally, would be determined by more temporary factors like the wind, and the distribution of boulders, rocks, and vegetation across the landscape. These short-term factors would correspond to perception and action processes in the determination of behavior.

This metaphor brings home the necessity of considering the interaction of all types of causal factors in the analysis of particular events. For example, if the purpose is to understand the ball's route, it is relatively pointless to concentrate the efforts on the processes determining the distribution of soil and strata. It is only through the interaction of these processes with the shapes of the underlying bedrock that they become helpful in understanding the course of the ball down the slope. Similarly, we argue that trying to understand phobias only by considering factors determining fear learning gives an incomplete analysis. Obviously, learning factors are involved, but they operate within an evolutionary context that not only determines some of their characteristics but also provides other factors that interact with learning to result in the behaviors we associate with phobias.

However, before we move to a detailed consideration of the evolutionary history of various phobic fears, it is necessary to discuss other characteristics of evolutionary arguments that are relevant for the context of psychopathology.

IMPLICATIONS OF EVOLUTIONARY ARGUMENTS

If we take seriously the claim that part of the causal factors behind phobias resides in mammalian evolution, a number of implications follow that can be traced to the Darwinian theory of evolution specifically, and to biological perspectives generally.

The Darwinian theory of evolution can be broken down into a few basic propositions. The first one is that there is between-individual variation in virtually any characteristic one chooses to study. The notion of a distribution of individuals across some behavioral dimension ranging from abnormal, deviant, or pathological to normal or positive variants is, of course, familiar to students of psychopathology.

The second principle is perhaps more controversial, because it states that for evolution to operate there must be at least a partial genetic basis for the between-individual variations. Thanks primarily to the Danish adoption studies, however, it has been clearly established that genetics has an important role to play in many types of psychopathology (see e.g., Mednick, Schulsinger, Higgins, & Bell, 1974). For phobias, data on twins suggests that there is a genetic component with regard to both the particular object and the intensity of fear, with a heredity index near .50 (Torgersen, 1979). Although conclusions from studies on twins are not as strong as conclusions on adoption studies, Torgersen's (1979) detailed results and interpretations are consistent with the preparedness perspective on phobias.

The third principle of Darwinian evolutionary theory suggests that natural selection chooses for those individuals in the population that are best fitted or adapted to the particular niche the population occupies. Thus they become more likely to influence the particular distribution of alleles (gene variants) in the gene pool for coming generations than do nonselected individuals. The concept of adaptation is a difficult one (Lewontin, 1978, 1982), and these difficulties are compounded when the object of study is psychopathology. Behaviors interpreted as reflecting psychopathology in some real sense are maladaptive. How then have they become represented in the gene pool in the first place?

At least two possibilities are evident. First, the behavior may reflect genetic transmission of an error, or a malfunctioning, in the complex chains of biochemical events bridging the gap from parent genes to offspring behavior, such as in Down's syndrome (see e.g., Plomin, DeFries, & McClearn, 1980). This case is straightforward and needs not invoke concepts of adaptation at all. Rather they can be understood as random accidents that may be kept in the gene pool because of some characteristics of gene transmission (e.g., Plomin et al., 1980).

The second case may be described as a mismatch between genetic readiness and the demands of the ecological niche. Generally, the gene pool reflects the mean expected ecological pressure. As genetic variability remains the best insurance of the gene pool to future ecological changes, there are mechanisms to maintain it (e.g., Dobzhansky, Ayala, Stebbins, & Valentine, 1977). Thus individuals on the extremes of the genetic distribution with regard to a particular trait may be "off scale" with regard to the typical expected environment. Although such individuals are likely to become the victims of stabilizing selection (Dobzhansky et al., 1977), during their lifetime they may appear "deviant" or "pathological."

Another way to achieve mismatches between genes and environment is through rapid environmental changes. Although humans are extremely adaptable, they have evolved in a particular ecology. The recent drastic transformation we have imposed on our living conditions has occurred during a tiny fraction of our existence as a species (Öhman & Dimberg, 1984). It is conceivable, therefore, that environmental changes may either reduce necessary ecological support for the development of some behavior, or introduce new situations where we lack biological readiness to cope. In fact, this is the type of argument used by Seligman (1971) with regard to phobias. He suggested that it is only for the present, largely man-made ecology that most phobic fear may be regarded as irrational, because the transformation of the environment has made threat from the objects of phobias obsolete.

BIOLOGY AND THE CLASSIFICATION OF BEHAVIOR

From the perspective of evolutionary biology, descriptive classification of the units studied is regarded as of paramount importance. This partly reflects a heritage from general biology, where description as an important ingredient of the scientific enterprise has been emphasized, and it partly reflects the insight that no unit evolves in isolation but owes its evolution to interactions with other units. This prompts a systems perspective, where various types of behaviors are viewed in relation to the behavior system in which they belong (see e.g., Scott, 1980). Thus the evolution of any behavior or behavior capacity represents a series of compromises and trade-offs with other behaviors and behavior systems, rather than the maximization of its individual adaptivity (Alexander, 1975). The emphasis on systems and exhaustive classification of behavior systems sets behavior evolutionists apart from the mainstream psychologists, who typically have payed only passing interest to this problem. Rather, psychologists have been content with the experimental analysis of whatever behavior they for more or less pragmatic reasons have chosen to study.

Because the type of fear may depend on the particular behavior system within which it occurs, it is necessary to delineate what behavior systems are relevant for a particular analysis. For the present purpose, a simple behavior-classification system proposed by the evolutionary biologist Mayr (1974) may be convenient. Mayr (1974) distinguished between two broad classes of behavior, noncommunicative and communicative. The former category refers to behaviors not eliciting any response from the environment; that is, it is directed at physical aspects of the surroundings. Communicative behavior, on the other hand, elicits active responses from the environment in the sense that it manipulates the behavior of other animals. If the other animal is of a different species, we are dealing with *interspecific behavior,* as in predation and predatory defense. If the other animal is of the same species as the animal emitting the behavior, we are dealing with *intraspecific behavior,* which includes all behavior that we typically refer to as "social."

Mayr's (1974) analysis results in three broad categories of behavior: noncommunicative, interspecific communicative, and intraspecific communicative. Fear may occur within any of these systems, so the question becomes whether we can generalize findings across systems. Psychologists' analyses of fear, for example, have relied heavily on studies of the acquisition of avoidance responses in shuttle boxes (see Mineka, 1979); that is, they have tested noncommunicative behaviors. To what extent can knowledge generated within this particular paradigm tell us anything about fear in the context of communicative behavior, as in predatory and social fears? Is it meaningful to apply the same fear concepts to these different contexts? To take another example, behavior classified as aggressive, that is, behavior including attacking, biting, injuring, and even killing other animals, occurs both within inter- and intraspecific behavior systems. Yet, depending on the system, it may show important differences in eliciting conditions, behavioral configurations, and physiological responses (e.g., Moyer, 1976). In fact, Lorenz (1966) explicitly restricted the term *aggression* to intraspecific agonistic behavior, excluding interspecific aggression, that is, aggression related to predation (see also Barash, 1977).

PHOBIAS AND BEHAVIOR SYSTEMS

The preceding discussion implies that a unitary fear concept covering all contexts where fear is observed is unlikely to be viable. The evolutionary perspective suggests that the function of fear is to protect the organism (e.g., by retreat) from actual or anticipated harmful or noxious circumstances. Fear, therefore, can be viewed as a flexibly organized ensemble of responses, which utilizes whatever environmental support is available to achieve this function (Archer, 1979). Thus the profile of activity across different response systems (Lang, 1978, in press) may differ among different fear contexts. Furthermore, because most responses of the ensemble are shared with other motivational systems, the odds of finding consistent and high correlations among responses are quite low (see e.g., Archer, 1979; Lang, 1968; and Öhman, in press, for a theoretical analysis).

Armed with this preliminary delineation of fear, we can examine phobic fear in the evolutionary context discussed in the previous section. It is clear that phobic fear may be elicited within any of the three behavior systems suggested by Mayr (1974). For example, fear of heights and small closed spaces would represent noncommunicative fear, fear of animals interspecific communicative fear, and social fears intraspecific communicative fear. In other words, this perspective provides a theoretical underpinning for Mark's (1969) distinction among (miscellaneous) specific phobias (for inanimate objects), animal phobias, and social phobias, which he based on differences in sex incidence, onset age, and psychophysiological characteristics.

The distinctiveness of these three categories was confirmed by Torgersen (1979), who isolated factors of "Nature fears," "Animal fears," and "Social fears" in a factor analysis based on items from different fear questionnaires. However, while most factor analyses of fear survey schedules appear to obtain animal and social fear factors (e.g., Bernstein & Allen, 1969; Braun & Reynolds, 1969; Landy & Gaupp, 1971; Lawlis, 1971), distinct factors covering fears of inanimate objects appears to be somewhat less frequently found (e.g., Bates, 1971; Braun & Reynolds, 1969; Miller, Barrett, Hampe, & Noble, 1972; Rubin, Katkin, Weiss, & Efran, 1968).

Further evidence for differences between these three classes of fears were provided by Öst and Hugdahl (1981) in a survey on severe clinical phobics. They reported that claustrophobia, a noncommunicative fear, was more likely to originate in conditioning experiences than were animal and social phobias. Animal phobics showed about equal prevalence of direct (conditioning) and indirect acquisition, whereas most of the social phobics has acquired their fear through conditioning and very few through instruction.

The thesis of this chapter is that this evolutionary-derived distinction between different types of phobias can be further elucidated by an analysis of the evolutionary origins of different fears. Because of space limitations, and because they are the most frequently studied, we have focused on the two types of communicative fears, animal and social phobias.

ANIMAL PHOBIAS (INTERSPECIFIC FEAR)

Natural Selection of Fear Responses

Fear responses must have an evolutionary history that extends far beyond the mammalian order. In fact, it can be argued that "active escape and avoidance reactions must have been among the first functional systems which evolved" (Archer, 1979, p. 77). While such responses are also important in noncommunicative behavior contexts, they take on a special evolutionary significance in interspecific, predatory behavior systems. To survive and breed, it is essential for any animal that it does not become an easy meal for a predator. Thus predatory strategies and antipredative, defensive behavior coevolve in an intricate arms race (Dawkins & Krebs, 1979) with the integrity of the gene pools of the involved species at stake. All animals that may fulfill the role of prey for some predator have repertoires of antipredation strategies, the foremost of which are active escape, immobility, and attack (e.g., Archer, 1979). Learning is a critical advance in this context, because through Pavlovian conditioning animals are able to activate their defense system anticipatory to the predator's strike, which provides an important adaptive edge (Hollis, 1982). However, it is important to note that this learning occurs in an evolutionary context. Rather than painfully chosing a correct response by trial and error, during life-threatening circumstances animals quickly learn to activate their natural protective responses, which are designed by evolution to fit the particular ecology. For example, Bolles (1970) demonstrated that the ease with which rats learned (noncommunicative) avoidance responses depended upon the extent to which the particular situation prompted use of some of the species' natural defense responses: running, jumping away, or freezing.

Types of Fear Responses

Although the particular set of predatory defense responses differs widely among animals, the physiological demands predation makes on the organism are remarkably similar (e.g., Hollis, 1982). Primarily they involve pronounced recruitment of the sympathetic branch of the autonomic nervous system as a support for the emergency use of the skeletal musculature in flight or fight (see Cannon, 1928). The overt motor responses are dependent on the species and on the particular situation (Archer, 1979; Hollis, 1982). Depending on which action is chosen, the particular pattern of conditioned autonomic activation may differ. For example, if the conditioned motor response is flight, heart rate acceleration is likely to be observed (e.g., Black, 1965; Black & Toledo, 1972). However, if the situation prompts the animal to evade detection by immobility, heart rate deceleration is likely (e.g., Obrist, Sutterer, & Howard, 1972), which in turn may be related to the dominantly outwardly directed attention of freezing animals (Hollis, 1982; see also Lacey & Lacey, 1970).

Fear of Reptiles

There are reasons to believe that fear of reptiles provides a prototype of mammalian predatory fear. The first mammals were small and vulnerable compared to the reptiles that preyed on them, and the asymmetry in brute force naturally prompted a strategy of flight or immobility instead of fight. Efficient escape and avoidance responses activated by reptilian stimului, therefore, must have been intensely selected for in the early evolution of mammals. Given that there were reptile predators of potential danger for many species around even after the demise of the dinosaurs, it is likely that genes favoring quick learning of avoidance and escape from reptilian stimuli were left in the gene pools of many mammals, unless the contrary was explicitly selected for. Furthermore, given the opportunism of evolution, it is not unlikely that similar defense strategies to new predator pressures were build around those originally designed for reptiles. Snakes and reptiles, therefore, may epitomize the deadly Evil as an archaic symbol for the Predator. Thus present-day snakes may be viewed as the scattered remnants of the once omnipotent "Dragons of Eden" (see Sagan, 1977).

Role of Learning in Fear of Predators

A pivotal question is whether fear of reptiles is in the gene pool, or whether some specific experience is necessary for the defense responses to emerge. Seligman's (1970, 1971) preparedness theory of course favors the latter view, because he suggests that organisms are biologically prepared to associate easily ecologically overlapping motivationally relevant events, such as snakes with fear and avoidance. It is clear that there are a number of stimuli and stimulus dimensions that are related to fear, escape, and avoidance in a great number of species (see Russell, 1979, for a review), but for every claim of innate fear there seems to be other research suggesting that learning has an important role to play. For example, in the case of primates, it has been claimed that fear of snakes is "innate" or "spontaneous" (e.g., Hebb, 1946; Morris & Morris, 1965). However, studies have shown that fear of snakes is manifested in virtually all wild-reared rhesus monkeys, but practically unheard of in laboratory-reared animals (Joslin, Fletcher, & Emlen, 1964; Mineka, Keir, & Price, 1980). Furthermore, research by Mineka and coworkers, which is reviewed in detail below, has decisively shown that learning from models provided by snake-fearing conspecifics is the critical factor behind the difference between wild- and laboratory-reared monkeys (Mineka, Davidson, Keir, & Cook, 1984). From these data it appears that the gene pool equips the rhesus individual with a tendency to easily develop fear of snakes, but that some precise learning experience is necessary for this tendency to manifest as overt fear and avoidance.

This arrangement makes evolutionary sense. As with imprinting, where experience inscribes the features of the parent into the offspring's memory, enabling the baby to recognize her or him (e.g., Colgan, 1982), the specifics of the predator is better conveyed by experience than the gene pool. In both these cases the specificity required is so high that it is inefficiently handled by genes. Similar predators may specialize on different preys, which means that all predators need not be avoided. Furthermore, the predation pressure on a particular species may change rapidly over time, providing an adaptive edge for learning as a mechanism to identify dangerous predators (Plotkin & Odling-Smee, 1979). Because avoidance and escape typically are metabolically taxing responses, there is an economy in not overusing them but rather having them finely tuned to the ecological demands. Furthermore, overuse of escape strategies to potential but not actual predators could keep the animal away from resourceful habitats that would be helpful in promoting the longevity of the particular gene pool. There are many evolutionary factors, therefore, that promote learning as the basis for predator fear (e.g., snake fear in the rhesus monkey, Mineka et al., 1984). However, this learning must be extremely efficient and biologically primed. The potential prey can not allow the predator to strike and let the associated pain activate the escape response. Rather, it must utilize whatever minimal information there is to suggest the danger involved, so that it can activate an avoidance response to any cue implying predator presence. Furthermore, once the predator is recognized as dangerous and fear evoking, there is an advantage to retaining this knowledge, because of the fatal consequences that are likely if forgetting occurs.

Stimulus Components Determining Fear Responses

While the issue of whether there is archetypical representation of snakes in memory must be left somewhat open (see Russell, 1979), it is clear that most predators announce their presence and life-threatening intents through a number of stimulus parameters that provide clues to the potential prey to start his escape. First, it appears that there is a reactive distance beyond which the predator is simply ignored (Russell, 1979). Most of us have seen movie scenes from African savannahs where herds of zebras are peacefully grazing in the relative vicinity of lazily resting lions. However, if the predator is moving, or if it appears suddenly and approaches rapidly, the prey begins defensive measures. Additional information to spot the predator may include specific visual cues, for example, eye and movement patterns, auditory and olfactory stimuli, and warning from conspecifics (see Russell, 1979, for review). The fear of predation may become linked with other more general environmental cues and thus contribute to the avoidance of particular locations. These avoided localities may include those previously associated with predatory attack or otherwise associated with predation, novel environments, and environments with special features, such as openness for species depending on hiding spaces in vegetation for their defense (see e.g., Archer, 1979; Russell, 1979).

Critical Periods of Acquisition of Animal Fears

Vulnerability for predation varies over the life cycle. Young primates are dependent on care and protection from parents (e.g., Öhman & Dimberg, 1984). However, as the child's ability for locomotion develops and his emotional dependence on parental presence lessens, he begins to explore his surroundings. Away from the parent's immediate protective attention, and lacking efficient defensive measures of his own, he is in a position where encounters with predators are especially likely to have fatal outcomes. Thus it is extremely important during this period that the child can learn from minimal input to avoid potentially disastrous predatory encounters and return to the relative safety zone defined by the parent.

Implications for Animal Phobias

A number of conclusions with clear implications for our understanding of animal phobias can be made from the discussion above. First, humans, like most mammals, have evolved a readiness to easily associate fear to stimuli suggesting the presence of a predator. For evolutionary reasons, snakes or rather reptiles may be regarded as a prototype for this type of fear stimuli.

Second, because this readiness is biologically determined, it is implied that it is genetically controlled and that individuals differ in their degree of readiness.

Third, the readiness concerns not an innate propensity to fear certain stimuli but ease of acquisition of fear responses to these stimuli, given that they occur in conjunction with other aversive events. Thus, as suggested by Seligman (1971; Seligman & Hager, 1972), only minimal input or training is needed for full-blown fear responses to emerge. Furthermore, because of the severe costs that would result from failure to utilize cues for quick avoidance, this learning should be very persistent. However, as learned responses, the fear behavior should eventually be reversible, that is, extinguishable.

Fourth, as the prototype fear response to threatening predators is escape, which involves rapid utilization of metabolic resources, immediate activation of the autonomic nervous system is needed, particularly its sympathetic branch. Thus one would expect simultaneous but independent activation of these output systems when predatory stimuli are encountered (see Black, 1971). Animal phobics, therefore, should display sympathetic activation when they are exposed to relevant fear stimuli. Because predation pressure has been a constant ingredient of mammalian evolution, this is part of normal life. Therefore, if no predatory stimuli or stimuli associated with predation through learning occur within the reactive distance, no evidence of enhanced activation should be discernible. In short, the fear responses are activated only when evoked by the relevant fear stimuli.

Fifth, because antipredatory defense responses are assumed to be organized around the ancient flight and avoidance responses to reptiles, their central nervous control is likely to extend into deep layers of the brain (called the reptilian brain by MacLean, e.g., 1970). Although some of this neural control has been transferred to limbic structures and even to neocortex with mammalian evolution, the fact that these types of fear responses partly reside in ancient brain areas relatively inaccessible from the neocortex may be one reason for its involuntary quality. Thus because of neural wiring, antipredator fear responses may have highly automatic affective components that are quite independent of the controlled processing routines of the more advanced brain loci. This, then, may be one important reason for the apparent "irrationality" of some human fears of animals.

Finally, fear response to predatory stimuli may be acquired with different degrees of ease at different ages. For example, there is reason to believe that in humans the preschool years, when the child is able to move away from the parent yet lacks efficient predator defense, is a particularly vulnerable period. Thus, to keep the young individual within protective distance from the parent, evolution is likely to have selected for fear and avoidance to stimuli even remotely associated with predators at this particular age. However, at an older age, with more efficient predatory defense and perhaps even preying on other animals, the pressure should be against acquiring fear too easily to undifferentiated animal stimuli.

SOCIAL PHOBIAS (INTRASPECIFIC FEAR)

A variety of evolutionary and ecological factors determine whether animal species extend their social life beyond merely meeting for mating (see Barash, 1977, for an excellent discussion). Such factors include characteristics of food (e.g., abundance and geographic dispersion), predation pressures, and type of care demanded by the young. Social living is ubiquitious among primates (e.g., Jolly, 1972), particularly among the most advanced triumvirate, gorillas, chimpanzees, and humans. Group living requires mutual coordination and organization of the behavior of the various group members, each of which in an evolutionary perspective may be expected to strive toward maximizing their own fitness. Thus there is always a potential conflict first, among social motives, where each individual's fitness gains most by cooperative efforts, for example, in predator defense and food finding, and second, individual motives where the group members compete for limited resources such as mating partners. To manage these complex interactions and potential conflicts, these species have typically evolved elaborate means for social control (see e.g., Hinde, 1974; Jolly, 1972; van Lawick-Goodall, 1971). Because these types of interactions, first, typically require an invariant relationship between stimulus and response to communicate effectively (Mayr, 1974), and second, occur in an ecology of face-to-face interaction that has been stable over time (Bowlby, 1969), it is plausible to argue that evolutionary history and biological makeup provide important causal factors for its control (Öhman & Dimberg, 1984).

Dominance Hierarchies

A prominent means of ordering animal social life is to establish new dominance relationships among group members. Such relationships simply imply that one group member more often bosses another than the other way around (e.g., Bernstein, 1981; Hinde, 1978). If more than two individuals are involved, relatively stable dominance or status hierarchies may be developed (e.g., Hinde, 1974, 1978; Jolly, 1972). In general, dominant group members have priority with regard to resources. Thus dominance is intimately related to between-individual competition within the group. Dominance is established through agonistic encounters, where the competing individuals typically measure their relative strength through the use of impressive displays designed to threaten and frighten the opponent. Thus, although animals occasionally get killed in this type of encounter (e.g., Barash, 1977), the fact that the combat is fought by help of ritualized displays increases the odds that both the combatants are leaving the battleground unhurt, at least physically. A typical outcome, therefore, is that one of the fighters gives up before the encounter is escalated into a real fight, by showing a display of fear and submissiveness and by leaving the field.

Dominance competition is especially likely when animals unfamiliar to each other are grouped together. Thus strangers typically evoke more aggressive displays than familiar animals (the "dear enemy" effect, see Colgan, 1982). Over time, as the group members take measure of each other, a hierarchy develops and may increase in consistency (e.g., Hinde, 1978), although it may not necessarily be strictly linear. Thus examples may be found where Animal A bosses Animal B, and the latter bosses Animal C, but where A may yield to C (e.g., Bernstein, 1981; Hinde, 1978). Furthermore, one dominance hierarchy may not be applicable to all situations, so that different dominance relationships may hold for food and mating, for example. Typically, relatively independent hierarchies hold for adult males and females. As juveniles reach puberty and adulthood, they have to fight their way into a rank among the adult animals. Puberty and early adulthood, therefore, is a stressful time for primates.

Once relatively stable hierarchies are established within a group, the number of agonistic incidents decreases, which provides important gains for group cohesiveness (e.g., Hinde, 1974; Jolly, 1972). In fact, in established groups of chimpanzees, for example, dominance and aggression seldom surface, unless there is a challenger to the male leader (Jolly, 1972; van Lawick-Goodall, 1971). The dominance hierarchy, therefore, is a device to control the potential conflicts between social and individual motives in the group. By defining the roles of the group members in mutual competition for resources, it increases group cohesion, and thus the groups functional value as a social unit.

Emotional Displays in Agonistic Encounters

Especially for primates with their elaborated neural control of the facial musculature (see e.g., Chevalier-Skolnikoff, 1973), the displays used in agonistic encounters have a decisive facial component. For example, a dominant chimpanzee threatens other group members by fixating them with wide open staring eyes, frowning brows, and a narrowly slit mouth with the corners somewhat lowered (e.g., Jolly, 1972; van Lawick-Goodall, 1971), an expression that in humans corresponds to an angry, silent glare (Ekman, 1972; also see Jolly, 1972, for good photographic examples). If the threat or attack is less confident the mouth may open with the teeth covered by the lips. Eye contact and gaze direction are obviously of central importance in this context, because they provide an efficient pointer to the recipient of the display. In humans, for example, staring promotes escape (Ellsworth, Carlsmith, & Henson, 1972), and consistent dominance hierarchies can be constructed on the basis of eye contact in human dyads (Strongman & Champness, 1968).

The threatening primate facial display is reinforced by an erect posture and general piloerection, which make the animal appear larger. However, especially with the open mouth display, ambivalence between attack and escape may be seen in alternating forward and withdrawal movements (e.g., Hinde, 1974).

These phasic, situation-evoked displays are supplemented by long-lasting dominance markers. Dominant primate males often have a self-confident, relaxed posture and gait, and a somewhat stiff-legged dignified walk (e.g., Hinde, 1974; Jolly, 1972). In some species, these behavioral characteristics may be seen in connection with physical changes, such as the impressive shoulder fur of dominant baboons.

A subordinate animal, on the other hand, acts very differently. As a response to the threat display, it may show a fear grimace in the form of a silent bare-teeth expression, with the eyes wide open, the brows relaxed or up, and the mouth corners drawn back, exposing the teeth (e.g., Jolly, 1972). The eyes may either fixate or evade the gaze of the threatener (gaze aversion serving as a cut-off signal for the threatening interaction, Exline, 1972). If the threat is intense, the eyes may widen even more, the mouth corner may draw further back to expose the gums, and the animal may scream and flee the situation. These fear expressions seem to correspond quite closely to the emotions of fear and terror as displayed in the human face (Ekman, 1972). The close interaction between threat faces and fear faces in controlling important group parameters such as mutual distance is graphically described in data presented by Weigel (1978) from the capuchin monkey.

The sequence of subordinated facial expressions from friendly appeasement to total submissiveness and flight is accompanied by appropriate postural adjustments. The animal may curve its spine and crouch in front of the threatener, and it may avert its gaze and turn its face away refusing to reciprocate the threat (e.g., Chevalier-Skolnikoff, 1982; Hinde, 1974). Because dominant males seldom attack females or juveniles, subordinate males may choose behavior that underlines their submissiveness (Barash, 1977). For example, they may present for mounting or mimic infant behavior.

In contrast to the self-confidence pervading the behavior of dominant males, the subordinate animals at the bottom of the hierarchy slink inconspicuously around at the periphery of the group, hunched over with curved spine, constantly vigilant for a potential attack (Hinde, 1974; Jolly, 1972; van Lawick-Goodall, 1971). Animals in this position are vulnerable and under stress in many different respects. Not only are they the last ones to receive food and mating, but they are also often inadvertently attacked by losers in skirmishes between dominant animals (see Chevalier-Skolnikoff, 1982, p. 316, for an example). In a way they are the victims of the conflict between social and individual motives referred to earlier. To take advantage of the gains of social living, they have to pay by becoming "trained losers" in the intragroup competition. Staying in the group obviously is making the best of a bad situation, and even subordinate animals may eventually make their way to the top, through intelligence if not through brute force (see van Lawick-Goodall, 1971).

Difference between Interspecific and Intraspecific Fear

By now it should be clear that there are important differences between inter- and intraspecific fear. Interspecific agonistic encounters, in contrast to the make-believe character of intraspecific conflicts, are serious and real, invariably involving real attack and defense behaviors, putting the life of the potential prey at stake. Thus interspecific fear has to be tightly organized as an escape or avoidance package that can be efficiently recruited by any animal cue suggesting the presence of a hunting predator. Part of its efficiency is that it is reflexive and automatic in its elicitation, which, of course, does not preclude the use of controlled processing resources in predatory defense. However, during fear stimulation, the automatic processing routines take precedence in the control of the fear response.

The expression of intraspecific fear, on the other hand, is much more loosely and conditionally concocted, with a less prominent and reflexive role for active avoidance behavior. Even when active flight is used, it consists of a short rush taking the target outside the immediate reach of the dominant threatener without expelling it from the protection of the group. Compared to the metabolical demands of a race against a predator, the intraspecific flight has relatively trivial metabolic consequences. Since the typical intraspecific fear reaction is crouching and relative immobility, the need to recruit a major autonomic response is much less here than in interspecific defense. Finally, in contrast to the reflexive automatic character of predator defense, the social interchange of agonistic intraspecific encounters has a deliberate, intentional flavor, involving, for example, cheating (Chevalier-Skolnikoff, 1982), which suggests an important role for controlled processing influences. For example, "animals under attack made fear grimaces and often turned their heads to look up at their attackers. They also occasionally reached up to grasp their attackers' face to orient them to receive their grimaces" (Chevalier-Skolnikoff, 1982, p. 317).

Implication for Social Fears

The foregoing discussion implies that social fears are the result of a bio-logically determined readiness to easily associate fear to certain classes of stimuli, and perhaps particularly those originating in the face. Again, it is important to point out that we are talking about readiness to learn rather than about biologically given responses. Dominant group members, for example, can also be expected to have some of this readiness, but because they lack a learning history of associating aggressive dominance displays with defeat and fear, they are not frightened by threat displays but instead intensify and prolong their own display to achieve eventual victory.

A second implication of the foregoing discussion is that social fears should be associated more with some social stimuli than with others, and that they should be particularly evoked in some specific contexts. Given the centrality of facial expressions, threatening facial displays and especially eyes fixating the subject should be central in social fears. Fears to these types of stimuli should, in general, be especially likely in contexts where domi-nance is uncertain or has to be established, that is, in contexts of social evaluation (e.g., Schlenker & Leary, 1982). Evolutionary considerations further suggest that the fear should be especially prominent in encounters with strangers, and in contexts of food and sex, because these are situations of limited resources likely to prompt dominance conflicts among primates.

Third, contrary to the automatic control of animal fears, social fears may be more dependent on controlled processing influences, although they do have an automatically controlled affective component. The controlled processing may involve appraisals both of the characteristics of threat-ening others and of one's own efficacy to withstand the threat; that is, both primary and secondary appraisal processes are involved (Lazarus *et al.*, 1980).

Fourth, encountering the feared social stimulus evokes an initial affective response primarily manifested as a facial gesture of fear and submissiveness. However, this initial response is not more or less automatically channeled into an avoidance response as in animal fears, but may instead be followed by several alternative responses more or less dependent on controlled pro-cessing, such as gaze aversion, awkward submissive smiles, learned verbal comments, or withdrawal. The conditional and partly deliberate nature of the social response repertoire prevents sympathetic autonomic activation from becoming as essential and invariable a component of the response profile as in animal phobias where metabolically taxing avoidance responses are more prominent. However, some sympathetic activation should be expected as part of the initial affective response.

Fifth, as social fears pervade the very center of social existence for socially highly dependent beings, they may be expected to have more pervasive effects than animal fears. Because, as we previously noted, the best thing to do in the unbearable situation of low-ranking animals is to stay in the group, social phobics may be expected to strive to cope with their fear and continue to live with it in unavoidable social situations. However, the lack of self-assertiveness that results from perceived failures in dominance conflicts is likely to give rise to low self-esteem and to generalized low self-efficacy expectations (Bandura, 1977a), which results in severe limitation of social life. Social phobias, therefore, are much more crippling than animal phobias, which are typically elicited only in quite easily avoidable situations. Furthermore, the vulnerability and stress associated with a position low in a dominance hierarchy may put the individual in a continual state of stress that may prompt elevated levels of physiological arousal even in nonsocial situations. Thus, in some respects social phobics would be expected to resemble patients with more generalized anxiety symptoms.

Sixth, social fears may be expected to have their origin in phases of life where dominance hierarchies are especially likely to become established. That is, socially fearful people should date their fear to adolescence and early adulthood, because this is the period of life where the adult hierarchies are established for both males and females. Because independent hierarchies typically exist for the two sexes, the sex distribution of social fears may be expected to be approximately equal.

Empirical Evaluation

ACQUISITION OF SNAKE FEARS IN RHESUS MONKEYS

As already noted, Mineka *et al.* (1980) reported that wild- but not laboratory-reared rhesus monkeys displayed fear when confronted with a real snake or with snake-like stimuli (toy or model snakes). This was evident in both avoidance behavior and ratings based on expressed emotional disturbance. In a second experiment, Mineka *et al.* (1980) attempted to extinguish the fear in the wild-reared monkeys and found it to be unusually persistent. The latency for the hungry monkeys to reach for food placed on the far side of an open box containing a snake decreased somewhat throughout seven extinction, or flooding, sessions, as did the number of trials required to reach a criterion of nonavoidance. However, the animals still showed more fear to the snake stimuli than to control stimuli in a post-test, with only moderate changes from a pre-test. Furthermore, the emotional disturbance behavior did not change at all across sessions, but it showed some change within session. All in all, only three of the eight monkeys studied were regarded as "clinical successes."

In a 6-months follow-up on these data, Mineka and Keir (1983) observed significant spontaneous recovery for both avoidance and emotional disturbance components of fear. Renewed and intensified flooding sessions again resulted in decreased latencies to reach for food across the snake box, with no change across session in disturbance behavior. Furthermore, even after this prolonged flooding, considerable avoidance of the snake stimuli was still apparent in the post-treatment behavioral test. Thus, it appears from these data that the snake fear displayed by wild-reared rhesus monkeys is unusually persistent and extremely hard to extinguish. However, as pointed out by Mineka and Keir (1983), this does not legitimize the conclusion that it is inextinguishable, because other procedures (e.g., modeling of fearlessness) may be more effective.

It is tempting to suggest that the difference between wild- and lab-reared monkeys observed by Mineka et al. (1980) reflects differential learning histories. This suggestion was confirmed by Mineka et al. (1984). They put lab-reared adolescent rhesus monkeys in a situation where they could observe their wild-reared parents display fear when exposed to a real snake and to snake-like stimuli. While the adolescents did not display differential behavior to snake stimuli and neutral stimuli in two different pre-test situations, their behavior closely mimicked that of their parents when they were exposed to these stimuli after the conditioning sessions, both with regard to avoidance and disturbance behaviors. The data clearly indicated that only limited exposure to the fearful model was sufficient to induce fear in the observer, and that this effect was not enhanced by further exposures to the model.

The work of Mineka and coworkers elegantly demonstrates that snake fear is rapidly acquired in rhesus monkeys. In fact, only a few exposures to a fearful model is sufficient for full-blown fear behavior to emerge. Furthermore, once acquired, this fear behavior is extremely resistant to extinction. Thus it conforms closely with what one would expect from the evolutionary considerations discussed in the section on animal phobias. Indeed, these data can be regarded as prototype examples of biologically prepared fear learning. The only reservation that may be voiced is that Mineka so far has not demonstrated that this effect is specific to snake or predator stimuli. Thus, although the possibility appears remote, one would like to see an empirical exclusion of the alternative that similar effects would result from observing a model conditioned to display fear to some evolutionary neutral object.

LABORATORY STUDIES OF FEAR ACQUISITION
IN HUMANS

Since the mid 1970s, substantial literature has emerged on human autonomic conditioning to fear-relevant stimuli, such as pictures of snakes and spiders (see Öhman, 1979a, for a review of the early studies). Because of human subject concerns, this research has examined only mild fear levels, where it becomes a potential issue whether fear is involved at all. Typically, responses innervated by the autonomic nervous system have been measured in subjects exposed to paired presentations of pictures of snakes, for example, and mildly aversive events such as loud noises or electric shocks to the fingers. Thus compared to Mineka's work, which incorporated both behavioral avoidance and emotional–expressive measures of fear as well as tests for generalization across different situations, studies on human autonomic conditioning is not explicitly connected to the fear intensities seen in phobics. On the other hand, by studying human fear reactions directly, this work is not hampered by the problems of cross-species comparisons. In some respects, therefore, it provides important extensions to Mineka's results.

Conditioning of Autonomic Responses to Animal Stimuli

Rachman (1977) argued that direct Pavlovian conditioning, where the phobic stimulus is explicitly paired with a trauma, cannot account for all instances of phobias. While it is true that a majority of clinically defined phobics report that their fear problem started with a traumatic event (Öst & Hugdahl, 1981; 1983), a substantial proportion of phobics do not report direct conditioning experiences. Furthermore, among fearful normal populations, a majority of subjects do not recall any specific traumatic event as the start of their fear (Kleinknecht, 1982; Murray & Foote, 1979; Rimm, Janda, Lancaster, Nahl, & Dittmar, 1977). On the basis of such evidence, as well as other considerations (see Rachman, 1978), Rachman (1977) suggested that there are three independent "pathways to fear": conditioning, vicarious experience, and instructions. All these pathways have been corroborated in laboratory studies of human autonomic responses to predator-relevant stimuli.

Öhman, Eriksson, and Olofsson (1975) presented pictures of snakes followed by shocks to one group of subjects, and pictures of houses followed by shocks to another, while skin conductance responses (SCRs) were measured. Two sets of control groups received unpaired presentations of pictures and shocks, or pictures alone, respectively, to control for shock sensitization effects and unconditioned effects of the pictures. Half of the conditioning groups were given one, and the other half five reinforced

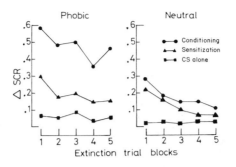

FIGURE 6.2 Extinction of skin conductance responses (SCR) in groups conditioned to phobic or neutral stimuli (Conditioning), given unpaired presentation of phobic or neutral stimuli (Sensitization) or given the conditioned stimulus alone (CS alone).

acquisition trials. Regardless of the number of acquisition trials, the subjects conditioned to snakes showed substantially more resistance to extinction than those conditioned to houses, which did not differ from any of the four control groups (see Figure 6.2). Thus, similar to the data of Mineka *et al.* (1984), responses acquired to snake stimuli were unusually persistent, and appeared full-blown after a single conditioning trial. This basic result has been replicated regularly in the Uppsala laboratory (see Hugdahl & Kärker, 1981; Hugdahl & Öhman, 1980; and the review in Öhman, 1979a). Figure 6.3 presents data collected at the University of Bergen, Norway, by Öhman, Alme, and Mykleburst (1981), using a conditioning paradigm incorporating an avoidance component. That is, different groups of subjects were exposed to pictures of snakes and spiders, or flowers and mushrooms, and one of the pictures was followed by a brief electric shock. If the subject was fast enough in pressing a microswitch when receiving the first shock, he could avoid four more shocks, which, in case of slow responses, followed within the next two seconds. The figure shows that the SCRs were clearly larger to the shocked than to the unshocked pictures in subjects exposed to snakes and spiders, whereas this difference was significantly smaller in those exposed to flowers and mushrooms.

   However, attempts to replicate these findings have met mixed success in other laboratories. Perhaps most bothersome were initial failures by Lang and coworkers at the University of Wisconsin (e.g., Cook, 1981; Hodes, 1981) to obtain differences between groups conditioned to animal and control stimuli in paradigms designed to closely replicate Öhman's (e.g., 1979) work. For example, while Hodes, Öhman, and Lang (1979) obtained reliable differences between groups conditioned to snakes and spiders on the one hand (phylogenetically fear-relevant stimuli) and hand weapons (ontogenetically fear-relevant stimuli) on the other, the difference between ani-

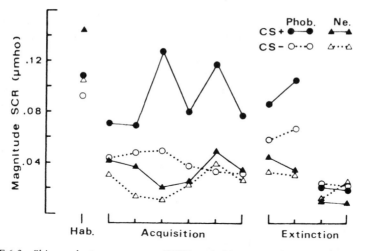

FIGURE 6.3   Skin conductance responses (SCR) to phobic or neutral stimuli signaling a train of electric shocks that could be terminated by a rapid motor response (CS+) or followed by nothing (CS−) (data from Öhman et al., 1981).

mal and control stimuli (household objects) was not significant. Similar failures were reported in work by Cook (1981) and Hodes (1981). However, Cook (1983) has convincingly demonstrated that these failures were due to the choice of UCS. Because of human subject concerns, Lang and coworkers had chosen aversive noise as the UCS.

Hodes (1981) argued that from an evolutionary perspective a tactile component might be essential, because if predators produce pain they are most likely to do it through insults to the skin. Consequently, he combined noise with a vibratory stimulus, and although he still failed to obtain reliable SCR differences between groups conditioned to snakes or spiders and to flowers or mushrooms, the tendencies of his data were much more similar to the Uppsala findings.

Cook (1983) first demonstrated a clear replication of the results of Öhman and coworkers by reporting significantly better resistance to extinction in an experimental group conditioned to snakes or spiders than in a control group conditioned to flowers or mushrooms, with electric shock UCSs. In a second experiment, Cook (1983) again demonstrated that this difference as a function of CS content was observed with a shock UCS, whereas as in most earlier Madison studies, CS content was ineffective with a noise UCS. This result provides further specificity to a previous finding by Öhman, Fredrikson, and Hugdahl (1978) and Öhman, Fredrikson, Hugdahl, and Rimmö (1976) that differences between animal and control stimuli were not obtained by nonaversive UCSs. Thus Cook's (1983) report that only noci-

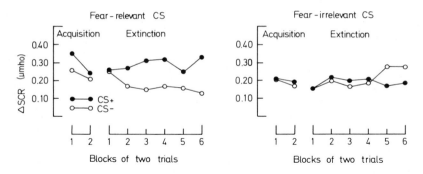

FIGURE 6.4   Skin conductance responses (SCR) to fear-relevant (or phobic) or fear-irrelevant (or neutral) stimuli in subjects having a model express fear after one stimulus (CS+) but
not after another (CS−) (data from Hygge & Öhman, 1978).

ceptive stimuli acting through the tactile modality are effective agrees with
the evolutionary perspective. Similar direct support is provided by the observation of larger resistance to extinction to phylogenetically fear-relevant
stimuli such as snakes and spiders than to ontogenetically fear-relevant
stimuli such as broken electrical cords (Hugdahl & Kärker, 1981) and hand
weapons (Hodes, Öhman, & Lang, 1979).

Vicarious Conditioning to Animal Stimuli in Humans

Mineka *et al.*'s (1984) findings on fear acquisition to snake stimuli in the
rhesus monkey were based on vicarious or observational learning. Similar
data were reported for humans by Hygge and Öhman (1978). Their subjects
either saw three animal stimuli (snakes, spiders, and rats) or three neutral
stimuli (flowers, mushrooms, and berries) arranged as a differential conditioning paradigm, where two stimuli occurred together and the third alone.
The subject was seated side-by-side with another ostensible subject, who in
fact was a confederate to the experimenter. This model expressed an intense
fear of the stimulus that occurred second in the pair. Even when this stimulus was removed in an extinction phase, the real subject continued to respond more to the stimulus that had preceded it than to the control stimulus
presented alone, if these stimuli were fear relevant, but not if they were
neutral (see Figure 6.4). These data, then, provide evidence that humans
acquire fear response through observing a model displaying fear more readily to animal stimuli than to neutral control stimuli, quite similar to what
was reported for other primates by Mineka *et al.* (1984).

Instructed Enhancement of Responses to Animal Stimuli

Most human behavior undoubtedly is acquired through symbolically transferred information (e.g., Bandura, 1977b). This is also true for human fears (e.g., Rachman, 1977). For example, Kleinknecht (1982) interrogated a group of tarantula enthusiasts about spider fears and found that, if they had experienced periods of fear of their pets, the fear was typically acquired through instructions and warnings.

An experimental analogue to this phenomenon was developed by Hugdahl and Öhman (1977), who threatened their subject with an electric shock after either one of two animal stimuli (snakes and spiders) or two neutral stimuli (flowers and mushrooms). For the former stimuli, significantly better differential responding between the two cues were observed than for the latter. These effects were replicated by Hugdahl (1978), who also reported that instructions were as efficient as electric shock UCSs in inducing SCR responding.

Kartsounis and Pickersgill (1981) reported similar effects for words that were generally rated as fear-relevant, although the particular subjects from which SCRs were obtained did not rate them as fearful. That is, differential responding was observed with, but not without, shock threat. Contrary to the previous studies, the shock threat used by Karsounis and Pickersgill (1981) was not contingent on a specific cue. Rather, as in a study by Öhman, Eriksson, Fredrikson, Hugdahl and Olofsson (1974), enhanced response to fear-relevant stimuli was observed merely as a consequence of anticipating noxious stimulation. Kartsounis and Pickersgill (1981) demonstrated that an aversive anticipation was necessary, since similar effects were not obtained with positive anticipation (pleasant music), nor was any enhancement seen for pleasant words with either aversive or pleasant anticipation (Pickersgill & Karsounis, 1982). Thus the effect was specific for fear-relevant words and noxious anticipation. These effects were further specified by Cook (1983). He found enhanced responding with cue-contingent shock threats to animal stimuli as compared with neutral stimuli, exactly as reported previously (Hugdahl, 1978; Hugdahl & Öhman, 1977). However, when the threat concerned an aversive noise, the opposite results were obtained. That is, with this type of threat, the instruction effects were larger for flowers and mushrooms than they were for snakes and spiders. Thus, again it was demonstrated that there is a connection between tactile UCSs and animal stimuli with regard to enhanced SCR responding.

Conditioned Heart Rate Accelerations

The data reviewed so far has relied entirely on SCR recordings. However, there is legitimate doubt as to whether such responses are primarily related to emotional states such as fear, their sympathetic innervation not-withstanding (Raskin, 1973). For example, Öhman (1979b, 1983) has pro-vided an integrated theoretical treatment of human SCR conditioning that utilizes notions of automatic and controlled processing in combination with the orienting response (OR) as key concepts in accounting for the data. This theoretical treatment then views SCR conditioning as more related to atten-tional processes than to fear. Although the OR probably has a role in the initiation of emotions (Öhman, in press), it is doubtful that OR indices such as SCRs have a specific relation to fear. To properly interpret the data on autonomic conditioning to fear-relevant stimuli as related to fear acquisi-tion, therefore, it would be highly desirable to supplement them with infor-mation from response systems with a less equivocal relationship to fear than the electrodermal system. Heart rate (HR) is an obvious candidate, because in spite of problems inherent in its dual innervation from both branches of the autonomic nervous system (e.g., Obrist, 1976), heart rate seems to accelerate in fear contexts (e.g., Lang, 1979; Lang, Melamed, & Hart, 1970), whereas it decelerates during orienting and external attention (e.g., Gra-ham, 1979; Lacey & Lacey, 1970).

Fredrikson and Öhman (1979) reported differential effects of snake or spider stimuli, on the one hand, and flower or mushroom stimuli, on the other, for SCR, and for another autonomic index, finger-pulse volume responses. For heart rate, however, both the animal and the neutral group showed primarily decelerative responses, with no significant conditioning effects. The only significant between-group effect pertained to a much larger HR acceleration to the UCS in the fear-relevant compared to the fear-irrelevant group. Somewhat more promising data were reported by Fred-rikson (1981), who observed a significant change in accelerative direction for the conditioned HR response to snake and spider material across trial blocks. However, because he did not include a control group with neutral stimuli, the interpretation of his results remains equivocal.

Two studies performed at the University of Bergen provided more promising, but not definitive, date. Figure 6.5 shows heart rate data from groups conditioned to snake and spider or to flower and mushroom stimuli in over thirty reinforced trials, a much more extensive acquisition phase than is usually employed (Öhman & Dimberg, 1978b, Note 3). Both groups showed reliable differential responding between the reinforced (CS+) and nonreinforced cue (CS−), but in opposite directions. The fear-relevant group essentially showed less deceleration to the CS+, resulting in maximal differential response in relative acceleration in the middle of the interstimu-lus interval. The neutral group, on the other hand, conformed to the typical findings (e.g., Bohlin & Kjellberg, 1979) in showing more deceleration to the CS+ than to the CS−, with maximal difference at the time that the

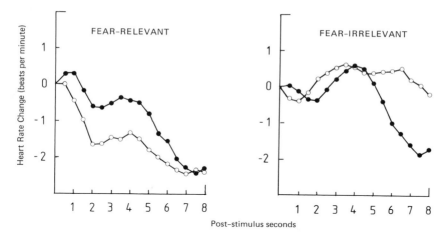

FIGURE 6.5   Changes in heart rate from pre-stimulus level for post-stimulus half-seconds to slides followed by electric shock (CS+; filled circles) or nothing (CS−; open circles) for groups of subjects exposed to fear-relevant or fear-irrelevant stimuli (data from Öhman & Dimberg, 1978b).

shock UCS was due. The opposite pattern of differential responding in these two groups is consistent with the hypothesis, which presumes accelerative conditioning to fear-relevant but decelerative conditioning to neutral stimuli, but the fact that there still was overall deceleration to the fear-relevant CS+ detracts from the impact of the finding. A second experiment (Öhman, Alme, & Mykleburst, 1981) sought to promote accelerative response. By having the subject perform a motor avoidance response (see Figure 6.3) to avoid more than one shock UCS, more acceleration was expected (Bohlin & Kjellberg, 1979; Simons, Öhman, & Lang, 1979). Similar effects were expected from the introduction of uncertainty in the CS–UCS relationship (Bohlin & Kjellberg, 1979). Thus the interstimulus interval varied between 6 and 9 s, and the probability of the UCS following the CS decreased from .8 on the first trial block to 0 during the last. Figure 6.6 shows that these efforts, if anything, were all too successful, because clear accelerative responding was obtained in both groups. However, whereas the HR response to the neutral CS+ showed the typical pronounced deceleration in anticipation of the affective UCS and the rapid motor response (Simons et al., 1979), no such deceleration was seen to the fear-relevant CS+, although motor performance did not differ between groups. These effects resulted in significantly higher HR in the fear-relevant than in the neutral group during this period, with significant between-group differences in response to CS+ but not in response to CS−. Taken together, these two experiments suggest an accelerative influence of possibly sympa-

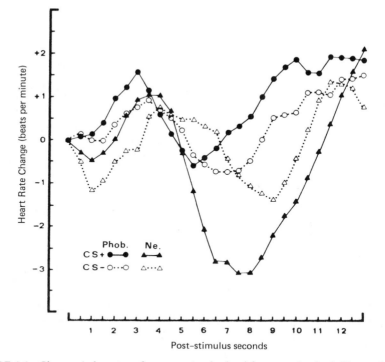

FIGURE 6.6   Changes in heart rate from pre-stimulus level for post-stimulus half-seconds to slides sometimes followed by a train of electric shocks that could be terminated by a rapid motor response (CS+) or followed by nothing (CS−) in group exposed to fear-relevant or fear-irrelevant stimuli. Data from non-shocked trials (from Öhman *et al.*, 1981).

thetic origin on the HR response conditioned to fear-relevant stimuli, whereas such an effect is not obvious in conditioned HR responses to neutral stimuli.

These suggestions have been confirmed and extended in Lang's Wisconsin laboratory. With a noise UCS, Cook (1981) found accelerative differential conditioning to snakes or spiders and decelerative conditioning to neutral stimuli, the effect being particularly strong for female subjects selected because of their high fear of snakes and spiders. Hodes (1981), in his study incorporating a tactile component to the noise UCS, reported similar findings evident for both sexes. Finally, Cook (1983) reported accelerative conditioning to fear-relevant but not to neutral stimuli with a shock UCS in two experiments.

Figure 6.7 presents pooled data from six experiments utilizing tactile UCS and carried out at the University of Wisconsin laboratory. For the

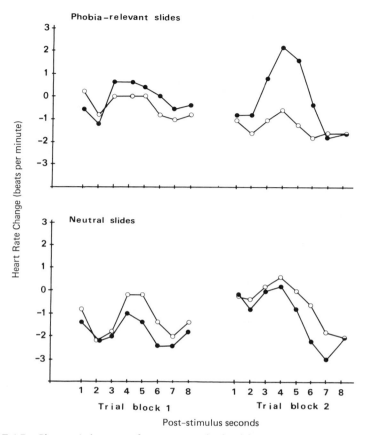

FIGURE 6.7   Changes in heart rate from pre-stimulus level for post-stimulus seconds to slide stimuli followed by electric shock (CS+) or nothing (CS−) in subjects exposed to fear-relevant or phobia-relevant and neutral stimuli (data from Cook, 1983, reprinted by permission of the author).

snake and spider groups, there is a conspicuous increase in differential accelerative response from the first to the second trial block, with no corresponding effect in the neutral group. This latter group, however, develops reliable differential response later in the interstimulus interval, but in a decelerative direction. Thus the two groups differ both with regard to the direction and point of maximal differential response, as did the two groups studied by Öhman and Dimberg in Bergen (see Figure 6.5). For the combined Wisconsin data there was also a significant UCS effect, so that somewhat clearer results were obtained with UCSs incorporating tactile elements.

The Wisconsin data clearly demonstrate that there is more than modification of orienting and attentional behavior involved in conditioning to animal (snake or spider) stimuli with electric shock UCS. This effect, however, may be somewhat fragile, and it seems to be modified by cognitive factors. Thus in his third experiment, where instructed acquisition was examined, Cook (1983) observed decelerative HR response curves with small differences between fear-relevant and neutral stimuli, during all phases of the experiments. That is, in a conditioning acquisition phase where shocks were presented, more deceleration was observed to the CS+ than to the CS− even for fear-relevant stimuli. During extinction, this effect was more pronounced for the fear-relevant than for the neutral group. These imply that the conditioned accelerative HR response to fear-relevant material can be overridden and changed to a general deceleration if a strong expectancy is induced in the subjects with the help of explicit contingency instructions. Thus these data may indicate that responses acquired through instructions differ from those acquired through direct conditioning (Rachman, 1977).

Automatic Control of Autonomic Responses to Animal Stimuli

A third theoretical prediction is that responses to potentially phobic stimuli should show evidence of automatic rather than voluntary control; that is, once acquired these responses should not be affected by conscious intentions as manipulated through verbal instructions to the subjects.

Early data from the Uppsala laboratory unequivocally supported this prediction (see Öhman & Hugdahl, 1979, for a review). Öhman, Erixon, and Löfgren (1975) found no effects from the instructions that no more UCSs would be presented on extinction of SCRs to pictures of snakes, whereas SCRs conditioned to pictures of houses extinguished immediately, regardless of instructions. Hugdahl and Öhman (1977) conditioned SCRs to either snake and spider or flower and mushroom pictures and then instructed half of the subjects in each group that no more UCSs would be presented. The instructions essentially abolished differential responding to the neutral stimuli, but they had no discernible statistical effect on SCRs to fear-relevant stimuli. After these demonstrations, instructed extinction was incorporated in the general procedures in studies performed by Hugdahl (1978) and Hygge and Öhman (1978). Thus in these studies all subjects were instructed that no more UCSs would be presented, yet significant differential responding remained to fear-relevant but not to neutral stimuli, regardless of whether the SCRs were acquired through direct conditioning, vicarious conditioning, or through contingency instructions.

Hodes (1981) obtained tendencies somewhat similar to the results reported by Hugdahl and Öhman (1977) in his experiment using a noise-vibrator UCS compound stimulus. However, as groups were small ($n = 6$) and the UCS ineffective in producing overall differences between fear-relevant and neutral stimuli, Hodes' data must be regarded as inconclusive. Using shock UCS, Cook (1983) found reliable resistance to extinction for SCR probability to fear-relevant but not to neutral CSs for subjects uninformed about extinction, whereas both groups instructed about extinction showed little resistance to extinction. These results clearly differed from those reported by Hugdahl and Öhman (1977). For SCR magnitude (the measure used by Hugdahl and Öhman), however, the informed subjects exposed to fear-relevant stimuli showed as much (or even more) resistance to extinction as uninformed subjects, whereas neither neutral group showed any resistance to extinction. However, these effects were not statistically reliable, possibly because of the small number of subjects per group ($n = 8$). In general, therefore, Cook's (1983) attempt at exact replication of the Hugdahl and Öhman study failed to obtain the same results.

Incongruent data were also reported by Dawson and Schell (1981, see also Dawson & Schell, 1985) in a more complicated multiple-cue paradigm designed to examine the relationship between awareness and conditioning to fear-relevant and neutral stimuli, while the subject performed a task designed to mask the CS–UCS contingency. Their experiment involved trial-by-trial ratings by the subjects of their shock expectancies. Half of their subjects were informed before acquisition that the UCS would be withheld in the middle of the experiment (that is, they received instructions about extinction). This instruction had no effect; no differences were observed between the groups conditioned to fear-relevant and neutral stimuli. With the help of subjective expectancy reports, Dawson and Schell (1981) were able to segregate the series of extinction trials into one part where the subjects still expected the shock UCS and another part in which their shock expectancies were extinguished. (Incidently, the point of expectancy extinction did not differ as a function of fear relevance.) However, when differential responding to the CS+ and the CS− was examined for the fear-relevant and the neutral groups after the point of expectancy extinction, reliable differentiation was observed in the former but not in the latter condition. Thus evidence for dissociations between verbal expectancies and autonomic response were observed for fear-relevant but not for neutral stimuli. To some extent, however, the impact of this finding is reduced by the fact that a similar tendency, albeit a nonsignificant one, was seen in the neutral group. Furthermore, the amount of differential responding did not differ significantly between the two groups.

McNally (1981) tried to reverse differential responding to fear-relevant stimuli by informing the subjects of the reversal of the contingency (see Grings, Schell, and Carey, 1973). He reported an immediate decrease in

SCR responding to the CS+ after the reversal instruction, but no reliable increase in the response to the CS− (which, according to the instruction, was now the CS+). The impacts of his findings, however, are reduced by the fact that he failed to obtain evidence of reliable conditioning during acquisition, and by the fact that he did not include a neutral control group.

Finally, in a previously described experiment, Öhman, Alme, and Mykleburst gave extinction instructions including removal of the shock electrodes, after the subject had been exposed to a gradually diluted CS−UCS contingency starting with a .8 reinforcement, which via .5 and .2 reinforcements slid to extinction. Twenty pure extinction trials were given during which differential responding was maintained before the instruction was given. However, after instruction, differential response disappeared completely, even in the fear-relevant group (see Figure 6.3).

Taken together, this set of results provides less firm empirical support for the prediction of automatic control of the responses to fear-relevant stimuli than for the predictions regarding UCS conditions and a conditioned heart rate response. While the Uppsala studies consistently failed to indicate any effect of extinction instructions on SCRs to fear-relevant stimuli, failures to replicate this finding have been frequently reported from other laboratories, with no hints about what the critical conditions for the effect might be. While some comforting tendencies or problems of interpretation are obvious in most of these studies, the present state of the art must be acknowledged as inconclusive. Given the centrality of this prediction for the analysis of phobias, empirical elucidation of the present state of confusion must be given high priority.

Conditioning to Facial Stimuli

According to the present analysis, animal and social phobias share an automatic affective response component the acquisition of which is biologically primed to certain classes of stimuli. Thus similar results to those reviewed in the previous sections would be expected if social stimuli signaling dominance and intraspecific aggression were paired with aversive events. In particular, fear should be much more readily conditioned to facial expressions of anger than to facial expressions of happiness, for example. Furthermore, the theoretical analysis suggests that this basic effect should have characteristics that in some respects differ from that seen with animal stimuli. For example, whereas snakes become permanently fear-evoking once they have been paired with aversion, this is not so for facial stimuli. Facial expressions are transient characteristics of an individual. For group-living animals, it is necessary to live close, or even seek proximity to, the dominant males. Thus they are not generally feared, but they are avoided when aggressive intents are disclosed through angry expressions. Further-more, only the group member who is the target of the display of anger needs to get out of the way. Thus the direction of the display of anger should be critical for the fear-evoking effects. This type of analysis suggests that group members learn which individuals are potentially dangerous. However, there is no need for a group member to let this learning be manifested as fear and avoidance except when the potentially dangerous individual expresses anger that is targeted toward him or her. These predic-tions have been supported in a program of research by Dimberg and Öhman (see Dimberg, 1983, for a review).

The basic prediction was confirmed by Öhman and Dimberg (1978a). They presented pictures of angry, neutral, or happy faces as signals for electric shock UCSs for three independent groups of subjects, while SCRs were measured. The subjects discriminated between two different persons expressing the same emotion by having one of them followed by the UCS. Responses did not differ between pictures during an initial habituation phase when the UCS was not presented. During acquisition, however, when shock followed one of the two persons with the same expression, differential responding emerged in all three groups. When the shock was withheld during extinction, differential responding collapsed immediately in the groups shocked when shown happy and neutral faces, but remained virtually intact over 16 extinction trials in those shown angry faces. Thus, similar to SCRs conditioned to snakes, SCRs conditioned to angry faces were much more resistant to extinction than those conditioned to happy or neutral stimuli, which is exactly in agreement with the prediction.

The evolutionary perspective suggests that this effect should be critically dependent on the direction of the angry face. Accordingly, Dimberg and Öhman (1983) conditioned one group of subjects to angry faces directed to the observer and another group to angry faces directed about 30° to the side of the observer. Significant resistance to extinction was obtained only in the former group. An angry face directed away appeared as inefficient as the happy faces in the previous study for inducing persistent response.

As outlined above (see also Öhman & Dimberg, 1984), subjects should learn that a particular stimulus person is potentially fear-evoking, but only show their fear when the person directs his display of anger specifically at them. This prediction was confirmed in a second experiment reported by Dimberg and Öhman (1983). They conditioned subjects to angry faces either directed at or away from the observer, and then shifted the condition from acquisition to extinction. That is, the subjects conditioned to a face looking away were now exposed to the same stimulus person directing his angry display at the observer, and vice versa. The critical condition was what direction the display had during extinction. Only the subjects exposed to the angry face directed at them showed significant resistance to extinction, even though they were conditioned to the face looking away. These results, then, suggest that the subjects learned something about the stimulus person that was manifested only when the anger was directed at them.

To further test this hypothesis, Dimberg (1984) kept the expression (angry or happy) constant across acquisition and extinction phases but shifted the person; that is, subjects were, for example, conditioned to Person A looking angry and then extinguished to Person B looking angry. The differential response achieved during acquisition was immediately lost when the person was changed. Thus the expression per se did not carry any effect at all, which strongly suggests that the effect was carried by the person. In further experiments, Dimberg (1984) demonstrated that similar effects held for emotion and direction of gaze; that is, the critical condition for resistance to extinction was that an angry face was present. However, he was also able to show that angry faces presented during acquisition contributed to resistance to extinction, whereas happy faces during extinction inhibited resistance. Thus subjects conditioned to a happy face looking away showed more resistance to extinction to the same stimulus person looking angry and directed at the observer than did subjects conditioned to the happy face directed at them. In other words, the inhibitory effect of the happy face was removed by having it directed away during acquisition.

To sum up, these experiments indicated that SCRs were conditioned to particular stimulus persons, with a facilitatory effect if the stimulus person looked angry and an inhibitory effect if he looked happy. However, the critical feature was what emotion was shown during extinction and which direction it had. Regardless of the characteristics of the acquisition phase, significant resistance to extinction was obtained only when the stimulus person directed the anger at the observer during this phase, exactly as expected from the evolutionary analysis (Öhman & Dimberg, 1984).

THE RESPONSES OF PHOBICS TO
FEAR-EVOKING SCENES

Our theoretical considerations have suggested that animal phobics should show clear evidence of subjective fear arousal, behavioral avoidance, and sympathetic physiological activation (including heart rate acceleration) when they are confronted with the feared object. This autonomic activation was postulated as part of a ready-made package of escape and avoidance in animal phobics. The previous demonstrations that the pairing of animal stimuli with aversive events, particularly when pain is mediated by the skin, provide support for this prediction. Another prediction that can be made from this general hypothesis is that subjects selected because of their high

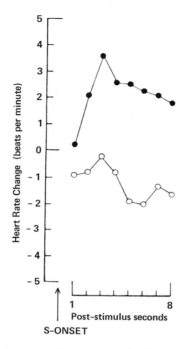

FIGURE 6.8   Changes in heart rate from pre-stimulus level for post-stimulus seconds for phobic subjects exposed to pictures of their feared (●) objects (e.g., snakes) or a control (○) picture (e.g., spiders) (adapted from Fredrikson, 1981; reprinted by permission of the author and the Society for Psychophysiological Research).

level of animal fears should show similar physiological responses when exposed to their fear stimulus.

Pictorial Stimuli

Figure 6.8 shows heart rate data for subjects selected for fear of snakes with no fear of spiders, or vice versa, when they were exposed to pictures of snakes and spiders presented in randomized order (Fredrikson, 1981). The heart rate response to the nonfeared animal stimulus is the deceleration typically seen to neutral or mildly pleasant stimuli, which provides an important component of the orienting response (e.g., Graham, 1979). The feared animal stimulus, on the other hand, provoked a quite marked heart rate acceleration, exactly in agreement with the present predictions (Fredrikson, 1981). These data essentially replicate previous reports by Hare (1973; Hare & Bleving, 1975), who reported heart rate accelerations to pictures of spiders in spider phobics, whereas decelerations were seen to neutral stimuli. Control subjects decelerated to both stimulus categories.

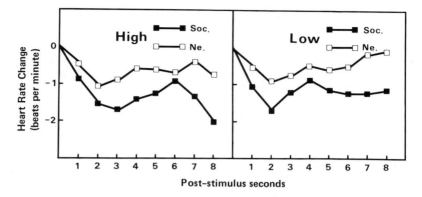

FIGURE 6.9   Changes in heart rate from pre-stimulus level for post-stimulus seconds to social or neutral slides in subjects selected to be high or low in public speaking fear (data from Dimberg *et al.*, 1984).

This clear evidence of heart rate accelerations to feared stimuli should not be expected in social phobics since this fear should be less related to vigorous avoidance behavior. To our knowledge, there is no data available in the literature on phasic physiological responses in socially anxious subjects when exposed to social stimuli. However, a recent Uppsala study (Dimberg, Fredrikson & Lundqvist, 1984) examined heart rate and skin conductance responses in subjects high or low in social fear. These subjects were exposed to social stimuli (mainly pictures of faces with a neutral expression), and to neutral control stimuli (pictures of mushrooms). The high-fear subjects showed significantly larger SCRs to the social than to the control stimuli, whereas the low fear subjects showed overall smaller responses with no differentiation between social and neutral stimuli. Heart rate data are displayed in Figure 6.9. Both groups showed overall decelerative responses that tended to be larger to the social than to the neutral stimuli. This tendency was especially pronounced for the socially fearful subjects on the first trial (not shown in Figure 6.9). However, the amount of deceleration did not differentiate the two groups. Thus, in agreement with theoretical expectations, accelerative heart rate responses to feared stimuli are seen in animal phobics whereas decelerative responses appear to be prominent in social phobics.

Exposure to Real Objects or Events

Further evidence suggesting differences in physiological activation patterns between animal and social phobics comes from studies examining tonic physiological changes during exposures to fear objects. Lang, Levin, Miller, and Kozak (1983) selected subjects fearful of either snakes or public speaking and had both groups participate in graded behavioral tests tapping fear of snakes and public speaking. Higher subjective arousal was reported both during anticipation and actual performance of the fear-relevant as compared to the fear-irrelevant task. Both behavioral tests were graded in seven levels, and the subjects were under instructions to stop whenever they felt overwhelming fear. There were no overall differences in the level at which avoidance occurred between type of task or between fear-relevant and fear-irrelevant tasks. However, females generally avoided more than males, and the snake phobics tended to avoid more than the socially anxious subjects. The proportion of avoiding subjects increased linearly for snake phobics exposed to the snake exposure task, whereas the socially anxious tended to quit primarily at the middle level of their relevant task.

Heart rate was generally somewhat higher in the snake phobics than in the socially anxious subjects. This was, of course, particularly obvious in the snake exposure test, where the nonavoiding snake phobics showed a reliable, linear increase across fear levels, resulting in overall higher heart rate than in the socially anxious group, which showed no trend over levels for the snake exposure test. The overall heart rate change was much larger to the speech test for both groups of subjects, and in fact, the snake phobics even tended to have a somewhat larger change than the socially anxious subjects. On the other hand, the speech test induced larger changes in skin conductance for social than for snake phobics. The snake phobics had better consistency across measures of fear (behavioral avoidance, verbal report of arousal, and heart rate and skin conductance changes); that is, for this group of subjects, the ones with the highest psychometrically assessed fear also tended to be highest in the various other fear measures. This relation did not hold for socially anxious subjects.

Overall, this pattern of results lead Lang et al. (1983) to conclude that the snake phobics displayed a consistent, relatively concordant set of fear responses organized primarily around behavioral avoidance, whereas avoidance was less prominent among the social phobics. Perhaps as a consequence of this fact, the physiological pattern was less integrated with self-report and behavioral domains in the latter group. The unexpected findings of as large a heart rate response in snake phobics as in social phobics during the speech test was partly attributed to the cognitive and motor demands of this task. The results from this study nicely confirm the theoretical notions advanced above, suggesting that animal phobia can be viewed primarily as an "avoidance-package," whereas social phobia is more loosely and conditionally concocted, having more to do with submissiveness and symbolic displays communicating fear than with a distinct urge to avoid.

Imagery of Fearful Scenes

Imagining a scene tends to induce patterns of responses similiar to actual exposure (see Lang, 1979, for a review). Lang, Melamed, and Hart (1970) provided a direct comparison between snake-fearful and socially fearful subjects when they imagined relevant scenes selected for each subject to represent varying fear intensities. Whereas the snake phobics showed a clear linear increase in subjective fear rating with increased scene intensity, and significant linear increases in heart rate, respiration variability, and skin conductance, the public speaking fearful subjects showed negatively accelerated changes with intensity for subjective ratings and heart rate, and no effect for skin conductance and respiration. Thus the snake phobics showed more consistent changes and tended to be more reactive than the social phobics, particularly for the scenes associated with the most fear.

Essentially similar findings were reported by Lang *et al.* (1983). To facilitate the observation of distinct response patterns, they used a procedure developed by Lang, Kozak, Miller, Levin, and McLean (1980) to train snake and social phobics to produce images involving response proposition elements. Again snake phobics showed overall larger heart rate changes than the social phobics, particularly when both groups imagined a snake scene. Replicating a previous report by Weerts and Lang (1978), both groups showed more heart rate change when imagining a relevant as compared to an irrelevant fear scene. However, the larger reactivity of the snake phobics resulted in their heart rate responses to the speech scene being equal to that shown by the socially anxious subjects to this scene. For the snake scene the snake phobics were significantly above the social phobics. A similar pattern was seen for skin conductance, with the snake phobics surpassing the socially anxious while imagining snake scenes, whereas the groups did not differ during imagery of public speaking. Lang *et al.* (1983) interpreted the results for the trained phobic groups during imagery of snake and speech scenes to be similar to the results shown when these populations of subjects actually were exposed to the scenes.

Tonic Physiological Levels during Fear-Irrelevant Stimulation

In the theoretical section, it was emphasized that animal fears are stimulus-elicited, and that lacking relevant predator cues within reactive distance, no evidence of high physiological arousal levels would be evident. For social phobias, on the other hand, fear is typically exhibited by an individual in a vulnerable position in the social hierarchy, who is therefore likely to show signs of anxious vigilance for potential attacks. It seems likely that social phobics may show evidence of enhanced physiological activation even in contexts unrelated to their primary fear, particularly as participation in any laboratory experiment involves an element of social evaluation.

This expectation is supported by data on tonic skin conductance changes. Thus, whereas animal phobics did not differ from normals, social phobics showed evidence of enhanced spontaneous skin conductance activity in the interstimulus intervals between loud tones (Lader, 1967). Similarly, Dimberg *et al.* (1984) reported a higher rate of spontaneous skin conductance activity between stimuli in their socially anxious subjects than in controls during the previously discussed experiment involving visually presented social and neutral stimuli. Reports from Lang's laboratory are conflicting in this respect, Lang *et al.* (1970) obtaining more spontaneous response in social than in animal phobics, whereas Weerts and Lang (1978) found no difference. Thus, on the whole, enhanced rate of spontaneous skin conductance response appears to be a relatively reliable associate of social fearfulness even in situations not primarily related to social stimuli, whereas it does not deviate from normal controls in snake phobics. It is particularly interesting that this finding concerns this particular measure, as it has been reliably associated both with free-floating anxiety (e.g., Lader & Wing, 1966) and vigilance performance (e.g., Katkin, 1975; Sostek, 1978).

DESCRIPTIVE CLINICAL OBSERVATIONS AND STUDIES

Animal Fears and Phobias

According to Marks (1969), animal phobias are isolated phobias for animals and insects. These phobias are isolated in the sense that they have few associated psychiatric symptoms and, in particular, in that they are typically not associated with elevated levels of more generalized overt anxiety (Marks, 1969).

At least among women, fear of animals is the most prevalent of all fear categories, being displayed by a little more than 40% of a female population (Costello, 1982). Furthermore, Costello (1982) demonstrated that animal fears tended to differ most from other fear categories (separation, mutilation, social, and nature fears) at more intense fear levels, including those being associated with behavioral avoidance. This resulted in substantially higher estimates of prevalence for animal (12.5%) than for mutilation and nature phobias (4.9% and 5.1%, respectively).

In clinical populations, Marks (1969) suggests phobias for birds and spiders to be especially common. Factor analyses of fear survey schedules typically isolate crawling and creeping animals such as snakes, spiders, worms, and various insects, as well as bats, rats, and mice, regardless of whether the analysis is based on normals (Bernstein & Allen, 1969; Braun &

Reynolds, 1969; Landy & Gaupp, 1971) or clinical samples (Lawlis, 1971; but see also Bates, 1971, who failed to obtain a clear-cut animal fear factor in 100 neurotic veterans).

The fact that birds and spiders are especially salient fear objects among phobics seeking professional help (Marks, 1969) can probably be accounted for by their prevalence even in urban environments. Thus the impact of a particular fear on the life of the individual is not only determined by its intensity, but also by how common the fear object is in the environment. Thus as long as the object (e.g., snakes) is very uncommon, it is easily avoided without any adverse consequences. However, if the objects occur in contexts to which the person has operant approach contingencies, avoidance is no longer a viable strategy. Therefore, an approach–avoidance conflict ensues (Hayes, 1976), and it becomes obvious that the fear has a negative impact on the individual's life which sets the stage for seeking professional help.

The onset of animal phobia appears to date almost exclusively from childhood, typically before the age of 7 years (Marks, 1969). "The selective age at which animal phobias began suggests a facilitatory phase for their acquisition, and once this is safely passed the mechanism which allowed these phobias to develop is no longer active" (Marks, 1969, p. 148). This selectivity is, as we have seen, readily predicted and explained from the present evolutionary perspective (see p. 137).

Marks (1969) reports that his sample of animal phobics from Maudsley Hospital in London has a very skewed sex ratio, with 95% of the patients being women. In agreement with this clinical observation, studies on fearful college students typically have obtained evidence of more fear in females, even if attempts are made to control for bias in verbal expression of fear (Cornelius & Averill, 1983; Katkin & Hoffman, 1976). However, Fredrikson, Hugdahl, and Öhman (1976) did not obtain sex differences in conditioning of SCRs to snake and spider pictures, nor are sex differences in fear typically found in children (Marks, 1969). This pattern of results prompted Fredrikson et al. (1976) to suggest that the actual conditioning mechanism may not differ between sexes, but that the difference observed in adult fear behavior can be attributed to social learning, with boys being exposed to a social pressure of fearlessness and bravery, and thus having to extinguish their fears.

In their sample of clinical phobics from Uppsala, Öst and Hugdahl (1981) reported that a little less than half of the sample attributed the onset of their animal fear to a traumatic conditioning episode, whereas slightly less than a third had vicarious conditioning experience, and about one sixth reported instruction and verbal warnings as the origin of their fear. Those with a conditioning origin rated themselves as more fearful on a specific fear questionnaire for their particular animal, and they tended to be more plagued by physiological than by cognitive symptoms (primarily negative thoughts).

Social Phobias

Social phobia denotes an intense fear of social situations, with the fear concentrated to "the people themselves or what they might think, rather than of a crowd 'en masse' in which the constituent individuals seem anonymous" (Marks, 1969, pp. 152–153). Thus, the social phobic is concerned about facing others, and particularly about being looked upon by others, while performing activities such as eating, drinking, or writing. He or she particularly fears acting in a way that may be humiliating or embarrassing.

Factor analysis of fear survey schedules almost invariably isolates a prominent social fear factor (e.g., Bates, 1971; Landy & Gaupp, 1971; Lawlis, 1971; Torgersen, 1979) that sometimes is split in two (e.g., Bernstein & Allen, 1969; Braun & Reynolds, 1969). When two factors emerge, one of them appears to denote situations likely to elicit social fear, such as "being a leader," "speaking before a group," "meeting authority," "entering a room where other people are seated," "meeting someone for the first time," "strangers," "feeling angry," and "angry people." The second factor denotes consequences or outcomes of such situations, typically associated with failure. Among the prominent items are "feeling disapproved of," "looking foolish," "being criticized or rejected," "making mistakes," and "losing control." According to Nichols (1974), the lack of self-confidence and self-assertiveness implied by such experiences are at the heart of social phobia. With the exception of Torgersen (1979), who found one very distinct factor of the situational type ("eating with strangers," "being watched writing, working and trembling"), the studies obtaining only one factor report a composite of situation and outcome factors (Bates, 1971; Landy & Gaupp, 1971).

Descriptively, this accords well with what one would expect from our evolutionary perspective. If social fears have their origin in a history of failures to assert oneself in competition for dominance, "meeting authority," "being a leader," and "facing an audience" must be the epitome of fright-inducing situations. Furthermore, submissiveness typically is induced by "angry people," and one must be careful not to "lose control" and display one's own "feeling of anger," because then the conflict may escalate. From the evolutionary perspective, dominance conflicts are particularly likely to arise when "strangers" are encountered, such as when one "meets somebody for the first time," and particularly when one has to enter a group of strangers ("entering a room where other people are seated"). Dominance is also activated when food is distributed, and social phobics typically complain of difficulties in eating in public (Marks, 1969), particularly with strangers in new environments. For individuals low in the dominance hierarchy, being looked at by others may signal an impending attack, and consequently is experienced as frightful, and as interfering with ongoing activities ("being looked at eating, writing, working, and trembling"). Particularly to tremble or show other signs of fear ("losing control") may be critical, since the implied submissiveness may indeed provoke dominant individuals to attack.

Social phobics show some associated psychiatric problems, particularly depression and more general anxiety (Marks, 1969). Thus not only is the object of fear more ubiquitous and difficult to avoid than that for animal phobics, but the general picture also appears more problematic than the typically isolated fear of animal phobics. From the theoretical discussion above, we would expect social phobics not to avoid social interaction completely but instead to attempt to cope with the fear, because staying close to the group has been critical for survival throughout our history as a species. In agreement with this expectation, "patients who report themselves to be socially anxious do not usually describe a pattern of social withdrawal. Rather they report frequent social interactions that they find painful" (Lang et al., 1983, p. 291).

In his Maudsley sample of social phobics, Marks (1969) described the age of onset as having a mean of 19 years, and typically ranging from after puberty at about 15 to 30 years. Similarly, Nichol's (1974) sample typically had an onset age ranging from late teenager and onward, beginning when the individual has to establish his own independent identity as an adult. Again, this is precisely what would be expected from the evolutionary perspective outlined above.

More than half of the social phobic sample of Öst and Hugdahl (1981) reported a traumatic incidence as the start of their phobia. One eighth reported vicarious experiences, and a substantial proportion (one fourth) could not recall how the phobia started. Social phobics with a conditioning history were more plagued by cognitive than physiological symptoms.

A Direct Comparison between Animal and Social Phobics

Many of the differences between animal and social phobias implied in the clinical description above were confirmed in a direct comparison between groups of patients treated for animal and social phobias by Öst and coworkers (Öst, 1978; Öst, Jerremalm, & Johansson, 1981). The pertinent data are shown in Table 6.1. The two groups were comparable with regard to age, general fear levels according to Fear Survey Schedule III (Wolpe & Lang, 1964), resting heart rate, and self-ratings of anxiety during a behavioral test.

TABLE 6.1

Comparison between Animal and Social Phobics

	Animal phobics (N = 40)	Social phobics (N = 41)	t
Age at treatment	32.1 (7.6) 15–45	34.4 (7.5) 21–51	1.36
Onset age	7.3 (2.8) 3–17	15.5 (6.4) 6–34	7.45★★★★
Duration	24.8 (7.8) 7–40	18.9 (9.4) 2–37	3.07★★★
Fear Survey Schedule (III)	163.4 (37.2)	171.45 (48.5)	0.84
Heart rate at rest	90.9 (16.4)	88.4 (12.4)	0.74
Mean heart rate during test	101.7 (18.7)	94.7 (15.1)	1.77★
Peak heart rate during test	108.9 (19.3)	99.9 (15.3)	2.22★★
Self-rated anxiety during test	5.9 (2.1)	6.7 (2.6)	1.35
Sex distribution	38F (95%); 2M (5%)	24F (59%); 17M (41%)	$\chi^2 = 7.16$★★★

★ $p < .10$; ★★ $p < .05$; ★★★ $p < .01$; ★★★★ $p < .001$

None of the testing situations demanded gross movements from the subjects. The animal phobics sat in a chair and pressed a button to advance a small trolley with a spider, snake, or rat in steps of 0.5 m each, starting 5 m away and coming closer to the patient for each step. The social phobics were simply instructed to initiate and maintain a conversation with a member of the opposite sex who sat down next to him or her.

The table shows that the largest difference between the two samples pertained to the age of onset, the animal phobics originating typically in the preschool years (70% before age 8) and the social phobics typically after puberty (73% after age 13). As a consequence of this difference, the samples also differed in the duration of the phobic problem. The mean heart rate during the behavioral test was marginally higher in the animal phobics (actually significant with an one-sided test), and the peak heart rate was clearly higher for this group, thus confirming the findings of Lang et al. (1983) and others. The sex distribution differed markedly between the samples, with far fewer males among the animal phobics, and a fairly balanced sex ratio for the social phobics.

Concluding Comments

The present theoretical analysis essentially provides a vulnerability-stress or psychobiological perspective (Öhman, 1981) on phobias. That is, it suggests that phobias are triggered through traumatic learning episodes in predisposed individuals. Individuals are differently predisposed to develop phobias as a result of an intricate interaction between biological makeup and environmental impacts throughout development (Delprato, 1980). Clearly, the evolutionary perspective entails that differences between individual's vulnerability to phobic disorders have a genetic basis. However, it is equally clear that this biological predisposition is modulated by experience. For example, even persons with a high degree of genetic vulnerability for animal phobias may be innoculated by graded, relaxed exposures to animals where no aversive consequences follow. Such pre-exposure without the UCS, or "latent inhibition," is highly effective in reducing subsequent conditioning to this particular stimulus (e.g., Rescorla & Holland, 1982). Thus if a vulnerable individual by help of latent inhibition is guided through the critical periods, he is likely not to become a phobic.

An important asset of the present theoretical perspective is that it articulates the similarities and differences among different types of phobias. The essential common component in all phobias is the automatic affective reaction (see Figure 6.1). It is suggested that any effective therapy for phobias must come to grips with the problem of reducing or annihilating this affective reaction, and this is probably what is achieved by the various exposure therapies.

We interpret the empirical evaluative section as providing quite strong support for the theoretical ideas developed in this chapter. Our evolutionary-based theory appears able to handle both animal and social phobias at a quite detailed empirical level, and to integrate large chunks of data from different contexts, including the clinical one. As far as we can see there is no data available that really seriously threatens the theory. However, so far this theory only deals with two types of phobias. It remains a challenging task to develop the evolutionary-learning framework to encompass other types of phobias, and particularly the sometimes perplexing clinical syndrome known as agoraphobia.

Acknowledgement

This chapter is dedicated to Peter J. Lang with friendship and admiration in recognition of his profound contributions to our understanding of fear. Its preparation was facilitated by grants to Arne Öhman from the Swedish Council for Humanities and Social Sciences and to Lars-Göran Öst from the Swedish Medical Research Council.

References

Agras, W. S., Sylvester, D., & Oliveau, D. (1969). The epidemiology of common fears and phobias. *Comprehensive Psychiatry, 10,* 151–156.

Alexander, R. D. (1975). The search for a general theory of behavior. *Behavioral Science, 20,* 77–100.

Archer, J. (1979). Behavioural aspects of fear. In W. Sluckin (Ed.) *Fear in animals and man.* New York: Van Nostrand Reinhold Company.

Bandura, A. (1977a). Self-efficacy: Toward a unifying theory of behavioral change. *Psychological Review, 84,* 191–215.

Bandura, A. (1977b). *Social learning theory.* Englewood Cliffs, NJ: Prentice-Hall.

Bandura, A. (1982). Self-efficacy mechanism in human agency. *American Psychologist, 37,* 122–147.

Barash, D. P. (1977). *Sociobiology and behavior.* New York: Elsevier.

Bates, H. D. (1971). Factorial structure and MMPI correlates of a fear survey schedule in a clinical population. *Behavioural Research and Therapy, 9,* 355–360.

Bernstein, I. S. (1981). Dominance: The baby and the bathwater. *Behavioral and Brain Sciences, 4,* 419–457.

Bernstein, D. A., & Allen, G. J. (1969). Fear survey schedule (II): Normative data and factor analyses based upon a large college sample. *Behavioural Research and Therapy, 7,* 403–407.

Black, A. H. (1965). Cardiac conditioning in curarized dogs: The relationship between heart rate and skeletal behavior. In W. F. Prokasy (Ed.) *Classical conditioning. A symposium.* New York: Appleton-Century-Crofts.

Black, A. H. (1971). Autonomic aversive conditioning in infrahuman subjects. In F. R. Brush (Ed.) *Aversive conditioning and learning.* New York: Academic Press.

Black, A. H., & de Toledo, L. (1972). The relationship among classically conditioned responses: Heart rate and skeletal behavior. In A. H. Black & W. F. Prokasy (Eds.) *Classical conditioning II: Current research and theory.* New York: Appleton-Century-Crofts.

Bohlin, G., & Kjellberg, A. (1979). Orienting activity in two-stimulus paradigms as reflected in heart rate. In H. D. Kimmel, E. H. van Olst, & J. F. Orlebeke (Eds.) *The orienting reflex in humans.* Hillsdale, NJ: Lawrence Erlbaum Associates.

Bolles, R. C. (1970). Species-specific defense reactions and avoidance learning. *Psychological Review, 77,* 32–48.

Bowlby, J. (1969). *Attachment and loss* (Vol. 1) *Attachment.* London: Hogarth Press.

Braun, P. R., & Reynolds, P. J. (1969). A factor analysis of a 100-item fear survey inventory. *Behaviour Research and Therapy, 7,* 399–402.

Cannon, W. B. (1928). The mechanism of emotional disturbance of bodily functions. *New England Journal of Medicine, 198,* 877–884.

Chevalier-Skolnikoff, S. (1973). Facial expression of emotion in nonhuman primates. In P. Ekman (Ed.) *Darwin and facial expression.* New York: Academic Press.

Chevalier-Skolnikoff, S. (1982). A cognitive analysis of facial behavior in old world monkeys, apes, and human beings. In C. T. Snowdon, C. H. Brown, & M. R. Petersen (Eds.) *Primate communication.* Cambridge: Cambridge University Press.

Colgan, P. (1982). *Comparative social recognition.* New York: John Wiley & Sons.

Cook, E. W. (1981). Classical conditioning, individual differences, and preparedness. Unpublished Master Thesis, Department of Psychology, University of Wisconsin, Madison.

Cook, E. W. (1983). Human classical conditioning and the preparedness hypothesis. Unpublished Doctoral Dissertation, Department of Psychology, University of Wisconsin, Madison.

Cornelius, R. R., & Averill, J. R. (1983). Sex differences in fear of spiders. *Journal of Personality and Social Psychology, 45,* 377–383.

Costello, C. G. (1982). Fears and phobias in women: A community study. *Journal of Abnormal Psychology, 91,* 280–286.

Dawkins, R., & Krebs, J. R. (1979). Arms races between and within species. *Proceedings of the Royal Society, B 205,* 489–511.

Dawson, M. E., & Schell, A. M. (1981). Electrodermal classical conditioning with potentially phobic CSs: Cognitive/autonomic dissociations? Paper presented at the meetings of the Society for Psychophysiological Research, Washington, DC.

Dawson, M. E., & Schell, A. M. (1985). Information processing and human autonomic classical conditioning. In P. K. Ackles, J. R. Jennings, & M. G. H. Coles (Eds.) *Advances in psychophysiology* (Vol. 1). Greenwich, CT: JAI Press.

Delprato, D. J. (1980). Heriditary determinants of fears and phobias: A critical review. *Behavior Therapy, 11,* 79–103.

Dimberg, U. (1983). Emotional conditioning to facial stimuli: A psychobiological analysis. *Acta Universitatis Upsaliensis, Abstracts of Uppsala dissertations from the faculty of Social Sciences, 29.* Uppsala, Sweden: Almqvist & Wiksell.

Dimberg, U. (1984). Facial expressions as excitatory and inhibitory stimuli for conditioned autonomic responses. Paper submitted for publication.

Dimberg, U., Fredrikson, M., & Lundqvist, O. (1984). Autonomic reactions to social and nonsocial stimuli in subjects high and low in public speaking fear. Paper submitted for publication.

Dimberg, U., & Öhman, A. (1983). The effects of directional facial cues on electrodermal conditioning to facial stimuli. *Psychophysiology, 20,* 160–167.

Dobshansky, T., Ayala, F. J., Stebbins, G. L., & Valentine, J. W. (1977). *Evolution.* San Francisco: W. H. Freeman & Co.

Ekman, P. (1972). Universals and cultural differences in facial expressions of emotion. In J. K. Cole (Ed.) *Nebraska Symposium on Motivation* (Vol. 19). Lincoln: University of Nebraska Press.

Ellsworth, P. C., Carlsmith, J. M., & Henson, A. (1972). The stare as a stimulus to flight in human subjects: A series of field experiments. *Journal of Personality and Social Psychology, 21,* 302–311.

Exline, R. V. (1972). Visual interaction: The glances of power and preference. In J. K. Cole (Ed.) *Nebraska Symposium on Motivation* (Vol. 19). Lincoln: University of Nebraska Press.

Eysenck, H. J. (1979). The conditioning model of neurosis. *Behavioral and Brain Sciences, 2,* 155–199.

Fredrikson, M. (1981). Orienting and defensive reactions to phobic and conditioned fear stimuli in phobics and normals. *Psychophysiology, 18,* 456–465.

Fredrikson, M., Hugdahl, K., & Öhman, A. (1976). Electrodermal conditioning to potentially phobic stimuli in male and female subjects. *Biological Psychology, 4,* 305–314.

Fredrikson, M., & Öhman, A. (1979). Cardiovascular and electrodermal responses conditioned to fear-relevant stimuli. *Psychophysiology, 16,* 1–7.

Graham, F. K. (1979). Distinguishing among orienting, defense, and startle reflexes. In H. D. Kimmel, E. H. van Olst, & J. F. Orlebeke (Eds.) *The orienting reflex in humans.* Hillsdale, NJ: Lawrence Erlbaum Associates.

Grings, W. W. (1973). Cognitive factors in electrodermal conditioning. *Psychological Bulletin, 79,* 200–210.

Grings, W. W., Schell, A. M., & Carey, C. A. (1973). Verbal control of an autonomic response in a cue reversal situation. *Journal of Experimental Psychology, 99,* 215–221.

Hare, R. D. (1973). Orienting and defensive responses to visual stimuli. *Psychophysiology, 10,* 453–464.

Hare, R. D., & Bleving, G. (1975). Defensive responses to phobic stimuli. *Biological Psychology, 3,* 1–13.

Harris, B. (1979). Whatever happened to little Albert? *American Psychologist, 34,* 151–160.

Hayes, S. C. (1976). The role of approach contingencies in phobic behavior. *Behavior Therapy, 7,* 28–36.

Hebb, D. O. (1946). On the nature of fear. *Psychological Review, 53,* 259–276.

Hinde, R. A. (1974). *Biological bases of human social behaviour.* New York: McGraw-Hill.

Hinde, R. A. (1978). Dominance and role—two concepts with dual meanings. *Journal of Social and Biological Structures, 1,* 27–38.

Hinde, R. A., & Stevenson-Hinde, J. (Eds.). (1973). *Constraints on learning.* London: Academic Press.

Hodes, R. L. (1981). A psychophysiological investigation of the classical conditioning model of fears and phobias. Unpublished Doctoral Dissertation, Department of Psychology, University of Wisconsin, Madison.

Hodes, R. L., Öhman, A., & Lang, P. J. (1979). "Ontogenetic" and "phylogemetic" fear relevance of the conditioned stimulus in electrodermal and heart rate conditioning. Unpublished manuscript, Department of Psychology, University of Wisconsin, Madison.

Hollis, K. L. (1982). Pavlovian conditioning of signal-centered action patterns and autonomic behavior: A biological analysis of function. In J. S. Rosenblatt, R. A. Hinde, C. Beer, & M.-C. Busnell (Eds.) *Advances in the study of behavior* (Vol. 12). New York: Academic Press.

Hugdahl, K. (1978). Electrodermal conditioning to potentially phobic stimuli: Effects of instructed extinction. *Behaviour Research and Therapy, 16,* 315–321.

Hugdahl, K., & Kärker, A.-C. (1981). Biological vs experiential factors in phobic conditioning. *Behaviour Research and Therapy, 19,* 109–115.

Hugdahl, K., & Öhman, A. (1977). Effects of instruction on acquistion and extinction of electrodermal responses to fear relevant stimuli. *Journal of Experimental Psychology: Human Learning and Memory, 3,* 608–618.

Hugdahl, K., & Öhman, A. (1980). Skin conductance conditioning to potentially phobic stimuli as a function of interstimulus interval and delay versus trace paradigm. *Psychophysiology, 17,* 348–355.

Hygge, S., & Öhman, A. (1978). Modeling processes in the acquisition of fears: Vicarious electrodermal conditioning to fear-relevant stimuli. *Journal of Personality and Social Psychology, 36,* 271–279.

Johnston, T. D. (1981). Contrasting approaches to a theory of learning. *Behavioral and Brain Sciences, 4,* 125–173.

Johnston, T. D. (1982). Selective costs and benefits in the evolution of learning. In J. S. Rosenblatt, R. A. Hinde, C. Beer, & M.-C. Busnel (Ed.) *Advances in the study of behavior* (Vol. 12). New York: Academic Press.

Johnston, T. D., & Turvey, M. T. (1980). A sketch of an ecological metatheory for theories of learning. In G. H. Bower (Ed.) *The psychology of learning and motivation* (Vol. 14). New York: Academic Press.

Jolly, A. (1972). *The evolution of primate behavior.* New York: MacMillan Co.

Joslin, J., Fletcher, H., & Emlen, J. A. (1964). A comparison of the responses to snakes of lab- and wild-reared rhesus monkeys. *Animal Behaviour, 12,* 348–352.

Kartsounis, L. D., & Pickersgill, M. J. (1981). Orienting responses to stimuli others fear. *British Journal of Clinical Psychology, 20,* 261–273.

Katkin, E. S. (1975). Electrodermal lability: A psychophysiological analysis of individual differences in response to stress. In I. G. Sarason, & C. D. Spielberger (Eds.) *Stress and anxiety* (Vol. 2). Washington, DC.: Hemisphere Publishing Company.

Katkin, E. S., & Hoffman, L. S. (1976). Sex differences and self-report of fear: A psychophysiological assessment. *Journal of Abnormal Psychology, 85,* 607–610.

Kleinknecht, R. A. (1982). The origins and remission of fear in a group of tarantula enthusiasts. *Behaviour Research and Therapy, 20,* 437–443.

LaBerge, D. (1981). Automatic information processing: A review. In J. Long & A. Baddeley (Eds.) *Attention and performance.* (Vol. IX). Hillsdale, NJ: Lawrence Erlbaum associates.

Lacey, J. I., & Lacey, B. C. (1970). Some autonomic-central nervous system interrelationships. In P. Black (Ed.) *Physiological correlates of emotion.* New York: Academic Press.

Lader, M. H. (1967). Palmar skin conductance measures in anxiety and phobic states. *Journal of Psychosomatic Research, 11*, 271–281.

Lader, M. H., & Wing, L. (1966). *Physiological measures, sedative drugs, and morbid anxiety.* London: Oxford University Press.

Landy, F. J., & Gaupp, L. A. (1971). A factor analysis of the fear survey schedule—III. *Behaviour Research and Therapy, 9*, 89–93.

Lang, P. J. (1968). Fear reduction and fear behavior: Problems in treating a construct. In J. M. Shlien (Ed.) *Research in psychotherapy* (Vol. III). Washington, DC.: American Psychological Association.

Lang, P. J. (1978). Anxiety: Toward a psychophysiological definition. In H. S. Akiskal & W. L. Webb (Eds.) *Psychiatric diagnosis: Exploration of biological predictors.* New York: Spectrum.

Lang, P. J. (1979). A bio-informational theory of emotional imagery. *Psychophysiology, 16*, 495–512.

Lang, P. J. (1984). Cognition in emotion: Concept and action. In C. Izard, J. Kagan, & R. Zajonc (Eds.) *Emotion, cognition, and behavior.* New York: Cambridge University Press.

Lang, P. J. (In press). The cognitive psychophysiology of emotion: Fear and anxiety. In A. H. Tuma & J. D. Maser (Eds.), *Anxiety and the anxiety disorders.* Hillsdale, NJ: Erlbaum.

Lang, P. J., Kozak, M. J., Miller, G. A., Levin, D. N., & McLean, A., Jr. (1980). Emotional imagery: Conceptual structure and pattern of somato-visceral response. *Psychophysiology, 17*, 179–192.

Lang, P. J., Levin, D. N., Miller, G. A., & Kozak, M. J. (1983). Fear behavior, fear imagery, and the psychophysiology of emotion: The problem of affective response integration. *Journal of Abnormal Psychology, 92*, 276–306.

Lang, P. J., Melamed, B. G., & Hart, J. D. (1970). A psychophysiological analysis of fear modification using an automated desensitization procedure. *Journal of Abnormal Psychology, 31*, 220–234.

Lawlis, G. F. (1971). Response styles of a patient population on the fear survey schedule. *Behaviour Research and Therapy, 9*, 95–192.

Lazarus, R. S., Averill, J. R., & Opton, E. M., Jr. (1970). Toward a cognitive theory of emotion. In M. Arnold (Ed.) *Feelings and emotions.* New York: Academic Press.

Lazarus, R. S., Kanner, A. D., & Folkman, S. (1980). Emotions: A cognitive-phenomenological analysis. In R. Plutchik & H. Kellerman (Eds.) *Emotion: Theory, research, and experience* (Vol. 1). *Theories of emotion.* New York: Academic Press.

Lewontin, R. C. (1978). Adaptation. *Scientific American, 239*(3), 157–169.

Lewontin, R. C. (1982). Organism and environment. In H. C. Plotkin (Ed.) *Learning, development and culture.* Chichester, England: John Wiley & Sons.

Lorenz, K. Z. (1966). *On aggression.* New York: Harcourt, Brace, and World.

MacLean, P. D. (1970). The limbic brain in relation to the psychoses. In P. Black (Ed.) *Physiological correlates of emotion.* New York: Academic Press.

McNally, R. J. (1981). Phobias and preparedness: Instructional reversal of electrodermal conditioning to fear-relevant stimuli. *Psychological Reports, 48*, 175–180.

Mandler, G. (1975). *Mind and emotion.* New York: John Wiley & Sons.

Marks, I. (1969). *Fears and phobias.* London: Heineman Medical Books.

Mayr, E. (1974). Behavior programs and evolutionary strategies. *American Scientist, 62*, 650–659.

Mednick, S. A., Schulsinger, F., Higgins, J., & Bell, B. (Eds.). (1974). *Genetics, environment, and psychopathology.* Amsterdam: North Holland.

Miller, S. M. (1979). Controllability and human stress: Method, evidence, and theory. *Behaviour Research and Therapy, 17*, 287–304.

Miller, S. M. (1981). Predictability and human stress: Toward a clarification of evidence and theory. In L. Berkowitz (Ed.) *Advances in experimental social psychology* (Vol. 14). New York: Academic Press.

Miller, L. C., Barrett, C. L., Hampe, E., & Noble, H. (1972). Factor structure of childhood fears. *Journal of Consulting and Clinical Psychology, 39,* 264–268.

Mineka, S. (1979). The role of fear in theories of avoidance learning, flooding, and extinction. *Psychological Bulletin, 86,* 985–1010.

Mineka, S., Davidson, M., Keir, R., & Cook, M. (1984). Observational conditioning of snake fear in rhesus monkeys. *Journal of Abnormal Psychology, 93,* 355–372.

Mineka, S., & Keir, R. (1983). The effects of flooding on reducing snake fear in rhesus monkeys. Six-month follow-up and further flooding. *Behaviour Research and Therapy, 21,* 527–536.

Mineka, S., Keir, R., & Price, V. (1980). Fear of snakes in wild- and laboratory-reared rhesus monkeys (Macaca mulatta). *Animal Learning and Behavior, 8,* 653–663.

Morris, R., & Morris, D. (1965). *Men and snakes.* London: Hutchinson.

Moyer, K. E. (1976). *The psychology of aggression.* New York: Harper & Row.

Murray, E. J., & Foote, F. (1979). The origins of fear of snakes. *Behaviour Research and Therapy, 17,* 489–493.

Nichols, K. A. (1974). Severe social anxiety. *British Journal of Medical Psychology, 47,* 301–306.

Obrist, P. A. (1976). The cardiovascular-behavioral interaction—as it appears today. *Psychophysiology, 13,* 95–107.

Obrist, P. A., Sutterer, J. R., & Howard, J. L. (1972). Preparatory cardiac changes: A psychobiological approach. In A. H. Black & W. F. Prokasy (Eds.) *Classical conditioning II: Current research and theory.* New York: Appleton-Century-Crofts.

Öhman, A. (1979a). Fear relevance, autonomic conditioning, and phobias: A laboratory model. In P. -O. Sjödén, S. Bates, & W. S. Dockens III (Eds.) *Trends in behavior therapy.* New York: Academic Press.

Öhman, A. (1979b). The orienting response, attention, and learning: An information-processing perspective. In H. D. Kimmel, E. H. van Olst, & J. F. Orlebeke (Eds.) *The orienting reflex in humans.* Hillsdale, NJ: Lawrence Erlbaum Associates.

Öhman, A. (1981). The role of experimental psychology in the scientific analysis of psychopathology. *International Journal of Psychology, 16,* 299–321.

Öhman, A. (1983). The orienting response during Pavlovian conditioning. In D. A. T. Siddle (Ed.), *Orienting and habituation: Perspectives in human research.* Chichester, England: John Wiley & Sons.

Öhman, A. (In press). The psychophysiology of emotion: An evolutionary-cognitive perspective. In P. K. Ackles, J. R. Jennings, & M. G. H. Coles (Eds.) *Advances in psychophysiology* (Vol. 2). Greenwich, CT: JAI Press.

Öhman, A., Alme, T., & Mykleburst, V. K. (1981). Unpublished data, Department of Somatic Psychology, University of Bergen, Bergen, Norway.

Öhman, A., & Dimberg, U. (1978a). Facial expressions as conditioned stimuli for electrodermal responses: A case of 'preparedness'? *Journal of Personality and Social Psychology, 36,* 1251–1258.

Öhman, A., & Dimberg, U. (1978b). Unpublished data, Department of Somatic Psychology, University of Bergen, Bergen, Norway.

Öhman, A., & Dimberg, U. (1984). An evolutionary perspective on human social behavior. In W. M. Waid (Ed.) *Sociophysiology.* New York: Springer Verlag.

Öhman, A., Eriksson, A., Fredrikson, M., Hugdahl, K. & Olofsson, C. (1974). Habituation of the electrodermal orienting reaction to potentially phobic and supposedly neutral stimuli in normal human subjects. *Biological Psychology, 2,* 85–93.

Öhman, A., Eriksson, A., & Olofsson, C. (1975). One-trial learning and superior resistance to extinction of autonomic responses conditioned to potentially phobic stimuli. *Journal of Comparative and Physiological Psychology, 88,* 619–627.

Öhman, A., Erixon, G., & Löfgren, I. (1975). Phobias and preparedness: Phobic versus neutral pictures as conditioned stimuli for human autonomic responses. *Journal of Abnormal Psychology, 84,* 41–45.

Öhman, A., Fredrikson, M., & Hugdahl, K. (1978). Orienting and defensive responding in the electrodermal system: Palmar-dorsal differences and recovery-rate during conditioning to potentially phobic stimuli. *Psychophysiology, 15,* 93–101.

Öhman, A., Fredrikson, M., Hugdahl, K., & Rimmö, P.-A. (1976). The premise of equipotentiality in human classical conditioning: Conditioned electrodermal responses to potentially phobic stimuli. *Journal of Experimental Psychology: General, 105,* 313–337.

Öhman, A., & Hugdahl, K. (1979). Instructional control of autonomic respondents: Fear-relevance as a critical factor. In N. Birbaumer & H. D. Kimmel (Eds.) *Biofeedback and self-regulation.* Hillsdale, NJ: Lawrence Erlbaum Associates.

Öst, L.-G. (1978). Fading vs. systematic desensitization in the treatment of snake and spider phobia. *Behaviour Research and Therapy, 16,* 379–389.

Öst, L.-G., & Hugdahl, K. (1981). Acquisition of phobias and anxiety response patterns in clinical patients. *Behaviour Research and Therapy, 19,* 439–447.

Öst, L.-G., & Hugdahl, K. (1983). Acquisition of agoraphobia, mode of onset and anxiety response patterns. *Behaviour Research and Therapy, 21,* 623–632.

Öst, L.-G., Jerremalm, A., & Johansson, J. (1981). Individual response patterns and the effects of different behavioral methods in the treatment of social phobia. *Behaviour Research and Therapy, 19,* 1–16.

Pickersgill, M. J., & Kartsounis, L. D. (1982). Orienting responses to pleasant stimuli when expecting pleasant or unpleasant events. *Current Psychological Research, 2,* 231–234.

Plomin, R., DeFries, J. C., & McClearn, G. E. (1980). *Behavioral genetics. A primer.* San Francisco: W. H. Freeman & Co.

Plotkin, H. C., & Odling-Smee, F. J. (1979). Learning, change, and evolution: An inquiry into the teleonomy of learning. In J. S. Rosenblatt, R. A. Hinde, C. Beer, & M.-C. Busnel (Eds.) *Advances in the study of behavior* (Vol. 10). New York: Academic Press.

Plotkin, H. C., & Odling-Smee, F. J. (1981). A multiple-level model of evolution and its implications for sociobiology. *Behavioral and Brain Sciences, 4,* 225–235.

Posner, M. I. (1978). *Chronometric explorations of mind.* Hillsdale, NJ: Lawrence Erlbaum Associates.

Rachman, S. (1977). The conditioning theory of fear-acquisition: A critical examination. *Behaviour Research and Therapy, 15,* 375–387.

Rachman, S. J. (1978). *Fear and courage.* San Francisco: W. H. Freeman & Co.

Rachman, S. J. (1981). The primacy of affect: Some theoretical implications. *Behaviour Research and Therapy, 19,* 279–290.

Raskin, D. C. (1973). Attention and arousal. In W. F. Prokasy & D. C. Raskin (Eds.) *Electrodermal activity in psychological research.* New York: Academic Press.

Rescorla, R. A., & Holland, P. C. (1982). Behavioral studies of associative learning in animals. *Annual Review of Psychology, 33,* 265–308.

Rimm, D. C., Janda, L. H., Lancaster, D. W., Nahl, M., & Dittmar, K. (1977). An exploratory investigation of the origin and maintenance of phobias. *Behaviour Research and Therapy, 15,* 231–238.

Rubin, B. M., Katkin, E. S., Weiss, B. W., & Efran, J. S. (1968). Factor analysis of a fear survey schedule. *Behaviour Research and Therapy, 6,* 65–75.

Russell, P. A. (1979). Fear-evoking stimuli. In W. Sluckin (Ed.) *Fear in animals and man*. New York: Van Nostrand Reynold Co.

Sagan, C. (1977). *The dragons of Eden: Speculations on the evolution of human intelligence*. London: Hodder & Stoughton.

Schlenker, B. R., & Leary, M. R. (1982). Social anxiety and self-presentation: A conceptualization and model. *Psychological Bulletin, 92*, 641–669.

Scott, J. P. (1980). The function of emotions in behavioral systems: A systems theory analysis. In R. Plutchik & H. Kellerman (Eds.) *Emotion: Theory, research, and experience*. (Vol. 1). *Theories of emotion*. New York: Academic Press.

Shiffrin, R. M., & Schneider, W. (1977). Controlled and automatic human information processing: II. Perceptual learning, automatic attending, and a general theory. *Psychological Review, 84*, 127–190.

Seligman, M. E. P. (1970). On the generality of the laws of learning. *Psychological Review, 77*, 406–418.

Seligman, M. E. P. (1971). Phobias and preparedness. *Behavior Therapy, 2*, 307–321.

Seligman, M. E. P., & Hager, J. E. (1972). (Eds.) *Biological boundaries of learning*. New York: Appleton-Century-Crofts.

Simons, R. F., Öhman, A., & Lang, P. J. (1979). Anticipation and response set: Cortical, cardiac, and electordermal correlates. *Psychophysiology, 16*, 222–233.

Sostek, A. J. (1978). Effects of electrodermal lability and payoff instructions on vigilance performance. *Psychophysiology, 15*, 561–568.

Strongman, K. T., & Champness, B. G. (1968). Dominance hierarchies and conflict in eye contact. *Acta Psychologica, 28*, 376–386.

Torgersen, S. (1979). The nature and origin of common phobic fears. *British Journal of Psychiatry, 134*, 343–351.

Van Lawick-Goodall, J. (1971). *In the shadow of man*. Boston: Houghton Mifflin.

Waddington, C. H. (1957). *The strategy of genes*. London: Allen & Unwin.

Watson, J. B., & Raynor, R. (1920). Conditioned emotional reactions. *Journal of Experimental Psychology, 3*, 1–14.

Weerts, T. C., & Lang, P. J. (1978). Psychophysiology of fear imagery: Differences between focal phobia and social performance anxiety. *Journal of Consulting and Clinical Psychology, 46*, 1157–1159.

Weigel, R. M. (1978). The facial expressions of the brown capuchin monkey (Cebus Apella). *Behaviour, 3–4*, 250–276.

Wolpe, J., & Lang, P. J. (1964). A fear survey schedule for use in behavior therapy. *Behaviour Research and Therapy, 2*, 27–30.

Zajonc, R. B. (1980). Feeling and thinking. Preferences need no inferences. *American Psychologist, 35*, 151–175.

PART *III*

SELECTED THEORETICAL ISSUES

One of the defining features of behavior therapy has been the use of experimental methodology to further our understanding of clinical problems. Whether it be the use of functional analysis, single-case experiments, or between-group experiments, assessment and methodology have played a unifying role among the diverse branches of behavior therapy.

There have been two ways in which experimental methodology has contributed to behavior therapy. First, behavior therapists have been at the forefront in developing outcome evaluations of behavioral interventions. Behavior therapists, through an extensive reliance on outcome evaluations, have introduced new interventions and revised old ones. This has led to the development of successful treatments for many clinical problems and the development of effective principles of behavior change.

Second, and sometimes overlooked, experimental methodology has contributed by advancing our understanding of the clinical problems themselves. Often the primary purpose of functional analyses and the experimental study of single cases is to identify the determinants of problem behavior. As Yates points out in Chapter 9, once determinants are accurately identified, various treatments can be employed effectively. The crucial contribution of assessment and methodology is to further our understanding of the problem so that effective treatments can be developed.

The three chapters in this section each indicate how assessment and methodology can be used to advance our understanding of specific problems. Donald Baer and Hikaru Deguchi provide a thorough theoretical and methodological analysis of imitation. Although modeling is an important component of many treatments, behavior therapists have not typically considered the extent to which differential effectiveness of modeling might be due to individual differences in the strength of imitative behavior. In evaluating theories of generalized imitation, Baer and Deguchi find that intermittent reinforcement and setting-event theories are incomplete. They suggest that a conditioned-reinforcement explanation provides the most complete account of the emergence and maintenance of generalized imitation.

Edward Carr and Mark Durand analyze severe behavior problems such as aggression, tantrums, and self-injury in developmentally disabled children. They propose that severe behavior problems function as a means either to seek positive reinforcement in the form of attention or to escape from aversive conditions such as teacher demands. A functional analysis for each individual case is critical in order to develop the appropriate intervention. Carr and Durand further outline a general theory that severe behavior problems can be usefully conceptualized as forms of communication. Thus, once it is clear what the child is attempting to communicate, behavior problems can be reduced by teaching more appropriate means of communicating.

Aubrey Yates illustrates the importance of evaluating basic assumptions by means of experimental analysis of individual cases in clinical biofeedback therapy. He analyzes common assumptions for the treatment of headaches, diabetes, asthma, and temporomandibular joint dysfunction (TMJD). Since the evidence is far from uniform for each assumption, the importance of individualized assessment for effective treatment is highlighted.

7

Generalized Imitation from a Radical-Behavioral Viewpoint

DONALD M. BAER
HIKARU DEGUCHI

Context

"Does the Savage speak? If he is not deaf why does he not speak?" (Itard, 1806/1932, p. 26).

At the end of the eighteenth century, Itard, educator of the Wild Boy of Aveyron, asked this simple question, and had already noticed the importance of imitation for the intellectual development of speech in a wild boy, Victor, captured in the woods of the Department of Aveyron in France. Itard attempted to "lead him to the use of speech by inducing the exercise of imitation through the imperious law of necessity" (p. 31). Itard, however, had little success in teaching verbal imitation:

> Nevertheless, I persisted, and still struggled for a long time against the obstinacy of the organ. Finally, however, seeing that the continuation of my efforts and the passing of time brought about no change, I resigned myself to the necessity of giving up any attempt to produce speech, and abandoned my pupil to incurable dumbness. (p. 187)

We see that normal children, unlike Victor, acquire new verbal behavior from others through observation. It is very difficult to believe that all our behaviors are taught directly by others, or learned by trial-and-error. Then it may be as inevitable for us as for Itard to conceptualize imitation as a crucial factor in the social and linguistic development of children. We also observe that many retarded and autistic children, who do not have the elaborate behavioral repertoires necessary to live independently in society, show poor or no imitative skills. Then it may also be inevitable for us to assume, as Itard did of Victor, that teaching imitation skills will be very helpful for them.

Indeed, we already assume that imitation is a useful mechanism in education and in therapy. Teaching by demonstration is such a commonplace technique in everyday interpersonal and educational interactions that it hardly needs exposition here. However, formal therapeutic attempts to change aberrant behavior by modeling—the so-called modeling therapies (e.g., Kirkland & Thelen, 1977; Rosenthal, 1976; Rosenthal & Bandura, 1978; Spiegler, 1983, Chap. 10)—are much more novel. Yet the practitioners of these therapies also seem to assume that imitation is a readily useful skill in their clients; their focus for technique development is primarily on what is to be modeled. Confronted with failure in an initial attempt, they are likely to add additional models, choose models with more appropriate status for their particular client, and display more clearly the good consequences that the models encounter after demonstrating the behavior that the observer is intended to acquire. Because modeling therapies rarely analyze further the conditions controlling when models are and are not imitated, their therapeutic outcomes may not be reliable.

In this chapter, we show that generalized imitation—imitation not supported directly by environmental contingencies—is best analyzed as a case of a behavior class maintained by a conditioned reinforcer. The conditioned reinforcer is hypothesized to be the class of stimulus similarities between the model's output and the observer's output. But whatever its hypothesized stimulus class may be, if a conditioned-reinforcer explanation is a sound analysis, it has serious implications for the practical application of modeling as a behavior-change technique. In particular, it suggests that this control of imitation is a relatively weak one, leaving the behavior open to control— and in particular, open to suppression—by a wealth of real-world events, many of them neither envisioned nor controllable within an office-therapy context. A review of the relevant literature will confirm this complexity and the sometime weakness that it confers on imitation as a behavior-change technique: It will show that modeling is an exceptionally powerful technique in the amount of information that can be conveyed efficiently, but a systematically undependable technique in getting that information acted upon, and acted upon durably, if it is used from the vantage point of only the office or clinic.

The conditions that control indirectly maintained imitation are the essence of the predominantly research-based controversy about generalized imitation. That controversy has been articulated primarily for its applicability to theories of normal language development and socialization, and for special-education applications such as the teaching of language and self-help skills to retarded persons; even so, its relevance to therapy, as in the modeling therapies, is no less central, even if (so far) less appreciated. We have tried to contribute a little to that appreciation by presenting the controversy and pressing farther toward its eventual resolution.

Historically, the function of imitation may have been too readily accepted as an explanation of the linguistic development and socialization of children, without enough understanding of the mechanisms or processes of imitation. Subsequently, diverse theories were proposed (Allport, 1924; Holt, 1931; Humphrey, 1921; Jersild, 1933; Miller & Dollard, 1941; Mowrer, 1960; Piaget, 1962), and significant disagreements still exist among recent imitation theorists (cf. Aronfreed, 1969; Baer & Sherman, 1964; Bandura, 1971, 1977; Clark, 1977; Flanders, 1968; Gewirtz & Stingle, 1968; Kohlberg, 1969; Kuhn, 1973; Whitehurst, 1978; Whitehurst & Vasta, 1975; Yando, Seitz, & Zigler, 1978). Further empirical understanding of the observational and imitative mechanisms by which people acquire verbal and nonverbal behavior patterns seems to be the first step toward resolving these disagreements enough to offer significant practical implications for childhood socialization, the development of language, and the roles of imitation in therapy. Understanding these mechanisms might be greatly facilitated by testing imitation in the laboratory: Establishing and controlling the phenomenon experimentally could develop some technology of teaching social and linguistic skills to delayed children, which Itard dreamed of but could not realize, and to clients of a much wider range of abilities, which the modern modeling therapies may assume too readily that they have realized.

Generalized Imitation

In the history of behavioral imitation research, a substantial advance has occurred in understanding its mechanisms. This review focuses on imitation and generalized imitation from a radical-behavioral perspective. First it considers early research into the nature of generalized imitation, and then it explores some of its subsequent behavioral explanations.

EARLY RESEARCH IN GENERALIZED IMITATION

One of the earliest efforts to establish and control imitation bore fruit in some quasi-experimental research involving a home-raised chimpanzee (Hayes & Hayes, 1952). The chimpanzee, Viki, was raised in the home of two psychologists; this provided her with many of the experiences common to young human children. Viki's behavior was carefully observed, from the moment of her adoption a few days after her birth, and recorded in a diary.

Between the ages of 17 and 34 months, Viki received imitation training. The training responses were selected from a pool of 70 items, all of which were simple, arbitrary, and usually meaningless responses. A response was modeled, paired with the instruction "Do this." A correct imitative response resulted in a small amount of her favorite food. Initially, frequent use of a putting-through procedure (Konorski & Miller, 1937) was necessary to establish the first several responses. However, beginning with the twelfth training item, new responses began to be imitated immediately, without any assistance. Eventually, 55 imitative responses were established directly. Throughout that training period, many other imitative behaviors were observed outside the training situation: for example, using a lipstick, using a hammer, and sharpening pencils.

Between 20 and 34 months, six problems were presented to Viki to test whether those problems could be solved simply by observing the experimenter's problem-solving behavior. Viki solved three of them after only a few demonstrations by the experimenter. In comparison, four normal children of Viki's age and a cage-raised chimpanzee were tested with some of those problems. Viki's results were comparable to those of the normal children. The caged chimpanzee, by contrast, succeeded very little.

Although Hayes and Hayes concluded that the imitative ability of a chimpanzee was determined by a combination of heredity and experience, their research provided a key to studying some environmental controls of imitation, especially the role of reinforcement in determining the appearance of novel imitations. Recent behavioral research on imitation has shared some other important procedural characteristics with the study by Hayes and Hayes.

A more thorough experimental paradigm for studying the role of reinforcement in the generalization of imitation in the laboratory was introduced by Baer and Sherman (1964). They showed that young children could be taught three specific imitations of a cowboy puppet, and could be controlled in their performance of these imitations, by contingent social reinforcement from that puppet. More important, they showed that a fourth response modeled by the puppet, bar-pressing, also was imitated without reinforcement when it was interspersed among the three other topographically different responses (head nodding, mouthing, and nonsense statements), imitations of which would be reinforced. When reinforcement was no longer given following the three directly taught imitations, or when these three models were no longer presented, imitation of both reinforced and nonreinforced responses decreased. The reinstatement of those conditions increased the nonreinforced bar-pressing imitation as well as the three reinforced ones. This generalized control of the modeled, untaught, and nonreinforced bar-pressing was called "generalized" imitation.

THE NATURE OF GENERALIZED IMITATION

In similar experimental paradigms, many studies have replicated and extended the phenomena of generalized imitation in various populations, for example, in normal (Brigham & Sherman, 1968), autistic (Metz, 1965), schizophrenic (Lovaas, Berberich, Perloff, & Schaeffer, 1966), and retarded children (Baer, Peterson, & Sherman, 1967).

Notably, these studies demonstrated that when enough imitations are established by contingent reinforcement (often with some additional techniques such as verbal and physical prompts), relatively novel modeled responses then are likely to be imitated without direct physical assistance, prompts, or reinforcement, even during their initial demonstrations by the model. This generalization of imitation has three characteristics that have led to the description of imitation as a response class:

1. Nonreinforced imitations are maintained as long as other imitations are reinforced, but decrease when reinforcement is no longer contingent on other imitations (Baer et al., 1967; Lovaas et al., 1966; Waxler & Yarrow, 1970).

2. Nonreinforced imitations persist despite continuous differential reinforcement (Baer et al., 1967; Steinman, 1970a, 1970b). In the typical experiment, some imitations always are reinforced and other imitations never are, yet persist. In the Baer et al. study (1967), nonreinforced imitations were stably maintained even after 100 training sessions in some of the subjects.

3. Accuracy of nonreinforced imitations increases when other imitations are reinforced in the course of developing generalized imitative skill (Brigham & Sherman, 1968; Lovaas et al., 1966; Schroeder & Baer, 1972). In the Lovaas et al. study (1966), imitative accuracy of nonreinforced Norwegian words increased as accurate imitations of English words were reinforced through a long period of imitative training, in two schizophrenic children. Brigham and Sherman (1968) replicated and extended this finding by demonstrating that the accuracy of nonreinforced Russian words covaried with that of some English words, which were directly manipulated by the reinforcement operation, in normal preschool children.

Thus, these covariations of two sets of behaviors (reinforced and nonreinforced imitations) in both quantity and quality allow the description of imitation as a functional response class.

Imitation, however, is not necessarily a large response class; it can consist of only restricted subclasses of behaviors. In fact, its range often seems to be restricted within the range of imitative topographies directly trained. For example, Baer *et al*. (1967) had reported difficulty in immediately obtaining generalization from motor imitation to vocal imitation, in previously non-imitative retarded children. Also, Steinman (1970a) demonstrated that generalized imitations topographically similar to reinforced imitations were more likely than imitations of topographically dissimilar responses, in normal children. Steinman chose 10 nonreinforced responses from two topographical types: hand and leg movements. When these two types of nonreinforced responses were interspersed among 10 reinforced hand movements, the nonreinforced hand movements were imitated more than the nonreinforced leg movements. However, it should be noted that the topography of responses trained directly may be relevant mainly to the initial development of or acquisition of imitation, rather than to the maintenance of imitation. For example, Garcia, Baer, and Firestone (1971) demonstrated that the development of generalized imitation in four previously nonimitative retarded persons remained within the topographical boundaries established by the responses that were trained, which were divided into three types: small-motor, large-motor, and short-vocal imitations. The effects of training small-motor imitations generalized to other small-motor untrained imitations, but not to other types of untrained imitations. The effects of subsequent training of large-motor imitations generalized to other untrained large-motor imitations, but not to vocal imitations; the small-motor imitations were maintained without further reinforcement of them. Nonreinforced vocal imitations increased only after vocal-imitation training was conducted, and the previously trained types of motor imitation were maintained without any reinforcement of them. Sherman, Clark, and Kelly (1977) obtained similar, although less clear, results with three normal preschool children. Thus, the topographical boundaries established in training may control the range of the initial development of generalized imitation, although the maintenance of established generalized imitation appears to be relatively independent of the topographical type currently being reinforced.

In summary, relatively new imitations emerge without direct training after enough imitations are trained directly or reinforced, in both previously nonimitative persons and normal children. The reinforcement imposed on some imitations controls other imitations in a similar manner. Thus, that kind of reinforcement seems to play a sufficient role in the establishment and maintenance of generalized imitation as a response class, although the range of the covariation appears to be restricted initially within the topographical boundaries trained or reinforced.

It is not clear from these results that reinforcement will always play a crucial role. Issues relevant to restricted generalization are discussed in detail later.

GENERALIZED IMITATION AS A RESPONSE CLASS

The fact that generalized imitation has the characteristics of a response class is of great importance for both educational practice and theoretical explanations of child development. If each imitative behavior needed to be directly trained and reinforced, enormous, unrealistic efforts by parents and teachers would be required to give children even a small amount of the skills necessary for daily life, and imitation then would fail to explain a wide range of social and linguistic development in children. Therefore, understanding the mechanisms by which imitation generalizes to new instances should be crucial for both the developing technology of behavior change and the theoretical understanding of child development.

The concept of response class has occasionally been used to explain such generalization, on the premise that each member of the class shares some common physical property or topographical elements, or some common function, such as environmental effect. For example, in the usual Skinner-box paradigm, bar-pressing behaviors share a common narrow range of topographies and a common environmental effect (the reinforcer). When the response class is defined in terms of common physical properties, that concept alone offers a familiar explanation of the covariation of its members. But Baer (1982) has pointed out that there may be few or no common physical properties among imitative behaviors, yet they still meet the descriptive definition of a response class. Consider an experimental case of two typical imitative responses: pick-up-cylinder, which is always reinforced, and open-the-book, which never is reinforced. These two responses have few common topographical elements, but when their stimulus controls are their own models, they can readily be identified as imitation. Thus, a response-class concept explained by common physical properties does not apply. Here, response class is not an explanation; it is only the observation that reinforcement of some members of the class controls the other members in a similar way. Thus, simply describing imitation as a response class does not contribute to understanding such complex cases. It is how the response class is molded and maintained that should be explained.

Procedure as Explanation

Perhaps the most parsimonious way to deal with the issue is to simply seek out procedural variables that can produce, maintain, or modify the class. The description of these procedures per se may prove to be a defensible explanation, depending on their *primitive* character (Baer, 1982, pp. 235–236), and on the complete identification of all the procedural variables. If the procedural variables identified are related to primitive terms that scientists within a scientific paradigm do not explain further (for example, reinforcement in many behavioral paradigms), it is thereby an effective explanation for those scientists (see Baer, 1982, p. 236 for further discussion). And some scientists may also be satisfied with identifying all the procedural variables and prerequisites needed to account for the observed variance in the phenomenon under study, whether or not they are identified as primitive. In this section, two examples of explanation by identifying procedural variables are assessed: explanation as schedule effects, which many behaviorists apparently consider primitive and thus satisfying; and setting-events or stimulus-control explanations, which most behaviorists should find problematic until a behavioral explanation of their function is produced.

SCHEDULE EFFECTS AS EXPLANATION

An example of a procedural explanation of generalized imitation is to note that a major procedural operation common among the studies that produce generalized imitation is intermittent reinforcement. Gewirtz and Stingle (1968) and Gewirtz (1971) have proposed that generalized imitation can be explained by the familiar general effects of intermittent reinforcement schedules, as seen repeatedly in many simpler response classes (e.g., bar pressing and key pecking). These simpler classes are well understood, experimentally; thus, for many behavior analysts, these procedures are primitive and thereby need no further analysis—they are the explanation of what they control. In the standard generalized imitation paradigm, nonreinforced imitations are interspersed randomly among reinforced imitations. Then, the class of "imitations" is intermittently reinforced. Here, Gewirtz explicitly assumed that an imitative response class is analogous to simple nonimitative response classes: Imitation is just a form of stimulus control over responses that are imitative only by virtue of that stimulus control. (No response is intrinsically imitative; any response becomes imitative when its controlling stimulus must be a topographically similar model.) Then generalized imitation is maintained in the same way that a nonimitative response class is maintained under an intermittent schedule. Thus, Gewirtz' thesis explains the maintenance of the largely unreinforced imitative response class without referring to any other complex behavioral process or any hypothetical construct.

Two problems arise. One problem is in the details of the maintenance of generalized imitation. In the typical generalized imitation procedure, one set of imitations is always (or intermittently) reinforced, but another set never is. Then the schedule is not simply an intermittent schedule, but rather a multiple (FR1 EXT or VR EXT) schedule; such a multiple schedule can and typically does result in discriminative behavior. Why does it not do so in this case? An imitative response class (as discussed earlier) is different from a bar-pressing or key-pecking class, in that members of the imitative response class usually have few common topographical elements. Gewirtz does not explicitly propose any common topographical property of the imitative response class; thus his arguments seem to imply an assumption of a functional identity between reinforced and nonreinforced imitations. Indeed, Gewirtz and Stingle (1968, p. 380) explicitly assumed no discrimination between the two sets as a necessary yet parsimonious assumption.

But this assumption needs testing. What if such tests show no functional identity (or even discrimination difficulty) between the two sets? Bufford (1971), studying verbal imitation in four retarded children, investigated the effects of systematically reducing the variety of reinforced words but not the probability of reinforcement, on the maintenance of nonreinforced verbal imitation. Reducing the variety of words to be reinforced from 50 to just 1, while maintaining a 1:1 ratio of reinforced-word trials to nonreinforced-word trials, produced no consistent changes in the imitation of 10 nonreinforced words. If the imitations of 50 of 60 different words are reinforced, perhaps it is difficult to discriminate the 10 that are not; but when the imitation of only 1 word of 11 is reinforced, and when that 1 occurs on half of all trials, should it not become more likely that the 10 that are not reinforced will be discriminated as such?

In studies by Steinman (1970a, 1970b) and Steinman and Boyce (1971), generalized imitation occurred even when (normal) children discriminated clearly which imitations would be reinforced and which would not be. When not-to-be-reinforced and to-be-reinforced imitations were modeled concurrently (double-model trials), these children consistently imitated the to-be-reinforced models; but the same not-to-be-reinforced responses were imitated when to-be-reinforced and not-to-be-reinforced responses were modeled separately (single-model trials). Strongly differential imitation occurred in the double-model trials, whether the sessions consisted of a mix of single- and double-model trials, or consisted of only double-model trials. These results argue that generalized imitation need not be based on a failure to discriminate nonreinforced from reinforced imitations—at least in the laboratory.

Another problem is that Gewirtz' thesis does not seem to explain the acquisition of new imitations. Intermittent reinforcement schedules grossly account for only the maintenance of the class already established through reinforcement and shaping. It should be noted that some members of the imitation response class, unlike the members of a bar-pressing response class, are not acquired under the same reinforcement that directly establishes and maintains other members; instead, new imitations can be and are acquired later, without shaping or reinforcement (Baer, 1982). Gewirtz (1971) dealt with the acquisition of new imitation by pointing out that an organism, through past experience, may acquire a learning set (Harlow, 1949) that could facilitate learning by observation (p. 295). However, this can hardly be a satisfactory explanation, because it explains generalized imitation by something—a learning set—that needs explanation as much as does generalized imitation. The term, *learning set,* merely describes the phenomenon as similar to observational learning or generalized imitation, not as analytic of it.

Gewirtz' description of imitation as a response class is factually correct: An imitative class is controlled by the reinforcement operation imposed on only some of its members. This is consistent with the anecdotal observation that children's imitation is only occasionally rewarded externally. In addition, Gewirtz' thesis has predictive value, in that knowledge gained in research on simple nonimitative response classes may well be generalizable to an imitative response class. For instance, the thesis seems to predict some behavioral changes of the class that are schedule specific, depending on the schedule of reinforcement adopted. Furnell and Thomas (1981) assessed the effects of two different reinforcement schedules on resistance to extinction in 12 previously nonimitative, severely subnormal children. After reliably establishing 10 imitative behaviors, 5 of which were continuously reinforced (FR1) and 5 of which were never reinforced, some children then encountered a VR4 schedule for the previously continuously reinforced imitations; the other children remained on the FR1 schedule. Then all reinforcement was withheld, and resistance to extinction in the VR4 group was approximately twice as great as in the FR1 group, for the previously reinforced training responses. These results are analogous to those in simple bar-pressing response classes. Performance of the generalized imitations by those two groups, however, was not significantly different: Furthermore, it exceeded their performance of the reinforced imitations, even after extinction of the reinforced imitations seemed complete. This qualitative difference between previously reinforced and generalized imitations suggests that some other variables are operating in generalized imitation, although Thomas and Furnell did not discuss this issue.

Thus, Gewirtz' thesis has testable and predictive value, and may also have practical implications, but does not seem to deal with the fact that generalized imitation appears without shaping and reinforcement. This theory persists despite generalized imitations being discriminated from reinforced imitations, and despite a possible quantitative difference between reinforced and nonreinforced imitation classes seen in extinction. The thesis explains only the maintenance of an already established imitative class, and only at a molar level: Explanation as schedule effects relates procedural variables to the primitive term *intermittent reinforcement* to describe the maintenance of the imitation class, but fails to identify equally primitive terms to describe the emergence of the class.

SETTING EVENTS AS EXPLANATION

Another example of a procedural explanation of generalized imitation is to find all the procedural variables that can experimentally modify the extent of generalization of generalized imitation, and then to consider these variables as explanatory of generalized imitation—as if they also accounted for its acquisition and its maintenance. Logically, the presence or absence of variables that modify the extent of generalized imitation cannot automatically be accepted as the cause of generalized imitation. For instance, a sudden, loud sound may stop an ongoing conversation between two persons, but the absence of the sound is probably not the major cause of that conversation: It is a single, uninteresting, and ineffective cause of the conversation. If, however, variables are closely related to or common in the typical generalized-imitation situation, their pursuit in the context of this logic may be reasonable, even if not analytic. Research of this kind has indeed explored the effects of manipulating extra-experimental variables that typically precede or coexist with variables such as modeling stimuli or reinforcing consequences, in either the pre-experimental or experimental environments, or both. The extra-experimental variables that have been studied can be classified into nonverbal and verbal categories.

Nonverbal Extra-Experimental Variables

Nonverbal extra-experimental variables refer here to variables that are not verbal instructions and can modify the extent to which imitation generalizes. This category can be subdivided into two types: diachronic and synchronic variables.

Diachronic Variables. *Diachronic variables,* in this context, are those in the pre-experimental history of generalized imitation that control the extent of its generalization. It has been demonstrated that the subject's earlier experience can affect differential performance of reinforced and nonreinforced imitations (Acker, Acker, & Pearson, 1973; Smeets, Striefel, & Gast, 1974). For example, in the Acker et al. study (1973), normal elementary school children with a reinforcement history of imitatively manipulating a toy bear were more likely to imitate both affectionate and aggressive nonreinforced responses with that bear than were children with a reinforcement history of either *verbal* affectionate or *verbal* aggressive imitation of that bear. In the Smeets *et al.* study (1974), two retarded children with a history of imitating a reinforced response repeatedly did not differentially imitate reinforced and nonreinforced responses in double-model trials; but three of the four retarded children without that history showed differential imitation in double-model trials.

Synchronic Variables. *Synchronic variables,* in this context, are the current extra-experimental variables that can control the breadth or rate of generalized imitation.

For example, the absence of the experimenter may reduce generalized imitation. In several studies (Peterson, Merwin, Moyer, & Whitehurst, 1971; Peterson & Whitehurst, 1971; Smeets & Striefel, 1973), nonreinforced imitations were modestly reduced in the experimenter's absence, but continued to be reliably imitated in the experimenter's presence. These experiments, however, employed no reinforced imitations: Their imitations were established simply by instructions to imitate. A partial exception is found in the Peterson *et al.* study (1971). When imitations in preschool children were established and maintained simply by instructions to imitate, with no reinforcement in the initial phase of the experiment, the absence of the experimenter greatly reduced these unreinforced imitations. In the next phase, some of the imitations were reinforced, which initially increased both reinforced and nonreinforced imitations, and then moderately reduced the nonreinforced imitations in four preschool children. However, these results by Peterson *et al.* may have some limitations, if they are to be considered explanatory of generalized imitation. Some of these effects may be sequence effects, especially since no reversal design was used to replicate the results. Thus, the generality of the effects of experimenter absence for the standard generalized imitation paradigm, in which some imitations are always reinforced, is uncertain. Future studies need to examine whether the effects of experimenter absence are reliable, and to compare the instructional control and standard generalized-imitation paradigms within individual-analysis designs.

Nonreinforced imitations can also be reduced by developing and presenting discriminative models or cues to distinguish reinforced from nonreinforced imitations. Bandura and Barab (1971) produced a moderate degree of differential imitation by employing two models, one of which always demonstrated reinforced responses and the other nonreinforced responses, for four severely retarded children. Bucher and Bowman (1974) created a small degree of differential imitation in retarded children by presenting a triangle cue just prior to all models of not-to-be-reinforced imitations, and produced a large degree of differential imitation by providing an alternative reinforced task in addition to the triangle cue, reminiscent of the double-model procedure of Steinman's studies.

Other studies also have shown that access to an alternative response that will be reinforced, concurrent with a model of a nonreinforced imitation, can reduce generalized imitation. When subjects are allowed to choose one of two responses, reinforced responses (either imitative or nonimitative) are more likely to be chosen than nonreinforced imitations (Bufford & Buchanan, 1974; Steinman, 1970a, 1970b). Bufford and Buchanan (1974) allowed four developmentally deviant children to choose between imitation and button pressing, in a multiple schedule in which imitation was reinforced in the presence of one light and bar pressing in the presence of another light. Their choices were systematically controlled by reversing the association of lights and contingencies: Children consistently imitated when imitation was reinforced, and pressed the button when it was reinforced.

Manipulating these diachronic and synchronic variables has created some discrimination between reinforced and nonreinforced imitations, although the degree of control often was not strong and varied across studies, depending on the variables manipulated. That is, each variable often reduced the probability of generalized imitation relative to the probability of reinforced imitation, but not necessarily to near-zero probability. The exception is seen only in those studies that made available a reinforced, competing, concurrent response (Bufford & Buchanan, 1974; Steinman, 1970a, 1970b); these studies demonstrated clearly differential imitation.

These results suggest that reinforcement history and setting factors such as discriminative cues, physical aspects of the models, and availability of competing responses can influence the generalization of imitation or its maintenance, but usually to a modest extent.

Verbal Extra-Experimental Variables

Verbal extra-experimental variables refer to explicit (and implicit) instructions that precede (or are juxtaposed with) the modeling stimulus. Instructions to imitate typically have been used either initially (Baer & Sherman, 1964; Brigham & Sherman, 1968; Bufford, 1971; Burgess, Burgess, & Esveldt, 1970; Martin, 1971; Waxler & Yarrow, 1970) or continuously (Peterson & Whitehurst, 1971; Smeets & Striefel, 1973; Steinman, 1970a; Steinman & Boyce, 1971). Exceptions are seen in studies by Metz (1965) and by Garcia *et al.* (1971), neither of which used any verbal instructions. These studies initially used physical prompts and putting-through procedures, which may be conceptualized as instructions. Therefore, the possibility arises that it is this use of instructions to imitate that establishes or maintains generalized imitation. (Even when instructions are discontinued, they may have aftereffects as implicit instructions, possibly enhanced by presenting a model and other variables that had always been associated with the instructions.)

In an effort to uncover the role of instructions in the generalization of imitation, various types of instructions have been manipulated. Some of them have created clearly differential imitation. In one of Steinman's studies (1970b), an instruction not to imitate nonreinforced responses greatly reduced nonreinforced imitation in six public-school children. Bufford (1971) similarly demonstrated that the instruction not to say nonreinforced words largely reduced nonreinforced imitation in both normal and retarded children. Also, Waxler and Yarrow (1970) decreased previously reinforced and nonreinforced imitations rapidly in nursery-school children, by telling them that imitation was not necessary (explicitly releasing them from an earlier instruction to imitate), in the context of no current reinforcement for any imitation, after imitations had been established by the initial instruction to imitate, with contingent reinforcement for doing so.

It is also interesting and instructive that researchers can easily establish imitation merely through the instruction "Do this," and can maintain those nonreinforced imitations without any external reinforcement of them, in already imitative children (Peterson *et al.,* 1971; Peterson & Whitehurst, 1971; Smeets & Striefel, 1973). This kind of generalized imitation can as easily be conceptualized as a special case of generalized instruction-following, probably originating in the child's pre-experimental history of compliance with adult commands, and also controlled by current reinforcement or punishment contingencies. A suggestive study in this matter was conducted by Oliver, Acker, and Oliver (1977). They demonstrated that normal kindergarten children with a reinforcement history for compliance with instructions were more likely to imitate nonreinforced responses than children with no such history or with a history of noncompliance with instructions. Thus, instructional variables seem to control generalized imitation powerfully.

Furthermore, some data suggest that extra-experimental variables that typically exist in the generalized-imitation researches may function as a set of implicit instructions to maintain responding. Several studies have shown that generalization to or maintenance of nonreinforced instances is not characteristic of only imitative behavior, and have done so in procedural paradigms similar to the standard generalized-imitation paradigm (Martin, 1971; Peterson, 1968; Wilcox, Meddock, & Steinman, 1973). Peterson (1968) found that nonimitative behaviors in a retarded girl could be maintained when those behaviors were interspersed among reinforced imitations. Martin (1971) replicated Peterson's finding and extended it by showing that nonreinforced imitations were maintained when nonimitative responses were reinforced, in four severely retarded children. In the Wilcox *et al.* study (1973), a successive visual-discrimination task was assigned to four normal preschool children. The procedure had some of the characteristics of the typical generalized-imitation procedure, in that nonreinforced trials were interspersed among reinforced trials with a constant intertrial interval, always in the presence of the experimenter. In spite of various procedures designed to enhance discrimination, differential responding was never produced. Such generalization to or maintenance of nonimitative nonreinforced responses may also be conceptualized as a type of instruction-following behavior.

These studies of nonverbal and verbal extra-experimental variables, especially if their effects are considered as additive, reinforce the setting–events hypothesis offered by Steinman (1977), which sees generalized imitation as an artifact produced by extra-experimental factors, including the reinforcement history, successive-discrimination procedures, implicit or explicit instructions, and social-setting conditions employed in the typical research studies.

Control by Other Antecedent and Consequent Events

It should not be concluded that the generalization of imitative or matching behavior is due only to instructions and such extra-experimental variables that Orne (1962) called demand characteristics, which are inherent in the typical experimental procedures. There is ample evidence against the hypothesis that control of generalized imitation results only from extra-experimental variables: Generalized imitation may be controlled by either antecedent (extra-experimental) or consequent (reinforcing) events. In Martin's study of generalized imitation in severely retarded children (1972), either the instruction "Do this" or the instruction and reinforcement of a subset of imitations could produce nonreinforced imitations. The instruction not to imitate did not at all decrease imitations of nonreinforced responses as long as some imitations were reinforced, but remarkably decreased them when reinforcement for imitations ended. Thus, when instructions and consequences are incongruent, imitative classes in all of these children were governed by their reinforcing consequences rather than these instructions about them.

Also, verbal release from either explicit or implicit instructions to choose imitation may not be effective for decreasing nonreinforced imitation when some imitations are reinforced, in contrast to Waxler and Yarrow's (1970) successful reduction of imitation by the verbal release from instruction in the context of no reinforcement for imitation. In Steinman's (1970b) study of normal public-school children, the instruction not to imitate nonreinforced responses resulted in near-perfect differential imitation. However, a similar instruction to choose any response the subject wanted largely recovered nonreinforced imitations. Similarly, Bufford (1971) demonstrated that instructions not to say nonreinforced words resulted in reduced nonreinforced imitation, but instruction to do anything the subjects wanted resulted in high rates of nonreinforced imitation in both retarded and normal children.

A high degree of social demand, similarly, may not be needed for producing the generalization and maintenance of responses. In the Baer and Sherman study (1964), generalized imitation appeared in the absence of the human experimenter when a cowboy puppet modeled the response while telling colorful stories to the child. Sherman, Saunders, and Brigham (1970) also showed the generalization of matching and mismatching behavior of preschool children to untrained stimuli, with no explicit instructions about the quality of response and with no experimenter present in that setting. Thus, demanding instructions to imitate or the presence of an experimenter may not always be crucial to generalization or maintenance when some imitations are reinforced.

Although the role of contingent reinforcement in the maintenance of imitative behavior has not always seemed consistent, it does not follow that contingent reinforcement is neither important nor necessary to its generalization or maintenance. Some studies have demonstrated considerable reduction of imitation by the use of DRO procedures (Baer & Sherman, 1964; Brigham & Sherman, 1968; Burgess, Burgess, & Esveldt, 1970), noncontingent reinforcement (Lovaas et al., 1966), or extinction (Waxler & Yarrow, 1970). In the Burgess et al. study (1970), a DRO-0 sec procedure, in which reinforcement was given immediately after the modeling of an English word, reduced those retarded children's imitation of English words (that had previously been either reinforced or nonreinforced) to near-zero levels. Lovaas et al. (1966) reported that imitation of English words was reduced by making reinforcement contingent only on time elapsed since the last reinforcement, that is, an FT schedule.

In some studies with normal children, however, DRO procedures and nonreinforcement of all imitations have failed to reduce previously well-established imitative behavior (Steinman, 1970a; Steinman & Boyce, 1971; Peterson & Whitehurst, 1971). Steinman (1970a) reported that DRO-15 sec, and even DRO-0 sec procedures did not reduce nonreinforced imitation in a preschool child. In the Steinman and Boyce study (1971), the DRO-0 sec schedule did not reduce imitation that had already been strongly established in three of four kindergarten children—but its lack of effectiveness was assessed for at most only five sessions. In the fourth child, imitation was reduced from 100% to about an 80% level in the course of five sessions.

However, in the Peterson and Whitehurst study (1971), imitation was maintained at a high rate in three preschool children (Experiment 1), despite delayed, predelivered, or no consequences over many sessions.

Close examination of the three studies that did not show the effectiveness of DRO or extinction procedures reveals that an instruction to imitate, "Do this," was used in every trial; in contrast, an instruction to imitate was used only initially in the five studies that reduced imitation with those procedures. Thus, continuous, every-trial instructions appear to be largely responsible for the ineffectiveness of DRO or extinction procedures in these studies. However, research using individual-analysis designs is needed to analyze the role of initial and continuous instructions in modulating the effects of DRO or extinction procedures.

These studies suggest the possibility that the generalization of imitation may be established and controlled by both antecedent stimulus controls including extra-experimental variables such as instructions, social-demand factors, and reinforcement, at least in the already-imitative children who have been studied in the laboratory. This theoretically commonplace two-source analysis of generalized imitation is capable of integrating the initially inconsistent data described in this paper. This question then becomes one of explaining the presumably acquired stimulus-control functions of such instructions and social-demand factors.

Limitations in the Setting–Events Explanation

Setting–events analyses of imitation face at least two difficulties:

1. These extra-experimental variables do not always account entirely for the generalization of imitation. They are only some of the variables that modify the generalization of already-established responses; they do not explain the quality of generalized imitation—why the behaviors that respond to novel stimuli always reproduce the stimuli, along the dimension of similarity. It is this response quality that is generalized or maintained. Thus it is important to analyze variables that control the establishment of generalized imitation, not just the variables that analyze response generalization, in order to complete an explanation by identification of all the procedural variables and by relating those to behavioral terms.

2. Variables that can modulate the extent of already-established generalized imitation are not automatically its major or initial cause. Any hypothesis that insists that children must always be coerced to imitate, explicitly or implicitly, will fail to explain a wide range of child development. Anecdotal observation agrees that the instructional and social-demand factors operative in experimental settings are not often salient in the natural environment. (Consider, for example, delayed imitation.) Also, it is not pragmatic

to develop only a technology that requires powerful social and instructional control. There are many occasions when choldren must and do learn new behaviors under no such control in daily life; those occasions, too, must be understood.

The present arguments, however, do not negate the setting–events and stimulus–control analyses of imitation. These studies of extra-experimental variables still have considerable predictive value, and thus should be treated positively. We suggest some of that value in the following sections.

Conditional Discriminative Stimuli. One positive response is to conceptualize extra-experimental variables as those that influence the range of generalized imitation, or the selection of imitative responses that are already established, rather than as the variables that establish imitation as a response class: These extra-experimental variables function as conditional discriminative stimuli (Lashley, 1938) that set the occasion for the reinforcement, punishment, or extinction of an imitative response class, or for potential modeling stimuli to function as discriminative for imitation. Furnell and Thomas (1976) offered an informative experiment in this context, using three previously nonimitative "subnormal" children. After establishing five reinforced and five generalized (untrained and nonreinforced) imitations in the presence of a large ball, discrimination training was conducted: Training responses now continued to be reinforced in the presence of the large ball, but were not reinforced in the presence of a small ball. With this training, the subjects came to imitate both trained and nontrained responses in the presence of the large ball, but not in the presence of the small ball. Additional generalization tests were carried out across six intermediate different-sized balls. Imitation rates decreased gradually as the ball size was reduced from the original large size. (It should be noted that the generalized imitations occurred at higher rates than the trained imitations across the different-sized balls, and their generalization curves were somewhat flatter than those of the trained imitations. This quantitative difference, considered together with that in Furnell and Thomas's later study [1981] reviewed previously, suggests that some additional factors were operating.) Thus, the large ball was a conditional discriminative stimulus that controlled when modeling stimuli would control imitation. Logically, conditional discriminative stimuli could be extra-experimental variables such as those just reviewed— presence or absence of an experimenter, availability of alternative responses, and instructions. These variables seem to be responsible at least partly for selective imitation in daily life.

Instruction-Following Behavior as a Response Class. Another positive response to the study of extra-experimental variables is to conceptualize instruction-following behavior as a parallel functional response class that can be controlled by reinforcement contingent on only one of its subsets: doing the same thing another does (Bucher, 1973; Martin, 1971). In other words, it is possible that an imitative response class is a subcategory of an instruction-following response class. Alternatively, it is possible that establishing an often nonimitative instruction-following class will create imitative subclasses that we may call modeling stimuli: "Do this" is more functionally considered a subclass of instructional stimuli such as "Do as I indicate." In the Martin study (1971), nonreinforced imitations were maintained when interspersed among reinforced nonimitative responses in two of four severely retarded children; and nonreinforced, nonimitative responses were maintained when interspersed among reinforced imitations in the other two children. In subsequent experimental phases, when DRO procedures were administered, nonreinforced imitative or nonimitative responses decreased greatly. Then, when responses that were not reinforced in the initial phases were reinforced, nonreinforced responses increased rapidly, and were maintained reliably. Bucher (1973) demonstrated a similar covariation of compliance and noncompliance behaviors in normal children: Nonreinforced compliance was miantained as long as some compliance behaviors were reinforced, but decreased when reinforcement for compliance was discontinued, especially when a competing task was reinforced. Occasionally, novel instructions were probed. Compliance to the novel instructions occurred at a level similar to that of the original, trained set of instructions, during both reinforcement and extinction conditions. Thus, the covariation of imitative and nonimitative compliant behaviors allows the classification of at least some imitation as a functional response class of instruction following.

This strategy of reclassifying imitation, however, may not be much of an explanation of its response-class characteristics. Like imitation as a response class, instruction-following behaviors have few or no common properties along a simple physical dimension. Therefore, the same argument against simply describing imitation as a response class is applied to instruction-following behavior. How such a complex response class is molded and maintained still needs to be explained. That type of research would lead to a better understanding of the establishment and maintenance of many complex response classes that appear to have important roles in human activities.

Summary

There is ample evidence to suggest that although various extra-experimental variables can control the generalization of imitation, it is very doubt-

ful that generalized imitation is due only to the extra-experimental variables:

1. Those variables do not themselves explain the initial generalization of
response quality without shaping and reinforcement.
2. This class of setting–event explanation fails to explain an important
part of child development if it insists that the child must always be coerced
to imitate, explicitly or implicitly. Social factors (extra-experimental variables) would be better conceptualized as influencing only the selectivity of
imitation. Also, further experiments may well be needed to analyze instruction-following behavior as a larger response class, in order to understand
the possible breadth of generalized imitation.

Consequently, the setting–events explanation seems incomplete for either identifying all the procedural variables establishing generalized imitation or demonstrating their extensive generality.

Indeed, the use of the setting event as explanatory seems little in harmony
with its intended function in theory. The setting event quite typically is a
measurable event that accounts for variance in some behavioral phenomenon, and is called a setting event rather than some more functional label
exactly because its function is still unknown. Setting events are invitations
to make an experimental analysis; they are not in themselves experimental
analyses. Usually they merely represent successful experiments in accounting for variance with a recognizable experimental procedure. That a procedure is recognizable and experimentable does not mean that it is theoretically or systematically primitive. If it were, it would have a different
categorization, and so would not need a label such as setting event.

FINAL COMMENT ON PROCEDURE
AS EXPLANATION

Although many procedural variables that establish, maintain, and modify
generalized imitation were examined here, it should be realized that the
controlling variables known to prevail in the laboratory may have only
limited generality. The variables operative in the natural environment may
be different, and clearly are also sufficient to produce generalized imitation.
Sidman (1960) noted the importance of determining whether a given set of
variables is relevant outside the confines of a particular experiment. Our
confidence may be increased by two different methods. Thorough, wide-
ranging systematic replications may extend the known generality of the
variables. In addition, we should see whether the procedural variables that
produce imitation in the generalized-imitation paradigm exist and seem to
operate similarly in the natural settings where imitation develops and func-

tions as a socializing process. Although this may be extremely laborious and difficult to prove experimentally, we should see at least that the procedural variables are compatible with the variables observed in the natural environment. This might be achieved by properly pointed systematic observations of infant and children. The interactive use of these two methods seems indispensable for at least a minimal understanding of imitation as a factor in child development.

In a pragmatic sense (James, 1907/1974), however, the issue of the generality of procedural variables in the natural environment may not be crucial even in developmental theory. An explanation through complete exploration of the procedural variables involved may prove ultimately to be satisfactory, if it allows the developmental and behavioral problems that we face to be solved sufficiently. The generality issue may become less urgent, if the collection of procedural variables validated in the laboratory should prove to be equal or even superior in practical control to the variables operative in the natural environment (which might be the same variables, in form). By the achievement of such powerful control of imitation, an explanation in the form of sufficient procedures may at least find its own place in the theories of child development.

Function as Explanation

Sufficient identification of procedural variables may often satisfy behaviorists and may stop them pursuing further explanation of why those variables produce a phenomenon of concern. Typically, though, behaviorists seek further explanation when they have difficulty relating those procedural variables directly to primitive or near-primitive terms in their paradigm.

In the case of generalized imitation, many procedural variables that can control generalized imitation have been reported. However, these procedural variables do not identify primitive behavioral terms for the emergence of generalized imitation, as the two examples just discussed (explanation as schedule effects and as setting events) show. Is there a more primitive level of explanation?

THE CONDITIONED-REINFORCEMENT EXPLANATION

One response to the question lies in pursuing the historical question of whether or not imitation can have a reinforcing function in itself. This question has captivated many imitation theorists (Baer & Sherman, 1964; Miller & Dollard, 1941; Mowrer, 1960; Parton & Fouts, 1969; Parton & Priefert, 1975); interestingly, their theories differ in important details as well as in their fundamental answers. One of the most recent hypotheses, that of Baer and Sherman (1964) and Baer, Peterson, and Sherman (1967), asked whether similarities between the model's stimuli and the observer's imitative responses were a class of response-produced discriminable physical stimuli that could acquire a conditioned reinforcing function through the repeated pairing of exemplars of this class and the explicit positive reinforcement used in establishing particular topographical imitations. If so, then any other responses that also produce exemplars from this class of similarities are thereby reinforced (see Skinner, 1957, and Vaughan & Michael, 1982, on automatic reinforcement). Reinforced under these circumstances, they not only increase in probability, given such models, but also become members of the imitative-response class. Thus they are acquired and maintained as long as some members of the class are explicitly (not automatically) reinforced. The automatic reinforcement process is a conditioned reinforcement process, and thus subject to extinction in the absence of some kind of support by the more durable explicit reinforcement process chosen by the experimenter (in part for just such durability.) The supposition of a reinforcing property of imitation or of similarity explains well the experimental formation of an imitative response class, and is consistent with anecdotal observations, in that imitation occurs in the absence of either social-demand factors or frequent contingent reinforcement in many scenes of the natural environment: Thus, this becomes one of the intuitively appealing theories of imitation.

The conditioned-reinforcement explanation, however, has been criticized on the bases of four reasonable points.

1. The explanation lacks firm empirical evidence, although its procedures have been proven effective many times. But while these procedures are its procedures, they may also be the procedures of alternative explanations.

2. If the automatic reinforcement process is a conditioned one dependent on some form of continuing contact with the explicit reinforcer, why are those specific models and their imitations that never contact the explicit reinforcer, and that are clearly discriminated by the imitator as different from the models and their imitations that do contact the explicit reinforcer, not extinguished?

3. Imitation is highly selective in daily life. If imitation has an automatic reinforcing function, it is constantly available; why do we not continue to imitate a wide range of responses across settings, models, and time?

4. Modeling stimuli are to some considerable extent dissimilar to the stimulus feedback generated by the imitative response.

These criticisms do not invalidate a conditioned reinforcement explanation; they only demonstrate that it is not completely developed, as stated so far. We attempt a more complete statement, first by offering new data, then by suggesting some future experiments aimed at better understanding, and finally by a fuller discussion of these issues.

Empirical Evidence

Indeed, behavioral research has not yet carefully examined the reinforcing function of imitation. One reason may have been the problem of experimental, independent manipulation of similarity as a consequential stimulus in a contingency. From an experimental viewpoint, a stimulus should meet at least two criteria: It should be amenable to both reliable measurement and independent manipulation. In imitation, similarity is created by and implicit in duplicating a modeled stimulus; then how can an experimenter manipulate similarity as a consequence of imitation, without directly manipulating the imitation itself?

Probably because of this difficulty, only a small body of research has been conducted to demonstrate the reinforcing function of similarity. Yet there are possible solutions to the problem. For example, behavioral similarity can be manipulated by using the paradigm of "being imitated": The experimenter duplicates a behavior of the child and thereby presents the child with a similarity not implicit in the child's behavior. In the Gladstone and Cooley study (1975), each of four preschool children was allowed to operate any one of three noise-makers (a desk bell, rubber horn, and cricket clicker), concurrently with imitating the experimenter in other ways, some of which were reinforced. However, if the child operated an experimentally designated one of the noise-makers, the experimenter matched that instance of the child's noise-making behavior, thereby producing behavioral similarity; the child's use of the other noisemakers resulted in nonimitative behaviors by the experimenter. All children came to use mainly the noisemaker that produced the experimenter's imitation of them.

Another example of manipulating similarity is seen in a "revised" match-to-sample format used by Parton and Fouts (1969). Matching-to-sample differs from imitating (or being imitated) mainly in that response topography in the match-to-sample format is uniform and nonfunctional (e.g., button pressing); in imitating, each behavior's topography is controlled by the topographies modeled. The revised match-to-sample format required preschool children to respond to either a left or right key to produce a comparison stimulus after a sample key was lit. Responding to one position of the two dark keys illuminated that key with the same color as the sample; responding to the other key lit the key with a different color. No other consequence was arranged. Over trials, the children developed a preference for the color-matching key. Thus, similarity was the functional consequence.

The logic of these experiments is that the nonmanipulable similarity produced by imitation may have a reinforcing function; and that manipulable similarity can be produced by other activities, such as being imitated and matching-to-sample, and may be found to have a reinforcing function. If the latter turns out to be true, the first may be true. In logical analysis, this approach is merely affirming a consequent; it increases the plausibility of the thesis (Sidman, 1960), but it also risks a well-known logical fallacy. Being imitated and matching-to-sample may not be the same as imitating, nor is being imitated necessarily the same as matching-to-sample. Then the similarities produced by those activities may not function in the same way as the similarity produced by imitating. Put another way: To say that behavior can be reinforced by similarity—by being imitated or by color-matching—does not prove that generalized imitation is reinforced by the similarity it accomplishes.

If imitation is considered a crucial factor in child development, it is important to know if it has or can have reinforcing function in itself, and if so, what maintains that function (if anything), and if not, what other maintenance functions are involved.

There does not seem to be any clear experimental demonstration of the reinforcing function of imitation itself in the literature. More important, the role of external (nonsimilarity) reinforcement in developing or maintaining a reinforcing function of similarity has never been demonstrated, even in the formats of being imitated or of matching-to-sample. The interesting approach is to treat imitation as a contingent response. As Premack (1959, 1962) convincingly demonstrated, contingent access to a high-probability response can reinforce a low-probability response. Bernstein and Ebbesen (1978) showed that when access to a response is externally restricted, it can then reinforce another response that gains access to it. Why not study the reinforcing property of imitation in this way, without requiring the independent manipulation of the similarity implicit in imitation? If imitation itself has a reinforcing function, contingent access even to generalized imitations that never yield explicit (nonsimilarity) reinforcers should be able to reinforce an arbitrary instrumental response (such as button pressing or lever pressing). Also, if reinforcement contingent on some members of an imitative class is responsible for acquisition and maintenance of other members that are never reinforced, then perhaps the reinforcing power of access to those generalized, never-reinforced imitations will change if the ongoing reinforcement for the other imitations is discontinued (Baer & Sherman, 1964).

We have conducted a series of experiments relevant to these issues. In this review, we summarize the essence of those experiments.

EXPERIMENTER

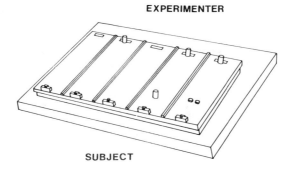

SUBJECT

FIGURE 7.1   The multiple-response apparatus and its seating arrangement.

As Figure 7.1 shows, the child subject sat in front of the multiple-response apparatus, and the experimenter sat behind it, facing the child. The child saw the apparatus as a five-paneled table. The center panel displayed a green light and a push-button, and each of the four other panels displayed a red light and a push-button. Each of these lights and push-buttons was located on the child's side of the panel. When any of the five lights was lit, pressing its push-button resulted in the sound of a chime. On some trials, the green light of the center panel was on, and the four red lights of the other panels were off; the child was taught to press only the push-button on the green–illuminated (center) panel. This push-button response was the only response that would ever be chained to an explicit reinforcer either directly or through an imitation of the experimenter. On other trials, all the red lights of the other four panels were on, and the green light of the center panel was off; the child was taught to press any of the four push-buttons in the red–illuminated panels. These four push-buttons were the instrumental responses of the preference study to be described; pressing them never led to an explicit reinforcer.

A multiple-response baseline of four types of activities, including imitation, was established in each of six preschool children. Access to each activity as a contingent response was gained by pressing the correct one of the four push-buttons in the red-light panels. Preference for each activity was measured in two contexts, depending on the condition: one condition in which access to reinforced imitations was gained by pressing the push-button of the green-light panel (when the green light was on); and another condition in which pressing the push-button of the green-light panel was reinforced directly, without access to reinforced imitations. Thus, occasions to engage in one of the four nonreinforced activities were interspersed among explicitly reinforced activities (button pressing or imitation). Each of these activities was pretrained in an activity-sampling phase. In this sampling and in the initial few sessions of the experiment, instructions from the experimenter about what activity could be performed were given after pressing one of the push-buttons; later in the experiment, these instructions were unnecessary, as the child could see from the stimuli present what activities were possible.

The four types of activities were as follows: *Nonreinforced Imitation* of an experimenter model, *Free Activity* following an experimenter model that could not be imitated (for lack of similar materials), mere *Observation* of an experimenter model that could not be imitated (for lack of any materials), and *Waiting* by both experimenter and child. Three of these four activities were controls for the stimulus features other than similarity (matching) that can operate in imitation. In the Nonreinforced Imitation Panel, two identical sets of objects were placed, one set for the experimenter and another for the subject (Figure 7.1). The experimenter modeled an action with one set; the subject could imitate the modeled response with the other set. In the Free Activity Panel, two different sets of objects were displayed; the experimenter modeled a given response with one set of objects, and the subject then could do anything the subject liked with the other, different set of objects. This was to assess whether manipulating objects nonimitatively was reinforcing. In the Observation Panel, only one set of objects appeared; this set was the experimenter's. The experimenter performed a response with this set; the subject could only observe the response (because of an absence of any objects on the subject's side). This was to see if observing modeled responses might be reinforcing. In the Waiting Panel, no objects were available. The experimenter did nothing, and the subject could only wait for 10 seconds. This controlled for intertrial intervals serving somehow as reinforcing or punishing time-outs.

Thus, the subject could always predict in which panel button pressing would lead to any activity, by observing the objects placed on (or absent from) each panel. Over trials, the placement of each of these activities varied at random among the two left-of-center and the two right-of-center panels. The center green-light panel was always the same.

Experiment 1 involved two conditions and two discrimination tests. Each session consisted of 14 trials, 6 in the center green-light panel, which would be reinforced, and 8 in the red-light panels, which would not be reinforced. In the baseline conditions, the preference for each activity, defined as the proportion of the eight responses given to each of the four red-light panels, was measured in the context of interspersed reinforcement of pressing the center-panel push-button, when its green light was on—the six reinforced trials. On these trials, the experimenter gave the subject praise and a plastic token backed up later by toys or stickers. In the eight nonreinforced trials, all of the four red lights were on at the same time. The subject could press any one of the corresponding four buttons for access to one of these four activities. No reinforcer was given for the execution of any activity in any red-light trials throughout the experiment. The nonreinforced red-light trials were interspersed among the reinforced green-light trials.

Figure 7.2 shows that Free Activity and Nonreinforced Imitation were generally preferred more than Observation and Waiting during the baseline conditions.

In the other experimental condition, imitations of six different responses were reinforced in the green-light trials, rather than the button-pressing that was reinforced in the baseline-condition trials. These were the Reinforced-Imitation conditions. A token was given only if the subject first pressed the green push-button while the light was on, and then correctly imitated the subsequently modeled response. These six responses did not include object manipulations, and were quite different in topography from the modeled responses used in the red-light trials. The green-light trials of reinforcing imitative responses were interspersed among the red-light trials, just as in the baseline conditions. As Figure 7.2 shows, the preference for Nonreinforced Imitation, in four of the six subjects (Ss 1, 2, 4, and 6), increased immediately in the Reinforced-Imitation conditions.

Two subjects, S3 and S5, did not show increased imitation in their first Reinforced Imitation conditions. For these two subjects, conditions that could increase their preference for the Imitation Panel were analyzed later.

After completing these conditions, one or both of two types of discrimination tests were conducted for all six subjects, to assess whether reinforced and nonreinforced imitations were discriminated: If they were not discriminated, increased preference for the Nonreinforced Imitation during the Reinforced Imitation conditions might be due to that. After each test session was completed, some toys or stickers were given without feedback on the subject's performance. Then, for a Type-1 test of discrimination between Reinforced and Nonreinforced Imitations, a reinforced and a nonreinforced response were modeled, one immediately after the other, while saying, "Do this (model) or do this (model)" (Steinman, 1970a, 1970b). The subject could choose one of the two modeled responses. Type-1 tests were conducted for all subjects except S1.

However, younger subjects (3-year-olds), who do not always understand Type-1 tests, were first given a Type-2 test. For a Type-2 test, the subject was instructed to guess which imitation would produce a token. The instruction was, "This one (model) or this one (model): Which one can you get a token for?" Whatever the child's response, no feedback or token was given.

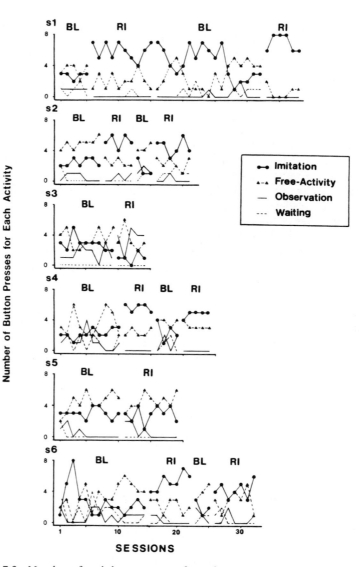

FIGURE 7.2 Number of push-button presses for each activity. BL represents the baseline condition and RI the Reinforced Imitation condition.

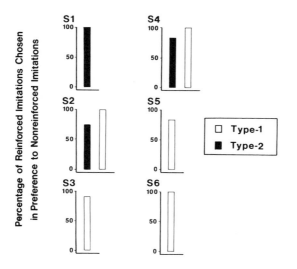

FIGURE 7.3   Preference for Reinforced Imitations (rather than Nonreinforced Imitations) in response to two types of instructions.

Prior to these two tests, each subject had been pretrained to choose one of two modeled responses (that were different from the responses used in the experiment); in this pretraining, subjects learned to wait until they had seen both models before imitating one of them, and to imitate only one of them.

In the Type-1 and Type-2 tests, as Figure 7.3 shows, the six subjects showed very clear discriminations between reinforced and nonreinforced imitations, ranging from 83% to 100% in the Type-1 tests, and from 75% to 100% in the Type-2 tests. In the two subjects (S2 and S4) who were given both types of test, the degree of discrimination improved in the second test, despite lack of feedback about correctness in predicting token delivery, and despite absence of the token.

In general, the proportions of button pressing for access to Nonreinforced Imitations increased and stayed at high rates as long as other imitations were being reinforced. When these other imitations were no longer available for reinforcement, the proportions of button-pressing for Nonreinforced Imitations decreased (usually quickly, sometimes slowly). The resumption of reinforcement of Reinforced Imitations again increased the proportions of Nonreinforced Imitations. This covariation occurred in spite of clear discrimination between reinforced and nonreinforced responses. Such clear discrimination weakens any explanation relying on difficulty of discriminating between the two classes of imitation. These results offer some evidence that the relative reinforcing value of Nonreinforced Imitation as a set of contingent responses may be increased by reinforcing other imitations. If this is generally true, the acquisition of novel untrained responses through imitation is explainable as an automatic reinforcement process (in the terms developed here), as long as other imitations are reinforced. Thus, these data support a conditioned-reinforcement analysis of the emergence and maintenance of the imitative response class.

Discrimination between Reinforced and Nonreinforced Imitations

Our experiments have presented some evidence that access to the opportunity to perform even nonreinforced imitations can have a conditionable reinforcing function. This function includes a reinforcing function modifiable by other contingencies on imitation operative at the time, and by the alternative responses that are available at the time (as we demonstrate later). However, an old problem is still unanswered: How can nonreinforced imitation function as a conditioned reinforcer, when such clear discrimination between Reinforced and Nonreinforced Imitations is shown by the subjects of these (and other) studies? If the automatic reinforcement process is a conditioned one dependent on some form of continuing contact with the explicit reinforcer, why do those imitations that never contact the explicit reinforcer, and are discriminated as different from the preferred imitations that do contact the explicit reinforcer, not extinguish?

One answer is that the demonstration of clear discrimination between the two sets is not proof that their individual similarities to their models have also been discriminated as nonreinforcing. A nonreinforced imitation consists of at least two stimulus components: One is the topography of the modeled response, and the other the similarity produced by imitating it. When children correctly choose which response they can get a token for imitating, after the experimenter demonstrates two responses, those discriminations presumably are made on the basis of the topographies modeled, rather than the similarity that will be produced; similarity is still absent at that time. Thus, a generalized behavioral similarity may well still be discriminative for reinforcement, as long as some imitations are reinforced (if some specific similarities remain discriminative for reinforcement). This is only a logical argument that supports the results just presented. Here the most important thing is to demonstrate the reinforcing function of access to the opportunity to perform Nonreinforced Imitations in spite of their discrimination from imitations that are reinforced explicitly.

Selective Imitation

Imitation is very selective in daily life. If imitation itself has a reinforcing function, why this selectivity? Parton (1976) pointed out that it is unreasonable to expect a change in the reinforcing efficacy of similarity because of a little additional conditioning in an experimental situation, because similarity is supposed to already have a long history of intermittent pairing with reinforcers in such children. But perhaps that argument conceptualizes a reinforcer as having a constant value. Note that in the baseline conditions of Experiment 1, Free Activity and Imitation were preferred relative to Observation and Waiting. That, we suggest, is the appropriate model of imitation as a reinforcer in daily life (and perhaps of all reinforcers in daily life): The reinforcing value of imitation is determined, at least in part, relative to the value of other activities available. No doubt the same is true of any of those other activities. In the baseline conditions of Experiment 1, access to any of the activities resulted only from corresponding button pressing. Then the differential use of those push-buttons presumably testified to a hierarchy of reinforcing effectiveness of those activities (especially since position preferences had been ruled out). We argue that rank in that hierarchy is relative, and that it is possible to change the relative reinforcing position of Nonreinforced Imitation in that hierarchy at any time, by additional conditioning, by restricting availability of the other activities, or by manipulating the stimulus controls for any of those activities.

The possibility of changing the response-preference hierarchy seen in Experiment 2 was pursued in the cases of S3 and S5, who had not shown any increased preference for Nonreinforced Imitations when other imitations began to be reinforced. First, it was asked whether the addition of object-manipulating responses to the class of Reinforced Imitations (which so far had never contained object-manipulating responses) would increase preference for the Nonreinforced Imitations, all of which were object manipulations. This procedure was labeled the Object-Manipulation Condition (OM). As Figure 7.4 shows, that addition did not influence preference for access to Nonreinforced Imitations in S3 and S5. Then, those additional object-manipulating responses were replaced with the original reinforced responses, and Free Activity was removed from the activities that could be chosen. Only occasions for Imitation, Observation, and Waiting were available in the red-light panels.

As Figure 7.4 shows, the absence of Free Activity increased these subjects' preference for Nonreinforced Imitation immediately, and its reintroduction decreased their preference for Nonreinforced Imitation. A second removal of Free Activity again increased their preference for Nonreinforced Imitation. Thus, the reinforcing power of Nonreinforced Imitations, at least in

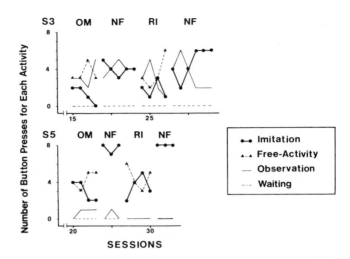

FIGURE 7.4   Number of push-button presses for each activity. OM represents the Object Manipulation Condition, RI represents the Reinforced Imitation Condition, and NF the No Free-Activity Condition.

the context of other imitations being reinforced, was altered relative to other activities, simply by removing one of those activities (a highly preferred one).

The reinforcement of other imitations, however, makes it somewhat difficult to interpret why the preference for Nonreinforced Imitations increased. The removal of Free Activity could increase that preference (1) simply because it made available more occasions to imitate, (2) because there was some functional relationship between Reinforced Imitation and Free Activity (for example, in terms of a preference for manipulating objects, which was possible in Free Activity but not in that set of Imitations), and (3) because some other imitations (object-manipulative imitations) were being reinforced (when the center panel was operative). The first possibility, however, is weakened by the fact that the removal of Free Activity did not increase their choices of Observation or for Waiting in both S3 and S5, and that S3's preference for Reinforced Imitation increased even though S3 had preferred Observation more than Reinforced Imitation in her previous hierarchy.

To test the second possibility, the availability of Observation was removed for S3. This operation, as Figure 7.5 shows, increased her preference only for Nonreinforced Imitation, not for Free Activity or Waiting. This relationship was replicated in a reversal design.

Such increase in preference for Nonreinforced Imitation by removing Observation suggests that the third possibility is most plausible. However,

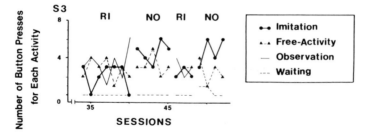

FIGURE 7.5   Number of push-button presses for each activity. RI represents the Reinforced Imitation Condition, and NO the No Observation Condition.

these results were gained only in the context of reinforcing some imitations; therefore, the hypothesis should be examined further by comparing results under conditions with and without reinforced imitations, and in individual-analysis designs.

At any rate, the present data show the modifiability of the reinforcing value of imitation by manipulating the availability of other concurrently available responses. This modifiability, in addition to setting factors such as the conditional discriminative stimuli described earlier, is strongly relevant to the selectivity of imitation in the natural environment, where numerous alternative responses are always available and numerous social factors are almost always present.

Stimulus Feedback and Similarity

The fourth criticism against the conditioned reinforcement thesis rests on the discrepancy between some modeling stimuli and the stimulus feedback generated by their imitative responses. Parton (1976) raised an example:

> In terms of visually guided behavior, it can be noted that the typical modeling exposure of grasping an object involves the infant and model facing each other with the object between them. In this circumstance the infant views the model's hand, fingers first, approaching the infant, but the infant's response involves extending the hand away from self with the fingers also pointing away. (p. 18)

Thus, the correct imitative behavior in this example should be visually different for the child from what the child sees in the model. That is, the child has to respond to the functional identity between the two different visual displays, in order to imitate correctly. Cognitive explanations have emphasized the role of some private, inferred ability to identify the functional similarity between the two stimuli. A behavioral account need not deny the ability, nor its typical privacy, but rather than infer it, would begin to postulate its appropriate curricula—the programs that teach it. At least, a

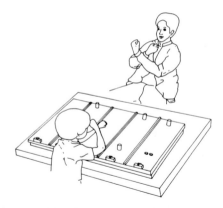

FIGURE 7.6   The "cross-arms" model seen from the child's viewpoint.

behavioral account would seek evidence of the learning process when it might well be ongoing.

In our experiments described earlier, one of the six reinforced models for imitation was "cross arms." The experimenter closed both his hands and crossed his forearms, with the back of his hands facing the subject. Five of seven children responding to this "cross-arms" model crossed their forearms with closed hands, but with the backs of their hands facing them. A completely correct imitative response would have the backs of their hands facing the experimenter, not them. Figure 7.6 illustrates this.

A possible explanation of their failures to demonstrate the perfectly correct imitation is their maximization of visual similarity. When the experimenter demonstrated "cross arms," the children saw the backs of the experimenter's hands and forearms. Possibly, they simply tried to reproduce the same visual display as perfectly as possible, by arranging their own hands so that they saw the backs of their hands also.

To test the generality of this phenomenon, another response was demonstrated to five children. The experimenter modeled raising his open hands with thumbs crossed and the back of his hands facing the child. Three of the five children crossed their thumbs with their backs facing them, not the experimenter—which a perfectly imitative response would require, if it were judged by a third party. Figure 7.7 illustrates this. Thus, it is entirely possible that much early developing imitative responding is executed to maximize visual similarity. How perfectly correct imitation (from the point view of a third party) comes to be processed in its later development still needs to be explained. Baer (1978) offered a preliminary explanation of how invisible-to-imitator models (for example, touch back of head) come to be imitated: It should be possible to learn the haptic stimulus correlates of the modeled stimulus—in less formal terms, to learn what it feels like to look

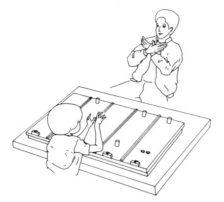

FIGURE 7.7   The "cross-thumbs" model seen from the child's viewpoint.

like a model, and, through sufficient exemplars, like any model. Accomplished imitators can observe a model, and then imitate it with their eyes closed. The question is how the haptic correlations that allow that are acquired. Better yet, how could we teach those correlations when they have not yet been acquired?

Although this argument is still thoroughly speculative, its future experimental analysis is possible. For example, with subjects like those just described, an experimenter could demonstrate "cross arms," systematically changing the direction of the palms, and teach the corresponding changes of the subject's palms, perhaps using a multielement or reversal design to show the functional relationship between teaching and subsequent behavior change. The generalization of training to similarly constructed untrained responses (like the "crossed-thumbs" model of Figure 7.7) could be probed, and, if absent, programmed, perhaps through the training of sufficiently numerous and diverse similarly constructed exemplars (e.g., Baer, 1981), perhaps with eyes-closed trials included to foster and accelerate the shift to haptic correlates of the visual displays. If such a conditioning history can be made responsible for this shift from visual to haptic control, explanation via the inference of a developing "cognitive" abstraction (such as role-taking or perspective-taking) is not necessary. If a too-early inference of that nature preempted empirical, experimental pursuit of how the process could be made to occur, it would in fact be counterproductive.

CONCLUSION

In reply to the four major criticisms of the conditioned-reinforcement explanation of generalized imitation, some empirical evidence was cited to demonstrate that access to nonreinforced imitations as a contingent response can modify an instrumental response, depending on the presence or absence of interspersed reinforced imitations. That reinforcing function of nonreinforced imitations was demonstrated in spite of clear discrimination between reinforced and nonreinforced imitations, yet was shown to depend on the unavailability of other competing (more powerfully reinforcing) activities. Consequently, the conditioned-reinforcement hypothesis is a prospective explanation of the currently known facts of generalized imitation. A major implication of that type of explanation is the fragility of control implicit in a conditioned-reinforcement mechanism, the correspondingly thorough control of numerous environmental and historical factors necessary to maximize it, and the typical vulnerability of any behavior so controlled to alternative forms of control—as the review of setting events known to be operative in generalized imitation makes clear. That implication has serious import for the modeling therapies: Far from being economical and efficient forms of behavior change, they may often become very expensive and demanding technologies, if their results are to be made reliable and durable. Their current applications deserve careful, intensive real-world monitoring and follow up.

References

Acker, L. E., Acker, M. A., & Pearson, D. (1973). Generalized imitative affection: Relationship to prior kinds of imitation training. *Journal of Experimental Child Psychology, 16,* 117–125.

Allport, F. H. (1924). *Social psychology.* Cambridge, MA: Riverside Press.

Aronfreed, J. (1969). The problem of imitation. In L. P. Lipsitt & H. W. Reese (Eds.), *Advances in child development and behavior* (Vol. 4, pp. 210–314). New York: Academic Press.

Baer, D. M. (1978). The analysis, refinement, and control of generalized motor imitation in profoundly retarded persons. Unpublished manuscript.

Baer, D. M. (1981). *How to plan for generalization.* Lawrence, KS: H & H Enterprises.

Baer, D. M. (1982). The imposition of structure on behavior and the demolition of behavioral structures. In D. Bernstein & H. Howe (Eds.), *Nebraska symposium on motivation* (Vol. 29, pp. 217–254). Lincoln: University of Nebraska Press.

Baer, D. M., Peterson, R. F., & Sherman, J. A. (1967). The development of imitation by reinforcing behavioral similarity to a model. *Journal of the Experimental Analysis of Behavior, 10,* 405–416.

Baer, D. M., & Sherman, J. A. (1964). Reinforcement control of generalized imitation in young children. *Journal of Experimental Child Psychology, 1,* 37–49.

Bandura, A. (Ed.). (1971). *Psychological modeling: Conflicting theories.* Chicago: Aldine-Atherton.

Bandura, A. (1977). *Social learning theory.* Englewood Cliffs, NJ: Prentice-Hall.

Bandura, A., & Barab, P. G. (1971). Conditions governing nonreinforced imitation. *Developmental Psychology, 5,* 244–255.

Bernstein, D. J., & Ebbesen, E. B. (1978). Reinforcement and substitution in humans: A multiple-response analysis. *Journal of the Experimental Analysis of Behavior, 30,* 243–253.

Brigham, T. A., & Sherman, J. A. (1968). An experimental analysis of verbal imitation in preschool children. *Journal of Applied Behavior Analysis, 1,* 151–158.

Bucher, B. (1973). Some variables affecting children's compliance with instructions. *Journal of Experimental Child Psychology, 15,* 10–21.

Bucher, B., & Bowman, E. A. (1974). The effects of a discriminative cue and an incompatible activity on generalized imitation. *Journal of Experimental Child Psychology, 18,* 22–33.

Bufford, R. K. (1971). Discrimination and instructions as factors in the control of nonreinforced imitation. *Journal of Experimental Child Psychology, 12,* 35–50.

Bufford, R. K., & Buchanan, J. (1974). An experimental demonstration of discriminated (nongeneralized) imitation. *Journal of Abnormal Child Psychology, 2,* 265–273.

Burgess, R. L., Burgess, J. M., & Esveldt, K. C. (1970). An analysis of generalized imitation. *Journal of Applied Behavior Analysis, 3,* 39–46.

Clark, R. (1977). What is the use of imitation? *Journal of Child Language, 4,* 341–358.

Flanders, J. P. (1968). A review of research on imitative behavior. *Psychological Bulletin, 69,* 316–337.

Furnell, J. R. G., & Thomas, G. V. (1976). Stimulus control of generalized imitation in subnormal children. *Journal of Experimental Child Psychology, 22,* 282–291.

Furnell, J. R. G., & Thomas, G. V. (1981). Intermittent reinforcement of imitation in subnormal children: Effect on resistance to extinction. *Behavior Analysis Letters, 1,* 117–122.

Garcia, E., Baer, D. M., & Firestone, I. (1971). The development of generalized imitation within topographically determined boundaries. *Journal of Applied Behavior Analysis, 4,* 101–112.

Gewirtz, J. L. (1971). The roles of overt responding and extrinsic reinforcement in "self-" and "vicarious-reinforcement" phenomena and in "observational learning" and imitation. In R. Glaser (Ed.), *The nature of reinforcement* (pp. 279–309). New York: Academic Press.

Gewirtz, J. L., & Stingle, K. G. (1968). The learning of generalized imitation as the basis for identification. *Psychological Review, 75,* 374–397.

Gladstone, B. W., & Cooley, J. (1975). Behavioral similarity as a reinforcer for preschool children. *Journal of the Experimental Analysis of Behavior, 23,* 357–368.

Harlow, H. F. (1949). The formation of learning sets. *Psychological Review, 56,* 51–65.

Hayes, K. J., & Hayes, C. (1952). Imitation in a home-raised chimpanzee. *Journal of Comparative & Physiological Psychology, 45,* 450–459.

Holt, E. B. (1931). *Animal drive and the learning process* (Vol. 1). New York: Holt, Rinehart, and Winston.

Humphrey, G. (1921). Imitation and the conditioned reflex. *Pedagogical Seminary, 28,* 1–21.

Itard, J. M. (1806/1932). *The wild boy of Aveyron.* New York: Appleton-Century-Crofts.

James, W. (1907/1974). *Pragmatism.* New York: New American Library.

Jersild, A. T. (1933). *Child psychology.* New York: Prentice-Hall.

Kirkland, K. D., & Thelen, M. H. (1977). Uses of modeling in child treatment. In B. B. Lahey & A. E. Kazdin (Eds.), *Advances in clinical child psychology* (Vol. 1, pp. 307–328). New York: Plenum Press.

Kohlberg, L. (1969). Stage and sequence: The cognitive-developmental approach to socialization. In D. A. Goslin (Ed.), *Handbook of socialization theory and research* (pp. 347–480). Chicago: Rand McNally.

Konorski, J., & Miller, S. (1937). On two types of conditioned reflex. *Journal of General Psychology, 16,* 264–272.

Kuhn, D. (1973). Imitation theory and research from a cognitive perspective. *Human Development, 16,* 157–180.

Lashley, K. S. (1938). Conditional reactions in the rat. *Journal of Psychology, 6,* 311–324.

Lovaas, O. I., Berberich, J. P., Perloff, B. F., & Schaeffer, B. (1966). Acquisition of imitative speech by schizophrenic children. *Science, 151,* 705–707.

Martin, J. A. (1971). The control of imitative and nonimitative behaviors in severely retarded children through "generalized-instruction following." *Journal of Experimental Child Psychology, 11,* 390–400.

Martin, J. A. (1972). The effects of incongruent instructions and consequences on imitation in retarded children. *Journal of Applied Behavior Analysis, 5,* 467–475.

Metz, J. R. (1965). Conditioning generalized imitation in autistic children. *Journal of Experimental Child Psychology, 2,* 389–399.

Miller, N. E., & Dollard, J. (1941). *Social learning and imitation.* New Haven: Yale University Press.

Mowrer, O. H. (1960). *Learning theory and the symbolic processes.* New York: Wiley.

Oliver, P. R., Acker, L. E., & Oliver, D. D. (1977). Effects of reinforcement histories of compliance and noncompliance on nonreinforced imitation. *Journal of Experimental Child Psychology, 23,* 180–190.

Orne, M. T. (1962). On the social psychology of the psychological experiment: With particular reference to demand characteristics and their implications. *American Psychologist, 17,* 776–783.

Parton, D. A. (1976). Learning to imitate in infancy. *Child Development, 47,* 14–31.

Parton, D. A., & Fouts, G. T. (1969). Effects of stimulus-response similarity and dissimilarity on children's matching performance. *Journal of Experimental Child Psychology, 8,* 461–468.

Parton, D. A., & Priefert, M. J. (1975). The value of being imitated. *Journal of Experimental Child Psychology, 20,* 286–295.

Peterson, R. F. (1968). Some experiments on the organization of a class of imitative behaviors. *Journal of Applied Behavior Analysis, 1,* 225–235.

Peterson, R. F., Merwin, M. R., Moyer, T. J., & Whitehurst, G. J. (1971). Generalized imitation: The effects of experimenter absence, differential reinforcement, and stimulus complexity. *Journal of Experimental Child Psychology, 12,* 114–128.

Peterson, R. F., & Whitehurst, G. J. (1971). A variable influencing the performance of nonreinforced imitative behavior. *Journal of Applied Behavior Analysis, 4,* 1–9.

Piaget, J. (1962). *Play, dreams, and imitation in childhood.* New York: Norton.

Premack, D. (1959). Toward empirical behavior laws: I. Positive reinforcement. *Psychological Review, 66,* 219–233.

Premack, D. (1962). Reversibility of the reinforcement relation. *Science, 136,* 255–257.

Rosenthal, T. L. (1976). Modeling therapies. In M. Hersen, R. M. Eisler, & P. M. Miller (Eds.), *Progress in behavior modification* (Vol. 2, pp. 53–97). New York: Academic Press.

Rosenthal, T. L., & Bandura, A. (1978). Psychological modeling: Theory and practice. In S. L. Garfield & A. E. Bergin (Eds.), *Handbook of psychotherapy and behavior change: An empirical analysis* (2nd Edition). New York: Wiley.

Schroeder, G. L., & Baer, D. M. (1972). Effects of concurrent and serial training on generalized vocal imitation in retarded children. *Developmental Psychology, 6,* 293–301.

Sherman, J. A., Clark, H. B., & Kelly, K. K. (1977). Imitative behavior of preschool children: The effects of reinforcement, instructions, and response similarity. In B. C. Etzel, J. M. LeBlanc, & D. M. Baer (Eds.), *New developments in behavioral research: Theory, method, and application. In honor of Sidney W. Bijou* (pp. 503–529). Hillsdale, NJ: Lawrence Erlbaum Associates.

Sherman, J. A., Saunders, R. R., & Brigham, T. A. (1970). Transfer of matching and mismatching behavior in preschool children. *Journal of Experimental Child Psychology, 1,* 123–134.

Sidman, M. (1960). *Tactics of scientific research.* New York: Basic Books.

Skinner, B. F. (1957). *Verbal behavior*. New York: Appleton-Century-Crofts.

Smeets, P. M., & Striefel, S. (1973). The effect of experimenter absence and response delay on nonreinforced imitation. *The Journal of Psychology, 84,* 119–127.

Smeets, P. M., Striefel, S., & Gast, D. L. (1974). Conditioning history and the imitation of reinforced and nonreinforced behaviors. *The Journal of General Psychology, 90,* 257–270.

Spiegler, M. D. (1983). *Contemporary behavior therapy* (Chapter 10: Modeling therapies, pp. 221–259). Palo Alto, CA: Mayfield.

Steinman, W. M. (1970a). Generalized imitation and the discrimination hypothesis. *Journal of Experimental Child Psychology, 10,* 79–99.

Steinman, W. M. (1970b). The social control of generalized imitation. *Journal of Applied Behavior Analysis, 3,* 159–167.

Steinman, W. M. (1977). Generalized imitation and the setting event concept. In B. C. Etzel, J. M. LeBlanc, D. M. Baer (Eds.), *New developments in behavioral research: Theory, method, and application. In honor of Sidney W. Bijou* (pp. 103–109). Hillsdale, NJ: Lawrence Erlbaum Associates.

Steinman, W. M., & Boyce, K. D. (1971). *Journal of Experimental Child Psychology, 11,* 251–265.

Vaughan, M. E., & Michael, J. L. (1982). Automatic reinforcement: An important but ignored concept. *Behaviorism, 10,* 217–227.

Waxler, C. Z. & Yarrow, M. R. (1970). Factors influencing imitative learning in preschool children. *Journal of Experimental Child Psychology, 9,* 115–130.

Whitehurst, G. J. (1978). Observational learning. In A. C. Cantania & T. A. Brigham (Eds.), *Handbook of applied behavior analysis: Social and instructional processes* (pp. 142–178). New York: Irvington.

Whitehurst, G. J., & Vasta, R. (1975). Is language acquired through imitation? *Journal of Psycholinguistic Research, 4,* 37–59.

Wilcox, B., Meddock, T. D., & Steinman, W. M. (1973). "Generalized imitation" on a nonimitative task: Effects of modeling and task history. *Journal of Experimental Child Psychology, 15,* 381–393.

Yando, R., Seitz, V., & Zigler, E. (1978). *Imitation: A developmental perspective.* New York: Wiley.

The Social–Communicative Basis of Severe Behavior Problems in Children

EDWARD G. CARR
V. MARK DURAND

Severe behavior disorders include problems such as self-injury, aggression, and tantrums. The literature in this area is vast and merits book-length exposition. Therefore, because of space limitations, we have chosen to concentrate on a circumscribed but nevertheless important subarea, namely, behavior disorders displayed by seriously handicapped children. These children typically receive labels such as retarded, autistic, and schizophrenic. Sometimes they are described in more general terms as developmentally disabled. Research and thinking in this subarea have advanced over the past two decades to the point at which it is now feasible to speak of general principles and offer guidelines for the construction of a theory of socially motivated behavior problems. The conceptual framework that has emerged is pertinent as well to other childhood disorders such as conduct problems. Therefore, where appropriate, we reference related research literature in order to highlight instances of convergent theorizing.

Our intent in this chapter is twofold. First, we wish to present evidence that the factors responsible for the maintenance of socially motivated behavior problems fall into two broad classes: escape behavior, controlled by negative reinforcement processes, and attention-seeking behavior, con-

219

trolled by positive reinforcement processes. Second, we wish to sketch the outline of a general theory of severe behavior problems in which the major assumption is that such problems may be usefully conceptualized as a primitive form of nonverbal communication.

Escape Hypothesis

This hypothesis states that self-injury, tantrums, and aggression are maintained by the termination of an aversive stimulus following the occurrence of any or all of these behavior problems. We develop the arguments in support of this hypothesis at some length since the role of escape variables in severe child psychopathology has been relatively less well explicated in the literature than the role of attention-seeking variables.

The first requirement is that an aversive stimulus be presented to the child. As we document below, the most common exemplars of this kind of stimulus are instructional demands. The process is as follows. An adult presents the aversive stimulus (demand) to the child. The child responds by behaving in an obnoxious manner. The adult then reacts by withdrawing the aversive stimulus at which point the child responds by ceasing to behave obnoxiously. In this sequence, the termination of instructional efforts by the adult is negatively reinforced by the cessation of the child's obnoxious behavior. Therefore, in the future, the adult will be more likely to respond to the child's misbehavior by withdrawing demands. Also, in this sequence, the child's obnoxious behavior is negatively reinforced by the withdrawal of adult demands. Therefore, in the future, the child will be more likely to respond to adult demands by misbehaving. Thus the central idea of the escape hypothesis is that a child and an adult exchange negative reinforcers, particularly within an instructional context. We next explore several ramifications of this hypothesis that bear on its validity.

IMPACT OF INSTRUCTIONAL DEMANDS

An escape hypothesis requires that behavior problems occur most frequently in the presence of aversive stimuli. If we postulate that demands are aversive, then two predictions follow. First, the absence of an aversive stimulus (i.e., no demands) should be correlated with lower rates of behavior problems than the presence of such a stimulus. Second, a high intensity aversive stimulus (i.e., difficult demands) should be correlated with greater levels of behavior problems than a low-intensity aversive stimulus (i.e., easy demands). The data bearing on each of these predictions are presented next.

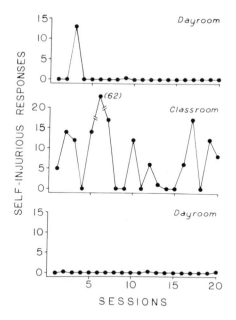

FIGURE 8.1   Frequency of self-injurious behavior exhibited by an autistic child in the absence of demands (Dayroom) and in the presence of demands (Classroom).

Consider first the impact of presence versus absence of demands. Figure 8.1 depicts the self-injurious behavior of a 12-year-old institutionalized autistic boy (Carr, Newsom, Binkoff, & Killion, 1976). The top and bottom panels show the child's performance on the ward (dayroom), a situation in which no instructional demands were made. The middle panel shows his performance in the classroom, a situation in which he was asked to label pictures as part of a vocabulary development exercise. Each day (session), the child was observed for 5 minutes on the ward, then 5 minutes in the classroom, and finally, 5 more minutes on the ward again. There was a 30-second break between the 5-minute observation periods. As is evident from the figure, this child rarely displayed self-injury on the ward. However, in the classroom, he displayed substantial rates of self-directed biting, scratching, and head banging. These effects have been systematically documented in three other studies of self-injury (Carr, Newsom, & Binkoff, 1976; Durand, 1982; Iwata, Dorsey, Slifer, Bauman, & Richman, 1982).

The findings just described are not unique to self-injury. Similar functional relationships have been documented with respect to aggression (Carr, Newsom, & Binkoff, 1980), tantrums (Carr & Newsom, in press), general social avoidance behaviors such as looking away or leaving one's seat (Richer, 1978), and self-stimulatory behavior (Durand & Carr, 1983).

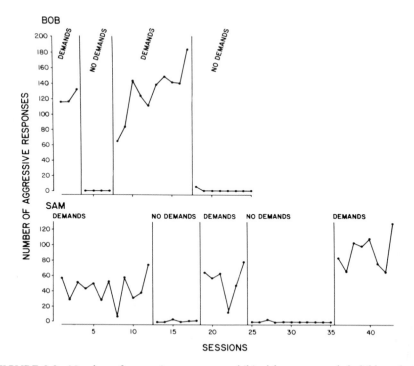

FIGURE 8.2 Number of aggressive responses exhibited by two retarded children during periods in which learning tasks were presented (Demands) or withheld (No Demands). From "Escape as a factor in the aggressive behavior of two retarded children" by E. G. Carr, C. D. Newsom, & J. A. Binkoff, 1980. *Journal of Applied Behavior Analysis, 13,* p.105. Copyright 1980 by the Society for the Experimental Analysis of Behavior. Reprinted by permission.

Figure 8.2 depicts the aggressive behavior of two retarded children in an instructional situation (Carr *et al.,* 1980). Bob was involved in learning readiness training and Sam, in self-care training. Each child displayed minimal levels of aggression in the absence of demands. In contrast, when confronted with demands, both children responded by scratching, kicking, biting, and pinching the teacher.

Consider next the second prediction, namely, that difficult demands will evoke high levels of behavior problems and easy demands, low levels. A study by Weeks and Gaylord-Ross (1981) is pertinent to this prediction. These investigators exposed two retarded children and one schizophrenic child to several visual discrimination and perceptual motor tasks that varied in difficulty. Self-injury, crying, and aggression occurred at higher rates during difficult tasks than during easy tasks. The relative difficulty of a task has also been identified as an important controlling variable for the three behaviors just noted in other investigations of behavior problems in retarded children (Durand & Carr, 1982b; Romanczyk, Colletti, & Plotkin, 1980). Finally, Churchill (1971) demonstrated that difficult demands produced a higher level of frustrative behavior (e.g., tantrums) and general social avoidance (e.g., looking away) than did easy tasks.

The studies reviewed are consistent with the notion that, for some children, demands may constitute aversive stimuli that evoke escape responses. Further, there is a continuum of aversiveness that ranges from a low level, in the case of no demands or easy demands, to a high level, in the case of difficult demands. As demand aversiveness increases, escape responses (i.e., behavior problems) become more frequent.

EFFECTS OF SAFETY SIGNAL STIMULI

Any stimulus that consistently signals the absence of an aversive event is technically referred to as a safety signal (Mowrer, 1960, p. 129). Typically, operant escape responding decreases in the presence of a safety signal (Azrin, Hake, Holz, & Hutchinson, 1965). Therefore, within an instructional context, an escape hypothesis would predict that whenever a child is provided with a reliable cue that demands (the aversive event) have terminated, escape responses (problem behavior) should decrease in frequency.

The effects of safety signal stimuli have been analyzed with respect to a variety of severe behavior problems. Figure 8.3 depicts the results of one such analysis carried out on tantrum behavior (Carr & Newsom, in press). Jim was an 8-year-old autistic child and Fred, an 11-year-old schizophrenic child. The task for Jim consisted of verbal imitation and for Fred, the acquisition of descriptive sentences. On the figure (left-hand panels), the label *Safety Signal* refers to a situation in which each child was cued that the session was over. The cue consisted of removing a work desk that the teacher and child had been using and placing it in a corner of the classroom. This stimulus event reliably signaled that the academic task had ended for the day. The abscissa depicts two time periods, the 6–10 minute period that represents the last 5 minutes   of the instructional session, and the 11–15 minute period that represents the 5 minute period that followed the removal of the work desk. Four separate sessions are represented in the figure. As is apparent, each child displayed high rates of tantrums (i.e., yelling, crying, and whining) during the instructional period but abruptly shifted to negligible tantrum rates once the safety signal was presented. The right-hand panels of Figure 8.3 show what happened when no discrete safety signal was presented. That is, at the end of the session (the completion of the tenth minute), the teacher stopped presenting demands but did not remove the

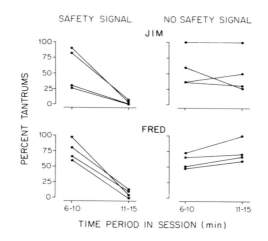

FIGURE 8.3   Percentage of intervals in which tantrums occurred for an autistic child (Jim) and a schizophrenic child (Fred). During Safety Signal sessions, each child was cued at the beginning of the eleventh minute of the instructional session that demands had terminated. During No Safety Signal sessions, the cue was omitted. From "Demand-related tantrums: Conceptualization and treatment" by E. G. Carr & C. D. Newsom, in press. *Behavior Modification*. Copyright © 1984 by Sage Publications, Inc. Reprinted by permission of Sage Publications, Inc.

work desk. Instead, the teacher continued to sit across the desk from the child. The data are clear in demonstrating that in the absence of a safety signal, the rate of the children's tantrums remained high. Presumably, this outcome occurred because the only cue available to signal the child that demands had ended was the absence of the demands themselves. The 5 minute period following the work session may not have been long enough to allow the child to discriminate the absence of demands. In other words, the lack of a discrete external cue (such as removal of the desk) may have prevented the child from readily discriminating that demands had ended and that therefore no further escape responses (tantrums) were necessary. The effects that we have described for tantrums have also been documented for aggression (Carr *et al.*, 1980) and self-injury (Carr *et al.*, 1976).

   With respect to self-injury, there is an additional interesting observation. Children who display this problem to a severe degree are sometimes placed in physical restraints as a protective measure. While in restraints, these children seldom receive any demands. In other words, restraints signal the absence of the aversive stimulus; that is, they constitute a safety signal. Basic research in learning theory suggests that safety signal stimuli can function as conditioned reinforcers (Bucher & Lovaas, 1968). Therefore, one would predict that it should be possible to condition an operant by using physical restraint as a reinforcer (Carr, 1977). Favell, McGimsey, & Jones (1978) demonstrated that increases in correct responding on a laboratory task (placing a marble in a hole) occurred when such responding produced physical restraint. The fact that restraints may come to function as conditioned reinforcers is further evidence in support of an escape conceptualization.

PATTERNING OF BEHAVIOR PROBLEMS

Basic research in animal learning suggests that if an organism is subjected to aversive stimuli on a regular schedule, then any escape responding that occurs should be organized into characteristic patterns. Consider a situation in which a child is given a 10-minute instructional session each day for a number of days. If one views demands as aversive stimuli, then it is possible to regard each session as a fixed-interval 10-minute schedule of escape. That is, each day, after a fixed interval of 10 minutes, the session ends, and any behavior problems that occur at that time would be negatively reinforced since they are correlated with the termination of aversive stimuli. Basic research has demonstrated that fixed-interval schedules of escape generate a behavior pattern in which responding gradually increases throughout the interval, the so-called fixed-interval scallop (Azrin et al., 1965; Hineline & Rachlin, 1969). The question can be raised as to whether behavior problems examined in the circumstances described above would also display the characteristic patterning. Figure 8.4 addresses this question. The data refer to the self-injurious behavior of a schizophrenic child who repeatedly hit himself in the face (Carr et al., 1976). The number of hits per minute were recorded during each third of a 10-minute instructional session. The figure represents the averaged data for several such sessions conducted over a number of days. The letter M refers to Mands, a condition in which a child was presented with several instructional demands. The letters F. T. refer to Free Time, a condition in which the child was not presented with demands. Finally, M + P.C. refers to Mands plus Positive Context, a condition in which an attempt was made to mitigate the presumed aversiveness of demands by presenting them in the context of entertaining stories. The important point to note is that during the Mands conditions (replicated in two separate experiments), the rate of self-injurious hitting accelerated from a low level during the first third of each session to a very high level during the final third of each session. In contrast, when demands were not presented (Free Time) or when steps were taken to reduce the presumed aversiveness of demands (Mands plus Positive Context), self-injury occurred at a low rate that remained stable across thirds of each session. In short, the pattern of behavior problems that emerged during a condition (i.e., Mands) in which demands were presented without any attempt to mitigate their aver-

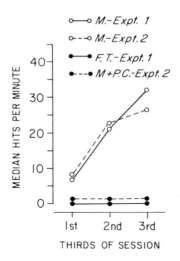

FIGURE 8.4   Median self-injurious acts per minute by a schizophrenic child during successive thirds of a session. The experimental conditions, which consisted of Mands (M), Free Time (F.T.), or Mands Plus Positive Context (M + P.C.), are explained in the text. From "Stimulus control of self-destructive behavior in a psychotic child" by E. G. Carr, C. D. Newsom, & J. A. Binkoff, 1976. *Journal of Abnormal Child Psychology, 4,* p. 149. Copyright 1976 by Plenum Publishing Corporation. Reprinted by permission.

siveness duplicated the fixed-interval scallop that is characteristic of escape schedules. When the same demands were presented in a positive context, behavioral scalloping did not occur, a fact that further supports a negative reinforcement interpretation of self-injury. We may note that Churchill (1971) also documented that general social avoidance (e.g., looking away) showed progressive increases during a difficult demand condition but not during an easy demand condition. It is unfortunate that the type of micro-analysis just described is so rare in the literature since it has the capability of providing a test of motivational hypotheses. In the present case, microanal-ysis revealed a patterning of behavior that was consistent with an escape hypothesis.

TIME-OUT STUDIES

Time-out studies provide the single most powerful test of the escape conceptualization of behavior problems. If demands are aversive and behav-ior problems function to terminate these stimuli, then one would expect that a time-out procedure administered contingent on behavior problems should increase, rather than decrease, the frequency of these problems. That is, time-out from an aversive stimulus constitutes negative reinforcement,

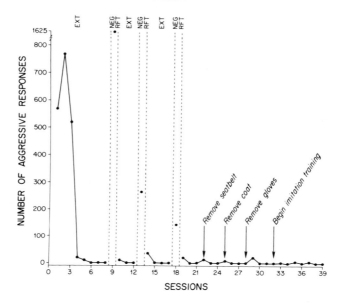

FIGURE 8.5 Number of aggressive responses exhibited by a retarded child during extinction (EXT), a condition in which the child was not allowed to leave the demand situation following aggressive behavior, and negative reinforcement (NEG RFT), a condition in which the child was allowed to leave the demand situation following aggressive behavior. From sessions 22 to 39, EXT remained in effect while the experimenter gradually removed articles of protective clothing designed to prevent injury from the child's agressive attacks, and faded in trials that involved training in nonverbal imitation. From "Escape as a factor in the aggressive behavior of two retarded children" by E. G. Carr, C. D. Newsom, & J. A. Binkoff, 1980. *Journal of Applied Behavior Analysis, 13,* p. 114. Copyright 1980 by the Society for the Experimental Analysis of Behavior. Reprinted by permission.

not punishment. Therefore, any behavior that accesses the time–out contingency will be strengthened through a process of negative reinforcement.

In a study cited earlier (Carr *et al.*, 1980), a retarded child was permitted to leave a demand situation each time he emitted a high frequency of aggressive behavior against the teacher. Procedurally, the intervention resembled time–out; however, as Figure 8.5 illustrates, the intervention functioned as negative reinforcement and was therefore labeled as such (NEG RFT). The child's aggression had been brought under control using an escape extinction procedure (EXT) described below. Control was so complete that the experimenter was able to gradually remove clothing that he was wearing to protect himself from the child, and was able to introduce new demands related to nonverbal imitation training. Nonetheless, when procedural time–out was employed (NEG RFT), the effect was to increase the frequency of aggression from a few responses per hour to hundreds per hour.

This figure makes plain the importance of distinguishing between behavior problems maintained by positive versus negative reinforcement. If aggressive behavior were always a form of attention-seeking (i.e., maintained by positive reinforcement), time-out might well prove an adequate control measure in most cases. The fact that aggression is apparently escape-motivated in some instances suggests that, on occasion, time-out may not only prove ineffective, it may clearly make the problem worse. In sum, then, the increase in aggression following procedural time-out suggests that demands may be aversive stimuli and that aggression may be a form of escape behavior.

The functional relationships described above have been observed for other behaviors in addition to aggression. Thus, Plummer, Baer, and LeBlanc (1977) applied procedural time-out to two autistic children in an instructional context in order to control a variety of disruptive behaviors such as tantrums and spitting. The effect of time-out was to produce a marked and systematic increase in the frequency of disruptive behavior. In another study, Solnick, Rincover, and Peterson (1977) applied time-out to the self-injurious and aggressive behaviors of two children, one of whom was autistic and the other, retarded. The treatment procedure was applied while each child participated in a receptive language training task. Time-out produced an increase in the frequency of both behavior problems.

The data are consistent with the notion that for some children, demands may indeed be aversive stimuli and that some behavior problems are a form of escape maintained by negative reinforcement resulting from the termination of demands.

REDUCING DEMAND AVERSIVENESS

Escape behavior is functional only when there are aversive stimuli in the environment. Therefore, any operation that serves to attenuate the aversiveness of a stimulus should bring about a reduction in escape behavior. Several studies are relevant to evaluating this implication of the escape hypothesis.

Consider the study already cited in which two retarded children were taught self-care and learning readiness skills (Carr et al., 1980). Figure 8.6 represents one set of findings from that study. In the Demands Condition, each child was praised for complying with adult demands. However, the use of praise alone was correlated with high rates of aggression. Therefore, an attempt was made to alter the nature of reinforcement given by identifying strongly preferred toys and foods for each child. When these reinforcing stimuli were used in addition to praise (Demands Plus Toys and Food Condition), the rate of aggression dropped precipitously and the remaining

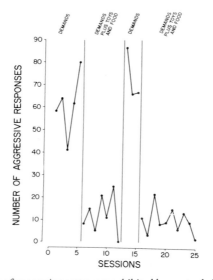

FIGURE 8.6   Number of aggressive responses exhibited by a retarded child during Demands, a condition in which correct responses were followed only by praise, and Demands Plus Toys and Food, a condition in which correct responses were followed by food and toys in addition to praise. From "Escape as a factor in the aggressive behavior of two retarded children" by E. G. Carr, C. D. Newsom, & J. A. Binkoff, 1980. *Journal of Applied Behavior Analysis, 13,* p. 109. Copyright 1980 by the Society for the Experimental Analysis of Behavior. Reprinted by permission.

aggressive responses were of lower intensity. One plausible mechanism for this effect may be that the addition of strong reinforcers to a demand situation reduces the overall aversiveness of the situation. Therefore, escape behavior is less functional. That is, successful escape would now not only remove the child from the demand situation (perhaps a desirable outcome for the child) but would also result in a very undesirable outcome, namely, the loss of preferred reinforcers that are obtainable only within the instructional situation. By pairing reinforcing stimuli (toys and foods) with aversive stimuli (demands), it is possible that overall aversiveness is reduced thereby undercutting the motivation for escape. Similar results have been obtained in the case of tantrums. Specifically, the use of highly preferred foods to reinforce compliance can produce a strong and sustained decrease in tantrum rates for developmentally disabled children (Carr & Newsom, in press).

The introduction of tangible reinforcers may not be the only way to mitigate the aversiveness of demands. In a study cited above (Carr *et al.,* 1976), an attempt was made to reduce aversiveness by embedding demands

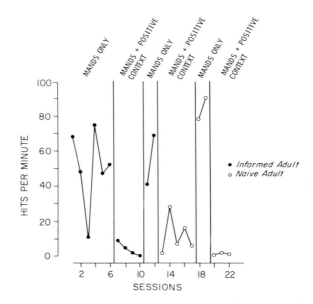

FIGURE 8.7 Number of self-injurious acts per minute exhibited by a schizophrenic child during Mands Only versus Mands Plus Positive Context. The two conditions are explained in the text. The filled circles are the data for sessions conducted by an adult who was knowledgeable about the rationale for the intervention, and the open circles are the data for sessions conducted by a naive adult. From "Stimulus control of self-destructive behavior in a psychotic child" by E. G. Carr, C. D. Newsom, & J. A. Binkoff, 1976. *Journal of Abnormal Child Psychology, 4,* p. 149. Copyright 1976 by Plenum Publishing Corporation. Reprinted by permission.

in a positive social context. In particular, a series of amusing, entertaining stories were introduced into the instructional situation and demands were presented periodically in between stories. The schizophrenic child who was involved in this intervention responded by smiling and laughing, and, most importantly, displayed a dramatic decrease in the level of self-injurious behavior. This result is illustrated in Figure 8.7 (i.e., the Mands plus Positive Context Condition). When the positive context was eliminated (Mands Only), self-injury increased once again to a high rate. It is plausible that the entertaining stories reduced the aversiveness of the demand situation thereby rendering behavior problems (self-injury) less functional.

Thus far we have discussed attempts to reduce aversiveness by altering the nature of reinforcement in the instructional situation. Presumably, one could also alter the nature of the demands themselves. In particular, any procedure that functions to reduce the difficulty of demands might be expected to result in fewer escape behaviors. A study by Weeks and Gaylord-

Ross (1981) is pertinent to this point. As noted earlier, these investigators found that self-injury was frequent when children were confronted with a difficult visual discrimination task. Interestingly, when an errorless learning procedure was applied to teach the discrimination, self-injury decreased to a low level. This result is significant since an errorless procedure would be expected to reduce task difficulty and, therefore, aversiveness.

The reinforcement and errorless learning interventions described above, though procedurally quite different from one another, share one important characteristic at a conceptual level: Each presumably acts to attenuate the aversive properties of the demand situation. Since escape behavior is maintained by the termination of aversive stimuli, one would predict that any reduction in aversiveness should result in fewer escape behaviors. The fact that this prediction is borne out is consistent with the notion that many behavior problems may be escape motivated.

ESCAPE EXTINCTION

If a problem behavior has been maintained by negative reinforcement resulting from successful escape, then it follows that if a child is not allowed to escape following emission of the problem behavior, that behavior should eventually decrease in frequency. In traditional extinction procedures, positive reinforcement is withdrawn for a specific behavior problem. In contrast, in the procedure just described, negative reinforcement is withdrawn. Because of this difference, the new procedure is technically referred to as *escape extinction* (Catania, 1968, p. 187).

The study cited earlier by Carr *et al.* (1980) and shown in Figure 8.5 provided a test of the escape extinction procedure. During escape extinction, the child was not permitted to leave the demand situation in spite of high levels of aggressive behavior. The figure illustrates that the initial effect of this procedure was to produce a large increase in aggression from approximately 600 acts during Session 1 to just under 800 acts in Session 2. This effect is analogous to the extinction burst phenomenon seen when traditional extinction procedures are employed to control behavior problems. Importantly, continued application of escape extinction resulted in a decrease in aggression to negligible levels. In other words, when a problem behavior is no longer effective in producing escape from demands, the problem diminishes.

The published literature provides other examples of the phenomenon we are describing. For example, Plummer *et al.* (1977) employed a procedure that they labeled, *paced instructions*. The essence of this procedure was that the teacher presented instructions to the child at regularly paced intervals and did so even if the child was being disruptive at the time. That is, the

child was not permitted to leave the demand situation contingent on disruptive behavior. The result was that a variety of disruptive behaviors, including tantrums, declined to a low level. In a related vein, Richer (1981) has
described a number of procedures that he refers to as *high intrusion*. The
essence of this method is for the adult to insist that the child complete a task
even if the child attempts to engage in avoidance behaviors. The apparent
result of this procedure is that the child acquiesces and terminates his or her
problem behavior.

Sometimes the procedures we have been describing are referred to as
working through, again a reference to the fact that the adult continues to
present demands in spite of disruptive behavior (Lovaas, 1981). At this
point, we may note that as the field of behavior modification has grown and
become more technically oriented, there has been a proliferation of terms
that, while descriptive, may all refer to the same treatment concept. Thus,
paced instructions, high intrusion, and working through are all terms that
are basically synonymous with escape extinction. It is our belief that, from
the standpoint of integrating the field theoretically, generic terms referring
to psychological processes should be substituted, whenever possible, for
technical terms referring to specific procedures. To sum up, several data
sources suggest that one can reduce the frequency of problem behavior by
preventing the child from leaving a demand situation contingent on such
behavior. This outcome is consistent with an escape hypothesis.

There is an important variant of escape extinction. Specifically, if a behavior problem is followed by an increase in the difficulty of demands or by
an increase in the number of demands, one would also expect an extinction
effect to occur. The reason is that the usual consequent, namely, complete
withdrawal of demands, is clearly not forthcoming in the two cases mentioned.

Consider first a procedure in which the difficulty of demands is manipulated contingent on the child's behavior. This procedure was used in a study
by Sailor, Guess, Rutherford, and Baer (1968). These investigators were
training a young retarded girl on a vocabulary task. Typically, the girl
responded to instructions with multiple tantrums. When the experimenter
altered the contingencies so that tantrums reliably produced easier tasks, the
rate of tantrums increased markedly, an effect that suggested the operation
of negative reinforcement. Most importantly, for present purposes, when
the experimenter rearranged the contingencies so that tantrums were now
followed by more difficult tasks, the tantrum rate decreased to a low level.
One could argue, based on these data, that tantrums represented an escape
behavior maintained by the negative reinforcement inherent in the reduction of demand difficulty. When tantrums failed to produce easier demands

but, in fact, produced more difficult demands, the behavior ceased to be an effective escape response and therefore decreased. In this case, escape extinction would be implicated. Alternatively, we must note that the decrease could be due to the punishing effects of increased task difficulty. Or, finally, the decrease may represent the combined effects of escape extinction and punishment. No attempt has yet been made to test these rival explanations.

Consider next a procedure in which the number of demands is manipulated. The best example of this approach is overcorrection. Although it is generally acknowledged that overcorrection functions as a punisher, it is quite possible that in some circumstances, escape extinction may be involved. Suppose, for example, that a child becomes aggressive in a demand situation and that such behavior regularly extricates the child from the situation. In this case, aggression will be maintained at a high level. Suppose now that the contingencies are changed so that each aggressive act is followed by a period of time in which the child is forced to practice repeatedly a prosocial form of behavior (i.e., positive practice overcorrection). In this case, aggression fails to produce the usual negative reinforcer (i.e., withdrawal of demands) but instead produces a sharp increase in the number of demands. Again, some combination of escape extinction and punishment may be involved although no research has been conducted to assess the separate contributions made by each process. Notwithstanding these interpretive difficulties, the widespread success of overcorrection (Foxx & Bechtel, 1983), particularly in instructional situations, provides indirect support for the idea that escape extinction may be a factor in the effective control of many behavior problems.

PROVIDING AN ALTERNATIVE ESCAPE RESPONSE

If a behavior problem reliably produces escape from a demand situation, then one would expect that providing an individual with an alternative means for escape should function to reduce the frequency of behavior problems. A test of this notion was provided in the study cited above by Carr *et al.* (1980). The aggressive behavior of a retarded boy was examined in two conditions. In one condition, the child was permitted to leave the demand situation following progressively higher levels of aggressive behavior. This condition is represented in Figure 8.8 by the label, Neg. rft.: Aggression. In the second condition, the child was permitted to leave following progressively higher levels of a tapping response. That is, the child would tap the back of one of his hands with the index finger of the other hand. When he did this a number of times, he was allowed to leave the session for about 1 minute. This response was intended to be a primitive but idiosyncratic form

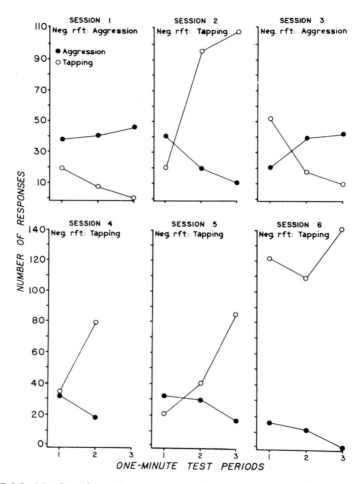

FIGURE 8.8 Number of agressive responses exhibited by a retarded child during 1-minute test periods that followed two types of experimental conditions. In one condition (Neg. rft.: Aggression), the child was permitted to escape from a demand situation contingent on successively increasing levels of aggression. In another condition (Neg. rft.: Tapping), escape was permitted contingent on successively increasing levels of tapping, a primitive form of sign language. From "Escape as a factor in the aggressive behavior of two retarded children" by E. G. Carr, C. D. Newsom, & J. A. Binkoff, 1980. *Journal of Applied Behavior Analysis, 13,* p. 112. Copyright 1980 by the Society for the Experimental Analysis of Behavior. Reprinted by permission.

of sign language (see Carr, 1979; 1982a, 1982b), enabling the child to indicate that he wanted to leave the session. This condition is represented in
Figure 8.8 by the label, Neg. rft.: Tapping. In short, during one condition,
aggression was negatively reinforced by allowing the child to escape from
demands whereas in the other condition, tapping was negatively reinforced
in the same manner. It is clear from the figure that when aggression produced escape, the rate of aggression rose to a high level. Most importantly,
however, when the child was taught an alternative escape response (tapping), not only did the rate of tapping gradually increase to a high level but
also the rate of aggression gradually decreased to a low level. In fact, there
was a strong inverse relationship between the rate of tapping and the rate of
aggression. We have speculated elsewhere (Carr & Lovaas, 1982) that to the
extent that an alternative escape response produces consistent access to negative reinforcement, one would expect that response alternative to gradually
replace the problem behavior. The reason for this is that in the natural
environment, problem behavior is likely to be negatively reinforced only on
a very inconsistent basis. Typically, reponses that are inconsistently reinforced are performed at a lower level than those that are consistently reinforced.

The data of Figure 8.8 represent an analogue study. In practice, one
would not wish to teach a child how to escape from an instructional session
since that would interfere with the child's education. However, the procedure we have described could also be applied in clinically relevant situations. For example, the child could be taught to sign or verbalize a desire to
leave the dining area following completion of dinner. This behavior would
be a more appropriate escape response than aggressing against an adult or
peer in order to be allowed to leave.

The observation that strengthening alternative escape responses can produce a decrease in behavior problems is an outcome consistent with the
escape hypothesis. Further, the fact that the effective alternative response
can be communicative in nature is an intriguing prospect that is taken up
again in detail at the end of this chapter.

CUMULATIVE NATURE OF THE EVIDENCE

No single piece of evidence that we have reviewed is sufficient to establish
the escape hypothesis as an explanation of severe behavior disorders. However, a consideration of the cumulative data presented suggests the viability
of the escape hypothesis both as an explanatory construct and as a useful
heuristic for designing treatment interventions.

RELATED RESEARCH LITERATURE

The processes we have described are not unique to developmentally disabled children. For example, demands have also been found to influence the behavior problems of emotionally disturbed children; that is, disruptive children of normal intelligence who are behind academically. In one study, Center, Deitz, and Kaufman (1982) presented such children with difficult task demands involving arithmetic problems. The children responded with a variety of inappropriate behaviors including making noises with objects, being out of their seats, and disturbing other students. In contrast, when the children were given easier tasks, inappropriate behavior occurred at a much lower level.

Instructional demands are not the only stimuli that are discriminative for behavior problems. The social behavior of peers may also influence the display of behavior problems. For example, an aggressive act performed by one child may set off aggression in another. A clear instance of this phenomenon can be seen in a study by Patterson, Littman, and Bricker (1967). These investigators found that normal preschool children who were victims of the aggressive behaviors of their peers would sometimes counterattack. If the counterattacks succeeded (i.e., their peers stopped attacking for the moment), the victims became increasingly more likely to aggress when attacked in the future. Apparently, the victims' counterattacks were negatively reinforced by terminating peer aggression.

In addition to demands and aggressive acts, a number of other stimuli have been identified that evoke behavior problems. For example, Patterson and his colleagues (Patterson, 1980; Patterson & Cobb, 1971) have noted that conduct problem children are likely to aggress against their brothers and sisters when these siblings yell at them or engage in other behaviors such as teasing, disapproval, or issuing negative commands (e.g., "Stop that!"). Likewise, parents who present noninstructional commands (e.g., "Clean your room.") may engender whining, threats, or other misbehavior from their conduct problem children (Forehand & McMahon, 1981; Patterson & Cobb, 1971).

The major conceptualization of behavior difficulties in conduct problem children centers on the notion of coercion (Patterson, 1982). Teasing, negative commands, yelling, hitting, and a number of other stimuli are viewed as aversive to the child. The child responds by displaying a variety of obnoxious behaviors that coerce others (parents, siblings) into withdrawing the aversive stimuli. The coercive behaviors are thereby strengthened through a process of negative reinforcement. Thus, they are more likely to be displayed in the future when, for example, the child is confronted with a sister who teases or a parent who issues commands.

Coercion has also been implicated in the control of problems as diverse as operant vomiting (Wolf, Birnbrauer, Williams, & Lawler, 1965), hyperactivity (Ross & Ross, 1976, p. 80), and asthmatic attacks (Creer, Weinberg, & Molk, 1974). Most importantly, the construct appears directly relevant to the analysis of severe behavior problems in developmentally disabled children presented earlier. Clearly, coercion is a notion that has generality far beyond the original population (conduct problem children) on which it was based. The fact that the behavior problems of developmentally disabled children can be viewed within the same conceptual framework as those of conduct problem children highlights a significant example of convergent theorizing within the field.

Attention Hypothesis

This hypothesis states that self-injury, tantrums, and aggression are maintained by positive social reinforcement delivered contingent upon performance of these behaviors. We may note two points at the outset. First, this hypothesis has already received a great deal of systematic analysis in the literature and there is thus no need to develop the argument in support of it to the same degree as was done for the escape hypothesis. Instead, we will highlight a few studies that appear especially pertinent to examining this hypothesis. Second, the convergent theorizing noted above with respect to the escape hypothesis is equally evident with respect to the attention hypothesis. Specifically, this hypothesis is isomorphic with the notion of the negative reinforcer trap proposed by Wahler (1976) and one aspect of coercion theory proposed by Patterson (1982). Although these two investigators developed their ideas based on work carried out with conduct problem children, it is clear that the same ideas are relevant to developmentally disabled children. The interactional paradigm is as follows. A child behaves in an obnoxious manner. An adult responds by providing a positive reinforcer such as attention. The child stops the obnoxious behavior. In this sequence, the child's obnoxious behavior is positively reinforced (by attention) and the adult's attending behavior is negatively reinforced (by the cessation of the child's obnoxious behavior). In other words, one party (the child) is positively reinforced, and the other party (the adult) is negatively reinforced. This exchange stands in contrast to the escape paradigm already described in which both parties are negatively reinforced. Several interventions have been applied to remedy this pattern of coercion and we will describe them next as they constitute tests, direct and indirect, of the attention hypothesis.

EXTINCTION AND CONTINGENT PRESENTATION
OF ATTENTION

If a problem behavior is maintained by attention, then one would predict that withholding attention following emission of the problem behavior should produce a decrease in the frequency of that behavior. This procedure is, of course, extinction. In addition, if attention is an important maintaining variable, one would expect that delivering attention contingent on a problem behavior should produce an increase in the level of the behavior. There are data bearing on both of these predictions. However, given the frequency with which researchers and clinicians alike have assumed that attention is a significant variable, it is impressive how few studies there are that directly test the attention notion in the manner just described.

Consider first the effects of contingent attention. Lovaas, Freitag, Gold, and Kassorla (1965) worked with a 9-year-old schizophrenic girl, who had a long history of self-injury. As part of an analysis of the problem, the investigators presented comforting comments each time the child banged her head or bit herself. The result was a clear increase in the frequency of self-injury, an effect that was partially replicated in a later study (Lovaas & Simmons, 1969). Martin and Foxx (1973) carried out a similar analysis on an aggressive, retarded client. Whenever the client, for example, slapped the experimenter, that person would deliver various warnings and comments (e.g., "Don't you ever do that again!"). The main effect of this procedure was a dramatic increase in the frequency of aggression.

Consider next the effects of extinction. Lovaas et al. (1965) found that ignoring self-injury in a noncontingent fashion (i.e., the experimenter stopped attending to all the child's behavior, both appropriate and inappropriate) had little effect on the behavior. However, the study by Martin and Foxx (1973) found clear effects when extinction was applied contingently. In that study, the experimenter withheld any comments or warnings even when attacked. This procedure resulted in low levels of aggression.

Although many investigators have noted that contingent application or withdrawal of attention can influence behavior problems, few have provided data that directly assess the frequency of attention and its relationship to behavior problems. Therefore, we conducted such a study in order to provide these data (Carr & McDowell, 1980). The client was a 10-year-old boy who was functioning in the borderline intelligence range (IQ 84). He exhibited a high frequency of scratching that produced sores all over his body. During extinction, the parents were asked not to make any comments when they saw him scratch. During a social attention condition, the parents were told to behave as usual, that is, to tell him to stop (e.g., "You'll make yourself ugly if you keep scratching!"). Figure 8.9 depicts the

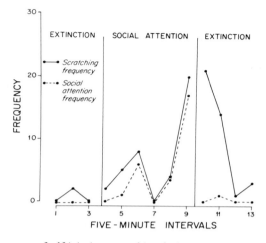

FIGURE 8.9   Frequency of self-injurious scratching during consecutive 5-minute observation intervals. In the extinction condition, the parents were instructed to ignore the child's scratching. In the social attention condition, the parents were instructed to tell the child to stop scratching each time that he engaged in the behavior. From "Social control of self-injurious behavior of organic etiology" by E. G. Carr, & J. J. McDowell, 1980. *Behavior Therapy, 11,* p. 405. Copyright 1980 by the Association for Advancement of Behavior Therapy. Reprinted by permission of the publisher and the author.

results. As was true for previous studies, the behavior decreased to low levels during extinction, and increased to high levels during social attention. Most importantly, the figure demonstrates the almost perfect correlation (Pearson $r = .98$) between the frequency of social attention and the frequency of scratching that occurred during the social attention condition.

The relationships noted above for developmentally disabled children have also been observed in other populations. For example, among normal children, extinction has proven effective in the control of both tantrums (Williams, 1959) and aggression (Brown & Elliott, 1965; Pinkston, Reese, LeBlanc, & Baer, 1973; Wahler, 1967).

In sum, the data on the effects of extinction and contingent attention generally provide clear support for the attention hypothesis.

TIME-OUT STUDIES

When the withdrawal of attention for a behavior problem is signaled (rather than unsignaled as in the case of extinction), the procedure is referred to as time-out (Harris & Ersner-Hershfield, 1978). The most common signal used involves the physical removal of the child from the situation in which the misbehavior occurs followed by the placement of the child in an isolation room. The procedure is carried out contingent on the emission of the problem behavior. Since time-out results in the withdrawal of attention, one would expect that any behavior maintained by that variable would decrease following the repeated application of time-out. In other words, time-out studies provide a test of the attention hypothesis.

In an extensive study, White, Nielsen, and Johnson (1972) attempted to control aggression, tantrums, and self-injury in a group of 20 retarded children. These investigators used varying durations of time-out applied contingent on each child's disruptive behaviors. In general, time-out effectively controlled the behavior problems. Similar findings have been obtained by other researchers working with developmentally disabled clients (Clark, Rowbury, Baer, & Baer, 1973; Hamilton, Stephens, & Allen, 1967; Tate & Baroff, 1966; Wolf, Risley, & Mees, 1964) although there have been occasional failures too (Risley, 1968). The behavior problems of normal children have also been controlled using this intervention (Hawkins, Peterson, Schweid, & Bijou, 1966; Zeilberger, Sampen, & Sloane, 1968).

Time-out studies have two interpretive problems not found in studies employing extinction. First, time-out not only removes the child from access to adult attention but also potentially denies access to a variety of tangible and activity reinforcers. Thus, the decelerative effects of the procedure cannot be unambiguously attributed to the withdrawal of attention per se. Second, the time-out environment is both barren and confining. Therefore, it is quite conceivable that it functions as an aversive stimulus. Thus, time-out effects may be due to the punishing aspects of the procedure rather than to the attention withdrawal aspects. There is typically no attempt made to disentangle these two variables. Notwithstanding these interpretive difficulties, the finding that time-out so often decreases the frequency of misbehavior is, at the very least, consistent with an attention hypothesis of behavior problems.

NONCONTINGENT SOCIAL ISOLATION

This procedure is a noncontingent form of time-out. That is, the child is placed in an isolation room for a period of time. The isolation, however, is not contingent on the occurrence of problem behavior. If an attention hypothesis has merit, one should find that this procedure suppresses behavior problems since the child cannot receive any form of attention while in isolation. All studies using this procedure have involved cases of self-injury.

Lovaas and Simmons (1969) employed 90-minute periods of noncontingent social isolation for the severe self-injurious behavior of two retarded boys. After an initial extinction burst, the self-injury slowly decreased to low levels. Similar results were obtained by Jones, Simmons, and Frankel

(1974) for a self-injurious autistic child. Using this procedure, Romanczyk and Goren (1975) produced a considerable reduction in the self-injurious behavior of their client but were unable to suppress the behavior permanently. However, these investigators were forced to intervene occasionally to protect the child. Such intervention may be seen as providing attention for the behavior problem and this of course would be expected to compromise the isolation procedure. Finally, Corte, Wolf, and Locke (1971) reported that noncontingent social isolation did not change the rate of self-injurious behavior for their two retarded clients. They noted, however, that the intervention was much less extensive than that reported in previous studies and the short duration may therefore have been responsible for the lack of success.

We may note at this point that the interpretive problems delineated earlier for contingent time-out, namely, the confounding of attention withdrawal and withdrawal of nonsocial reinforcers, and the possible punitive aspects of isolation, also apply to noncontingent time-out. Nonetheless, the general success of noncontingent social isolation is, at the least, consistent with an attention hypothesis.

Communication Hypothesis

Our discussion thus far has suggested that behavior problems may serve multiple social functions. Interestingly, researchers who study communication (rather than behavior problems) have frequently noted that language too may serve multiple social functions (Halliday, 1975; Skinner, 1957). In this sense, communicative responses and behavior problems are similar. We would like to go one step further and suggest that this similarity is not fortuitous and that, in fact, behavior problems can be a form of communication. In other words, we are proposing that a communication hypothesis may be used to subsume and integrate the escape and attention hypotheses of behavior problems.

The notion that nonverbal behavior may have a communicative function has been present in the clinical literature, particularly family therapy, for some time (see Haley, 1963; Minuchin, 1974; Satir, 1967; Watzlawick, Beavin, & Jackson, 1967). However, the idea has not been applied in a systematic way, at either an empirical or theoretical level, to the analysis and remediation of severe behavior problems. We believe that such an extension may be useful. Therefore, in what follows, we develop the communication hypothesis in several ways. First, we examine its conceptual roots in philosophy and developmental psychology. Next, we review relevant research in the area of developmental disabilities. Our review is a short one since the literature here is not extensive. The main impact of the hypothesis is heuristic. That is, it leads to a new view of behavior problems. The heuristic aspects, particularly their relation to theory and treatments are considered last.

PHILOSOPHICAL BACKGROUND

The notion that some nonverbal behavior, particularly crying, may constitute a protocommunicative act dates back at least to the ancient Greeks. Thus, in the *Laws,* Plato (circa 348 BC/1960) observed,

> new born beings, have from the very first a way of screaming. . . . So when the nurse would discover its desires she guesses from these indications what to offer it; if the child is quiet when something is offered it, she thinks she has found the right thing, but the wrong if it cries and screams. (p. 174)

In this vignette, the caretaker is responding to the child's screaming, not as an aberrant behavior, but rather as a primitive form of communication. The adult's task becomes one of trying to guess what the child is asking for and then providing the desired item.

Centuries later, the French philosopher, Rousseau, made the same point more directly. In his educational treatise, *Émile,* Rousseau observed, "when children begin to speak, they cry less. This is a natural progression. One language is substituted for another. As soon as they can say with words . . . why would they say it with cries?" (1762/1979, p. 77). Rousseau implies quite clearly that a child's nonverbal behavior may have a communicative dimension. As the child acquires more sophisticated means of communication (e.g., speech), the more primitive means (e.g., crying) gradually become less prominent. There is an important clinical implication here. Specifically, if a child is retarded and fails to acquire speech or acquires only minimal levels of communicative speech, then one would expect that the primitive behaviors would remain. Such behaviors might then constitute the major, if not only, means of communication for the child.

ROOTS IN DEVELOPMENTAL PSYCHOLOGY

Pragmatics is that portion of psycholinguistics that deals with the social–communicative functions of language. Pragmatic analysis of the language of normal children has suggested that a variety of nonverbal behaviors may have communicative functions. Thus, Bates and her coworkers (Bates, 1976; Bates, Benigni, Bretherton, Camaioni, & Volterra, 1977; Bates, Camaioni, & Volterra, 1975) introduced the notion of the protodeclarative and protoimperative. These linguistic entities occur before the child has acquired speech, and yet, they appear to function communicatively. Specifically, the protodeclarative serves an attention-seeking function while the protoimperative serves as a means for obtaining desired objects.

Consider first the protodeclarative. A child may exhibit a variety of showing, giving, and pointing behaviors in the presence of an adult. For instance, a child may show the adult a toy truck while looking at the adult. The adult looks at the child and says, "Yes, what a nice truck you have!" These ritualized exchanges may take a variety of forms but what they all share in common is their efficacy in generating and maintaining adult attention. Likewise, for the protoimperative, the child employs a variety of nonverbal behaviors to communicate. For example, the child sees a toy truck that is out of reach on a shelf and responds by looking back and forth between the truck and the adult, all the while with hand extended toward the truck. The adult responds by taking the truck down from the shelf and handing it to the child. Again, a ritualized nonverbal exchange produces a desirable outcome. In this case, however, the child receives an object rather than verbal attention.

Other psycholinguists have noted communicative functions similar to those described by Bates. Halliday (1975), for example, postulated instrumental and regulatory functions of nonverbal behavior that directly parallel the protoimperative and protodeclarative respectively. It is interesting, if not surprising, that the categories we have been describing are virtually isomorphic with the notion of mands and tacts developed by behaviorists (Skinner, 1957), a point that has been explicated in some detail (Hart, 1980). Specifically, a *mand* corresponds to the protoimperative, and a *tact,* to the protodeclarative, although as Skinner uses these terms, they generally apply to speech rather than nonverbal communication.

Showing, giving, and pointing, as well as related behaviors appear to have communicative import. However, these behaviors are not problematic. The question now becomes whether the pragmatic viewpoint alluded to can be extended to the analysis of other nonverbal acts, in particular, those behaviors that adults find disturbing. Several studies with normal children suggest that this extension can be made. The most elaborate analyses have been carried out on infant crying and we therefore examine this literature next.

In a detailed study, Wolff (1969) identified a number of situations in which infants displayed socially oriented cries. For example, by the third week of life, many infants would exhibit cries that their mothers labeled as "faking." That is, the mothers inferred that the crying was not based on distress but was simply a means of getting attention. Such cries frequently resulted in the mothers' picking up their children and talking to or comforting them. Also, Wolff found that the offering of certain foods reliably set off fussing and crying. To the extent that such activity resulted in withdrawal of the food, the behavior would appear to be escape motivated. By 2 to 3 months of age, infants were observed to start crying whenever a favorite toy was removed and stopped when the toy was returned. Again, crying influenced the adult in predictable ways.

The social effects noted by Wolff (1969) were examined more systematically in a later paper by Bell and Ainsworth (1972). These investigators performed a longitudinal study of infant crying during the first year of life. A major finding was that crying became increasingly socially oriented as the infant grew older so that the behavior was eventually emitted most frequently when the children were in close proximity to their mothers, and least frequently when their mothers were out of the vicinity and could not be seen or heard by the children. When the children cried, the most frequent maternal response was to pick up and hold the child, followed (in order of probability), by vocalizing and interacting, feeding, approaching and touching, and offering toys. Infant crying clearly had the effect of promoting maternal proximity and appeared to have both protodeclarative and protoimperative functions as per Bates' analysis. Most importantly, Bell and Ainsworth found a substantial negative correlation between infant communication and crying by the end of the first year. That is, babies who had developed communicative competence involving facial expression, gesture, and noncrying vocalization tended to be the ones who cried the least. This type of finding has prompted Bruner (1979, p. 268) to conclude that "There is a progressive development of these primitive procedures for communicating, and typically they are replaced by less primitive ones until eventually they are replaced by standard linguistic procedures". Bruner states, and Bell and Ainsworth imply, that infant cries may be a primitive form of communication from which speech eventually emerges. This characterization is one that meshes well with Rousseau's observation, cited above, that crying and speech are functionally the same, the former being a communicative precursor of the latter.

Finally, we may note a study by Brownlee and Bakeman (1981) that explored aggression in toddlers. These investigators found that certain aggressive acts had reliable social consequences. For example, when one child hit another with an open hand, the other child typically broke off further contact, leading the investigators to speculate that aggression functioned to communicate the notion, "Leave me alone." That is, the behavior appeared to be escape-motivated. In contrast, hitting that involved objects (e.g., a low intensity hit that employed a stuffed animal) promoted pleasant social interaction, especially play, leading to the speculation that such behavior functioned communicatively to express the notion, "Hey, wanna play?" That is, the behavior appeared to be attention seeking. Most importantly, these observations held for 2-year-olds but not 3-year-olds. Children who were 3 years of age appeared to rely more on verbal modes of expression rather than aggressive behavior in order to influence their peers. This fact is consistent with the idea that the nonverbal behavior (aggression) may have been ontogenetically related to subsequent verbal expression. Specifically, the verbal mode of communication replaced the more primitive nonverbal mode. Again, the literature on behavior problems in normal children is congruent with a communication hypothesis.

RELATED RESEARCH IN DEVELOPMENTAL DISABILITIES

The notion that nonverbal behavior may have communicative functions has been extended to developmentally disabled children. In particular, behavior problems such as tantrums and persistent crying are sometimes described as protoimperatives, that is, behaviors that function to recruit adult assistance in order to obtain a desired object or activity (Kanner, 1943; Reichle & Yoder, 1979; Schaeffer, 1978). Other nonverbal behaviors are described as serving a protest function, enabling children to escape, for example, from having to eat undesired foods or participate in instructional routines. In the case of mentally retarded children, a variety of nonverbal behaviors have been observed to function as protodeclaratives, effectively eliciting adult attention (Schaeffer, 1978). In short, investigators have begun to view many nonverbal behaviors, including those that are problematic, as serving social–communicative functions.

If behavior problems are social–communicative in nature, then one would anticipate that intervention programs stressing broad communication training could have the effect of replacing behavior problems. Specifically, a communication hypothesis would predict that as a child acquires more sophisticated and effective means of communication (e.g., speech or sign language), primitive communicative responses (e.g., behavior problems) should decline. The literature in developmental disabilities by and large supports this prediction. For example, consider a study by Casey (1978). This investigator trained the parents of four autistic children to reinforce spontaneous sign language. Following intervention, communicative signing increased and, most importantly, behavior problems, including tantrums, aggression, and self-injury, decreased. These findings, namely, the inverse relationship between the training of communicative signs and the frequency of tantrums have been noted in other studies as well (Ellsworth, 1975; Rowe & Rapp, 1980).

The literature on normal children already reviewed suggested that increases in communicative competence are correlated with decreases in a variety of behavior problems. The same correlations have been found in the case of developmentally disabled children. Talkington, Hall, and Altman

(1971) compared matched groups of noncommunicating and communicating retarded individuals with respect to several measures of aggression. The noncommunicating group received substantially higher aggression ratings. The authors speculated that the noncommunicating individuals had no verbal means of eliciting adult attention in frustrating situations and therefore resorted to nonverbal behavior, particularly aggression, as a way of attracting attention. In contrast, the communicating clients had verbal skills that presumably provided a nonaggressive means for eliciting attention. Therefore, aggression was infrequent in this group. Similar findings have been obtained with respect to self-injury. Shodell and Reiter (1968), for example, found that self-injury was more frequent for nonverbal autistic children. They hypothesized that children who lack verbal skills exhibit self-injury for communicative purposes. Therefore, they suggested that the development of verbal communicative skills could lead to reductions in self-injurious behavior.

The results of the studies reviewed are consistent with a communication hypothesis. For several reasons, however, they do not constitute strong tests of such an hypothesis. First, the observations made in several of the studies (Ellsworth, 1975; Rowe & Rapp, 1980) were anecdotal. Second, the data presented in other studies (Shodell & Reiter, 1968; Talkington et al., 1971) were purely correlational, leaving open the possibility that the observed relationships between behavior problems and communicative competence was in fact due to a third (extraneous) variable. Finally, in the study in which communicative skill was experimentally manipulated (Casey, 1978), the manipulation was undertaken in the context of a multifaceted intervention program that stressed the development of many different kinds of language activity. Because of the complex nature of the intervention, it was not possible to determine which aspect of the intervention was responsible for the decrease in behavior problems. Notwithstanding these limitations, the literature we have reviewed is suggestive enough to warrant a more direct experimental test of the communication hypothesis. We outline one such test in what follows.

DIFFERENTIAL REINFORCEMENT OF COMMUNICATIVE BEHAVIOR (DRC)

An appropriate test of a communication hypothesis involves two elements. First, it is necessary to perform an assessment of the social function of the behavior problem. Second, it is necessary to teach the child a communicative response that is functionally equivalent to the behavior problem. If the hypothesis has merit, one should see a decrease in the frequency of the behavior problem when functionally equivalent responses are taught but no decrease when functionally nonequivalent responses are taught. This logic forms the basis of our current research program (Carr & Durand, 1983; Durand & Carr, 1982a), a portion of which is described next.

We examined behavior problems in the context of an instructional situation. There are good reasons for doing so. First, systematic instruction offers the best hope for treatment gains. Second, behavior problems often disrupt systematic instruction thereby minimizing treatment gains. As noted above, two broad classes of motivating factors are particularly salient in the control of disruptive behavior: escape and attention. We constructed our assessment procedures with this fact in mind.

We worked with a number of autistic, retarded, and schizophrenic children, all of whom displayed various combinations of self-injury, tantrums, and aggression. In order to assess for escape-motivated problems, we manipulated the level of difficulty of the instructional tasks. Difficult tasks were selected so as to generate only 25% correct responding. Easy tasks were selected that generated 100% correct responding. In order to assess for attention-motivated problems, we manipulated the level of adult attention. In the low attention situation, the adult spent most of the session teaching other children and attended to the target child only 33% of the time. In the high attention situation, the adult spent all of the session interacting directly with the target child; that is, the child was attended to 100% of the time. This type of assessment produced several replicable patterns of disruptive behavior. Generally, all children were well behaved when adults provided them with high attention and easy tasks. Some children were disruptive only when confronted with low adult attention (i.e., attention pattern). Others were disruptive only when confronted with difficult tasks (i.e., escape pattern). A few were disruptive when confronted with either difficult tasks or low adult attention.

A communication hypothesis implies a specific treatment, namely, that children should be provided with an alternative communicative response that serves the same social function as the behavior problem. Thus, escape-motivated behavior could plausibly be dealt with by teaching the child to emit a verbal response such as "Help me" or "I don't understand" whenever confronted with a difficult task. This response should elicit teacher assistance thereby decreasing task difficulty and consequent failure. Research reviewed earlier suggests that procedures that produce decreases in task difficulty minimize escape responding. Attention-seeking behavior could plausibly be dealt with by teaching the child to emit a verbal response such as, "Am I doing good work?" whenever confronted with low rates of teacher attention. This response should elicit teacher attention thereby altering the stimulus situation (i.e., low attention) responsible for disruptive behavior. Our data, based on a sample of seven children, show that behav-

ior problems can be reduced to negligible levels following the training
procedure just outlined. Since the procedure involves reinforcing specific
communicative acts, we refer to it as the differential reinforcement of communicative behavior, or DRC.

Our analysis includes a control procedure that is very important from a
theoretical perspective. Specifically, we also examined the effects of training
communicative responses that were not functionally equivalent to the behavior problems. That is, children exhibiting escape behavior were also
taught (in a separate condition) the attention-seeking phrase, and children
exhibiting attention-seeking behavior were also taught the escape phrase.
During conditions in which children emitted communicative responses that
were functionally nonequivalent to the behavior problems, such problems
remained frequent. In other words, suppression of behavior problems following communication training occurred only if the communicative acts
that were trained were functionally equivalent to the problem behavior.
This fact emphasizes the extreme importance of performing a functional
analysis of the social motivation of behavior problems before implementing
a DRC-type intervention. The necessity for functional equivalence is consistent with and directly supports a communication hypothesis of behavior
problems.

RECONCEPTUALIZING CHILDREN'S BEHAVIOR
PROBLEMS: FORM AND FUNCTION

A major part of child behavior therapy has been concerned with the
question: "How shall we eliminate aberrant behavior?" When one labels a
behavior as aberrant, bizarre, psychotic, or maladaptive, one's inclination
is to suppress the behavior. This attitude reflects itself in the treatment
literature that is dominated by descriptions of decelerative techniques. Of
course, it is true that many behavior problems are so severe that they pose a
threat to others or to the target children themselves. Therefore, we are often
forced, in the short term, to use techniques that are designed solely to
decelerate behavior problems. A number of these techniques were discussed
earlier in this chapter. These measures, however, should be viewed as temporary emergency procedures only.

Ultimately, we must consider the possibility that the long-term treatment
of behavior problems may require a conceptualization that differs from the
current view that behavior problems are aberrant and maladaptive. Our
discussion above suggests that in many instances behavior problems may be
usefully reconceptualized as communicative. That is, we are proposing that

these behaviors be viewed as adaptive and functional. Specifically, they help children whose communicative skills are poor to influence important aspects of the social situation.

If behavior problems are adaptive and functional, why then are they labeled as problems? We would suggest that the difficulty lies in a discrepancy between form and function. Specifically, adults do not accept certain behavior forms such as aggression, tantrums, and self-injury, as appropriate means for eliciting attention or assistance. Children are expected to ask (verbally) for these adult-mediated events. In other words, what is wrong with behavior problems is their form. Their function (i.e., social communication) is fine. Seen in this light, the central task of intervention agents must be to preserve the communicative functions inherent in behavior problems by instating new socially appropriate forms that are functionally equivalent to the undesirable behaviors (Carr, 1982b, in press; Carr & Lovaas, 1982; Donnellan, Mirenda, Mesaros, & Fassbender, 1983; Durand, 1982; Neel, Billingsley, McCarty, Symonds, Lambert, Lewis-Smith, & Hanashiro, 1983; Voeltz & Evans, 1983). Our job is clearly not to eliminate all attempts to communicate by routinely suppressing every behavior problem without asking what social function such behavior may serve for the individual.

The procedure that we have referred to as DRC represents one means for replacing behavior problems with socially appropriate forms serving the same function as the problem behavior. Since there are a multitude of reasons why a child might solicit assistance or attention from adults, the DRC procedure can constitute an important strategy for enhancing the communicative repertoires of children who frequently exhibit behavior problems. That is, a child could be taught a large number of communicative phrases to deal with various social situations.

What we are proposing is a linkage between communicative development and the remediation of behavior problems. Currently, the field is divided into two frequently nonoverlapping groups of treatment specialists. There are educators whose major role is to facilitate the development of social and communicative skills, and there are clinical psychologists whose major role has been to manage crises, particularly those involving severe behavior problems. This division is artificial and potentially nonproductive. We (psychologists) must stop defining ourselves solely as crisis managers and, instead, view ourselves primarily as educators. The long-term successful remediation of behavior problems may best be pursued via an attempt to combine the technology of behavior modification with the conceptual framework of developmental psychology. This synthesis can be a useful treatment heuristic as well as a means for theoretical integration.

Acknowledgment

We would like to thank June Lindquist for her helpful comments on earlier drafts of this manuscript.

References

Azrin, N. H., Hake, D. F., Holz, W. C., & Hutchinson, R. R. (1965). Motivational aspects of escape from punishment. *Journal of the Experimental Analysis of Behavior, 8,* 31–44.

Bates, E. (1976). *Language and context.* New York: Academic Press.

Bates, E., Benigni, L., Bretherton, I., Camaioni, L., & Volterra, V. (1977). From gesture to the first word: On cognitive and social prerequisites. In M. Lewis and L. Rosenbaum (Eds.) *Conversation and the development of language* (pp. 247–307). New York: Wiley.

Bates, E., Camaioni, L., & Volterra, V. (1975). The acquisition of performatives prior to speech. *Merrill-Palmer Quarterly, 21,* 205–226.

Bell, S. M., & Ainsworth, M. D. S. (1972). Infant crying and maternal responsiveness. *Child Development, 43,* 1171–1190.

Brown, P., & Elliott, R. (1965). Control of aggression in a nursery school class. *Journal of Experimental Child Psychology, 2,* 103–107.

Brownlee, J. R., & Bakeman, R. (1981). Hitting in toddler-peer interaction. *Child Development, 52,* 1076–1079.

Bruner, J. (1979). Learning how to do things with words. In D. Aaronson and R. W. Reiber (Eds.), *Psycholinguistic Research* (pp. 265–284). Hillsdale, NJ: Lawrence Erlbaum.

Bucher, B., & Lovaas, O. I. (1968). Use of aversive stimulation in behavior modification. In M. R. Jones (Ed.), *Miami symposium on the prediction of behavior, 1967: Aversive stimulation* (pp. 77–145). Coral Gables, FL: University of Miami Press.

Carr, E. G. (1977). The motivation of self-injurious behavior: A review of some hypotheses. *Psychological Bulletin, 84,* 800–816.

Carr, E. G. (1979). Teaching autistic children to use sign language: Some research issues. *Journal of Autism and Developmental Disorders, 9,* 345–359.

Carr, E. G. (1982a). *How to teach sign language to developmentally disabled children.* Lawrence, KS: H & H Enterprises.

Carr, E. G. (1982b). Sign language. In R. L. Koegel, A. Rincover, and A. L. Egel (Eds.), *Educating and understanding autistic children* (pp. 142–157). San Diego: College Hill Press.

Carr, E. G. (in press). Behavioral approaches to language and communication. In E. Schopler and G. Mesibov (Eds.), *Current issues in autism: Volume 3. Communication problems in autism.* New York: Plenum.

Carr, E. G., & Durand, V. M. (1983, August). *The application of pragmatics to the conceptualization and treatment of severe behavior problems in children.* Invited address presented at the meeting of the American Psychological Association, Anaheim, CA.

Carr, E. G., & Lovaas, O. I. (1982). Contingent electric shock as a treatment for severe behavior problems. In S. Axelrod and J. Apsche (Eds.), *Punishment: Its effects on human behavior* (pp. 221–245). New York: Academic Press.

Carr, E. G., & McDowell, J. J. (1980). Social control of self-injurious behavior of organic etiology. *Behavior Therapy, 11,* 402–409.

Carr, E. G., & Newsom, C. D. (in press). Demand-related tantrums: Conceptualization and treatment. *Behavior Modification.*

Carr, E. G., Newsom, C. D., & Binkoff, J. A. (1976). Stimulus control of self-destructive behavior in a psychotic child. *Journal of Abnormal Child Psychology, 4,* 139–153.

Carr, E. G., Newsom, C. D., & Binkoff, J. A. (1980). Escape as a factor in the aggressive behavior of two retarded children. *Journal of Applied Behavior Analysis, 13,* 101–117.

Carr, E. G., Newsom, C. D., Binkoff, J. A., & Killion, J. (1976, August). Stimulus variables involved in the control of self-destructive behavior. In T. R. Risley (Chair), *Current behavioral research with autistic children.* Symposium conducted at the meeting of the American Psychological Association, Washington, DC.

Casey, L. O. (1978). Development of communicative behavior in autistic children: A parent program using manual signs. *Journal of Autism and Childhood Schizophrenia, 8,* 45–59.

Catania, A. C. (Ed.). (1968). *Contemporary research in operant behavior.* Glenview, IL: Scott, Foresman.

Center, D. B., Deitz, S. M., & Kaufman, M. E. (1982). Student ability, task difficulty, and inappropriate classroom behavior. *Behavior Modification, 6,* 355–374.

Churchill, D. W. (1971). Effects of success and failure in psychotic children. *Archives of General Psychiatry, 25,* 208–214.

Clark, H. B., Rowbury, T., Baer, A. M., & Baer, D. M. (1973). Timeout as a punishing stimulus in continuous and intermittent schedules. *Journal of Applied Behavior Analysis, 6,* 443–455.

Corte, H. E., Wolf, M. M., & Locke, B. J. (1971). A comparison of procedures for eliminating self-injurious behavior of retarded adolescents. *Journal of Applied Behavior Analysis, 4,* 201–213.

Creer, T. L., Weinberg, E., & Molk, L. (1974). Managing a hospital behavior problem: Malingering. *Journal of Behavior Therapy and Experimental Psychiatry, 5,* 259–262.

Donnellan, A. M., Mirenda, P. L., Mesaros, R. A., & Fassbender, L. L. (1983, November). *A strategy for analyzing the communicative functions of behavior.* Paper presented at the meeting of The Association for the Severely Handicapped, San Francisco.

Durand, V. M. (1982). Analysis and intervention of self-injurious behavior. *Journal of the Association of the Severely Handicapped, 7,* 44–53.

Durand, V. M., & Carr, E. G. (1982a, August). Differential reinforcement of communicative behavior. In R. L. Koegel (Chair), *Research on clinical intervention with autistic and psychotic children.* Symposium conducted at the meeting of the American Psychological Association, Washington, DC.

Durand, V. M., & Carr, E. G. (1982b, November). *Contextual determinants of disruptive behavior.* Paper presented at the meeting of the Association for Advancement of Behavior Therapy, Los Angeles, CA.

Durand, V. M., & Carr, E. G. (1983, August). *The functional significance of "self-stimulatory" behavior.* Paper presented at the meeting of the American Psychological Association, Anaheim, CA.

Ellsworth, S. (1975). If only Jimmy could speak. *Hearing and Speech Action, 43*(6), 6–10.

Favell, J. E., McGimsey, J. F., & Jones, M. L. (1978). The use of physical restraint in the treatment of self-injury and as positive reinforcement. *Journal of Applied Behavior Analysis, 11,* 225–241.

Forehand, R. L., & McMahon, R. J. (1981). *Helping the noncompliant child.* New York: Guilford.

Foxx, R. M., & Bechtel, D. R. (1983). Overcorrection: A review and analysis. In S. Axelrod and J. Apsche (Eds.), *Punishment: Its effects on human behavior* (pp. 133–220). New York: Academic Press.

Haley, J. (1963). *Strategies of psychotherapy.* New York: Grune & Stratton.

Halliday, M. A. K. (1975). *Learning how to mean: Explorations in the development of language.* London: Edward Arnold.

Hamilton, J., Stephens, L., & Allen, P. (1967). Controlling aggressive and destructive behavior in severely retarded institutionalized residents. *American Journal of Mental Deficiency,* *71,* 852–856.

Harris, S. L., & Ersner-Hershfield, R. (1978). Behavioral suppression of seriously disruptive behavior in psychotic and retarded patients: A review of punishment and its alternatives. *Psychological Bulletin, 85,* 1352–1375.

Hart, B. (1980). Pragmatics and language development. In B. B. Lahey and A. E. Kazdin (Eds.), *Advances in clinical child psychology, Volume 3* (pp. 383–427). New York: Plenum.

Hawkins, R. P., Peterson, R. F., Schweid, E., & Bijou, S. W. (1966). Amelioration of problem parent-child relations with the parent in a therapeutic role. *Journal of Experimental Child Psychology, 4,* 99–107.

Hineline, P. H., & Rachlin, H. (1969). Notes on fixed-ratio and fixed-interval escape responding in the pigeon. *Journal of the Experimental Analysis of Behavior, 12,* 397–401.

Iwata, B. A., Dorsey, M. F., Slifer, K. J., Bauman, K. E., & Richman, G. S. (1982). Toward a functional analysis of self-injury. *Analysis and Intervention in Developmental Disabilities, 2,* 3–20.

Jones, F. H., Simmons, J. Q., & Frankel, F. (1974). An extinction procedure for eliminating self-destructive behavior in a 9-year-old autistic girl. *Journal of Autism and Childhood Schizophrenia, 4,* 241–250.

Kanner, L. (1943). Autistic disturbances of affective contact. *Nervous Child, 2,* 217–250.

Lovaas, O. I. (1981). *Teaching developmentally disabled children.* Baltimore: University Park Press.

Lovaas, O. I., Freitag, G., Gold, V. J., & Kassorla, I. C. (1965). Experimental studies in childhood schizophrenia: Analysis of self-destructive behavior. *Journal of Experimental Child Psychology, 2,* 67–84.

Lovaas, O. I., & Simmons, J. Q. (1969). Manipulation of self-destruction in three retarded children. *Journal of Applied Behavior Analysis, 2,* 143–157.

Martin, P. L., & Foxx, R. M. (1973). Victim control of the aggression of an institutionalized retardate. *Journal of Behavior Therapy and Experimental Psychiatry, 4,* 161–165.

Minuchin, S. (1974). *Families and family therapy.* Cambridge, MA: Harvard University Press.

Mowrer, O. H. (1960). *Learning theory and behavior.* New York: John Wiley.

Neel, R. S., Billingsley, F. F., McCarty, F., Symonds, D., Lambert, C., Lewis-Smith, N., & Hanashiro, R. (1983). *Innovative model program for autistic children and their teachers.* Unpublished manuscript, University of Washington, Seattle.

Patterson, G. R. (1980). Mothers: The unacknowledged victims. *Monographs of the Society for Research in Child Development, 45* (5, Whole No. 186).

Patterson, G. R. (1982). *Coercive family process.* Eugene, OR: Castalia.

Patterson, G. R., & Cobb, J. A. (1971). A dyadic analysis of "aggressive" behaviors: An additional step toward a theory of aggression. In J. P. Hill (Ed.), *Minnesota symposia on child psychology: Vol. 5.* Minneapolis: University of Minnesota Press.

Patterson, G. R., Littman, R. A., & Bricker, W. (1967). Assertive behavior in children: A step toward a theory of aggression. *Monographs of the Society for Research in Child Development, 32* (5, Whole No. 113).

Pinkston, E. M., Reese, N. H., LeBlanc, J. M. & Baer, D. M. (1973). Independent control of a preschool child's aggression and peer interaction by contingent teacher attention. *Journal of Applied Behavior Analysis, 6,* 115–124.

Plato, (1960). *The laws* (A. E. Taylor, Trans.). London: J. M. Dent. (Original work published circa 348 BC).

Plummer, S., Baer, D. M., & LeBlanc, J. M. (1977). Functional considerations in the use of procedural timeout and an effective alternative. *Journal of Applied Behavior Analysis, 10,* 689–706.

Reichle, J. E., & Yoder, D. E. (1979). Assessment and early stimulation of communication in the severely and profoundly mentally retarded. In R. L. York and E. Edgar (Eds.), *Teaching the severely handicapped. Volume 4* (pp. 180–218). Seattle: American Association for the Education of the Severely/Profoundly Handicapped.

Richer, J. (1978). The partial noncommunication of culture to autistic children—An application of human ethology. In M. Rutter and E. Schopler (Eds.), *Autism—A reappraisal of concepts and treatment* (pp. 47–61). New York: Plenum.

Richer, J. (1981). *Development of social avoidance in autistic children.* Paper presented at the International Human Ethology Workshop: The Behaviour of Human Infants, Erice, Italy.

Risley, T. R. (1968). The effects and side effects of punishment with an autistic child. *Journal of Applied Behavior Analysis, 1,* 21–34.

Romanczyk, R. G., Colletti, G., & Plotkin, R. (1980). Punishment of self-injurious behavior: Issues of behavior analysis, generalization and the right to treatment. *Child Behavior Therapy, 2,* 37–54.

Romanczyk, R. G., & Goren, E. R. (1975). Severe self-injurious behavior: The problem of clinical control. *Journal of Consulting and Clinical Psychology, 43,* 730–739.

Ross, D. M., & Ross, S. A. (1976). *Hyperactivity: Research, theory, action.* New York: Wiley.

Rousseau, J. J. (1979). *Émile* (A. Bloom, Trans.). New York: Basic Books. (Original work published 1762).

Rowe, J. A., & Rapp, D. L. (1980). Tantrums: Remediation through communication. *Child Care, Health, and Development, 6,* 197–208.

Sailor, W., Guess, D., Rutherford, G., & Baer, D. M. (1968). Control of tantrum behavior by operant techniques during experimental verbal training. *Journal of Applied Behavior Analysis, 1,* 237–243.

Satir, V. (1967). *Conjoint family therapy.* Palo Alto, CA: Science and Behavior Books.

Schaeffer, B. (1978). Teaching spontaneous sign language to nonverbal children: Theory and method. *Sign Language Studies, 21,* 317–352.

Shodell, M. J., & Reiter, H. H. (1968). Self-mutilative behavior in verbal and nonverbal schizophrenic children. *Archives of General Psychiatry, 19,* 453–455.

Skinner, B. F. (1957). *Verbal behavior.* New York: Appelton-Century-Crofts.

Solnick, J. V., Rincover, A., & Peterson, C. R. (1977). Some determinants of the reinforcing and punishing effects of timeout. *Journal of Applied Behavior Analysis, 10,* 415–424.

Talkington, L. W., Hall, S., & Altman, R. (1971). Communication deficits and aggression in the mentally retarded. *American Journal of Mental Deficiency, 76,* 235–237.

Tate, B. G., & Baroff, G. S. (1966). Aversive control of self-injurious behavior in a psychotic boy. *Behaviour Research and Therapy, 4,* 281–287.

Voeltz, L. M., & Evans, I. M. (1983). Educational validity: Procedures to evaluate outcomes in programs for severely handicapped learners. *Journal of the Association for the Severely Handicapped, 8,* 3–15.

Wahler, R. G. (1967). Child-child interactions in free field settings: Some experimental analyses. *Journal of Experimental Child Psychology, 5,* 123–141.

Wahler, R. G. (1976). Deviant child behavior within the family: Developmental speculations and behavior change strategies. In H. Leitenberg (Ed.), *Handbook of behavior modification and behavior therapy* (pp. 516–543). Englewood Cliffs, NJ: Prentice-Hall.

Watzlawick, P., Beavin, J. H., & Jackson, D. D. (1967). *Pragmatics of human communication.* New York: W. W. Norton.

Weeks, M., & Gaylord-Ross, R. (1981). Task difficulty and aberrant behavior in severely handicapped students. *Journal of Applied Behavior Analysis, 14,* 449–463.

White, G. D., Nielsen, G., & Johnson, S. M. (1972). Timeout duration and the suppression of deviant behavior in children. *Journal of Applied Behavior Analysis, 5,* 111–120.

Williams, C. D. (1959). The elimination of tantrum behavior by extinction procedures. *Journal of Abnormal and Social Psychology, 59,* 269.

Wolf, M. M., Birnbrauer, J. S., Williams, T., & Lawler, J. (1965). A note on apparent extinction of the vomiting behavior of a retarded child. In L. Ullman and L. Krasner (Eds.), *Case studies in behavior modification* (pp. 364–366). New York: Holt, Rinehart, & Winston.

Wolf, M. M., Risley, T. R., & Mees, H. L. (1964). Application of operant conditioning procedures to the behavior problems of an autistic child. *Behaviour Research and Therapy, 1,* 305–312.

Wolff, P. H. (1969). The natural history of crying and other vocalizations in early infancy. In B. M. Foss (Ed.), *Determinants of infant behavior, Volume 4* (pp. 81–109). London: Methuen.

Zeilberger, J., Sampen, S. E., & Sloane, H. N., Jr. (1968). Modification of a child's behavior problems in the home with the mother as therapist. *Journal of Applied Behavior Analysis, 1,* 47–53.

The Relevance of Fundamental Research to Clinical Applications of Biofeedback

AUBREY J. YATES

Development of Clinical Behavior Therapy

During its developmental stage, behavior therapy was mainly conducted within academic settings, its protagonists were able to pick and choose among the problems they investigated, and relatively unlimited time was available to conduct what became known as "experimental investigations of the single case." In due course, as clinical training programs proliferated, behavior therapy became a professional lifestyle for many therapists and the clinical behavior therapist became as much a part of the therapeutic scenery as the psychoanalyst or psychodynamic psychologist.

On several occasions (Yates, 1975, Ch. 1, 1981, 1983) the question has been raised as to what clinical behavior therapists actually do in their clinical practice that unequivocally distinguishes them from other clinical psychologists and justifies their use of the term *clinical behavior therapist*. The answer to this question remains unclear as to date no adequate survey appears to have been conducted. The following account must therefore be regarded as somewhat speculative rather than based on hard evidence.

The Application of Clinical Behavior Therapy

However the therapist may prefer to advertise himself (whether behavior therapist, psychodynamic psychotherapist, or just clinical psychologist), several stages appear to be involved in dealing with a presenting client. Within the behavior therapy model, the first stage requires an evaluation of the nature of the client's problem. This has come to be termed *behavior analysis* and encompasses a very wide range of possible investigatory activities (Hersen & Bellack, 1981) leading to the selection of target behaviors for modification. Shapiro (1961a,b, 1966) suggested that this evaluation phase should consist not in the application of standardized tests to produce diagnostic labels but of an experimental investigation to determine precisely the nature of the difficulty that brought the client to seek help. The experimental investigation would involve the formulation of precise hypotheses that would be rigorously tested until the presenting difficulty was clearly understood. From this standpoint it was then a short step to the conclusion that the same approach could be utilized to change the maladaptive behaviors in such a way as to enable the client to cope with his situation. Behavior therapy thus was originally essentially a methodological prescription rather than the application of a theoretical model or of techniques of a standardized kind. It provided a unique way of approaching the task of elucidating the nature of the problem of the presenting client. In a very real sense, it provided an answer to the question posed earlier: What, if anything, clearly distinguishes a clinical behavior therapist from other therapists? In addition, it provided a unique way of evaluating the results of behavior therapy since, within this framework, the validity of behavior therapy would be determined not by whether the client was cured or even improved but rather by whether his behavior changed in a way that was predicted from operations derived from hypotheses that in turn resulted from the behavioral analysis.

The fact that behavior therapy was not derived from nor supportive of any particular theoretical model does not lead to the conclusion that the practice of behavior therapy does not involve the use of theory. Some forms of behavior therapy (e.g., strict Skinnerian operant conditioning) do tend to avoid the use of unobservable theoretical constructs, but this is certainly not true of the majority of behavior therapists. Thus Yates (1958) made use of Hull's constructs of $_sH_R$, D, I_R, and $_sI_R$ to derive a therapeutic approach to the treatment of multiple tics. The explicit use of theoretical constructs in clinical work is, however, relatively rare. More often, the clinician works within a set of assumptions that vary according to the nature of the presenting problem. These assumptions are often unspecified, and the clinician may even be unaware of them, yet they may influence profoundly the way in which he approaches the therapy of the presenting client. The use of such assumptions is nowhere more clearly evident than in the clinical application of biofeedback to psychophysiological (formerly termed "psychosomatic") problems such as headaches and asthma. Thus in the case of a client presenting with a complaint of tension headaches, if the clinician is guided by the assumption (based on his knowledge of the biofeedback literature) that tension headaches are associated with (caused by?) excessively high levels of frontalis muscle activity and that if the client can be helped to reduce the level of that activity there will be a reduction in the frequency and severity of the tension headaches, it is very likely he will institute a therapy program involving training the client, with the assistance of feedback, to reduce frontalis muscle activity and maintain it at a low level. However, the important point to note is that the assumption under which the therapy is instituted is usually not based on any empirical evidence collected by the clinician himself but rather arises from his knowledge of the research literature, or his clinical impressions of his own results.

If the assumption is, however, invalid, then it is likely that the frontalis muscle relaxation training will lead to inconsistent therapeutic results across a range of clients all bearing the same label (tension headaches); or it will work with some (or even all) of the clients bearing such a label but not for the reasons that would be valid if the assumptions were correct. In either case, of course, the therapeutic approach, if it is based on an assumption that is invalid, will be less effective than if it is based on a valid assumption.

I hope to show in this chapter how important it is that clinicians examine very carefully and try to be fully aware of the assumptions (both general and specific) underlying their clinical therapy decisions; that they should examine and keep updated their knowledge of the empirical evidence relating to those assumptions and be prepared to modify their approach if the assumptions are shown to be invalid; that they should endeavor, in the course of their clinical work, to collect hard evidence from the behavior of their own clients in therapy relating to the validity of the assumptions underlying the therapeutic approach being applied to a particular client; and that this evidence is best collected by the technique known as the "experimental investigation of the single case."

Four substantive areas (tension–migraine headaches, diabetes, asthma, and temporomandibular joint dysfunction syndrome) are used to illustrate the importance of identifying and testing the assumptions that appear to underly current clinical biofeedback therapy approaches to these problems. In some instances the assumptions have been clearly stated and tested, but in others the assumptions have been much less clearly stated and not tested at all. The significance of some recent work on an old problem area of general significance for clinical biofeedback work (the relationship between symptomatology and physiological patterns of responding) is also considered.

The Role of Assumptions in Clinical Biofeedback Therapy

TENSION HEADACHES, MIGRAINE HEADACHES, AND THE SPECIFICITY ASSUMPTION

Two conflicting assumptions appear to underly much of the research that has been applied to psychophysiological disorders, and these assumptions appear to have been adopted uncritically by clinical biofeedback therapists. These assumptions were first stated unequivocally by Yates (1975), who labeled them as the *specificity assumption* and the *generality assumption*. The *specificity assumption* implies that if a specific disorder (e.g., tension headache) is associated with (caused by?) a specific physiological dysfunction (e.g., elevated level of frontalis muscle activity), there will be a reduction in the severity of the disorder if the client is successfully trained by way of biofeedback to reduce and maintain at a low level the excessively high frontalis muscle activity. The *generality assumption* implies, however, that specific disorders have an underlying common factor, anxiety. Hence, any biofeedback technique that counteracts anxiety will have beneficial effects on the specific disorder. Thus the training need not be directed at a physiological system that is directly implicated in the specific disorder. The training may be directed at any specific physiological response system because generalization is expected to occur to all or most other physiological systems, producing general relaxation that is antagonistic to the anxiety underlying the specific disorder. This assumption underlies a very wide range of biofeedback approaches to specific disorders. As a direct comparison with the specificity assumption, frontalis muscle relaxation training has been used in the biofeedback therapy of such diverse disorders as alcoholism (e.g., Steffen, 1975), diabetes (Fowler, Budzynski, & VandenBergh, 1976), asthma (e.g., Davis, Saunders, Creer, & Chai, 1973), and general anxiety (e.g., Lavallée, Lamontagne, Pinard, Annable, & Tétreault, 1977).

The history of biofeedback-oriented research into tension and migraine headaches is an object lesson in the pervading influence of assumptions that are unspecified and often unrecognized in clinical therapy of these disorders. As pointed out already, the assumption underlying the biofeedback therapy of tension headaches was that these headaches are uniquely defined by (and possibly caused by) excessive levels of frontalis muscle activity. On the other hand, the assumption underlying the biofeedback therapy of migraine headaches was that these headaches are uniquely defined by (and possibly

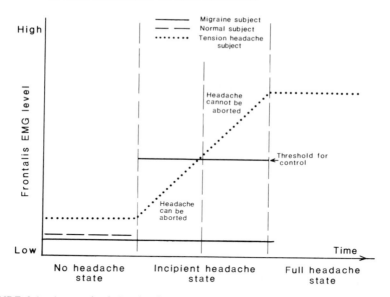

FIGURE 9.1 Assumed relationship between frontalis EMG levels and onset of a tension headache.

caused by) excessive dilation of the superficial temporal artery. In the one case, an abnormality of muscle function was implicated; in the other, an abnormality of blood flow. The most important point, however, relates to the consequent assumption that training in frontalis muscle activity reduction is an appropriate therapy for tension headaches but not for migraine headaches, whereas training in voluntary control of blood volume and flow (originally, warming of the fingers; more recently, direct control of blood flow in the temporal artery) is an appropriate therapy for migraine headaches but not for tension headaches. On the basis of these assumptions, it was believed by clinicians that specific and different therapies for tension and migraine headaches were necessary. The validity of these assumptions is now examined in more detail.

Figure 9.1 shows the expectations generated by the specificity assumption for changes in frontalis muscle levels in tension and migraine headache clients as either kind of headache develops from a no–headache starting point. It has been assumed in the figure that the resting no–headache levels of tension headache clients will be higher than the levels of migraine headache clients or normal control subjects. As tension headache clients develop a headache, the prediction is that frontalis muscle activity levels will increase and become maximal when the tension headache is at its worst (i.e., there will be a correlation between subjective reports of variations in severity of headache and frontalis muscle activity levels). As migraine headache clients develop a headache, on the other hand, no such elevation of levels of frontalis muscle activity should occur. Although not shown graphically in Figure 9.1, a fall in frontalis muscle activity levels should parallel subjective reports of a reduction of the severity of a tension headache episode—but this should not occur, of course, in the case of migraine headaches. A similar correspondence should be found in subjects who have occasional tension headaches but who are not regarded as having a clinical condition. It is interesting to note that the common alternative term for tension headaches is "muscular contraction headaches."

These expectations, based on the specificity model, were clearly spelled out in detail by Philips (1978), who also examined the evidence relating to them. Of the seven expectations derived from the specificity assumption that she detailed, not one received unequivocal support from her own experiments. It is not necessary here to review in detail the empirical literature relating to these assumptions and the expectations arising from them, since many comprehensive reviews are available (e.g., Andrasik, Blanchard, Arena, Saunders, & Barron, 1982; Andrasik & Holroyd, 1980; Blanchard & Andrasik, 1982; Blanchard, Andrasik, Ahles, Teders, & O'Keefe, 1980; Reading, 1982a,b, to list but a few). Suffice it to point out that the most critical expectation of all (that high levels of frontalis muscle activity will be found in tension headache but not in migraine headache clients) has received little or no support (e.g., Bakal & Kaganov, 1977). Indeed the evidence suggests that both in the headache-free and the headache state, levels of frontalis muscle activity in migraine clients are as high if not higher than the levels found in tension headache clients. One possible implication of these findings is that tension headache and migraine clients differ mainly on a dimension of severity with additional symptoms being manifested as severity increases, migraine being regarded as the more severe form of tension headache (but it should be noted that this conclusion has itself to be regarded as an assumption that unless properly verified, may trigger off clinical procedures that in due course will be found to be invalid).

A number of additional comments are warranted. Even if the expected relationships between report of a tension headache episode and frontalis muscle activity levels had been found (and migraine clients had significantly lower levels), the training procedures commonly followed would not necessarily have been the most logical ones. As Philips (1978) pointed out, since the training involves relaxation of the frontalis muscle and since such training usually takes place when the client is not experiencing a tension headache, the procedure only makes sense on the assumption that in the resting no-tension-headache state the client will have elevated levels of frontalis muscle activity. But reference to Figure 9.1 shows that even this rationale does not necessarily lead to the conclusion that the appropriate training is relaxation training unless further assumptions are invoked. The model in Figure 9.1 assumes that a threshold is involved below which a developing tension headache can be aborted but above which it cannot (in much the same way that an epileptic attack may be inevitable once a threshold of brain excitation is passed). The critical period therefore would lie in the time preceding the achievement of the threshold, and the most important training could well involve the ability of the client to detect increases in level of frontalis muscle activity rather than decreases (which it is assumed training in reduction of activity would achieve). Thus in order to train the client in this ability it might be desirable not just to institute relaxation training but to train him to achieve complete control of all aspects of frontalis muscle activity. A program of such training might involve trials in which the client is required to increase level of frontalis muscle activity to various specified levels, to hold the activity level for specified periods of time, and only then to relax the muscle. In this way the client would achieve more sophisticated control over all aspects of the activity of the frontalis muscle but in particular would be able to detect increases of activity before the critical threshold was passed and thus abort an attack by then applying appropriate relaxation procedures. This point remains generally valid even though it is irrelevant now to the therapy of tension headaches because the more general assumption has been so severely undermined.

It is not necessary to pursue here in any detail the similar events that have undermined the biofeedback therapy of migraine headaches. The assumption underlying the therapy of tension headaches had some degree of plausibility; that underlying the therapy of migraine headaches had very little, being based upon a casual observation and an extraordinarily implausible hydraulic model of blood flow as if increasing blood flow in the periphery (finger) would reduce blood flow in the superficial temporal artery. Furthermore, the assumption ignored the crucial fact that in many migraine headaches a two-stage process is involved. In the first stage, vasoconstriction occurs in the superficial temporal artery, associated with the prodromal symptoms of migraine (the visual symptoms). This is succeeded by vasodilation, a massive rebound effect that produces the headache pain. But if the underlying hydraulic assumption were true (which, fortunately, it is not), then application of the finger-warming technique should exacerbate the headache if it is applied during the prodromal (vasoconstriction) phase, since it would increase vasoconstriction in the superficial temporal artery. The finger-warming procedure should only be applied when the second (dilation) phase has started. Yet in all of the clinical reports on the use of finger-warming training for migraine headaches, no consideration has been given to this crucial distinction.

DIABETES AND BLOOD GLUCOSE LEVELS
UNDER STRESS

Since diabetes mellitus is a disorder involving the danger of hyperglyce-
mia, the control of blood glucose levels (BGL) is of great importance and
may be achieved by control of diet or insulin administration. However, it is
generally accepted that medical control of diabetes may be affected to a
significant degree by stress factors. For example, control of diabetes may be
readily achieved within a hospital setting by a combination of diet and
insulin regimen. While the dietary and insulin regimen may be adequate to
control the illness outside the hospital setting, failures of maintenance of
control occur in some patients in spite of evidence that they are carefully
following the prescribed regimen. The possibility thus arises that real-life
stress factors (within the family situation, at work, and so on) may from
time to time override the dietary–insulin control, leading to adverse physiological consequences. The development of portable BGL measurement instruments and the importance of maintaining stable levels of BGL within
the normal range have led to diabetics purchasing such machines and monitoring their BGLs once or twice a day. One assumption underlying such
activities is that if the effects of stress are measurable, steps could be taken to
deal with the stress and eliminate it as a disturbing factor in BGL maintenance.

The effect of stress on BGL is, however, by no means clear. Some studies
have concluded that stress increases BGL (e.g., Baker, Barcai, Kaye, &
Haque, 1969; Koch & Molnar, 1974), but others have concluded that stress
decreases BGL (e.g., Hinkle & Wolf, 1952; VandenBergh, Sussman, &
Titus, 1966; VandenBergh, Sussman, & Vaughn, 1967). However, a serious
criticism of most studies of the relationship between stress and BGL is the
failure to distinguish adequately between BGLs in baseline and in stress
conditions. In most studies relating BGLs to stress, only a very short baseline is run before the stress task is introduced. If, however, an unfamiliar
baseline condition is more stressful to a diabetic than to a nondiabetic, then
the apparent greater change in the diabetic under stress may simply be a
residue of the general response to a stressful unfamiliar situation and not a
specific response to the stress task at all. Of equal importance would be a
careful examination of the relationship between the supposed objective indi-
cator of response to a stressful situation (BGL) and subjective estimates of
stress level (SESL) taken during baseline, stress, and post-stress stages
(though this relationship will not be considered here).

Figure 9.2 shows the results obtained with a single diabetic patient. Three
45-minute baseline sessions were run on successive days in as objectively
low stress a situation as it was possible to devise. BGL readings were taken

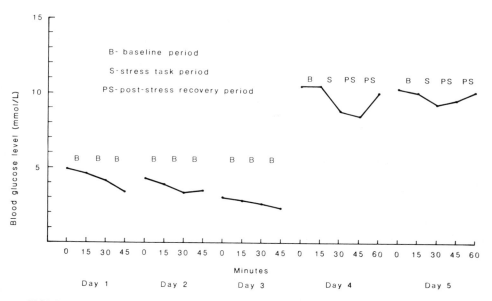

FIGURE 9.2   Blood glucose levels in diabetic subject during three baseline and two stress task levels.

at the start of the baseline and then at 15-minute intervals. On the following 2 days each session consisted of a 15-minute baseline, a 15-minute cognitive stress task, and two 15-minute post-stress recovery baseline periods. BGL readings were taken at the start and end of the baseline (the latter being the start of the stress period), at the end of the stress period (which also served as the start of the post-stress periods), and at the end of the first and second post-stress periods. The stress task consisted of a digit–symbol substitution task in which the patient had to complete one operation every 2 s with a metronome set at that rate.

Consider first the three baseline sessions. A progressively decreasing BGL is apparent both within each session and across sessions. How can these data be interpreted? Normal BGL levels fall between about 3 and 8 mmol/L, so the patient's level appears "normal" at the start of the first session. But the consistent fall within each session and the decrease from the start of one session to the next suggest that this objectively low stress situation, being unfamiliar to the patient, was in fact stressful initially but was less so on Days 2 and 3. The implication therefore is that the starting level of 4.9 mmol/L on Day 1 was the result of an increase in BGL due to stress and that the level at the end of Day 3 (2.3 mmol/L) represented the patient's normal non-stress BGL level. Thus the data indicate clearly the importance of taking significantly long and repeated low-stress baseline sessions prior to evaluating the effects of stress. The results also suggest that the effect of stress for this diabetic is to increase BGL. (It should be remembered, of course, that the "natural" non-stress BGL in this patient is an insulin–diet controlled level and that the "natural" level in the absence of such control would probably be many times higher. It should also be pointed out that in all sessions, close control was exercised over time of testing in relation to time and calorie content of meals and time of last insulin injection.)

Turning to the two stress sessions, it will be immediately evident that an unexpected result has been obtained. The main purpose of the three baseline sessions was to ensure that, on the stress days, any general stress effects would by then have been minimized, and it was expected that the 15-minute baseline on Day 4 would therefore be at roughly the same level as the final level on Day 3 (i.e., about 2.5 mmol/L). In fact, however, the starting baseline level on Day 4 was 10.5 mmol/L (as it was on Day 5 as well). How is this discrepancy to be explained? It turns out that by the end of Day 3 the patient's BGL had dropped so low that he was in some danger of becoming severely hypoglycemic, and indeed he reported that he was well aware of this. As a consequence, he significantly reduced his insulin dosage with the direct consequence of a significant rise (indeed, probably an overshoot) of his BGL in the baseline sessions on Days 4 and 5. In spite of this uncontrollable event, the effects of the introduction of stress are clear-cut. A significant decrease in BGL occurred during the stress period; this was maintained for some time into the post-stress recovery period, but a significant degree of recovery occurred during the later stage of the recovery period. The pattern of BGL on Day 5 parallels that on Day 4 with an indication that less stress is experienced on Day 5 because the patient is now more familiar with the stress task and better able to cope with it.

Thus the results obtained across the 3 baseline and 2 stress days appear reliable and make sense; the stress results are not invalidated by the perturbation produced by the change in insulin dose. However, it is obvious that a major problem arises from these data. The baseline data suggest that the response to stress is an increase in BGL whereas the stress data suggest that the response to stress is a decrease in BGL. The point to be made by this illustrative example is that the discrepancy is not a matter for despair but for further systematic investigation along the lines advocated by Shapiro (1961a,b, 1966) in his delineation of the "experimental investigation of the single case." The basic question that needs to be answered is: Why did the baseline general stress apparently lead to an increase in BGL but the specific stress task apparently lead to a decrease in BGL? Several hypotheses can be put forward to account for the conflicting results. It has been suggested

(Bradley, 1982) that if stress is imposed when the patient's BGL is high, it will go higher (and if imposed when BGL is low, it will decrease). The results in Figure 9.2 do not support such an explanation. Another possibility is that general stress (apprehension, uncertainty about what is going to happen) will produce increases in BGL, whereas a specific stress task will produce decreases. Yet another possibility is that whether stress increases or decreases, BGL depends on whether the stress is introduced suddenly or builds up gradually. Within the present frame of reference, all of these possibilities can be systematically investigated by the clinician with the single presenting patient. It should be pointed out also that with the use of the portable BGL equipment the data shown in Figure 9.2 could have been collected as easily in a clinical therapeutic setting as in the laboratory setting in which they were actually collected. Thus, if the clinician wishes to know whether, for example, stress (however operationally defined—in the therapy setting, the cause of stress may be family relationships) is affecting day-to-day stability of BGL, it is imperative that he collect data systematically. A failure to collect baseline data in the above example would have led to gross misinterpretation of the stress data.

ASTHMA AND THE FRACTIONATION OF RESPONSE UNDER STRESS

Bronchial asthma is a term applied to a symptom complex involving over-reactivity of the respiratory system and specifically constriction of the bronchial tubes resulting in bronchospasm. Its major characteristic is hypersensitivity of the airways and its most common clinical sign is wheezing. As with diabetes, there is evidence that stress may induce or exacerbate an attack, and hence biofeedback-oriented therapy has often been conducted on the basis of the generality assumption, the aim being to increase general relaxation and thus counteract anxiety. Although the frontalis muscle is not specifically implicated in asthmatic episodes, therapy has frequently utilized frontalis muscle activity reduction training as a means of increasing the ability to relax generally, although the dependent variable measured is usually some aspect of pulmonary functioning such as forced expiratory volume. Other studies have utilized the specificity assumption and attempted directly to influence airways constriction. In clinical therapy and in research it is almost always assumed that pulmonary functioning should be the focus of attention.

This is, however, to ignore other important evidence. In fact, a triad of disturbed functions in asthmatics suggests that the autonomic nervous system may be generally implicated in asthma. It has been consistently found that asthmatics tend to have both higher heart rates and finger temperature

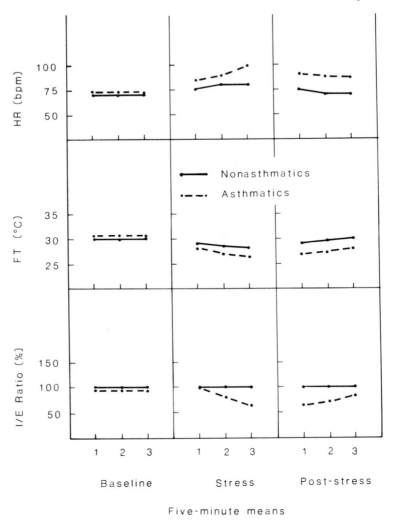

FIGURE 9.3   HR, FT, and I/E levels in baseline, stress, and post-stress recovery periods in asthmatics and nonasthmatics.

than nonasthmatics, as well as having a different inhalation–exhalation (I/E) ratio in the breathing cycle (the latter being due to the longer time asthmatics take to exhale as compared with the time to inhale) (Hahn, 1966; Hahn & Clark, 1967; Ziegler, 1951). As in the case of diabetes research, however, the meaning of this triadic response pattern is unclear because baseline levels (including adaptation) have not been clearly separated out from levels under stress. Figure 9.3 shows the hypothetical results for heart rate, finger temperature, and I/E ratio in a baseline, stress, and post-stress session analogous to the one depicted in Figure 9.2 for diabetics (the equivalent of Figure 9.2 for the preceding successive baseline sessions could readily be constructed also). The interesting point to note is that a fractionated response is predicted. Thus, during the baseline period, it is assumed that (if sufficient baseline adaptation sessions have been run) there will be no differences in HR, FT, and I/E in asthmatics and nonasthmatics. During the stress period both groups will show an increase in HR, but the increase will be greater in the asthmatics. Likewise both groups will show a decrease in FT (since FT tends to drop under stress) but the asthmatics will show a greater fall. In relation to the I/E ratio it is predicted that asthmatics will show a marked drop (exhalation time will be prolonged under stress) but the I/E ratio will be unchanged in the nonasthmatic group. In the post-stress period the asthmatics will be slow to return to their pre-stress levels as compared with the nonasthmatics.

Clearly, if such patterns of response could be demonstrated, they would have potentially important implications for therapy. For such a result would suggest a more general involvement of the autonomic nervous system with the distorted breathing pattern being an end product that could be averted if therapy were to be directed toward more precise control of the autonomic nervous system as a whole (this would not necessarily be best achieved by general relaxation training). However, the important point to note once again is that the predicted data shown in Figure 9.3 are unsupported by empirical evidence, for carefully controlled studies have not yet been carried out. The clinician working with asthmatics currently must draw on inadequate data. Results obtained with one asthmatic patient are shown in Figure 9.4. In the baseline preceding the stress task (the digit–symbol substitution task) the patient's HR was high, increased during stress, and returned to baseline in the post-stress period. However, the predicted fractionation of response was not found. The I/E ratio was low during baseline but did not decrease further during the stress task. Nevertheless, the systematic investigation of the three response systems enables the pattern of responding before, during, and after induced stress to be examined in detail and specific hypotheses to be tested.

THE TMJD SYNDROME: MUSCULAR HYPERACTIVITY AND SUBJECTIVE PAIN AND DISCOMFORT

The etiology and treatment of the temporomandibular joint dysfunction (TMJD) syndrome has evolved in three phases according to whether the

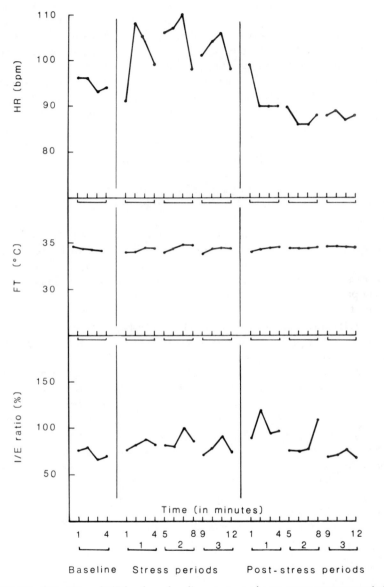

FIGURE 9.4   HR, FT, and I/E levels on baseline, stress, and post-stress recovery periods in an asthmatic patient.

symptoms of pain and dysfunction have been attributed to (1) the loss of occlusal support of the dentition, (2) temporomandibular joint articulation dysfunction, or (3) hypertonicity of the masticatory muscles. According to the psychophysiologic theory proposed by Laskin (1969), which he calls the "myofascial pain–dysfunction syndrome," masticatory muscle spasm is the primary factor responsible for the symptoms that include pain and tenderness in the TMJ area and muscles of mastication, TMJ sounds during movements, and limitations of mandibular movements (Rugh & Solberg, 1976). Increased muscle tone appears to be a concomitant of most types of mandibular dysfunction and the biofeedback approach to the treatment of the TMJD syndrome appears to be based on the specificity assumption, that is, that muscle hyperactivity is the cause of the pain and dysfunction. Thus treatment studies have examined biofeedback reduction of tension in the masseter muscle in single case designs (Carlsson & Gale, 1976; Carlsson, Gale, & Öhman, 1975) and general versus specific relaxation training (Moss, Wedding, & Sanders, 1983; Stenn, Mothersill, & Brooke, 1979).

An important question that has not yet been fully explored is the relationship between changes in level of EMG activity and changes in subjective estimates of pain and dysfunction during attacks. Thus in deciding to treat a TMJD patient with biofeedback-assisted masseter or temporalis muscle reduction training, the assumption of the clinician appears to be clearly one of specificity of association: That is, the severity of the clinical disorder is correlated with levels of masseter or temporalis muscle activity so that if the patient is trained to control (i.e., reduce) the level of activity in those muscles, there will be a corresponding reduction in the frequency and severity of clinical attacks. There is, however, little or no evidence that such a correlation exists; and bearing in mind the fate of the specificity assumption in the case of tension and migraine headaches, there is considerable doubt as to its validity. An alternative hypothesis would suggest that the disorder is correlated with specific levels of muscle activity *or* with specific levels of pain and discomfort, but that these two variables may not be congruent with each other.

The resolution of this issue requires detailed and careful experiments on the relationship between these two variables in the resting state and in stress, in the same way described for diabetes and asthma. Three plausible hypotheses may be formulated in relation to the functional characteristics of TMJ dysfunction:

HYPOTHESIS 1. In a resting level (baseline) condition, the level of EMG activity in the temporalis and masseter muscle region will be significantly higher in TMJD patients than in non-TMJD subjects.

HYPOTHESIS 2.   In a resting level (baseline) condition, the reported level of subjective pain and discomfort in the temporalis and masseter muscle region will be significantly higher in TMJD patients than in non-TMJD subjects.

HYPOTHESIS 3.   When subjects are required to produce and then maintain a specified level of masticatory muscle tension, TMJD patients will report higher levels of pain and discomfort in the temporalis and masseter muscle region than non-TMJD subjects.

Hypotheses 1 and 2 may readily be tested. Hypothesis 3 may be tested by making use of the clench test in which maximal clench ability is first tested by asking the subject to place the mandible in the position of maximum intercuspation of the occluding teeth and hold the maximum clench for a brief period of time, recording both EMG level and subjective levels of pain and dscomfort. The average EMG level over this period is then used to define 25, 50, 75, and 100% clench levels to be achieved and sustained on subsequent trials. These levels would be displayed on a graphics terminal and the subject asked to align a marker with the indicated clench level and maintain that level for varying periods of time. It is well established that maintaining such clench levels (even if well short of the maximum time) is highly stressful. One possible set of results in which a specified clench magnitude is maintained for either 10 seconds or 30 seconds is shown in Figure 9.5. While some discomfort is produced in normal subjects by this technique, it would be expected that quite dramatic results would be found with TMJD patients. The design would enable the relationship between EMG levels and subjective pain and discomfort levels to be determined. Although the changes in the graph are shown as being linear in nature, a curvilinear relationship might well be found. The importance of determining this relationship lies particularly in its significance for an approach to treatment. While most therapeutic procedures have assumed that the patients should be trained in voluntary reduction of EMG levels, an alternative approach might seek to train the patient in control of subjective pain and discomfort levels by a kind of systematic desensitization procedure in which the data obtained in Figure 9.5 are used to establish a starting point for generating and tolerating a level of pain and discomfort that can be withstood for some time with the possibility that the level may gradually reduce over repeated practice trials. Equally important, the experiment described would determine the validity of the specificity assumption in the case of the TMJD syndrome.

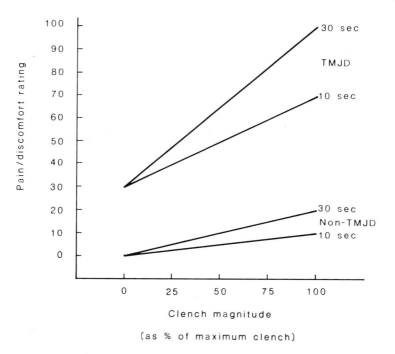

FIGURE 9.5   Pain and discomfort ratings of TMJD and non-TMJD subjects as a function of magnitude and duration of mandible clench.

The Significance of Individual Differences in Clinical Biofeedback Therapy

In illustrating and discussing the actual and expected levels and changes in physiological functioning in baseline and stress conditions of headache patients, diabetics, asthmatics, and TMJD patients, it has become evident that much can be gained by making careful assessments of level of functioning over several prolonged baseline sessions before introducing the stress sessions, and that it is beneficial to analyze carefully individual records. The implication is that careful detailed examination of both objective and subjective indices of stress may be very important in deciding on the treatment approach to be applied in individual cases. This conclusion is strongly supported by evidence presented by Pennebaker (1982). In a series of studies, he has examined the relationships among "symptoms" (such as racing heart, sweating hands, shortness of breath or heavy breathing, tense muscles, etc.), "emotions" (guilt feelings, tenseness, fear, anger, etc.), and physiological functions (heart rate, blood pressure, finger temperature, etc.). Such studies as these in the past have yielded little evidence of significant patterns of relationships (hence, for example, the warning to hypertensive patients not to discontinue medication just because they seem subjectively to be symptom-free). Studies by Pennebaker and his colleagues have, however, shown convincingly that significant patterns may be present if data are analyzed separately for each individual, and that these patterns are both idiosyncratic and reliable from one occasion to another. In one study, for example, which is of particular interest in the context of this chapter because it used diabetics as the subjects (Pennebaker, Cox, Gonder-Frederick, Wunsch, Evans, & Pohl, 1981), 30 insulin-dependent diabetics sampled their BGL seven times daily over 2 weeks. Immediately prior to sampling BGL the patients checked 19 symptoms or emotions thought to be relevant to BGL for most patients and were allowed to nominate up to 4 additional individual items. The symptoms included trembling, pounding heart, flushed face, light-headedness, queasy stomach, and so on. The results indicated individual patterns of relationship between BGL and symptomatology.

These findings of Pennebaker and his colleagues suggest the existence of individual patterns of physiological–symptomatic responses that are highly replicable. There is no reason to doubt that this is so, but evidence from my laboratory suggests that idiosyncratic variations in these patterns can occur. Figure 9.6 shows the drift effect for a male and a female on successive days in a room temperature of 20°C. The male pattern over the 2 days in fact showed no drift and was very similar on both days. The female showed a massive drift effect on both days but inexplicably started at a significantly lower level on the second day. Such a difference may well be readily explainable in a female by hormonal changes, but such variations have been found in a number of males as well. In each case, the outside temperature and time of testing were the same, the subject's activity and clothing were similar on both days, and 15 minutes adaptation in 25°C was provided before the subject entered the experimental room. In these circumstances, a variation in a male of 5°C from the starting temperature becomes very large. Such variations pose a problem because they act as noise in the experimental condition itself. More important, however, in light of Pennebaker's results and the general framework of this chapter, these individual patterns of behavior are obviously of interest in their own right and have significance for clinical work. We return, in fact, full circle to the argument made by Shapiro for the clinical psychologist to treat the presenting client within the framework of the "experimental investigation of the single case." Shapiro (1961a,b, 1966) argued that no action should be taken in respect of a presenting patient unless the action was intended to test a specific question.

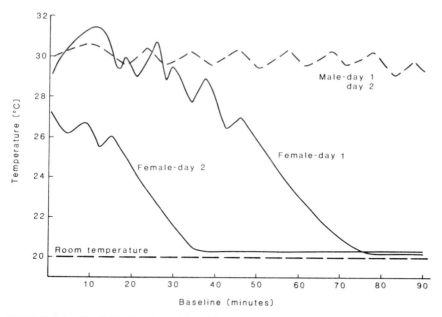

FIGURE 9.6   The drift effect in peripheral finger temperature and individualized patterns of responding.

Initially the questions would relate to what is now called behavioral analysis; subsequently to the development of ways of changing the patient's behavior (or assisting him to change it himself). Whenever, in the process of doing this, the results do not fit (as in the data relating to Days 3 and 4 in Figure 9.2) a new specific question must be formulated. In light of the evidence and viewpoint presented in this chapter, Shapiro's prescription remains as valid as it was when first presented 30 years ago. It is encouraging to see that it is beginning to be taken up more widely in clinical psychology generally (Meyer & Turkat, 1979; Turkat & Meyer, 1982).

Conclusion

Behavior therapy began in part as a reaction against the tendency to classify presenting clients into categories that had few of no implications for etiology or treatment, that tended to label them irrevocably, and that did not adequately reflect the individual nature of each patient's problem. Behavior therapy, in its early stages particularly, stressed the need for a systematic, experimentally based approach to the task of defining the nature of the presenting problem. Subsequent developments in psychophysiology led to an increasing emphasis on the physiological concomitants of disorders such as asthma and diabetes, while the advent of biofeedback produced a stress on individual voluntary control of physiological functions believed to be implicated in the disorder. However, the tendency within clinical biofeedback was to apply standard solutions to standard (classified) patients. The material reviewed in this chapter suggests that a synthesis of individual investigation and psychophysiological measurement can be achieved by the working clinician, which, in terms of generating more rationally based therapeutic procedures, will represent a considerable advance on present practices.

References

Andrasik, F., Blanchard, E. B., Arena, J. G., Saunders, N. L., & Barron, K. D. (1982). Psychophysiology of recurrent headache: Methodological issues and new empirical findings. *Behavior Therapy, 13,* 407–429.

Andrasik, F., & Holroyd, K. A. (1980). A test of specific and nonspecific effects in the biofeedback treatment of tension headache. *Journal of Consulting and Clinical Psychology, 48,* 575–586.

Bakal, D. A., & Kaganov, J. A. (1977). Muscle contraction and migraine headaches: Psychophysiologic comparison. *Headache, 17,* 208–214.

Baker, L., Barcai, A., Kaye, R., & Haque, N. (1969). Beta adrenergic blockade and juvenile diabetes: Acute studies and long-term therapeutic trial. *Journal of Pediatrics, 75,* 19–29

Blanchard, E. B., & Andrasik, F. (1982). Psychological assessment and treatment of headache: Recent developments and emerging issues. *Journal of Consulting and Clinical Psychology, 50,* 859–879.

Blanchard, E. B., Andrasik, F., Ahles, T. A., Teders, S. J., & O'Keefe, D. (1980). Migraine and tension headache: A meta-analytic review. *Behavior Therapy, 11,* 613–631.

Bradley, C. (1982). Psychophysiological aspects of the management of diabetes mellitus. *International Journal of Mental Health, 11,* 117–132.

Carlsson, S. G., & Gale, E. N. (1976). Biofeedback treatment for muscle pain associated with temporomandibular joint. *Journal of Behavior Therapy and Experimental Psychiatry, 7,* 383–385.

Carlsson, S. G., Gale, E. N., & Öhman, A. (1975). Treatment of temporomandibular joint syndrome with biofeedback training. *Journal of the American Dental Association, 91,* 602–605.

Davis, M. H., Saunders, D. R., Creer, T. L., & Chai, H. (1973). Relaxation training facilitated by biofeedback apparatus as a supplemental treatment in bronchial asthma. *Journal of Psychosomatic Research, 17,* 121–128.

Fowler, J. E., Budzynski, T. H., & VandenBergh, R. L. (1976). Effects of an EMG biofeedback relaxation program on the control of diabetes: A case study. *Biofeedback and Self-Regulation, 1,* 105–112.

Hahn, W. W. (1966). Autonomic responses of asthmatic children. *Psychosomatic Medicine, 28,* 323–332.

Hahn, W. W., & Clark, J. A. (1967). Psychophysiological reactivity of asthmatic children. *Psychosomatic Medicine, 29,* 526–536.

Hersen, M., & Bellack, A. S. (Eds.). (1981). *Behavioral assessment: A practical handbook* (2nd Ed.). New York: Pergamon.

Hinkle, L. E., & Wolf, S. (1952). Importance of life stress in course and management of diabetes mellitus. *Journal of the American Medical Association, 148,* 513–520.

Koch, M. F., & Molnar, G. D. (1974). Psychiatric aspects of patients with unstable diabetes mellitus. *Psychosomatic Medicine, 36,* 57–68.

Laskin, D. M. (1969). Etiology of the pain-dysfunction syndrome. *Journal of the American Dental Assoication, 79,* 147–153.

Lavallée, Y.-J., Lamontagne, Y., Pinard, G., Annable, L., & Tétreault, L. (1977). Effects of EMG feedback, diazepam and their combination on chronic anxiety. *Journal of Psychosomatic Research, 21,* 65–71.

Meyer, V., & Turkat, I. D. (1979). Behavioral analysis of clinical cases. *Journal of Behavioral Assessment, 1,* 259–270.

Moss, R. A., Wedding, D., & Sanders, S. H. (1983). The comparative efficacy of relaxation training and masseter EMG feedback in the treatment of TMJ dysfunction. *Journal of Oral Rehabilitation, 10,* 9–17.

Pennebaker, J. W. (1982). *The psychology of physical symptoms.* New York: Springer-Verlag.

Pennebaker, J. W., Cox, D. J., Gonder-Frederick, L., Wunsch, M. G., Evans, W. S., & Pohl, S. (1981). Physical symptoms related to blood glucose in insulin-dependent diabetics. *Psychosomatic Medicine, 43,* 489–500.

Philips, C. (1978). Tension headache-theoretical problems. *Behaviour Research and Therapy, 16,* 249–261.

Reading, C. (1982a). Psychophysiological approaches to the classification and treatment of headache. In C. J. Main (Ed.). *Clinical psychology and medicine: A behavioral perspective* (pp. 231–249). New York: Plenum.

Reading, C. (1982b). Experimental investigations of psychophysiological basis of headache and its treatment using biofeedback. In C. J. Main (Ed.). *Clinical psychology and medicine: A behavioral perspective* (pp. 251–270). New York: Plenum.

Rugh, J. D., & Solberg, W. K. (1976). Psychological implications in temporomandibular pain and dysfunction. *Oral Sciences Review, 7,* 3–30.

Shapiro, M. B. (1961a). A method of measuring psychological changes specific to the individual psychiatric patient. *British Journal of Medical Psychology, 34,* 151–155.

Shapiro, M. B. (1961b). The single case in fundamental clinical psychological research. *British Journal of Medical Psychology, 34,* 255–262.

Shapiro, M. B. (1966). The single case in clinical-psychological research. *Journal of General Psychology, 74,* 3–23.

Steffen, J. J. (1975). Electromyographically induced relaxation in the treatment of chronic alcohol abuse. *Journal of Consulting and Clinical Psychology, 43,* 275.

Stenn, P. G., Mothersill, K. J., & Brooke, R. I. (1979). Biofeedback and a cognitive behavioral approach to treatment of myofascial pain dysfunction syndrome. *Behavior Therapy, 10,* 29–36.

Turkat, I. D., & Meyer, V. (1982). The behavior-analytic approach. In P. Wachtel (Ed.). *Resistance: Psychodynamic and behavioral approaches* (pp 157–184). New York: Plenum.

VandenBergh, R. L., Sussman, K. E., & Titus, C. C. (1966). Effects of hypnotically induced acute emotional stress on carbohydrate and lipid metabolism in patients with diabetes mellitus. *Psychosomatic Medicine, 28,* 382–390.

VandenBergh, R. L., Sussman, K. E., & Vaughn, G. D. (1967). Effects of combined physical-anticipatory stress on carbohydrate lipid metabolism in patients with diabetes mellitus. *Psychosomatics, 8,* 16–19.

Yates, A. J. (1958). The application of learning theory to the treatment of tics. *Journal of Abnormal and Social Psychology, 56,* 175–182.

Yates, A. J. (1975). *Theory and practice in behavior therapy*. New York: Wiley.
Yates, A. J. (1981). Behavior therapy: Past, present, future—imperfect? *Clinical Psychology Review, 1,* 269–291.
Yates, A. J. (1983). Behavior therapy and psychodynamic psychotherapy: Basic conflict or reconciliation and integration? *British Journal of Clinical Psychology, 22,* 107–125.
Ziegler, R. F. (1951). *Electrocardiographic studies in normal infants and children*. Springfield, IL: C. C. Thomas.

PART *IV*

THEORIES OF DEPRESSION

The trend in theorizing about depression is toward recognizing a wide range of relevant factors. Behavior theorists are broadening their views to include cognitive factors, and cognitive theorists are broadening their views to recognize the influence of behavioral factors. The emerging consensus is that depression is a complicated, multidimensional problem that will require many years of additional research before it can be understood.

Arthur W. Staats and Elaine M. Heiby present a comprehensive analysis of depression in terms of the concepts of social behaviorism. This theory specifies antecedent conditions, complex personality processes, and reinforcement processes as relevant to the development of depression. Staats and Heiby show how a wide range of research can potentially be explained by their theory and also point out the possible implications of the general theory for phenomena other than depression.

Peter M. Lewinsohn, Harry Hoberman, Linda Teri, and Martin Hautzinger also present a comprehensive theory of depression, one focusing on the interactive effects of a variety of behavioral, cognitive, and social factors. Their model is testable and represents an updating of an established and highly influential theoretical position.

L. Rowell Huesmann and Sharon Morikawa present a chapter on Martin Seligman's learned helplessness model of *depression. The large amount of empirical research that has been conducted on depression as a result of Seligman's work is noted. The chapter provides a rigorous review of these data and, while doubt is cast on the importance of the concept of perceived independence of response and outcome, support is found for the importance of attributional factors.*

Lauren B. Alloy, Caroline Clements, and Gregory Kolden provide a comprehensive discussion of the cognitive styles that may predispose people to become depressed when stressful life circumstances are experienced. The most recent cognitive research is reviewed, and, of special interest for the readers of this volume, implications for prevention and therapy are considered. The chapter shows how knowledge of the cognitive processes in depression can be integrated with clinical and behavioral data to provide a comprehensive theoretical understanding of depression.

10

Paradigmatic Behaviorism's Theory of Depression: Unified, Explanatory, and Heuristic

ARTHUR W. STAATS
ELAINE M. HEIBY

Psychology has been called a preparadigmatic science, characterized by a great separatism among its various bodies of knowledge. A theory has been proposed to unify the various levels of knowledge—ranging from the basic principles of conditioning, which are related to biological study, to the very complex phenomena of personality, and individual, and social behavior (see Staats, 1975, 1981). To cover the range of events dealt with across the very diversified science of psychology, it is necessary for such a unified theory to be able to indicate how its principles apply to a variety of areas in broad strokes. In each area treated, the theory may at first be a heuristic foundation. But the proof of the pudding also occurs in systematic and detailed analyses that come to grips with subject matter in specific problem areas, first in theoretical analyses and later in research and applied projections. The present paper may thus be considered to serve two goals. First, it is a treatment of the important problem area of depression. Second, the treatment is accomplished within the more general structure of the unified theory and as such shows how the more generally stated theory can serve as the basis for more profound treatments. Third, the methodology for constructing unified theory in psychology is exemplified, in the context of deal-

279

ing with an issue that is central in contemporary psychology (Staats, 1983).

A theory of depression is outlined herein whose principles derive from the position called social (and, more recently, paradigmatic) behaviorism. The general position states that there have been various sources of knowledge of abnormal psychology that have remained separate and antagonistic. This disadvantageous fragmentation occurs in the study of depression, where there is traditional clinical knowledge; a literature concerning unipolar, nonpsychotic depression that is based upon behavior modification and behavior therapy developments (to which the present authors have contributed); and a more recent focus upon behavioral–cognitive variables in a less systematically structured theoretical framework. Several reviews of the depression literature (Blaney, 1977; Heiby, 1979; Mathews, 1977) point out that the contemporary models of depression (e.g., Beck, 1967; Ferster, 1966, 1973; Lewinsohn, 1974; Rehm, 1977; Seligman, 1978) have failed to integrate the separate findings in the behavioral and cognitive fields. And the models have failed to include the knowledge of depression that has derived from nonbehavioral sources.

A theory of depression is developed herein that addresses the several types of knowledge, composing a first unified theory in this area that is broad, on the one hand, but is also explanatory and heuristic, with implications for further developments in abnormal psychology, psychological measurement (assessment), and clinical treatment.

The Theory of Abnormal Psychology

Standard behaviorism is a two-level theory. Its basic, and central, level consists of the elementary principles of conditioning. The first and second generation behaviorists (e.g., Pavlov, Thorndike, Hull, Skinner) concentrated their work in this level. The other level of the theory involves that direct application of the first level to the consideration of selected aspects of human behavior. Although the first and second generation behaviorists did not extensively develop the second level, later research working in the framework did so, especially in the fields of behavior therapy and behavior modification. As will be seen, however, there are many concerns of interest to psychology that do not fall into the two-level formulation of standard behaviorism, concerns that are of interest to abnormal and clinical psychology and other areas of psychology concerned with human behavior.

Paradigmatic behaviorism has been projected as a third-generation behaviorism, in part on the basis of the fact that it is a multilevel theoretical effort. While it is based upon a theory of the elementary principles of conditioning, it has taken the position that the elementary principles need development in a series of levels before complex human behavior—important to abnormal and clinical psychology, and to personality measurement—can be dealt with in an adequate way. It is relevant to sketch out some of these levels as a foundation for a theory of depression.

THE BASIC LEVEL OF THEORY

There have been various basic theories of learning, composed to deal with the facts of the animal laboratory. Each has had the problem of relating the two major principles of classical and instrumental conditioning (reinforcement). Some theorists have solved the problem by stating that reinforcement is the only principle of learning (see Hull, 1943). Skinner (1938) resolved the problem by recognizing the two principles and stipulating that they are entirely separate and independent of one another, and further by emphasizing the importance of, and restricting his study to, instrumental conditioning. The classical conditioning of emotions in his theory is given a peripheral role, having no causative effect upon behavior (Skinner, 1975). In his view behavior is solely a function of instrumental reinforcement contingencies.

Paradigmatic behaviorism's three-function learning theory, composed in the context of human behavior also, states that the classical conditioning of emotional responses and the instrumental conditioning of behavior are intimately related. This can be summarized by saying that there are stimuli that elicit emotional responses (central nervous system responses with peripheral indices such as smooth muscle responding in the viscera, glandular responses, and so on). When an emotion-eliciting stimulus is paired with some other, neutral stimulus, the latter will come to elicit an emotional response also, exemplifying classical conditioning. It is important to recognize that such emotion-elicitors in classical conditioning are the same stimuli as those that serve as reinforcers to produce instrumental conditioning. For example, food elicits an emotional response. But when food is presented following an instrumental response the response will be strengthened, which is the definition of a reinforcing stimulus. The three-function learning theory states that a stimulus that elicits an emotional response—which has emotional value—will because of that also be a reinforcing stimulus (either positive or negative, as the case may be). Importantly, when a stimulus is given emotional value through classical conditioning procedures, then it will also become a reinforcing stimulus. It may be added, as a central third function, that humans (and lower animals as well) learn to approach stimuli that elicit positive emotional responses and to avoid stimuli that elicit negative emotional responses. We learn a very large class of positive behaviors to positive emotional stimuli, and a very large class of negative behaviors under the control of stimuli that elicit a negative emotional response. Emotional stimuli will thus be what are usually called discriminative stimuli (in operant theory), directive stimuli (in paradigmatic behaviorism), or incentives (in traditional usage). The three functions of stimuli (emotional, reinforcing, and directive) are related, and depend upon the emotional value of the stimulus. The three-function character of this basic theory is very important in considering human behavior, as we demonstrate herein.

THE PERSONALITY LEVEL OF THE THEORY

The traditional conception of personality is that it is a process or structure within the individual that determines the characteristic ways in which the individual behaves (e.g., Allport, 1937). Based upon this conception, it becomes very central to be able to measure personality, for in this way one can gain predictive and controlling power in working with human problems.

Standard behaviorism, on the other hand, has denied the existence of an internal personality process that determines human behavior. In this view, personality is simply the total of one's behavior, which is a function of the behavioral contingencies in the situation. The traditional concept of personality is considered to be another mentalistic construct with no explanatory power. Thus, traditional measurements of personality have been rejected. Any individual differences in human behavior have been assumed to be explainable by differences in environmental variables. Personality, therefore, has been considered an effect, not a causal process as posited in traditional approaches.

Paradigmatic behaviorism very early stated that the standard behaviorism position was not well considered. There are individual differences that have a causal role in the individual's behavior. Two people placed in the same environmental situation will behave differently, irrespective of the behavioral contingencies in the situation. They come to the situation with different characteristics and it is necessary to have a personality level of study in a theory that is able to account for such differences in behavior. It may be added that the personality theory must be objective and abide by the demands of an objective psychological methodology. And the personality theory must be explicit; simply saying in a general manner that individual differences in behavior are due to differences in learning history is not adequate. A fundamental characteristic of paradigmatic behaviorism is its demand for analytic specification, not general, assumptive statements.

In the paradigmatic behaviorism approach, personality consists of what have been called basic behavioral repertoires or, simply, personality repertoires. Very early the child begins to learn complex systems of behaviors.

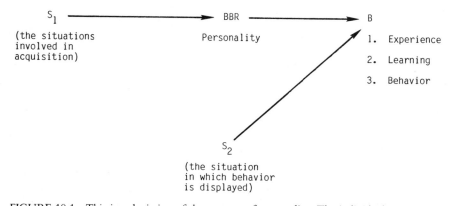

FIGURE 10.1   This is a depiction of the concept of personality. The individual experiences various situations that result in the formation of three basic behavioral repertoires (BBRs) that constitute the individual's personality. These situations may have occurred over an extensive period of time, up until the occurrence of S_2, the presently acting situation (or the present living conditions) for the individual. S_2 and the BBRs in conjunction will determine the nature of the individual's experience, learning, and behavior in that situation. It should be noted that the experience, learning, and behavior (and that latter's effects upon the environment) will result in further development of the individual's BBRs, in a continuing interactional development.

These behavioral systems begin with relatively simple structures and few elements, but they are elaborated in a cumulative–hierarchical way where past acquisitions of skills are basic to the further acquisition of new units in the developing personality repertoires. The behavior of the individual in any situation is therefore always a function of the personality repertoires that the individual brings to the situation, as well as the situation itself. Very importantly, the basic behavioral repertoires determine how the individual will experience a situation, how she or he will behave in that situation, and what she or he will learn in that situation (Staats, 1968a, 1968b, 1971b, 1975). This conception may be schematized as in Figure 10.1.

Stated in this way paradigmatic behaviorism indicates the avenues that must be developed to turn this terse abstraction into an explanatory theory. For one thing, the basic behavioral repertoires (BBRs) must be defined. In addition, the manner in which these personality repertoires are learned and the principles involved must also be stipulated. Furthermore, the principles by which the personality repertoires help determine how the individual behaves in interaction with the elements of the later situation must also be explicated.

These stipulations are by no means complete, but a prototypical framework has been formulated within paradigmatic behaviorism utilizing various sources of knowledge inside and outside of the approach (see Staats,

1963, 1968a, 1971a, 1971b, 1975, 1980, 1981). It should be noted in providing specification that the personality repertoires may be conceptualized to fall into three general areas: the emotional–motivational, the language–cognitive, and the sensory–motor. The basis for this conception was built from below, by research extending the elementary principles of conditioning to the study of human behavior, as will be noted briefly in describing the three areas of personality.[1]

THE LANGUAGE–COGNITIVE REPERTOIRE

Beginning with the investigation of human problem solving and reasoning (Staats, 1956, 1957) it became apparent that basic to these cognitive phenomena was language—and a major focus of study became that of how language is learned. Other behaviorists (see Mowrer, 1954; Osgood, 1953; Skinner, 1957; Watson, 1930) had made theoretical analyses of the learning of some of the aspects of language. Paradigmatic behaviorism made additional analyses, began the experimental study of both classical conditioning and instrumental conditioning in learning language, and indicated how the principles interact in this area of human behavior (Staats, 1957, 1961, 1963, 1968a; Staats, Finley, Minke, & Wolfe, 1964; Staats, Minke, Finley, Wolfe, & Brooks, 1964; Staats & Staats, 1957; Staats, Staats, & Biggs, 1958; Staats, Staats, & Crawford, 1962). It should be indicated that this included how language is involved in emotional arousal and emotional learning (see Staats, 1961, 1963, 1968a, for summaries of the research), in image arousal (see Staats, 1961, 1963, 1968a; Staats & Lohr, 1979), and in eliciting behavior (Staats, 1968a; Staats, Brewer, & Gross, 1970; Staats & Burns, 1981). Moreover, the experimental–longitudinal study of language learning involved work with individual children conducted over considerable periods, with specific procedures and methods by which to make systematic observation of behavioral outcomes involved in training-produced development. Thus, the early acquisition of language was also studied (see Staats, 1963, 1968a, 1971a, for summaries).

However, the theoretical approach, unlike the other behavioristic analyses, developed a concern with the *function* of the language skills once they are acquired, not just with the learning of the skills. The fact is that language is involved in reasoning and problem solving—which was the topic of

---

[1] It should be noted that the three proposed repertoires of personality constitute a substantive, functional classification system of behavior. This is in contrast to the triple-response mode conception such as that proposed by Rachman and Hodgson (1974) which involves measurement of one emotional phenomenon along three dimensions: verbal, motoric, and physiological. Although similar terminology is involved in that conception and the present one, the latter is a theory of personality, the former is only a theory of the indexes of emotion.

interest of Staats' first study (1956). Language is also basic to the individual's communication, school learning, self-direction, self-reinforcement, and many human social behaviors. This conception recognizes that language skills underlie many of the cognitive characteristics of the individual—that intelligence, as an important example, largely consists of language skills. The conception that it is important to study language function as well as language learning (see Staats, 1963, 1968a) provided the basis for the next step in the theoretical development—that is, that the individual's language repertoires were essential components of personality, such as intelligence. Analysis of intelligence tests, with detailed consideration of specific items, showed clearly that primarily language repertoires were being measured and that training that produced language repertoire development in children increased their measured intelligence (see Staats, 1963, 1968a, 1971a, 1975; Staats, et al., 1970; Staats & Burns, 1981).

THE SENSORY–MOTOR REPERTOIRE

Similarly, since most basic research in learning has been done with animals, there was very little study of the development of sensory–motor skills in humans by the first- or second-generation behaviorists. Sensory–motor repertoires, however, are considered in the present view to be one of the three major areas of personality. In addition to the experimental–longitudinal study of language development mentioned above, Staats applied the same methods to the development of procedures to promote the sensory–motor skill development in children, first his own, in experimental–naturalistic studies. This included early visual tracking of skills, standing, walking, catching a ball, swimming, feeding, and toilet skills (both for defecation as well as nocturnal urination), and descriptions of this type of training were employed in Staats' general works (1963, pp. 369–379), presaging later, more formal behavior modification works of various behavior modifiers. In the area of the sensory–motor skills of imitation of writing the alphabet, maze problem solving, and geometric drawing, this experimental–longitudinal research was continued into detailed study (see Staats, 1968a, 1975; Staats et al., 1970; Staats & Burns, 1981). The point is that individual differences in such sensory–motor skills are considered to be personality differences in the approach.

THE EMOTIONAL–MOTIVATIONAL REPERTOIRE

The third area of personality is that of the emotional–motivational system. It has been said already that stimuli that elicit a positive emotional response will serve as positive reinforcers for the individual and also have directive (incentive) value in tending to elicit the large class of positive behaviors the individual has learned. The same principles apply to negative emotional stimuli. This basic theory says that what stimuli have emotional value for the individual will be an imporant determinant of the individual's behavior. Emotional stimuli are largely learned, in complex conditioning histories. The stimuli may be physical objects or events, people or the actions (verbal or nonverbal) of people, or stimuli produced by oneself (such as one's appearance, thoughts, images, and other self-stimulation as well as overt performance). There are stimuli that occur in the family; in recreation, work, social situations, politics, religion; in music, art, and the theatre; in daydreaming; in competing; and so on, that elicit emotional responses in individuals. For the normal human being there are thousands of stimulus events that will elicit an emotional response of either a positive or negative type. These myriad stimuli constitute that individual's emotional–motivational system. The emotional–motivational systems of two individuals can differ in that some stimuli, on the basis of past learning variables, will elicit an emotional response in one individual and not the other, and vice versa. Differences may also reside in the positive or negative nature of the emotional response elicited, as well as in differences in the strength of response and in the relative strengths of responses. As an example of the latter, an attractive woman may elicit an equally strong positive emotional response in two men. For one of the men, however, there may be other stimuli in his emotional–motivational system that elicit a positive emotional response that is as strong or stronger—for example, love of work, family attachments, recreational stimuli, and the like. These men will as a consequence have different emotional–motivational personalities (and will respond differently). Moreover, conditions of deprivation for a class of positive emotional stimuli will have effects upon the absolute and relative strengths of the class of stimuli in the individual's emotional–motivational system. For example, when the individual has been deprived of food, all food stimuli in the individual's system will be stronger, both absolutely and relative to other classes of emotional stimuli, such as sexual stimuli or recreational stimuli. Personality (and behavior) differences thus may result from deprivation differences.

A central point, however, is that the nature of the individual's emotional–motivational system can be considered to be unique and different from anyone else's, because no two individuals will have learned precisely the same system, which contains many thousands of elements. And no two individuals will face the same deprivation–satiation conditions. There will, however, be similarities between individuals because of similarities of experiences—similarities of family, socio-economic class, ethnic group, occupation, political and religious persuasion, and so on.

It should be stressed that the three basic behavioral repertoires are called basic, and constitute personality processes, because they partly determine what the individual experiences and learns, and how the individual behaves. Take, for example, a woman who has learned a very positive emotional response to classical music of various kinds, constituting part of her emotional–motivational system. When she is confronted with the sounds made by a symphony orchestra, the experience will be emotionally positive. As a consequence of her personality and her experience of the symphony, she will thus learn a positive emotional response to an escort who has taken her to the concert. She will be more likely to accept a future date from her escort, other things equal. A quite different experience, learning, and behavior will occur to another young woman for whom classical music has no positive emotional value, or has negative emotional value. It is suggested that personality characteristics like intelligence, sociability, introversion, orderliness, gender-identification, and so on are in part constituted of characteristics of the three basic behavioral repertoires. It has been shown that personality characteristics such as interests (Staats, Gross, Guay, & Carlson, 1973) and values (Staats & Burns, 1982) may be considered parts of the emotional–motivational system and follow the principles of the theory in determining behavior. And it has been shown (Staats, 1968; Staats et al., 1970; Staats & Burns, 1981) that aspects of the sensory–motor and language–cognitive basic behavioral repertoires are constituents of other types of personality. The next section suggests that the determination of behavior by the personality repertoires extends also into the realm of abnormal psychology.

Abnormal Personality

Introduction of the concept of personality into the behavioristic theory of paradigmatic behaviorism provides a foundation for the consideration of abnormal personality in a manner not possible in other behavioral approaches. To elaborate, paradigmatic behaviorism has said that abnormal behavior may involve deficits and inappropriate aspects of any or all of the three personality repertoires (Staats, 1975, Chap. 8). In this theory, like traditional approaches, determinants of abnormal behavior can reside in personality problems. There are deficits and inappropriatenesses in the language–cognitive repertoires involved in schizophrenia, childhood autism, paranoia, dyslexia, learning disabilities, and mental retardation. There are deficits and inappropriatenesses in the emotional–motivational repertoire involved in fetishes, phobias, anxiety neuroses, sex identity crossings, sexual deviations of various kinds, as well as schizophrenia and autism. Deficits

and inappropriatenesses in sensory–motor behaviors occur in aggressive
personalities, mental retardation, schizophrenia and autism, some sexual
problems, sex identity crossings, and so on. The more complete theory of
abnormal psychology may be schematized as in Figure 10.2.

As the figure indicates, the individual's learning environment may have
been either deficit or inappropriate, resulting in the development of deficient or inappropriate personality repertoires. (This is not to say that the
environment totally imposed these characteristics on the individual. As
soon as the individual acquires his beginning basic behavioral repertoires,
part of what he experiences and learns will be a function of what he has
contributed to each situation and what situations he has selected to approach
and take part in.) There may be deficits and inappropriate aspects of each of
the three personality repertoires. Moreover, the later situations in which the
individual participates (S_2 in the diagram) may be either deficient or inappropriate in nature. In some cases the later situation is the primary cause of
the abnormal behavior. More usually, it will be an interaction among the
personality repertoires and the later situation that will determine the abnormal experiences, learning, and behavior of the individual.[2]

An important part of this model of abnormal behavior is what it indicates
regarding sites for psychological study. First, unlike standard behaviorism,
it says that there may be a difference between the symptoms of the abnormality and the underlying causative abnormal personality repertoires. As
one example, an autistic child may display the symptomatic behaviors of
self-stimulation and simple repetitive movements. Part of the underlying
causation, however, may involve deficits in the three personality repertoires
such that the usual solitary activities—reading, daydreaming, playing
games, and so on—are not available to the autistic child. Considering the
self-stimulation a symptom involves a different conception than considering it to be a central problem, and different treatment is called for. (It should
be noted that there are behavioral treatments of autistic children that aim to
remedy skill deficits, although in the present view the treatments are incomplete.) It has also been said "All treatment of neurotic disorders is concerned
with habits existing at present; their historical development is largely irrelevant" (Eysenck, 1960, p. 11). Paradigmatic behaviorism says in contrast

---

[2] This interaction is one reason why, in the present view, it is important to indicate in
abnormal psychology theories that abnormality is culturally defined. For example, a child who
cannot read, a language–cognitive deficit, is considered to be abnormal in our culture but not
in some other cultures, where very few people read. This cultural definition of abnormality
will affect the nature and course of abnormality. In our culture the child without reading skills
will be subjected to further problems as a result, and is likely to develop other abnormal
characteristics. In a culture in which illiteracy is the norm, the deficit in reading skills will be
unnoticed and generate no further abnormalities.

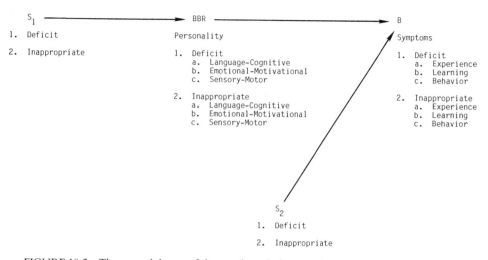

FIGURE 10.2   The general theory of abnormal psychology. Deficit or inappropriate environments (which also involve the effects produced by the individual's behavior and choice) produce deficit or inappropriate aspects of the three basic personality repertoires (BBRs). In interaction with later situations, which may also be deficit or inappropriate in nature, the abnormal personality repertoires produce deficit or inappropriate experience, learning, and behavior, some of which are considered to be symptomatic of the several psychopathologies.

that a centrally important site of study for abnormal psychology concerns the original learning of the personality repertoires.

The general model therefore says that it is important to study the behaviors that are involved in the symptoms of abnormal behavior. They may be problems in and of themselves, for example. But it is important, also, to study (1) the basic personality repertoires, (2) the conditions of learning of these repertoires, and (3) the conditions involved in the person's present environment. This model, unlike contemporary behavioral approaches, provides a basis for an interest in systematic stipulation and measurement of personality, behavioral symptoms, and environmental determinants and interactions; as well as an interest in methods for changing both the personality repertoires, the individual's behavior, and the individual's life situation for therapeutic purposes.

The above discussion provides a general illustration of the model. An elaboration of the model in the specific area of depression follows.

Depression: Description and Analysis

The paradigmatic behaviorism conception of abnormal psychology (Staats, 1975) has been presented as a heuristic theory. The approach con-

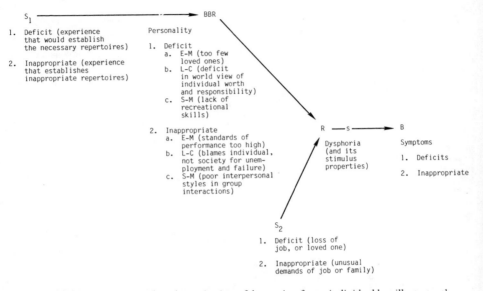

FIGURE 10.3   This is not the schematization of depression for an individual but illustrates the several sites of causes and effects in depression generally. There are original learning conditions (S_1) that produce aspects of the BBRs that result in the production of dysphoria. The individual's present life circumstances (S_2) may also contain elements that by themselves, or in interaction with the BBRs produce dysphoria. The dysphoric state (and the BBRs and present environment) produce the symptoms of depression, and the dysphoric state, as well as the BBRs, is a personality process.

siders the heuristic value of the theory to be central, something to be proved by its contributions to systematic and detailed analysis of the essential types of psychopathology, by research that supports the analyses, and ultimately by diagnostic and treatment methods that derive from the analyses. The present paper has the purpose, primarily, of providing a specific elaboration of a theory of nonpsychotic depression, which aims to have this heuristic value. This section presents a general description of the theoretical model of depression, along with illustrations of a clinical nature that will characterize the several sites of interest that the model indicates. A later section indicates more particularly how the theoretical model can be employed to organize the behavioral literature on depression.

The model is shown in Figure 10.3. As can be seen, it is an elaboration of the general model of abnormal behavior depicted in Figure 10.2. In depression—although not in the case of all psychopathologies—the symptoms are primarily distinct and different from the personality processes and current environmental conditions that are causative. As will be indicated more fully, depression may be seen to involve deficits and inappropriate aspects in the personality repertoires that in conjunction with environmental events evoke a negative emotional state of dysphoria that in turn elicits the symptoms or sets the circumstances by which they will occur. The direct cause of the symptoms of depression is here hypothesized to be the dysphoria, which is brought on by the individual's personality repertoires and the current environmental conditions that confront the individual. This theory of depression is quite different from the behavioral and behavioral–cognitive views that place themselves in an operant framework of learning principles. The paradigmatic behaviorism theory provides a foundation for unification with traditional knowledge in this area, yet it is based upon learning principles and an objective, analytic methodology, and therefore connects to the basic foundations of study in psychology. The following sections more clearly outline the theory; later sections indicate how the theoretical model can be employed to organize the behavioral literature on depression.

THE SYMPTOMS OF DEPRESSION

The presentation of social behaviorism's theory of depression can commence with reference to the diagnostic description of the psychopathology, using the American Psychiatric Association's Diagnostic and Statistical Manual of Mental Disorders (American Psychiatric Association, 1980, p. 223). The symptoms of Major Depressive Episode include dysphoric mood, depression, and loss of interest or pleasure in all or almost all usual activities and pastimes. "This disturbance is prominent, relatively persistent, and associated with other symptoms of the depressive syndrome" such as "appetite disturbance, change in weight, sleep disturbance, psychomotor agitation or retardation, decreased energy, feelings of worthlessness or guilt, difficulty concentrating or thinking, and thoughts of death or suicide or suicidal attempts" (APA, 1980, p. 210).

As will be further explicated, the symptoms listed above may be considered to be of two types of depths or generality. Very centrally, depression is characterized by a negative mood or affect. In the present view that is the immediate cause of such other symptoms as the loss of interest and pleasure as well as those that are overt and open to observation, such as decreased food consumption, loss of concentration, and so on. (As with the other figures, Figure 10.3 is a summarized abstracted model with only a few examples that do not have matching terms for all the nuances of the psychopathology.)

In the paradigmatic behaviorism conception the depressive's dysphoria is a function of the individual's personality repertoires or, more precisely, of the personal experiences that the repertoires result in or produce, as are described in a later section. The individual, however, may also have dysphoric experience that results from occurrences in his life situation (S_2), as the next section indicates. The characteristic symptoms produced may be seen to be a function of the individual's basic personality repertoires and the environmental circumstances encountered as well as the dysphoria (negative emotional state) these two classes of events produce. For example, an individual who has learned strong religious values against suicide is less likely, other things equal, to demonstrate suicidal behavioral symptoms than an equally depressed person whose values accept such actions. An important principle of the conception is that the symptoms of depression arise from personality–environment interactions involving deficits or inappropriate aspects of either or both. But the description, comparison, and categorization of symptoms in constructing an abnormal psychology remain as one of the central sites of study. It is necessary that any abnormal psychology indicate what the role of the study of symptoms is in the task and how the symptoms relate to the events considered causal in the theory.

ENVIRONMENTAL EVENTS PRECIPITATING AND MAINTAINING DEPRESSION

That the present environment of the individual is an important area of causation in considering the onset and persistence of depression has been recognized in the traditional literature. For example, "The precipitating events in depressions tend to be things like the death of a loved one, rejection in a love relationship, losing one's job or enforced retirement . . . , failure to be admitted to college . . . , or, more rarely, appointment to new responsibilities or the receipt of great honors" (London, 1968, p. 403).

The environment in which the individual finds himself or herself may be deficient—such as in the loss of one's job or a loved one, or the loved one's affection; in being placed in the military or in prison; or in going away to college (which removes many formerly important emotional–motivational stimuli). The environment may also be inappropriate—such as occurs when there are unusual demands made upon the individual by his family, his job, the military, or whatever. As an example, the individual may acquire a new boss in his place of work who dislikes the individual and who makes unreasonable demands, who withholds usual rewards and recognition, and who creates special problems for the individual.

It is important to realize that the theoretical model stipulates that ordinarily it is not the environment alone that is the determinant of depression. The environment interacts with the personal characteristics of the individual in determining whether or not the symptoms of major depression will be displayed. While it is true that such environmental events as death of a loved one, rejection in love, or loss of a job can be expected to produce dysphoria, as do many other conditions encountered in life, such events do not always produce the unusually extended clinical depression. Many people experience dysphoria from the problems and losses encountered for an appropriate period and then recover to take up their life patterns again.

What is it that makes it so that some people do not recover in an appropriate manner or length of time from such precipitating events (S_2 in Figure 10.3)? In the paradigmatic behaviorism analysis, the other interacting determinant resides in the individual's basic behavioral repertoires. Everyone experiences grief with the loss of a child, for example. But most parents suffering such a loss—although remembering the loss forever with sadness—nevertheless do not settle into a clinical depression. Normally, there will be other important elements in the parent's emotional–motivational system. There are the stimuli of work, recreation, social activities, other children and relatives, one's spouse, and so on. When these also have strong emotional value they will be reinforcers and they will act as incentives in attracting the behavior of the individual. They will prevent the symptomatic behaviors of depression from developing past an appropriate point of persistance and intensity. On the other hand, let us take the case of a woman who only has one child, who has few friends, no activities and recreations that elicit a strong emotional response, little emotional satisfaction in sex and marriage, a weak emotional response to her husband, household responsibilities that are a burden rather than a joy, and strong satisfaction only in the person and doings of the child. Loss of the child in such a case may be catastrophic and produce a dysphoria that yields a deep, sustained, and unremitting picture of depression.

PERSONALITY DETERMINANTS OF DEPRESSION

As the last example indicates, it is usually not the environment alone that is the determinant of the dysphoria of depression (although the contribution of the environment may be considered to involve a continuum of importance). The individual's personal characteristics are also important, and this means that another important site of study resides in the study of personality as it interacts with environmental causes in producing depression. Paradigmatic behaviorism's theory says that there are three areas of personality: the emotional–motivational, the language–cognitive, and the sensory–motor. We can take the example of the mother bereft from the loss of a child to illustrate the case where deficits in the emotional–motivational personality system are a root cause of depressive dysphoria. The individual's emotional–motivational system may also be problematical (abnormal) because it is inappropriate in some respects. For example, the individual's standards of performance may be too high to allow for achievement, so that an environment that offers a full measure of positive emotional–motivational stimulation for most people nevertheless will yield deprivation and dysphoria in that individual. For example, this can occur in one's professional life because the individual has been so successful that his or her standards have continued to go up, to the point where there is nothing left to bring satisfaction. Emotional–motivational stimuli other than of a professional type must then be available, and if they are not the individual may experience emotional–motivational loss, that is, dysphoria.

In the language–cognitive area there may also be inappropriate aspects of personality that are etiologically causative. Let us take an example of a working man who has lost his job. The individual, let us say, then suffers great losses in emotional–motivational stimulation. Without funds he is unable to drink with his buddies and engage in other social events. His wife must work, which provides negative emotional–motivational stimulation as well as the withdrawal of aspects of her affection and esteem and that of his children. These losses can themselves produce a dysphoric state. But, let us say, the working man has a rigid belief in individual responsibility for success in the American society. Moreover, in the past he has many times argued that it is not the fault of society when people are down and out, but is the fault of the people themselves. When these statements are applied to himself the result may be a deep and lasting dysphoria that finds expression in the symptomatic "feelings of inadequacy, loss of self-esteem, or self-deprecation." "Exaggerated expressions of guilt are certainly common among depressed people . . . " (London, 1968, p. 402). Mowrer's (1966) view of depression agrees with the classic analytic view that guilt is a cause, but he added that depressed people had a history of misconduct to be guilty about. It should be emphasized here that guilt is a product of the language–cognitive system. Of people with the same conduct, or misconduct, some will say self-recriminatory things and produce negative emotionality and others will not—depending upon the language–cognitive repertoires they have learned that determine what they consider to be righteous. Their belief systems interpret the events involved, that is, produce guilt, and thus are causative.

Looked at from the other side, we may see that the unemployed worker who considers himself to be inadequate and guilty for his unemployment also has a deficit in hig language–cognitive system. That is, if he had a world view that included an understanding of the economics of recessions and depressions, of the political and geopolitical reasons involved, and so on, the unemployed worker could see that his unemployment is not his fault and that he is not guilty for the personal and familial losses that have occurred. Another person who suffers the same environmental circumstances, but with a different world view, may experience anger instead of dysphoria and be motivated to social action—rather than to the symptoms of depression. Again we see that dysphoria results from an interaction.

Finally, there are deficits and inappropriatenesses in the sensory–motor repertoires that are also involved in depression. On the deficit side, limitations in the individual's sensory–motor skills may place limits upon the individual's adaptability in the face of environmental losses. Let us take the housewife whose life is centered on a child or children. When they are gone, there is a gap that must be filled. The housewife who has previously developed athletic, dance, art, or music skills may reactivate them in a program of activity that replaces the children who have gone. The lost sources of positive emotional experience are replaced by other sources. The housewife who lacks those sensory–motor skills does not have that avenue, and other things being equal will suffer more from the loss. Let us take the following example of inappropriate sensory–motor (including social) behavior as a determinant of depression. "Sometimes the patient will engage in sort of premanic activity in which he tries to surround himself with people, and his efforts to win friends become frantic—so frenzied, in fact, that they often alienate the very people he is trying to win over" (McMahon, 1976, p. 248). In this example the frenzied behavior has an effect upon the social environment that results in the loss of emotional–motivational stimuli that further helps determine the onset of the dysphoria. There is some empirical support for the notion that depressive behavior is aversive to others (e.g., Lewinsohn, Mischel, Chaplin, & Barton, 1980). As another example, lack of physical skills in lovemaking or sports may be evaluated by the individual himself in a way that produces dysphoria.

The Behavior Interaction Principle and Symptom Effects

The behavioral interaction principle (Staats, 1963, 1968a, 1971b)—which has counterparts in the more recent person–situation interactionism and the reciprocal determinism concepts of social learning theory—has also been employed in considering abnormal behavior (see Bandura, 1968; Staats, 1963, 1971a, 1975; Staats & Butterfield, 1965). In the present context it may be said that the symptoms of depression themselves have effects upon the development and maintenance of the pathology. As an example, the loss of effectiveness (in study, work, and other activities) that comes about from the depressive's dysphoria, in turn has the effect of deepening the dysphoria. That is, on top of the other inducers of the dysphoria the individual also experiences a decrement in his own effectiveness as well as the negative social responses to his ineffectiveness, an additional loss. This type of interaction can be considered to be widespread in this problem.

The Behavior Competition Principle

This principle is important in the etiological development of depression as well as in the way that will be mentioned here. As with the above-stated principle, space limitations preclude the extensive coverage the importance of the topic demands. The principle is that abnormal and normal behaviors are frequently in a competitive relationship (Staats, 1975). Symptoms in depression can be used to illustrate the principle; for example, thoughts of suicide and brooding about past events are behaviors that are in competition with interest in and enjoyment of pleasurable events and activities. The abnormal behavior displaces the normal. The individual experiencing dysphoria cannot at the same time experience joy. The converse may be expected in a treatment program. Sometimes treatment may involve removing the abnormal behavior, other times it may be desirable to strengthen the normal behavior that is in competition with the abnormal behavior. For example, one treatment of depression could involve an athletic recreation program, since the emotional responses elicited could displace the dysphoria. In the present example, the reference is to symptomatic behaviors, but the same rationale extends to the personality repertoires.

THE ORIGINAL LEARNING OF PERSONALITY AS AN ETIOLOGICAL CAUSE

Another site of concern in Figure 10.3 has to do with the acquisition of the basic behavioral (personality) repertoires. There have been references in the classic dynamic literature to experiential factors that are causative in producing personality characteristics predisposing one to depression. "These patients have been sensitized to the traumatic event by losses they have sustained in the past, by insecurities, and by unendurable situations of stress to which they were exposed in their childhood." (Gutheil, 1959, p. 349). Cameron says that "The adult who develops a neurotic depression under stress is one whose major points of fixation lie somewhere in this period of weaning from an oral infantile dependence toward a dawning independence. He carries within him . . . basic conflict over dependent needs and the fear of becoming helplessly dependent" (1963, p. 429). London puts it thus:

> Dynamic theorists are more prone to regard depression as a learned pattern of response to the threat of losing the source of satisfaction of dependency needs. This would be most likely to happen, of course, to people who developed exaggerated dependency needs in childhood, perhaps by being repeatedly threatened with the loss of nurture if they did not comply with parental demands. (London, 1968, p. 403)

Standard behaviorism has rejected dynamic explanations of human behavior. Paradigmatic behaviorism, in contrast, recognizes these as beginning attempts to consider early experiences as independent variables in the causation of human behavior. This is not to say that the assessment of human experience by dynamic psychologists was well or completely conducted, or that they formulated a theoretical system that could serve as the basis for continued growth in this direction. On the contrary, the paradigmatic behaviorism position is that the dynamic theorists' attempts to consider how experience affects personality were too simple and sometimes incorrect. This was also true of the personality constructs of id, ego, and superego, and other like attempts. And these developments were not related to the complexities of behavior that humans display. A fundamental weakness was that dynamic theory was not stated in a way that could grow with the findings that the general field of psychology has made; it never developed a good or detailed understanding of learning.

In the view of paradigmatic behaviorism the types of clinical observation on which the psychodynamic approach has been based are nevertheless important sources of knowledge, and the conceptions of the psychopathologies must be formulated so these sources of knowledge can be employed. But, the social behaviorism conception has been derived from the basic science and it is thus capable of utilizing further developments in that basic knowledge. When the conception, for example, states that the individual's language–cognitive personality repertoire is involved in producing depression, the theory of language–cognitive personality ties into the psychology of language–cognition. To illustrate, with respect to Figure 10.3, how does the depressive learn such aphorisms in his language–cognitive system as "Those who are out of work don't want to work." More basically, how does one learn one's language? Understanding the individual's personal philosophy and how it was learned may be a clinical task necessary to treating the individual case. But that understanding demands that the clinician have an understanding of how that aspect of the personality repertoires can be important in producing depression, and how it is important therefore to understand how such repertoires can be changed. The basic etiological study of depression, therefore lies in the general psychological study of the manner in which the language–cognitive, the emotional–motivational, and the sensory–motor repertoires are learned and with the principles by which the personality repertoires and the person's life circumstances (in interaction) produce dysphoria as well as the principles by which dysphoria produces symptoms. The implications of this model are that we need greatly expanded study of the personality repertoires and how they are learned. This calls for a theory that unifies various fields of psychology.

THE DYSPHORIA AND THE SYMPTOMS
IT PRODUCES

Central questions are raised by the last statements; questions that the theory indicates will require study. By way of explanation, it may be said that the traditional view of personality is that personality determines behavior. But the principles by which the effects occur are not explicized. Paradigmatic behaviorism demands that explication, and this demand is true of the dysphoric state. The paradigmatic behaviorism theory is that the depressive's dysphoric state represents an enduring negative emotional response. The theory, moreover, states that the negative emotional state will further elicit a class of behaviors: verbal and other motor behaviors. The experience of a negative emotional state, for example, will tend to elicit a large class of words that have a negative meaning (Staats, 1961, 1963, pp. 154–157), words that will be described as feelings of worthlessness, thoughts of suicide, and so on. The dysphoric state will also produce difficulty in thinking and concentrating because the state will elicit those negative meaning words so strongly that they interfere with the trains of language responses that would ordinarily be elicited by the other affairs of life. The particular words that the negative emotional state elicits will be a function of the individual's learned language–cognitive repertoires, commonly called ideas, opinions, knowledge, and so on.

The experience of the negative emotional state will also further elicit other motor symptoms of depression such as sleep disturbances, agitation, irritability, inability to work, and so on. The negative emotional state will also interfere with eating, because it will detract from the positive emotional response value that food ordinarily elicits, which controls eating behavior. The same thing is true of other ordinarily positive emotional stimuli. That is, the positive emotional value of recreation (movies, parties, reading), hobbies, perhaps sex, and so on, that ordinarily insures that the behavior of participating will be well reinforced, will be diminished by the dysphoria. As a result the behaviors will weaken, and this is also symptomatic of depression.

It may be added that environmental losses and the like generally produce a negative emotional state. But the behaviors (symptoms) that the negative emotional state will elicit in different individuals will not be the same. Two individuals may experience rejection of a loved person, as an example. In one case, the experience will elicit negative-meaning verbal behaviors that will be called anger, because they are directed toward the rejecting person. In the other individual the negative-meaning verbal behaviors will be directed toward the rejected person himself and will be called depression. Schachter (1970) has said that the external cues determine whether the person will experience an emotional state as negative or positive. The paradigmatic behaviorism position adds a different principle, that is, that individuals learn to respond differently to the same type of environmental loss or other negative-emotion-producing circumstance—and their differences in learned behavior provide the definition of what specific emotional response is involved, for example, anger versus sadness.

The sites of study that have been specified thus far in the theory are utilized in briefly examining some of the behavioral and behavioral–cognitive literature in terms of the theory. Then some additional elaborations are made to introduce new theoretical elements with value for explaining additional aspects of depression.

ENVIRONMENTAL (S_2) VARIABLES

The environmental factors that affect aspects of the personality repertoires of the depressive are readily observable and can be manipulated in experimental and sometimes clinical settings. Of five major environmental variables that have been hypothesized by behavioral psychologists to occasion an episode of depression, four have been studied and there is very mixed support. This is not surprising since investigations based on standard behaviorism conceptions customarily isolate an environmental variable without considering the environmental–personality interactions that predict depression. Nevertheless, there are important findings relevant to developing the present theory.

It has been suggested that excessively low reinforcement (ratio strain) (Ferster, 1973) is an environmental variable that produces depression. This is still awaiting investigation. Case studies (e.g., Moss & Boren, 1972), however, do provide anecdotal support that these variables play some role in the determination of depression and suggest further research may be promising. For example, ratio strain may be a factor in depression that occurs in college freshmen who are reacting to a major increase in the amount of studying required to obtain a grade that was more easily obtained in high school. It should be noted, however, that ratio strain refers to weakened instrumental responding, not to dysphoria, and without the latter, weak responding would not constitute depression.

It has also been said that depression results from learned helplessness, where behavior ceases because it is not reinforced. (The principle is actually very much like Ferster's analysis of depression.) In any event, such research (e.g., Miller & Seligman, 1975) has failed to demonstrate that this environmental variable is related to depression (Heiby, 1979). Seligman and his colleagues (Abramson, Seligman, & Teasdale, 1978) have revised the learned helplessness hypothesis to include variables involving some of the language–cognitive personality repertoires, in the present view, by maintaining that attributional style is the critical determinant of depression. In the original learned helplessness hypothesis, mere exposure to an uncontrollable event, such as a spouse dying of terminal cancer, was posited to result in the grieving individual behaving as if no events were controllable and therefore being helpless and depressed. In the revised hypothesis, whether or not the event actually is controllable is irrelevant. Instead, helplessness or depression is viewed as a function of one's beliefs regarding controllability. The support for the revised hypotheses is discussed in the language–cognitive section below.

Both Ferster (1973) and Lewinsohn (1974) propose that depressive behavior is acquired and maintained by contingent environmental reinforcement. The notion of secondary gain as an etiologic factor in depression has a long anecdotal history in the psychiatric and psychological literature (e.g., Freedman, Kaplan, & Sadock, 1976). A person who attempts to obtain social support through behaving in a depressive manner may become dependent upon others to alleviate despondency through the provision of such special attention and support. Correlational evidence has suggested that a depressive environment is characterized by an increase in the frequency of certain types of positive reinforcement, such as sympathy, but has not related these reinforcers to specific contingencies controlling depressive behavior (e.g., Rehm & Plakosh, 1975; Sheslow & Erickson, 1975). Single-subject reversal design studies have indicated that, once the symptomatic behaviors of depression are extinguished, they can be reinstituted and maintained if followed by positive reinforcement (e.g., Liberman, 1970; Liberman & Raskin, 1971; Reisinger, 1972).

The environmental variable receiving the greatest empirical support also was proposed by both Ferster (1973) and Lewinsohn (1974) and involves the acquisition and maintenance of depressive behavior following a reduction in sources of environmental reinforcement that, in effect, places much of the individual's adaptive behavior on an extinction schedule. The notion that depression is a reaction to a loss is by no means a new one (Freud, 1933). The Freudian explanation of depression, of course, involves an assumption of oral fixation and subsequent regression for which is substituted the principle that extinction follows loss of reinforcement. Although an oversimplification is involved, putting the Freudian hypothesis of loss in reinforcement terms has encouraged empirical validation, which is a productive outcome.

Ferster (1973) also posited that punishment of large classes of behaviors was an environmental determinant of depression. The punishment, however, was considered to work through its effects upon the adaptive behaviors of the individual. As in the other cases already described, the concern here is with explaining the diminished activity of the depressive patient through referring to the direct action of reinforcement conditions. It is the symptom of the depressive's lack of active, striving behavior that assumes the central role in this approach to depression, as in the learned helplessness approach.

It should be understood that most of the behavioral (and behavior–cognitive) literature dealing with depression has been conducted within a particular learning theory and a particular view of behavior—actually, the operant behaviorism view. Centrally, the operant approach focuses upon instrumental behavior and the effects of reinforcement conditions upon behavior. Dysphoria, while brought on by loss of reinforcement and by punishment, in the operant view is an epiphenomenon that can parallel changes in behavior but has no effects upon behavior—and an explanation of human behavior does not have to treat emotions, positive or negative. Thus, in this view, it is the instrumental behavioral symptoms of depression that are focal— especially those involving the decreased activity, work, studying, socializing, talking, and so on, as well as the increase in maladaptive behaviors such as crying, irritability, anger, thoughts of suicide, and so on. The operant theory of depression involves centrally those environmental variables, such as ratio strain, extinction, punishment, uncontrollable environment, that can decrease the frequency of adaptive behaviors and those environmental variables, such as positive reinforcement, that can increase the frequency of maladaptive behaviors. This theory of depression suggests that treatment should attempt to increase the frequency of adaptive instrumental behaviors and lessen the frequency of maladaptive behaviors, using procedures involving direct reinforcement of the behaviors themselves. Theorists who employ this theory framework, even when they recognize clinically that a dysphoric condition is involved in depression, are not systematically concerned with dysphoria as a cause because there is no place in the theory for recognizing how an emotional state can affect overt instrumental behavior (Skinner, 1975). Not considering dysphoria and language–cognitive phenomena as causal in depression is a severe weakness of this approach.

Research conducted within this framework, however, has been productive within the limitations of its interest. Thus, it is recognized that case studies of depressives commonly include descriptions of excessive complaining over losses and failure to obtain reinforcement (e.g., Burgess, 1969). Correlational studies demonstrate the lowered activity level; depressed individuals engage in fewer pleasurable activities than do nondepressives (e.g., Lewinsohn & Graf, 1973; Lewinsohn and McPhillamy, 1974). Retrospective studies suggest that depressed individuals experienced a reduction in reinforcement (or at least in positive life circumstances) prior to the onset of the depression (e.g., Leff, Roatch, & Bunney, 1970; Lewinsohn

& Talkington, 1979; Mueller, Edwards, & Yarvis, 1977; Paykel, 1969; Roy, 1981; Slater & DePue, 1981). Other studies have demonstrated that severity of depression increases with a concurrent decrease in sources of reinforcement (positive life circumstances) and decreases with concurrent increases in such sources (Hammen & Glass, 1975; Hersen, Eisler, Alford, & Agras, 1973; Reisinger, 1972). An environmental reduction in sources of positive stimulation, however, does not always occasion depression and is not a sufficient predictor in and of itself. Hammen and Cochran (1981), for example, demonstrated that severe recent losses of sources of reinforcement do not necessarily result in depression. Similarly, Lloyd (1980) found that many depressives do not report significant losses. These are contradicting findings when one stays within the operant framework. Moreover, it is not clear usually in these studies whether the losses are response-contingent, that is, that a reinforcement effect is involved.

Thus, valuable research has been generated within this framework. But it is also unclear and inconsistent. The approach does not distinguish losses that elicit dysphoria from the loss of response-contingent reinforcement. Moreover, without a concept of personality there is no explanation of why there are individual differences in response to the same environmental conditions of loss. The findings can be more useful when it is realized that environmental losses can interact with personality and thereby constitute an antecedent for depression onset.

BASIC BEHAVIORAL REPERTOIRES (PERSONALITY)

Without a concept of personality, standard behaviorism's studies have not been addressed to understanding the person's own contribution to the onset and maintenance of depression. We may nevertheless see that research has been conducted that can be interpreted to involve the several personality repertoires.

The Sensory–Motor Repertoire

Lewinsohn (1974) proposed that possession of poor social skills is an antecedent to depression because poor social skills typically lead to a low rate of positive social reinforcement. (Actually, it is not only the reinforcement value of the social stimulation that is central in depression but the loss of positive emotion elicitation, which contributes to dysphoria.) The depression literature has failed to distinguish between poor social skills due to a skills deficit (as in lacking assertiveness) or to inappropriate behavior (as in being overly aggressive or overly self disclosing). This lack of specification detracts from the theoretical structure. It should also be noted that social skills are not constituted solely of sensory–motor behaviors, but also of the two other personality repertoires, and this represents another weakness of Lewinsohn's theory.

Studies comparing the quality of social skill in depressives and nondepressives report mixed results. It is difficult to interpret these studies because numerous different measures of social skill have been implemented. Depressives have been found to exhibit a lower rate of speech during verbal interchanges (Hinchliffe, Lancashire, & Roberts, 1971; Libet & Lewinsohn, 1973), elicit fewer positive reactions from others (Coyne, 1976; Libet & Lewinsohn, 1973), perform more ambiguous nonverbal communication (Prakchin, Craig, Papageorges, & Reith, 1977), and receive global ratings of greater dependency and lower social competence (Lewinsohn, Mischel, Chaplin, & Barton, 1980; Gotlib, 1982). This is what the paradigmatic behaviorism theory would expect; that is, poor social skills gain for the depressed individual little in positive emotion elicitation and abundant negative emotion elicitation of both response–contingent and nonresponse–contingent types. However, it is true that none of these studies measures social skill prior to the onset of depression or after the depressive behavior dissipates. Because depression is partly defined in terms of psychomotor retardation and decreased social activity, it is not surprising that depressives appear less skilled than their nondepressed counterparts.

In order to identify a social skills deficit or inappropriate social behavior that is etiological in depression, it is necessary to demonstrate dysfunctional social skills prior to depression onset as well as support the expectation that dysfunctional social skills can elicit social responses from others whose negative emotional value deepens the dysphoria. Dysfunctional social skills cannot be a sufficient antecedent, or those with such deficiencies would be chronically depressed, and all those with such deficits would be depressed. It may be added that Tanner, Weissman, & Prusoff (1975) evaluated longitudinal data comparing social adjustment for two groups with a history of depression and found no relation between social skill and frequency of depression. Shrader, Craighead and Shrader (1978) take the contrary view that depressives do not possess poor social skill abilities but only exhibit a difference in performance of those social behaviors. It may be concluded that the evidence that depressives exhibit a dysfunctional instrumental repertoire is still weak. This is the case the paradigmatic behaviorism theory suggests, because in manifestation as well as in causative circumstances depression is not a unitary disorder. Poor social skills can be experienced as a severe problem. But lack of social skills is only one of various problems that may produce the negative affective conditions that underlie the symptoms of depression. Approaches that assume an oversimplified etiology, that hypothesize the same causative agent in all patients, and that do not recognize personality differences in response to problems, inevitably must produce confused and inconsistent findings.

The Language–Cognitive Repertoire

Research on cognitive factors in depression has included variables regarding inappropriate causal attributions of unpleasant events, unrealistic performance expectations, and negative self-evaluations. In terms of paradigmatic behaviorism, what are called cognitive factors frequently include characteristics that would more appropriately be considered as emotional–motivational in nature. Thus the literature is not clear-cut in these areas.

Seligman and his colleagues (Abramson et al., 1978) revised the learned helplessness hypothesis (based primarily on Weiner's [1978] attributional model) to exclude environmental determinants of depression and replace the response–outcome–independence cause of depression with what in the present theory is the language–cognitive variable of making inappropriate attributions regarding the cause of unpleasant experiences. That is, Abramson et al. hypothesize that depression onset is a function of attributing all unpleasant events as being beyond one's own control and caused by internal (one's own characteristics), stable (permanent), and global (generalizes to all unpleasant events) factors. In other words, they hypothesize that the person who makes the contradictory conclusion of being responsible for what are perceived to be uncontrollable, unpleasant events (and really beyond the responsibility of anyone) will become depressed. Again, the issue of why such persons are not chronically depressed is not addressed since their attribution characteristics are considered to be stable.

The research evaluating the attribution hypothesis has produced mixed results. Several studies found that depressives, compared to nondepressives, are more likely to attribute unpleasant events to global, stable, and internal causes (Raps, Peterson, Reinhard, Abramson, & Seligman, 1982; Seligman, Abramson, Semmel, & von Baeyer, 1979). Some studies support that internal attributions for failure are more likely in depressives (Nelson & Craighead, 1981) while other studies found depressives were not more likely to report internal attributions for negative outcomes (Golin, Sweene, & Shaeffer, 1981; Hammen, Krantz, & Cockran, 1981) or did so inconsistently (Zuroff, 1981). Again such research has produced mixed results, which is what the present approach would expect when the complex disorder is considered in an oversimplified, unitary manner.

One study may be interpreted as evidence for the type of environment–personality interaction that has been described herein. Hammen and de Mayo (1982) found that some negative environmental events are more related to depression than are others. Undesirable events that the subject assesses as controllable were found to be more associated with depression than were negative events deemed to be beyond control. The depressed subjects attributed the former events to be internally (self) caused and global. This is in contrast to undesirable events for which the subject reports no controllability. Undesirable, uncontrollable events were rated as equally upsetting but due to external causes, and these events were less associated with depression. Thus, self-blame (internal attributions) is more likely to occur if the event is not only undesirable but could have been affected by the subject. In other words, it is unlikely that depressives make the same attribution for all unpleasant events as Abramson, *et al.* (1978) would predict; otherwise the depressive would assume responsibility for such common events as poor weather, and his failure would be all encompassing. Instead, the data suggest selectivity for depressives, that self-degradation for failure occurs only in the case of controllable negative events.

There is additional evidence that supports the concept of varying conditions for self-blame. In a longitudinal study repeatedly assessing unpleasant events and subsequent reactions, Coyne, Alduin and Lazarus (1981) found that individuals already depressed at the outset and during the course of the study did not engage in self-blame for unpleasant events more than did their nondepressed counterparts. Peterson, Schwartz, & Seligman (1981) found that blame directed at one's entire character (thus implying permanence) was correlated with current depression, but blame directed at one's isolated behavior was not so correlated. Furthermore, characterological blame was not related to subsequent onset of depression. This suggests that studies manipulating self-blame alone cannot predict depression onset. It is suggested, again, that the problem of such studies is they assume self-blame to be a general characteristic, and to be generally a factor in depression. As has already been indicated, the latter is not a rule and self-blame need not be a general characteristic. Following the example previously given, the unemployed man may blame himself in this sphere, but not do so generally. The present theory stresses that the individual's language–cognitive repertoire is complex, as is the individual's environmental experience, and the two interact.

Beck (1967) hypothesizes a "negative triad" in which he states that depression is a function of a negative view of the self, the world, and the future. These more inclusive negative views are purported to be maintained by a memory deficit that involves distorting environmental feedback in order to exaggerate the negative and ignore the positive. For Beck, the depression-prone individual fails to attend to events or feedback that contradict these negative assumptions. The depressives' habitual errors of logic that Beck proposed include arbitrary inference, selective abstraction, overgeneralization, and personalization, as ways of lessening positive stimuli and increasing negative stimuli. The present theory would qualify such statements, again, in terms of generality and being the only cause.

Additional self-control hypotheses are related to this analysis and when appropriately interpreted also contribute to the framework being developed herein. These hypotheses may be seen to involve both the language–cognitive and emotional–motivational personality repertoires and agree with predictions derived from paradigmatic behaviorism theory. Negative evaluations of one's performance and a failure to discriminate positive events are variables posited to antecede depression by a number of self-control theorists and researchers (Heiby, 1979, 1981, 1983b, 1983c; Jackson, 1972; Mathews, 1977; Rehm, 1977). What is called the self-control hypothesis suggests that deficits in evaluation and discrimination of positively valenced events may result in a dysfunctionally low frequency of self-reinforcement (LFSR). (This may affect other sources of emotional–motivational stimulation as will be discussed in a following section.) A LFSR is hypothesized to antecede and in part contribute to depression, which in the present terms must refer to the instrumental symptoms of depression. It is reasoned that some portion of human behavior is a function of self-presented reinforcement. It is also assumed that adaptive, nondepressed functioning depends upon obtaining some unspecified minimum amount of positive reinforcement.[3] The source of the reinforcement may be from externally-controlled contingencies (material or social) or from self-controlled contingencies (covert or overt). It is further hypothesized that the adaptive functioning of an individual who engages in a LFSR is relatively more dependent upon externally-controlled contingencies. Therefore, the individual with a LFSR may fluctuate in adaptive functioning as the environment fluctuates in sources of reinforcement, whereas the individual with a high frequency of self-reinforcement (HFSR) may exhibit more consistent adaptive functioning because such functioning is less dependent upon changing environmental contingencies. The individual with a LFSR may appear to have a fluctuating sense of self-esteem and self-confidence and be predisposed to depression when changes in environmental contingencies occur (reduction in environmental sources of reinforcement, Ferster [1966], Bandura [1969]). This actually involves a theoretical lacuna, since the analysis never explains how self-reinforcement, low or high, is related to self-esteem and self-confidence. Studies investigating the effect of a LFSR per se will be reviewed in the following section, which concerns the emotional–motiva-

[3] The notion that the human is a hedonistic being whose behavior is influenced by pleasure has been commonly assumed in many personality theories since Freud's (1933) introduction of the pleasure principle. Useful as this conception has been, it has very different heuristic characteristics than a theory that closely links findings ranging from the animal laboratory to clinical practice, in a multilevel theory structure with detailed and explicit principles.

tional repertoire. The language–cognitive components of a LFSR will be considered here.

Both the Beck negative triad and self-control literature provide consistent support for the hypothesis that individuals who are depressed exhibit concurrent negative expectations and a tendency to report fewer recent positive events than nondepressives. Numerous studies have shown that depressives, as compared to nondepressives, are more likely to rate their objectively comparable performance on experimental tasks as inferior (Heiby, 1981; Loeb, Beck, Diggory, & Tuthill, 1967; Lobitz & Post, 1979; Rozensky, Rehm, Pry, & Roth, 1977). When asked to recall the frequency of recently experienced positive and negative outcomes on an experimental task, depressives report a lower frequency of positive outcomes than do nondepressives (DeMonbreun & Craighead, 1977; Dobson & Shaw, 1981; Gotlib, 1981; Nelson & Craighead, 1977; Wener & Rehm, 1975). DeMonbreun and Craighead measured both immediate perception and recall of feedback and found that depressives negatively distort recall but are accurate in reporting the frequency of immediate feedback, suggesting that a memory rather than discrimination deficit is in effect. Perhaps the memory deficit involves errors of logic as Beck proposed or inappropriate attention and rumination over negative occurrences that inflates estimates of frequency of unpleasant events.

A few studies compared depressives' and nondepressives' estimates of positive events to the actual rate and found that depressives do indeed report a lower frequency than do nondepressives but that the depressives' estimates were more accurate and reflective of actual experience (Hoehn–Hyde, Schlottman, & Rush, 1982; Lewinsohn et al., 1980; Miller & Seligman, 1975; Miller, Seligman, & Kurlander, 1975). These results suggest that lower estimates of positive events reported by other researchers may be low by virtue of being more realistic than the estimates of the nondepressives. In other words, depressives may be lacking an adaptive skill of distorting the memory of recent events to exaggerate the positive. Jenkins and Ward (1965) demonstrated that nondepressives identify a positive contingency for behavior when such a contingency is actually not operative. (Unfortunately, no depressives were evaluated in the study.) A couple of studies compared depressives and nondepressives and found the nondepressives were more likely to report that success contingencies exist when indeed they do not (Golin, Terrel, & Johnson, 1977). This suggests that normative, nondepressed functioning is partly a consequence of distortion toward optimism; that is, in the present theory, a habit of labeling things in positive emotional words. These various studies provide important findings, although they have not previously been integrated into a coherent theoretical framework as is the present aim.

It is important to indicate that although social behaviorism, among the behavioral approaches, suggested the turn toward the cognitive (see Staats, 1968a, 1972), the turn, when it occurred, has involved the theoretical language and methodology of operant theory or social learning theory—neither of which rests upon or requires the type of behavioral analysis demanded by social behaviorism. We can see this clearly in the present case. What does it mean for example to say that adaptive functioning depends on a minimum of positive reinforcement? Does that refer to adaptive instrumental behaviors, which is the only type that reinforcement is pertinent to? It is also said that a low self-esteem is related to a LFSR. Does that mean that self-esteem is an instrumental behavior and that the person with a LFSR does not reinforce his self-esteem? In more general terms how is self-reinforcement related to self-esteem? Perhaps low self-esteem produces LFSR, not the reverse. Actually, in the present view the relationship is one of sameness—for example, that which is called self-esteem consists of self-referring statements that elicit a positive emotional response (Staats, 1968a, 1975), which is a type of "self-reinforcement."

The fact is there is a lack of analysis in presently popular cognitive concepts amongst modern behavioral clinicians. This vagueness has drawbacks when considered in terms of paradigmatic behaviorism. For example, such a concept as self-reinforcement, which actually derived from explicit early learning analyses (Mowrer, 1960; Staats, 1963, pp. 95–98) is left by most contemporary theorists as an unanalyzed category, without specification of the repertoire mechanisms by which self-reinforcement takes place. We must ask what are the cognitive mechanisms of self-reinforcement? If we do not explicize what they are then we cannot understand them or state how they must be changed to affect treatment. In contrast to this lack of specification, in paradigmatic behaviorism the mechanisms of self-reinforcement have been given specific analysis in terms of the repertoires that underlie the process. For example, as is indicated further on, much of self-reinforcement depends upon language repertoires, particularly what has been called the verbal–emotional repertoire (the very large group of words that elicit emotional responses). Paradigmatic behaviorism suggests that the phenomena of self-reinforcement cannot be understood without reference to the verbal–emotional repertoire (Staats, 1968a, 1972, 1975). Another central self-reinforcement mechanism depends upon self-elicited images, which again depends upon a verbal repertoire, the verbal–image repertoire (the large group of words that elicit image responses; see Staats [1968a], Staats & Lohr [1979]). Referring again to the previous example, positive or negative views of the self, as in Beck's analysis, must also be understood in terms of their repertoire constituents (see Staats, 1963, 1968a, 1972, 1975), if we desire an explanatory theory with which to treat clinical problems. The social behaviorism approach is characterized by its demand for analysis into the causal mechanisms of human behavior in a hierarchical theory structure of multiple levels (Staats, 1981). That is the method by which the basic knowledge of learning and the applied knowledge of clinical and abnormal psychology can be tied together. When the links between the levels are not indicated, the reasoning is loose and there are not avenues by which the knowledge from the one area can contribute to the other. The next section exemplifies further the analytic specification of paradigmatic behaviorism.

Emotional–Motivational System

There are several points that must be made in the present theory elaboration, to clarify its principles. First, there is overlap between the language–cognitive and the emotional–motivational personality systems (and the sensory–motor as well). For example, an important part of the language–cognitive system resides in the fact that there are many single words that elicit emotional responses in all of us. (As indicated, this is called the verbal–emotional subrepertoire in social behaviorism's language–cognitive theory.) And words may be joined in groups such that they will elicit emotional responses. Emotional words can serve: (1) as unconditioned stimuli to condition emotional responses to other stimuli with which the words are paired (Staats & Staats, 1957; Staats & Staats, 1958) and thereby produce new emotional stimuli through classical conditioning; (2) as reinforcers of instrumental behavior (Finley & Staats, 1967; Harms & Staats, 1978); and (3) as directive (incentive) stimuli (Staats & Burns, 1982; Staats & Warren, 1974). Such words are thus part of the language–cognitive system and also the emotional–motivational system—which is a way of indicating that the personality repertoires are not separate and independent, not different in fundamental principles, but are only useful classifications of aspects of what is really an integrated human personality system. In the present context it is relevant to note this, since elements of the preceding discussion—such as self-reinforcement—are just as relevant to the emotional–motivational system as to the language–cognitive system.

Most contemporary behavior therapists and behavior modifiers employ as their basic learning theory the principles of the operant conditioning approach (which, with the exception of modeling, are the same for social learning theorists). In this approach the reinforcing function of stimuli is emphasized, but the directing (or incentive or discriminative) function is almost entirely ignored in considering human behavior, and the emotion-eliciting and emotion-conditioning function is not recognized. In contrast, in the three-function learning theory (see Staats, 1968b, 1970, 1975) the emotional function is considered central and determines both the reinforcing and incentive value of the stimulus. This difference is important in considering such a topic as self-reinforcement. In the contemporary use of this concept the reinforcing function is not distinguish from the emotion-eliciting function. However, frequently when a person is said to provide a reinforcing stimulus to him or herself, the important and only function of such self-stimulation is actually the experience of emotionality. There may be no contingency relationship to a preceding behavior to provide a reason for considering the process as reinforcement. To call the process self-reinforcement is then very misleading, and the attempt to consider the process in operant terms is in error. This has been a typical error in considering depression.

When a person is dysphoric it is the absence of the experience of positive emotional stimulation and the experience of negative emotional stimulation that is involved—not the lack of reinforcement contingencies. Reinforcement, or its absence, will have been involved in producing deficient and inappropriate personality repertoires. But depression has as its central element dysphoria. And that is an emotional, not a reinforcement, process. Whether reinforcement typically plays a central role in producing symptoms of depression, as an operant approach suggests, is very dubious. All the symptomatic behaviors of depression—for example, thoughts of suicide—can be elicited by the negative emotionality that is experienced, and the symptoms may never have been reinforced. The present theory is that true depression is not maintained by instrumental reinforcement, because dysphoria cannot be produced by positive reinforcement, although certain complicating symptoms may be maintained by their consequences. Depression symptoms are produced primarily by dysphoria, and that is an emotional response.

Part of the purpose of the present paper is to unify behavioral research within a paradigmatic behaviorism framework—and this applies to such things as the concept of self-reinforcement as a mechanism in depression. In pursuit of this goal, it may be said that self-stimuli can be of an emotional nature. When they are, they may or may not function as reinforcing and directive (incentive) stimuli. Thus, the concept of self-produced reinforcement is by itself inadequate and must more appropriately be considered as the application of self-administered affective–reinforcing–directive stimuli. Low and high frequency of self-reinforcement (LFSR and HFSR), a personal characteristic that has been employed in the present context, is treated in the next section, with the more appropriate concept of low and high frequency of self-affective–reinforcing–directive stimulation (LFSARD and HFSARD). Some people, it may be noted, richly supply themselves with positive affective–reinforcing–directive (A–R–D) stimuli, and others do not. This may be referred to in terms of people with systems of HFSARD in the one case and LFSARD in the other.

To continue, the self-control hypothesis in the consideration of depression directly involves the concept of "self-reinforcement." The hypothesis more appropriately should state that one variable associated with depression is a dysfunctionally low level of self-administered emotional stimuli (LFSARD). A LFSARD may be a consequence of inappropriate, learned, negative self-evaluations, which may be associated with a memory deficit of positive events in the language–cognitive repertoire as well as with actual skill dysfunctions in the language–cognitive and sensory–motor repertoires that additionally lead to negative self-labeling. For example, if parental values have eschewed self-recognition and have equated such expression with boastfulness, then a developing individual may not acquire self-language by which to provide self-satisfaction and self-reward and by which to set up incentives (plans) in the manner of a more self-confident individual. The result may be the loss of experience by the individual without a positive self-language (self-concept), which impedes the development of social and other skills, further leading to what is here called a LFSARD system (see Staats, 1963, pp. 262–264; 1975, pp. 155–158).

Further, there is consistent evidence that many depressives exhibit LFSARD characteristics and at least one study that demonstrates that LFSARD can function as both an antecedent to and a subsequent characteristic of depression. Depressives, compared to nondepressives, exhibit a lower frequency of self-produced A–R–D stimuli on a wide variety of experimental tasks (Heiby, 1979; Nelson & Craighead, 1977; Rozensky et al., 1977) as well as in natural settings (Heiby, 1982a, 1982b, 1983a). LFSARD characteristics appear to be a generalized rather than situation-specific skill deficit and are amenable to measurement by a self-report attitude scale (Heiby, 1982a, 1982b, 1983b, 1983c). Depressives exhibiting LFSARD characteristics are not universally negative in evaluating and reinforcing the behavior of others (Lobitz & Post, 1979) suggesting that these depressives are inappropriate specifically regarding self-stimulation in self-evaluation and self-praise. Furthermore, LFSARD characteristics have been associated with general psychopathology but deficits in recall of positive self-stimulation appear to be specific to depression (Gotlib, 1981). A supportive finding is that HFSARD characteristics have been associated with a lack of psychopathology (Barling & Fincham, 1979).

As with all response-defined variables hypothesized to antecede depression, most of the evidence derives from subjects who are depressed, which confounds the question of whether the variable is a determinant or simply a symptom of depression. At least two studies, however, address the question of whether what are here called LFSARD characteristics actually ante-cede depression onset. In an analogue study, Heiby (1983b) found that nondepressives with LFSARD characteristics exhibit a greater dysphoric reaction to a decrease in experimenter-controlled reinforcement than do nondepressives with HFSARD personalities. This study provides evidence that LFSARD is not simply a symptom of depression but may be exhibited without concommitant depressive symptoms. In another study, it was found that persons exhibiting LFSARD stimulation are more likely to ex-hibit dysphoria than are persons exhibiting HFSARD stimulation when faced with similar naturally occurring environmental losses of reinforce-ment (Heiby, 1983a). Furthermore, it was found that some cases of de-pression occurred in people with LFSARD and HFSARD characteristics without environmental losses, suggesting that yet other determinants of depression were operating. Heiby concluded that subtypes of depression exist that may be defined in terms of differences in etiologic factors and, perhaps, variations in response to treatment in the self-reinforcement indi-vidual differences being discussed. The notion of subtypes of depression was suggested by Craighead (1980). Heiby (1982a, 1982b, 1983a) suggests that the interaction of conditions that result in an inappropriately low self-reinforcement characteristic along with a deficit in environmental sources of reinforcement may result in one such subtype. Others have also suggested that subtypes according to whether the individual exhibits dysfunctional social skills or self-control skills may also prove useful in identifying etiol-ogy and selecting the most effective treatment (Blatt, Quinlan, Chevron, McDonald, & Zuroff, 1982; Gotlib, 1982; Rehm, Fuchs, Roth, Kornblith, & Romano, 1979). It is suggested, however, that the multi-elements of the present theory, including its specific, elaborated analysis of interactive pro-cesses, both within the personality repertoires and between these repertoires and the environment, provide the framework of a rich, multi-etiological typology of depression.

ENVIRONMENTAL (S_1) AND BEHAVIOR (B) VARIABLES

The behavioral approach has not directed itself to the study of the original learning conditions responsible for the development of depression. This lack of interest can be seen to be due to several reasons. One reason, it is suggested, has been the reification of the methodology of our early develop-ment of behavior modification and behavior therapy treatment procedures. At the beginning it was necessary to select relatively simple and straightfor-ward types of behavior problems; ones that were self-evident and that were the whole problem, not a symptom of a more complex problem. Although this was an appropriate beginning strategy, it should not be considered to be the complete exploitation of the potential of learning analysis. This reification has been abetted by the rejection of the notion that some problem behaviors are symptoms of more complex problems (Bergin, 1966; Davison, 1967; Eysenck & Rachman, 1965; Grossberg, 1964), by the notion that behavior modification should be a technology rather than seek deeper theoretical understanding (Tryon, 1974), and by the notion that the behavioral approach to clinical treatment must be ahistorical. As an example of the latter, Eysenck stated, "All treatment of neurotic disorders is concerned with habits existing at *present;* their historical development is largely irrelevant" (1960, p. 11). Skinner's functional analysis of behavior implied the same thing, as indicated by Lovaas (1966, pp. 111–112) and Mischel, who stated, "The focus of . . . behavior theory is on what the person is doing in the 'here and now' rather than on reconstruction of his psychic history" (1971, p. 86), a statement that mirrors Eysenck's position.

While valuable at an early time, in the contemporary period this has been a very limiting view, and one that has separated the behavioral approach from both traditional psychodynamic approaches and personality-oriented approaches (Staats, 1970, 1975). Moreover, this position interferes with an approach based upon the utilization of learning principles with which to understand the development of normal and abnormal personality processes. To understand depression, or any other psychopathological state, an analysis of the learning of personality must be a central concern. Ultimately, specific and detailed study of the original learning of the personality repertoires will be required, and this tenet is an important part of the paradigmatic behaviorism conception. Only through such an understanding will we be able to gain knowledge by which to prevent the development of personality factors that are conducive to the occurrence of depression, and to treat depression once it has occurred.

The standard behaviorism point of view has also detracted from an interest in systematically studying the clinical knowledge of psychopathology. Radical behaviorists have rejected the concept of personality and the idea that behaviors can be symptomatic of personality problems (Mischel, 1972, p. 323; Skinner, 1969, pp. 77-78). This conceptual framework has not provided an impetus for the diagnostic study of the behaviors (experience, learning, and behavior) that define depression (or most other psychopathological states). Social behaviorism's analysis of abnormal psychology, however, suggests that an important aspect of dealing with and understanding abnormal behavior lies in the systematic study of the available knowledge of the phenomena involved. The source of knowledge in this area is largely traditional psychiatric or clinical. This should be recognized openly, so that this area of knowledge can be utilized openly by behaviorists using methods of analysis such as those exemplified in the present behavioral approach. As of now, however, this stands as an area of study indicated by the present theoretical model, but not yet developed within general behavioral psychology. See Staats (1975) and Burns (1980) for a general discussion of this topic.

DYSPHORIA

As has been indicated, the focus in behavioral and behavioral–cognitive conceptualizations has not been on the dysphoric state or its role in producing depression. There has, however, been an attempt to measure dysphoria by Schwartz and his colleagues (Schwartz, Fair, Salt, Mandel, & Klerman, 1976). They found the dysphoric mood to be consistently related to increased EMG activity in the facial corrugator and depressor muscles, and they suggested that this facial response is an unconditioned component of dysphoric mood. There are numerous studies demonstrating that specific self-statements are highly correlated with self-reported dysphoric mood. Statements reflecting low achievement and affection expectancies (Gurtman, 1982) as well as a lack of competence and an indication of personal failure (Coleman, 1975; Harrell, Chambless, & Calhoun, 1981; Nelson & Craighead, 1981) have been shown to result in greater dysphoric mood in both depressives and nondepressives. The data, even examined in this preliminary way, support the paradigmatic behaviorism theory of depression, which states that dysphoria is produced by personality processes as well as environmental occurrences. In this theory it is important to study the nature of the dysphoric state, physiologically as well as behaviorally, in another departure from radical behaviorism.

Bipolar Depression: The Mirror Image

Although this distinction has not been treated by behavioral and cognitive–behavioral approaches to depression, traditionally another side is recognized to exist for many patients who experience depressive episodes. In the past the diagnostic category was named manic–depression; a more modern term is bipolar depression, another is to describe the psychopathology as falling generally into the category of affective disorders with manic and depressive phases. The essential feature of the positive phase involves an elevated, excessive, euphoric mood. The associated symptoms are hyperactivity, excessive planning of and "participation in multiple activities (e.g., sexual, occupational, political, religious)."

> Almost invariably there is increased sociability [which exceeds the usual]. . . . [There are] buying sprees, reckless driving, foolish business investments, and sexual behavior

unusual for the individual. . . . Manic speech is typically loud, rapid, and difficult to interrupt. . . . Frequently there is flight of ideas, i.e., a nearly continuous flow of accelerated speech (APA, 1980, pp. 206–207).

Clinical observations have identified individuals who will have alternating episodes of mania and depression, which is the basis for traditionally considering there to be two types of manifestation of the same disease. In recent times bipolar depression has been distinguished from unipolar depression. Bipolar depression is considered to involve greater familial prevalence (Gershon, Bunney, Neckman, Van Erdewegh, & DeBauche, 1976), and to have a greater incidence in monozygotic, as opposed to dyzygotic, twins (Allen, 1976). Because of this and other types of suggestive evidence, bipolar depression is thought by many to be a genetic and biological problem.

The paradigmatic behaviorism theory, on the other hand, provides a basis for considering how mania and depression are related types of behavior disorder, independent of biological causes. This theory does not attempt to rule out the possibility of biological causes. Rather, the theory provides a set of principles and an analysis with which to understand the phenomena involved in behavioral terms. To begin this analysis, it should be recognized that the individual's behavior can result in the production of positive A–R–D consequences, as well as the negative consequences that have been the focus of interest in the account thus far. In the same way that environmental losses can elicit a dysphoric (negative emotional) state, positive occurrences can elicit a euphoric state. This is all very usual, and all of us have experienced such states. For example, when we have an evening when we have been very knowledgeable and intelligent in a social gathering, and have gained social attention and approval, we may experience a euphoric emotional state. The business person who has pulled off an unusually astute and lucrative deal will experience such a state, as will a person who finds a bargain in some important sphere of shopping. When such things happen, the euphoric state itself will be a determinent of subsequent behaviors. The business person may have a drink to celebrate, and she or he may then regale others with the importance of the deal and the skill with which it was conducted, and hence with the ability that she or he has shown. Resulting praise strengthens behavior and positive emotion, which in turn predispose the individual to enter into subsequent business deals. We see this process in many people in a rising real estate or stock market, where individuals enter into deals with an increasing rate. We have a situation that involves repeated sequences of circumstances eliciting an emotional response leading to positive behaviors that produce a further positive emotional response, and so on. It is not uncommon for people in this manner to experience such a euphoric state that when it dissipates, may also leave the individual feeling relatively down.

An important element to add to this analysis is that there are individuals whose personality repertoire development gives them two characteristics that intensify this process. First, they have developed skills for gaining consequences that, while very positive, are not merited by the realities of life. As an example, we may find an individual who has verbal and social skills such that he can convince others to invest in business deals that are not worthy of support. Their investment will be a very positive consequence that will elicit a euphoric state in the individual. Second, these skills will be complicated by deficits in the individual's language–cognitive repertoires that would provide cautionary descriptions of possible dire results further down the line. In the presence of the euphoric state by itself the individual is then likely to enter into additional deals that will further elicit euphoria, in a cumulative process. These may involve a type of manic state. The cases of this type of development that hurt a number of people—as in the collapse of super-successful but shaky business empires—gain attention in the news-papers. But the same process occurs in a less spectacular scope and can be identified in a clinical circumstance as a run-of-the-mill manic state.

This analysis and the theoretical model already developed include princi-ples by which to understand the link between the positive and negative states of affective disorders or bipolar depression. That is, because the indi-vidual's instrumental behaviors do not create real success, but only immedi-ate and ephemeral success, the environmental occurrences that follow in-volve losses. These may be losses of a financial sort, social approval, material possessions, or liberty (when one is imprisoned). At such a point, the dynamics become the same as for general depression. The depression process is the same whether the individual's success has been built upon inadequate skills and unrealistic expectations or whether the individual has displayed great skill in constructing an important set of environ-mental events, only to see the situation collapse—as in the case of a Napoleon.

On the basis of this theory we can see that the classification of mania as an affect disorder represents an inadequate analysis of what is involved. This psychopathology may focally involve disorders of the language–cognitive and sensory–motor personality repertoires. The etiological circumstances may be the exaggerations of language descriptions and of self-promotion, on the one hand, and the deficits in language–cognitive repertoires that involve cautionary, negative, realistic descriptions, on the other. An analy-sis of these latter repertoires has been presented, as the following excerpt indicates.

An important aspect of [how] verbal behavior [can determine the individual's other behavior involves] the existence of verbal aversive stimuli that control avoidant behavior. The cautious man who "anticipates" the aversive consequences of certain actions, the socially sensitive man who "anticipates" socially aversive consequences of certain actions, and so on, would seem to do so, at least in part, because of training that had established for them effective verbal aversive stimuli, as well as the necessary reasoning verbal response sequences. From this interpretation it would seem to follow that the overcautious, timid man's behavior may be, in part, a function of a superabundance of this type of training. The irresponsible, reckless, wild individual, on the other hand, may suffer from a deficit in the relevant training. (Staats, 1963, p. 398)

This analysis, it may also be indicated, posits a relationship between manic psychopathologies and sociopathic problems—in that both can involve related deficits and inappropriate elements in the language–cognitive repertoires. The two, however, differ in other repertoires.

In conclusion, it may be said that this is the first behavioral theory that includes an analysis of manic–depressive psychopathology, and it is the first theory that provides an explanatory account of the positive and negative phases of the disorder in terms of behavioral principles. As such it would be expected that there would be various implications of the theory. For example, the language–cognitive repertoires of manic–depressive patients should be studied and compared to those of unipolar depressives. A specific hypothesis that results from the theory and these empirical hypotheses is that manic–depressives as a group will differ from unipolar depressives with respect to their self-concept (and self-reinforcement) repertoires—at least in their manic and between-phase states. Moreover, it would be of interest to study any differences in the self-concept (and self-reinforcement) repertoires of manic–depressives as a function of the phase of the psychopathology as well as during drug treatment. Psychological tests should be composed to describe and measure the language–cognitive characteristics of manic–depressives. The basic conception involved here calls for theoretical–empirical elaboration.

Exogenous and Endogenous Depression

One of the major considerations of depression has been that some depressions are exogenous, that is, determined by external factors, and the etiology of some depressions are endogenous, that is, determined by physiological dysfunctions (Van Praag, Ulleman, & Spitz, 1965). It should therefore be indicated that the paradigmatic behaviorism theory can give explicit analysis of an endogenous–exogenous dimension, in such a way that it is unified with considerations of this type of psychopathology. We have already discussed various exogenous causes of depression. It is necessary, however, to clarify what is meant by endogenous. First, in the present theory the term *endogenous* refers to any independent variable, that leads to or produces dysphoria, that is part of the person as distinguished from the external environment. Thus, developments in the individual's personality repertoires that contribute to depression would be considered to be endogenous in nature (even though personality was learned in a long personal history). In addition, however, the individual could have a metabolic aberration or an illness that as an endogenous cause would directly produce a dysphoric state, aside from either deficits or inappropriate aspects of the individual's personality repertoires, and aside from any external environmental precipitants.

In addition, however, a theory of depression calls for the understanding of the interaction of endogenous and exogenous etiological events. That is, endogenous factors of both a biological type and a personality type will ordinarily have an environmental effect. For example, a medical problem may incapacitate the individual and produce various environmental–social problems that lead to dysphoria, as will serious personality problems. On the other hand, environmental losses are physical stressors for the individual and ordinarily will have physiological effects—ranging from immune system suppression to hypertension. These "endogenous" factors can in turn result in losses that will be identified as exogenous precipitants of depression. We can see here the principles of complex exogenous-endogenous interaction.

We can see also within this theory why medical prescriptions that directly elevate the patient's mood can be effective. Mood elevation can treat depression by removing the dysphoria, whether the etiology is physiological (endogenous), a problem of personality (endogenous), or an environmental problem (exogenous). Unless the drug treatment ameliorates a primary physiological problem, however, the treatment will only be symptomatic, for the problem will be there when the effects of the drug wear off. If either the patient's personality or environment is a primary cause of the depression, then these problems will require remediation if the drug treatment of dysphoria is to be lasting.

In any event, although these topics cannot be developed herein, it is suggested that the present theory provides a clear and specific framework for considering what exogenous and endogenous depression means, in a way that can be related to other concerns with depression. The theory leaves open the possibility that there may be endogenous causes of a primary physiological sort. Since the biological evidence at this point is only suggestive, the theory calls for specificity in this realm as in the others.

Accentuating the Positive: Prevention through
Social as well as Personality Factors

The study of psychopathology typically focuses on the abnormal, the undesirable, as the cause of problems. We study individuals and design instruments by which to detect pathology. The present theory, for example, discusses deficits and inappropriate aspects of the individual's personality repertoires and environmental circumstances. A dimension that is missing in these efforts is the analysis of the positive, in understanding, assessing, and treating psychopathology. For in considering whether an individual will develop depression when exposed to losses we must also consider possible strong points in the individual's personality repertoires or environmental circumstances.

It is not possible here to consider the implications of this concept in any detail. It can be said, however, that there are personality and environmental pluses as well as minuses, and the pluses may be decisive in whether or not depression will develop. In terms of personality, we have already illustrated how a person with a rich emotional–motivational personality system will withstand environmental loss better than a person with a usual or impoverished emotional–motivational system. As examples of environmental pluses, let us first take the case of the factory worker who loses his job and who considers his loss to be evidence of personal inadequacy. He will be less likely to develop a depression if he has a friend who has a political–economic philosophy that places the blame on societal rather than personal factors. This friend may turn the factory worker's self-recriminations into language-cognitive ruminations that produce anger and social activism instead of depression. The child who loses a loved father or mother may emerge more rapidly from a depression through the contacts of a Big Brother or Big Sister program. The importance of social support groups should be indicated within the present framework (see Albee, 1983), as well as treatment through individual psychotherapy and drug prescription.

> The rapid growth of support groups [for people experiencing such things as marital problems, for children of divorced, alcoholic, or psychotic parents, for school dropouts, for parents of handicapped children, and so on] . . . is one of the most encouraging developments of recent years in the mental-health field. But we need more and larger self-help organizations. Research has made it very clear that individuals who have the support of such organizations are much better off emotionally than those who face their problems alone (Albee, 1985, p. 64).

The important point to emphasize here is that the present theory is not one of just individual frailty and predisposition to psychological problems. The theory is placed into a broader conceptual framework that includes the social context (Staats, 1975) and the necessity for consideration of human problems in that broad manner, in a way that recognizes the social contributions to psychopathology and the potential for the treatment of such problems with social interventions. Moreover, the present theory of depression, with its basis in personality development through learning and in the importance of social conditions as precipitators of depression, provides a foundation for the consideration of prevention as the preferred alternative to treatment. These features make the paradigmatic behaviorism theory of psychopathology (see also Staats, 1975) generally a very appropriate conceptual foundation for the contemporary social-factors–prevention orientation (see Albee, 1982, 1983), and for community psychology generally.

Implications

The paradigmatic behaviorism theory that has been presented herein opens new avenues for the analysis of depression that can be further elaborated and developed. The theory says that there will be a number of etiological subtypes of the category of depression, in contrast to uni-factor simplistic theories. While every true depressive will suffer the pain of negative emotionality, the causes of the dysphoric state may reside in any of the deficient or inappropriate aspects of the three personality repertoires, in their interaction, in the environmental events that confront the individual, or in interactions between the personality repertoires and the environmental events, and between the individual's behavior and resulting environmental occurrences. Ordinarily, of course, the original acquisition of the personality repertoires is a central cause. Since there are multiple ways in which the personality repertoires may be either deficient or inappropriate, and there are many environmental events that may interact with the personality repertoires to produce depressive emotional states, there are a large number of subtypes of depression that are possible. The present theory, with its enhanced detail and specification of etiology, can serve as the foundation for new lines of research to analyze what is now largely an indiscriminate categorization.

The theory that has been set forth contains a number of implications, some of which may be mentioned herein, although a serious treatment is beyond the limitations of one article. One of the implications is methodological, unification of experimental and clinical knowledge as well as behavioral and nonbehavioral knowledge (see Staats, 1983). In the present case the realization that there are various personality determinants and past and present environmental determinants of depression militates against research based upon the implicit assumption that the psychopathology called depression is unitary in a personalistic way other than in the dysphoric affect. Thus, while it may be relevant to consider that some depressives are so because they have negative aspects of their language–cognitive system (Beck, 1967), this cannot be assumed to be the general cause of depression. Similarly, although an environment that does not systematically apply reinforcement could (along with other circumstances) produce learned helplessness and depression, the present theory states this is only one of various causal circumstances. As another example, although deficits in social skills could be a cause, this is only one of various possible causes. The nature of depression, it must be noted, suggests that methods of research that are based upon constituting one group of depressives in the search for causes is likely to produce invalid or unstable results.

The present theory suggests, rather, that we must be prepared to see depression as a unitary category in the dysphoric affect sense, but in no other. The possible determinants of depression appear to be capable of large variability. The theory tells us that there are various sites for research on causal circumstances and, it may be added, for the development of diagnostic and treatment methods. Some of these sites have been in part addressed by research, although typically in a fashion that deals only with a part or subaspect of the processes involved. Thus we can see that Beck's "negative triad" deals with some aspects of the language–cognitive system (and the emotional–motivational) system. But it does not deal with other equally important aspects. Moreover, Beck's theory does not tell us generally what the language–cognitive system (or the emotional–motivational system) is and thus we cannot see the relationship of depression as defined in his way with other aspects of the study of psychology, or even with other types of psychopathology. We cannot, for example, ask the theory to indicate to us how the language–cognitive system is learned, how the negative triad is learned, or how to relate the negative triad concept to the lack of social skills of some depressives, to deficits in other aspects of the personality repertoires, and the like. It is a general characteristic of psychology to attempt to deal with every area or phenomenon as if it existed by itself and is amenable to treatment within a highly specialized conception relevant only to the area or phenomenon (Kimble, 1984; Koch, 1981; Staats, 1981). We can see clearly how this strategy breaks down in the face of a pathological phenomenon as complex as depression.

One of the things that is notable when one enters the study of depression is that there is little in the way of integration of the various hypotheses, concepts, and findings. It is suggested that this is so because there has been no theoretical structure whose aim is to provide a broad framework within which such integration can occur. Rather, as indicated above, each theorist has begun from a limited set of phenomena and a limited conceptualization. The present approach is that it is necessary for a theory of depression to take account of a large proportion of the phenomena and concepts that the various approaches have produced. Rather than considering the various findings and approaches to be in competition, the view is that they are pieces of the puzzle that must be fitted together. In this way, the present theory is an exemplification of a methodology for constructing unified theory (see Staats, 1981, 1983).

One of the concerns that arises within the context of any theory relates to its heuristic value, its value in suggesting new avenues of theory, research, and clinical activities. Since the theory presented herein is only a skeleton, one avenue of advancement is clear, that is, the elaboration of the principles and concepts that have been presented. The present paper exemplifies heuristic potential in other ways as well. As an example, it should be noted that the theory of depression is placed within a structure that is related to a broad theory of psychopathology and of general psychology, and this calls for interrelating our consideration of other diagnostic categories within the concepts and principles of the theory.

New avenues of research are thereby suggested. As an example, while depression is unitary in terms of dysphoria, the personality–environmental interactions may differ in multiple ways, and research must be conducted to characterize those differences. This can be done also in that the analysis suggests that specific personality–environment interactions for these can be the basis for research hypotheses. For example, it has been said that there is an interaction between the environmental event of the loss of job and the individual's conception regarding the blame for such personal failures. Individuals who believe in individual responsibility for personal failure should be more depressed following job loss than individuals without such beliefs, or individuals who believe that it is the society's fault. This analysis suggests a study of people who have lost their jobs: the subjects should be separated into the above three groups, and the proportions of depression should be tabulated in each group. The present analysis has also said there is an interaction between the environmental loss of a loved one and the personality characteristics involving the emotional–motivational system in terms of the breadth of other potent elements in the system—those with narrow focus on the loved one being more susceptible to depression. This analysis could serve very readily as an hypothesis in the above type of study. Let us take another example that has to do with the instrumental skill aspect of the three personality repertoires. Social skills have been of interest in depression research, as has been indicated, but not within the type of theoretical analysis that has been presented herein. The theoretical analysis, by placing the importance of social skills in the theoretical structure involving other variables has implications for improving the type of research conducted. That is, social skills constitute part of a personality system that is involved in a personality–environment interaction, the realization of which can sharpen research to judge the importance of social skills. For example, a deficit in social skills can be expected to be of importance in those cases involving a personality–environment interaction where its presence or absence will play a causative role. Let us take, as the environmental event, adolescents who go away to college. Those who have good social skills would be expected to regain more easily the losses in emotional–motivational elements the move might entail. Under such circumstances social skills will be more crucial than in a socially stable environmental situation. Recognizing the personality–environment interactions in the type of experiments described above would be expected to yield improved precision, reliability, and analysis in the study of depression. Research could also be designed to study other implications of the theory, for example, the interactions between the personality systems. To illustrate, there are individuals with narrow emotional–motivational systems who suffer losses in loved persons. Of those individuals, let us say some will have well-developed social skills and some will not. The latter, in the present analysis, will be more likely to develop depression than the former. What would be involved, in terms of experimental design, would be a three-fold interaction involving the occurrence or nonoccurrence of the environmental loss, the narrow or broad emotional–motivational system, and the rich or sparse social skills. The understanding of depression, it is suggested, demands this type of interactional analysis and the research that such analyses will provide.

At the clinical level of interest there are two types of focus that may be mentioned. First, there is the problem of constructing instruments that are based upon the theory, for the theory suggests much broader assessment sites than have typically been the basis for test construction. For example, the general nature of the three personality systems becomes focal. Moreover, the manner in which the three personality repertoires interact to predispose the individual to depression also needs specification for clinical purposes. When someone is depressed, displaying the typical dysphoria, it is necessary to determine which of the personality repertoires and what environmental events are involved. Treatment procedures will depend upon that knowledge. In the present view we need to begin constructing treatment procedures that follow from the increase in knowledge the theory projects, and that utilize diagnostic instruments formulated on the basis of the theory (see Leduc & Dumais, 1983).

Conclusion

One cannot fully assess the value of a theory in advance of the evaluation of its heuristic implications. But there are some characteristics of the present theory that should be considered before the fact, as it were. First, the theory is more comprehensive than is usual, and yet at the same time it presents analysis in increased detail in terms of suggesting empirical operations. Second, the theory has broader implications in that it is part of a more general theory. Because of its structure, validation of the theory of depression will validate its more basic levels of study, for example, its more general personality theory, which in turn is based upon the theories of language–cognition, emotion–motivation, and instrumental skill learning. These three basic theories in turn are based on the basic learning theory that integrates the principles of classical and instrumental conditioning. The theory advances in steps from the basic level to the advanced level of abnormal psychology. It is a psychodynamic theory in that it gives a causal role to personality problems in the etiology of abnormal behavior. But it is an indigenous psychodynamic theory—not one derived from psychiatry—and its roots are established very generally in psychology.

It is suggested that in our diverse field of psychology, a theory that shows the capability of providing the products of unification should be considered also for this characteristic. In the present case the theory shows promise for bringing together previously separated areas of knowledge in the field of depression. In addition, the theory provides the possibility of unification on yet deeper levels of theory construction. Finally, it raises also the possibility that such multilevel theory structures are possible, and advantageous, in psychology. It is time that psychology began considering its various theories in terms of how they provide for such products, as well as the method of theory construction each theory employs. The disorganized science of psychology desperately needs unifying theory structures. The present effort exemplifies the possibilities in one area of study, and suggests that the theory involved (Staats, 1975) and the methodology of the theory construction (Staats, 1983) have very general heuristic potential. The general behavioral theories (behaviorisms) are used as framework theories within which new developments in behavior therapy, behavior analysis, cognitive-behavioral therapy, and behavioral assessment are projected. Skinner's operant behaviorism and Bandura's social learning theory have tended in recent years to be monopolies of influence in this respect. It is time to break the monopoly; to compare and examine the several framework theories. The history of the development of behavioral psychology does not support contemporary monopoly; moreover, the present theory demonstrates the productivity of employing paradigmatic behaviorism as a framework theory. This suggests that behavioral psychologists should use this framework widely and deeply in pursuing their various creative tasks.

Acknowledgment

The authors express appreciation to the Social Science Research Institute and the Psychology Department for help in preparing the present manuscript, and Arthur Staats is additionally grateful to the institute for the support of his time in the present work.

References

Abramson, L., Seligman, M., & Teasdale, J. (1978). Learned helplessness in humans: Critique and reformulation. *Journal of Abnormal Psychology, 87*, 49–74.

Albee, G. (1983). The answer is prevention. *Psychology Today, 19*, 60–64.

Albee, G. (1985). Psychopathology, prevention, and the just society. *Journal of Primary Prevention, 4*, 5–40.

Allen, M. G. (1976). Twin studies of affective illness. *Archives of General Psychiatry, 33*, 1476–1478.

Allport, G. W. (1937). *Personality: A psychological interpretation.* NY: Holt.

American Psychiatric Association (APA) (1980). *Diagnostic and statistical manual: Mental disorders,* 3rd ed. (DSM-III). Washington DC: American Psychiatric Association.

Bandura, A. (1968). A social learning interpretation of psychological dysfunctions. In P. London and D. Rosenhan (Eds.), *Foundations of abnormal psychology.* New York: Holt, Rinehart, and Winston.

Bandura, A. (1969). *Principles of behavior modification.* New York: Holt, Rinehart, and Winston.

Bandura, A. (1978). The self system in reciprocal determinism. *American Psychologist, 33*, 334–358.

Barling, J., & Fincham, F. (1979). Psychological adjustment and self-reinforcement style. *The Journal of Genetic Psychology, 135*, 287–289.

Beck, A. (1967). *Depression: Clinical, experimental, and theoretical aspects.* New York: Hoeber.

Bergin, A. E. (1966). Some implications of psycho-therapy for research for therapeutic practice. *Journal of Abnormal Psychology, 71*, 235–246.

Blaney, P. (1977). Contemporary theories of depression: Critique and comparison. *Journal of Abnormal Psychology, 86*, 203–223.

Blatt, S., Quinlan, D., Chevron, E., McDonald, C., & Zuroff, D. (1982). Dependency and self-criticism: Psychological dimensions of depression. *Journal of Consulting and Clinical Psychology, 50*, 113–124.

Burgess, E. (1969). The modification of depressive behaviors. In R. Rubin & C. Franks (Eds.), *Advances in behavior therapy* (pp. 193–200). New York: Academic Press.

Burns, G. L. (1980). Indirect measurement and behavior assessment: A case for social behaviorism psychometrics. *Behavioral Assessment, 2*, 197–206.

Cameron, N. (1963). *Personality development and psychopathology: A dynamic approach.* Boston: Houghton-Mifflin.

Coleman, R. (1975). Manipulation of self-esteem as a determinant of mood of elated and depressed women. *Journal of Abnormal Psychology, 84*, 693–700.

Coyne, J. (1976). Depression and the response to others. *Journal of Abnormal Psychology, 85*, 186–193.

Coyne, J., Aldwin, C., & Lazarus, R. (1981). Depression and coping in stressful episodes. *Journal of Abnormal Psychology, 90*, 439–447.

Craighead, W. E. (1980). Away from a unitary model of depression. *Behavior Therapy, 11*, 122–128.

Davison, G. C. (1967). Some problems of logic and conceptualization in behavior therapy research and theory. Paper presented at the first annual meeting of the Association for the Advancement of the Behavioral Therapies. American Psychological Association, Washington DC.

De Monbruen, B., & Craighead, W. E. (1977). Distortion of perception and recall of positive and neutral feedback in depression. *Cognitive Therapy and Research, 1*, 311–329.

Dobson, K., & Shaw, B. (1981). The effects of self-correction on cognitive distortions in depression. *Cognitive Therapy and Research, 5*, 391–403.

Eysenck, H. J. (Eds.) (1960). *Behavior therapy and the neuroses.* London: Pergamon.

Eysenck, H. J., & Rachman, S. (1965). *The causes and cures of neurosis.* London: Routledge & Kegan Paul.

Ferster, C. (1966). Animal behavior and mental illness. *Psychological Record, 16*, 345–356.

Ferster, C. (1973). A functional analysis of depression. *American Psychologist, 28*, 857–870.

Finley, J. R., & Staats, A. W. (1967). Evaluative meaning words as reinforcing stimuli. *Journal of Verbal Learning and Verbal Behavior, 6*, 193–197.

Freud, S. (1933). *The complete introductory lectures on psychoanalysis.* NY: W. W. Norton & Co., Inc.

Freedman, A., Kaplan, H., & Sadock, B. (1976). Modern synopsis of comprehensive textbook of Psychiatry/II. Baltimore: The Williams & Wilkins Co.

Gershon, E. S., Bunney, W. E., Neckman, J. F., Van Erdewegh, M., & DeBauche, B. A. (1976). The inheritance of affective disorders: A review of data and hypotheses. *Behavior Genetics, 6*, 227–261.

Golin, S., Sweeney, P., & Shaeffer, D. (1981). The causality of causal attributions in depression: A cross-lagged panel correlational analysis. *Journal of Abnormal Psychology, 90*, 14–22.

Golin, S., Terrell, F., & Johnson, B. (1977). Depression and the illusion of control. *Journal of Abnormal Psychology, 86*, 440–442.

Gotlib, I. (1981). Self-reinforcement and recall: Differential deficits in depressed and nondepressed psychiatric patients. *Journal of Abnormal Psychology, 90*, 521–530.

Gotlib, I. (1982). Self-reinforcement and depression in interpersonal interaction: The role of performance level. *Journal of Abnormal Psychology, 91*, 3–13.

Grossberg, J. M. (1964). Behavior therapy: A review. *Psychological Bulletin, 62*, 73–88.

Gurtman, M. (1982). The relationship of expectancies for need attainment to depression and hopelessness in college students. Unpublished manuscript.

Gutheil, E. A. (1959). Reactive depressions. In S. Arieti (Ed.), *American handbook of psychiatry.* New York: Basic Books.

Hammen, C., & Cochran, S. (1981). Cognitive correlates of life stress and depression in college students. *Journal of Abnormal Psychology, 90*, 23–27.

Hammen, C., & de Mayo, R. (1982). Cognitive correlates of teacher stress and depressive symptoms: Implications of attributional models of depression. *Journal of Abnormal Psychology, 91*, 96–101.

Hammen, C., & Glass, D. (1975). Depression, activity, and evaluation of reinforcement. *Journal of Abnormal Psychology, 84*, 718–721.

Hammen, C., Krantz, S., & Cochran, S. (1981). Relationships between depression and causal attributions about stressful life events. *Cognitive Therapy and Research, 5*, 351–358.

Harms, J. Y., & Staats, A. W. (1978). Food deprivation and conditioned reinforcing value of food words: Interaction for Pavlovian and instrumental conditioning. *Bulletin of the Psychonomic Society, 12*(4), 294–296.

Harrell, T., Chambless, D., & Calhoun, J. (1981). Correlational relationships between self-statements and affective states. *Cognitive Therapy and Research, 5,* 159–173.

Heiby, E. (1979). Conditions which occasion depression: A review of three behavioral models. *Psychological Reports, 45,* 683–714.

Heiby, E. (1981). Depression and frequency of self-reinforcement. *Behavior Therapy, 12,* 549–555.

Heiby, E. (1982a). A self-reinforcement questionnaire. *Behaviour Research and Therapy, 20,* 397–401.

Heiby, E. (1982b). Prediction of mood change: An analog for a subtype of depression. Presentation at the 16th Annual Convention of the Association for Advancement of Behavior Therapy, November.

Heiby, E. (1983a). Toward the prediction of mood change. *Behavior Therapy, 14,* 110–115.

Heiby, E. (1983b). Depression as a function of self- and environmentally controlled reinforcement. *Behavior Therapy. 14,* 430–433.

Heiby, E. (1983c). The assessment of frequency of self-reinforcement. *Journal of Personality and Social Psychology. 44,* 1304–1307.

Hersen, M., Eisler, R., Alford, G., & Agras, W. (1973). Effects of token economy on neurotic depression: An experimental analysis. *Behavior Therapy, 4,* 932–937.

Hinchcliffe, M., Lancashire, M., & Roberts, F. (1971). Depression: Defense mechanisms in speech. *British Journal of Psychiatry, 118,* 471–472.

Hoehn-Hyde, D., Schlottman, R., & Rush, A. (1982). Perception of social interactions in depressed psychiatric patients. *Journal of Consulting and Clinical Psychology, 50,* 209–212.

Hull, C. L. (1943). *Principles of behavior.* NY: Appleton-Century.

Jackson, B. (1972). Treatment of depression by self-reinforcement. *Behavior Therapy, 3,* 298–307.

Jenkins, H., & Ward, W. (1965). Judgment of contingency between responses and outcomes. *Psychological Monographs: General and Applied, 79,* No. 1 (Whole No. 594).

Kimble, Gregory A. (1984). Psychology's two cultures. *American Psychologist, 39,* 833–839.

Koch, S. (1981). The nature and limits of psychological knowledge. *American Psychologist, 36,* 257–269.

Leduc, A., & Dumais, A. (1983). Une innovation dans la programmation d'interventions aupres de beneficiaires du C. H. Robert Giffard, *Revue de modification du comportement, 13,* 53–65.

Leff, M., Roatch, J., & Bunney, W. (1970). Environmental factors preceding the onset of severe depression. *Psychiatry, 33,* 293–311.

Lewinsohn, P. (1974). A behavioral approach to depression. In R. Friedman & M. Katz (Eds.), *The psychology of depression: Contemporary theory and research* (pp. 157–185). New York: Wiley.

Lewinsohn, P., & Graf, M. (1973). Pleasant activities and depression. *Journal of Consulting and Clinical Psychology, 41,* 261–268.

Lewinsohn, P., & Libet, J. (1972). Pleasant events, activity schedules, and depression. *Journal of Abnormal Psychology, 79,* 292–295.

Lewinsohn, P., & MacPhillamy, D. (1974). The relationship between age and engagement in pleasant activities. *Journal of Gerontology, 41,* 258–261.

Lewinsohn, P., Mischel, W., Chaplin, W., & Barton, R. (1980). Social competence and depression: The role of illusory self-perceptions. *Journal of Abnormal Psychology, 89,* 203–212.

Lewinsohn, P., & Talkington, J. (1979). Studies on the measurement of unpleasant events and relations with depression. *Applied Psychological Measurement, 3,* 83–101.

Liberman, R. (1970). Behavioral approaches to family and couple therapy. *American Journal of Orthopsychiatry, 40,* 106–118.

Liberman, R., & Raskin, D. (1971). Depression: A behavioral formulation. *Archives of General Psychiatry, 24,* 525–533.

328 ARTHUR W. STAATS AND ELAINE M. HEIBY

Libet, J., & Lewinsohn, P. (1973). Concept of social skill with special reference to the behavior of depressed persons. *Journal of Consulting and Clinical Psychology*, *40*, 304–312.

Lloyd, C. (1980). Life events and depressive disorder reviewed. *Archives of General Psychiatry*, *37*, 529–535.

Lobitz, W., & Post, R. (1979). Parameters of self-reinforcement and depression. *Journal of Abnormal Psychology*, *88*, 33–41.

Loeb, A., Beck, A., Diggory, J., & Tuthill, R. (1967). Expectancy, level of aspiration, performance, and self-evaluation in depression. *Proceedings, 75th Annual Convention APA*, *75*, 193–194.

London, P. (1968). The major psychological disorders. In P. London (Ed.), *Foundations of abnormal psychology*. NY: Holt, Rinehart, & Winston.

Lovaas, O. I. (1966). A behavior therapy approach to the treatment of childhood schizophrenia. In J. P. Hill (Ed.), *Minnesota symposium on child psychology, Vol. I*. Minneapolis: University of Minnesota Press.

McMahon, F. B. (1976). *Abnormal behavior*. Englewood Cliffs, NJ: Prentice-Hall.

Mathews, C. (1977). A review of behavioral theories of depression and a self-regulation model for depression. *Psychotherapy: Theory, Research, and Practice*, *14*, 79–85.

Miller, W., & Seligman, M. (1975). Depression and learned helplessness in man. *Journal of Abnormal Psychology*, *84*, 228–238.

Miller, W., Seligman, M., & Kurlander, H. (1975). Learned helplessness, depression, and anxiety. *Journal of Nervous and Mental Disease*, *161*, 347–357.

Mischel, W. (1971). *Introduction to personality*. New York: Holt, Rinehart, & Winston.

Mischel, W. (1972). Direct versus indirect personality assessment: Evidence and implications. *Journal of Consulting and Clinical Psychology*, *38*, 319–324.

Moss, G., & Boren, J. (1972). Depression as a model for behavioral analysis. *Comprehensive Psychiatry*, *13*, 581–590.

Mowrer, O. H. (1954). The psychologist looks at language. *American Psychologist*, *9*, 660–694.

Mowrer, O. H. (1960). *Learning theory and the symbolic processes*. New York: Wiley.

Mowrer, O. H. (1966). *Abnormal reactions or actions? An autobiographical answer*. Dubuque, IA: William C. Brown Company.

Mueller, D., Edwards, D., & Yarvis, R. (1977). Stressful life events and psychiatric symptomatology: Change or undesirability? *Journal of Health and Social Behavior*, *18*, 307–317.

Nelson, R., & Craighead, W. (1977). Selective recall of positive and negative feedback, self-control behaviors, and depression. *Journal of Abnormal Psychology*, *86*, 379–388.

Nelson, R., & Craighead, W. (1981). Tests of a self-control model of depression. *Behavior Therapy*, *12*, 123–129.

Osgood, C. E. (1953). *Method and theory in experimental psychology*. New York: Oxford University Press.

Paykel, E. (1969). Life events and depression. *Archives of General Psychiatry*, *21*, 753–760.

Peterson, C., Schwartz, S., & Seligman, M. (1981). Self-blame and depressive symptoms. *Journal of Personality and Social Psychology*, *41*, 253–259.

Prakchin, K., Craig, K., Papageorges, D., & Reith, G. (1977). Nonverbal communication deficits and responses to performance feedback in depression. *Journal of Abnormal Psychology*, *86*, 224–234.

Rachman, S., & Hodgson, R. (1974). Synchrony and desynchrony in fear and avoidance. *Behaviour Research and Therapy*, *12*, 311–318.

Raps, C., Peterson, C., Reinhard, K., Abramson, L., & Seligman, M. (1982). Attributional style among depressed patients. *Journal of Abnormal Psychology*, *91*, 102–108.

Rehm, L. (1977). A self-control model of depression. *Behavior Therapy*, *8*, 787–804.

Rehm, L., Fuchs, C., Roth, D., Kornblith, S., & Romano, J. (1979). A comparison of self-control and assertion skills treatments of depression. *Behavior Therapy*, *10*, 429–442.

Rehm, L., & Plakosh, P. (1975). Preference for immediate reinforcement in depression. *Journal of Behavior Therapy and Experimental Psychiatry*, *6*, 101–103.

Reisinger, J. (1972). The treatment of "anxiety depression" via positive reinforcement and response cost. *Journal of Applied Behavior Analysis, 5,* 125–130.

Roy, A. (1981). Role of past loss in depression. *Archives of General Psychiatry, 38,* 301–302.

Rozensky, R., Rehm, L., Pry, G., & Roth, D. (1977). Depression and self-reinforcement behavior in hospitalized patients. *Journal of Behavior Therapy and Experimental Psychiatry, 8,* 31–34.

Schacter, S. (1970). The assumption of identity and peripheral-centralist controversies in motivation and emotion. In M. B. Arnold (Ed.), *Feelings and emotions.* NY: Academic Press.

Schrader, S., Craighead, E., & Schrader, R. (1978). Reinforcement patterns in depression. *Behavior Therapy, 9,* 1–14.

Schwartz, G., Fair, P., Salt, P., Mandel, M., & Klerman, G. (1976). Facial muscle patterning to affective imagery in depressed and nondepressed subjects. *Science, 192,* 489–491.

Seligman, M. (1978). Comment and integration. *Journal of Abnormal Psychology, 87,* 165–179.

Seligman, M., Abramson, L., Semmel, A., & von Baeyer, C. (1979). Depressive attributional style. *Journal of Abnormal Psychology, 88,* 242–247.

Shaffer, M., & Lewinsohn, P. (1971). Interpersonal behaviors in the home of depressed versus nondepressed psychiatric and normal controls: A test of several hypotheses. Paper presented at the meeting of the Western Psychological Association, April.

Sheslow, D., & Erickson, M. (1975). Analysis of activity preference in depressed and nondepressed college students. *Journal of Counseling Psychology, 22,* 329–332.

Skinner, B. F. (1938). *The behavior of organisms.* New York: Appleton.

Skinner, B. F. (1957). *Verbal behavior.* New York: Appleton-Century-Crofts.

Skinner, B. F. (1969). *Contingencies of reinforcement.* New York: Appleton-Century-Crofts.

Skinner, B. F. (1975). The steep and thorny way to a science of behavior. *American Psychologist, 30,* 42–49.

Slater, J., & DePue, R. (1981). The contribution of environmental events and social support to serious suicide attempts in primary depressive disorder. *Journal of Abnormal Psychology, 90,* 275–285.

Staats, A. W. (1956). A behavioristic study of verbal and instrumental response hierarchies and their relationship to human problem solving. Unpublished doctoral dissertation, University of California at Los Angeles.

Staats, A. W. (1957). Learning theory and "opposite speech." *Journal of Abnormal and Social Psychology, 55,* 268–269.

Staats, A. W. (1961). Verbal habit families, concepts, and the operant conditioning of word classes. *Psychological Review, 68,* 190–204.

Staats, A. W. (with contributions by C. K. Staats). (1963). *Complex human behavior.* New York: Holt, Rinehart, & Winston.

Staats, A. W. (1968a). *Learning, language, and cognition.* New York: Holt, Rinehart, & Winston.

Staats, A. W. (1968b). Social behaviorism and human motivation: Principles of the attitude-reinforcer-discriminative system. In A. G. Greenwald, T. C. Brock, and T. M. Ostrom (Eds.), *Psychological foundations of attitudes.* NY: Academic Press.

Staats, A. W. (1971a). Linguistic–mentalistic theory versus an explanatory S-R learning theory of language development. In D. I. Slobin (Ed.), *The ontogenesis of grammar.* New York: Academic Press.

Staats, A. W. (1971b). *Child learning, intelligence, and personality.* New York: Harper & Row.

Staats, A. W. (1972). Language behavior therapy: A derivative of social behaviorism. *Behavior Therapy, 3,* 165–192.

Staats, A. W. (1975). *Social behaviorism.* Homewood, IL: Dorsey Press.

Staats, A. W. (1980). 'Behavioral interaction' and 'interactional psychology' theories of personality: Similarities, differences, and the need for unification. *British Journal of Psychology, 71,* 205–220.

Staats, A. W. (1981). Paradigmatic behaviorism, unified theory, unified theory construction methods, and the zeitgeist of separatism. *American Psychologist, 36,* 239–256.

Staats, A. W. (1983). *Psychology's crisis of disunity*. New York: Praeger.

Staats, A. W., Brewer, B. A., & Gross, M. C. (1970). Learning and cognitive development: Representative samples, cumulative-hierarchical learning, and experimental-longitudinal methods. *Monographs of the Society for Research in Child Development, 35*, (8, Whole No. 141).

Staats, A. W., & Burns, G. L. (1981). Intelligence and child development: What intelligence is and how it is learned and functions. *Genetic Psychology Monographs, 104*, 237–301.

Staats, A. W., & Burns, G. L. (1982). Emotional personality repertoire as cause of behavior: Specification of personality and interaction principles. *Journal of Personality and Social Psychology, 43*, 873–881.

Staats, A. W., & Butterfield, W. H. (1965). Treatment of nonreading in a culturally-deprived juvenile delinquent: An application of reinforcement principles. *Child Development, 36*, 925–942.

Staats, A. W., Finley, J. R., Minke, K. A., & Wolf, M. M. (1964). Reinforcement variables in the control of unit reading responses. *Journal of the Experimental Analysis of Behavior, 7*, 139–149.

Staats, A. W., Gross, M. C., Guay, P. F., & Carlson, C. C. (1973). Personality and social systems and attitude-reinforcer-discriminative theory: Interest (attitude) formation, function, and measurement. *Journal of Personality and Social Psychology, 26*, 251–261.

Staats, A. W., & Lohr, J. M. (1979). Images, language, emotions, and personality: Social behaviorism's theory. *Journal of Mental Imagery, 3*, 85–106.

Staats, A. W., Minke, K. A., Finley, J. R., Wolf, M. M., & Brooks, L. O. (1964). A reinforcer system and experimental procedure for the laboratory study of reading acquisition. *Child Development, 35*, 209–231.

Staats, A. W., & Staats, C. K. (1958). Attitudes established by classical conditioning. *Journal of Abnormal and Social Psychology, 57*, 37–40.

Staats, A. W., Staats, C. K., & Biggs, D. A. (1958). Meaning of verbal stimuli changed by conditioning. *American Journal of Psychology, 71*, 429–431.

Staats, A. W., Staats, C. K., & Crawford, H. L. (1962). First-order conditioning of a GSR and the parallel conditioning of a meaning response. *Journal of General Psychology, 67*, 159–167.

Staats, A. W., & Warren, D. R. (1974). Motivation and three-function learning: Deprivation-satiation and approach-avoidance to food words. *Journal of Experimental Psychology, 103*, 1191–1199.

Staats, C. K., & Staats, A. W. (1957). Meaning established by classical conditioning. *Journal of Experimental Psychology, 54*, 74–80.

Tanner, J., Weissman, M., & Prusoff, B. (1975). Social adjustment and clinical relapse in depressed outpatients. *Comprehensive Psychiatry, 16*, 547–556.

Tryon, W. W. (1974). A reply to Staats' language behavior therapy: A derivative of social behaviorism. *Behavior Therapy, 5*, 273–276.

Van Praag, H. M., Ulleman, A. M., & Spitz, J. C. (1965). The vital syndrome interview. *Psychiatrica, Neurologia et Neurochurgia, 68*, 329–346.

Watson, J. B. (1930). *Behaviorism* (rev. ed.). Chicago: University of Chicago Press.

Weiner, B. (1978). *Achievement motivation and attribution theory*. Morristown, NJ: General Learning Press.

Wener, A., & Rehm, L. (1975). Depressive affect: A test of behavioral hypotheses. *Journal of Abnormal Psychology, 84*, 221–227.

Zuroff, D. (1981). Depression and attribution: Some new data and a review of old data. *Cognitive Therapy and Research, 5*, 273–281.

An Integrative Theory
of Depression

PETER M. LEWINSOHN
HARRY HOBERMAN
LINDA TERI
MARTIN HAUTZINGER

Introduction

Over the last 15 years there has been a dramatic proliferation of theories of the etiology of depression. Contemporary theories of depression generally postulate a unitary and linear mechanism that is assumed to be causal of depression. According to these theories, if a given phenomenon (X) is present, an episode of depression should occur; that is, X is sufficient and necessary for the occurrence of depression. In part, the variety of theoretical models reflects the heterogeneity of the symptomatology of depressed individuals, with different theorists emphasizing different dimensions of the depressive experience as being critical to the onset of the disorder.

Currently, the most influential theoretical approaches in the etiology of depression may roughly be divided into the following emphases: reinforcement, interpersonal interaction, cognitions, and biochemical factors. Early models of depression based on reinforcement include those of Skinner (1953), Ferster (1965), and Lazarus (1968). Lewinsohn (1975; Lewinsohn, Weinstein, and Shaw, 1969) places the focus of causality on the quality of an individual's interactions with his or her environment; a decrease in response–contingent reinforcement (a decrease in pleasant events or an in-

331

crease in unpleasant events) is assumed to lead to dysphoria, which is seen as the key manifestation of depression. McLean (1976), Coyne (1976b), and Weissman and her associates (Klerman & Weissman, 1982; Weissman & Paykel, 1974) emphasize the importance of interpersonal interactions and relationships. Cognitive perspectives of depression are represented by the writings of Beck (1967; Beck, Rush, Shaw, & Emery, 1979), Ellis and Harper (1961), Rehm (1977), and Seligman (1975), who suggest that depression results from negative cognitive structures that distort an individual's experience in a negative manner. Seligman emphasizes a perceived lack of control over the environment and aspects of the individual's attributional style in the onset of depression (Abramson, Seligman, & Teasdale, 1978). Ellis and Harper (1961) hypothesize that individual's irrational beliefs cause them to overreact emotionally to situations and to become depressed. Rehm (1977), and Kanfer and Hagerman (1981) view the concept of self-control as critical, so that depression is related to the manner in which people self-monitor, evaluate, and reward their behavior.

Biochemical theories of depression have focused on changes in the levels of neurotransmitters in areas of the brain subserving emotionality, sleep regulation, and motor activity. Thus, Schildkraut (1965), Bunney and Davis (1965) and Schildkraut and Kety (1967) advanced the biogenic amine hypothesis. According to this hypothesis, depression is associated with a functional deficit of one or more neurotransmitter amines at critical synapses in the central nervous system.

Clearly, a rich and varied collection of theories of unipopular depression have been proposed, and for each some supportive experimental evidence exists. (A complete review of research findings for the different psychosocial theories is presented in Blaney [1977]; Doerfler [1981]; and Lewinsohn, Teri, & Hoberman [1982].) Biochemical theories are reviewed in Sachar (1975) and Zis and Goodwin (1982). However, it seems fair to say that in any given study the theoretical predictions have accounted for only a relatively small proportion of the total variance. Moreover, many of these studies suffer from serious methodological problems (Blaney, 1977; Doerfler, 1981; Eastman, 1976). Perhaps most importantly, causal relationships have rarely been tested, let alone proven. The experimental research on depression has relied almost exclusively on studies that examine the covariation of depression level with theory-indicated variables. For example, while characteristic thought and behavior patterns have been shown to be associated with depression (e.g., Lewinsohn, Steinmetz, Larson, & Franklin, 1981), it is impossible to know whether these correlational findings are of etiological significance. Certain critical phenomena may indeed precede the onset of depression, and in some way contribute to its occurrence, but it is equally possible that the cognitive and behavioral changes are in fact the consequences of being depressed. From the point of view of developing an accurate understanding of the etiology of depression, the current state of affairs is tantalizing but confusing.

Two interrelated steps would seem to be necessary in order to obtain greater clarity about the etiology of depression. The first would involve a change in research methodology. While considerable progress has been made in the delineation of the psychological abnormalities associated with depression, most of these findings are based on studies of people who are already depressed. Consequently, it is impossible to determine whether the distinguishing characteristics of depressives antedate or result from the disorder. As several writers have pointed out (e.g., Hirschfeld & Cross, 1982; Lloyd, 1980) longitudinal, prospective studies are essential for understanding whether variables are antecedents, concomitants, or consequences of depression. It is abundantly clear that a number of factors do covary with depression; the issue now is to identify the temporal, if not causal, relationship between these factors and depressive disorders. The second step would involve a change in the conceptualization of the nature of etiological agents in psychopathology. As already discussed, most theorists have consistently advocated unidimensional, linear models of depressive onset. Such an approach to conceptualizing the causation of disorders, mental or physical, has been criticized on a number of accounts by contemporary epidemiologists; there is a substantial body of empirical evidence and theoretical justification that suggests that disorders have more than one cause (Kleinbaum, Kupper, & Morganstern, 1982). Further, writers such as Susser (1966) have suggested that the most common causes of pathological conditions may be contributory, not necessary, nor by themselves, sufficient. By accepting a multidetermined model of depression, theorists would thereby allow for a synthesis of the variety of factors shown to be associated with depression.

More multifaceted theoretical statements on the etiology of depression have been presented. Foremost among these writers have been Akiskal and McKinney (1973, 1975). In a series of papers, Akiskal and McKinney have suggested that all of the different theoretically privileged variables (chemical, experiential, and behavioral) can be seen to induce depression by affecting a common pathway perhaps in the diencephalon.

Akiskal and McKinney's view would seem to be that all of the depression theorists may be right, with a heterogeneity of causes producing the same end result, namely a depressive episode. Billings and Moos (1982) have also proposed an integrative framework for summarizing the available data on depression. They too emphasize a multiplicity of causes in the onset of depression and view depression as resulting from the interplay of stressors, personal and environmental resources, and an individual's appraisal and coping responses to the specific stressor. A somewhat different view of the causation of depression has been postulated by Craighead (1981). While agreeing with the two aforementioned groups of theorists as to the multiplicity of etiological factors in depression, Craighead also suggests that it may be more clinically useful to view the end result of the depressive process as polydimensional rather than unitary. Thus, the different phenomenological dimensions of depression may each have their own causes and etiological patterns. This conceptualization implies that there may well be subtypes of depressives who correspond to the variety of causal factors indicated by the various theories of depression, for example, negative cognition depressives, low positive reinforcement depressives, learned helplessness depressives, and so on. Although these integrative perspectives on depression differ somewhat from one another, they represent important contributions to a more sophisticated understanding of the etiology of depression.

Although these more recent theoretical statements represent important contributions, they also possess certain limitations. To begin with, they are far more descriptive than explanatory. While these theories suggest that theoretically privileged variables can and should be integrated with one another, they fail to provide an adequate explanation of how such variables might interact with one another and what the nature of the etiological mechanisms might be. Further, these theories fail to show how the multiple-cause models account for the diverse phenomena and findings known about depression.

The purpose of this article is severalfold. First, an attempt is made to identify the significant research findings on depression that an adequate theory of depression needs to be able to explain. Second, a new theory of the etiology of depression is presented which attempts to provide an explanation of the environmental and personal mechanisms that interact to produce an episode of depression. Finally, the heuristic value of the new theory in explaining the various findings about depression are explored.

Key Findings Any Theory of Depression Should Explain

Perhaps the primary value of a theoretical model for depression is to provide a cohesive and internally consistent framework for integrating the available knowledge about depression and to generate new and testable hypotheses. Our current theorizing is heavily influenced by certain findings that we feel have expecially important theoretical implications. These include

1. The symptom heterogeneity of depression.
2. The centrality of dysphoria in depression.
3. The multiplicity of the behavioral and cognitive changes that are associated with depression.
4. The high prevalence (point and lifetime) and incidence of depression in the general population.
5. The relationship between age and the prevalence of depression.
6. The elevated prevalence of depression in females and in persons who have had a previous episode of depression.
7. The fact that persons with a previous history of depression do not differ from controls on depression-related variables.
8. The time-limited nature of depression.
9. Effectiveness of many different kinds of interventions and the non-specificity of treatment effects.
10. The unique role of stress and of low social supports as triggers (precipitating factors) for the occurrence of depression.

THE SYMPTOM HETEROGENEITY OF THE DEPRESSION SYNDROME

On the basis of well-designed descriptive studies and reviews of the clinical literature (Levitt & Lubin, 1975) a fairly concise picture of the depression syndrome has emerged. It is clear that:

1. The depression syndrome is constituted by a large number of diverse symptoms that include emotional (e.g., feelings of dysphoria, sadness), cognitive (e.g., feelings of guilt, low self-esteem, difficulties with memory and concentration), behavioral (e.g., passivity, psychomotor retardation, social–interactional problems, agitation), and somatic (e.g., sleeplessness, headaches, aches and pains, loss of energy, fatigue) manifestations.

2. Individual patients differ in the number and the degree of severity with which they experience these symptoms.

Even though it is possible and convenient to reduce the large number of depression symptoms to a smaller number of clusters by means of statistical procedures (e.g., Grinker, Miller, Sabshin, Nunn, & Nunnally, 1961; Paykel, Prusoff & Klerman, 1971; Rosenthal & Gudeman, 1967), the fact remains that there are large individual differences in the specific symptoms shown by depressed individuals. These individual differences are clearly recognized by DSM-III (APA, 1980) with its stipulation that to meet criteria for a diagnosis of depression, patients must show *n* out of *N* symptoms. There have also been numerous attempts to account for this individual variation in depression symptoms by postulating the existence of subtypes of depression, such as the endogenous versus reactive categorization (Feinberg & Carroll, 1982; Gillespie, 1929), the anxious, hostile, retarded, and agitated subtypes (Overall & Hollister, 1980), and distinctions based on pharmacotherapy response (Overall & Hollister, 1966). Unfortunately, these attempts have been relatively unsuccessful and no generally acceptable typology for unipolar depression has yet emerged. In addition, none of these typologies are based on singly or jointly sufficient features and they do not generate subgroups of depressed patients who are homogeneous with respect to the defining characteristics. Rather, these categorizations are based on the fact that, to some extent, all depression symptoms are intercorrelated (that is, of course, the reason they are included in the depression syndrome) and that some symptoms are more highly correlated with some than with other symptoms. (For excellent reviews of the difficulties that have been encountered in generating a depression typology, the reader is referred to papers by Andreason [1982] and Akiskal, Hirschfeld, and Yerevanian [1983].)

Thus, no compelling evidence has been provided to reject the arguments by Lewis (1938) and Kendell (1976) that the various states of depression can most parsimoniously be conceptualized as being on a continuum with severe forms at one end and milder forms at the other end, and with individual patients manifesting different (and at this point unpredictable) combinations of these symptoms. A theory of depression must include a mechanism that allows for this highly variegated symptom pattern and for the large individual differences in symptomatology.

CENTRALITY OF DYSPHORIA IN DEPRESSION

Another key finding that has emerged from descriptive studies is that dysphoria is the only depression symptom that comes close to being invariant; that is, it appears in almost all depressed patients. Dysphoria has been reported to be present in more than 90% of depressed patients (Ayd, 1961; Levitt & Lubin, 1975; Woodruff, Murphy, & Herjanic, 1967). The unique importance of dysphoria for the definition of the depression syndrome is clearly recognized by DSM-III, which comes close to making persistent dysphoria a necessary condition for a diagnosis of depression. If dysphoria is a key manifestation of depression, it should be given a central position in depression theory.

THE MULTIPLICITY OF THE BEHAVIORAL AND COGNITIVE CHANGES WHICH ARE ASSOCIATED WITH DEPRESSION

Another important finding from depression research is the pervasiveness of the impact of depression on the individual's functioning. These largely negative repercussions occur in multiple spheres, affecting behavior, cognitions, and biochemical functioning.

At the level of overt behavior, people who are depressed are less active (Libet & Lewinsohn, 1973); tend not to enjoy pleasant activities (MacPhillamy & Lewinsohn, 1974), and consequently are probably less motivated; are more sensitive to aversive contingencies (Lewinsohn, Lobitz, & Wilson, 1973; Lewinsohn & Talkington, 1979) and therefore are probably more likely to avoid situations; manifest social skill difficulties that affect their behavior in social interactions (Gotlib, 1982; Hautzinger, 1980; Hinchcliffe, Hooper, & Roberts, 1978; Libet & Lewinsohn, 1973; Youngren & Lewinsohn, 1980); have a negative social impact (Coyne, 1976a; Hammen & Peters, 1977; 1978; Lewinsohn, Mischel, Chaplin, & Barton, 1980); and have fewer close friends and intimates (Brown & Harris, 1978; Costello, 1982). Not surprisingly, their adjustment in important life roles is seriously reduced (Weissman & Paykel, 1974).

At the level of cognitions, depressed individuals have higher expectancies for negative outcomes and lower expectancies for positive outcomes (Lewinsohn, Larson, & Muñoz, 1982), subscribe to irrational beliefs (Muñoz, 1977; Nelson, 1977), and blame themselves for failures (Seligman, Abramson, Semmel, & von Baeyer, 1979). Depressed individuals also have enhanced recall for hedonically negative information (Kuiper, 1978; Lloyd & Lishman, 1975; Wener & Rehm, 1975).

Clearly, to be depressed puts a severe load on the individual's ability to cope. Theories of depression need to account for the seriousness and for the pervasiveness of these effects. Apparently all areas of functioning are affected in a global way.

THE HIGH PREVALENCE (POINT AND LIFE TIME) OF DEPRESSION IN THE GENERAL POPULATION

While specific estimates vary somewhat, probably due to different methods of assessment and sampling procedures, it is clear that, compared with most other disorders, depression is a very common problem. It has been called the common cold of mental disorders (Seligman, 1975). On the basis of the available information it may safely be estimated that at least 4% of the adult population is sufficiently depressed at any given time to meet rigorous diagnostic criteria (Lehmann, 1971; Weissman & Myers, 1978), and that approximately 10% of the population will develop an episode of depression within a one year period (Amenson & Lewinsohn, 1981). The lifetime prevalence of depression (i.e., the percentage of individuals likely to experience an episode of depression at some time during their lifetime) may be estimated to be between 25–50% (Amenson & Lewinsohn, 1981; Myers & Weissman, 1980).

The very high rate of occurrence of depression strongly suggests that its antecedents or its predisposing characteristics must be common or multiple.

THE RELATIONSHIP BETWEEN AGE AND THE PREVALENCE OF DEPRESSION

While the available data are relatively weak and conclusions therefore must be tentative, it appears that the prevalence of depression is relatively low in early childhood (Kashani & Simonds, 1979). The prevalence of depression increases during adolescence and probably peaks between the ages of 20 and 40 (Lewinsohn, Hautzinger, & Duncan, 1984). Beyond this age the prevalence of depression seems to remain stable and perhaps even to decrease slightly (Teri & Lewinsohn, 1981). This counter-intuitive decrease of depression beyond a certain age has been found in several studies (Comstock & Helsing, 1976; Craig & Van Natta, 1979; Hirschfeld & Cross, 1982; Teri & Lewinsohn, 1981). Theories of depression, therefore, must allow for what appears to be a curvilinear relationship between age and depression.

THE ELEVATED PREVALENCE OF DEPRESSION IN FEMALES AND IN PERSONS WHO HAVE HAD A PREVIOUS EPISODE OF DEPRESSION

The elevated prevalence of depression among females is probably one of the best-documented findings in the depression literature with two to three times as many females as males reported to have depression (Weissman & Klerman, 1977). This finding extends across the entire adult age span (Teri & Lewinsohn, 1985).

Epidemiological findings have placed this finding in a somewhat new perspective. Amenson and Lewinsohn (1981) in a longitudinal, prospective study of approximately 1000 community participants replicating the elevated prevalence, found that the incidence of new cases of depression (i.e., in people without a previous history of depression) was quite comparable for men (7.1%) and for women (6.9%). Women did not have longer lasting episodes than men, nor did they become depressed earlier in life. The major gender difference was obtained for persons with a history of previous depression. Women with a history of previous depression were much more likely to become depressed again than were men with a history of previous depression (21.8% vs. 12.9%) This increased susceptibility for women to become depressed again was present even after the effects of a host of potentially relevant psychosocial factors were statistically removed. Thus for men a history of previous depression doubled their risk for depression; for women the risk factor tripled. In related findings, Keller, Shapiro, Lavori, and Wolfe (1982) and Gonzales, Lewinsohn, and Clarke (1985) also found that about 30% of depressed patients who were recovered after treatment had another episode within one year. The finding that some segments of the population are more vulnerable for depression suggests the importance of including a predisposing factor or vulnerability construct in depression theory.

THE FACT THAT PERSONS WITH A PREVIOUS HISTORY OF DEPRESSION DO NOT DIFFER FROM CONTROLS ON DEPRESSION-RELATED VARIABLES

A number of studies (Hamilton & Abramson, 1983; Lewinsohn, et al., 1981; Youngren, 1978; Youngren & Lewinsohn, 1980; Zeiss & Lewinsohn, 1985) indicate that persons with a history of depression do not show depression-related cognitive and behavioral manifestations after they are depressed. The correlates of depression do not seem to represent stable characteristics of such persons. Yet, as pointed out earlier, these same individuals are at substantially elevated risk for future depression. What may be suggested by these findings is that not only do people differ in their vulnerability to depression but this vulnerability may only be activated under certain conditions.

THE TIME-LIMITED NATURE OF DEPRESSION

Two additional findings seem especially salient for depression theory: (1) Most people have relatively short-lived episodes; and (2) Most people are able to terminate their depression without professional assistance.

In a study on the duration of episodes of depression, the frequency distribution of episode duration values was found to be very skewed (Lewinsohn, Fenn, Stanton, & Franklin, 1985); about 25% of episodes of unipolar depression last less than one month; 50% last less than 3 months; and only 25% one year or longer. The fact that most episodes are of relatively short duration confirms clinical observation (Beck, 1967) that depression usually is a time-limited disorder. Furthermore, most people who experience an episode of depression do not seek treatment (Vernon & Roberts, 1982). The psychological processes that enable people to terminate their depression in such a short period of time are being studied (Hautzinger & Hoffman, 1979; Parker & Brown, 1979), and the findings suggest that a range of different strategies are employed. Clearly, treatment is not a necessary condition for depression improvement. At the same time, there are a substantial number of individuals (approximately 25–30%) who do have long episodes or who do not seem to benefit from treatment (Weissman, Prusoff, & Klerman, 1978).

The fact that some people are able to effectively use a wide range of behaviors to terminate their depression suggests that depression can be influenced from many directions. Consequently, a theory of depression probably needs multiple points of entry for potential reversal.

THE EFFECTIVENESS OF MANY DIFFERENT KINDS OF INTERVENTIONS AND THE NONSPECIFICITY OF TREATMENT EFFECTS

An impressively wide array of different interventions have been found to be efficacious for depression. Cognitive therapy is aimed at changing depressive thought processes (e.g., Beck et al., 1979; Fuchs & Rehm, 1977); behavioral treatments are aimed at improving social skills (Hersen, Bellack, & Himmelhoch, 1980; Sanchez, Lewinsohn, & Larson, 1980; Zeiss, 1977), increasing pleasant activities, teaching time management and relaxation skills (Lewinsohn, 1976), or training in general problem-solving skills (McLean & Hakstian, 1979); and antidepressant medications (Rush, Beck, Kovacs, & Hollon, 1977; Morris & Beck, 1974) are aimed at restoring a theorized biochemical imbalance. In spite of this theoretically provocative diversity, empirical support for the therapeutic efficacy of all of these treatments has been provided (Lewinsohn & Hoberman, 1982; Paykel, 1982; Rehm, 1981; Rehm & Kornblith, 1979) and differences between treatment outcomes have generally been small and often not significant (e.g., Wilson, Goldin, & Charbonneau-Powis, 1983).

These studies pose several interesting challenges for depression theory. Since most of the treatments were theoretically derived, that is, specifically designed to modify the specific conditions assumed by the theory to be a critical antecedent for depression, how can they all be effective? Furthermore, the treatments while effective in ameliorating depression, do not seem to be specific in impacting hypothesized target behaviors (and cognitions) at which they are aimed (e.g., Zeiss, Lewinsohn, & Munoz, 1979).

These findings suggest that a theory of depression should allow for multiple points of causal entry and multiple modes of improving depression. Further, the findings suggest that the functional systems (i.e., cognitive, behavioral, and somatic) that are affected by depression, tend to change together; that is, they move en masse.

STRESS AND LOW SOCIAL SUPPORTS AS TRIGGERS
OF DEPRESSION

The association among stress, weak social supports, and depression has, of course, been known for some time (Paykel *et al.*, 1969). Recent prospective studies (e.g., Lewinsohn & Hoberman, 1982) have gone a step farther in showing that the occurrence of stressful life events actually precedes the occurrence of depression. In particular the literature suggests that stressors related to marital distress, social exits, and work problems bear an especially strong relationship to the later development of depression. The central importance of stress in the chain of events leading to depression has been recognized by several theorists (Aneshensel & Frerichs, 1982; Billings & Moos, 1982; Brown & Harris, 1978).

Current Psychological Theories of Depression

Having identified what we consider to be the most salient research findings that a theory of unipolar depression needs to address, it is now appropriate to move toward an elaboration of a model of the etiology of depression. Before presenting the structure of this new theory, however, it is important to briefly reconsider the bases of the two major types of psychological theories of depression. Cognitive theories of depression, particularly those of Beck (1967) and Abramson *et al.*, (1978), are fairly explicit in postulating that certain depressogenic cognitive patterns cause people to interpret their experiences in ways that cause them to become depressed. These predisposing cognitive patterns are assumed to be relatively stable characteristics of the person; that is, individuals who become depressed possess a stable depressogenic cognitive style that predisposes them to depressive episodes. Thus Beck (1967, p. 290) has stated: "During the developmental period, the depression-prone individual acquires certain negative attitudes regarding himself, the outside world, and his future . . . The idiosyncratic attitudes represent persistent cognitive patterns, designated as schemas." Similarly, Seligman has reported on a prospective study that attempted to assess whether students who possess a depressogenic attributional style would score as more depressed after a later failure; that is, it was predicted that the "combination of a *preexisting* internal, stable, and global way of construing causality for negative events followed by an actual encounter with failure will be sufficient to cause depression. (1981, p. 125; emphasis added).

Unfortunately, the available research has failed to demonstrate that individuals who become depressed can be distinguished on the basis of the kinds of preexisting cognitive styles suggested by Beck and other cognitive theorists. While patterns of depressive cognitions do indeed co-occur with dys-phoria—that is, they definitely are concomitants of depression—there is accumulating evidence that these patterns are not apparent either before or after a depressive episode. Lewinsohn *et al.,* (1981) reported on the results of a longitudinal, prospective study of the onset of depression. All participants were assessed on a number of cognitions (expectations for positive and negative outcomes, attributions, and irrational negative beliefs) at the be-ginning of the study and were later evaluated to determine if an episode of depression occurred. Participants who became depressed during the course of the study were compared with those who did not become depressed and with those who were depressed at entry into the study. The results of this study indicated that persons who were later to become depressed did not differ on the cognitive measures from those who remained undepressed. The types of cognitions endorsed by the major cognitive theories were found to be concomitants but not antecedents of depression. Additionally, the cognitive patterns of persons who had been depressed at some time in the past (but who were not depressed during the course of the study) were not distinguishable from those who remained undepressed. Thus individ-uals who have been depressed or who are about to become depressed are not characterized by a stable depressogenic cognitive style. Similarly, Peterson, Schwartz, and Seligman (1981) found no evidence for a particular attribu-tional style to be predictive of later depressive symptoms, and, also consis-tent with our findings, Wilkinson and Blackburn (1981) showed that the cognitions of recovered depressed patients could not be differentiated from those of normal or psychiatric controls. In short, there is little evidence for the contention in cognitive theories that a particular cognitive content is a causal factor in the initial development of a depressive episode.

Behavioral or reinforcement theories of depression have postulated the nature of person–environment interactions as causing depression. In partic-ular, theories such as Lewinsohn's (Lewinsohn, Youngren, & Grosscup, 1979) have emphasized that changes in the quality of a person's reinforce-ment (e.g., a decrease in positive or an increase in negative reinforcement) lead to depression. As was indicated earlier, such changes do indeed covary with depression. However, in the results of a longitudinal, prospective study by Lewinsohn and Hoberman (1982), neither the frequency of pleas-ant nor unpleasant events predicted the later occurrence of depression, sug-gesting that the number of such events are not antecedents of depressive episodes. With regard to reinforcement, only the aversiveness of unpleasant events emerged as predicting later depression and the number of macro-stressors (which could be considered a measure of negative reinforcement) predicted depressive onset. Thus it is clear that the premises of the reinforce-ment theory of depression were not entirely supported.

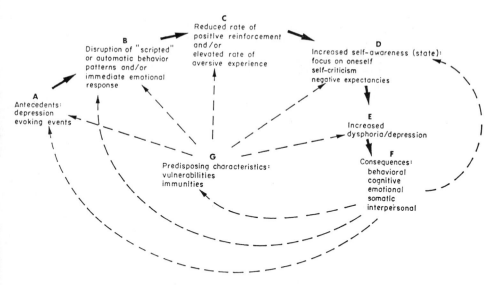

FIGURE 11.1   Schematic representation of variables involved in the occurence of unipolar depression.

An Integrative Theory of Depression

The findings that major predictions of cognitive and reinforcement theories have not been demonstrated to be antecedents for depression provides cause for thought. Can it be that neither cognitions nor the quality of person–environment interactions are related to the etiology and maintenance of depression? We think not. Rather, we propose that cognitions and reinforcement are both important variables in the onset of depression. However, we would argue that past cognitive and reinforcement positions have offered too simplistic views; in particular, we contend that while the cognitive models have overemphasized cognitive dispositional factors, the reinforcement models have, in turn, overemphasized situational factors. Consequently, we offer a model of the etiology and maintenance of depression that attempts to capture what we see as the complexity and interactive nature of psychopathogenic factors. This model is presented schematically in Figure 11.1. The model represents an attempt to integrate the findings of our epidemiological and treatment outcome studies with an increasing body of work in social psychology in the phenomenon of self-awareness (e.g., Carver, Blaney & Scheier, 1979a,b; Duvall & Wicklund, 1972; Scheier, Carver, & Gibbons, 1981). The proposed etiological model should be regarded as tentative and not etched in concrete. It simply represents the phenomena and conditions that we think are often involved in the development and maintenance of depression. We do not imply that the chain of causation is fixed and invariant; rather, the model attempts to incorporate a number of different characteristics and processes that can influence and in turn are influenced by the occurrence of depression.

We view the occurrence of depression as a product of both environmental and dispositional factors. More specifically, we see depression as the end result of environmentally initiated changes in behavior, affect, and cognitions. In accord with previous behavioral theories of depression, we view environmental or situational factors as the primary triggers of the depressogenic process. Like cognitive theorists, we view cognitions as significant moderators of the effects of the environment, that is, as critical for determining whether situational conditions are going to result in depression. In particular, we believe that when attention is shifted increasingly toward the self versus the environment as a consequence of the individual's unsuccessful efforts to cope with disruptive life conditions, the preconditions for depression are set in motion.

The chain of events leading to the occurrence of depression is postulated to begin with the occurrence of an evoking event or antecedent (**A**), which is empirically defined as any event that increases the probability for the future occurrence of depression. In the literature to date, all of these evoking events fall under the general rubric of stressors, including macrostressors (e.g., losing one's job), microstressors (e.g., being criticized), and chronic difficulties (e.g., marital discord). The relationship between such stressors and depression is a well-documented finding in the depression literature. Both retrospective studies (e.g., Brown & Harris, 1978; Costello, 1982; and Paykel *et al.*, 1969) and prospective studies (Lewinsohn & Alexander, 1983; Lewinsohn & Hoberman, 1982; Lewinsohn & Teri, 1984) have demonstrated an increase in the incidence of life events, or the presence of chronic difficulties, in the months preceding an episode of depression. In particular, the literature suggests that stressors related to marital distress, social exits, and work problems exhibit an especially strong relationship to the later development of depression.

ANTECEDENTS OF THE OCCURRENCE OF DEPRESSION

The occurrence of antecedents are assumed to initiate the depressogenic process to the extent that they disrupt substantial, important, and relatively automatic behavior patterns of an individual (**B**). Langer (1978) has suggested that much of everyday behavior is "scripted" (e.g., Schank & Abelson, 1975) and consequently automatic, requiring very little mental effort. An implication of Langer's position is that much of what occurs to people on an everyday basis is generally expected and predictable (or at least is perceived that way). Thus as Coyne (1982) has postulated, most individuals get by in their lives with well-established behavior patterns because of the regularities in their environment. The presence of a stressor or chronic difficulty acts to disrupt the regularity of an individual's life, particularly those aspects of the individual's behavioral repertoire that are typical and crucial to a person's everyday interactions with the environment. Stressful life events are assumed to lead to depression to the extent that they are disruptive of personal relationships, job tasks, and automatic behaviors. Thus promotion, moving to a new (albeit better) job or environment, could become an **A,** as can rejection or the ending of a relationship unless the person is able to quickly develop other behavior patterns to replace those that have been disrupted.

A further consequence of the presence of an evoking event and its subsequent disruption of patterned behavior is an initial negative emotional reaction. The degree or intensity of this initial negative affect will be a function of the salience or importance of the evoking event or the degree of disruption of everyday behavior (Taylor & Fiske, 1978).

Such disruptions and the emotional upset they typically engender are assumed to be related to the occurrence of depression to the extent that they lead to a reduction of positive reinforcement or to an elevated rate of aversive experience (**C**); that is, they shift the balance of the quality of a person's interactions with the environment in a negative direction (e.g., Lewinsohn et al., 1979).

As the effects of evoking events exert their impact on an individual's obtained level of reinforcement, persons attempt to reduce that impact (Coyne, Aldwin, & Lazarus, 1981). In fact, these endeavors to cope with the deleterious effects of stressors are conceptualized as being an important component of the stress process (Lazarus & Launier, 1978). Stressors and their effects are rarely discrete experiences and depending upon the salience of the evoking event and the degree of life disruption, individuals typically are forced to deal with such events over a period of time. These efforts will be successful to different degrees, depending upon both environmental and dispositional factors (**G**).

The inability to reverse the impact of the stress (e.g., through decreasing negative reinforcement or increasing positive reinforcement and consequently, producing a resumption of patterned behavior or neutral or positive affect) is hypothesized to lead to a heightened state of self-awareness (**D**). We would suggest that two phenomena will focus a person's attention on him or herself. First, the initial negative emotional response that follows the evoking event and the subsequent emotional impact of the person's inability to reverse the impact of the stress increases self-awareness. As Wegner and Giuliano (1980) have demonstrated, physiological arousal elicits self-focused attention. In addition we hypothesize that a reduction in positive reinforcement or increase in negative experience will also produce an increment in self-focused attention.

The concept of self-awareness or self-focused attention was introduced by Duval and Wicklund (1972) who suggested that attention at a specific point in time can be directed in either of two directions—outwardly, toward the environment, or inwardly, toward the self—and that certain events will increase the degree to which attention will be focused on the self or be externally focused. One of Duval and Wicklund's major points was that when attention is focused internally (that is when a state of self-awareness exists), individuals become more aware of their thoughts, feelings, values, and standards. A reconceptualization of self-focused attention by Carver and Scheier (1981) suggests that self-awareness produces a heightened consciousness of whatever self-elements are salient in a specific situation. A substantial literature has accumulated that explores a variety of effects of self-focused attention. It is this body of research that forms the basis for the assumption that self-awareness, a cognitive process, is the critical factor in mediating the effects of reduced positive reinforcement on depression.

As has been noted by several investigators (Ganellen & Blaney, 1981; Ingram & Smith, 1984; Smith & Greenberg, 1981; Teasdale, 1983), the effects of increasing self-awareness are amazingly similar to many of the cognitive and behavioral phenomena of depression. First, increased self-awareness has been shown to cause individuals to become increasingly self-critical (Duval & Wicklund, 1972) and to produce an increase in the discrepancy between ratings of ideal self and the perceived self (Ickes, Wicklund, & Ferris, 1973). Second, when a state of self-awareness is induced, individuals are increasingly likely to attend to performance norms or standards for behavior (Carver & Scheier, 1983). Thus, as individuals attempt to cope with their disrupted lives, they will compare themselves to certain standards. If the comparison to standards is unfavorable (as it is likely to be in initial coping efforts and over time with unsuccessful coping efforts) Carver and Scheier's (1983) theory of self-attention predicts that a negative affective reaction will ensue. A third consequence of heightened self-awareness will be to impact on an individual's attributions for events. Conditions of heightened self-awareness result in greater acceptance of responsibility for outcomes, that is, internal attributions (Buss & Scheier, 1976; Duval & Wicklund, 1972; Hull & Levy, 1979). Self-focused attention also potentiates negative expectancies (Carver, Blaney, & Scheier, 1979a, 1979b). In short, self-focused attention produces many of the cognitive alterations that have been emphasized by cognitive theorists.

Self-focused attention also has behavioral consequences. Increased self-awareness in the face of negative outcome expectancies has been shown to be associated with behavioral withdrawal (Carver et al. 1979, 1979b) and with social difficulties (Christensen, 1982; Fenigstein, 1979). Research has also shown that under conditions of self-focused attention, negative expectancies lead to reduced effort and persistence (e.g., Carver et al., 1979a, 1979b; Kernis, Zuckerman, Cohen, & Spadafora, 1982; Scheier & Carver, 1977) and reducing self-awareness increases performance (Brockner & Hulton, 1978). Another important consequence of a heightened state of self-awareness is an intensification or magnification of affective reactions. Experimentally induced self-focused attention has been shown (Scheier & Carver, 1977) to produce more extreme depression or elation following mood-induction procedures and to produce negative affect in psychiatric patients (Gibbons, Smith, Brehm, & Schroeder, 1980).

In short, the elicitation of a state of self-awareness increases the individual's awareness of his or her failure to live up to his or her expected standards of coping, and engenders a state of self-denigration, behavioral withdrawal, and dysphoria.

We hypothesize that feeling increasingly self-aware (**D**) and dysphoric (**E**) breaks through an individual's self-protective and self-enhancing self-perceptions (e.g., Alloy & Abramson, 1979; Lewinsohn, et al. 1980) and thus leads to many of the cognitive, behavioral, and emotional changes (**F**) that have been shown to be correlated with depression. These changes (**F**) are presumed to be quite consequential and to play an important role in the maintenance and exacerbation of the depressive state. The negative effects of dysphoria on a host of cognitive processes have been shown on a series of studies (Clark & Teasdale, 1982; Davis, 1979; Derry & Kuiper, 1981; Isen, Shalker, Clark, & Karp, 1978; Lloyd & Lishman, 1975; Natale & Hantas, 1982; Rogers, Kuiper, & Kirker, 1977; Teasdale, 1983; Teasdale & Fogarty, 1979; Teasdale & Russell, 1983; Teasdale & Taylor, 1981; Teasdale, Taylor, Fogarty, 1980). Briefly these studies have shown that in a state of dysphoria negative thoughts and memories become more accessible and that negative information about the self is processed more efficiently, a complete reversal from the way information about the self is processed in nondepressed individuals. In other words, the induction of depressed mood drastically changes the way in which subjects interpret their previous and their current experiences and augments the dysphoria.

Thus, as dysphoria escalates we would argue that a very basic transition occurs in cognitions regarding the self. Specifically, we suggest that the self-schema is changed. Research in cognitive social psychology has indicated that knowledge is structured in schemas or schemata. A *schema* is defined as a structured body of information that is stored in long-term memory and that is capable of organizing and clustering new incoming environmental and personal information (Davis, 1979). The self–schema (Derry & Kuiper, 1981; Rogers *et al.*, 1977) is assumed to be the particular body of information about the individual that interacts with incoming data so as to organize the processing and retention of self–related information. It is this self–schema that we hypothesize has changed. Specific instances of this change in the self–schema are hypothesized to represent negative self–evaluations, low rates of self–reinforcement, pessimism about the future, internal and global attributions for failure experiences, cognitive distortion of the type described by Beck *et al.*, (1979), and preoccupation with negative experiences from the past.

We also hypothesize that being self–aware and dysphoric acts to reduce the individual's social competence and contributes to the negative impact on others (Coyne, 1976a; Hammen & Peters, 1978). Consistent with this focus on self–awareness, Jacobson and Anderson (1982), for example, found that depressed subjects are more likely to refer to themselves in social conversation when self–references were not directly solicited. They suggest that depressed people are preoccupied with themselves and that they therefore focus on themselves even at times when the normal flow of conversation suggests a more natural focus on the interacting partner. We suggest that it is these types of behaviors that cause depressed people to elicit social rejection in social interaction (Coyne, 1976a; Hammen & Peters, 1978; Strack & Coyne, 1983). Our hypothesis that many of the social skill deficits shown by depressed individuals are secondary to being depressed is consistent with observations that social skill of recovered depressed persons is indistinguishable from that of nondepressed persons (Zeiss & Lewinsohn, 1985; Youngren, personal communication, 1977).

In short, then, an episode of depression is likely to result as a consequence of a chain of events beginning with the occurrence of antecedent–eliciting events leading to a heightened state of self–focused attention. In turn, a continuing increase in self–awareness provides a basis for a large number of affective, behavioral, and cognitive transformations that exacerbate dysphoria and act to induce and maintain an episode of depression.

IMMUNITIES AND VULNERABILITIES

Additionally, the proposed model allows for predisposing characteristics of various kinds either to increase or to decrease the risk for a depressive episode. The need to incorporate a moderator variable of this kind is dictated by the fact that there seem to be individual differences and environmental variables that systematically increase (vulnerabilities) or decrease (immunities) the probability for the occurrence of depression. These vulnerabilities and immunities are assumed to be relatively stable characteristics of the person or of the person's environment. The concept of vulnerability was first introduced by Zubin (1976). The central idea was that under a given set of circumstances some individuals are more (or less) likely to develop a psychopathological disorder. Predisposing characteristics are assumed to influence not only the probability for the occurrence of a depressive episode but also to influence whether an episode is going to be of short or long duration.

On the basis of our own research as well as that of other researchers in the field, the following person and environment characteristics can be suggested to act as predisposing vulnerabilities: (1) being female, (2) being age 20–40, (3) having a previous history of depression, (4) having low coping skills, (5) having increased sensitivity to aversive events, (6) being poor, (7) being highly self-conscious (Fenigstein, Scheier & Buss, 1975) (8) having a low threshold for the evocation of the depressogenic self-schemata, (9) having low self-esteem, (10) being high on interpersonal dependency (Hirschfeld, Klerman, Chodoff, Korchin, & Barrett, 1976), and (11) having children below the age of 7 (Brown & Harris, 1978). The following may be hypothesized to act as protective immunities: high learned resourcefulness (Rosenbaum, 1980); high self-perceived social competence (Lewinsohn *et al.*, 1980); high frequency of pleasant events; and the availability of a close and intimate confidant (Brown & Harris, 1978).

As indicated in Figure 11.1, predisposing characteristics are assumed to affect all elements of the model. While an accounting of the many ways in which each of the suggested predisposing characteristics can affect the path of depressive onset is beyond the limit of this paper, a few illustrative examples can be provided. An individual with good coping skills would be more likely to be able to reverse the depressogenic cycle by implementing new behaviors to deal with the disruption (**B**), or by decreasing self-awareness by finding distractions and thereby staying focused on external events. The ease with which the individual can become angry may also in this context constitute an immunity in that by becoming angry the individual remains focused on external events and avoids becoming self-aware.

The behavior of the significant others in the person's environment may constitute a vulnerability to the extent that they selectively reinforce the depressed individual's symptoms and complaints. Under such conditions one would expect the depression to become an operant; that is, it is now being maintained by the environment and therefore will perpetuate and become part of the individual's life style. Conversely, the action of significant others may act as an immunity for an episode of depression to the extent that they are able to provide help with restoring disrupted behavior patterns or call attention to instances of competence, for example.

FEEDBACK LOOPS

The model allows for additional "feedback loops" that are seen as important for determining the level of severity and the duration of an episode of depression. Thus, becoming depressed (**F**) and thinking and behaving in the depressed mode would be expected to interfere with the individual's problem-solving skills (**G**) and, consequently, their ability to reverse the disruption (**B**) and the effects of the disruption (**C**). Similarly, when an individual has become depressed, his or her behavior becomes more complaining, less friendly, more withdrawn and passive, and more aversive to others (Coyne, 1976a; Hammen & Peters, 1977). This may serve to increase the likelihood for the occurrence of additional depression–evoking events (**A**); for example, the spouse becomes more dissatisfied and threatens to leave the patient; the boss begins questioning the patient's competence. Being depressed (**F**) would also be expected to reduce the individual's energy level and enjoyment of pleasant activities, to increase sensitivity to aversive events and self-awareness, and consequently to influence the overall ability to reverse the depressogenic chain.

The feedback loops set the stage for a vicious cycle but also for a benign cycle. By reversing any of the components of the model, the depression will be progressively and increasingly ameliorated.

Explanatory Power of the Model

We believe that our model, in addition to taking into account much of what is empirically known about depression, provides potential explanations for a number of important aspects of depression. For example, the model allows for the heterogeneity and the multiplicity of depression symptoms because the effects of increased self-awareness and of dysphoria appear to be so global and include such a wide range of behavioral, physiological, and cognitive manifestations. The model allows for many points of entry into the chain of events leading to depression and thus allows for a multiplicity of causes, each of which is contributory but none of which is essential.

The model suggests that the prevalence and incidence of depression should be high because there are so many points of entry and because there probably are many relatively common (e.g., everyday) antecedents. Conversely, our model implies that while episodes of depression are common, most will be of a short duration because there are a large number of person–initiated and environmental changes that can act to reverse the depresso-genic cycle.

The model assigns a central role to dysphoria because dysphoria is as-sumed to be necessary for the evocation of the consequences (**F**), that is, the shift into the depressive mode of thinking and behaving. While there has been some debate about whether depression can exist in the absence of dysphoria (the so-called "masked depressions," for example, Glaser, 1967; Sugar, 1967; Toolan, 1969), our assumption is that without dysphoria only a very incomplete syndrome will exist since neither the changes in process-ing of information about the self nor the depression–induced social behavior changes will have occurred.

People can ameliorate their depression by changing the consequences of depression, distracting themselves, reducing self-awareness, increasing pleasant activities, decreasing unpleasant activities, trying to enhance one's general coping skills and becoming more effective in eliminating the disrup-tion or perhaps even the antecedent events, or moving to a different envi-ronment that does not have the antecedent event and that calls for behavior patterns that are part of the individual's nondepressive repertoire.

The fact that any number of psychological, biological, and eclectic inter-ventions for depression are successful may be explained by the large number of person-initiated and environmental changes that can act to reverse the depressogenic cycle. Interventions would be expected to be effective to the extent that they affect one of the links of the model in a crucial and powerful way or because the intervention impacts many of the points and thus has a large cumulative effect. Because the feedback loops are so extensive, there are many ways to get a reverse process started. The fact that most current therapies are actually multimodal is consistent with this argument. There is, of course, no reason why a person can't do all of these things by them-selves—and most people do (Parker & Brown, 1979; Rippere, 1977; Vernon & Roberts, 1982).

The model also is capable of generating relatively specific and testable predictions. To wit, our model predicts that (1) the likelihood that anteced-ents increase the probability for depression should be proportional to the degree to which they disrupt important behavior patterns; (2) disruptions should increase the probability for the occurrence of depression to the extent that they result in a decrease in positive and an increase in negative person–environment interactions; and (3) a reduced rate of positive reinforcement or an elevated rate of aversive experience increases self-awareness.

Theories of unipolar depression are important not only because of the prevalence and seriousness of the clinical syndrome, but, at a more general level, because of their potential relevance for larger theories of behavior.

Depression clearly involves interactions between overt and covert behavior; among emotions, cognitions, and behavior; and between current situational conditions and the more remote effects of the individual's past. Thus, theories of depression provide a testing ground for many of the more important issues in psychology.

Concluding Comments

We want to emphasize that our conceptualization is meant to be a working model. We do not expect that the directions of all of the arrows in Figure 11.1 will necessarily be correct. We may have suggested too many or too few linkages; future research will hopefully clarify these issues. A primary virtue of the model is that it is testable and that it emphasizes the importance of the temporal study of the chain of events and the processes that lead to depression.

This is certainly an exciting time in depression theory. Through the mid-60s what might be considered the first phase of psychological theories of depression was dominated by psychoanalytic thinking and was a relatively static period during which people in the field felt they had most of the answers. During the late 60s and through the 70s (Phase 2), linear theories focused on a single causal agent to the exclusion of others. These theories stimulated a great deal of productive conceptual and empirical activity. The field is now moving into the next phase that promises to do justice to the complexity of the clinical phenomena of depression and of the underlying psychological processes. These newer theories appear to be multifactorial. They assume that a number of different causes are important, none of which are necessary or sufficient but all of which interact in important ways.

Acknowledgment

The preparation of this chapter was partially supported by a grant from the National Institute of Mental Health (MH 35672). Portions of this paper were presented at the 1982 Meetings of the American Psychological Association and at the 1983 Convention of the Association for the Advancement of Behavior Therapy.

References

Abramson, L. Y., Seligman, M. E., & Teasdale, J. D. (1978). Learned helplessness in humans: Critique and reformation. *Journal of Abnormal Psychology, 7*, 49–74.

Akiskal, H. S., Herschfeld, R. M. A., & Yerevanian, B. I. (1983). The relationship of personality to affective disorders. *Archives of General Psychiatry, 40*, 801–810.

Akiskal, H. S., & McKinney, W. T. (1973). Depressive disorders: Toward a unified hypothesis. *Science, 182*, 20–29.

Akiskal, H. S., & McKinney, W. T. (1975). Overview of recent research in depression, integration of ten conceptual models into a comprehensive clinical frame. *Archives of General Psychiatry, 32,* 285.

Alloy, L. B., & Abramson, L. Y. (1979). Judgment of contingency in depressed and nondepressed students: Sadder but wiser? *Journal of Experimental Psychology, 90,* 1–13.

Amenson, C. S., & Lewinsohn, P. M. (1981). An investigation into the observed sex difference in prevalence of unipolar depression. *Journal of Abnormal Psychology, 90,* 1–13.

American Psychiatric Association. (1980). *Diagnostic and Statistical Manual of Mental Disorders* (3rd ed.). Washington, DC: Author.

Andreason, N. C. (1982). Concepts, diagnosis and classification. In E. S. Paykel (Ed.), *Handbook of affective disorders* (pp. 24–44). London: Churchill-Livingstone.

Aneshensel, C. S., & Frerichs, R. R. (1982). Stress, support, and depression: A longitudinal causal model. *Journal of Community Psychology, 10,* 363–376.

Ayd, F. J., Jr. (1961) *Recognizing the depressed patient.* NY: Grune & Stratton.

Beck, A. T. (1967). *Depression: Clinical, experimental and theoretical aspects.* NY: Harper & Row.

Beck, A. T., Rush, A. J., Shaw, B. F., & Emery, G. (1979). *Cognitive therapy of depression.* NY: Guilford Press.

Billings, A. G., & Moos, R. N. (1982). Psychosocial theory and research on depression: An integrative framework and review. *Clinical Psychology Review, 2,* 213–237.

Blaney, P. H. (1977). Contemporary theories of depression: Critique and comparison. *Journal of Abnormal Psychology, 86,* 203–223.

Brockner, J., & Hulton, A. J. B. (1978). How to reverse the vicious cycle of low self-esteem: The importance of attentional focus. *Journal of Experimental Social Psychology, 14,* 564–578.

Brown, G. W., & Harris, T. (1978). *Social origins of depression: A study of psychiatric disorder in women.* NY: Free Press.

Bunney, W. E., & Davis, J. M. (1965). Nonrepinephrine in depressed reactions. *Archives of General Psychiatry, 13,* 483–494.

Buss, A., & Scheier, M. (1976). Self-consciousness, self-awareness and self-attribution. *Journal of Research in Personality, 10,* 463–468.

Carver, C. S., Blaney, P. H., & Scheier, M. F. (1979a). Focus of attention, chronic expectancy, and responses to a feared stimulus. *Journal of Personality and Social Psychology, 37,* 1186–1195.

Carver, C. S., Blaney, P. H., & Scheier, M. F. (1979b). Reassertion and giving up: The interactive role of self-directed attention and outcome expectancy. *Journal of Personality and Social Psychology, 37,* 1859–1870.

Carver, C. S., & Scheier, M. F. (1978). Self-focusing effects of dispositional self-consciousness, mirror presence, and audience presence. *Journal of Personality and Social Psychology, 36,* 324–332.

Carver, C. S., Scheier, M. F. (1981). *Attention and self-regulation: A control-theory approach to human behavior.* NY: Springer.

Carver, C. S., & Scheier, M. F. (1983). A control theory approach to human behavior, and implications for problems of self-management. In P. Kendall (Ed.), *Advances in cognitive–behavioral research and therapy* (Vol. 2, pp. 127–194). NY: Academic Press.

Christensen, D. (1982). The relationship between self-consciousness and interpersonal effectiveness and a new scale to measure individual differences in self-consciousness. *Personality and Individual Differences, 3,* 177–188.

Clark, D. M., & Teasdale, J. D. (1982). Diurnal variation in clinical depression and accessibility of memories of positive and negative experiences. *Journal of Abnormal Psychology, 91,* 87–95.

Comstock, G. W., & Helsing, K. J. (1976). Symptoms of depression in two communities. *Psychological Medicine, 6,* 551–563.

Costello, C. G. (1982). Social factors associated with depression: A retrospective community study. *Psychological Medicine, 12,* 329–339.

Coyne, J. C. (1976a). Depression and the response of others. *Journal of Abnormal Psychology, 85,* 186–193.

Coyne, J. C. (1976b). Toward an interactional description of depression. *Psychiatry, 39,* 28–40.

Coyne, J. C. (1982). A critique of cognitions as causal entities with particular reference to depression. *Cognitive Therapy and Research, 6,* 3–13.

Coyne, J. C., Aldwin, C., & Lazarus, R. S. (1981). Depression and coping in stressful episodes. *Journal of Abnormal Psychology, 90,* 439–447.

Craig, T., & Van Natta, P. A. (1979). Influence of demographic characteristics on two measures of depressive symptoms. *Archives of General Psychiatry, 35,* 149–154.

Craighead, W. E. (1981). Behavior therapy for depression: Issues resulting from treatment studies. In L. P. Rehm (Ed.), *Behavior therapy for depression: Present status and future directions.* NY: Academic Press.

Davis, H. (1979). The self-schema and subjective organization of personal information in depression. *Cognitive Therapy and Research, 3,* 415–425.

Derry, P. A., & Kuiper, N. A. (1981). Schematic processing and self-reference in clinical depression. *Journal of Abnormal Psychology, 90,* 286–297.

Doerfler, L. A. (1981). Psychological research on depression: A methodological review. *Clinical Psychology Review, 1,* 119–137.

Duval, S., & Wicklund, R. (1972). *A theory of objective self-awareness.* NY: Academic Press.

Eastman, C. (1976). Behavioral formulations of depression. *Psychological Review, 83,* 277–291.

Ellis, A., & Harper, R. A. (1961). *A guide to rational living.* Hollywood, CA: Wilshire.

Feinberg, M., & Carroll, B. J. (1982). Separation of subtypes of depression using discriminant analyses I. Separation of unipolar endogenous depression from nonendogenous depression. *British Journal of Psychiatry, 140,* 384–391.

Fenigstein, A. (1979). Self-consciousness, self-attention, and social interaction. *Journal of Personality and Social Psychology, 37,* 75–86.

Fenigstein, A., Scheier, M. F., & Buss, A. H. (1975). Public and private self-consciousness assessment and theory. *Journal of Consulting and Clinical Psychology, 43,* 522–527.

Ferster, C. B. (1965). Classification of behavior pathology. In L. Krasner & S. P. Ullman (Eds.), *Research in behavior modification* (pp. 6–26). NY: Holt, Rinehart, & Winston.

Fuchs, C. Z., & Rehm, C. P. (1977). A self-control behavior therapy program for depression. *Journal of Consulting and Clinical Psychology, 45,* 206–215.

Ganellen, R., & Blaney, P. H. (1981, August). *A cognitive model of depressive onset.* In New theoretical approaches to the psychology of depression. Annual convention of the American Psychological Association, Los Angeles.

Gibbons, F., Smith, T., Brehm, S., & Schroeder, D. (1980). *Self-awareness and self-confrontation: The role of focus of attention in the process of psychotherapy.* Unpublished manuscript, University of Kansas, Lawrence.

Gillespie, R. D. (1929). The clinical differentiation of types of depression. *Guy's Hospital Reports, 75,* 306–344.

Glaser, K. (1967). Masked depression in children and adolescents. *American Journal of Psychotherapy, 21,* 565–574.

Gonzales, L., Lewinsohn, P. M., & Clarke, G. (1985). Longitudinal follow-up of unipolar depressives: An investigation of predictors of relapse. Journal of Consulting and Clinical Psychology, in press.

Gotlib, I. H. (1982). Self-reinforcement and depression in interpersonal interaction: The role of performance level. *Journal of Abnormal Psychology, 91,* 3–13.

Grinker, R. R., Sr., Miller, J., Sabshin, M., Nunn, R., & Nunnally, J. C. (1961). *The phenomena of depressions.* NY: Hoeber.

Hamilton, E. W., & Abramson, L. U. (1983). Cognitive patterns and major depressive disorder: A longitudinal study in a hospital setting. *Journal of Abnormal Psychology, 92,* 173–184.

Hammen, C. L., & Peters, S. D. (1977). Differential responses to male and female depressive reactions. *Journal of Consulting and Clinical Psychology, 45,* 994–1001.

Hammen, C. L., & Peters, S. D. (1978). Interpersonal consequences of depression: Responses to men and women enacting a depressed role. *Journal of Abnormal Psychology, 87,* 322–332.

Hautzinger, M. (1980). *Verbalverhalten Depressiver und ihrer Socialpartner.* Dissertation, Technischen Universitat Berlin.

Hautzinger, M., & Hoffman, N. (Eds.). (1979). *Depression und Umwelt.* Salzburg, Austria: Otto Muller Verlag.

Hersen, M., Bellack, A. S., & Himmelhoch, J. M. (1980). Skills training with unipolar depressed women. In J. P. Curran & P. M. Monti (Eds.), *Social competence and psychiatric disorders: Theory and practice.* NY: Guilford.

Hinchcliffe, M. K., Hooper, D., & Roberts, F. J. (1978). *The melancholy marriage.* NY: John Wiley and Sons.

Hirschfeld, R. M., & Cross, C. K. (1982). Epidemiology of affective disorders: Psychosocial risk factors. *Archives of General Psychiatry, 39,* 35–45.

Hirschfeld, R., Klerman, G. L., Chodoff, P., Korchin, S., & Barret, J. (1976). Dependency, self-esteem, clinical depression. *Journal of the American Academy of Psychoanalysis, 4,* 373–388.

Hull, J. G., & Levy, A. S. (1979). The organizational functioning of the self: An alternative to the Duval and Wicklund model of self-awareness. *Personality and Social Psychology, 37,* 756–768.

Ickes, J., Wicklund, A., & Ferris, C. (1973). Objective self-awareness and self-esteem. *Journal of Experimental Social Psychology, 9,* 202–219.

Ingram, R. E., & Smith, T. S. (1984). Depression and internal versus external locus of attention. *Cognitive Therapy and Research, 8,* 139–152.

Isen, A. M., Shalker, T. E., Clark, M., & Karp, L. (1978). Affect, accessibility of material in memory, and behavior: A cognitive loop? *Journal of Personality and Social Psychology, 36,* 1–12.

Kanfer, F. H., & Hagerman, S. (1981). The role of self-regulation. In L. Rehm (Ed.), *Behavior therapy for depression: Present status and future directions.* (Chap. 4). NY: Academic Press.

Kashani, J. G., & Simonds, J. (1979). The incidence of depression in children. *American Journal of Psychiatry, 136,* 1203–1205.

Keller, M. B., Shapiro, R. W., Lavori, P. W., & Wolfe, N. (1982). Relapse in major depressive disorder: Analysis of the life table. *Archives of General Psychiatry, 39,* 911–915.

Kendell, R. E. (1976). The classification of depression: A review of contemporary confusions. *British Journal of Psychiatry, 129,* 15–28.

Kernis, M. H., Zuckerman, M., Cohen, A., & Spadafora, S. (1982). Persistence following failure: The interactive role of self-awareness and the attributional basis for negative expectancies. *Journal of Personality and Social Psychology, 43,* 1184–1191.

Kleinbaum, D. G., Kupper, L. L., & Morganstern, H. (1982). *Epidemiologic research: Principles and quantitative methods.* Belmont, CA: Lifetime Learning.

Klerman, G. L., & Weissman, M. M. (1982). Interpersonal psychotherapy: Theory and research. In A. J. Rush (Ed.), *Short-term psychotherapies for depression.* NY: Guilford Press.

Kuiper, N. A. (1978). Depression and causal attributions for success and failure. *Journal of Personality and Social Psychology, 36,* 236–246.

Langer, E. J. (1978). Rethinking the role of thought in social interaction. In J. Harvey, W.

Ickes, & R. F. Kidd (Eds.), *New directions in attribution research* (Vol. 2). Hillsdale, NJ: Erlbaum.

Lazarus, A. A. (1968). Learning theory and the treatment of depression. *Behavior Research and Therapy, 6,* 83–89.

Lazarus, R. S., & Launier, R. (1978). Stress-related transactions between person and environment. In L. A. Pervin & M. Lewis (Eds.), *Internal and external determinants of behavior.* NY: Plenum.

Lehman, H. E. (1971). Epidemiology of depressive disorders. In R. R. Fieve (Ed.), *Depression in the 70's: Modern theory and research.* Princeton, NJ: Excerpta Medica.

Levitt, E. G., & Lubin, B. (1975). *Depression.* NY: Springer.

Lewinsohn, P. M. (1975). The behavioral study and treatment of depression. In M. Hersen, R. M. Eisler, & P. M. Miller (Eds.), *Progress in behavioral modification* (Vol. 1). NY: Academic Press.

Lewinsohn, P. M. (1976). Activity schedules in the treatment of depression. In C. E. Thoresen & J. D. Krumboltz (Eds.), *Counseling methods* (pp. 74–83). NY: Holt, Rinehart, & Winston.

Lewinsohn, P. M., & Alexander, C. (1983). *Depression and learned helplessness.* Paper presented at the Annual Meeting of the Association for the Advancement of Behavior Therapy, Washington, DC.

Lewinsohn, P. M., Fenn, D., Stanton, A., & Franklin, J. (1985). *The relationship of age of onset to duration of episode in unipolar depression.* Unpublished manuscript, University of Oregon, Eugene.

Lewinsohn, P. M., Hautzinger, M., & Duncan, E. (1984). *Is there an age elevated risk for unipolar depression?* Unpublished mimeo, University of Oregon, Eugene.

Lewinsohn, P. M., & Hoberman, H. M. (1982). Depression. In A. S. Bellack, M. Hersen, & A. E. Kazdin (Eds.), *International handbook of behavior modification and therapy.* NY: Plenum.

Lewinsohn, P. M., Larson, D. W., & Muñoz, R. F. (1982). Measurement of expectancies and other cognitions in depressed individuals. *Cognitive Therapy and Research, 6,* 437–446.

Lewinsohn, P. M., Lobitz, W. C., & Wilson, S. (1973). Sensitivity of depressed individuals to aversive stimuli. *Journal of Abnormal Psychology, 81,* 259–263.

Lewinsohn, P. M., Mischel, W., Chaplin, W., & Barton, R. (1980). Social competence & depression: The role of illusory self-perceptions. *Journal of Abnormal Psychology, 89,* 203–212.

Lewinsohn, P. M., Steinmetz, J., Larson, D., & Franklin, J. (1981). Depression related cognitions: Antecedent or consequence? *Journal of Abnormal Psychology, 90,* 213–219.

Lewinsohn, P. M., & Talkington, J. (1979). Studies on the measurement of unpleasant events and relations with depression. *Applied Psychological Measurement, 3,* 83–101.

Lewinsohn, P. M., Teri, L., & Hoberman, H. (1983). Depression: A perspective on etiology, treatment, and life span issues. In M. Rosenbaum, D. Franks, & Y. Jaffe (Eds.), *Perspectives on behavior therapy in the eighties.* NY: Springer.

Lewinsohn, P. M., Weinstein, M., & Shaw, D. (1969). Depression: A clinical–research approach. In R. D. Rubin & C. M. Frank (Eds.), *Advances in behavior therapy.* NY: Academic Press.

Lewinsohn, P. M., Youngren, M. A., & Grosscup, S. J. (1979). Reinforcement and depression. In R. A. DePue (Ed.), *The psychobiology of depressive disorders: Implications for the effects of stress.* NY: Academic Press.

Lewis, A. J. (1938). States of depression: Their clinical and etiological differentiation. *British Medical Journal, 2,* 875–878.

Libet, J., & Lewinsohn, P. M. (1973). The concept of social skill with special references to the behavior of depressed persons. *Journal of Consulting and Clinical Psychology, 40,* 304–312.

Lloyd, C. (1980). Life events and depressive disorder reviewed: Events as predisposing factors. *Archives of General Psychiatry, 37,* 529–535.

Lloyd, G., & Lishman, W. A. (1975). Effect of depression on the speed of recall of pleasant and unpleasant experiences. *Psychological Medicine, 5,* 173–180.

MacPhillamy, D. J., & Lewinsohn, P. M. (1974). Depression as a function of levels of desired and obtained pleasure. *Journal of Abnormal Psychology, 83,* 651–657.

McLean, P. D. (1976). Therapeutic decision making in the behavioral treatment of depression. In P. O. Davidson (Ed.), *The behavioral management of anxiety, depression, and pain.* NY: Bruner/Mazel.

McLean, P. D. (1979). *Matching of treatments to subject characteristics.* Paper presented at the NIMH conference "Research recommendations for the behavioral treatment of depression," Pittsburgh, PA.

McLean, P. D., & Hakstian, A. R. (1979). Clinical depression: Comparative efficacy of outpatient treatments. *Journal of Clinical and Counseling Psychology, 47,* 818–836.

Morris, J. B., & Beck, A. T. (1974). The efficacy of anti-depressant drugs: A review of research (1958 to 1972). *Archives of General Psychiatry, 30,* 667–674.

Muñoz, R. F. (1977). A cognitive approach to the assessment and treatment of depression. *Dissertation Abstracts International, 38,* 2873B.

Myers, J. K., & Weissman, M. M. (1980). Use of a self-report symptom scale to detect depression in a community sample. *American Journal of Psychiatry, 137,* 1081–1084.

Natale, M., & Hantas, M. (1982). Effect of temporary mood states on selective memory about the self. *Journal of Personality and Social Psychology, 42,* 927–934.

Nelson, R. E. (1977). Irrational beliefs in depression. *Journal of Consulting and Clinical Psychology, 45,* 1190–1191.

Overall, J. E., & Hollister, L. E. (1966). Nosology and depression and differential response to drugs. *The Journal of the American Medical Association, 195,* 946–948.

Overall, J. E., & Hollister, L. E. (1980). Phenomenological classification of depressive disorders. *Journal of Clinical Psychology, 36,* 372–376.

Parker, G., & Brown, L. (1979). Repertoires of response to potential precipitants of depression. *Australian and New Zealand Journal of Psychiatry, 13,* 327–333.

Paykel, E. S. (Ed.). (1982). *Handbook of affective disorders.* Edinburgh, Scotland: Churchill-Livingston.

Paykel, E. S., Myers, J. K., Dienelt, M. N., Klerman, G. L., Lindenthal, J. J., & Pepper, M. P. (1969). Life events and depression: A controlled study. *Archives of General Psychiatry, 21,* 753–760.

Paykel, E. A., Prusoff, B., & Klerman, G. L. (1971). The endogenous–neurotic continuum in depression: Rater independence and factor distributions. *Journal of Psychiatric Research, 8,* 73–90.

Peterson, C., Schwartz, S., & Seligman, M. E. P. (1981). Self-blame and depressive symptoms. *Journal of Personality and Social Psychology, 41,* 253–259.

Rehm, L. P. (1977). A self-control model of depression. *Behavior Therapy, 8,* 787–804.

Rehm, L. P., & Kornblith, G. I. (1979). Behavior therapy for depression: A review of recent developments. In M. Hersen, R. M. Eisler, & P. M. Miller (Eds.), *Progress in behavior modification* (Vol. 7). NY: Academic Press.

Rippere, V. (1977). Common sense beliefs about depression and antidepressive behavior: A study of social consensus. *Behavior Research and Therapy, 15,* 465–473.

Rogers, T. B., Kuiper, N. A., & Kirker, W. S. (1977). Self-reference and the encoding of personal information. *Journal of Personality and Social Psychology, 35,* 677–688.

Rosenbaum, M. (1980). A schedule for assessing self-control behaviors: Preliminary findings. *Behavior Therapy, 11,* 109–121.

Rosenthal, S. H., & Gudeman, J. E. (1967). The endogenous depressive pattern: An empirical investigation. *Archives of General Psychiatry, 16,* 241–249.

Rush, A. J., Beck, A. T., Kovacs, M., & Hollon, S. (1977). Comparative efficacy of cognitive therapy and pharmacotherapy in the treatment of depressed outpatients. *Cognitive Therapy and Research, 1,* 17–37.

Sachar, E. J. (1975). Neuroendocrine abnormalities in depressive illness. In E. J. Sachar (Ed.), *Topics in psychoendocrinology* (pp. 135–156). NY: Grune & Stratton.

Sanchez, V. C., Lewinsohn, P. M., & Larson, D. W. (1980). Assertion training: Effectiveness in the treatment of depression. *Journal of Clinical Psychology, 36,* 526–529.

Schank, R., & Ableson, R. P. (1975). *Scripts, plans and knowledge.* Prepared for presentation at the 4th International Conference on Artificial Intelligence. Tbilisi, USSR.

Scheier, M. F., & Carver, C. S. (1977). *Learned helplessness or egotism: Do expectancies matter?* Carnegie-Mellon University, Pittsburgh.

Scheier, M. F., Carver, C. S., & Gibbons, F. X. (1981). Self-focused attention and reactions to fear. *Journal of Research in Personality, 15,* 1–15.

Schildkraut, J. J. (1965). The catecholamine hypothesis of affective disorders: A review of supporting evidence. *American Journal of Psychiatry, 122,* 509–522.

Schildkraut, J. J., & Kety, S. S. (1967). Biogenic amines and emotion. *Science, 156,* 21–30.

Seligman, M. E. P. (1975). *Helplessness.* San Francisco, CA: W. H. Freeman.

Seligman, M. E. P. (1981). A learned helplessness point of view. In L. P. Rehm (Ed.), *Behavior therapy for depression* (pp. 123–142). NY: Academic Press.

Seligman, M. E. P., Abramson, L. Y., Semmel, A., & Baeyer, C. von. (1979). Depressive attributional style. *Journal of Abnormal Psychology, 88,* 242–247.

Skinner, B. F. (1953). *Science and human behavior.* NY: Macmillan.

Smith, T. W., & Greenberg, J. (1981). Depression and self-focused attention. *Motivation and Emotion, 5,* 323–329.

Strack, S., & Coyne, J. C. (1983). Social confirmation of dysphoria: Shared and private reactions. *Journal of Personality and Social Psychology, 44,* 798–806.

Sugar, M. (1967). Disguised depressions in adolescents. In G. L. Usden (Ed.), *Adolescence: Care and counseling* (pp. 77–93). Philadelphia: J. P. Lippincott.

Susser, M. (1966). *Causal thinking in the health sciences: Concepts and strategies of epidemiology.* NY: Oxford University Press.

Taylor, S. E., & Fiske, S. T. (1978). Getting inside the head: Methodologies for process analysis in attribution and social cognition. In J. Harvey, W. Ickes, & R. Kidd (Eds.), *New directions in attributional research* (Vol. 3). Hillsdale, NJ: Erlbaum.

Teasdale, J. D. (1983). Affect and accessibility. *Phil. Trans. R. Soc. Lond., B302,* 403–412.

Teasdale, J. D., & Fogarty, S. J. (1979). Differential effects of induced mood on retrieval of pleasant and unpleasant events from episodic memory. *Journal of Abnormal Psychology, 88,* 248–257.

Teasdale, J. D., & Russell, M. L. (1983). Differential effects of induced mood on the recall of positive, negative, and neutral words. *British Journal of Clinical Psychology, 22,* 163–171.

Teasdale, J. D., & Taylor, R. (1981). Induced mood and accessibility of memories: An effect of mood state or of mood induction procedure? *British Journal of Clinical Psychology, 20,* 426–442.

Teasdale, J. D., Taylor, R., & Fogarty, S. J. (1980). Effects of induced elation–depression on the accessibility of memories of happy and unhappy experiences. *Behavior Research and Therapy, 18,* 339–346.

Teri, L., & Lewinsohn, P. M. (1985). Depression and age: The relationship of age, gender, and method of assessment on the symptom pattern of depression. Unpublished mimeo, University of Oregon, Eugene.

Toolan, J. M. (1969). Depression in children and adolescents. In G. Caplan & S. LeBovici (Eds.), *Adolescence: Psychosocial perspective*. NY: Basic Books.

Vernon, S. W., & Roberts, R. E. (1982). Prevalence of treated and untreated psychiatric disorders in three ethnic groups. *Social Science & Medicine, 16*, 1575–1582.

Wegner, D. N., & Giuliano, T. (1980). Arousal-induced attention to self. *Journal of Personality and Social Psychology, 38*, 719–726.

Weissman, M. M., & Klerman, G. (1977). Sex differences and the epidemiology of depression. *Archives of General Psychiatry, 34*, 98–111.

Weissman, M. M., & Myers, J. K. (1978). Affective disorders in a US urban community. *Archives of General Psychiatry, 35*, 1304–1311.

Weissman, M. M., & Paykel, E. S. (1974). *The depressed woman*. Chicago: University of Chicago Press.

Weissman, M. M., Prusoff, B. A., & Klerman, G. L. (1978). Personality and the prediction of long-term outcome of depression. *American Journal of Psychiatry, 135*, 797–800.

Wener, A. E., & Rehm, L. P. (1975). Depressive affect: A test of behavioral hypotheses. *Journal of Abnormal Psychology, 84*, 221–227.

Wilkinson, I. M., & Blackburn, I. M. (1981). Cognitive style in depressed and recovered depressed patients. *British Journal of Clinical Psychology, 20*, 283–292.

Wilson, P. H., Goldin, J. C., & Charbonneau-Powis, M. (1983). Comparative efficacy of behavioral and cognitive treatments of depression. *Cognitive Therapy and Research, 7*, 111–124.

Woodruff, R. A., Jr., Murphy, G. E., & Herjanic, M. (1967). The natural history of affective disorders. I. Symptoms of 72 patients at the time of index hospital admission. *Journal of Psychiatric Research, 5*, 255–263.

Youngren, M. A. (1978). *The functional relationship of depression and problematic interpersonal behavior*. Unpublished doctoral dissertation, University of Oregon, Eugene.

Youngren, M. A., & Lewinsohn, P. M. (1980). The functional relationship between depression and problematic interpersonal behavior. *Journal of Abnormal Psychology, 89*, 333–341.

Zeiss, A. M. (1977). Interpersonal behavior problems of the depressed: A study of outpatient treatment. *Dissertation Abstracts International, 38*, 2895B–28956B.

Zeiss, A. M., Lewinsohn, P. M., & Muñoz, R. (1979). Nonspecific improvement effects in depression using interpersonal, cognitive, and pleasant events focused treatments. *Journal of Consulting and Clinical Psychology, 47*, 427–439.

Zeiss, A. M., & Lewinsohn, P. M. (in preparation). *Social skill of formerly depressed individuals*. University of Oregon, Eugene.

Zis, A. P., & Goodwin, F. K. (1982). The amine hypothesis. In E. S. Paykel (Ed.), *Handbook of affective disorders* (pp. 179–190). NY: Guilford Press.

Zubin, J. (1976). The role of vulnerability in the etiology of schizophrenic episodes. In L. J. West & D. E. Flinn (Eds.), *Treatment of schizophrenia: Progress and prospects*. NY: Grune & Stratton.

Learned Helplessness and Depression: Cognitive Factors in Treatment and Inoculation

L. ROWELL HUESMANN
SHARON MORIKAWA

Few behavioral theories have stimulated as much research over the past decade as Seligman's (1974, 1975) learned helplessness model of depression. Not only has this research provided insight into the components that may be effective in behavioral treatments of depressed mood, but also the research has helped to elucidate the importance of cognitions in the development of depression. Cognitions play a critical intervening role in the revised model of learned helplessness (Abramson, Seligman, & Teasdale, 1978). Yet, in this chapter we will argue that even this revision has major flaws. The central feature of the original helplessness theory was that a learned perception of noncontingency between behavior and outcome leads to behavioral helplessness and the symptoms of depression. On this basis, inoculations preventing the learning of noncontingency or treatments producing an unlearning should be effective therapy. However, the accumulating evidence seems to suggest that a perception of noncontingency is neither a necessary nor sufficient condition for helplessness and depression. Rather, an individual's cognitive interpretation of what happens to him or her is critical. That is, the extent to which changes induced in behavior will affect mood also depends strongly on the cognitive attributions about those changes.

Learned Helplessness in Infrahumans

The term *learned helplessness* was first coined by Seligman and his colleagues (Overmeier & Seligman, 1967; Seligman & Maier, 1967) to describe the behavior of dogs in a particular escape/avoidance conditioning paradigm. Dogs exposed to shocks that no behavior could terminate showed severe deficits in learning future escape/avoidance responses. While about 95% of the experimentally naive dogs learned to escape or avoid a shock in a new situation, almost 70% of the experimental dogs did not learn. They appeared uncomfortable but passively accepted the shocks. These results were easily reproduced in many infrahuman species (Maier & Seligman, 1976; Seligman, 1975), suggesting a very robust phenomenon. A wide variety of variations in methodology had little effect on the results.

Seligman and his colleagues attributed the results to the "uncontrollability" of the initial shocks. By uncontrollable Seligman (1975, p. 16–17) meant that the probability of a shock was the same regardless of what response the dog emitted. In other words, the outcome was independent of the response. One should note that while the term *uncontrollable* is generally used without any qualifiers, it almost always means that the shock is uncontrollable by the organism receiving it. How can one be sure that learning and performance deficits are caused by the uncontrollability of the shock in the previous situation? Logically, one cannot be sure. One can only eliminate other explanations or dimensions of difference between the experimental and control groups as explanations by equating these dimensions across groups. It was in this way that Seligman and his colleagues demonstrated that it was not the amount or pattern of previous shocks per se that was causing the helplessness. They proved this by yoking experimental dogs to control dogs in an initial shock situation. The experimental and control dogs received exactly the same pattern and number of shocks. However, a control dog could terminate each shock to itself and its yoked partner by pressing the panel with its nose. A panel press by the experimental dog had no effect. Thus, the shocks to both animals were controllable by the control dog and uncontrollable by the experimental dog. The experimental dogs displayed the usual helplessness deficits, but the control dogs did not. While other methodological or psychological interpretations of the cause of the difference between the escapable and inescapable groups are possible (e.g., see Costello, 1978; Levis, 1976), it was certainly reasonable, given these results, for Seligman to adopt the theory that the locus of the helplessness effect in animals was exposure to an uncontrollable aversive stimulus.

Almost immediately, the learned helplessness paradigm was adopted as an explanation of human helplessness and depression. The reasons are not mysterious. The behavior of helpless animals seemed to mimic the behavior of depressed humans. The learned helplessness model was a relatively parsimonious model that made specific, testable predictions about behavior. Perhaps most important, the helplessness model suggested that certain straightforward therapy techniques would relieve depression. Yet, there are many pitfalls readily apparent in extrapolating the results of the animal experiments to humans. Seligman, himself, (1975, p. 27) has said "the history of comparative psychology is littered with invalidated experiments and discredited theories that have made this assumption without warrant." There are several different aspects of the extrapolation that must be separated in the case of learned helplessness. First, can helplessness be learned by humans and is it frequently learned? Second, if learned helplessness occurs in humans, is it a result of exposure to uncontrollable aversive stimulation? Third, is clinical depression in humans often, frequently, or sometimes a result of learned helplessness? Fourth, is exposure to uncontrollable aversive stimulation a necessary or sufficient condition for depressed mood? Finally, do the inoculation and alleviation treatments suggested by the learned helplessness theory ameliorate depression in humans?

Learned Helplessness in Humans

If by *helplessness* one simply means a passive acceptance of whatever happens to one's self without an effort to either improve one's lot or to avoid negative consequences, one can certainly find numerous examples of helplessness in human behavior. In certain situations (e.g., after a devastating personal loss, in prisons or concentration camps, or among the chronically unemployed) such behaviors may even become commonplace. The question of interest, though, is are these behaviors learned, and, if so, are they learned by exposure to uncontrollable aversive stimulation? No matter how many analogues are drawn between the behavior of dogs exposed to uncontrollable shock and the behavior of humans in certain situations, it cannot be validly argued that the behavior stems from the same cause. Rather, experimental investigations with humans are required.

A large number of such experiments now exist. Broadly they fall into two groups: (1) those using normal subjects and directed at demonstrating that temporary helplessness can be induced in humans, and (2) those using groups of subjects varying in depressed mood and directed at demonstrating an analogy between depression and learned helplessness. Of the former, the best known and most representative experiment is one by Hiroto (1974; Hiroto & Seligman, 1975) in which experimental and control subjects were exposed to an uncontrollable loud, aversive noise. A control subject could terminate the loud noise to both him or herself and the yoked control by pressing an appropriate pattern of buttons; an experimental subject could not. Hiroto found that on a subsequent avoidance task, experimental subjects were poor at learning to escape or avoid the loud noise, indicating a helplessness effect. Hiroto also demonstrated deficits in avoidance learning when the initial task was quite different from the avoidance task, namely, when the initial task for the experimental group involved attempting to solve insoluble problems. These experiments and the numerous others following a similar paradigm (Klein, Fencil-Morse, & Seligman, 1976; Klein & Seligman, 1976; Miller & Seligman, 1975; Oakes & Curtis, 1982; Roth & Bootzin, 1974; Tennen, Drum, Gillen, & Stanton, 1982) demonstrated that temporary performance deficits could be induced in humans with procedures that resemble those used in animal helplessness studies. However, they do not prove that the perceived uncontrollability of the aversive stimulus is a necessary or sufficient condition for the helplessness. Moreover, the results with humans are not as robust as those with animals. Experiments in which performance deficits are not obtained are seldom published, but these authors are aware of a number of such studies.

The evidence that exposure to uncontrollable aversive stimulation significantly lowers mood also is not as powerful as many seem to believe. In their 1979 review, Miller and Norman found six studies that investigated mood deficits in humans following the typical helplessness induction procedure. A few such studies found that a helplessness induction unequivocally lowered mood (e.g., Gatchel & Proctor, 1976). Other studies, however, found no differences between groups (e.g., Cole & Coyne, 1977; Klein, et al., 1976; Klein & Seligman, 1976; Oakes & Curtis, 1982; Tennen et al., 1982) or found differences on anxiety and hostility instead of differences on depression (e.g., Miller & Seligman, 1975). Still others have reported equivocal results (Roth & Kubal, 1975; Teasdale, 1978; Willis & Blaney, 1978; Wortman, Panciera, Shusterman, & Hibscher, 1976).

The second type of experiment with humans, those comparing subjects differing initially on affective mood, also has yielded ambiguous results. The typical paradigm in these studies has been to compare the mood and performance deficits displayed by normal subjects who experience a helplessness induction with the deficits displayed by depressed subjects (Klein & Seligman, 1976; Klein et al., 1976; Miller & Seligman, 1975; Price, Tryon, & Raps, 1978; Sacco & Hokanson, 1978; Teasdale, 1978). While most of these studies demonstrated some similarities between normal and depressed subjects, it is not known what these similarities indicate. The two groups may be performing similarly for entirely different reasons. Furthermore, even if they are performing poorly for the same reasons, as Huesmann (1981) has pointed out, it is fallacious to conclude that a particular characteristic (e.g., expectation of noncontingency) is a cause of a pathology simply because it occurs among individuals with that pathology.

Cognitive Processes and Learned Helplessness

The experiments with humans, taken as a whole, suggest that no straight-forward extrapolation of animal-learned helplessness can explain human depression. Performance and learning deficits in humans often follow prior exposure to an uncontrollable aversive stimulus; but the reasons are not clear. Mood changes seldom follow a helplessness induction, and, when they do follow, they cannot be shown to be a consequence of uncontrollability. Similar conclusions have been reached by a number of other theoreticians (Blaney, 1977; Buchwald, Coyne, & Cole, 1978; Costello, 1978; Golin & Terrell, 1977; Huesmann, 1978; Wortman & Brehm, 1975). The central problem seems to be that the cognitive response of an individual to the induction situation can completely change the effect of a helplessness induction.

With infrahuman species, only a simple cognitive schema was required to explain learned helplessness. Seligman assumed that the repeated presentation of noncontingent aversive stimulation led to an internalized expectation of noncontingency which, in turn, produced the helpless behavior in new situations. However, Seligman and his colleagues (1978) have recognized that such a model of cognitive processing is unrealistically simple for humans. The response of an individual to a so-called uncontrollable aversive stimulus will depend upon that individual's analysis and understanding of the situation. The cognitive processes involved in such an analysis may be extremely complex. There is no possibility for an animal without the facility for symbolic representation and logical analysis to analyze the reason that its responses do not change the aversive stimulation it receives. Any human, however, with the facility for symbolic representation and logical analysis will wonder why the tone cannot be stopped no matter what he or she does on the silly button-pushing task that some psychologist is making him or her do. The subject may decide that the tone is uncontrollable and random, that the tone is being controlled by the experimenter, or that the tone is controllable but that he or she cannot figure out how. The aversiveness of the tone may also depend on the cognitive reaction of the subject. If this situation is viewed as a test of perseverance, tolerance for the tone may be greater. Regardless of which of these or many other interpretations the subject makes about the task situation, the effect of the procedure, if any, on the subject's mood and future performance could also depend on his or her pre-existing cognitions about him or herself.

In response to both the empirical failures of the learned helplessness model to predict human behavior and to the model's obvious shortcomings in representing the complexity of human cognition, Abramson *et al.,* (1978) proposed their revised model of how at least some types of human depression are caused by exposure to uncontrollable aversive stimulation. In their revision they drew heavily on the social–cognitive literature concerning the role of attributions as mediators between stimulus events and behavioral responses (e.g., Harvey, Ickes, & Kidd, 1976, 1977; Jones et al., 1972; Weiner, 1974). They agreed that the effectiveness of an exposure to uncontrollable aversive stimulation in producing performance and mood deficits would depend on the subject's attributions about the situation. These attributions, in turn, might depend on the relatively stable characteristics of a subject's personality, for example, locus of control orientation. More specifically, they proposed that three dimensions of the subject's attributions about the cause of uncontrollable aversive stimulation are critical. Does the subject perceive the cause as internal (e.g., lack of intelligence) or external (e.g., the test is biased)? Does the subject perceive the cause as stable (e.g., I have poor vision) or unstable (e.g., I forgot my glasses)? Does the subject perceive the cause as generalizing to many situations (global) or as situationally determined (specific)? Abramson et al. (1978) argued that exposure to uncontrollable aversive stimulation coupled with the wrong type of attributions for the cause (e.g., to internal, global, stable factors) produces the symptoms of helplessness and some type of depression.

There are numerous problems with this reformulation that have been cogently elucidated elsewhere (Buchwald et al., 1978; Huesmann, 1978; Wortman & Dintzer, 1978). In many respects the theory is unfalsifiable. If a helplessness induction does not produce the predicted deficits, one can always argue it is because the wrong attributions were made. If the deficits do occur, it is assumed that the right attributions were made. However, perhaps the most important challenge that faces the theory is the argument that the occurrence of an uncontrollable aversive stimulus and the perception of response–outcome independence are superfluous; only the attributions matter. Beck (1967) and Rizley (1978) have argued that subjects' attributions about negative events are a prime determinant of whether or not depressive moods will occur. Whether or not the negative event is uncontrollable does not matter except to the extent that it can affect attributions about one's self. Thus, in some cases an uncontrollable aversive event could be less depressing than a controllable one.

Some experimental evidence exists to support such a view. For example, Rizley (1978) reported that depressed subjects believed they had greater influence over other people (e.g., more control) than less depressed subjects. Blaney (1977) reported similar results about control. Alloy and Abramson (1982) discovered that, following a helplessness induction, normal subjects showed a "robust illusion of control" in situations in which events were noncontingent but associated with success. Both normal and depressed subjects who were not given the helplessness induction judged control accurately. In other words, the helplessness induction engendered an illusion of control rather than taught that control was not possible.

Hanusa and Schulz (1977) and Wortman *et al.* (1976), as well as others, found that subjects exposed to a helplessness induction who attributed their failure to inadequate ability performed better on a post-test than those who attributed their failure to task difficulty. Both factors seem equally uncontrollable. However, according to the the Abramson *et al.* (1978) revision of the learned helplessness model, an attribution to an internal, stable factor (ability) should not produce a facilitation effect. On the other hand, if one views the attributions themselves as central, one can see the subjects' facilitated performance as compensation for the threat to self-esteem posed by the attribution of failure to ability.

There are also significant data that challange the core tenet of learned helplessness theory that a perception of uncontrollability produces helplessness. Oakes and Curtis (1982), using a target shooting task (with a light gun), found that the significant performance deficits evidenced in the noncontingent feedback condition were not related to the subjects' perception of noncontingency. Tennen *et al.* (1982) reported similar results with a different experimental paradigm. These authors' conclusions have been challenged by others (Alloy, 1982; Silver, Wortman, & Klos, 1982), and there are certain discrepancies in their results. Nevertheless, these results are only part of a growing body of literature suggesting that a perception of uncontrollability is not critical. Willis and Blaney (1978) found that depressed and nondepressed individuals did not differ on measures of perceived noncontingency. They also found no evidence of a perception of noncontingency among nondepressed individuals who were made helpless. Similar results were obtained for the depressed subjects in McNitt and Thornton's (1978) study. In fact, experimental evidence exists to support the opposite view. Rizley (1978) and Blaney (1977) reported that depressed subjects believed they had greater control (i.e., greater influence over others) than less depressed subjects. Alloy and Abramson (1982) discovered that, following a helplessness induction, nondepressed subjects showed a "robust illusion of control" when events were noncontingent but associated with success. Since nondepressed and depressed subjects not given the helplessness induction judged control accurately in Alloy and Abramson's study, the induction had engendered an illusion of control rather than uncontrollability.

The whole notion of uncontrollability is the source of much confusion in the learned helplessness literature. According to the theory, in order to inoculate against helplessness, individuals should be trained to attribute their failure to an external, unstable, and specific cause, that is, luck. In other words, *helplessness,* which has been defined as "deficits produced by an exposure to uncontrollable outcomes" (Overmeier & Seligman, 1967; Seligman & Maier, 1967), should be prevented by attributions to luck, which is an uncontrollable cause. Perhaps it is the identification of an uncontrollable cause as luck versus an unknown uncontrollable cause that qualifies the former as an inoculation method. Regardless, Abramson *et al*. (1978) did not address this problem.

Treatment and Inoculation

The issue of whether or not exposure to an uncontrollable aversive stimulus is a necessary or sufficient condition for at least some depressions becomes most important when one attempts to design inoculation and alleviation procedures for depression. Investigations in these areas may provide some of the best evidence to settle questions about the validity of the learned helplessness model of depression. If response–outcome independence is critical to helplessness and depression in humans, then inoculation and treatment methods based on correcting a perception of uncontrollability should have a substantial effect. On the other hand, changing an individual's attributional style should have little effect on depression unless attributions are being made about the cause of uncontrollable aversive stimulation.

A major distinction must be drawn between helplessness treatment procedures that are designed to inoculate a subject against helplessness and those that are designed to alleviate helplessness deficts. An alleviation procedure that has proven effective with learned–helpless animals is to force them to make a response that terminates an aversive stimulus. Thus, Seligman (1975) and his colleagues (Seligman, Maier, & Geer, 1968), using leashes, dragged their helpless dogs across the shuttle box to terminate shock. After numerous trials, the dogs finally performed the escape/avoidance response on their own. Seligman argued that these results are consistent with the theory that perceived uncontrollability is the key to helplessness. Such an argument is rather optimistic. These results are open to numerous other interpretations (Costello, 1978). The most simple interpretation, usually the first that should be adopted, is that a specific instrumental avoidance response that had been extinguished is relearned through shaping. More generous extrapolations must be considered highly speculative.

A similar criticism could be leveled at Seligman's (1975) initial experiments on inoculating animals against learned helplessness. The experiments showed that if dogs first learned an escape response in a shuttle box, the usual inescapable shock treatment did not produce helplessness. However, the simplest interpretation of this result is that the animals' original escape response never completely extinguished. It is speculation to assert that the initial experience teaches dogs a cognition that they can control shock and that this cognition prevents the formation of the opposite cognition, that is, that they have no control over shock.

support to the role of attributions in the learned helplessness model of depression. The authors followed the helplessness induction task with a treatment task consisting of having subjects make certain attributions for their success on a social intelligence test. In so doing, Miller and Norman manipulated the subjects' attributions for the success task and not their attributions regarding why they failed on the helplessness task. Training these subjects to attribute their success to internal factors improved mood and performance in both the clinically depressed and the previously clinically depressed group that received the helplessness induction. However, it is not known if the attribution training proved effective because (1) the currently depressed subjects really were helpless without the benefit of an induction, and the treatment counteracted their natural helplessness, or (2) learned helplessness was irrelevant to the study, and the attribution for success manipulation would have improved anyone's mood, performance, and expectancies for success.

Interventions to alleviate helplessness also have been attempted outside the laboratory on subjects who have been diagnosed as acting helpless and depressed. These interventions have been directed primarily at changing the subject's attitudes and attributions. The authors of these studies have often written that they are attempting to alleviate learned helplessness, but, of course, it can only be supposition that the helplessness of the subjects was learned in a manner consistent with Seligman's theory.

Dweck and Reppucci (1973) identified children who routinely gave up easily on academic tasks in the face of failure as helpless. Upon further examination they found that these children either tended to take little responsibility for the outcome of their actions or tended to attribute the outcome to lack of ability. However, nonhelpless children who did not give up easily on an insolvable task tended to attribute the outcome of their behavior to effort. Dweck (1975) described the former group of children as "learned helpless" because they believed that outcome was independent of effort and that no matter how hard they tried, failure was inevitable. These children were said to give up in order to avoid or minimize a sense of failure.

Based on the finding that helpless grade school children possess a particular attributional style, Dweck (1975) conducted a treatment study that included attribution training in addition to the usual treatment of exposure to a success experience. Children identified as helpless by teachers and other school personnel were placed in one of two treatment conditions: exposure to success only or exposure to success plus attribution training. Subjects in the success only group were given a variety of success experiences but no attribution training. Subjects in the attribution group were given two or three failure trials per day accompanied by indirect instructions to attribute the failure to lack of effort. More specifically, when the subject failed, the experimenter stated, "that means you should have tried harder." Results showed that helpless children receiving the success only treatment continued to display marked performance deficits. In contrast, helpless children taught to attribute failure to lack of effort persisted, maintained, and even improved their performance following failure.

Unfortunately, in this study the differential effectiveness of the two pure types of treatment methods, attribution training versus exposure to success, cannot be assessed. Subjects were either placed in an exposure to success only treatment group or an exposure to success plus attribution training group. In addition, the children in the success only group received continuous successes (continuous reinforcement) whereas children in the combined treatment group received both successes and failures (partial reinforcement) in order to facilitate attribution training. Therefore, the superior persistence and performance of children in the combined treatment group may have been due to the longer lasting effects of a partial reinforcement schedule rather than the attribution training.

A number of other researchers have replicated and extended Dweck's (1975) findings (Chapin & Dyck, 1976; Fowler & Peterson, 1981; Rhodes, 1977). Taken together, these studies indicate that persistence in reading can be increased by exposing children to failures and convincing them to attribute those failures to lack of effort. However, it is highly speculative to assume that this treatment amounts to reversing learned helplessness performance deficits. Furthermore, there is little evidence that these treatments changed the children's perceptions of their control over their reinforcements.

On the whole, alleviation studies have demonstrated that changing an individual's attributions about success and failure can affect the persistence of the individual's behaviors that are relevant to that success and failure. However, these studies provide little evidence that such persistence generalizes much or that general mood is affected much by the training. Also, they provide little evidence that a generalized perception of noncontingency is a critical variable in human helplessness.

INOCULATIONS AGAINST HELPLESSNESS IN HUMANS

Considerably fewer studies have examined how to inoculate humans against helplessness. Teasdale's (1978) alleviation study indirectly included a test of immunization. On the basis of immunization experiments with animals (Seligman, 1975), one might have expected that the subject's success at pre-induction problem solving would have mitigated the induction of helplessness. However, it did not, even though only five minutes elapsed between pre-induction problem solving and the helplessness induction.

Generally, inoculation procedures have not proven very successful. The more successful experiments seem to have been those that provided prior success experiences. For example, Douglas and Anisman (1975) found that prior exposure to success on a cognitive task prevented failure on the helplessness task from interfering with performance on a final cognitive task. Since then, various versions of this basically simple design have been created to induce control and inoculate against helplessness. Dyck and Breen (1978) added the variable of task importance to success and failure experiences prior to learned helplessness. As expected, subjects given prior exposure to a success experience on a task, performed superior to those given prior exposure to a failure experience. When the task was high in importance, failure subjects performed much poorer than immunized subjects on a final anagram task. Eckelman and Dyck (1979) added the variable of stimulus specificity (both situation and task) to their study on immunization against helplessness via a success experience. Subjects immunized in the same setting and on a similar task to the final setting and task showed the greatest immunization. Diminishing degrees of immunization were found when similarities first in setting and then in task decreased.

Jones, Nation, and Massad (1977) investigated the effect of different schedules of success in inoculating subjects against helplessness deficits. These researchers found that a 50% rather than 100% schedule of success on anagram problems prior to the learned helplessness induction was most effective in lessening performance deficits on a final anagram test. While these studies indicate that at least some degree of inoculation against performance deficits can be obtained by pre-exposure to success experiences, they do not address the question of the role of uncontrollability in helplessness deficits. Perhaps the most direct attempt at inoculation, that is, teaching subjects that they could control an aversive stimulus, was carried out by Thornton and Powell (1974). Using a direct extension of Seligman's procedure with dogs, they taught human subjects that they could escape shock prior to exposing them to inescapable shock. This procedure produced no detectable immunization.

Only a few inoculation studies have investigated the effect of manipulating attributions prior to the helplessness induction. Stein (1980) found that training subjects to attribute success and failure to effort and lack of effort was not effective in preventing helplessness deficits when failure and success experiences alternated during attribution training. It is difficult to know, though, whether this immunization failure reflects a failure of the attribution training procedure to alter attributions or a failure of altered attributions to affect performance.

Finally, in our own laboratory we discovered that we can affect how a subject's mood will change during a helplessness induction by manipulating attributions prior to the induction. However, the mood change seems to depend only on the attribution and not on the induction of helplessness. In this study, three groups of subjects were exposed to an inescapable noise induction procedure. One group received prior instructions emphasizing the internal, stable, and global dimensions of the task; the second received instructions emphasizing the external, unstable, and specific characteristics; and the third received no attribution manipulation. Following a helplessness induction, the group receiving no attribution manipulation showed that they did not differ in mood from a control group that received no helplessness induction However, the two groups that received attribution manipulations showed more depressed moods. Apparently, the attribution manipulation itself lowered the subject's mood independently of the content of the attributions adopted by the subjects. These results, like most of the other results from alleviation and inoculation studies, suggest that mood changes can be induced by changing attributions about success and failure, but that the changes are not dependent in any direct way on the subject learning or unlearning that he or she can control his or her reinforcements.

Summary

Seldom has a theory in psychology stimulated as much research as Seligman's learned helplessness theory. Since one of the primary functions of any theory is to stimulate research, the learned helplessness theory must be counted as a success on these grounds alone. However, beyond such a stimulating effect, Seligman's thinking has provided a firm basis on which a number of new theoretical positions have been built and has suggested a number of practical applications. Among the most interesting of these have been the attempts to inoculate against depression on the basis of helplessness theory.

Inoculation and alleviation procedures based on the learned helplessness model of depression have met varying degrees of success in preventing and alleviating helplessness and depression. When successful, the success seems to stem directly from changing the subject's cognitions and from the way these cognitions cause the subject to view success and failure. There is little evidence that learning that aversive outcomes are controllable is either a necessary or sufficient condition for inoculation or alleviation. Such results cast general doubt on the central tenet of the learned helplessness theory of depression; that is, a subject's perception of response-outcome independence is at the root of depression. A more plausible model seems to be that a person's attributions and cognitions about one's self and about one's behaviors are critical in their own right.

References

Abramson, L. Y., Seligman, M. E. P., & Teasdale, J. D. (1978). Learned helplessness in humans: Critique and reformulation. *Journal of Abnormal Psychology, 87,* 49–74.

Alloy, L. B. (1982). The role of perceptions and attributions for response-outcome noncontingency in learned helplessness: A commentary and discussion. *Journal of Personality, 50:4,* 443–479.

Alloy, L. B., & Abramson, L. Y. (1982). Learned helplessness, depression, and the illusion of control. *Journal of Personality and Social Psychology, 42,* 1114–1126.

Beck, A. T. (1967). *Depression: Clinical, experimental, and theoretical aspects.* New York: Harper & Row.

Blaney, P. H. (1977). Contemporary theories of depression: Critique and comparison. *Journal of Abnormal Psychology, 86,* 203–223.

Buchwald, A. M., Coyne, J. C., & Cole, C. S. (1978). A critical evaluation of the learned helplessness model of depression. *Journal of Abnormal Psychology, 87,* 180–193.

Chapin, M., & Dyck, D. G. (1976). Persistence in children's reading behavior as a function of N length and attribution retraining. *Journal of Abnormal Psychology, 85,* 511–515.

Cole, C. S., & Coyne, J. C. (1977). Situational specificity of laboratory-induced learned helplessness. *Journal of Abnormal Psychology, 86,* 615–623.

Costello, C. G. (1978). A critical review of Seligman's laboratory experiments on learned helplessness and depression in humans. *Journal of Abnormal Psychology, 87,* 21–31.

Douglas, D., & Anisman, H. (1975). Helplessness or expectation incongruency: Effects of aversive stimulation on subsequent performance. *Journal of Experimental Psychology: Human Perception and Performance, 1,* 411–417.

Dweck, C. S. (1975). The role of expectations and attributions in the alleviation of learned helplessness. *Journal of Personality and Social Psychology, 31,* 674–685.

Dweck, C. S., & Reppucci, N. D. (1973). Learned helplessness and reinforcement responsibility in children. *Journal of Personality and Social Psychology, 25,* 109–116.

Dyck, D. G., & Breen, L. J. (1978). Learned helplessness, immunization, and importance of task in humans. *Psychological Reports, 43,* 315–321.

Eckelman, J. D., & Dyck, D. G. (1979). Task- and setting-related cues in immunization against learned helplessness. *American Journal of Psychology, 92,* 653–667.

Fowler, J. W., & Peterson, P. L. (1981). Increasing reading persistence and altering attributional style of learned helpless children. *Journal of Educational Psychology, 73,* 251–260.

Gatchel, R., & Proctor, J. (1976). Physiological correlates of learned helplessness in man. *Journal of Abnormal Psychology, 85,* 24–34.

Golin, S., & Terrell, F. (1977). Motivational and associative aspects of mild depression in skill and chance. *Journal of Abnormal Psychology, 86,* 389–401.

Hanusa, B. H., & Schulz, R. (1977). Attributional mediators of learned helplessness. *Journal of Personality and Social Psychology, 35,* 602–611.

Harvey, J. H., Ickes, W. J., & Kidd, R. F. (Eds.). (1976). *New directions in attribution research* (Vol. 1). Hinsdale, NJ: Erlbaum.

Harvey, J. H., Ickes, W. J., & Kidd, R. F. (Eds.). (1977). *New directions in attribution research* (Vol. 2). Hinsdale, NJ: Erlbaum.

Hiroto, D. S. (1974). Locus of control and learned helplessness. *Journal of Experimental Psychology, 102*, 187–193.

Hiroto, D. S., & Seligman, M. E. P. (1975). Generality of learned helplessness in man. *Journal of Personality and Social Psychology, 31*, 311–327.

Huesmann, L. R. (1978). Cognitive processes and models of depression. *Journal of Abnormal Psychology, 87*, 194–198.

Huesmann, L. R. (1981). Experimental methods in research in psychopathology. In P. C. Kendall and J. N. Butcher (Eds.), *Handbook of research methods in clinical psychology.* New York: Wiley.

Jones, E. E., Kanouse, D. E., Kelly, H. H., Nisbett, R. E., Valins, S., & Weiner, B. (1972). *Attribution: Perceiving the causes of behavior.* Morristown, NJ: General Learning Press.

Jones, S. L., Nation, J. R., & Massad, P. (1977). Immunization against learned helplessness in man. *Journal of Abnormal Psychology, 86*, 75–83.

Kilpatrick-Tabak, B., & Roth, S. (1978). An attempt to reverse performance deficits associated with depression and experimentally-induced helplessness. *Journal of Abnormal Psychology, 87*, 141–154.

Klein, D. C., Fencil-Morse, E., & Seligman, M. E. P. (1976). Learned helplessness depression, and the attribution of failure. *Journal of Personality and Social Psychology, 33*, 508–516.

Klein, D. C., & Seligman, M. E. P. (1976). Reversal of performance deficits and perceptual deficits in learned helplessness and depression. *Journal of Abnormal Psychology, 85*, 11–26.

Levis, D. J. (1976). Learned helplessness: A reply and an alternative S–R interpretation. *Journal of Experimental Psychology: General, 105*, 47–65.

McNitt, P. C. & Thornton, D. W. (1978). Depression and perceived reinforcement: A reconsideration. *Journal of Abnormal Psychology, 87*(1), 137–140.

Maier, S. F., & Seligman, M. E. P. (1976). Learned helplessness: Theory & evidence. *Journal of Experimental Psychology: General, 105*, 3–46.

Miller, I. W., & Norman, W. H. (1979). Learned helplessness in humans: A review and attribution-theory model. *Psychological Bulletin, 86*, 93–118.

Miller, I. W., & Norman, W. H. (1981). Effects of attributions for success on the alleviation of learned helplessness and depression. *Journal of Abnormal Psychology, 90*, 113–124.

Miller, W. R., & Seligman, M. E. P. (1975). Depression and learned helplessness in man. *Journal of Abnormal Psychology, 84*, 228–238.

Nation, J. R., & Massad, P. (1978). Persistence training: A partial reinforcement procedure for reversing learned helplessness and depression. *Journal of Experimental Psychology: General, 107*, 436–451.

Oakes, W. F., & Curtis, N. (1982). Learned helplessness: Not dependent upon cognitions, attributions, or other such phenomenal experiences. *Journal of Personality, 50*:4, 387–407.

Overmeier, J. B., & Seligman, M. E. P. (1967). Effects of inescapable shock upon subsequent escape and avoidance learning. *Journal of Comparative and Physiological Psychology, 63*, 28–33.

Price, K. P., Tryon, W. W., & Raps, C. S. (1978). Learned helplessness and depression in a clinical population: A test of two behavioral hypotheses. *Journal of Abnormal Psychology, 87*, 113–121.

Raps, C. S., Reinhard, K. E., & Seligman, M. E. P. (1980). Reversal of cognitive and affective deficits associated with depression and learned helplessness by mood elevation in patients. *Journal of Abnormal Psychology, 89*, 342–349.

Rhodes, W. A. (1977). Generalization of attribution retraining *Dissertation Abstracts International, 38*, 2882B. (University Microfilms No. 77–26, 737).

Rizley, R. (1978). Depression and distortion in the attribution of causality. *Journal of Abnormal Psychology, 87*, 32–49.

Roth, S., & Bootzin, R. R. (1974). Effects of experimentally induced expectancies of external control: An investigation of learned helplessness. *Journal of Personality and Social Psychology, 29,* 253–264.

Roth, S., & Kubal, L. (1975). Tasks of differing importance: Facilitation and learned helplessness. *Journal of Personality and Social Psychology, 32,* 680–691.

Sacco, W. P., & Hokanson, J. E. (1978). Expectations of success and anagram performance of depressives in a public and private setting. *Journal of Abnormal Psychology, 87,* 122–130.

Seligman, M. E. P. (1974). Depression and learned helplessness. In R. J. Friedman & M. M. Katz (Eds.), *The psychology of depression: Contemporary theory and research.* Washington, DC: Winston-Wiley.

Seligman, M. E. P. (1975). *Helplessness: On depression, development, and death.* San Francisco: Freeman.

Seligman, M. E. P., & Maier, S. F. (1967). Failure to escape traumatic shock. *Journal of Experimental Psychology, 74,* 1–9.

Seligman, M. E. P., Maier, S. F., & Geer, J. H. (1968). The alleviation of learned helplessness in the dog. *Journal of Abnormal Psychology, 73,* 256–262.

Silver, R. L., Wortman, C. B., & Klos, D. S. (1982). Cognitions, affect, and behavior following uncontrollable outcomes: A response to current human helplessness research. *Journal of Personality, 50:4,* 480–514.

Stein, N. (1980). Inoculation against learned helplessness. *Psychological Reports, 47,* 1143–1151.

Tennen, H., Drum, P. E., Gillen, R., & Stanton, A. (1982). Learned helplessness and the detection of contingency: A direct test. *Journal of Personality, 50:4,* 426–442.

Teasdale, J. D. (1978). Effects of real and recalled success on learned helplessness and depression. *Journal of Abnormal Psychology, 87,* 155–164.

Thornton, J. W., & Powell, G. D. (1974). Immunization to and alleviation of learned helplessness in man. *American Journal of Psychology, 87,* 351–367.

Weiner, B. (Ed.). (1974). *Achievement motivation and attribution theory.* Morristown, NJ: General Learning Press.

Willis, M. H., & Blaney, P. H. (1978). Three tests of the learned helplessness model of depression. *Journal of Abnormal Psychology, 87,* 131–136.

Wortman, C. B., & Brehm, J. W. (1975). Responses to uncontrollable outcomes: An integration of reactance theory and the learned helplessness model. In L. Berkowitz (Ed.), *Advances in experimental social psychology* (Vol. 8) New York: Academic Press.

Wortman, C. B., & Dintzer, L. (1978). Is an attributional analysis of the learned helplessness phenomenon viable?: A critique of the Abramson–Seligman–Teasdale Reformulation. *Journal of Abnormal Psychology 87,* 75–90.

Wortman, C. B., Panciera, L., Shusterman, L., & Hibscher, J. (1976). Attributions of causality and reactions to uncontrollable outcomes. *Journal of Experimental Social Psychology, 12,* 301–316.

13

The Cognitive Diathesis–Stress Theories of Depression: Therapeutic Implications*

LAUREN B. ALLOY
CAROLINE CLEMENTS
GREGORY KOLDEN

Introduction

Beginning in the early 1970s, with the advent of the cognitive revolution in psychology, many clinical theorists shifted from a motivational–affective perspective to a cognitive approach to the study of psychopathology. From the cognitive perspective, psychopathological individuals are characterized by the maladaptive content or form of their beliefs and thought processes. Perhaps the majority of research and theorizing about psychopathological individuals' dysfunctional cognitive processes has been in the area of depression. Clinicians and experimental psychologists alike have emphasized the role of negative and distorted cognitions in the etiology, maintenance, and treatment of depression.

In this chapter, we have focused on the two predominant cognitive etiological theories of depression—Beck's cognitive model (Beck, 1967, 1976; Beck, Rush, Shaw, & Emery, 1979) and the reformulated theory of learned

* Preparation of this chapter was supported by a grant from the John D. and Catherine T. MacArthur Foundation to Lauren B. Alloy.

helplessness and depression (Abramson, Seligman, & Teasdale, 1978)—and discuss the implications of these etiological models for the therapy and prevention of depression. We emphasize that these two models share similar formal properties in that both may be conceptualized as cognitive diathesis–stress models of depression in which individuals with particular negative cognitive styles are hypothesized to be vulnerable to depression when confronted with negative life events. The causal sequences predicted to lead to depressive symptoms by these two cognitive theories suggest multiple points of clinical intervention for remediating or preventing depressive disorders. Thus, in this chapter, we have derived and explicated the therapeutic predictions of the cognitive theories. We attempt to integrate basic work from cognitive and social psychology on cognitive processes and structures and their modification with current therapeutic techniques for depression within the theoretical context provided by these models. Our overall purpose is to provide a conceptual framework that will stimulate and guide further research into therapeutic strategies based on the cognitive etiological theories of depression.

Cognitive Etiological Theories of Depression: Description and Formal Properties

Although Beck's theory and the reformulated learned helplessness theory differ with respect to the specific nature of the cognitions hypothesized to lead to depression, the two models share similar formal properties with regard to the logical and sequential relations between cognitive constructs featured in the models and depressive symptomatology. Thus, before describing the basic postulates of the cognitive theories, it is useful to distinguish among the logical concepts of necessary cause, sufficient cause, and contributory cause in regard to the occurrence of depressive symptoms (see Halberstadt, Andrews, Metalsky, & Abramson, 1984). *Necessary causes* refer to those etiological factors that must be present in order for the symptoms of the syndrome of depression to become manifest. *Sufficient causes* refer to those etiological factors that, once present, assure manifestation of the depressive syndrome. That is, a necessary cause of disorder suggests that whenever symptoms are manifest, the hypothesized etiological factor must have been present, whereas a sufficient cause of disorder suggests that if the etiological factor is present, then the symptoms will occur. Finally, *contributory causes* refer to those etiological factors that serve to increase the probability that depressive symptoms will become manifest. However, they are neither necessary nor sufficient for symptom expression.

Halberstadt *et al.* (1984) suggest that in addition to varying in their logical

relationships to the occurrence of symptoms, causes may also be distinguished according to their sequential relationships to symptom onset. *Distal
causes* may be defined as operative quite early in the etiological sequence
culminating in the occurrence of symptoms. At this point in the causal
sequence, there is little or no manifestation of depressive symptoms. *Proximal causes,* on the other hand, operate relatively late in the causal pathway
and may occur immediately prior to or concurrent with symptoms of the
depressive syndrome.

THE REFORMULATED THEORY OF LEARNED
HELPLESSNESS AND DEPRESSION

The reformulated learned helplessness theory of depression is explicit in
its statement of the formal and sequential relationships between causal constructs and depressive symptoms, and hence, we present this theory first.
The original helplessness model (Seligman, 1975), postulated that the expectation that outcomes are uncontrollable leads to the cognitive, motivational, and emotional symptoms of depression. Abramson *et al.* (1978)
revised the original model to overcome several inadequacies in its application to depression including the sufficient conditions for explaining depressed affect and the symptoms of low self-esteem and self-blame as well
as the inability to account for variations in the intensity, chronicity, and
generality of depression (see Alloy, 1982a for a detailed discussion of the
historical development of helplessness theory).

According to Abramson *et al.* (1978), the expectation that highly desired
outcomes are unlikely to occur or that highly aversive outcomes are probable and that no response one can make will change the probability of these
outcomes—the expectation of hopelessness—is a proximal sufficient cause
of depression. It is important to emphasize that the reformulated helplessness theory postulates that the expectation of hopelessness is a sufficient, but
not a necessary, cause of depression and thus it explicitly recognizes the
heterogeneity of this disorder (Alloy, 1982a; Craighead, 1980; Depue &
Monroe, 1978; Glazer, Clarkin, & Hunt, 1981; Halberstadt *et al.,* 1984).
Depression may be the result of other etiological factors such as genetic
predisposition, biochemical vulnerability, or interpersonal processes. However, whenever the expectation of hopelessness is present, depressive symptoms should ensue.

The reformulated helplessness theory also specifies a causal chain of
events hypothesized to culminate in the expectation of hopelessness (see
Figure 13.1). The causal sequence begins with the occurrence of negative life
events and ends with the onset of depressive symptoms. Each causal event
in the chain leading to the expectation of hopelessness (the proximal suffi-

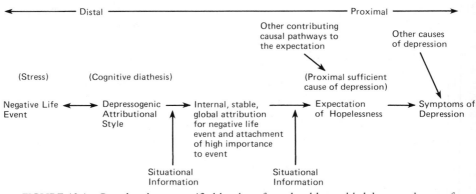

FIGURE 13.1   Causal pathway specified by the reformulated learned helplessness theory of depression (adapted from Halberstadt *et al.*, 1984).

cient cause) is a contributory cause of depression because it increases the likelihood of, but is neither necessary nor sufficient for, the production of symptoms (see Halberstadt *et al.*, 1984). The kinds of causal attributions people make for particular negative life events and the degree of importance they attach to these events are proximal contributory causes of depression.[1] Abramson *et al.* argued that the expectation of hopelessness, and thus, depressive symptoms are more likely to occur when negative life events are attributed to *internal* (i.e., due to something about me), *stable* (i.e., enduring), and *global* (i.e., general across many outcomes) factors and viewed as important than when they are attributed to external, unstable, and specific factors and perceived as unimportant. The causal attributions an individual makes for a negative life event increase the probability of, but are not sufficient for, the occurrence of the expectation of hopelessness, and thus depression, because situational information may intervene between the attribution and the expectation (see Figure 13.1) to contradict the original attribution formed. Similarly, causal attributions are not necessary causes of the expectation of hopelessness and depressive symptoms because other factors may also increase the likelihood that an individual will form this expectation (e.g., lack of social support; see Brown & Harris, 1978; see Figure 13.1).

Abramson *et al.* (1978) speculated that some individuals possess a depressogenic attributional style, which consists of a generalized tendency to attribute negative events to internal, stable, and global factors and to view negative events as very important. According to Abramson *et al.*, people

---

[1] While causal attributions for particular negative life events are distal to depression, Halberstadt *et al.* (1984) referred to them as proximal contributory causes to distinguish them from other more distal contributory causes of depression (i.e., attributional styles).

who exhibit the hypothesized depressive attributional style should have a higher probability than people who do not to attribute any particular negative event they experience to internal, stable, and global factors and view the event as very important, thereby increasing the probability of forming an expectation of hopelessness, and thus, depressive symptoms (see Figure 13.1). However, in the absence of stress (i.e., in the presence of positive life events or the absence of negative life events) people exhibiting the depressive attributional style will be no more likely than people not exhibiting this style to form the expectation of hopelessness, and hence a depressive reaction. Therefore, a depressogenic attributional style may be viewed as a distal contributory cause of depression onset that operates in the presence, but not the absence, of negative life events. In this context, then, it serves as a cognitive diathesis to depression that places individuals at risk for depressive symptoms when confronted by stressful life events.

Although the original statement of the reformulated helplessness theory (Abramson et al., 1978) failed to specify how situational information guides the causal attribution process, work in social psychology (e.g., Kelley, 1967; McArthur, 1972) indicates that the kinds of situational information people confront also partially determine the causal attributions they make for particular events (see Figure 13.1). This line of work suggests that people will tend to attribute an outcome to the events with which it covaries. Therefore, an individual would be predicted to make an internal, stable, and global attribution for an outcome when that outcome is low in consensus (i.e., the outcome has not happened to other people), high in consistency (i.e., the outcome has occurred frequently to that person in the past), and low in distinctiveness (i.e., the outcome is similar to others that have happened to the person; Kelley, 1967). Alloy and Tabachnik (1984) have described the manner in which prior expectations or attributional styles and current situational information interact to determine causal attributions for particular life events (see also Metalsky & Abramson, 1981). In sum, the reformulated theory of learned helplessness and depression posits a specific causal chain of events that is likely to culminate in a proximal, sufficient cause of depression. Each link in the causal pathway only contributes to, but is neither necessary nor sufficient for, the formation of the expectation of hopelessness, and hence, depressive symptoms.

BECK'S COGNITIVE MODEL

Although Beck's model is much less explicit than the reformulated helplessness theory in describing the logical and sequential relations between hypothesized causal factors and depression, we believe its formal structure is similar to that of helplessness theory. Three cognitive constructs are postulated to account for the development of the syndrome of depression in Beck's cognitive model: schemata, cognitive errors, and the cognitive triad.

Schemata represent relatively enduring, cognitive organizing structures that guide the processing of situational information (Beck, 1967; Beck *et al.*, 1979; Rush & Giles, 1982). Schemata are postulated to develop through interactions with the environment and to be initially derived from childhood experience, reinforced by ongoing experience, and relatively trait-like and enduring. According to Beck (1967), depressogenic schemata are negative in content and consist of immature and absolute and rigid attitudes concerning the self and its relation to the world. Dysfunctional schematic information processing is posited to constitute a predisposing or vulnerability factor in the development of the depressive syndrome. Thus, negative content schemata constitute the cognitive diathesis in Beck's cognitive etiological model of depression (see Beck *et al.*, 1979; Kuiper, Olinger, & MacDonald, in press; Rush & Giles, 1982, for extended discussion; Alloy, Clements, Kolden, Greenberg, & Guttman, 1985; Davis, 1979a, 1979b; Davis & Unruh, 1981; Derry & Kuiper, 1981; Greenberg & Alloy, 1985a, 1985b; Kuiper & Derry, 1980; Kuiper *et al.*, in press, for empirical work on depressives' schemata).

Beck hypothesizes that when activated by stress (negative life events), depressogenic schemata lead to systematic cognitive errors in the logic or form of depressives' thinking. According to Beck, depressives' perceptions and inferences are unrealistic, extreme, and distorted in a negative direction. These cognitive distortions are viewed as relatively automatic and involuntary products of depressogenic schematic processing and consist of the following forms of logical errors: arbitrary inference, selective abstraction, overgeneralization, magnification and minimization, personalization, and absolutistic, dichotomous thinking (see Beck *et al.*, 1979, for a complete explication of these cognitive errors).

Hollon and Beck (1979) note that depressives differ from nondepressives not only in how they process information, but also in what they think. As the result of depressogenic schema-based cognitive distortions, the content of depressives' thinking is dominated by a negative view of the self, the world, and the future—the *negative cognitive triad*. Depressed individuals view themselves as inadequate, worthless, and lacking attributes necessary for the attainment of happiness and contentment. They perceive their world as unreasonably demanding and filled with obstacles preventing them from reaching important life goals. They expect that their future will be colored by continued suffering and hardship leading to unremitting frustration, deprivation, and failure. In short, depressives' cognitions are characterized by a systematic bias against the self that logically precedes and is fundamental to their negative views of the self, world, and future (Rush & Giles, 1982).

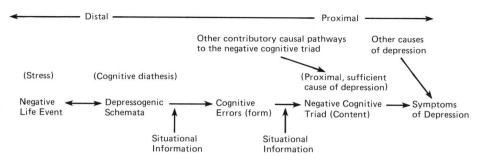

FIGURE 13.2   Causal pathway specified by Beck's cognitive model.

We suggest that, like the reformulated helplessness theory, Beck's cognitive model postulates a sequential causal pathway culminating in a proximal, sufficient cause of depressive symptomatology (see Figure 13.2). In Beck's model, the proximal, sufficient cause of depression is the negative cognitive triad. It is interesting that both cognitive etiological models view an expectation of a hopeless future as a sufficient cause of depression. The formation of the negative cognitive triad is made more probable, in Beck's model, by the occurrence of cognitive distortions or errors (proximal, contributory causes) that, in turn, are typically the result of the negative, maladaptive cognitive schemata (distal, contributory causes—see Figure 13.2). Again, situational information may intervene between the operation of schemata and the production of cognitive distortions or between cognitive errors and the formation of the negative cognitive triad to countermand the development of the cognitive triad, and hence, the onset of depressive symptoms.

In sum, we argue that the two major cognitive etiological theories of depression are best conceptualized as cognitive diathesis–stress models. These theories postulate that when confronted with equivalent stress (similar negative life events), people who consistently display the relevant cognitive diathesis should be more likely to experience a depressive reaction than people who do not display this predisposition. On the other hand, in situations where stress is relatively nonexistent (in the presence of positive life events or absence of negative life events), people possessing the cognitive diathesis should be no more likely to develop depressive symptoms than people not possessing this risk factor. Moreover, the cognitive diathesis–stress theories of depression are sufficiency models and not necessity models. They acknowledge the possibility, either explicitly (helplessness theory) or implicitly (Beck's model) that people might become depressed for reasons other than those specified in the cognitive models and thus recognize the heterogeneity of the depressive disorders (Craighead, 1980; Depue & Monroe, 1978). In essence, it could be said that the cognitive theories posit the existence of an etiological subtype of depression—cognitive depression—defined by its proximal sufficient causes (negative views of the self, world, and future). This subtype may cut across current diagnostic categories of clinical depression (e.g., major, intermittent, endogenous) and may be found in subsyndromal form in nonclinical populations as well (see Akiskal, Khani, & Scott-Strauss, 1979; Depue *et al.*, 1981; Seligman, 1978).

EMPIRICAL EVIDENCE PERTAINING TO THE
COGNITIVE ETIOLOGICAL MODELS OF DEPRESSION

In the last decade, investigators have been actively investigating the validity of the cognitive theories with a variety of research strategies. The majority of studies have compared the cognitive styles and processes of depressed and nondepressed people at one point in time (see Abramson, Metalsky, & Alloy, 1985; Blaney, 1977; Coyne & Gotlib, 1983; Halberstadt *et al.*, 1984; and Hollon & Beck, 1979 for reviews). While the findings of these studies have been mixed, most are supportive of an association between particular negative beliefs or cognitive styles and depressive symptoms. However, most of the work to date has not adequately tested the notion that cognitions and cognitive factors are causally related to the depressive syndrome. In the last few years, researchers have begun to utilize longitudinal–prospective designs that are more appropriate for examining the causality issue (e.g., Cutrona, 1983; Eaves & Rush, 1984; Golin, Sweeney, & Shaffer, 1981; Hamilton & Abramson, 1983; Kayne, Alloy, Romer, & Crocker, 1985; Lewinsohn, Steinmetz, Larson, & Franklin, 1981; Metalsky, Abramson, Seligman, Semmel, & Peterson, 1982; O'Hara, Rehm, & Campbell, 1982; Peterson, Schwartz, & Seligman, 1981; Weintraub, Segal, & Beck, 1974). Unfortunately, many of these longitudinal studies suffer from important conceptual and methodological limitations including failure to assess stress, failure to appreciate the heterogeneity of depression, derivation of incorrect predictions from the cognitive models, and inadequate or nonoptimal measurement techniques; therefore, they do not adequately test the validity of the etiological hypotheses of the cognitive diathesis–stress theories (see Abramson *et al.*, 1985 and Kayne *et al.*, 1985 for a detailed discussion of the inadequacies of prior research). Interestingly, the prospective studies that have explicitly measured stress as well as the cognitive diatheses featured in the cognitive theories (Cutrona, 1983; Kayne *et al.*, 1985; Metalsky *et al.*, 1982; O'Hara *et al.*, 1982) have supported the validity of these models.

Concepts of Cognitive Diathesis and Stress in Cognitive Models of Depression

COGNITIVE DIATHESIS

Both major cognitive etiological models of depression propose that when confronted by stress, individuals with a cognitive diathesis for depression are more likely to develop a depressive episode than those not possessing this diathesis. A diathesis is simply a predisposition to disorder; thus, a cognitive diathesis refers to risk factors for disorder that are belief-based or attitudinal in nature. According to Beck, individuals who are vulnerable to depression process current information in a biased way because they assimilate environmental experiences to their negative, depressogenic schemata. Similarly, the depressogenic attributional style viewed as the diathesis for depression in the reformulated helplessness theory, biases the interpretation of situational information regarding the causes of life events (i.e., consensus, consistency, and distinctiveness information—Kelley, 1967; McArthur, 1972), which increases the probability that an individual will form internal, stable, and global attributions for these events, and therefore, the expectation of hopelessness. Because attributional styles share most of the properties of the schemata featured in Beck's model, they may be viewed as causal schemata that organize people's implicit beliefs about how causes and different classes of events covary (see Alloy & Tabachnik, 1984; Kelley, 1972; Orvis, Cunningham, & Kelley, 1975).

Work in cognitive and social psychology on the schematic bases of information processing may be useful in providing conceptual clarity about the cognitive diathesis components of the cognitive theories of depression. A basic assumption of cognitive and social psychologists is that people both make sense of and impose sense upon the world (see Alloy & Tabachnik, 1984). Contemporary developments in these fields emphasize the ubiquity with which people go beyond the information given and use schemata or generalized knowledge about the self and the world in the perception, interpretation, and comprehension of everyday experience (e.g., Bobrow & Norman, 1975; Bower, Black, & Turner, 1979; Bransford & Johnson, 1972, 1973; Cantor & Mischel, 1977, 1979; Hastie, 1981; Markus, 1977; Rumelhart, 1975; Schank & Abelson, 1977; Taylor & Crocker, 1980; Thorndyke, 1977; Zadney & Gerard, 1974). Although the term *schema* has been defined in a number of ways by psychologists (e.g., Hastie, 1981; Neisser, 1967; 1976; Taylor & Crocker, 1980), it is generally used to refer to an organized representation of prior knowledge in memory that guides the processing of current information. *Schemata* specify the defining features and relevant attributes of a stimulus or content domain as well as the interrelations among these defining features and attributes (see Crocker, Fiske, & Taylor, 1984; Fiske & Linville, 1980; Hastie, 1981; Rumelhart & Ortony, 1977). As enduring cognitive structures, they act as patterns for selecting, encoding, retrieving, and interpreting the stimuli that confront an individual, and thus, they serve a function of cognitive economy (Rosch, 1975). According to this view, schemata are not "fixed and lifeless" (cf. Bartlett, 1932) but are dynamic and often modified by the very information whose processing they guide.

Because the quantity and variety of information available at any time is greater than any person could process or attend to, individuals must be selective in what they notice, learn, remember, or infer in any situation (Neisser, 1967). Cognitive knowledge structures facilitate processing of information in nonrandom ways. Information that is inconsistent with the general organization of the schema is often ignored or forgotten; other aspects of the information are elaborated in a way that makes them consistent with the schema (e.g., Bartlett, 1932; Bower, Black, & Turner, 1979; Bransford & Johnson, 1972; Bruner & Postman, 1949; Owens, Bower, & Black, 1979). Thus, although schemata facilitate perception, comprehension, recall, and problem solving (Taylor & Crocker, 1980), an important consequence of their operation is bias and distortion. From the perspective of work in cognitive and social psychology then, depressogenic schemata and attributional styles serve as diatheses to depression in the cognitive models by negatively biasing the perception and interpretation of life experiences in a manner that increases the probability that the negative cognitive triad or the expectation of hopelessness will be formed, and therefore, that depressive symptoms will occur.

STRESS

Since 1970, concepts of psychosocial stress have gained importance as contributors to psychological problems. Although conceptual and definitional debates abound (Hinkle, 1974; Lazarus, Cohen, Folkman, Kanner, & Schaefer, 1980; Mason, 1975; Monroe, 1982a, 1982b; Selye, 1975), a growing body of empirical evidence supports an association between psychosocial stress and disorder (Barrett, 1979; Depue, 1979; Dohrenwend & Dohrenwend, 1974, 1981; Goldberger & Breznitz, 1982; Rabkin & Struening, 1976). Specifically, the evidence for stressful life events as predictors of depression is particularly compelling (Lloyd, 1980; Paykel, 1982).

In general, proponents of the cognitive models have paid considerably less attention to the construct of stress than to the construct of diathesis in delineating causal pathways to depression. For example, these theories have been either silent or relatively inarticulate about the kinds of life events that are most important for depression onset (e.g., the occurrence of major life events versus the cumulative effect of minor hassles—see Kanner, Coyne, Schaefer, & Lazarus, 1981; Monroe, 1983; or of chronic stressful circumstances versus episodic events—see Monroe, 1983; Rose, Jenkins, & Hurst, 1978). However, similar to much research in the field of life stress (e.g., Lazarus, 1981; Lazarus, Coyne, & Folkman, 1982; Lazarus & Launier, 1978; Mason, 1975; Meichenbaum & Jaremko, 1983; Paykel, 1979; Sarason, Johnson, & Siegel, 1978), the cognitive theories of depression are distinguished by their emphasis on people's appraisals of and inferences derived from negative life events rather than the mere occurrence of such events as a determinant of depressive reactions.

According to the cognitive theories of depression, negative life events act as triggers of depressive symptoms by initiating a causal sequence leading to symptom onset in individuals predisposed to this disorder by virtue of possessing depressogenic self or causal schemata. In this context, stressful life events may be viewed as occupying two roles in the cognitive etiological theories of depression: a passive and an active role. In their passive role, life experiences provide the occasion for the operation of the cognitive diathesis in the models. That is, they constitute the situational information that is filtered through and interpreted by the negative content, depressogenic schemata, and attributional styles. In their active role, negative life events may activate or prime depressogenic self or causal schemata so that they become accessible in memory and can bias the processing of situational information (Riskind & Rholes, 1984). *Accessibility* is a term used in cognitive and social psychology to refer to the ease with which a schema or concept can be retrieved from long-term memory and placed in short-term working memory (Higgins & King, 1981; Higgins, Rholes, & Jones, 1977; Srull & Wyer, 1980; Tversky & Kahneman, 1973). Negativistic schema-based attitudes may be enduring but latent characteristics of depression-prone individuals that are not always more dominant or cognitively accessible than other neutral or positive content patterns of thinking. Instead, these latent schemata or attributional styles may get activated or cognitively primed in stressful situations (situations of negative life events) and once activated and thus accessible, they will tend to produce negative attributions and thinking patterns and hence, the symptoms of depression. Moreover, primed depressogenic schemata may not only guide the processing of negative life events, but may also bias the interpretation of more ambiguous or positive life experiences in a negative direction.

The capacity of a life event to prime depressogenic cognitive schemata may be a function of both the characteristic level of accessibility of such schemata in the individual and the degree of congruence or match between the life event and the content embodied in the schemata (Riskind & Rholes,

1984). Indeed, Beck (1967; Beck & Rush, 1978) argues that though depressive schemata may be latent at a given time, they are triggered by situations analogous to the experiences responsible for embedding them in the first place (e.g., a divorce may activate the concept of irreversible loss that followed death of a parent in childhood). Similarly, from the perspective of the reformulated helplessness theory, events that are likely to instigate attributional processing may be likely to activate depressogenic causal schemata. Evidence from social psychology suggests that spontaneous attributional analyses are most apt to be triggered by experiences of failure or loss of control as well as unexpected events (Pittman & Pittman, 1980; Pyszczynski & Greenberg, 1981; Swann, Stephenson, & Pittman, 1981; Wong & Weiner, 1981). Negative or uncontrollable events that are embedded in a situational context that suggests internal, stable, and global causes of the events may be especially likely to activate depressogenic attributional styles and thus induce the expectation of hopelessness. In sum, stressful life events both activate depressogenic cognitive diatheses and are acted on by these diatheses in the cognitive etiological models of depression (hence, the bidirectional arrows between negative life events and schemata or attributional styles in Figures 13.1 and 13.2).

Cognitive Diathesis–Stress Models:
Therapeutic Implications

A distinction may be drawn between theories of etiology, theories of intervention, and procedures or techniques of intervention (Hollon & Beck, 1979). The cognitive diathesis–stress models of depression presented above are theories of etiology. The causal pathways postulated to result in symptom onset by these theories, however, serve as an organizing rationale for the derivation of theories and techniques of intervention. While, of course, there need be no logical congruence between factors that contribute to the onset of a particular disorder (etiological factors) and those that contribute to its remediation (interventive factors), knowledge of etiological factors can be generally assumed to lead to therapeutic strategies that are specifically effective for a given disorder. Thus, the cognitive theories suggest therapeutic techniques that may be especially effective for the cognitive subtype of depression. Because each step in the causal pathways of the cognitive models is hypothesized to contribute to the probability of symptom occurrence, each step suggests a point for therapeutic intervention. Moreover, due to the sequential nature of the cognitive models, these theories not only suggest points of intervention for remediating current depressive episodes, but also points for prevention of depression by decreasing vulnerability to depressive episodes and immunizing against the development of depression-proneness (Halberstadt et al., 1984).

THE COMMUNITY PREVENTION ANALOGY

Halberstadt et al. (1984) suggest that a conceptualization for clinical intervention utilizing a community mental health prevention model (Rappaport, 1977; Zax & Cowen, 1976) that is generalized to the level of individuals provides a heuristic framework for organizing general treatment and preventive strategies. The three types of prevention are termed primary, secondary, and tertiary. *Primary prevention,* at the individual level, concerns the promotion of psychological health and well-being of individuals in the general population. As related to depression, primary prevention pertains to the promotion of nondepression and the enhancement of invulnerability to depressive reactions. *Secondary prevention,* at the individual level, concerns the application of clinical intervention strategies for individuals at high risk for mental disorder. As related to depression, secondary prevention pertains to reducing the prevalence of the depressive clinical syndrome in individuals identified as vulnerable to, or prone to, depression. *Tertiary prevention,* at the individual level, concerns the application of clinical intervention strategies to remediate or ameliorate a mental disorder once it has become manifest. As related to depression, tertiary prevention pertains to clinical intervention with individuals manifesting the clinical syndrome of depression in order to reduce the duration or severity of the episode. In the sections that follow, we have briefly discussed the predictions of the cognitive etiological models for clinical strategies aimed at tertiary, secondary, and primary prevention of depression.[2] We propose that basic work from cognitive and social psychology on belief change and schema change suggests many clinical techniques that are currently incorporated in cognitive therapy for depression (Beck et al., 1979) as well as some that are not.

TERTIARY PREVENTION: REMEDIATING CURRENT DEPRESSIVE EPISODES

The primary goal of tertiary prevention is the treatment of current depressive disorders in order to produce symptom relief. The cognitive etiological models of depression each posit a proximal sufficient cause of depression—the expectation of hopelessness (helplessness theory) or the expectation of hopelessness (negative expectations about the future) plus negative beliefs about the self and the world (Beck's model). According to

---

[2] We discuss these three types of prevention in reverse order, as their focus becomes increasingly distant from the occurrence of depressive symptoms.

these theories, then, any therapeutic technique that undermines the expectation of hopelessness or negative views of the self and the world should be effective in remediating current depressive symptoms. The negative cognitive triad could be attacked directly or alternatively, because the cognitive theories also suggest proximal contributory causes (internal, stable, and global attributions for negative events and cognitive errors or distortions, respectively) that increase the likelihood of the negative cognitive triad, these negative beliefs should also be undermined by strategies aimed at reducing dysfunctional attributions or cognitive errors. Finally, the cognitive models hypothesize that negative life events contribute to the maintenance of the expectation of hopelessness or negative cognitive triad by repeatedly activating depressogenic schemata or attributional styles (cognitive diatheses) and by providing continual stressful experiences available for negative interpretation. Thus, therapeutic interventions aimed at modifying the depression-provoking environment should also be effective in relieving depressive symptoms. In sum, the following points for tertiary intervention can be derived from the causal pathways specified in the cognitive models of depression: (1) reverse the patient's expectation of hopelessness and negative views of him or herself and the environment; (2) decrease the occurrence of internal, stable, and global attributions for negative events and cognitive distortions; and (3) lessen the stressfulness of the patient's environment.

It follows from the cognitive theories of depression that a reduction of negative life events and an increase of positive life events should undermine the stress component of the cognitive diathesis–stress models and hence, will diminish the probability that a patient will exhibit negative perceptions of the self, world, and future and, in turn, depression. In cases where a depressed person happens to be in a severely stressful or unresponsive environment, the primary target for change may be the ungratifying environment itself. Therapeutic procedures designed to modify a depressogenic environment might range from aiding a person to obtain an education or leave an unhappy marriage to more widespread sociopolitical changes such as reducing hunger and unemployment. Along these lines, Beck's cognitive–behavioral therapy of depression (Beck et al., 1979) as well as other behavioral therapy programs (e.g., Lewinsohn, 1974, 1976; Rehm, 1977) include behavioral procedures designed to diminish the aversiveness of a patient's environment. The scheduling of pleasant activities is often used to increase a depressed person's positive reinforcement while the technique of breaking down a task into more manageable "chunks" is employed to increase the depressive's experiences of mastery or success (Evans & Hollon, in press). In some cases, however, depressives' behavior may be contributing to the negative feedback they receive from the environment. Lewinsohn (1974) has provided evidence that depressed patients may suffer social skills deficits and the interpersonal (e.g., Coates & Wortman, 1980; Coyne, 1976; Gotlib & Robinson, 1982; Howes & Hokanson, 1979) theories of depression emphasize the maladaptive interaction patterns exhibited by depressives in personal relationships. In such cases, behavioral techniques involving social skills training and role playing procedures to overcome social deficits may be an effective way to alter the stressfulness of the depressive's environment.

Both cognitive theories of depression posit that an expectation of a hopeless future is a proximal, sufficient cause of depression, and therefore, changing this expectation to one of hopefulness should ameliorate depressive symptoms. According to the reformulated helplessness theory, the expectation of hopelessness consists of the beliefs that highly valued outcomes are improbable or highly aversive outcomes are very probable and that one is helpless to change the likelihood of these outcomes. Therefore, either modifying a depressed patient's belief in his or her lack of control or his or her belief about the probability of outcomes should reduce the expectation of hopelessness and, in turn, depressive symptoms. Abramson, Alloy, and Rosoff (1981) suggested that depressed individuals may sometimes fail to learn about control because they have low rates of initiating voluntary cognitive and overt responses and are less likely to try the appropriate controlling response in a given situation. Seligman and his colleagues (Klein & Seligman, 1976: Seligman, Maier, & Geer, 1968) found that forcibly exposing people or animals to the contingency between their responses and outcomes can reverse a belief in helplessness. These considerations suggest that behavioral procedures such as activity scheduling and particularly, the scheduling of mastery activities, may enhance the salience of the dependency between a depressed patient's efforts and successful outcomes and hence, the perception of control.

The belief that important goals are unattainable is the second component of the expectation of hopelessness. Both theory and research indicate that depressed individuals may set unrealistic goals for themselves (Bandura, 1971; Diggony, 1966; Golin & Terrell, 1977; Rehm, 1977), and therefore, redirecting a depressed patient's attention to more realistic goals may be an appropriate point of intervention. Along these lines, Beck's cognitive–behavior therapy (Beck et al., 1979) includes a technique of "graded task assignment," which consists of encouraging patients to engage in a series of steps or tasks that gradually increase in difficulty or complexity. As the patients master the easier steps, they move on to more complex tasks. By helping depressives construct more specific and achievable behavioral goals, graded task assignment may alter their expectations of hopelessness.

According to the reformulated helplessness theory, attributing negative outcomes to stable and global causal factors will also increase the likelihood of forming an expectation of hopelessness. Two general approaches should be effective in modifying depressogenic attributions for negative events according to the reformulated helplessness theory: (1) change the depressed person's interpretation of available situational information; and (2) alter the nature of the situational information the depressed person is confronting.

Beck's cognitive therapy (Beck et al., 1979) includes a number of techniques designed to challenge depressogenic interpretations of available situational feedback. The basic strategy that underlies cognitive therapy is one of "collaborative empiricism" (Hollon & Beck, 1979) between patient and therapist. The depressed patient is encouraged to formulate his or her beliefs, assumptions, and interpretations as hypotheses to be tested. Patient and therapist then serve as active collaborators in the careful review of evidence already available and in the design and execution of systematic empirical tests of the various beliefs. In taking an empirical approach, the patient generates evidence from his or her own experiences that can disconfirm depressogenic beliefs if they are faulty. In the specific case of overly stable and global attributions for negative events, the technique of "reattribution training" (Beck et al., 1979) in which possible alternative attributions are generated and rated for their plausibility may be appropriate. The patient would then be encouraged to seek out additional information including consistency (Does this event always happen to me?) and distinctiveness (Does this event happen to me in many areas of my life?) information in order to decide between alternatives. Social psychological evidence (Ross, Lepper, Strack, & Steinmetz, 1977; Sherman, Skov, Hervitz, & Stock, 1981), which indicates that the act of simply generating a plausible causal explanation for an event increases the salience and subjective likelihood of the causal scenario, suggests that it is important for depressed patients to generate alternative attributions themselves in utilizing the reattribution training technique. In addition, situational information has been shown to have greater impact on perceptions and attributions when it is concrete and vivid rather than pallid and abstract (Nisbett & Ross, 1980). This finding suggests that in vivo tests of attributional hypotheses may be more effective in modifying depressives' dysfunctional explanations than imaginal tests. On the other hand, if empirical tests of the depressed patient's causal explanations do uncover situational information converging on stable and global causes of negative outcomes, strategies of the kind described above that are aimed at modifying the environmental feedback the patient confronts may be a more appropriate means for altering attributions.

In addition to a perception of a hopeless future, Beck's cognitive theory also hypothesizes that a negative view of oneself and the world are important proximal, sufficient causes of depression. The negative content of these self and environmental perceptions are, in turn, made more likely by the presumed logical errors in depressed persons' thinking processes. Consequently, clinical interventions aimed at combating cognitive distortions and negative perceptions of the self and world should also be effective means of remediating depressive symptoms.

People often evaluate themselves by drawing comparisons between themselves and others (e.g., Festinger, 1954; Schachter, 1959). Beck's cognitive theory suggests that depressives' negative self perceptions are the result of unfavorable social comparisons. Similarly, the reformulated helplessness theory postulates that low self-esteem and self-worth are more likely when individuals attribute negative outcomes to internal, rather than external, causes and believe that they cannot obtain desired outcomes that others can. According to Kelley (1967), people will be more likely to make internal attributions for events that happen to themselves but not others (events having low consensus) and Tabachnik, Crocker, and Alloy (1983, 1984) found that depressed individuals perceive less consensus for events, traits, and behaviors than do nondepressives. Depressives' perceptions of low consensus could be the result of self-derogation (as Beck predicts) or as Alloy and her colleagues (Martin, Abramson, & Alloy, 1984; Tabachnik *et al.*, 1983) have found, of overly optimistic beliefs about others' capabilities. These considerations suggest that when a depressed patient makes an internal attribution for a negative outcome or exhibits self-views that are negative in content, the accuracy of these interpretations may be tested by encouraging the patient to seek out additional information about the performance of relevant others in the situation. A group therapy experience with other depressed patients may be especially helpful in this regard (Tabachnik *et al.*, 1983). On the other hand, if the situational consensus information supports an internal attribution for the negative outcome or negative self-perceptions, then problem-solving skills training to increase the patient's competence may be the most appropriate strategy for altering self-perceptions. Similar kinds of hypothesis-testing techniques (Beck *et al.*, 1979) may be effective in reversing depressives' negative views of the world, as well.

To the extent that cognitive distortions contribute to the negative cognitive triad, clinical interventions designed to correct these errors in reasoning should also be effective ways of reducing depressive symptoms. In addition to prospective hypothesis testing, Beck's cognitive therapy for depression (Beck *et al.*, 1979) employs several specific strategies for identifying and disconfirming cognitive errors. These include patient–therapist collaboration in identifying negatively valenced automatic thoughts, self-monitoring of situations and contexts in which these thoughts occur, evaluating the processes by which these automatic thoughts are generated, and identifying the underlying assumptions (schemata) that give rise to these thoughts (Beck *et al.,* 1979; Evans & Hollon, in press; Hollon & Beck, 1979).

Although the cognitive theories of depression emphasize the role of distorted thought processes in the etiology and maintenance of depression, in the last five years a growing body of research has suggested that depressed people's perceptions and inferences in situations relevant to the self are actually more accurate or realistic than those of nondepressed people (e.g., Abramson & Alloy, 1981; Abramson *et al.,* 1981; Alloy, 1982b; Alloy & Abramson, 1979, 1982; Alloy, Abramson, & Kossman, 1985; Alloy, Abramson, & Viscusi, 1981; Alloy, Ahrens, & Kayne, 1985; Golin, Terrell, & Johnson, 1977; Golin, Terrell, Weitz, & Drost, 1979; Lewinsohn, Mischel, Chaplain, & Barton, 1980; Martin *et al.,* 1984; Nelson & Craighead, 1977; Rozensky, Rehm, Pry, & Roth, 1977; Tabachnik *et al.,* 1983). These studies have documented pervasive self-enhancing biases and illusions in nondepressive cognition. Moreover, they suggest that an important property of depressives' self-relevant perceptions and judgments is the relative absence of biases and distortions that would allow depressives to perceive themselves in an optimistic fashion.

The work on depressive realism (Mischel, 1979) poses two problems for the cognitive therapy of depression (Evans & Hollon, in press; Kayne & Alloy, in press): (1) If normal, nondepressed individuals succumb to cognitive distortions, yet are not depressed, should depressed patients be taught to distort reality in an optimistic fashion in order to bring about symptom relief? and (2) If depressives' self-perceptions are more realistic than those of nondepressives, would efforts to enhance reality testing, which Beck believes constitutes the primary active component in cognitive therapy, increase depressive symptoms rather than alleviate them? Sufficient evidence now exists that cognitive therapy is an effective treatment for depression (Beck, Hollon, Bedrosian, & Young, in press; Blackburn, Bishop, Glen, Whalley, & Christie, 1981; Kovacs, Rush, Beck, & Hollon, 1981; Rush, Beck, Kovacs, & Hollon, 1977; Shaw, 1977; Taylor & Marshall, 1977); however, little evidence is yet available concerning how cognitive therapy works. The findings of depressive realism and nondepressive distortion suggest that cognitive therapy may be effective because it trains depressed patients to construct for themselves the sort of optimistic and adaptive illusions that nondepressives typically construct. Alternatively, cognitive therapy may, indeed, work by sharpening the reality-testing skills of depressed patients so that their information processing is more systematic and normative than that of most nondepressives (see Evans & Hollon, in press, and Kayne & Alloy, in press for a more detailed discussion of the implications of the work on depressive realism for cognitive therapy of depression). Clearly, further research is needed to clarify the active components of cognitive therapy and the mechanisms by which it produces change in depressed patients.

SECONDARY PREVENTION:
REDUCING DEPRESSION-PRONENESS

Secondary prevention strategies address factors leading to the onset of new cases of disorder. Both cognitive models of depression posit distal, contributory causes—depressogenic schemata (Beck's model) or attributional styles (helplessness theory)—that place individuals at risk for the development of a depressive disorder. In addition, in both theories, negative life events are hypothesized to activate these latent diatheses and provide stressful information available for negative interpretation. Thus, secondary prevention strategies derived from these models would be aimed at altering depressogenic schemata or attributional styles before these diatheses are activated by stress and can contribute to the onset of depressive symptoms. Modification of self or causal schemata in already depressed individuals would also be appropriate as a means of reducing the likelihood of relapse or future episodes. Alternatively, secondary prevention efforts might be directed toward lessening the stressfulness of events in the depression-prone individual's environment, thereby, decreasing the probability that the cognitive diatheses become activated.

While cognitive therapy for depression (Beck et al., 1979) has not been developed specifically to meet the aims of secondary prevention, many of its procedures and techniques would appear to be relevant for effecting change in depressogenic self or causal schemata. Work in cognitive and social psychology suggests several general principles for facilitating changes in schemata or belief systems. Hence, the application of these principles to cognitive–behavior therapy may enhance the effectiveness of many of the techniques currently in use.

Schemata have been hypothesized to change in two ways in response to new information (Crocker et al., 1984; Fiske & Dyer, 1982): (1) They can develop through increasing exposure to instantiating experiences. That is, an evolving schema expands and changes to fit the variety of schema-relevant exemplars to which the individual is exposed. (2) Schemata can be altered through exposure to incongruent information (i.e., information that is improbable given the schema). It is this second type of schema change that is relevant to the aims of secondary prevention; schema development through exposure to exemplars is more appropriate to the goals of primary prevention (promotion of nondepressogenic schemata). Ross (1977) has suggested three processes by which incongruent information may produce change in belief systems. First, individuals may be exposed to numerous and repeated instances of belief disconfirmation so that existing beliefs are overwhelmed by the sheer weight of contradictory evidence. Second, an existing schema can be replaced by an alternative belief system that accounts for most of the information currently explained within the existing system as well as new, inconsistent evidence. The third process involves the education of the individual with regard to the nature of the distorting processes that might be active in the assimilation of new information into an existing schema. Ross refers to this type of educational training as cognitive process training. Interestingly, cognitive therapy (Beck *et al.*, 1979) has, quite independently, utilized each of the three processes Ross identified in general belief change. For example, cognitive techniques such as prospective hypothesis testing of specific negative beliefs and the challenging of assumptions underlying specific beliefs are designed to provide depressed patients with numerous instances of schema-incongruent evidence. Procedures such as reattribution training, on the other hand, provide depressives with alternative, nondepressive ways of interpreting environmental experiences. Finally, significant portions of initial cognitive therapy sessions are devoted to providing patients with a basic cognitive rationale in order to produce insight into the manner in which thoughts influence affect and behavior (Beck *et al.*, 1979; Evans & Hollon, in press). Although these cognitive interventions have typically been employed for the purpose of symptom alleviation in already depressed individuals, we would suggest that they might also be particularly appropriate for modification of depressogenic schemata in depression-prone persons.

Crocker *et al.* (1984) have described several features of both schemata and situational information that may influence the degree to which these knowledge structures change when confronted by incongruent data. According to Crocker *et al.*, schemata differ in the extent to which they are disconfirmable in response to contrary evidence. A schema may be logically disconfirmable or practically disconfirmable. A schema is *logically disconfirmable* to the extent that its defining attributes clearly specify which features of situational information ought and ought not to occur. A schema is *practically disconfirmable* to the extent that the likelihood of actually encountering incongruent environmental feedback is high or low. These considerations suggest that cognitive interventions such as collaborative hypothesis testing should be conducted in a manner so as to insure that depression-prone individuals are aided in specifying clear, concise predictions derived from their depressogenic schemata about the kinds of environmental evidence they should and should not encounter (i.e., logical disconfirmability). Once such precise, schema-based hypotheses have been formulated, the clinician should strive to set up situations for testing these hypotheses that have high probability of providing the depression-prone person with contradictory evidence (e.g., situations in which success rather than failure is probable; ractical disconfirmability).

In addition to features of the schema itself, the characteristics of incongruent information encountered in the environment may also contribute to schema change. Qualities of incongruent information that are likely to influence schema reform include: (1) the degree of discrepancy between incongruent information and the schema (Judd & Harackiewicz, 1980; Judd & Kulik, 1980; Sherif & Havland, 1961); (2) the degree of ambiguity present in the incongruent information (Cohen, 1981; Lord, Ross, & Lepper, 1979; Owens *et al.*, 1979); and (3) the extent to which incongruent information is dispersed or concentrated (Crocker & Weber, 1983; Weber & Crocker, 1983). In general, the more discrepant environmental feedback is from the data incorporated in a schema, the more likely it is that the schema will change in response to this information. However, when information is too discrepant, it is likely to be rejected and seen as irrelevant to the schema and hence, produce no change. Incongruent information should be optimally or moderately discrepant in order to induce maximum schema reform. This general principle fits well with clinical intuition. Even in psychodynamic psychotherapy, which is not explicitly focused on cognitive change, great importance is placed on providing interpretations of clients' behaviors that are neither too close nor too far from clients' current levels of personal insight. Secondary prevention strategies for depression might also strive to present moderately incongruent schema-relevant experiences in efforts to effect modification in depressogenic schemata or attributional styles. The techniques of collaborative, behavioral experimentation might be particularly adaptable to this end.

Incongruent information must also be unambiguous in order to produce alteration of a schema. Ambiguous information, regardless of its congruence with the content of a knowledge structure, will be likely to be assimilated into the schema rather than modify the schema. Situational information is ambiguous to the extent that it is not clearly and vividly related to defining attributes of the schema (e.g., prototypic exemplars of the schema). Therefore, clinical interventions aimed at modifying depressogenic self and causal schemata might seek to maximize the vividness and diagnosticity of schema-incongruent situational evidence that depression-prone individuals encounter. Self-monitoring techniques with therapist feedback and in vivo hypothesis testing strategies may be particularly useful in this regard. Inconsistent evidence may also be concentrated in a few incongruent instances or dispersed across many incongruent instances. Incongruent information that is distributed across many experiences is more likely to lead to schema change than incongruent information that is concentrated in a few experiences; when contradictory data are encountered in concentrated form, individuals are likely to form exceptions to or subcategories of their schemata (Crocker & Weber, 1983; Weber & Crocker, 1983). Clinical techniques designed to promote secondary prevention of depression might be cognizant of this basic principle, and therefore, expose depression-prone persons to a few experiences that are incongruent with their negative schemata or attributional styles across many sessions of therapy, rather than to many experiences in a few sessions of therapy.

In both cognitive etiological models of depression, negative life events serve to activate maladaptive schemata or attributional styles (cognitive diatheses). Once schema activation has occurred, these experiences are also continuously available for negative interpretation. Therefore, a final set of strategies for reducing vulnerability to depression might involve the identification and neutralization of life experiences that are likely to prime depressogenic self and causal schemata. Earlier (see section on Stress) we suggested that events that are congruent with the content embodied in a schema or that are analogous to prototypic exemplars of the schema would be particularly apt to activate that schema. Identification of these depression-provoking events for a given individual might be accomplished through careful self-monitoring of the situations, environmental contexts, and surrounding events in which the individual finds that he or she typically becomes depressed. Once such depression triggers are ascertained, secondary prevention efforts could be addressed either toward decreasing their probability of occurrence (see section on Tertiary Prevention for methods for reducing the stressfulness of the environment) or toward the development of cognitive coping skills that may reduce the likelihood that these events will activate dysfunctional schemata or attributional styles in the future. Lazarus and his colleagues (e.g., Lazarus, 1981; Lazarus et al., 1982; Lazarus & Launier, 1978) have emphasized the degree to which the stressfulness of an experience is determined by a person's appraisals of his or her ability to cope with the event. Thus, cognitive techniques such as reattribution training that are aimed at providing depression-prone individuals with healthy, nondepressogenic reinterpretations of life events might promote coping skills and consequently reduce the likelihood of depressogenic schema activation.

PRIMARY PREVENTION:
PROMOTING NONDEPRESSION

Primary prevention involves the promotion of psychological well-being. Within a cognitive diathesis–stress framework, the goal of primary prevention strategies is to eliminate factors leading to depression-proneness (depressogenic diatheses) and concomitantly, to inculcate nondepressive cognitive styles in the population. This type of prevention is primarily community-based in approach in that it does not attempt either to identify depressed cases or persons at risk for depression, but rather promotes the psychological health of the community as a whole. To date, very little research has been conducted on the determinants of cognitive styles that would be relevant to primary prevention strategies. Research in learning–cognitive, social, and developmental psychology, however, provides some suggestions as to how individuals may develop both depressogenic and nondepressogenic cognitive styles or schemata.

Rumelhart and Norman (1976) have suggested that new schemata are constructed when existing memory structures are inadequate for information processing. New schemata are originally formed on a gross level and are refined through congruent and incongruent experiential data or through feedback from others. Initially, an individual is exposed to a large body of information about a particular topic or domain. The schema itself is then created so that this body of knowledge can be effectively organized. Finally, through continued interaction with the environment, the schema is further refined by assimilating and accommodating to new, schema-relevant information (Rumelhart & Norman, 1976). Primary prevention of depression might occur, then, either by: (1) ameliorating or modifying early stresses in an individual's environmental history so that a nondepressogenic information base is available for incorporation into a schema; or (2) by modeling and reinforcing nondepressive cognitions and behaviors that promote the formation of healthy, positively valenced schemata.

Researchers in the learned helplessness tradition have begun to investigate both of these means of fostering the development of nondepressogenic attributional styles and perceptions of control. One line of inquiry has focused on the latter strategy and has examined the manner in which children model and internalize the preexisting cognitive styles of significant others. For example, Dweck and her associates (Dweck & Licht, 1980) have identified two cognitive orientations in children affecting emotional reactions and performance—helplessness and mastery orientations. When confronted with failure, children with helplessness orientations tend to attribute the failure to lack of ability (an internal, stable, and global factor), give up readily, and exhibit sad affect, self-devaluation, and decreased expectations for future success. Children with mastery orientations, on the other hand, tend to attribute failure to lack of effort (an internal, but unstable and specific cause), persist on tasks, and show positive affect and high expectations for future success. Given the well-replicated finding that men are less vulnerable to depression than women (Weissman & Klerman, 1977), it is interesting that boys are more likely to exhibit the mastery orientation than girls.

Dweck, Davidson, Nelson, and Enna (1978) examined the hypothesis that these mastery and helplessness orientations may be learned through interactions with significant others. They found that teachers provide different kinds of feedback to boys than girls following success and failure in the classroom. Teachers tend to suggest that failure is due to lack of ability in their interactions with girls, whereas boys are told that their failure is due to lack of effort. A follow-up experiment demonstrated that when girls are given the type of feedback boys normally receive in the classroom, the girls begin to attribute their failures to lack of effort, whereas feedback of the sort girls typically receive led boys to attribute failures to inability. Parental feedback and attributional styles may also influence the kind of attributional style their child develops (Seligman *et al.*, 1984).

Seligman and his colleagues have focused on the first strategy described above for fostering nondepression-proneness and have investigated the manner in which early experiences with instrumental control may immunize individuals against the effects of later helplessness-inducing experiences (Alloy & Bersh, 1979; Alloy & Seligman, 1979; Seligman, 1975; Seligman & Maier, 1967). For example, Hannum, Rosellini, and Seligman (cited in Seligman, 1975) found that rats that received early experience with control over noxious stimuli (shocks) as weanlings, were immune to helplessness behavioral deficits as adults when confronted with inescapable shocks. Similarly, Mineka (1985) reported that young monkeys who experience control over appetitive reinforcers (e.g., food and treats) exhibit less fear when confronted with novel situations and are more socially adept in interacting with other monkeys. Human infants who experience control in the early mother–child relationship have also been found to experience less stranger anxiety and to interact more effectively with peers in early school settings than those who do not experience control (Ainsworth & Bell, 1973; Main, 1973).

Clearly, further research is needed into the determinants of nondepressive cognitive styles and environments. However, the findings to date, suggest two broad educational approaches for primary prevention programs for depression. First, comprehensive public education through the mass media could be directed toward communicating the precursors of depression and depression-proneness to members of the general community. Second, special effort could be addressed to the development of programs that would foster parenting and teaching practices that provide models for and reinforcement of adaptive, cognitive styles in children.

Conclusion

In this chapter, we have presented the cognitive diathesis-stress theories of depression and some of their implications for therapy and prevention. Although a number of controlled outcome studies have demonstrated the efficacy of packages of cognitive and behavioral procedures of the sort derived from the cognitive theories of depression (Evans & Hollon, in press; Hollon & Beck, 1979), the efficacy of these techniques has not been demonstrated in isolation from other techniques or in the context of the cognitive etiological models. Given that the cognitive theories predict that clinical intervention at specific points in the causal pathways identified by these models will result in changes in particular problem behaviors and cognitions, future therapy research will need to ascertain whether these techniques do, in fact, produce changes at the points identified and through the psychological processes specified by the cognitive models. In addition, further research is required to determine which intervention strategies are useful in reversing current depressive episodes, which reduce depression-proneness, and which promote nondepression.

References

Abramson, L. Y., & Alloy, L. B. (1981). Depression, nondepression, and cognitive illusions: A reply to Schwartz. *Journal of Experimental Psychology: General, 110,* 436–447.

Abramson, L. Y., Alloy, L. B., & Rosoff, R. (1981). Depression and the generation of complex hypotheses in the judgment of contingency. *Behavior Research and Therapy, 19,* 35–45.

Abramson, L. Y., Metalsky, G. I., & Alloy, L. B. (1985). *The reformulated helplessness theory of depression: Does the research test the theory?* Manuscript under editorial review.

Abramson, L. Y., Seligman, M. E. P., & Teasdale, J. (1978). Learned helplessness in humans: Critique and reformulation. *Journal of Abnormal Psychology, 87,* 49–74.

Ainsworth, M. D., & Bell, S. M. (1973). *Mother–infant interaction and the development of competence.* In K. Connolly & J. Brunner (Eds.), New York: Academic Press.

Akiskal, H. S., Khani, M., & Scott-Strauss, A. (1979). Cyclothymic temperamental disorders. *Psychiatric Clinics of North America, 2,* 527–554.

Alloy, L. B. (1982a). The role of perceptions and attributions for response-outcome noncontingency in learned helplessness: A commentary and discussion. *Journal of Personality, 4,* 445–479.

Alloy, L. B. (1982b). Depression: On the absence of self-serving cognitive biases. Paper presented at the meeting of the American Psychological Association, Washington, DC.

Alloy, L. B., & Abramson, L. Y. (1979). Judgment of contingency in depressed and nondepressed students: Sadder but wiser? *Journal of Experimental Psychology: General, 108,* 441–485.

Alloy, L. B., & Abramson, L. Y. (1982). Learned helplessness, depression, and the illusion of control. *Journal of Personality and Social Psychology, 42,* 1114–1126.

Alloy, L. B., Abramson, L. Y., & Kossman, D. (1985). The judgment of predictability in depressed and nondepressed college students. In F. R. Brush & J. B. Overmier (Eds.),

Affect, conditioning, and cognition: Essays on the determinants of behavior. Hillsdale, NJ: Erlbaum.

Alloy, L. B., Abramson, L. Y., & Viscusi, D. (1981). Induced mood and the illusion of control. *Journal of Personality and Social Psychology, 41,* 1129–1140.

Alloy, L. B., Ahrens, A. H., & Kayne, N. T. (1985). Depression, predictions, and causal schemata I: Biased use of statistically relevant information in predictions for self and others. Manuscript under editorial review.

Alloy, L. B., & Bersh, P. J. (1979). Partial control and learned helplessness in rats: Control over shock intensity prevents interference with subsequent escape. *Animal Learning & Behavior, 7,* 157–164.

Alloy, L. B., Clements, C., Kolden, G., Greenberg, M. S., & Guttman, J. (1985). *Depression, anxiety, and self-schemata: A test of Beck's theory.* Manuscript in preparation.

Alloy, L. B., & Seligman, M. E. P. (1979). On the cognitive component of learned helplessness and depression. In G. H. Bower (Ed.), *The psychology of learning and motivation* (Vol. 13). New York: Academic Press.

Alloy, L. B., & Tabachnik, N. (1984). The assessment of covariation by humans and animals: The joint influence of prior expectations and current situational information. *Psychological Review, 91,* 112–149.

Bandura, A. (1971). Vicarious and self-reinforcement processes. In R. Glaser (Ed.), *The nature of reinforcement.* New York: Academic Press.

Barrett, J. E., Ed. (1979). *Stress and mental disorder.* New York: Raven Press.

Bartlett, F. C. (1932). *Remembering.* Cambridge: Cambridge University Press.

Beck, A. T. (1967). *Depression: Clinical, experimental, and theoretical aspects.* New York: Hoeber.

Beck, A. T. (1976). *Cognitive therapy and the emotional disorders.* New York: International Universities Press.

Beck, A. T., Hollon, S. D., Bedrosian, R. C., & Young, J. (in press). Treatment of depression with cognitive therapy and amitriptyline. *Archives of General Psychiatry.*

Beck, A. T., & Rush, A. J. (1978). Cognitive approaches to depression and suicide. In G. Serban (Ed.), *Cognitive defects in development of mental illness.* New York: Bruner/Mazel.

Beck, A. T., Rush, A. J., Shaw, B. F., & Emery, G. (1979). *Cognitive therapy of depression: A treatment manual.* New York: Guilford.

Blackburn, I. M., Bishop, S., Glen, A. I. M., Whalley, L. J., & Christie, T. E. (1981). The efficacy of cognitive therapy in depression: A treatment trial using cognitive therapy and pharmacotherapy, each alone and in combination. *British Journal of Psychiatry, 139,* 181–189.

Blaney, P. H. (1977). Contemporary theories of depression: Critique and comparison. *Journal of Abnormal Psychology, 86,* 203–223.

Bobrow, D. G., & Norman, D. A. (1975). Some principles of memory schemata. In D. G. Bobrow & A. M. Collins (Eds.), *Representation and understanding: Studies in cognitive science.* New York: Academic Press.

Bower, G. H., Black, J. B., & Turner, T. J. (1979). Scripts in memory for text. *Cognitive Psychology, 11,* 177–220.

Bransford, J. D., & Johnson, M. K. (1972). Contextual prerequisites for understanding: Some investigations of comprehension and recall. *Journal of Verbal Learning and Verbal Behavior, 11,* 717–721.

Bransford, J. D., & Johnson, M. K. (1973). Consideration of some problems of comprehension. In W. G. Chase (Ed.), *Visual information processing.* New York: Academic Press.

Brown, G. W., & Harris, T. (1978). *Social origins of depression.* New York: The Free Press.

Bruner, J. S., & Postman, L. (1949). On the perception of incongruity: A paradigm. *Journal of Personality, 18,* 206–223.

Cantor, N., & Mischel, W. (1977). Traits as prototypes: Effects on recognition memory. *Journal of Personality and Social Psychology, 35,* 38–48.

Cantor, N., & Mischel, W. (1979). Prototypes in person perception. In L. Berkowitz (Ed.), *Advances in experimental social psychology* (Vol. 2). New York: Academic Press.

Coates, D., & Wortman, C. B. (1980). Depression maintenance and interpersonal control. In A. Baum and J. Singer (Eds.), *Advances in environmental psychology* (Vol. 2). Hillsdale, NJ: Erlbaum.

Cohen, C. E. (1981). Person categories and social perception: Testing some boundaries of the processing effects of prior knowledge. *Journal of Personality and Social Psychology, 40,* 441–452.

Coyne, J. C. (1976). Toward an interactional description of depression. *Psychiatry, 39,* 28–40.

Coyne, J. C., & Gotlib, I. H. (1983). The role of cognition in depression: A critical appraisal. *Psychological Bulletin, 94,* 472–505.

Craighead, W. E. (1980). Away from a unitary model of depression. *Behavior Therapy, 11,* 122–128.

Crocker, J., Fiske, S. T., & Taylor, S. E. (1984). Schematic bases of belief change. In J. R. Eiser (Ed.), *Attitudinal judgment.* New York: Springer.

Crocker, J., & Weber, R. (1983). Cognitive structure and stereotype change. In R. P. Bagozzi & A. M. Thibaut (Eds.), *Advances in consumer research* (Vol. 10).

Cutrona, C. E. (1983). Causal attributions and perinatal depression. *Journal of Abnormal Psychology, 92,* 161–172.

Davis, H. (1979a). Self-reference and the encoding of personal information in depression. *Cognitive Therapy and Research, 3,* 97–110.

Davis, H. (1979b). The self-schema and subjective organization of personal information in depression. *Cognitive Therapy and Research, 3,* 415–425.

Davis, H., & Unruh, W. R. (1981). The development of the self-schema in adult depression. *Journal of Abnormal Psychology, 90,* 125–133.

Depue, R. A., Ed. (1979). *The psychology of the depressive disorders: Implications for the effects of stress.* New York: Academic Press.

Depue, R. A., & Monroe, S. M. (1978). Learned helplessness in the perspective of the depressive disorders. *Journal of Abnormal Psychology, 87,* 3–20.

Depue, R. A., Slater, J., Wolfstetter-Kausch, H., Klein, D., Goplerud, E., & Farr, D. (1981). A behavioral paradigm for identifying persons at risk for bipolar depressive disorder: A conceptual framework and five validation studies. *Journal of Abnormal Psychology, 90,* 381–438.

Derry, P. A., & Kuiper, N. A. (1981). Schematic processing and self-reference in clinical depression. *Journal of Abnormal Psychology, 90,* 286–297.

Diggony, J. C. (1966). *Self evaluation—Concepts and studies.* New York: Wiley.

Dohrenwend, B. S., & Dohrenwend, B. P., Eds. (1974). *Stressful life events: Their nature and effects.* New York: Wiley.

Dohrenwend, B. S., & Dohrenwend, B. P., Eds. (1981). *Stressful life events and their contexts.* New York: Neale Watson Academic Publications.

Dweck, C. S., Davidson, W., Nelson, S., & Enna, B. (1978). Sex differences in learned helplessness: II. The contingencies of evaluative feedback in the classroom and III. An experimental analysis. *Developmental Psychology, 14,* 268–276.

Dweck, C. S., & Licht, B. G. (1980). Learned helplessness and intellectual achievement. In J. Garber and M. E. P. Seligman (Eds.), *Human helplessness: Theory and application.* New York: Academic Press.

Eaves, G., & Rush, A. J. (1984). Cognitive patterns in symptomatic and remitted unipolar major depression. *Journal of Abnormal Psychology, 93,* 31–40.

Evans, M. D., & Hollon, S. D. (in press). Patterns of personal and causal inference: Implications for the cognitive therapy of depression. In L. B. Alloy (Ed.), *Cognitive processes in depression*. New York: Guilford.

Festinger, L. (1954). A theory of social comparison processes. *Human Relations, 7*, 117–140.

Fiske, S. T., & Dyer, L. (1982). Cognitive analyses of involvement in persuasion. *Persuasion and cognitive processing*. Symposium of the American Psychological Association, Washington, DC.

Fiske, S. T., & Linville, P. W. (1980). What does the schema concept buy us? *Personality and Social Psychology Bulletin, 6*, 540–547.

Glazer, H. I., Clarkin, J. F., & Hunt, A. F. (1981). Assessment of depression. In J. F. Clarkin & H. I. Glazer (Eds.), *Depression: Behavioral and directive intervention strategies*. New York: Garland.

Goldberger, L., & Breznitz, S., Eds. (1982). *Handbook of stress*. New York: The Free Press.

Golin, S., Sweeney, P. D., & Schaeffer, D. E. (1981). The causality of causal attributions in depression; A cross-lagged panel correlational analysis. *Journal of Abnormal Psychology, 90*, 14–22.

Golin, S., & Terrell, F. (1977). Motivational and associative aspects of mild depression in skill and chance tasks. *Journal of Abnormal Psychology, 86*, 389–401.

Golin, S., Terrell, F., & Johnson, B. (1977). Depression and the illusion of control. *Journal of Abnormal Psychology, 86*, 440–442.

Golin, S., Terrell, F., Weitz, J., & Drost, P. L. (1979). The illusion of control among depressed patients. *Journal of Abnormal Psychology, 88*, 454–457.

Gotlib, I. H., & Robinson, L. A. (1982). Responses to depressed individuals: Discrepancies between self-report and observer-rated behavior. *Journal of Abnormal Psychology, 91*, 231–240.

Greenberg, M. S., & Alloy, L. B. (1985a). *Depression vs. anxiety: Schematic processing of self- and other-referent information*. Manuscript in preparation.

Greenberg, M. S., & Alloy, L. B. (1985b). *Depression vs. anxiety: Schematic processing of world- and future-referent information*. Manuscript in preparation.

Halberstadt, L. J., Andrews, D., Metalsky, G. I., & Abramson, L. Y. (1984). Helplessness, hopelessness, and depression: A review of progress and future directions. In N. S. Endler & J. Hunt (Eds.), *Personality and behavior disorders*. New York: Wiley.

Hamilton, E. W., & Abramson, L. Y. (1983). Cognitive patterns and major depressive disorder: A longitudinal study in a hospital setting. *Journal of Abnormal Psychology, 92*, 173–184.

Hastie, R. (1981). Schematic principles in human memory. In E. T. Higgins, P. Herman, & M. Zanna (Eds.), *Social Cognition*. Hillsdale, NJ: Erlbaum.

Higgins, E. T., & King, G. (1981). Accessibility of social constructs: Information-processing consequences of individual and contextual variability. In N. Cantor and J. F. Kihlstrom (Eds.), *Personality, cognition, and social interaction*. Hillsdale, NJ: Erlbaum.

Higgins, E. T., Rholes, W. S., & Jones, C. R. (1977). Category accessibility and impression formation. *Journal of Experimental Social Psychology, 13*, 141–154.

Hinkle, L. E. (1974). The concept of stress in the biological and social sciences. *International Journal of Psychiatry in Medicine, 5*, 335–357.

Hollon, S. D., & Beck, A. T. (1979). Cognitive therapy for depression. In P. C. Kendall and S. D. Hollon (Eds.), *Cognitive–behavioral interventions: Theory, research and procedures*. New York: Academic Press.

Howes, M. J., & Hokanson, J. E. (1979). Conversational and social responses to depressive interpersonal behavior. *Journal of Abnormal Psychology, 88*, 625–634.

Judd, C. M., & Harackiewicz, J. M. (1980). Contrast effects in attitude judgment: An examination of the accentuation hypothesis. *Journal of Personality and Social Psychology, 38,* 390–398.

Judd, C. M., & Kulik, J. A. (1980). Schematic effects of social attitudes and recall. *Journal of Personality and Social Psychology, 38,* 569–578.

Kanner, A. D., Coyne, J. C., Schaefer, C., & Lazarus, R. S. (1981). Comparison of two modes of stress measurement: Daily hassles and uplifts versus major life events. *Journal of Behavioral Medicine, 4,* 1–39.

Kayne, N. T., Alloy, L. B., Romer, D., & Crocker, J. (1985). Predicting depressive reactions in the classroom: A test of a cognitive diathesis-stress theory with causal modeling techniques. Manuscript under editorial review.

Kayne, N. T., & Alloy, L. B. (in press). Clinician and patient as aberrant actuaries: Expectation-based distortions in assessment of covariation. In L. Y. Abramson (Ed.), *Attribution processes and clinical psychology.* New York: Guilford.

Kelley, H. H. (1967). Attribution theory in social psychology. In D. Levine (Ed.), *Nebraska symposium on motivation* (Vol. 15). Lincoln: University of Nebraska Press.

Kelley, H. H. (1972). Causal schemata and the attribution process. In E. E. Jones, D. E. Kanouse, H. H. Kelley, R. E. Nisbett, S. Valins, and B. Weiner (Eds.), *Attribution: Perceiving the causes of behavior.* Morristown, NJ: General Learning Press.

Klein, D. C., & Seligman, M. E. P. (1976). Reversal of performance deficits and perceptual deficits in learned helplessness and depression. *Journal of Abnormal Psychology, 85,* 11–26.

Kovacs, M., Rush, A. J., Beck, A. T., & Hollon, S. D. (1981). Depressed outpatients treated with cognitive therapy or pharmacotherapy: A one year followup. *Archives of General Psychiatry, 38,* 33–39.

Kuiper, N. A., & Derry, P. A. (1980). The self as a cognitive prototype: An application to person perception and depression. In N. Cantor and J. F. Kihlstrom (Eds.), *Personality, cognition, and social interaction.* Hillsdale, NJ: Erlbaum.

Kuiper, N. A., Olinger, L. J., & MacDonald, M. R. (in press). Depressive schemata and the processing of personal and social information. In L. B. Alloy (Ed.), *Cognitive processes in depression.* New York: Guilford.

Lazarus, R. S. (1981). The stress and coping paradigm. In C. Eisdorfer, D. Cohen, A. Kleinman, and P. Maxim (Eds.), *Models for clinical psychopathology.* New York: Spectrum.

Lazarus, R. S., Cohen, J. B., Folkman, S., Kanner, A., & Schaefer, C. (1980). Psychological stress and adaptation: Some unresolved issues. In H. Selye (Ed.), *Selye's guide to stress research* (Vol. 1). New York: Van Nostrand.

Lazarus, R. S., Coyne, J. C., & Folkman, S. (1982). Cognition, emotion, and motivation: The doctoring of Humpty-Dumpty. In R. W. J. Neufeld (Ed.), *Psychological stress and psychopathology.* New York: McGraw-Hill.

Lazarus, R. S., & Launier, R. (1978). Stress-related transactions between person and environment. In L. A. Pervin and M. Lewis (Eds.), *Perspectives in interactional psychology.* New York: Plenum Press.

Lewinsohn, P. M. (1974). A behavioral approach to depression. In R. J. Friedman and M. M. Katz (Eds.), *The psychology of depression: Contemporary theory and research.* Washington, DC: Winston.

Lewinsohn, P. M. (1976). Activity schedules in the treatment of depression. In J. D. Krumboltz and C. E. Thoresen (Eds.), *Counseling methods.* New York: Holt, Rinehart, and Winston.

Lewinsohn, P. M., Mischel, W., Chaplain, W., & Barton, R. (1980). Social competence and depression: The role of illusory self-perception? *Journal of Abnormal Psychology, 89,* 203–212.

Lewinsohn, P. M., Steinmetz, J. L., Larson, D. W., & Franklin, J. (1981). Depression-related cognitions: Antecedent or consequence? *Journal of Abnormal Psychology*, *90*, 213–219.

Lloyd, C. (1980). Life events and depressive disorder reviewed: II. Events as precipitating factors. *Archives of General Psychiatry*, *37*, 542–548.

Lord, C., Ross, L., & Lepper, M. R. (1979). Biased assimilation and attitude polarization: The effects of prior theories on subsequently considered evidence. *Journal of Personality and Social Psychology*, *37*, 2098–2109.

McArthur, L. A. (1972). The how and what of why: Some determinants and consequences of causal attributions. *Journal of Personality and Social Psychology*, *22*, 171–193.

Main, M. (1973). Exploration, play and level of cognitive functioning as related to child–mother attachment. Unpublished doctoral dissertation. The Johns Hopkins University.

Markus, H. (1977). Self-schemata and processing information about the self. *Journal of Personality and Social Psychology*, *35*, 63–78.

Martin, D., Abramson, L. Y., & Alloy, L. B. (1984). The illusion of control for self and others in depressed and nondepressed college students. *Journal of Personality and Social Psychology*, *46*, 125–136.

Mason, J. (1975). A historical view of the stress field (Parts I and II.) *Journal of Human Stress*, *15*, 6–12, 22–36.

Metalsky, G. I., & Abramson, L. Y. (1981). Attributional styles: Toward a framework for conceptualization and assessment. In P. C. Kendall and S. D. Hollon (Eds.), *Cognitive–behavioral interventions: Assessment methods*. New York: Academic Press.

Metalsky, G. I., Abramson, L. Y., Seligman, M. E. P., Semmel, A., & Peterson, C. (1982). Attributional styles and life events in the classroom: Vulnerability and invulnerability to depressive mood reactions. *Journal of Personality and Social Psychology*, *43*, 612–617.

Meichenbaum, D., & Jaremko, M., Eds. (1983). *Stress reduction and prevention*. New York: Plenum.

Mineka, S. (1985). In F. R. Brush & J. B. Overmier (Eds.), *Affect, conditioning, and cognition: Essays on the determinants of behavior*. Hillsdale, NJ: Erlbaum.

Mischel, W. (1979). On the interface of cognition and personality: Beyond the person–situation debate. *American Psychologist*, *34*, 740–754.

Monroe, S. M. (1982a). Assessment of life events: Retrospective versus concurrent strategies. *Archives of General Psychiatry*, *39*, 606–610.

Monroe, S. M. (1982b). Life events assessment: Current practices, emerging trends. *Clinical Psychology Review*, *2*, 435–452.

Monroe, S. M. (1983). Social support and disorder: Toward an untangling of cause and effect. *American Journal of Community Psychology*, *11*, 81–97.

Monroe, S. M. (1983). Major and minor life events as predictors of disorder: Further issues and findings. *Journal of Behavioral Medicine*, *6*, 189–205.

Neisser, U. (1967). *Cognitive psychology*. New York: Appleton-Century-Crofts.

Neisser, U. (1976). *Cognition and reality: Principles and implications of cognitive psychology*. San Francisco: Freeman.

Nelson, R. E., & Craighead, W. E. (1977). Selective recall of positive and negative feedback, self control behaviors, and depression. *Journal of Abnormal Psychology*, *86*, 379–388.

Nisbett, R., & Ross, L. (1980). *Human inference: Strategies and shortcomings*. Englewood, NJ: Prentice-Hall.

O'Hara, M., Rehm, L. P., & Campbell, S. R. (1982). Predicting depressive symptomatology: Cognitive–behavioral models and postpartum depression. *Journal of Abnormal Psychology*, *91*, 457–461.

Orvis, B. R., Cunningham, J. D., & Kelley, H. H. (1975). A closer examination of causal inference: The roles of consensus, distinctiveness, and consistency information. *Journal of Personality and Social Psychology*, *32*, 605–616.

Owens, J., Bower, G. H., & Black, J. B. (1979). The "soap opera" effect in story recall. *Memory and Cognition, 7,* 185–191.

Paykel, E. S. (1979). Recent life events in the development of the depressive disorders. In R. A. Depue (Ed.), *The psychobiology of the depressive disorders: Implications for the effects of stress.* New York: Academic Press.

Paykel, E. S. (1982). Life events and early environment. In E. S. Paykel (Ed.), *Handbook of affective disorders.* New York: Guilford.

Peterson, C., Shwartz, S. M., & Seligman, M. E. P. (1981). Self blame and depressive symptoms. *Journal of Personality and Social Psychology, 41,* 253–259.

Pittman, T. S., & Pittman, N. L. (1980). Deprivation of control and the attribution process. *Journal of Personality and Social Psychology, 39,* 377–389.

Pyszczynski, T. A., & Greenberg, J. (1981). Role of disconfirmed expectancies in the instigation of attributional processing. *Journal of Personality and Social Psychology, 40,* 31–38.

Rabkin, J. G., & Struening, E. L. (1976). Life events, stress, and illness. *Science, 194,* 1013–1020.

Rappaport, J. (1977). *Community psychology: Values, research, and action.* New York: Holt, Rinehart, & Winston.

Rehm, L. P. (1977). A self-control model of depression. *Behavior Therapy, 8,* 787–804.

Riskind, J. H., & Rholes, W. S. (1984). Cognitive accessibility and the capacity of cognitions to predict future depression: A theoretical note. *Cognitive Therapy and Research, 8,* 1–12.

Rosch, E. (1975). Cognitive reference points. *Cognitive Psychology, 7,* 532–547.

Rose, R. M., Jenkins, C. D., & Hurst, M. W. (1978). *Air traffic controller health change study: A prospective investigation of physical, psychological and work-related changes.* Galveston: University of Texas Medical Branch.

Ross, L. (1977). The intuitive psychologist and his shortcomings. In L. Berkowitz (Ed.), *Advances in experimental social psychology.* (Volume 10). New York: Academic Press.

Ross, L., Lepper, M. R., Strack, F., & Steinmetz, J. (1977). Social explanation and social expectation: Effects of real and hypothetical explanations on subjective likelihood. *Journal of Personality and Social Psychology, 35,* 817–829.

Rozensky, R. H., Rehm, L. P., Pry, G. G., & Roth, D. (1977). Depression and self-reinforcement behavior in hospitalized patients. *Journal of Behavior Therapy and Experimental Psychiatry, 8,* 35–38.

Rumelhart, D. E. (1975). Notes on a schema for stories. In D. G. Bobrow and A. Collins (Eds.), *Representation and understanding: Studies in cognitive science.* New York: Academic Press.

Rumelhart, D. E., & Norman, D. A. (1976). *Accretion, tuning and restructuring: Three modes of learning.* Technical report, Center for Information Processing. La Jolla, California.

Rumelhart, D. E., & Ortony, A. (1977). The representation of knowledge in memory. In R. C. Anderson, F. J. Spiro, & W. E. Montague (Eds.), *Schooling and the acquisition of knowledge.* Hillsdale, NJ: Erlbaum.

Rush, A. J., Beck, A. T., Kovacs, M., & Hollon, S. (1977). Comparative efficacy of cognitive therapy and pharmacotherapy in the treatment of depressed out-patients. *Cognitive Therapy and Research, 1,* 17–37.

Rush, A. J., & Giles, D. E. (1982). Cognitive therapy: Theory and research. In A. J. Rush (Ed.), *Short-term psychotherapies for depression.* New York: Guilford.

Sarason, I. G., Johnson, J. H., & Siegel, J. M. (1978). Assessing the impact of life changes: Development of the life experiences survey. *Journal of Consulting and Clinical Psychology, 46,* 932–946.

Schachter, S. (1959). *The psychology of affiliation.* Stanford, CA: Stanford University Press.

Schank, R., & Abelson, R. (1977). *Scripts, plans, goals and understanding: An inquiry into human knowledge structures.* Hillsdale, NJ: Erlbaum.

Seligman, M. E. P. (1975). *Helplessness: On depression, development, and death*. San Francisco: Freeman.

Seligman, M. E. P. (1978). Comment and integration. *Journal of Abnormal Psychology, 87*, 165–179.

Seligman, M. E. P., & Maier, S. F. (1967). Failure to escape traumatic shock. *Journal of Experimental Psychology, 74*, 1–9.

Seligman, M. E. P., Maier, S. F., & Geer, J. (1968). The alleviation of learned helplessness in the dog. *Journal of Abnormal Psychology, 73*, 256–262.

Seligman, M. E. P., Peterson, C., Kaslow, N. J., Tanenbaum, R. L., Alloy, L. B., & Abramson, L. Y. (1984). Attributional style and depressive symptoms among children. *Journal of Abnormal Psychology, 93*, 235–238.

Selye, H. (1975). Confusion and controversy in the stress field. *Journal of Human Stress, 1*, 37–44.

Shaw, B. F. (1977). Comparison of cognitive therapy and behavior therapy in the treatment of depression. *Journal of Consulting and Clinical Psychology, 45*, 543–551.

Sherif, M. & Hovland, C. I. (1961). *Social judgment: Assimilation and contrast effects in communication and attitude change*. New Haven: Yale University Press.

Sherman, S. J., Skov, R. B., Hervitz, E. F., & Stock, C. B. (1981). The effects of explaining hypothetical future events: From possibility to probability to actuality and beyond. *Journal of Experimental Social Psychology, 17*, 142–158.

Srull, T. K. & Wyer, R. S., Jr. (1980). Category accessibility and social perception: Some implications for the study of person memory and interpersonal judgments. *Journal of Personality and Social Psychology, 38*, 841–856.

Swann, W. B., Jr., Stephenson, B., & Pittman, T. S. (1981). Curiosity and control: On the determinants of the search for social knowledge. *Journal of Personality and Social Psychology, 40*, 635–642.

Tabachnik, N., Crocker, J., & Alloy, L. B. (1983). Depression, social comparison, and the false consensus effect. *Journal of Personality and Social Psychology, 45*, 688–699.

Taylor, F. G., & Marshall, W. L. (1977). Experimental analysis of a cognitive–behavioral therapy for depression. *Cognitive Therapy and Research, 1*, 59–72.

Taylor, S. E., & Crocker, J. (1980). Schematic bases of information processing. In E. T. Higgins, P. Herman, and M. Zanna (Eds.), *Social Cognition*. Hillsdale, NJ: Erlbaum.

Thorndyke, P. W. (1977). Cognitive structures in comprehension and memory of narrative discourse. *Cognitive Psychology, 9*, 77–110.

Tversky, A., & Kahneman, D. (1973). Availability: A heuristic for judging frequency and probability. *Cognitive Psychology, 5*, 207–232.

Weber, R., & Crocker, J. (1983). Cognitive processes in the revision of stereotypic beliefs. *Journal of Personality and Social Psychology, 45*, 961–977.

Weintraub, M., Segal, R. M., & Beck, A. T. (1974). An investigation of cognition and affect in the depressive experiences of normal men. *Journal of Consulting and Clinical Psychology, 42*, 911.

Weissman, M., & Klerman, G. L. (1977). Sex differences and the epidemiology of depression. *Archives of General Psychiatry, 34*, 98–111.

Wong, P. T., & Weiner, B. (1981). When people ask "why" questions, and the heuristics of attributional search. *Journal of Personality and Social Psychology, 40*, 650–663.

Zadney, J., & Gerard, H. B. (1974). Attributed intentions and information selectivity. *Journal of Experimental Social Psychology, 10*, 34–52.

Zax, M., & Cowen, E. (1976). *Abnormal psychology: Changing conceptions*. New York: Holt, Rinehart, & Winston.

AUTHOR INDEX

SUBJECT INDEX

A

Affect, 37–39, 42–43
Aggressive behavior, 132, 222, 224, 227, 228, 233, 236, 240, 245, 288
Agoraphobia, 114, 119
Animal behavior, 10–11, 50–51, 91–94, 138–148, 181–183
Anxiety, *see* Fear/anxiety
Anxiety sensitivity, 108, 112–114, 119–120
Archetype, 72
ARD system, 310, 311, 315
Asthma, 257, 265–267
Attention-seeking behavior, 219, 228, 237–241
Attribution, 17, 25, 300, 304, 309, 366–368, 370–373, 381–383
Autism, 183, 219, 228, 241, 246, 247, 287, 288
Automatic processing, 20–22, 124
Autonomic nervous system, 125, 134
Avoidance behavior, 35, 40, 50, 53, 57, 58, 59, 108, 124, 133, 362, 364
and symptom maintenance, 62–66

B

Basic behavioral repertoire, 302–312
Behavior analysis, 6, 256
Behavior disorder, 219–254

Behavior therapy, 35
and clinical work, 256–258
and cognition, 8–10
and experimentation, 177
history, 4–5, 255, 280, 312–313
scope, 6
shortcomings, 7
Behaviorism, 5–10, 15–19, 280, 282, 288, 296–297, 301, 313
Biofeedback, 255–276
and individual differences, 271–273
Bipolar depression, 314–317

C

Classical conditioning, 7, 36, 49, 53, 55, 57, 63, 84–85, 88–89, 110–112, 114–115, 133, 145–148, 284, 309
Pavlovian A conditioning, 89
Pavlovian B conditioning, 90
Cognition
and behavior change, 40–42
and behavior therapy, 1–2, 8–10
and behaviorism, 15–19
and depression, 305–309, 332, 334, 337, 341–342, 366–368, 379–410
and fear, 111
and imitation, 211
and mental processes, 8–10
and social behaviorism, 284–285
and theories of emotion, 37–39